COMMUNIST INTERNATIONAL ECONOMICS

COMMUNIST
INTERNATIONAL
ECONOMICS

P. J. D. WILES

FREDERICK A. PRAEGER, *PUBLISHERS*
NEW YORK · WASHINGTON

BOOKS THAT MATTER

Published in the United States of America in 1969
by Frederick A. Praeger, Inc., Publishers
111 Fourth Avenue, New York, N.Y. 10003

Library of Congress Catalog Card Number: 68–16098

Printed in the United States of America

TO H. B. M.

If we can make the unlikely supposition that A and B are both 'socialistic' States, the exchange will then be in form exactly the same as that between individuals. The ratio of exchange must be arranged by treaty, and will be a high act of State, so that any attempt to determine it would be practically impossible.

—C. F. Bastable,
The Theory of International Values
(4th ed., London 1903), p. 28.

CONTENTS

PREFACE

This book tries to build out the theory and the generalized description of international economics, as given in advanced textbooks of that subject, to include Communism; or alternatively to build out Sovietological economics to include all international aspects.

In the attempt I have covered all the most important modern developments of either subject known to me: the 'activation' of subordinates in a command economy, the special position of small countries, the special position of underdeveloped countries, trade in technology, blocs of countries, etc. etc. There are only three conscious omissions. The first is factor-price equalization. This question seems so absolutely remote from the Soviet-type economy, and indeed from all practical application in a market economy, that I have, not without relief, omitted it altogether. The second is the Communist analysis of the West, both imperialist and underdeveloped. Crucial for world peace and prosperity as this is, it belongs rather to general ideology than to foreign trade. The third great omission is the banks that Communist countries establish on foreign soil. Chinese banks in Hong Kong, Soviet banks in Paris, London and Beirut—the list is endless. Only a very long-winded researcher with very special connections could say anything of value about them. Some of the other problems receive chapters or sections to themselves; others—e.g. underdeveloped countries and small countries—are simply treated at every point where normal analysis seems to rest on the assumption that a country is large, or developed, or both.

Two shifts of emphasis have been made from that usual in a textbook. The first has been to get away from visible trade as the center of everything. Trade in services, factor-movements, aid, international planning and the agreement *not* to trade have all been brought nearer the center of the picture. 'International economics' is a far better title and subject than 'international trade.' Secondly I have tried, at whatever cost in generality and respectability, to stress that foreign economic relations are a political act. If in so doing I have trespassed beyond the borders of economics I make no apology: such borders, like international ones, exist only to be trampled upon.

I have not, then, hesitated before rigorous and abstract reasoning, but have still not ventured far from real problems, being, truth to say, not only giddy but bored at these Icarian heights. It is with mathematical (not statistical) economics as Kant felt about metaphysics: the thing has an 'accursed fertility'. Decapitate one algebraical model of the economy, and you will find seven more in the next issue of the journal, with empty boxes opening up to disclose an infinite vista of—empty boxes. I firmly believe that the descriptive basis of economics is nothing like *solid* enough to support these cathedrals of the mind: consider the fearful discrepancies between the recorded exports of A to B and the recorded imports of B from A.[1] Nor is this basis anything like *wide* enough: consider that virtually every fact in this book has been hitherto neglected by virtually every textbook of international trade (in this connexion it should be stated that the epigraph has been chosen for no other purpose than to illustrate this point). Partly, then, from incapacity, but far more of set policy, I have confined abstract reasoning to short excursions in particular places: i.e. to small and interesting questions on which it is likely to throw immediate light.

One should state one's linguistic incapacities. This book has been written on the free use of sources in English, French and Swedish but only in a few Communist languages: German, Russian, Spanish, and much too little Polish.

My thanks are due to the Wenner-Gren Foundation for making it economically possible to concentrate on this work for one year; and to Gunnar Myrdal for suggesting the project, and for setting a shining example of how an economist ought to choose questions and answer them; may he, however, forgive me for not adopting many of his detailed views. I must also thank the innumerable learned seminars who have listened to draft passages and pointed out the fallacies; and especially class U 337 of 1965 at the City College of New York. Moreover Drs. Holzman and Pryor have been kind enough to read many chapters—may my indebtedness not inhibit their reviewing.

This book could not have been written in American—in so far as it is—without the devoted accuracy of my wife, and at one remove that of her erstwhile English teacher Miss M. E. Kane, both New Englanders. But the final choice of dialect has been mine.

---

[1] Oskar Morgenstern, *On the Accuracy of Economic Observations*, Princeton 1963.

Postscript

THE passage to print is slow, and certain 'stop press' items should be alluded to here.

(i) A most interesting Hungarian article[1] confirms the generally vague and arbitrary nature of 'world prices,' as described in pp. 236–7. It adds that there are certain 'hard' items easy to sell in the West but still underpriced *vis-à-vis* CMEA demand; and that these are subject to special bilateral balancing between STEs. We further learn that the agreed 'world price' takes account of a phantom freight charge from the frontier of the importer (not the exporter) to the main capitalist supplier: the importing STE pays the exporting STE one-half of this amount. Compare clause 3 in Mr. Pryor's document, p. 236.

(ii) Further, recent developments in the USSR, Hungary and Czechoslovakia call for qualifications to pp. 170–4 and 544–7. It is stated there, correctly, that rationality of prices and outputs is an import: that the whole practical and much of the theoretical reform movement began in foreign trade. Yet in these three countries the actual decentralization of decision has proceeded most slowly in imports and exports. There is no mystery: decentralization allows home demand priority, and so worsens the b.o.p. The failure to decentralize export decisions is, then, only a Soviet-type export drive, and the continued physical allocation of imports is a way to ensure import-substitution. Needless to say there is least change in the structure of export decision in inter-STE trade, where foreign demand is least volatile.

[1] Ferenc Bartha in *Kulkereskedelem*, 9/1967; cf. Harry Trend's summary in Radio Free Europe Research, February 23/1968.

GLOSSARY AND ABBREVIATIONS

ACC	Advanced capitalist country. See Chapter II, Section 7.
active money	money having most of its normal market functions: see 'passive money'.
bilateralism	is in this book confined to financial arrangements whereby countries do not convert each other's money. See 'reciprocity' and Chapter X, Section 1.
'body'	only intermediate planning authority, between the center and the enterprise.
b.o.p.	balance of payments.
CB	'Current Background': translations from Chinese publications issued by the United States Consulate-General, Hong Kong.
CIA	Central Intelligence Agency (of the United States).
CMEA	Council of Mutual Economic Aid, often called 'Comecon'. See Chapter XII.
CoCom	the Co-ordinating Committee of the North Atlantic Treaty Organization's embargo.
Cominform	Information Bureau of the Communist and Workers' Parties. See 'Dates'.
command economy	one in which legal commands, not profit, are the mainspring of economic activity.
Communist countries	The Soviet-type countries, q.v., plus Yugoslavia.
DDR	Deutsche Demokratische Republik (East Germany).
ECMM	'Extracts from China Mainland Magazines': translations as under 'CB'.
ECSC	European Coal and Steel Community, Luxembourg.
GATT	General Agreement on Trade and Tariffs.
GKES	Gosudarstvenni Komitet Ekonomicheskikh Svyazei (State Committee on Economic Relations: see appendix to Chapter XIV).
IBEC	International Bank for Economic Cooperation, Moscow.
IBRD	International Bank for Reconstruction and Development, Washington.
IMF	International Monetary Fund, Washington.
kolkhoz	collective farm.
md.	milliard, a thousand million. I have preferred this word, standard in East European languages, to the ambiguous 'billion'.

ME	market economy: includes all economies not STEs, even Yugoslavia.
MFN	most-favored nation.
mn.	million.
Munich Bulletin	Strictly 'Bulletin for the Study of the USSR', published by the Institut zur Erforschung der UdSSR, Munich.
n.m.p.	net material product, the Communist national income concept. Excludes services other than trade and most transport, but includes the materials used by the excluded services.
n.n.i.o.	net national income originating. See Chapter XV, Section 10.
OECD	Organization for Economic Cooperation and Development, Paris.
PAG	Preisausgleich, q.v.
participation rate	the proportion between the average of (visible and invisible) exports and imports and the net national income.
passive money	money mainly used for accounting purposes, without effect on resource allocation or income distribution: E.g., in a command economy. See 'active money'.
p.p.p.	purchasing power parity.
Preisausgleich	the budgetary measures taken in an STE, q.v., to skim the profits of importers and make good the losses of exporters in home currency. See Chapter VI, Section 5.
reciprocity	equal volumes of (visible and invisible) trade between two countries. See 'bilateralism'.
SCMP	'Survey of the China Mainland Press': translations from the daily press as under 'CB'.
sortament	the variety of types of a given article produced.
Soviet-type countries	USSR, Albania, Bulgaria, China, Cuba, Czechoslovakia, DDR, Hungary, Mongolia, North Korea, North Vietnam, Poland, Rumania.
sovkhoz	state farm.
STE	Soviet-type economy.
sovnarkhoz	see Chapter XI, Section 1.
UDC	underdeveloped country. See Chapter II, Section 7.
valuta	Russian and Rumanian word for foreign exchange. Adopted here as the most euphonious neologism for the 'foreign-exchange' form of a Soviet-type currency. See Chapter VI, Section 5.

SOME DATES RELEVANT TO THE STUDY OF
COMMUNIST INTERNATIONAL ECONOMICS

March	1947	UN Economic Commission for Europe founded.
June–July	1947	Marshall Plan conference in Paris. Molotov arrives with large delegation, but leaves early. Czechoslovakia and Poland decide to apply for aid; Stalin forbids them.
July	1947	Organization (at first Committee) of European Economic Cooperation founded.
September	1947	Cominform founded. Includes Communist Parties of: USSR, Poland, Czechoslovakia, Rumania, Bulgaria, Hungary, Yugoslavia, Italy, France.
November	1947	Benelux begins to operate.
Late	1947	United States embargo begins.
February	1948	Communist coup in Czechoslovakia.
June	1948	Yugoslavia expelled from Cominform.
January 25	1949	Communique on foundation of CMEA: USSR, Czechoslovakia, Poland, Hungary, Rumania, Bulgaria.
February	1949	Albania joins CMEA but not Cominform.
October 1	1949	Chinese Communists declare foundation of republic.
November	1949	Last plenary session of Cominform.
January	1950	CoCom founded.
March	1950	Ruble appreciated; gold basis re-asserted.
June 25	1950	Korean War begins.
September	1950	DDR joins CMEA, but not Cominform.
October	1951	United States passes Battle Act.
August	1952	ECSC founded.
	1953	East German reparations end.
March 4	1953	Stalin dies. Malenkov's 'New Course' begins.
June 17	1953	Revolt in the DDR.
July 27	1953	Armistice in Korea.
July	1953	Imre Nagy, as Hungarian Premier, attacks autarky (Ch. I, sec. 11).
	1954	Communist capital exports to UDCs begin; Mixed companies liquidated.
May	1954	French defeat at Dienbienphu.
July 20	1954	North Vietnamese Republic founded.
Summer	1954	'New Course' ends.
October	1954	Hungarian article on comparative costs published (Ch. I, sec. 11).

October	1955/6	Leontief's *Studies on the Structure of the American Economy* translated and circulated in Moscow (as described by Leontief in *Foreign Affairs*, Jan. 1960).
February	1955	Malenkov resigns as premier.
July 1953–April 1955		Imre Nagy's first premiership in Hungary.
May	1955	Khrushchev's first visit to Belgrade.
	1956	First year of Chinese visible trade surplus with USSR; Yugoslavia and China enter CMEA as observers.
February	1956	XX Congress in USSR: Khrushchev's Secret Speech.
April	1956	Cominform disbanded.
October	1956	Gomulka returns to power in Poland.
November	1956	Hungarian Revolution.
March	1957	Treaty of Rome signed: Common Market begins.
April	1957	'Non-commercial' exchange rates established in Eastern Europe.
May	1958	Chinese 'Great Leap Forward' and attack on Yugoslavia.
June	1958	Yugoslav *rafroidissement* with USSR; observer status with CMEA ceases.
Summer	1960	Soviet experts withdrawn from China.
January 1	1961	Ruble devalued.
December	1961	Open break between USSR and Albania; ambassadors withdrawn. China and Albania absent from CMEA meeting. From this meeting China's attendance (as observer) variable. Albania (as member) always absent.
June	1962	Session of CMEA creates council of Ministers Resident. Rumanian-Soviet quarrel begins. Mongolia joins CMEA.
September	1962	Khrushchev proposes to make CMEA supra-national.
September	1962	Liberman's first great revisionist article in *Pravda*.
April	1963	New non-commercial rates begin.
April	1963	Rumanian quarrel with CMEA becomes open.
July	1964	Intermetall founded (Chapter XI, Section 3).
September 17	1964	Yugoslavia gets associated status with CMEA.

COMMUNIST INTERNATIONAL ECONOMICS

CHAPTER I

THE MARXIST TRADITION

Capitalist economics is about socialism, and socialist economics is about capitalism.

—OSKAR LANGE

A Bankers' Conspiracy! The idea is absurd. I only wish there were one.

—J. M. KEYNES

I

THIS chapter examines the traditional Marxist doctrine of international economics and its influence on practice. The *terminus ad quem* is Stalin's death in 1953, after which Marxism is heavily infiltrated with common sense and Western theory. Our task is a light one: though the notion that Communist governments pay only lip service to Marxism is quite wrong, and though in innumerable matters of domestic policy we can trace the strong, detailed influence of Marx and Engels, let alone Lenin, the ideology really has little to say about *international* economics. It is rather about *world* economics, i.e., it purports to analyse and predict the economic and political development of the world. It has almost nothing to say on what a given nation's commercial policy should be and most conspicuously lacks a theory of international values.

The notion of 'the world economy' is originally German. There is no real English translation of *Weltwirtschaft*. To this day, Anglo-Saxon universities do not offer courses, or harbor institutes, so entitled. But the Institut für Weltwirtschaft in Kiel dates from 1911–14. Thus, just when Marxism, that heresy of *Deutschtum*, was beginning to struggle with theories of imperialism, the German establishment was moving in the same direction. The very phrase 'international economics' is still almost unknown to Marxism, but not to the Americanized Germany of today.

But German or Marxist, what does *Weltwirtschaft, Mirovaya Ekonomika*, really mean? I can well remember the professor of international trade at a German (capitalist) oral exam asking 'What are world ports?' (*Was sind Welthäfen?*) The correct answer was, evidently, places like Le Havre and Southampton. Did he not simply mean big ports, ports with international, as opposed to coastal, connections? What is the point of saying 'world'? Since every port of the world belongs to some nation there is no logical point. But in practice those who study 'international economics' are more or less pure analytical economists who stress national separateness, while *Weltwirtschaft* is political economy, even economic history. What it loses on factor-price equalization it gains on imperialism. Like all German or Marxist social science, it has a much surer grasp of what really matters, but a tendency to meaningless phrase-making. Stalin's doctrine of 'two world markets' (Section 12, below) is a case in point.[1]

It seems that the first Marxist work of international economics, as opposed to monographs on imperialism or on the practical procedures of Soviet trading bodies, was published by a Pole in 1954.[2] It is difficult for the Western reader to appreciate Mr. Łychowski's courage and achievement. Polish Marxists and ex-Marxists assure me—and the basis for their assertion seems to be firmer than mere chauvinism—that there was literally no single

---

[1] Cf. the excellent account in Erich Klinkmüller and Maria Ruban, *Die Wirtschaftliche Zusammenarbeit der Ostblockstaaten*, Berlin, 1960, pp. 24–30.

[2] Tadeusz Łychowski, *Zagadnienia Obrotu Międzynarodowego* (Warsaw, 1954). A prior, incomplete version [*Handel Międzynarodowy* (Warsaw, 1951)] circulated in cyclostyle. I am indebted here to Mr. Seweryn Bialer, now of Columbia University. At that time a coming young Communist functionary, he edited Mr. Łychowski's book.

connected work on Marxist international economics in any language until his book appeared. Actually, to set up a Marxist theory of international values would have been a 'creative development' of Marxism, the making of which is the privilege of great leaders alone. So we can demand no great new thing of this book. But it seems entirely fair to take its great deficiencies as truly representing the deficiencies of Marxism itself.

Not long after Łychowski's pioneering effort rational Westernized economic thought began to make heavy inroads, and precisely and primarily in international economics. Only in Marx' homeland is the weight of tradition strong enough, and the number of 'gute Marxkenner' great enough, for further specifically Marxian development to have occurred in this field. We shall return below to Kohlmey's genuinely innovating application of Marxism.[1] It is also important that intellectual freedom in the DDR has increased since Stalin's death, but not enough for economics to Westernize itself. This too must have directed Dr. Kohlmey's great abilities towards their obsolescent goal.

2

These matters apart, a first point of crucial importance for the Western economist to grasp is that his own economics rests upon a particular political theory. Democracy and utilitarianism have stamped indelibly his theory of value and resource allocation, and the conflict between individualism and *Western* collectivism has been fought within these bounds. The British Utilitarians were, of course, originally collectivists, but only in the sense that the state was a reliable means to the good of the individual. If Bentham's opinion evolved away from this stand, Edwin Chadwick's and Sidney Webb's did not. It is almost accidental that when utilitarianism finally conquered the keep of the economic castle—the theory of value—its champion, W. S. Jevons, was of the individualist wing. Certainly the Fabians, also Utilitarians and, in a way, democrats, but above all Western collectivists, had nothing against him.

But what of those different kinds of collectivists, for whom the state, or at least the collective, is an end, not a means, for whom it is false that 'collective happiness is the sum of individual

---

[1] Günther Kohlmey, 'Karl Marx' Theorie von den Internationalen Werten', in *Jahrbuch des Instituts für Wirtschafts-wissenschaften*, Band 5, Akademie-Verlag, Berlin, 1962.

happinesses'?[1] They felt themselves ill served by such a theory of value. Communism has stuck to the labor theory, which, though not *per se* collectivist, has received overtones of that coloring from Marx. Fascism is far more collectivist, since it makes the individual a mere biological link in the only valid unit: the racial chain. But in economics it was less intellectualized and simply dispensed with all theory. Nevertheless, it certainly showed no respect for '*bourgeois economics*'.

Above all, such ideologies have resisted individualist theories of foreign trade. The notion that the relations between states, even merely the economic relations between states, should be subject to the unguided decisions of politically unmotivated individuals seems in their light preposterous. Marx himself could not conceive of a nonpolitical theory of foreign trade:

> I treat the system of bourgeois economy and the following categories: capital, landed property, hired labor, government, foreign trade, the world market. Under the first three rubrics I study the economic conditions of life of the three great classes into which present-day bourgeois society is divided. *The mutual link between the three further rubrics leaps to the eye* [italics added].[2]

The Western student of international trade sees instinctively an individual merchant or firm or investor operating across a frontier and an exchange rate. Even when we insert tariffs, exchange control and devaluation, the whole thing is still seen in terms of individual interests. The government's intervention is thought of as a mere canalizer; the micro-initiative still rests with the free citizen. And the grounds for the intervention are thought of as individual economic welfare. The 'state-as-end' economist on the other hand sees two states. He sees therefore a political act. The act may be quite routine and uninteresting and may have purely economic ends. But it is still the act of a sovereign power, and non-economic considerations always come in.

The very word 'international' is misleading. It leads us to think

---

[1] Under Full Communism (Section 11), the State and even the Party will wither away. But mystical veneration goes to them both in fact, and above all to 'the Collective', whatever that means, which will remain supreme. There is not in the longest of long runs to be any individualism; man is to remain forever a cog on the wheel of society. The perfect freedom and anarchy of Full Communism are not individualistic either. The freedom is merely Hegel's realized necessity; the anarchy presupposes the Rousseauian unanimity of a perfectly virtuous citizenry. The phrase in quotation marks is that of the Chinese philosopher Feng Ting. His book, *The Communist Philosophy of Life*, was attacked in 1965 as revisionist precisely because he was basically a Utilitarian, to whom Communism was a means. See CB 750 and SCMP 3407. It is highly significant that Feng Ting's heresy is official in Yugoslavia. Cf. *Komunist*, Belgrade, Aug. 8, 1965, p. 6 (tr. in *Hinter dem Eisernen Vorhang*, 11, 1965, p. 10).

[2] Karl Marx, *Preface to the Critique of Political Economy*. Translated here from the Polish in Tadeusz Łychowski, *Handel Międzynarodowy*, Part I.

of businesses or people, who happen to live in particular places and, say, to speak different languages; some of their trade happens to be among their kith and kin, and some of it happens to go further afield. Substitute now 'inter-state', and a whole new set of images is conjured up: a set far more appropriate to the seventeenth, eighteenth or twentieth centuries. This has, too, interesting consequences for the enforcement of international contracts. According to ordinary international law a state enjoys legal immunity only when it acts 'as a sovereign body', a concept which excludes trade. Soviet-type foreign trade enterprises are recognized by Communism as not enjoying such immunity. It continues however to be claimed for ships, even when engaged in trade or fishing.[1]

Interferences with trade between market economies (MEs) are often motivated by international power politics, and even individuals show more spontaneous political motivation than in home markets.[2] State trading and public foreign aid are fundamentally 'Soviet-type' activities after practiced by MEs. *Per contra*, the state-as-end economist's obsession with politics often reaches ridiculous heights of paranoia—and so does that of the Western politician contemplating Communist trade. If American capitalists bought Cuban real estate it was because it was profitable to each one individually. If the Russians are selling oil it is because they have a surplus. Our explanation must always base itself on what happens to be the case. Sentiment, conspiracy, power-lust all have their place: so does the capitalist's desire to get rich quick, and the Communist's desire to do the best he can for his economy.

Mercantilism shows how unnecessary it is for the ideology of a market economy to be individualistic. To this way of thinking state power was the end of politics and a war of all against all was the natural condition of international affairs. The state was the end and the private capitalist the means. It was merely considered inefficient for the state to run industry or even whole colonies;[3] but the way in which private people ran them was most strictly controlled for the supposed benefit of the state. Writers very often argued for a prosperous population, but primarily because tax yields would rise. All political and economic theories rest upon some

[1] Cf. M. M. Boguslavski, *Immunitet Gosudarstva*, Moscow, 1962; T. Davletshin in *Munich Bulletin*, December, 1966.

[2] Thus Britons boycott South African sherry, and *per contra* I have met a South African importer, British born, who always bought British mining equipment though he knew that Swedish was cheaper and better. Foreign investment is, of course, very largely governed by political sympathy, often in the complete absence of government controls.

[3] Eli Heckscher, *Mercantilism*, trans. Mendel Shapiro (London, 1955), Chapter II.

metaphor, mostly misleading. The Mercantilist metaphor would be of an economy or polity (it does not matter which, for the doctrine made no distinction) like a herd of sheep. The sheep are each individually motivated (the desire for gain) to eat the grass and grow; no compulsion is required for that. But their *raison d'être* is not their own welfare: it is to be sheared (taxed). And in many ways they cannot be trusted, so the shepherd sends his dogs (e.g., Colbert's *réglements*) among them to keep them in the right pastures. These are, of course, so far as possible, other people's pastures.

Thus Mercantilism relied on the market mechanism, partly on principle and partly because it had to in the absence of an administrative machine. Its use of controls regulated but in no way abolished private initiative, so we are bound to call it an ME with state intervention. But the spirit and policy of such interventions were perfectly different from those of today: to enrich the state and wage economic warfare against other states.

The fundamental metaphor for Smith and the free traders hardly contained a term for the state at all. We may rather speak of the glass balls in Marshall's bowl, where the bowl is the whole world and the balls are individuals. They find their level under the pull of gravity (the profit motive), but are delayed by various frictions. *Among* these frictions is the state's control of foreign trade; it ranks on a par with the poor-law, the legal impediments to the sale of land, the remnants of feudalism and the guild system, etc., etc. Although Smith was not *sensu stricto* a Utilitarian, he was close enough to them, and his fundamental metaphor suited individualist Utilitarianism well enough.

Western thought bears innumerable traces of this period. The 'state-as-means' collectivism, subsequently grafted on to *laissez-faire* economics, has hardly changed the basic image. We may now best think of several smaller bowls, all full of glass balls of varying sizes; and a *deus ex machina* who moves certain balls from one bowl to another and observes the results. These still come about through gravity and friction; thus *laissez-faire* is still basic, and is subjected only to a few specified external shocks. So broadly viewed the economics of List or Keynes is not very different from that of Smith. It is, for instance, striking that Keynes and his followers have produced virtually nothing on economic warfare. The old, and ridiculous, dictum of Cannan, that there is no such thing as the economics of war,[1] remains more true than we think. For the great

[1] Edwin Cannan, *An Economist's Protest* (London, 1927), p. 49.

efflorescence of planning economics, especially in Britain, during World War II concerned fiscal policy and rationing, not war. Even the Keynesian view of Hjalmar Schacht's prewar policy treats it in terms of full employment and high gold reserves alone.[1]

Now in fact the Nazis, whatever the personal attitude of their employee Schacht, were pure Mercantilists. This applies both to their theorizing about colonies and to their behavior in Eastern Europe. It applies also to Mussolini's behavior in his colonies and in Albania. So right-wing collectivism may be dismissed as having been already discussed: if the basic Fascist theory of the state was far from resembling that of Mercantilism, the resulting economics was much the same. Moreover, there has been a strong revival of Mercantilist *behavior* in democratic capitalist countries since about 1870. This showed itself in protectionism at home, imperial preference, the political direction of foreign investment, and diplomatic intervention on a massive scale in underdeveloped countries (UDCs). Even before 1870 free trade was supported by Britain alone, and most of the steam behind this too was Mercantilist: it was to her economic and strategic advantage as a state. For the most part contemporary Western economics shut its eyes to the political motivation behind all this.

3

Thus political preconceptions dominate and should dominate all theories of international trade. It is merely discreditable that in the case of orthodox Western economics these preconceptions are unconscious. Marxism in particular is more honest and less blinkered.

But in another way it is very much more blinkered. For it has really nothing more to offer than a pre-revolutionary analysis of the capitalist world, a theory of imperialism. There was, and—as we shall see—is, nothing we can properly call a Marxist theory of post-revolutionary foreign trade. Be that as it may, the pre-revolutionary analysis runs as follows. Relations between rich countries, which have capitalists, and poor countries, which do not, are class relations. International trade is like domestic trade: a search for surplus value. In the initial period of 'free-trade capitalism' the nation-state is little involved: capitalists clash as individuals. This is also the period of exploitation merely through trade, not through foreign investment

[1] F. A. Burchardt in *The Economics of Full Employment*, Oxford University Institute of Statistics (Oxford, 1946).

and armed force as well (cf. Section 5, below). In the later phase of imperialism, capitalism[1] has been more or less 'nationalized', and the capitalists, united under the banners of their financiers,[2] do indeed represent national interests. Thus developed capitalism, causing imperialism, causes war. We may now accurately speak of the capitalist state as the executive organ of the *bourgeoisie*, and of advanced capitalist countries (ACCs) exploiting UDCs: the *bourgeoisie* in the former perverting to their own side some of the upper-level proletariat at home and the 'comprador' *bourgeoisie* overseas.

Marxism, then, is uninterested in trade between countries on the same level of development, even though it forms much the majority of all trade. It is really fair to say that there is no doctrine on these, politically uninteresting, exchanges. The doctrine is also too abusive and hostile to be a serious analysis even in political terms. But still it made in its time an immense advance on Western thinking by merely recognizing the existence of UDCs and imperialism. Until recently, development economics—let alone development-and-trade economics—did not exist in the West. A UDC was just a poor capitalist country, and probably on its way to becoming a rich one. As to imperialism, there is still nothing about that. For the subject belongs to political economy, and it is of the essence of Western economics since John Stuart Mill to purify all politics away. If in the domestic sphere Western economics may justly feel superior, even in its contributions to planning, in the international sphere it is but a pot, facing a black kettle.

4

So much for the political theory. Turning now to economics, the main point to grasp is that one cannot turn to economics. Nothing in Marxism is purely economic; everything is at least partly political. No important exchange or production is a purely economic act. There is always an involuntary element with a winner and a loser. The idea that both parties might gain from, say, an employment contract or an international exchange is bourgeois philistinism: it refers either to trivial events or to none. For events

---

[1] Note the curious Marxist confusion of capitalism with industrialism. The previous period of non-industrial, capitalist, imperialism (Mercantilism, of course) finds no place in the Marxian scheme of history at all. It is, apparently, just the tail-end of 'feudalism'.

[2] Who are held to have all entrepreneurs in mere production firmly under control, along with the government. The exact means of this control are never laid bare—a fatal flaw which is, however, not our concern.

in which no one exploits anyone and the March of the Dialectic is not hastened or retarded, are *ipso facto* trivial, e.g., when one capitalist lends money to another of equal size. Everything else is charged with a historical significance usually invisible to the non-Marxist. Moreover, there is, especially among vulgar Marxists, a constant suggestion of political intent, over and above all political effect, the absurdity of which was effectively lampooned by Keynes in our title quotation.

All this is a prejudice, not a conscious doctrine explicitly stated in a recognized classic. We are, then, contemplating the psychology, not the logic, of Marxist economics. I state merely as an empirical fact that no Marxist thinker can imagine an international exchange without origin in, or effect on, the international power structure. There is a parallel here to the exchange of labor and wages. The employment relation is of course inherently exploitative, owing to Marx' own theory of value; its nature characterizes the historical stage at which society has arrived. Anything so important as international exchange must similarly be exploitative.

Now to exploit another man is to take, through the normal market or productive process, something that is his due, not yours. You may rely on legal force for this, or simply on the market; you may even practice various institutionalized forms of fraud. Thus slavery, which rests on force, is exploitation, and so is capitalism or 'wage-slavery', where the market operates almost independently and the law is a mere back-stop. Mr. Łychowski's Phoenicians, below, practiced so grand and general a fraud, profiting from their institutional position, that they too were exploiters. The notion only excludes the private burglar or embezzler, operating *against* society.

Our purpose here is not polemical but descriptive, so we shall not enter into any rebuttal of this type of argument—should one be possible. We need only note that in international economics the charge of exploitation is particularly difficult to sustain. For one thing there is no supranational sovereign whose law might enforce it—a thing considered very necessary in domestic markets. For another, Communist countries, as we shall see, feel free to criticize as exploitative the terms of trade between ACCs and UDCs, but use world prices themselves!

Marginalist definitions of exploitation we shall also pass by.[1] They are not important enough within marginalism, and have no

---

[1] Cf. Gordon F. Bloom in *Quarterly Journal of Economics* (1940–41) and P. J. D. Wiles, 'Ausbeutung', *Enzyklopädisches Wörterbuch* (Herder, 1966).

connection with international trade. However, exploitation is basic to all Marxism, so it is not surprising that the doctrine's main technical application to international economics is to the terms of trade. Since some countries are more powerful than others, the terms of trade *must* be exploitative.

5

There appear to be an orthodox and an unorthodox Marxist explanation of this so-called *non-equivalent exchange* under capitalism. The orthodox version is conveniently set out by Łychowski, following Marx. In ancient times, he begins, there was mainly subsistence production and 'the equivalent form of value (the value of the commodity in which the value of another commodity exchanged for it expressed itself in direct exchange) existed still in a simple and undeveloped form'. Owing to the irregularity of barter, equivalent forms of value were very variable and sharp traders like the Phoenicians were in an excellent position to cheat. They did so on a grand scale, and only through this cheating was there non-equivalent exchange.[1]

Later:

In every country a certain average intensity of labor reigns, below which labor in the production of any commodity uses up more time than is socially necessary, and on that account it is not counted as labor of normal quality. . . . The average intensity of labor varies from country to country: here it is greater, there less. These national averages thus form a scale, in which the unit of measurement is the average unit of universal labor. So more intensive national labor produces more value in comparison with less intensive, which expresses itself in a larger money sum (Marx, *Kapital*, Dietz Verlag, 1952, I/586). . . . The same truth can be expressed differently, namely that *the same international values express on the world market different inputs of labor*, in accordance with their intensity. . . .

Marx, speaking of trade between more and less industrially developed countries, established that truth in the following words: 'In the measure in which the labor of the advanced country is paid as labor of higher specific weight, the rate of profit rises, while labor which is not paid as of high quality, is sold as just labor. This same relation can be found in a country to which goods are exported and from which they are imported: namely that *it gives more embodied labor in natura than it receives*, but at the same time it gets the goods cheaper than it could have produced them itself' (*Kapital*, III/xiv/5).

In these remarks of Marx are contained the whole inner substance of international trade in the period of free-trade capitalism. We shall try to draw from them the following conclusions.

    1. Capitalist trade in the free-trade era consists *per se*—even where it is not

[1] Łychowski, *Handel Międzynarodowy*, I, 9–10.

accompanied by capital export—in the exploitation of the unindustrialized by the industrialized country, an exploitation based on the purchase by the latter of a *greater quantity of labor* in the former, than *at that same price* the capitalist country gives in exchange.

2. On the other hand, in so far as ... that trade is accompanied by the export of capital, then the exploitation is doubled. For not only does the industrial country get out of the backward country 'more embodied labor in return', *but in addition it transfers to itself a part of the surplus value* produced with the help of its capital *by the labor of the population of the backward country.*[1]

'Intensity', 'quality' and 'specific weight' are awkward expressions that Marx nowhere defines. But if we read further on in this passage we find that he must mean intellectual and physical effort, which he seems to have thought to increase with economic progress. He then collects himself and remembers the effects of capital and technology, thus:

But the law of value is still more greatly modified in its international application by the fact that more *productive* national labor also counts as more intensive, so that often the more productive country is not forced by competition to lower the sale prices of its goods down to their values.[2]

It is fair to say, incidentally, that this passage contains the whole of Ricardo, who himself tried to explain non-equivalent exchange, but without reference to exploitation. It would therefore have been orthodox to use comparative costs. But Łychowski characteristically omits it, and we have had to wait for Kohlmey to take this step, in 1962 (see Section 11).

Be that as it may, we here hit directly upon the most fundamental of all the many flaws of the labor theory of value: its basic unit is admitted to vary in quality, but the variations are nowhere explained or even described. If I understand Marx correctly, he is saying that there is an international hierarchy of labor intensity, and that the bottommost 'simple abstract undifferentiated labor', which receives only its subsistence and on which the theory of value rests, is mostly to be found in UDCs. More 'intense' labor is paid more. But there is essentially only one currency in the world: gold.[3] Now price, as opposed to value, rests simply on cost, not labor time.[4] It follows that the prices of ACC exports are higher to the extent that they have to cover these higher wages. In this way the UDCs pay for the high wages embodied in ACC exports: their gold buys few labor-hours. But the ACCs pay out the same amount of gold for

[1] Ibid., pp. 42–44. Italics and references to *Das Kapital* are Łychowski's.
[2] *Das Kapital*, Dietz Verlag, 1952, I/586 sqq.
[3] Cf. the title quotation to Chapter VI here.
[4] Karl Marx, *Das Kapital*, Chapter III, Section 9.

the product of many labor-hours. Note that unless we posit higher wages in ACCs the argument breaks down. For if labor in ACCs continues to be paid at subsistence level technical progress there simply shifts the terms of trade in favor of UDCs. Their exports buy more goods, and the same amount of ACC labor as before. In modern Western parlance, A is guilty of non-equivalent exchange with B when the double factor terms of trade move in A's favor, even though the single factor terms of trade may move in favor of both parties, and the commodity terms in favor of B.

It is possible, indeed highly probable, that another student of Marx would interpret these passages differently.[1] But it is dangerous, and often unprofitable, to move from what a historic figure actually said to 'what he really meant'. Whatever he precisely meant, the doctrine of non-equivalent exchange is impossibly stupid. It implies that everybody, wherever he lives, is exploiting everyone else, wherever he lives, who gets lower real wages so long as there is trade between them. If there is no trade both parties are worse off, but there is no exploitation. Non-exploitative trade between such parties, whether they live in the same or in different countries, means that prices are so fixed as to ensure equal real wages. They will not, of course, be fixed like this except by planning, national or international as the case may be; for if a rich country satisfies part of its demand for a product by imports from a poor country, part by its own more efficient production, it must in order to avoid exploitation pay at two different prices. The doctrine also implies that it pays a poor country to arrange to be exploited, i.e., to engage in international trade. It further follows that the more efficient Soviet-type economies (STEs) are exploiting the less efficient ones, and the UDCs, if they trade at world prices—which they do (cf. Section 10 below).

It is no doubt for all these reasons that we hear so little nowadays about non-equivalent exchange. But in the 'late classical period' of Marxism—say up to 1954—this doctrine was still part of the canon. How used Communist authors to handle this hot potato, especially the fact that STEs use world prices between themselves? Łychowski simply skirts the problem. Indeed, it would require an attentive and suspicious reader to extract from his text that the STEs do use world prices; in the far-off days of 1954 it was still 'not done' to admit this fact[2]:

[1] I am indebted here to Dr. Murray Wolfson, who is not, however, responsible for the text.
[2] Prof. Bialer confirms what is evident from the silence of the literature; the fact was not spoken of in Warsaw University seminars on foreign trade.

The level of so-called world prices serves the formation of prices in the mutual exchanges of these countries merely for orientation. Criticizing in his last work a certain proposal to establish prices of grain and cotton in internal Soviet trade Stalin pointed among other things to the fact that 'cotton is in general much dearer than grain, for which fact there witness *also* [Łychowski's italics] the prices of cotton and grain on the world market' [Joseph Stalin, *Economic Problems of Socialism in the USSR* (Moscow, 1952)]. So also in the agreements establishing prices in exchanges between the countries of socialism and democracy, 'world' prices play in a certain measure the role of one of the indicators, whereas the proper basis of price formation (and of the relative prices of the articles exchanged) is the 'desire to arrive at mutual aid and to attain on both sides an expansion of the economy' that guides each country of this type. . . .

'The trade of the USSR'—writes the Soviet author I. Ivanov [I. Ivanov, *Vneshnyaya Torgovlya SSSR* (10/1952)]—'with the people's democracies is concluded on the basis of uniform conditions of delivery, according to uniform fair prices fixed for a long period. In the trade of democratic countries the possibility of nonequivalent exchange is excluded. This trade is carried out according to long-term agreements which guarantee to a country for considerable periods the machines . . . necessary for its economic development, and guarantee the disposal of its production. . . .'[1]

Yet all this time detailed agreements were being signed, wholly dependent on world prices, like the one quoted in Chapter IX, Section 18.

6

So much for the official doctrine. But as usual the Yugoslavs had their home-made version. This was produced by their Minister of Foreign Trade during the Tito-Stalin split, Mr. Popović.[2] He proves Tito's case against Stalin as a trading partner out of *Das Kapital*. Now as Marx so rightly said, although he did not know he was saying it, the labor theory of value is wholly false. It does not even explain the stable average prices of particular commodities in a given state of the arts. Mr. Popović quotes his celebrated self-destruction in *Kapital*:

The organic composition of the capital invested in different branches of production[3] differs; so these capitals produce very different quantities of surplus value. Therefore, the rates of profit[4] that rule in the various branches of industry are

---

[1] Łychowski, *Zagadnienia . . .*, pp. 457–8.

[2] Milentije Popović, *Über die wirtschaftlichen Beziehungen zwischen sozialistischen Staaten* (Mainz, 1950).

[3] In technically backward branches, says Marx—who identifies capital-intensity with technical progress—most capital is employed in living labor (V), little sunk in machinery, buildings or raw materials (C). But since only labor produces surplus value (M), and the rate of surplus value per laborer (M/V) is constant throughout the economy, it follows that the backward branches produce more surplus value.—P.J.D.W.

[4] Profit in Marx is surplus value divided by total capital employed [M/(C + V)].—P.J.D.W.

originally very different. These different rates of profit are equated by competition into a single general rate of profit, which is the average of all these different rates. The profit that accrues to a capital of given size in accordance with this general rate is called the average profit. . . . Although the capitalists of the various production branches recoup in the sale of their commodities the capital values used up in the production of these commodities, they do not cash the surplus value produced in their own branch during the output of these commodities, but only so much surplus value and therefore profit as falls to the lot of each aliquot part of the total capital out of the total surplus value and total profit produced by society's total capital in all production branches taken together.[1]

Now this passage gives about the only explanation a Marxist can give of why the profit rate is in fact everywhere nearly equal; competition makes it so. But this admitted fact is completely incompatible with the statement that living labor is the only source of value in general and profit in particular. For then the more labor-intensive the enterprise the more profitable it must be. The result is that the labor theory of value can only be saved in one of two ways: to allow that surplus value per labor-day is not the same in all branches of production, or to make the theory purely macro-economic and use it only to explain the national total of surplus value. In each case the theory ceases altogether to explain individual prices.

We need not here speak of all the other objections to the labor theory of value: its incapacity to account for monopoly, land rent, wage differentials, or interest; its confusion of the average with the margin, etc. Enough that at least this particular objection to it was recognized, in so devastating a fashion, by Marx, as indeed it had previously been by Ricardo.[2] Engels gave the matter great publicity,[3] and the above passage was published by him, as *the* solution to the problem, from the unfinished manuscript Marx had left. Most Marxists in official positions have sheered away from this problem; indeed, the labor theory of value hardly claims their attention at all now, even apart from this particular embarrassment.

Mr. Popović, however, has excellent reasons for dragging out the skeleton. It serves him as a basis for a terms-of-trade theory the extremism of which would make Mr. Prebisch turn pale. Popović continues in his own words:

Under the conditions of a capitalist economy then not only is labor exploited by capital. In addition to this basic form of exploitation an extra profit is extracted from backward production branches for the benefit of more advanced branches. . . .

[1] Marx, op. cit., Book III, Chapter XII.
[2] Who for exactly the same reason retreated at the end of his life from any belief in the labor theory: Marion Bowley, *Nassau Senior* (London, 1937), pp. 81–5.
[3] Karl Popper, *The Open Society and Its Enemies* (Princeton, N.J., 1950), II, p. 20.

This is wholly valid also for the formation of the world average profit and the world market prices. . . . From these national prices and on the basis of world competition the world average profit and the world price are formed on the world market in mutual competition. Only on the basis of a world price formed in this way is it decided how great the share shall be in the world profit that goes to each competing producer (i.e., each single national economy). . . . On the world market come commodities from countries with different national organic compositions of capital, i.e., countries of different technical equipment and economic development. So those countries in which the organic composition of capital exceeds the world average at the time . . . draw an extra profit at the expense of those where the composition is lower. . . . Capitalist relations in the world economy not only have degraded a whole series of countries to backwardness and kept them there, but make this disproportion worse.[1]

Thus each country ought to retain its surplus value, reckoning to itself the world rate of surplus value and the local number of workers. This means an immense transfer of surplus value to UDCs (among which Popović reckons his own country), where capital has not yet ousted labor. The crucial error in all this is evident equally to both a Marxist and an orthodox economist: the rate of profit is equalized only by competition, i.e., by the free flow of capital. But capital does not flow freely between nations, and most particularly it did not do so between Yugoslavia and other nations in 1939–49. The Popović corollary, as we may call it, to *Das Kapital*, III, Chapter XII, applies only to areas like, say, the sterling or franc areas, which really are one capital market. Therefore, confining ourselves now to the Marxist analysis, there is a shortage of capital in the Yugoslavia of 1949, even by Soviet standards. So production is extremely labor-intensive, which might indicate that surplus value is generated in immense quantities (and appropriated, of course, by the state). But not so, since productivity is also very low, and surplus value, of course, is the difference between productivity and subsistence. It is, indeed, nowhere stated in Marx, but it is very strictly in accordance with his logic, that the rate of surplus value, which for some mystical reason he made equal all over a given country, does differ from country to country in accordance with its stage of development. After all he explicitly made the rate differ by time as the economy developed; how then not also by place?

It is implicit, then, in Marx that the world rates of both profit and, still more, surplus value are mere statistical abstractions. Therefore things do not exchange according to their labor value across national boundaries, even in principle, except where capital flows freely. It is not our business to inquire why Mr. Popović did not

[1] Op. cit., p. 8.

use Marx' own doctrine of non-equivalent exchange, which would have suited him just as well.

7

Now, in fact, a Ricardian theory of international values would have been forced on Marx had he seriously thought about international trade, and in the quotations given above he himself came very near to it indeed. His doctrine of the differing intensities and productivities of labor, *ad hoc* as it may be, and difficult to reconcile with that of the differing 'organic composition of capital', clearly states the principle of comparative costs in all its Ricardian nakedness: a poor country does better to trade with a rich country, even though it thereby exchanges many labor-hours against a few. If only Marx could have refrained from calling this process exploitative!

It is under the circumstances most unfortunate that Marxists, whose own master stood upon the very threshold of the truth, should dismiss Ricardo so cavalierly. After all, Ricardo faced exactly Marx' problem: he merely was more worried about it and went a little further in the same direction. Nevertheless, Mr. Łychowski, perhaps the best and most comprehensive of these writers, deals with comparative costs in one page, in a four-page discussion of Ricardo.[1] The theory is not explained at all, and its truth or falsehood, let alone its applicability to socialism, are not discussed in one word. The passage ends: 'The whole theory of "comparative costs" therefore arises out of the situation ruling at the beginning of the nineteenth century, in which England was the leader in industrial production: a leadership which Ricardo wanted to fix "for ever".' This is the result of the disastrous Marxist habit of seeing everything in political and subjective terms, as if there were no such thing as social *science*. What the author undoubtedly has in mind is not international trade in general, but the exchange of manufactures with raw materials in particular. This, as we shall see in Section 9 below, he knows *a priori* to be disadvantageous to colonies.[2]

We should deal here proleptically with the objection that 'comparative costs isn't dynamic'. Of course it is not. What it is, is

---

[1] Łychowski, *Zagadnienia . . .*, pp. 54–8. The book has 560 pages.
[2] Cf. ibid., p. 458. As late as 1957 the very influential Czechoslovak economist Cerniansky, the doyen of Marxist theorists in this field, dismissed Ricardo in exactly the same way (Pryor in *Soviet Studies*, July 1962, p. 50).

something to dynamize; where 'dynamize' means 'make more complicated', 'bring nearer to reality', or 'diminish the *ceteris paribus* clause of'. We should thank heaven for a static theory, correct on its own assumptions, that may safely be dynamized by varying those assumptions; and not hanker after some rubbish or other that, making no sense as it stands, *a fortiori* makes less sense when complications are introduced. The serious student should have no patience with the confusion between 'static' and 'wrong'.

8

The doctrine of non-equivalent exchange has one important practical conclusion, whether we use Marx' or Popović's argument: Inter-STE trade must not be based on world market prices *but upon such prices as will eventually everywhere equalize real wages* (or for that matter wages plus surplus value). Naturally Łychowski dare not draw this conclusion, since in 1954 Poland is still a satellite; and perhaps anyway as a moderately advanced country Poland might not wish it to be drawn. But Popović draws it most gleefully; indeed, he claims that Yugoslavia treated Albania in this manner before the split.[1] To ask for such prices is effectually to ask for enormous subsidies—only, of course, he would not call them by that word, since his whole claim is that Yugoslavia was subsidizing the more advanced STEs. It seems irrelevant to him that productivity levels differ from country to country. For instance, if Bulgaria's exports in 1937 cost her 76.4 million labor-days while her imports cost their producer 27.6 million labor-days, he only comments: 'The appropriation of an extra profit from underdeveloped countries is an economic process that inevitably unfolds itself as a result of capitalist relations on the capitalist world market.'[2]

It is interesting to speculate on what would have happened had this directive been applied. One is reminded of Robert Owen's 'labor exchanges'[3] in which various co-operatives sold products at their labor, not their scarcity, values. They were destroyed, of course, by people flocking in to buy whatever was cheaper than on the open market and by the unsalability of all the rest. It is not to be supposed that Party discipline, applied to sovereign states, would

[1] Op. cit., pp. 57–60. Cf. Chapter XIV here, Table III. The actual prices paid in Soviet-Yugoslav trade were indeed about equal to world prices: *Economist*, April 16, 1949, p. 699.
[2] Ibid., pp. 11–12.
[3] G. D. H. Cole, *A Century of Co-operation* (Manchester, Eng., 1945), pp. 29–31.

have long prevented a similar collapse here. But in Owen's scheme at least each product had one price, according to its average labor cost in many co-operatives; which accords with Marx' later insistence that only 'socially necessary labor-time' determines value. In the Popović scheme, on the other hand, Yugoslavia would have been selling many commodities in competition with other STEs, and having lower productivity in each would have had to enjoy price discrimination in each. Objectively, Popović was not demanding special prices for commodities but for countries. No wonder 'non-equivalent exchange' never became a practical guide to policy![1]

It must certainly not be thought that Popović's extremism was the only opinion in Yugoslavia. Thus Dedijer writes:

> There were people in our country who considered it incorrect for trade between socialist countries to be carried on at world prices, because the underdeveloped country (in this case Yugoslavia) would be an unequal partner, its lower productivity of labor would compel it to give extra profit to the more developed country (in this case the Soviet Union). But none of us objected seriously. . . .[2]

Neither Dedijer nor Popović suggests that the world market price criterion itself was distorted in favor of the USSR.

As we have seen, the Yugoslavs allege that, as the more advanced country, they treated Albania quite differently. I have only found Dedijer's version of this treatment.[3] It is far from clear, but states that both countries sold each other goods at their domestic prices, and that 'the difference in prices' (presumably at the official rate of exchange) was covered by a price-equalization fund fed by a Yugoslav credit. This can only have worked in Albania's favor if the official rate of exchange for the lek was more absurd than that for the dinar—which it presumably was. Similarly, Yugoslavia financed the difference between domestic and foreign prices of Albanian copper sold to third countries.[4] If I have correctly understood these procedures, they were in fact based neither on calculations of the Popović type, nor on Marxist reasoning, but on chance.

---

[1] The Popović argument has much in common with the French proposals to the UN Conference on Trade and Development, 1964 (cf. Michael L. Hoffman in *Lloyds Bank Review*, July, 1954). It is possible that the richer European STEs (DDR and Czechoslovakia) subsidize the poorer ones (Bulgaria and Hungary) through the terms of trade (see below, Chapter IX, Section 23).

[2] Vladimir Dedijer, *Tito Speaks* (London, 1953), p. 276. Cf. p. 310.

[3] Ibid., pp. 310–13.

[4] Dedijer also lists large credits (cf. Table XIV/3 here), gifts and technical aid. He further states that Yugoslav-Albanian mixed companies paid ground rent, unlike the Soviet-Yugoslav ones.

9

So much for the absence of a general theory of international values. But perhaps as important, and certainly of much greater practical influence, has been the Marxian attachment to a particular commodity structure of foreign trade: one ought not to be a net exporter, nor a very great exporter, of raw materials. We deal with the present practice of forcing a particular structure in Chapter VIII. The tradition, however, is very deeply rooted in Marxism and must be examined here. We saw in the footnotes to Section 6 that Marx and all his followers identify technical progress with a rising 'organic composition of capital', i.e. the ratio of capital that employs living labor in each enterprise to the capital employing dead labor, where raw materials are included in the latter. The notion that inventions might save capital was rejected until the most recent times. It fell to Rudolf Hilferding and Otto Bauer[1] to extend this doctrine to international trade. A tariff, they said, or any external event, did good to a country if it brought about more exports and fewer imports with a high organic composition. Imperialism was, and commercial policy should be, directed towards this end.[2]

Now since bought-in materials are dead labor as defined, but also a larger and larger part of costs as we approach the consumer, it would seem to follow that we should export finished goods, not the products of heavy industry. Indeed an economy that lived by buying very expensive imports and re-exporting them with a small dealer's margin would show the highest organic composition of capital. This 'creative extension of Marxism', then, offends against common sense while at the same time failing to prove what it seeks to.

Apart from bad theory the hostility to raw material exports appears to derive from nineteenth-century experience, the transitoriness of which has not been noticed. For in the nineteenth century colonies had little capital, and did export raw materials, so that in fact raw materials were labor-intensive. In return the imperialist powers did send them only manufactures, which were in fact thus more capital-

[1] Quoted here from Hoselitz in *Journal of Political Economy*, 1949, p. 235. But I have not been able to find so much emphasis on the organic composition of capital as Mr. Hoselitz implies in one of his main references: Hilferding's *Finanzkapital*, Vienna, 1910, Ch. 21. Hilferding also uses a parallel, incompatible and quite acceptable line of argument from mere profit maximization.

[2] It is no accident, then, that Engels, who lived well before Hilferding, supported List's policies for Germany. It is even no accident that Marx supported free trade for Britain—Hoselitz, op. cit.

intensive. But this was somewhat in contrast to previous centuries, when the nascent imperialism of Europe exchanged silver against Indian silk and Damascene steel. Moreover, even in the nineteenth century there was also an exchange of manufactures for raw materials among ACCs, but this trade, though greater in volume, was not politically interesting and so did not figure in Marxist economics. The swapping of raw materials for manufactures has thus become completely identified in the Marxist mind with the colony-metropolis relation, and industrialization is without question and in all circumstances the royal road to national sovereignty. Nearly all commercial quarrels between STEs today have their roots in these same doctrines, which are so much taken to be self-evident that they have never to my knowledge been demonstrated or even analysed by Communists.

Now it is obvious that if a country is to be politically sovereign it needs (a) a rounded economy, (b) not too great dependence on foreign trade in general, (c) many markets of about equal size and (d) a large number of exportable commodities, on no one of which it relies too much. But it cannot be inferred that its foreign trade should have any particular commodity structure. Such wholly sovereign ACCs as Australia and Canada, even very nearly the United States, violate the Marxist canon. One would not wish to call Hong Kong, on the other hand, an even potentially sovereign power; indeed, by the 1960s, raw material exports have become almost uncharacteristic of UDCs. How often must the Indian government sigh for the old days when it had raw material surpluses! How very much more independent it would be if it still had them! How great a diplomatic weapon is the United States wheat surplus!— and specifically when it is offered to UDCs, which should by Marxist theory not be requiring wheat but machinery. In fact, however, it is easier to industrialize India than to feed her. Communism has even presented us with the remarkable spectacle of an industrialized country running into trouble by over-concentration on one export (Czechoslovakia, machinery, 1962-63).[1]

This whole part of the Marxist political economy is then an illegitimate generalization from the nineteenth century. Historically, it was inevitable that the imperialism of that epoch should rest upon colonial exports of raw materials: what else could colonies export, when industrialization was still new in the world as a whole? There is no such inevitability today, nor are extractive industries within ACCs

[1] For a strictly economic analysis cf. Chapter V, Section 12, and Chapter VIII, Section 15.

less capital-intensive than manufactures—should that be an advantage in the first place. Modern imperialism and neo-colonialism, whether practiced by ACCs or STEs, rest upon no particular commodity structure of trade.

10

We have not heard the last of these doctrines, even though economic rationality has begun seriously to emasculate Marxist thought. 'Structure snobbery' is still rampant in the world, and in many versions independent of the strict Marxist version of non-equivalent exchange (Chapter VIII, below). As to this latter doctrine, even though Popović may have been the last Marxist actually to believe it (and the first to use it), it is too good a stick in the hands of a poor country ever to be formally thrown away. The Rumanians have recently revived it, and similar doctrines are constantly preached by UDCs. The whole Prebisch doctrine of the terms of trade is very similar to that of non-equivalent exchange (cf. Chapter VIII, Section 6). It does, however, at least admit the validity of comparative-cost theory, and so is a great deal more sophisticated than the Marxist version that may or may not have influenced it.

In the same way, from their published documents, it seems that the Chinese never use the strict argument from non-equivalent exchange against the Russians. There is, however, a great lag between what STEs do amongst each other and what they say about the actions of ACCs. Here old stereotypes and rhetoric prevail. If any one thing is the *raison d'être* of Communism it is the notion that the 'exploitation of man by man' persists inevitably under capitalism. It must do so not only internally, upon the labor market, but also externally, between ACCs and UDCs. It is not too much to say that if this belief could be destroyed the Cold War would come to an end.

The doctrine of non-equivalent exchange continues therefore to flourish in this field, even though STE-UDC trade is conducted at world prices. Out of many quotations I select two:

Foreign trade is an important source of enrichment by industrially developed countries and of their monopolies on the account of nonequivalent exchange with economically less developed countries.[1]

The fundamental point of the theory of 'comparative cost' does not withstand criticism from the standpoint of the formation of international value. As is well known, the development of a world market brings about the formation of a single

[1] V. Panov, *Voprosy Ekonomiki*, March, 1963.

international value around which the prices at which commodities are sold on the world market fluctuate. Under capitalism and particularly under imperialism international values lead to non-equivalent exchange when those countries having production cost lower than the international value, sell their commodities at a price higher than their national value, while less developed countries having a labor productivity below the average, sell their commodities at a price lower than their national value.[1]

II

In contrast the STEs need among themselves rational criteria, not convenient propaganda. They were particularly hampered by the peculiar sort of heavy-industry autarky imposed on them by Stalin, who did not see that several STEs living in pretended amity needed a quite different attitude to foreign trade from that of the solitary, threatened, pre-war USSR. Autarky itself we postpone until Chapter XV. Suffice it here that the cosmopolitan theorists Marx and Engels, and the cosmopolitan practitioners Lenin and Trotsky, had no place for autarky (cf. Section 12 below). Empirically necessary or not, it was due to Stalin alone, and the weight of Marxist cosmopolitanism was certain to break it down after he died.

The demand that each small STE set up its own many-sided heavy industry was a particularly irrational form of autarky, and it was this that set off the Hungarian protest of 1954. In that year Imre Nagy, the premier of the first liberal Communist government since 1928, denounced autarky.[2] He was supported by the celebrated article of Liska and Máriás,[3] which gave theoretical underpinning to the attack on autarky by recognizing the principle of comparative costs. The authors had the great good luck that Ricardo himself had believed in the labor theory of value, and thus expressed himself in quasi-Marxist terms. So the step forward that they were able to make was not wholly heterodox.

All the sophisticated criteria for foreign trade came into being after this article, and as we see in Chapter VII, Section 7 they mostly compare the export directly with the import-substitute which is its true opportunity cost. This is of course very precisely Ricardo's achievement, and the true importance of the law of comparative costs. From denying this law the Communists have swung right

---

[1] V. G. Solodovnikov, *Burzhuazniye Teorii i Problemy Ekonomicheskogo Razvitiya Slabo-sazvitykh Stran* (Moscow, 1961), pp. 38 sqq.

[2] *For a Lasting Peace, For a People's Democracy* (Bucharest, July 17, 1953). Nagy's first premiership (1953–55) is not to be confused with his second, during the 1956 revolution.

[3] Tibor Liska and Antal Máriás in *Közgazdasagi Szemle* (1/1954). For English extracts, see UN Economic Commission for Europe, *Economic Survey of Europe in* 1954 (Geneva, 1955).

round to using it consciously, whereas in a free market it may be ignored because it will be obeyed anyhow.

Liska and Máriás did not get off scot-free, of course. In late 1955, after Nagy had fallen, a counter-attacker delivered himself thus: 'The socialist market is an *organized* market; this fundamentally excludes the validity of the principle of comparative cost on the new world market. The principle of comparative cost can be valid only in the framework of the anarchy of production.'[1]

A longer and more learned, though technically much inferior, incorporation of comparative costs into Marxism is presented by Günther Kohlmey.[2] Mr. Kohlmey is a perfectly orthodox Marxist, to whom I owe many of the *Marx-zitate* which embellish this chapter. It is impressive with what ease he can show that Marx, in a few *obiter dicta* reproduced here, actually accepted Ricardo. In addition to those quoted above, this one is particularly impressive:

Even Ricardo's theory contemplates—what Say does not notice—that three labor-days in one country can be exchanged against one in another. The law of value undergoes substantial modifications at this point. Or as inside a country qualified labor, complicated labor, is related to unqualified and simple labor, so can the labor-days of different countries be related. In this case the richer country exploits the poorer, even when the latter gains by the exchange, as J. St. Mill has also explained in his 'Some Unsettled Questions'.[3]

Łychowski's dismissal of comparative costs appears then to be a piece of Vulgar Marxism from the Stalinist period. That leaves, however, most of the *damnosa hereditas* intact. Dr. Kohlmey is innocent of marginalism, and operates with a world value that is a weighted average of national values. The notion of exploitation, too, dies hard. Thus Kohlmey quotes Marx as above on the benefits of being exploited, and then explains Ricardo's doctrine of comparative costs at approving length, with an example. His least productive country emerges, like the others, richer from trade. But Kohlmey has so arranged his arithmetic that it benefits least, and then says (op. cit., p. 49): 'But notice that the relative advantages are usually different. In general the less productive national economies should (*dürften*) gain least.' He attempts absolutely no proof of this proposition.

But 'comparative costs' is a mere corollary of general capitalist economic principles. Marxists, with their historicist bias, have

---

[1] T. Kiss, *Közgazdasagi Szemle*, 6/1957, quoted here from Bela Balassa, *The Hungarian Experience in Economic Planning* (New Haven, Conn., 1959), p. 265. On the whole genesis of foreign trade criteria cf. Pryor, op. cit. 1962.

[2] Op. cit. It is interesting that in his earlier book on foreign trade the author avoids this problem altogether: *Der Demokratische Weltmarkt*, (East Berlin, 1956).

[3] Karl Marx, *Theorien uber den Mehrwert* (Dietz, Berlin, 1956), Volume 3, pp. 279 sqq.

always tended to recognize the validity of those principles for capitalism, and Mr. Kiss (above) even extends this toleration to comparative costs. How about inter-STE trade? Would the principle apply there too? We face here the ideological question: is inter-STE trade 'commodity turnover'? In 'commodity turnover' the seller legally owns and freely disposes of the product,[1] being subject to no superior socialist authority. This is, of course, ideologically inferior, and would not be tolerated in, indeed is excluded by definition from, transactions within the nationalized sector of a single STE. These are 'product exchanges': the output is simply transferred to its planned recipient under order, and the producer—whom we must not now call seller—receives accounting money in return. Indeed, under Full Communism he will receive nothing in return. In any case neither party, but the state or society as a whole, owns the product.[2]

To put it another way, how far does the law of value operate between socialist countries? The 'law of value' is seldom defined by Marxists, doubtless because of the embarrassing fact that it refers to actual prices, which on their own admission do not correspond to unit labor values. But they evidently use it to mean perfect competition: profit maximization, free entry, many sellers and buyers, perfect information, freely-formed prices. All of this they hold, in defiance of Yugoslav experience, to be possible only when the means of production are privately owned. 'Imperialism', i.e., the tendency to monopoly,[3] itself interferes with the 'law of value'. Is the inter-STE market simply a further instance of still greater interference or is it something else?

Note the metaphysical preoccupation with ownership, and the implication that somehow resource allocation questions should be solved not merely by different methods but with different results under socialism. Behind the verbiage, however, the orthodox answer has been substantially correct: the law of value operates on the inter-STE market, but not in a regulatory way. It is hemmed in by central planning.[4] Specifically, 'socialist brotherhood' prevents

---

[1] P. J. D. Wiles, The Political Economy of Communism (Cambridge, Mass., 1962), Chapter 3.

[2] I give here the orthodox position. 'Commodity turnover under Socialism' has recently become ideologically fashionable.

[3] Nothing in Marxism strictly corresponds to the Western 'imperfect competition'. Polypolistic imperfections are not dignified by a special phrase, indeed, not spoken of. The word 'monopoly' has lost all memory of the original Greek, and simply means a large business. The 'competition of monopolies' thus means our 'oligopoly'. 'Imperialism', in so far as it has any strict economic meaning, is international oligopoly.

[4] This was Stalin's answer, op. cit. Cf. Łychowski, Zagadnienia..., pp. 456–7; Kohlmey, ... Weltmarkt..., pp. 203–9; Klinkmüller and Ruban, ... Zusammenarbeit..., pp. 87–90.

STEs from exploiting market conditions against each other, and the mere fact that they are so few in number makes the market very imperfect.

Thus the ideology was in tune with the facts, but the facts themselves were very far from satisfactory. Nor did the language used permit them to be described in any detail. For as to the actual extent to which the 'law of value' operates, one can only say: read this book; the thing is not to be summed up in a sentence or a formula. So criticism and reform were extremely difficult to develop except by throwing the ideology over. This is what has happened. For the subsequent, increasingly non-Marxist, development of the Communist theory of international values see Chapter VII, below. Today in Poland and Hungary the subject is almost excessively sophisticated, and even the orthodox Bulgarians are prepared to fly Mr. Tom Kronsjö (Chapter VII, Section 15) to Sofia. The conservative Russians themselves are now able to clothe Ricardo in Aesopian but quite unmistakable language: 'The equality of countries practising exchange, their mutual gain, does not depend on whether the quantity of national labor contained in the commodities exchanged is equal or not. The economic gain, i.e., the economic effect, is determined by the difference between the cost of one's own production of a good and the cost of production of the commodity by exporting which one can obtain the same good.'[1] By 1964, when the author visited Poland a second time, he found it necessary to explain exactly why he was reading Łychowski: 'Ah, you have a *historical* chapter . . . oh well.'

12

Mainly, then, the traditional doctrine broke down over inter-STE trade. One could rub along without a rational allocation theory so long as at least the ideology was in order. In the cruel world market an STE might indeed be exploited, might indeed even be forced to exploit. But it is really too much for one proletarian country to exploit another; but if we do not use world prices what *are* we to do? The tradition—Marx, Engels, Lenin—was silent. Stalin also was silent. It was even doubtful that there ought to be Communist countries other than the USSR. In 1917–23 the Russian Soviet Federal Socialist Republic had spread Communism by annexation, or, strictly, forcible federation. This was the origin of the other

[1] O. Bogomolov, *Voprosy Ekonomiki*, November, 1963.

'Union Republics' in the 'Union of Soviet Socialist Republics'. More or less by design, this federation had stopped short within the boundaries of Tsarist Russia. Then in 1924 Mongolia became the first People's Democracy. To my knowledge, neither her existence as a separate state nor the conduct of trade with her gave rise to any deep ideological ruminations. During World War II, in 1942, Moshe Pijade declared the area of Yugoslavia under his control to be a Soviet Socialist Republic. The compliment was certainly not taken up by Stalin, but such ideas continued to sway the Yugoslav Communist leaders in 1945, and were only abandoned after the split in 1948. In the course of that split Stalin too denounced them as 'primitive and fallacious'.[1] Indeed, already in 1945, faced with unlimited opportunities of annexation, he had only retaken the Baltic states and a few other border areas to all of which the USSR had historic claims.

So when in 1945 the People's Democracies were formed, the ideology of their existence, let alone of trade with them, had to be worked out from scratch. Moreover, it had to be done under Stalin, and at that under the later, more conservative, more paranoid Stalin. Of what he in fact did, nearly every page here is witness. That he permitted any ideological considerations to govern him is unclear. He seems to have proceeded quite empirically.

Truth to tell, Marxism has little to say about 'Socialism'. It analyses capitalism very fully, and then leaps on to 'Communism' (the end-stage we here call Full Communism) about which it has a great deal, though nothing systematic, to say. The popular Western notion that Marx provided no blueprint for after the revolution applies only to the intervening stage of 'Socialism'. Here, precisely, temperament and historical circumstance made Stalin the expert. His main objects seem to have been to preserve separate nation-states and Soviet hegemony over them. This may seem a strange policy, but it had its logic. The desire for Soviet hegemony needs, presumably, no explanation. The refusal to complete it by annexation has several logical motives. It made possible very heavy reparations from ex-enemy satellites. It looked better to outsiders. It made it possible to exploit local patriotism. It kept unreliable elements outside the Soviet borders. It was reversible if it turned out that the USSR had bitten off more than she could chew. It gave the USSR more votes at the United Nations, etc., etc.

[1] Stephen Clissold, *Whirlwind* (London, 1948), pp. 82, 240; Elliot R. Goodman, *The Soviet Design for a World State* (New York, 1960), pp. 328–32.

As to strict economics, wherever we turn in the period 1945–54 we see procedures typical of Stalin but owing almost nothing to Marxism. Exorbitant reparations, mixed companies, various forms of chicanery, the preference for informal pressures over formal imperialism, the refusal to draw up a binding international plan, bilateralism, autarky, the use of world prices—there is no ideology here. It was Popović who addressed himself to those issues as a Marxist; Stalin muddled through; Łychowski had to slide over them.

It might be thought that the doctrine of 'two world markets' was a serious ideological contribution. This was proclaimed by Stalin in 1952,[1] and simply stated that there was now more than one socialist country, so there was a socialist world market. This was separate from the old, capitalist, one not only because of the United States' embargo but mainly because of socialist brotherhood.

I cannot find that this proclamation was an important event in Marxist *Dogmengeschichte*, for all the splash it made. Even though the doctrine was unofficially leaked all over the bloc as early as 1951,[2] it was still a mere description of *faits* long *accomplis* and very obvious. Stalin placed it in the context of a prediction of further imperialist wars among capitalist states—which he based in part on the shrinkage of the world market available to them. We may also speculate that the doctrine finally sanctified the existence of separate states under socialism, and—perhaps through absence of mind—served to cut these states off from the UDCs, which belonged to the first world market. But neither in this nor in any other section of his short last work had Stalin any serious pronouncement on trade between STEs. Nor does he at all insist on price differences between the two markets. Rather the contrary, as Łychowski's quotation from him (above, Section 5) shows, he expects prices to be about the same.

13

Marxist tradition is far more explicit and far less easy to shrug off when we turn to eschatology: the moneyless, egalitarian, uniform, highly productive, stateless society of Full Communism. As I have explained elsewhere,[3] there remains in this society a single, central, voluntary 'social organization' which efficiently plans everything. It is not the 'state', since it has no police power, but through it the perfectly rational and perfectly unanimous citizenry distribute themselves among their tasks, and allocate directly to each other the

---

[1] Op. cit., p. 5. [3] Wiles, op. cit., Chapter XVII.
[2] By the circulation of a draft of Stalin's *Economic Problems* . . . . I owe this and much other information to Mr. Seweryn Bialer, whom I interviewed in March, 1965.

fruits of their labors: i.e., there is no longer a retail market or a labor market; the consumer and the worker are inside the system. How do separate countries fit into this? There is no doubt at all that under Full Communism they must disappear. It is, of course, obvious that all capitalist countries must disappear, for until they do so Communist countries require armaments and a state machine. But it is scarcely less important to get rid of separate Communist countries. It has not to my knowledge been discussed among Marxists, but it would seem a plausible and orthodox extension of the doctrine to say that a frontier as such entails a state machine.

World government, then, or rather world not-quite-government, is the end-state of humanity. This follows not only from the political and economic eschatology but also from the general Communist overestimate of classes and incomprehension of nationalism. The myths that 'the workers have no fatherland', or that 'the Soviet Union is the workers' fatherland', or that 'peaceful co-existence is a higher form of class struggle', are extremely deeply rooted in the Communist psyche. Not Yugoslavia, not Albania, not Poland, not Hungary, not Rumania, perhaps not even China has caused this myth seriously to be questioned. These incidents are all temporary deviations from the path of history, which however crookedly leads us to the Brotherhood of Man.[1]

Full Communism, then, is by definition universal. As Soviet propagandists pointed out in 1958, each particular Chinese People's Commune can stop paying money and distribute equal wages in kind; but that is not Full Communism since they have to trade, and this trade must be centrally planned by something above them. It follows that nearly all, or as the present writer holds,[2] all the domestic production of the Communes must also be centrally planned. So the nature of this 'something above them', and the degree to which it penetrates the Commune's domestic affairs, are more important for Full Communism than the abolition of money in the villages. Moreover, and equally important, independent Communes do not ensure that equality of living standard and uniformity of social environment that is a *sine qua non* for Full Communism.

---

[1] Among the non-economic features of world-wide Full Communism is that there is one language, an amalgam of all major world languages (Goodman, op. cit., Chapter 9). This book is an indispensable source for the international aspects of Full Communism generally. Not only Communist economists, of course, have seen world government as the end-state of humanity. Implicitly Adam Smith did so, and the free traders that followed him. No less remarkably, and much more explicitly, so did List (*Das nationale System der politischen Oekonomie* [Stuttgart, 1841]). Among non-economists, the idea was very widespread during the Enlightenment.   [2] See Chapter XI here.

The anti-Chinese People's Commune arguments of 1958 are thus a paradigm for anti-country arguments in general. A country is like a Commune: its independence leads to (a) international inequality and (b) 'commodity turnover' between states, both of them undesirable.

Postscript to section 6, p. 16

The Chinese have never used the argument of non-equivalent exchange, it seems. Evidently not wishing to disturb trade negotiations, they made no discoverable adverse comment until in 1964 Mao Tse-tung himself condemned Soviet trading practices. Their attacks since then have been sharp but not ideological. USSR is merely a 'bully,' a 'capitalist' and a 'monopolist' in its dealings with other STEs.[1] Indeed it charges *above* world market prices, like a monopolist—with the clear implication that such prices would have been all right. But Che Guevara, forced to take Cuba back to producing sugar, was a better Marxist for all his wild, personalist courage; he used very precisely the language of non-equivalent exchange against USSR.[2]

[1] *Peking Review*, May 8 and November 27, 1964. In one glorious instance a Chinese writer uses the work of—presumably—Horst Mendershausen himself, exaggerations and all, and refers to the RAND Corporation as 'an institute abroad' (New China News Agency May 8, 1967 = SCMP 3937, p. 37).

[2] *Hoy*, Havana, February 26, 1965. Cf. Michael Kaser, *Comecon* (2nd ed., Oxford 1967), p. 218.

CHAPTER II

INSTITUTIONS AND DEFINITIONS

I

IT is appropriate at this point, where the non-Marxist part of our work begins, to belabor the reader with most of the theoretical and institutional definitions we shall use. This chapter is principally aimed at the non-Sovietologist; who should be warned that we are describing the classical system, before the recent changes.

A *Soviet-type economy* (STE) may for most purposes be imagined as one in which an immense public corporation monopolizes all productive activity. It sells its consumer goods and services in shops for money, charging what prices it pleases, making here a profit and there a loss; for it happens not to be a 'rational' corporation, interested either in maximizing its profits or in following 'welfare' rules. It makes its own investment goods, financing them largely out of the profit margin on its consumer goods. Thus, investment finance is almost entirely 'ploughback', though there is also a little borrowing from the public. The corporation pays wages, which are thus the principal source of finance for consumption; and workers are as free to change jobs as consumers are to choose between shops and goods. Thus there is at each end *worker's choice* and *consumer's choice*, but neither party is *sovereign*, except, of course, in the trivial sense of being able freely to adapt itself to conditions he cannot alter. True sovereignty rests with the corporation, in the sense that it invests exactly as it pleases, and makes pretty much what consumer goods it pleases, varying its profit rate to get the stuff sold. It also obtains pretty much the employment pattern it pleases, varying its wage-rates to that end. There is formally no direction of labor, but in practice it is fairly common.

The treasury of the corporation is identical with the government's ministry of finance. So armaments can be assimilated to the status of investment goods. The varying profit rates on consumer goods might just as well be called indirect taxes, and, in fact, the major part is called the turnover tax, which, unlike such taxes in other countries, is set according to the 'method of differences': i.e., it is the *ex post* difference between the average cost of a product and the price that will clear the market for the quantity the corporation happens to have decided to make. For the corporation likes to clear the market, or at least to clear its stocks. So if stocks pile up it reduces its price with only moderate delay. But if the price is too low and a queue forms there will be more delay in raising it, as the corporation cares little about such trivial inconveniences; after all, they affect its customers, not itself. After deducting the turnover tax, the remainder of the profit is called profit; and in principle it all flows, along with the amortization quotas, into the central treasury. In practice, however, the privilege is granted of withholding some of both at the point where they are earned.

Capital, unlike labor, is invariably 'directed', i.e., allocated by the treasury to the points it designates. It must be amortized. Otherwise in principle no charge is made for the use of capital, since there is only one large corporation and it is extremely centralized. Necessity, however, has dictated many exceptions to this (see Chapter III). Land is entirely 'directed', and there is no rent for it.

The ordinary unit of production is still called the enterprise. However, it is not an independent firm but rather a branch establishment. It has in principle no inviolable rights, and in the incorrigible informality of the system, whatever rights the law temporarily assures it are very commonly taken away *ad hoc*, by administrative fiat. Its outputs and inputs, the enterprises to which it shall sell and from which it shall buy, and all the relevant prices and techniques, are supposed to be set by the central plan in the form of *targets*. But since this task is superhuman, the 'corporation HQ' only sets a very general plan. The targets are handed down in very broad categories, which are broken down into further detail by intermediate planning *bodies*. In this sense 'body' is a technical term in this book. Mainly, Communist 'bodies' have been either ministries, organized on the 'production' principle, or *Sovnarkhozy*, organized on the

'territorial' principle. The former sit in the capital city and administer enterprises producing a particular product, wherever located.
The latter sit in provincial centres and administer all enterprises in
the area, whatever they produce. The independent rights of 'bodies'
are, of course, very ill defined. Some fine detail in the plan is left
to the enterprise itself (see Section 3, below, on 'indicators').

2

The STE is thus a *command economy*. The definition of this is that
the enterprise receives orders and does not bargain, since it is a
branch establishment, not a firm. But in the STE the enterprise is
roughly the limit of the command system. Another type of command economy is the promised Utopia of the Communist future,
Full Communism. In this the consumer and the worker come under
the umbrella of the central plan, i.e., are also commanded; and
money ceases to be used. The whole economy is like one family or
monastery.

The principal use of money in the STE has already been given:
to persuade (not command) the worker to work where he is wanted
and the consumer to consume what has been produced. This is
active money. However, money is also used as a unit of account
between the branches of the great corporation. Now, as we have
seen, these transactions are in principle subject exclusively to central
command. Could these commands be expressed in sufficient detail
they might just as well, even for audit purposes, be given in physical
terms, and all prices would be like the fifth wheel in a coach: we
should be dealing with absolutely *passive money*. But such detail is,
to repeat, impossible, and it is convenient to express certain commands in terms of general monetary volumes, with prices, but not
outputs, for the component details. Convenient, but not absolutely
necessary: even the inevitability of such decentralization does not
make money necessary, as other tricks can be thought of and are
used. However, in so far as monetary aggregates are used without
detailed specification, prices do influence inter-enterprise transactions, though mostly in a queer and limited way.

Truth to tell, the survival of money inside the corporation is in
part a historical accident. It had been active throughout the economy
under the NEP (see Glossary), and Stalin held that to abolish it was
Trotskyism. It serves also this purpose, that costs of finished consumer goods can be built up quite naturally, by normal accountancy

as elsewhere, out of wage and raw-material costs all along the line. Each raw material cost is itself, of course, some other enterprise's wage cost, and depreciation and (where charged) interest also enter normally. The enterprise is supposed to account for its actions independently in this queer money, and this is known as *khozraschet*. *Khozraschet* implies, but does not insist upon, the balancing of revenue with outgo; but not the maximization of profit. Thus, to use the language of the next paragraph, loss avoidance is an indicator and a criterion of some importance, but profit is not.

3

A planner is said to be influenced by *criteria*: e.g., micro-rationality, autarky, rapid growth, equality of income, armed might, the development of unpopulated areas, greater capital-intensity, etc., etc. All his principles are called here by this one name, and many of them are perfectly absurd—not only in STEs. Where the center devolves decisions on the enterprise it lays down principles upon which the latter shall proceed, and these are called *indicators*. In a *free market*, profit is the usual, but not the sole, criterion-cum-indicator (we hardly know which to call it) of the sole sovereign body, the enterprise or firm. This remains so in a *regulated market*. This is defined as a market in which the government gives no positive orders, but forbids or taxes a number of things.[1] The initiative remains with the enterprise, which continues to pursue profit. The only difference is that it has been subjected to certain restraints. But the enterprise, or establishment, in a command economy is very different. It has only such initiative as may have been from time to time devolved to it, and even that is governed by the indicators the government has laid down. It cannot choose its own indicators, and profit may or may not be among the ones it is given. Thus in market economies the enterprise has on the whole a single indicator or target, in the command economy very many indeed—and they usually contradict each other.

Profit has yet another function in free and regulated markets: to be an *activator*. It is, indeed, much the most important motive for economic activity under these conditions. But a command economy, as its name implies, is by definition distinguished through the choice of another activator. The prime motive for economic

---

[1] The distinction between prohibition or licensing (physical regulation) and taxes or subsidies (monetary regulation) is interesting but secondary, and does not concern us here.

activity is that the plan is law. A command economy is conceivable in which there is nothing 'in it' for anybody, but the law—or social persuasion of a milder kind—is the sole activator. Indeed, Full Communism is supposed to be like this: what Communists euphemistically call 'material interestedness in production', or, more crudely, human selfishness, disappears. Instead of bonuses, piece-work, and generally differentiated earnings everyone gets an income appropriate to his needs, i.e., an almost equal one, and does what he is told solely because he identifies his own interest with the common interest. There is, of course, no actual law, because the state has withered away. As things are, however, in the present stage, called 'Socialism', the law's commands have to be supplemented by a second activator: plan-fulfillment bonuses. These bonuses are not at all the same thing as profit, except only where profit happens to be the criterion or indicator. In that (practically unimportant) case it is harmless to equate plan-fulfillment bonuses with profit-sharing.

An enterprise's central plan targets and various indicators are likely to point in different directions. In the absence of further instructions, i.e., yet other super-indicators and super-targets, the director then tends to follow his own interest, i.e., maximize his bonus and minimize the danger of prosecution. This will probably mean going bald-headed for one of the plan targets (typically value or weight of output in some broad category), to the neglect of all the other targets (typically input maxima) and indicators (typically details of output). This is simply because the system of activation characteristically attaches greatest material bonus and greatest legal penalty to the single target, over-all output. The broader details of output may or may not figure in the targets, but the finer ones are, of course, always left to the indicators. All these details together are called the *sortament*. Perhaps the principal problem in the length and breadth of an STE is the universal and appalling failure to produce a correct *sortament*.

4

I have defended elsewhere[1] my unashamed and old-fashioned use of the concept *rationality*. It means in this book: doing the things we want done in the cheapest possible way. This phrase could, of course, be interpreted at book length, but the more details one considers the less convinced one is that there is anything obscure or

[1] P. J. D. Wiles, *The Political Economy of Communism*, Chapter V.

misleading, for serious and practical use, in the simple classical notion. There are heavily diminishing returns to refinement. Let us then be bloody, bold and resolute, and confine ourselves to this brief interpretation:

A. 'What we want done' means satisfying the tastes of consumers out of their given incomes, provided these tastes are not self-destructive (alcohol) or dangerous to others (private guns). The ministry of defense is treated as a single consumer. In ordinary practical circumstances when we reallocate resources more or less rationally we do not much affect the distribution of income between all these consumers, say, by altering relative wages. That is to say, 'what we want done' is not much altered by our trying to get it done at lower cost. Our definition of rationality is thus not very circular.

B. Apart from such obvious things as taxing alcohol and licensing private guns, what room does this rationality concept allow the government? It should interfere, say with industrial location or foreign trade, out of defense considerations. It should interfere, in a market economy, to keep employment full; for that is a thing that each individual wants but none can separately ensure. It should interfere wherever the decision-making unit is too small to internalize all the effects of its actions, so that external economies and diseconomies arise to which it is indifferent. Examples of this are the old clichés of factory smoke and land drainage; also such large and complicated matters as the choice between road and rail in suburban transport.

C. Other exercises of planner's sovereignty are irrational. For instance, it is no business of the planner to choose between two consumer goods, in the silence of the above considerations; e.g., between whiskey and gin, or cotton and wool. Such action cannot be shown to produce 'what we want' and is therefore irrational. The same applies to the planner's choice between investment projects, or, once the desirable degree of autarky is obtained, between foreign and domestic trade in particular things.

Micro-rationality is thus hardly a matter for the government. There should be *general* rules against alcohol or imports or present consumption or whatever it is, to establish the macro-rational proportions that the government can defend as being wise policy. This latter phrase, incidentally, is a very important qualification upon government interference with free choice even at the macro-level. For the rest, the consumer knows best 'what we want'. Thus an economy should be of mixed rationality.

5

A completely socialized economy might avoid such planning irrationalities in at least three ways. The first is the *perfect competition* of small socialist enterprises. It is in this general direction that Yugoslavia moves, though her markets remain exceedingly imperfect. This is also Lerner's solution.[1] It is no part of Marx' own vision,[2] and is rightly rejected as unorthodox by all proper Communists. The second is to simulate perfect competition by modern mathematical means: *perfect computation*.[3] Now rationality itself was no part of Marx' own vision; indeed, it is incompatible with the labor theory of value. So again we cannot call perfect computation really Marxist. But at least it is centralized, grandiose and futuristic; therefore, psychologically right. It also makes it possible to abolish, if not prices, then at least money as Marx understood it; which he did most definitely predict and recommend. Also it comes in two handy sizes. One starts, like the existing STE, from money wage-rates in a free labor market and money prices in a free retail market, and ensures that the one great nationalized corporation shall rationally respond to them. The other, like Full Communism, abolishes money at these stages, too, and includes in the direct computations the supply curves of labor and demand curves for goods that lie behind the wage-rates and prices.

Our third possible combination of rationality with socialism is *perfect central adjustment*, the solution recommended by Lange before the war.[4] The center sets all prices and instructs the enterprise to react according to some rule. When the upshot indicates that change is desirable, the center gives orders for adjustments. Thus it attains rationality *à tâtons*, since at all times it is consciously pursuing consumer satisfaction and obeys the Lerner rules to that end. This model, then, like perfect competition, requires money.

The actual STE we have described is best called *imperfect computation*, though it contains strong elements of imperfect central adjustment and even of imperfect competition. The computation, that is, is largely arbitrary and based on a knowledge of consumer wants that is both too little and too late. Under Stalin it did not even

[1] Abba P. Lerner, *The Economics of Control* (New York, 1946).
[2] Wiles, op. cit., Chapter XVIII.
[3] Ibid., Chapter X; L. Smolinski and P. J. D. Wiles, in *Problems of Communism* (November-December, 1963); and see below, Chapter XI.
[4] Oskar Lange, *On the Economic Theory of Socialism* (Minneapolis, Minn., 1948); Wiles, op. cit., Chapter X.

pretend to be trying to satisfy the consumer, not even on the micro-level. The variable turnover tax took up the slack at retail level. Within the 'one great corporation' the passivity of money and the incomplete accounting for costs again made computation imperfect.

6

There are innumerable *practical exceptions* to the model of the STE here propounded. Happily, few of them affect foreign trade, so we may simply list the bigger ones, and thus avert the charge of over-simplification.

A. Most of agriculture is on the cooperative system. The kolkhoz, or in China the People's Commune, is planned in far less detail than the state factory, shop, construction enterprise or, indeed, farm. Only most, not all, of its output is subject to direct command. To some extent the state uses market incentives upon it, and to some extent leaves it free to deal directly with the consumer on a free market. But all agricultural exports and imports pass through the state procurement organs and, therefore, through the command system.

B. Some of agriculture (most of it in Poland) is on the individual peasant system. Little of its output is subject to direct command (except in Poland), much more of it is sold voluntarily or near-voluntarily to the state, and much more again directly to the consumer.

C. Labor is often (usually in China) directed. Indeed, the labor market is only free in the formal economic theory of the system. Although labor turnover is no greater than in advanced capitalist countries, the authorities find this situation unacceptable and constantly try to diminish it. Masses of labor are also extra-legally directed during *ad hoc* campaigns, and some groups are permanently subject to legal direction. Notable among these are those passing out of secondary schools and universities, whose first job is assigned to them for about three years, and kolkhoz members, who acquire membership by birth and may not leave the farm without permission. From the standpoint of Marxist ideology the free labor market is an embarrassment about which the less said the better.

D. There are large black markets in every field; theft and corruption are the order of the day (though perhaps less so in China). These things significantly affect agriculture and residential construction, but probably do not force us to change our model designation. In particular it is much to be doubted if smuggling is as great as in market economies. Corruption may or may not be disfunctional—a

large and neglected subject from which we must regretfully turn aside.
E. The most interesting and promising exception, though not
until 1966 the most practically important, is decentralization. This
does *not* mean a mere geographical shift of the 'bodies' out of the
capital city, as, for instance, Khrushchev's substitution of sovnarkhozy for ministries. It means that enterprises, and reasonably small
enterprises at that, not great amalgamations, have freedom of action.
In other words, where they previously had targets they now have
indicators, and profit bulks larger among these latter. Moreover,
they are no longer strictly held to clients named in the plan, so may
to some extent shop around, i.e., compete. Money becomes, of
course, active in the inter-enterprise sector, prices are made more
rational, and charges are introduced for land and long-term capital.

This movement embraces, with wide individual differences, every
single STE of which I have knowledge, including Albania and
China. Despite its immense future interest and importance, I have
rather neglected it. It may well be that in a few years Sovietological
economics will cease to exist as such, because of the predominance
of market elements in Communist economies. The Soviet economy
would then be no more peculiar than the Yugoslav, which this book
mostly neglects. But as this goes to press, decentralization is more
talked about than practiced. It is easier for a revisionist Communist
professor to publish a splendid new proposal than for him to get
the Minister to act on it. It is easier for his Western colleague to
read his article than to find out what the Minister is doing. Indeed,
does the Minister know? He has innumerable subordinates who do
not necessarily obey him, and there is no official statistical measure
of decentralization. The very records upon which such figures
might be based do not exist.

In any case the central planners' hold on foreign trade is still very
great. Decentralized contact with the outside world is described
where it happens (Chapter XVIII, Section 16), and so is the great
influence of world prices upon the *centralized* price reforms of
Eastern European STEs (Chapter VII). The macro-monetary
consequences of decentralization are touched upon in Chapter III,
Section 12. For the rest I have not speculated upon what may
shortly be.

7

Turning now to international economics, we define a *country* thus:
(*a*) An area within which labor flows *more* freely than across the

boundaries. A country normally but not necessarily has also the following attributes:

(b) It constitutes a sovereign state,[1] with a foreign policy and the political machinery to coerce its own inhabitants.

(c) It has a separate currency, the quantity of which it can, though it may not, control separately from international monetary flows. It therefore has a central bank.[2]

(d) Goods cross the boundaries more easily than labor.[3]

(e) The flow of long-term capital across its boundaries is a little stickier than within them.

I have not found it necessary to make the customary breach with reality and assume that short-term capital is as shy to migrate as labor. A premise so flatly at variance with the facts, and, moreover, directly contradictory to the basis of monetary theory (see c above), could scarcely be called a simplifying one. The ones chosen, however, seem to me to be very realistic. This position may be described as semi-Ricardian. It is surely immune from the root-and-branch criticisms of Williams,[4] which strike seriously only at the assumed international immobility of capital. I note in passing that the Ricardian assumptions are indeed historically relative; but they have become much more true since Ricardo made them, indeed, mainly in the period since Williams attacked them (1929). They did not, indeed, apply to the Hanseatic League, as Williams points out; but then the League operated in an area where there were no countries, and it was perfectly unjust to complain of Ricardo's irrelevance to such a situation. In the early nineteenth century labor was still often more mobile internationally than nationally. But modern countries, especially STEs, exhibit all the characteristics named. We shall not, of course, neglect international movements of labor, but we can safely abstract from them when convenient.

If a country's economic model is not that of an STE it is a *market economy* (ME). MEs are divided into *advanced capitalist countries*

---

[1] As politics looms so large in this book I have been careful to call the area and its population 'country', and the governmental machine 'state' throughout. The word 'nation', implying that the population is in some way homogeneous and patriotic, has been eschewed, except in the slightly pejorative phrase 'nation-state'. 'International' means inter-country or inter-state.

[2] Good examples of countries without a separate currency or central bank are Eire and pre-1955 Cuba. Both were sovereign states, but significantly it was possible to doubt their sovereignty in economic matters, and labor flowed easily to or from the dominant power.

[3] There are, of course, many exceptions. For instance, it is easier to import Italian miners into France than Chianti; and the managers of international firms cross boundaries more easily than their products.

[4] J. H. Williams in *Economic Journal* (1929).

(ACCs) and *underdeveloped countries* (UDCs). This distinction has innumerable practical and theoretical applications, whereas that between underdeveloped and more developed STEs has, in international questions, very few and is not worth emphasizing. The following countries only are neither ACCs, UDCs, nor STEs, and the applicability to them of any sentence is left to the reader's discretion: Yugoslavia, Spain, Greece, Mexico, Argentina, Uruguay, Iceland, South Africa and Portugal. Thus the unclassifiables amount to a mere 7% of all countries.

8

However different their ideology and internal institutions, *STEs still trade like capitalists*. Indeed, more than that: owing to its internal institutional model *the STE more closely resembles a large firm than a country*. These two insights are perhaps the most fundamental of all in understanding the international economics of Communism.[1]

They 'trade like capitalists' in the sense that they operate, among themselves as well as when facing outwards to MEs, on a market, however imperfect (cf. Chapter I, Section 11). When they face MEs, they do so on the world market, and they are no more forced to trade bilaterally than is any large firm trading with any other. Bilateralism between MEs and STEs arose from the currency inconvertibility of the *former* (Chapter XI). But later STEs also insisted on it, seemingly through sheer intellectual error. Between STEs on the other hand the large-enterprise analogy breaks down; there is not one market but a series of bilateral ones, as many as there are pairs of STEs, and each pair conducts what I have elsewhere called an 'advanced higgle',[2] i.e., an immensely complicated bargain between two diversified bureaucracies over many interdependent variables. If the Council for Mutual Economic Assistance (CMEA) were a supra-national central planner then, of course, it would own all the things traded and there would be 'product exchange' (cf. p. 24) among its members. But the CMEA is nothing of the sort (Chapter XII). The prices at which trade is conducted are, it happens, basically those of the capitalist world market (Chapter IX).

As might occur in any irrationally conducted large enterprise, the

---

[1] The two best short accounts of Soviet-type foreign trade are by Franklyn Holzman: in *Comparisons of the United States and Soviet Economies* (U.S.G.P.O., Washington, 1959), Part II, and in Henry Rosovky (ed.), *Essays in Honor of Alexander Gerschenkron* (Harvard, 1965).

[2] *Price, Cost and Output*, 2nd ed., (New York, 1963), p. 26.

branches trade with each other regardless of outside prices, and inter-branch costing is very imperfect. But the STE goes much further. It exports only to import (Chapter XV, Section 13), and is thus, above all, concerned with its foreign currency (valuta) balance. Export-import is thus basically a single venture; producers do not export for their own separate profit, nor do all the ultimate buyers of foreign goods and services import them for that reason. Until recently no one cared about the domestic currency operations of the Ministry of Foreign Trade, either on the macro- or on the micro-level. The domestic macro-balance was often very negative, because while the full domestic price was paid for exports, imports were under-priced. But so long as the valuta balance was in order there was no cause for alarm, and the Treasury happily made up to the ministry its domestic loss.

The whole operation of export-import involves no exchange of foreign for domestic money. The Ministry of Foreign Trade buys exports from exporters and sells imports to importers; its domestic currency balance is made up to it if necessary. It also sells exports to foreigners and buys imports from them; and this balance it must finance by borrowing or lending abroad at short term, just like any ordinary country. The only exchangers of money via the rate of exchange are tourists, diplomats etc.; they do this, of course, with the state bank, not the ministry.

Micro-economically, the breakage of the link between the two currencies is much more serious than tariffs or exchange controls. It means that there need be no relation at all between foreign and domestic prices. Nor did the Marxist governments of STEs, insensitive to all rationality questions, until recently see any reason to re-establish artificially the link that their institutions had broken.

In Soviet parlance, we have been describing the government's foreign-trade monopoly and foreign-currency monopoly. The Soviet textbooks rightly lay great stress on these as the basis of the country's international economic position.

The individual country, then, resembles a single enterprise, not only vis-à-vis its own workers and consumers but also on the international market. General Motors is economically larger than Albania,[1] and doubtless has as much difficulty in knowing what its various branches are up to. Nevertheless, the relation between headquarters and these branches is essentially one of command in

---

[1] Indeed, its industrial production exceeded that of the DDR in 1959: Frederick Pryor, *The Communist Foreign Trade System* (London, 1953), p. 78.

both cases, so that speculation and liquidity preference are ruled out. Moreover, the volume of employment is simply what the government orders it to be, so that movements in aggregate demand, generated by the balance of payments or by anything else, have only monetary, not real, multiplier effects.[1] *Foreign trade, then, is not subject to any Keynesian analysis* (see Chapter III).

This is as much as to say that the government is the only entrepreneur, and is not going to feel doubt about its own intentions to invest in one project, to withhold decision on another project. Nor has it any fear of spontaneous under-consumption, say, a buyer's strike, let alone of one generated by unemployment in the investment sector. It is not that any of these things is absolutely inconceivable; in particular the widely-separated bureaus of an inefficient, non-Communist STE (could such a thing be imagined) might, indeed, doubt each other's intentions to the point of not investing themselves. It is that such doubt would be extremely easy to remove and under Communist rule never arises, so great is the pressure for growth and the clamor for scarce investment funds.

But foreign trade does have input-output effects, i.e., the lack of imports may make it materially impossible for all factories to function. In Chapter IV we pursue this matter and are tempted to diagnose a similar but neglected effect in an ME.

---

[1] To say that there are no real multiplier effects is not, of course, to deny the permanent existence of Malthusian unemployment in, say, Poland, or even, latterly, of technological unemployment in the USSR. Over these a Soviet-type government has much less control.

CHAPTER III

INFLATION AND THE SOVIET-TYPE ECONOMY

I

THE notion that money should originate inside a country is new: it always used to come in from abroad. In the sixteenth to eighteenth centuries—to go no further back—this was obvious. If the king had no gold or silver mine in his territories all his money was of foreign origin. Had economics then been a serious subject, textbooks would have presented 'the quantity of money' after 'international trade'. Without organically incorporating this element in our total vision, we cannot understand Mercantilism.

As long as the gold standard lasted, the existence of banks and paper money did not really change this. Moreover, textbooks *were* written in the nineteenth century, and many of them *did* do violence, by their order of presentation, to the basic facts. These facts were especially evident in the case of that then neglected subject, colonial money. Imperial powers extended to their colonies not so much the gold standard as their own paper money and branches of their own banks. When in the 'thirties Keynes said that so great an influence of foreign trade upon the quantity of money was like the tail wagging the dog, it was not only a protest; it was a needed assertion of which ought now to be dog and which tail.

The contrast between the micro- and the macro-theory of money is therefore very absolute. The former has, indeed, logical priority, and should 'come at the beginning of the book'. The latter is, *except in STEs*, an integral part of a larger subject: international-trade-and-the-quantity-of-money. Of course, for simplicity it is inevitable that we must begin to theorize about some aspects of trade as if it were barter, and about some aspects of money as if the economy were closed. But this cannot take us far, except in an STE. This chapter is, then, almost unnecessary: its role is to show what does not happen.

2

We contemplated, in Chapter II, the essential nature of a STE. How, then, does it look with regard to banking, taxes, the quantity of money and foreign trade? There is still a central bank and a treasury; so we can still speak of 'the monetary authorities'. Much more of the national income and of the total money circulation flows through the treasury than in an ME; in particular, enterprise profits are in principle at its disposal, while amortization quotas go back to the relevant ministry. The enterprise may only keep a part of them, and even that is seen as a privilege. However, in detail, the treasury operates very much like any other treasury. In particular, budget surpluses and deficits are de- and inflationary, and are financed by contraction or expansion of the 'national debt'. The national debt is mainly what the government owes the central bank, but in addition there are bond sales, forced and unforced, to the public, and foreign capital transactions.[1] However, in practice the budget is always nearly balanced, and the simplest Gladstonian, or pre-Keynesian, views prevail on this subject. Although the ignorance and crudity of these views are a terrible hindrance to Communist understanding of ACCs,[2] it is of little consequence at home, since macro-monetary movements have no effect on employment in a command economy. Inflation has seldom, in fact, been caused by deficits or cured by surpluses.

An STE, then, is entirely non-Keynesian. The planners decide the volume of output, even if not all its details, irrespective of

[1] Enterprises (in fact, solely foreign trade enterprises) also lend and borrow abroad: but only at short and medium term and in minimal amounts (cf. Chapter XIV). The treasury also borrows from the public at home, through savings banks. These transactions, also rather small, figure as normal current items in the budget. As in any other economy, they are in- or deflationary only in so far as they affect the public's hoarding.

[2] For Marx' view of Say's Law, cf. Joan V. Robinson, *An Essay on Marxian Economics* (London, 1942), Chapters 6 and 10. For modern Communist views of Keynes cf. L. Al'ter in *Problems of Economics*, June 1961, March 1962; P. Oldak, ibid., August 1961; V. Cheprakov, ibid., May 1963.

aggregate demand. If the latter were, indeed, too low it would be a fairly serious matter: things would pile up in the shops and, eventually, production would have to cease or new warehouses would have to be built. But this would be a gross and stupid failure of planning, and besides a quite unlikely one; for defense and investment expenditure are always high, and tend naturally to exceed public and private saving. Since of these latter, public saving (the 'above-the-line'[1] budget surplus) is far the greater, the total can be very simply adjusted by taxation. Deflationary unemployment is thus theoretically possible in an STE, but in such a case the planners' heads should be examined.

The model is, then, such that particular goods are sometimes— latterly often—overproduced. This is principally because their quality is so bad, and prices are very sticky; but the higher standard of living is also important, since it raises the mere number of types of good to be planned and makes consumers less willing to spend their money. This leads to frictional unemployment in a given factory, cured by a management shake-up, a planner's order to produce something different, or possibly a subsidy and lower prices (see below). As to micro-economic underproduction, it causes principally queues.

There is thus, indeed, a virtue in excess aggregate demand: it smooths the planner's task. For the queue is an adjustment the consumer has to make, while over-production forces adjustment on the planner. As I have said elsewhere:

> The principal protagonist of excess demand in the USSR seems to have been A. I. Mikoyan. Cf. *Pravda*, February 18, 1956; but there are many similar passages in the speeches of Mikoyan and his subordinates, reaching right back into Stalin's lifetime. When I was in Poland in summer 1956 the desirability of excess demand was known as 'the Mikoyan doctrine'. As the man chiefly responsible for both domestic and foreign trade he would naturally recognize its stimulating effect, since it is on the trade organs that rests the burden of selling the shoddy qualities and arbitrary quantities that the production plan provides. The doctrine is strongly attacked by Chernyak and Stanislavsky in, of all places, *Partiinaya Zhizn'* (Party Life) 12/1956. Evidently it was at this time being debated on a very high level, perhaps in connection with the annual retail price reductions. These undoubtedly caused grave inconvenience through excess demand. The grossest case was that of potatoes in 1954. Since 1954 there have been no annual price reductions.[2]

This kind of trouble, then, is truly frictional. Macro-monetary

---

[1] In British, not Soviet, terminology. The Soviet budget is very rudimentary, and does not draw this line.

[2] P. J. D. Wiles, *The Political Economy of Communism* (Cambridge, Mass., 1962), pp. 261–2. Khrushchev himself condemned the Mikoyan doctrine, without giving it that name, at the 22nd Party Congress.

movements can seriously affect total output only where the command economy does not operate: on the black, kolkhoz, and second-hand markets. When there is inflation old durables are dragged out of cupboards, peasant grandmothers hoe in their plots until sundown, craftsmen of all kinds steal materials at their workplace and go 'moonlighting'. These are very small matters, however, so small that we may without unrealism imagine always a 'perfect' STE: agriculture consists entirely of sovkhozy and the official deliveries of kolkhozy, and there is no kolkhoz, black or second-hand market, or theft. Then all output is according to central order and money flows do not affect it. The multiplier, as we see in Chapter IV, is equal to one.

3

This goes even for unplanned money flows, such as will still arise from a good harvest or an exogenous improvement in the terms or balance of trade. Then the multiplier still operates as a description of the flow of extra money: it passes from hand to hand and, a bit sticking to the fingers here and a bit there, it eventually all leaks away into saving. The process is, of course, not instantaneous,[1] and lags may still vary between round and round; but *the multiplier is a purely monetary phenomenon*; *there is no output or employment multiplier at all*. We may compare the multiplier effect of additional inflation in a fully employed ME with exchange control. Only in an STE the multiplier is without 'real' consequences even if it is directed toward deflation.

4

Turning now to the banks and 'monetary' institutions, there is no stock exchange or bill market (though there are inconvertible private savings deposits); so there are no open-market operations as known in MEs. Yet the central bank is recognizably a bank, and can be described in Western terms. The system may be described as one-tier, branch central banking, or in one word a *monobank*. Other banks exist, principally for investment, agriculture and foreign trade. They cannot create money, but are in essence specialized funds, lending or simply allocating only the amounts they receive from the

---

[1] See Chapter IV, Section 1, below.

treasury. They cannot borrow from the central bank; so there is not even the pale shadow of a money market. For our purposes they may be neglected—even, at present, the foreign trade bank. Nearly all current transactions, and all money-creating transactions, flow through the central bank. Its lending policy may be described as a very extreme version of 'qualitative controls' coupled with 'needs of trade'. Thus 'ruble control' or, better translated, 'ruble audit',[1] is the principle whereby no check is cleared unless the underlying transaction can be shown to the bank's satisfaction to have been in accordance with the plan. The detail into which the bank must go would make a French or Latin American banker blench, but the notion that a bank must discriminate between customers and transactions on the grounds of public policy is not, of course, new in MEs. The real distinction between qualitative controls in MEs and STEs is that in the former the enterprise is still pursuing private profit. Retaining all initiative, it is only deflected, not commanded, by the bank's tutelage: 'control' means 'canalization'. But in the STE the initiative resides with the planner, not the enterprise. The latter does what it is told, and the bank checks that it has done so. Neither has much initiative, and in particular the bank is dispensable—someone else could have 'checked'.

5

Inflation, as we have seen, is neither directly caused nor directly controlled by the treasury. Yet it is fairly prevalent. It is caused by the bank's 'needs of trade' (i.e., needs of the plan) policy. For it follows from the exceedingly passive role forced upon it by the planning system that the bank must finance nearly every transaction the plan appears to demand. True, each enterprise does have a cash plan, a profit plan, and a cost plan, but they are not as important as the output plan, even when the latter is, as nowadays, increasingly expressed in money terms. Now the three former plans are often found to be unfulfillable for various reasons. They may have been simply miscalculated, or the enterprise may be inefficient, or there may be an accumulation of unsold stocks, or wage-creep,[2] or an

---

[1] In European languages other than English *controller*, *kontrollieren*, *kontrolirovat'*, etc., mean to check, not to govern. It is thus a considerably weaker concept, and should never be translated 'control'.

[2] It may well be asked what anything so bourgeois as wage-creep is doing in this list. The answer is that the labor market is competitive, even though wages are centrally fixed. So when, as is normal, there is excess demand, managers take advantage of every loophole in the law, and also straightforwardly break the law, in order to attract labor.

act of God. In any case the bank dare not refuse to make up the difference, for that would prejudice the output plan.

Of course, the output plan itself is often the reason why the financial plans are violated: in the case of marginal mines and *sovkhozy* that ought to be closed down, or of an unsalable *sortament* arbitrarily chosen in preference to a salable one. In particular there is *planner's tension*: the output plans are perpetually screwed up a little above the actual capacity of the enterprise. The causes of this are the vaulting economic ambition of the government and the criteria of personal promotion in the economic hierarchy. A manager, whether of an enterprise or of some intermediate planning organ, gets ahead by pressuring his subordinates to produce more in physical terms. This causes them to cut corners in every conceivable way, mostly by raising costs, lowering quality and choosing the easiest, rather than the most wanted, *sortament*.

In a general way planner's tension is the Soviet-type equivalent of inflation, since it may be defined as excessive planners' demand in physical terms. But it is also a principal cause of straightforward excessive monetary demand, since as we have seen it leads to neglect of costs—and therefore to ever new bank loans.

But that is not the banker's business. Interference with the output plan, which public opinion regards as somehow independent of the financial plans, gets him into political trouble, and anyway he shares, in a quiet bankerly way, the general Communist scale of values: output before all. So he makes the erring enterprise a loan— which it is scarcely ever in a position to pay back. If it is repaid, or if a budget surplus offsets it, there is, of course, no permanent inflation. But a Communist government tends to take such loans rather lightly.

In a word, we have been speaking of the *impossibility of Soviet-type bankruptcy*. A procedure exists in the statute books of every STE, but it is literally never applied. Even the Yugoslavs, it would appear, bankrupted only private enterprises until 1965. Perpetual loss-makers are either subsidized by the treasury, or forcibly amalgamated with profit-makers, or kept alive by bank loans; preferably one of the two latter, since it is a fixed Communist principle to keep budgetary expenditure down, and pass fiscal burdens to other bodies. In each case the inefficiency that caused the loss continues, or at least is far more slowly corrected than it would have been by bankruptcy. This keeps up output in the short run, and the quantity of money in the long run.

6

The second reason for the prevalence of unrepayable bank loans is that they are not considered to be real money. We come here to the sharp nineteenth-century distinction that Communists still make between 'notes' or 'currency' and 'checks' or 'credit'. It is in keeping with the Gladstonian simplicities of Communist theories on these subjects that the note issue is thought of as far more important than bank deposits, even to the point that the very name of money is denied to bank credit in an STE, though it is allowed when capitalist conditions are being described.[1] Now even in an underdeveloped capitalist banking system there is no distinction of importance between these interchangeable kinds of money. But in an STE the Communist dichotomy is for the most part right. For in principle all intermediate transactions are financed by checks on banks, while all final transactions (wage payments and purchases in shops) are financed by notes. Thus *active money is notes and passive money is checks*. Check money is centered in the single bank so that the government can see what is going on; it is the accounting money of the socialist sector. For precisely this reason the cash plan is taken far more seriously than the credit plan. The cash plan, after all, is much the same as the personal income plan, a deadly serious matter. Cash may be hoarded and dishoarded by anyone, but credit is already under control. Again, enterprises are forbidden to pay each other in cash. In this way 'ruble audit' is enhanced.

7

Now the banking system, being subject to no open-market pressures, is not forced to, and does not, maintain any liquidity ratio between deposits and notes. Such liquidity ratios operate, of course, only in two-tier systems, where the commercial banks use the notes of the central bank as a liquid reserve. No individual bank uses its own notes in this way, and an STE's central bank is no exception to this logic. It is, thus, in no very obvious way that the volume of currency determines that of credit. They are separately planned.

So the volume of notes is adjusted to the liquidity preference of the population and the output of consumer goods, but this tells us

[1] Y. E. Shenger, *Ocherki Sovetskogo Kredita* (Moscow, 1961), pp. 119 ff.; V. M. Batyrev, *Denezhnoye Obrashchenie v SSSR* (Moscow, 1959), pp. 228–9; Lin Chi-k'en in *Ching-chi Yen-chiu* (*Economic Research*) (2/1963 = SCMM 356). Cf. G. Garvy in *Soviet Planning*, ed. Jane Degras and Alec Nove (Oxford, 1964), p. 72.

precious little about the right volume of bank deposits, which must depend on the amount of inter-enterprise activity they have to finance. Communists claim that the note circulation determines the volume of bank deposits, not vice versa.[1] But, in fact, if investment or defense expenditures rise, or if the need for inter-enterprise finance is increased by vertical disintegration, the right ratio of credit to currency increases. Above all, in the case that here concerns us, unrepaid credit issues to deficitary enterprises have a very direct causal effect on currency issues. For the effect of the loan is that more high-cost production is being financed. But in any economy, most of the costs of production turn out to be eventually somebody's personal income—if not in the loss-making enterprise then in the enterprises from which it buys its inputs. So the extra credit becomes extra currency; i.e., passive money generates active money.

We said above that the borrowing enterprise was scarcely ever in a position to pay back the credit, and it follows, of course, that the volume of currency also remains inflated. For the enterprise could only repay out of a future improvement in its financial affairs, but that is not a very likely event. 'Planner's tension' (i.e., the over-ambitious output targets set by the planners) will continue to impose an unrealistic view of costs; yet the planners do not commonly grant relief by raising prices. For one enterprise's price is the next enterprise's cost, and this will merely shift the violation of the financial plans, and the necessity for bank loans, to the next enterprise. In particular cases, where the 'next enterprise' is profitable, this is, of course, worth doing and, indeed, done. It simplifies accountancy, tightens financial discipline, and may even give acceptable guidance to planners with an eye on rationality. But it does not lower real costs at any point, nor raise the net revenues of the whole nationalized sector.

8

So, broadly speaking, either (a) the bank's unplanned loan is never repaid, but, on the contrary, more of the same are continually made, inflation is perpetual, the output plan is enforced as it was, and the real distribution of resources is unchanged; or (b) the planners genuinely reduce tension, and also make such other minor substitutions in the output plan as will increase profits at constant prices; or (c) wholesale prices are so adjusted as to abolish the loss,

[1] Garvy, op. cit., p. 62.

i.e., the turnover tax is lowered; or (d) consumer prices are raised; or (e) wages are lowered. In these last three ways the financial burden is placed outside the nationalized sector, on the government or the consumer. Now, in fact, the turnover tax cannot readily be lowered, for that leads to budgetary imbalance, which is again inflationary. We may juggle with individual tax rates, as with individual enterprise prices, but a diminution of their total yield is a macro-economic change in real terms, i.e., a shift from investment to consumption.

(a) and (b) we have already discussed, so that leaves wages and consumer prices. The perpetual flow of inflationary bank loans can indeed be stanched by raising the nationalized sector's revenue from the consumer, but only if costs are constant. Wages are ultimately almost the only cost, so that means lower real incomes. So a rise in retail prices (d) is deflationary, i.e. reduces excess demand, and vice versa: a thing not always paradoxical even in an ME. Now in fact the most savage restraint on personal real incomes is fairly easy in an STE. At rare intervals, to be sure, it leads to a Pilsen, a Poznań or an East German revolution: each of which events was touched off, though not, of course, solely caused, by the government's personal-income policy.[1] But for the most part the restraint works. It even works so well that the government can (e) lower money incomes while keeping prices constant— the lowering is disguised as the 'introduction of technologically based norms' instead of the old 'empirical' or 'historically based' wage rates. This, then, by lowering the costs of the whole national- ized sector, renders new bank loans unnecessary.[2] The input of labor per unit of consumption rises, but otherwise the distribution of resources remains unchanged, and the inflation stops.

The government's principal weapon against inflation, then, is neither the rate of interest (see below—an impossible candidate); nor the budget (see above—this weapon might well be used but is not); but personal-income policy. I.e. its agency is not the 'mone- tary authorities'—neither the bank nor the treasury—but the Party, the trade unions, and the economic bureaucracy. Since khozraschet is only a relative independence, and the treasuries

[1] Kronstadt and the Hungarian Revolution had other proximate causes. But here, too, and, indeed, all the time, discontent with personal-income policy is very high indeed.

[2] As Full Communism approaches, social services grow and wages diminish, even in money terms. It is then open to the government to deflate by cutting social services and relinquishing the unnecessary tax revenue to the nationalized sector. This also, of course, is a cut in living standards. In the case of a kolkhoz the government lowers the compulsory delivery price; or raises the quantity to be delivered at the old price, so reducing the pro- fitable sales of surpluses in the free market.

of each enterprise are directly connected with that of the state, all such outgoes as kolkhoz purchases and socialist wages may be treated like state payments. Just as one of the weapons of fiscal policy in an ME is the lowering of civil servants' salaries, so in an STE we lower all salaries and the revenues of kolkhozy.

9

In an ME, inflation is in a sense a real, not a monetary, phenomenon. It is an excess of real demand over real supply, and can only be cured by a movement in one or the other. This is as much as to say that Say's Law is not true. In the wholesale markets of an STE, money is passive, and the word 'inflation', or at least the words 'excess demand', have no meaning. But money is not passive in the retail market, and queues or rising prices show a real attempt to consume more than is being produced. We need not, therefore, be surprised that an STE must take unpleasant, 'real' measures to cure inflation, such as reducing wages or raising prices. The difference from an ME is that the thing is not so necessary. Supply will not react much whatever happens. In particular, inflation is neither increasing or diminishing investment nor keeping exports back or sucking imports in; these are subject to the command economy, and the marginal propensity to import is, as we have seen, zero. The government might almost as well, and often does, let inflation rip.

10

The rate of interest could not, of course, be used by the bank. First, it would be un-Marxist. Secondly, the rate of interest is, after all, a price like other prices, and in a command economy all supply and demand curves ought to be of zero elasticity—indeed, it is wrong to speak of them. This is just another way of saying that physical orders have absolute priority. Thirdly, long-term capital is, on ideological grounds, never lent and borrowed by the bank but allocated free of charge by the treasury.

Devastating as this case may seem to be, the central bank does, after all, make a charge on all short-term loans.[1] Only the charge

---

[1] A basic amount of circulating capital is allocated free of charge by the treasury to each enterprise according to centrally-defined norms, just as if it were long-term capital. We may compare the capitalist practice of borrowing a similar sum at long term. All extra circulating capital must be borrowed from the bank. In Hungary there has been a charge on long-term capital since January 1, 1964, and in the DDR since 1966.

is a quite invariable one, which it has never entered anyone's head to use against inflation. The charge is there to prevent waste, and its existence implies a certain activity in the nominally passive money, a certain elasticity in the nominally non-existent demand curve for short funds. So deflation by varying the rate on short-term funds is not unthinkable: it is simply never practiced. It would, of course, have far less effect than the already rather small effects it has in an ME. For the elasticity of demand for stocks, since it should in a command economy be zero, must, in fact, be very small; and the short rate has no effect whatsoever on the long rate, since long-term capital comes out of the budget free of charge.[1]

11

Such, however, is not the case externally. There is no technical reason why the Gosbank should not set up shop in the international short-loan market and offset a bad harvest by drawing in funds. It has, indeed, especially good opportunities for so doing through the Soviet banks in foreign countries, such as Moscow Narodny Bank in London and Beirut, or the Banque Commerciale pour l'Europe du Nord in Paris. Such a hypothetical use of bank rates abroad would have no connection at all with the 'bank rate'—if we may call it that—at home. It would be as if in an ME there were two quite separate bank rates, one for foreigners and one for residents; and the latter were frozen at some conventional level while the former varied actively with supply and demand.

The banks of STEs, having from time to time short-term funds available, do, in fact, operate on capitalist money markets. They were among the first customers for Euro-dollars. More strikingly, the Moscow Narodny Bank in London is one of several foreign banks that finance British local authorities, in competition with the Public Works Loan Board.[2]

12

In the semi-decentralized STE of the near future (Chapter II, Section 6), macro-monetary controls will be much more important. Although there will still be over-all output targets, the enterprise's

[1] In Hungary and the DDR the long rate is, of course, the concern of the treasury, not the bank. Variations in this rate would similarly meet a very inelastic demand indeed.
[2] Notably Dawley Urban District Council in Shropshire. See *The Observer* (London), March 4, 1961.

micro-economic freedom will be so great that they may not be enforceable. For a command to produce X tons of 'steel' is meaningless unless it is backed by commands to produce Y tons of this kind of steel pipe and Z tons of the other kind. 'Steel' is a metaphysical entity: there are only steel pipes of this or that dimension and alloy. So if the enterprise is truly free to choose between qualities, i.e., vary Y and Z by bargaining with its customers, there can and must be no guarantee that it will produce X. As a target, X is only meaningful if the restraint is legally enforced that $Y + Z$ must $= X$. But in that case the enterprise's micro-freedom is severely curtailed.

It is, therefore, probable that even in principle macro-targets will lose much of their legal force; let alone what may happen in practice if subordinate officials become persuaded of the need for genuine decentralization. Then the macro-volume of activity will be the *ex post* sum of all micro-contracts, and the government's principal lever on these latter will be fiscal and monetary policy, much as in a pure ME. This will be particularly true of the volume of investment. Communist local authorities and enterprises are so anxious, for various reasons, to invest, that even methods of command hardly suffice to hold them in check. Monetary restraints would have to be forceful indeed, as we see in the Czechoslovak case (Chapter V, Section 12). Mere fluctuations in the rates of interest would not suffice; there would have to be a budget surplus, an incomes policy, and a number of exemplary bankruptcies.

Where macro-monetary measures operate the economy becomes 'Keynesian' in the sense used above. The multiplier becomes greater than one, and in particular the balance of trade has a genuine multiplier, as opposed to merely an inflationary, effect. This is so even if the government's monopoly of valuta and foreign trade continues. It may continue, *more sovietico*—or for that matter *more britannico*—to devalue its currency at intervals, and meanwhile subsidize exports and tax imports (Chapter VI). But the absence of a direct currency link with the outside world is not enough to prevent the Keynesian effects of movements in the balance of trade, any more than it was in Britain under exchange control.

What has been prophesied above for Czechoslovakia (and Hungary, we might add, and perhaps Bulgaria—for these are now the three most decentralized STEs) can be illustrated from the Yugoslav present. For Yugoslavia is not so different, and her workers' councils are not so important, but that she can be roughly described as a very decentralized STE. Since the political reforms of 1965 the principles of the market have been taken much more seriously, though they are nominally unchanged and it is incorrect to speak of economic reforms. The true reform dates from 1950, since when there has been perpetual inflation, which is far more characteristic of market than of command socialism. Excess demand worsens the balance of payments through its normal effects on imports and exports. The foreign-trade multiplier and the marginal propensity to import have real effects, the budget should indeed be running a surplus (though Marxist prejudices still inhibit this), bank restraint is constantly preached (characteristically, through direct quantitative restrictions on lending, not through a higher bank rate),[1] and bankruptcy is becoming a reality. All this is in addition to an old-style incomes policy (which in Yugoslavia must work through the workers' councils); while a price freeze is conspicuous, for the first time, by its absence.

Another case of a 'very decentralized STE' was the USSR of the NEP. The Scissors Crisis of 1923, notably, was solved by the Gosbank's orthodox credit restriction, which caused state industrial enterprises to run down their stocks and reduce their prices. Though mainly an internal crisis, concerned with the terms of trade between state industry and private agriculture, it had its balance-of-payments side. The Gosbank wanted to collect gold, and succeeded in so doing. Cf. Chapter VI, Section 1.

[1] There are now many banks, and an 'open' bill market connects them. Not even Czechoslovakia intends to go this far.

CHAPTER IV

A PRODUCTION-ORIENTED VIEW OF THE BALANCE OF PAYMENTS

I

THIS chapter presents the additions and corrections that seem to be required in Western international trade theory in order to accommodate the STE. We have essentially one correction to make (Section 5): in the formulation of the foreign trade multiplier; and one addition (Section 7): applying the input-output analysis to imports. The title to this chapter conveniently describes them both.

Why do planned increases in exports form no part of the Western pharmacopoeia for a balance-of-payments crisis? The thing seems so obvious to the student of an STE, and to recommend it is, indeed, one of the principal contributions such a student can make to the better running of a market economy.[1] 'Increase in exports' is under-

[1] For an excellent short defense of export subsidies in purely Western terms, cf. P. Streeten in *AICC Economic Review* (New Delhi), April 1, 1963. Mr. Streeten makes many of the same points as myself.

stood to include 'increase in import substitutes' unless it is expressly stated to the contrary.

The first reason for this lacuna is theoretical error. It is not the most important reason, but theoretical error is the principal begetter of other theory; so the reader must excuse a few prefatory paragraphs of seeming irrelevance. It is essential to the argument of this chapter that the instantaneous multiplier is actually wrong, that it is not an admissible alternative formulation to the lagged multiplier. If the multiplier shows the total effect on national income of an initial injection of money into the income stream, it can no more be instantaneous than any cause can be simultaneous with its effect. When Keynes used the equations:[1]

$$\Delta Y = \Delta I + \Delta C$$
$$\therefore \frac{\Delta Y}{\Delta I} = \frac{1}{1 - \dfrac{\Delta C}{\Delta Y}}$$

where Y = income
I = investment
C = consumption

he was in actual error, confusing *ex post* with *ex ante* and timeless correlation with cause and effect. Only an iterative series, of the type used below, is acceptable. That the iterative, *ex ante*, mathematics leads us to the same answer as the simultaneous, *ex post*, mathematics does not validate the latter; it is simply an unfortunate and confusing coincidence. Mathematics is a *language* that *describes*. If the result is right but the description is wrong, then it is a coincidence, which can happen in any language. We do not call such coincidence proof when we use words; no more is it proof when we use symbols.[2] Keynes' mathematical 'proof' has the logical status of a pun.

If the reader finds this too dogmatic let him look honestly at the confusion resulting from Keynes' mathematics. A chain of reasoning that comes out right accidentally, starting from wrong premises, is almost bound to let us down if we try to use it for further results. That is certainly the case here. Thus let the public dishoard in order to consume, or let the government remit taxes on consumers while keeping expenditure unchanged. Then there is an initial ΔC, which,

---

[1] J. M. Keynes, *The General Theory of Employment, Interest, and Money* (London, 1936), p. 115.

[2] It is no accident that the inventor of the multiplier used an iterative series: R. F. Kahn in *Economic Journal* (1931).

of course, has a multiplier effect—the new expenditure creates
incomes, the recipients in their turn save a little and pass on the rest,
the recipients of which . . ., etc., etc. According to Keynes' algebra
we must now write:

$$\frac{\Delta Y}{\Delta C}[\text{the multiplier}] = \frac{1}{1 - \dfrac{\Delta I}{\Delta Y}}$$

which is simply wrong. So wrong is it that Keynes never dared directly
to discuss the multiplier effects of new consumption, and treated all
budget deficits as if they were investment—'honorary investment'
in D. H. Robertson's phrase. In contrast, in the iterative formula,
the nature of the first term is not laid down by the symbol used.
It can be any sum of money, x, injected into the income stream in
any way we please:

$$x + cx + c^2x \ldots = x\left(\frac{1}{1-c}\right),$$

where c is the marginal propensity to consume, and the right-hand
side of the equation is the total increase in the national income.

The lapse of time between each term in this series is, of course,
determined by the income-velocity of circulation of marginal money
(v); and no apology is offered for using this concept, derided by
some. For our future purposes, moreover, we need a much more
detailed account of c than the elementary textbooks give. Extra
income goes on taxes (t), savings (s), home consumption (h), and
imports (i), these being all marginal propensities. As a general rule,
h and t are of the same order of magnitude in ACCs: 30 or 40%
each. The others vary more, but i might be about 20% and s about
10%. Now $c \equiv h + i$; the leaks are t, s and i; only h multiplies.
With a long lag it is true that all the leaks generate domestic expenditure: t prompts the government to spend more in the succeeding
fiscal year, s is dissaved, i reflects back on our own exports. But in
the short run this may all be neglected. Moreover, within one
twelve-month or other short period we can only count as many
terms of the multiplier as actually occur. If $v = 4$, the series reads:

$$\Delta Y = x + hx + h^2x + h^3x = x\frac{h^v - 1}{h - 1};$$

$$\frac{\Delta Y}{x} = \frac{1 - h^v}{1 - h}.$$

With $h = 0.35$, this gives a 'twelve-month multiplier' of 1.5.

Moreover, the multiplier is in essence a monetary phenomenon. When there is surplus capacity it has a real effect also, indeed, two separate real effects. Since the increased income is 'earned' by factors, employment will increase, but by less than income since factor prices rise; and since the increased income is spent on products, output will increase but again by less than income since output prices rise. So if the monetary multiplier is $\Delta Y/x$, the input multiplier is $\Delta Y/wx$, and the output multiplier is $\Delta Y/px$, where w is the index of factor prices and p is the index of product prices. It is normally assumed that $\Delta Y/wx > \Delta Y/px$ owing to diminishing returns, or $p > w$. But that might not be so, especially now that labor is so often a fixed cost. When there is full employment, $\Delta Y/wx = 0$, by definition, but $\Delta Y/px$ may still slightly exceed that value if productivity rises, and $\Delta Y/x$ will have about the same value as with unemployment. The leaks differ in size: with rising prices s is usually smaller, and with inelastic home supplies i is usually bigger—but the essence of the concept is unchanged.

2

It is permissible to speak of a monetary multiplier in an STE, since there also money goes round, exports generate incomes, and imports are deflationary. Only, since inflation does not affect the planners, it does not affect production or employment (except in the negligible free sector). Full employment is, indeed, the rule in an STE, but if by some chance the planners had ordered surplus capacity the foreign-trade multiplier would not alter the position. In the possible future semi-decentralized STE things will be more normal, but we are interested here in the actual state of affairs as described in Chapter III.

It may be objected that micro-economically a lack of demand is not met by filling the warehouses, nor by a sale at low prices, but by output change, i.e., plan change; and that this can give rise to short-run unemployment. Is not this, then, ordinary deflation, and might not an import surplus in particular cause such a small 'slump'? Our previous answer must suffice. Such unemployment does not spread much, nor last long, even in an advanced Communist country where the consumer can afford to pick and choose. The command economy puts ample powers in the hands of the authorities, which they do, in fact, use. It is wise to note the possibility, but foolish to base analysis upon it.

3

We can now come to the point. Mr. Gerald Meier states flatly that no real or structural change can in the short run affect the balance of payments:[1]

In demonstrating that there will be no change in the balance on current account as long as any increase in desired investment is matched by a concurrent increase of desired saving, the preceding analysis reiterates the fundamental principle that external imbalance can be avoided if the investment is financed by non-inflationary methods. As long as investment expenditure is not increased by inflationary means, it will not cause any balance of payments deficit during the operation of the investment even though the investment itself may entail some increase in imports. For, regardless of its character, the output created by the investment allows aggregate supply to keep pace with aggregate demand, thereby removing pressure on the balance of payments. *When the output is either export-creating or import-saving, it will directly improve the balance of payments.* But the remaining alternative—an expansion in output for the domestic market—will also be import-saving, even though the substitution of domestic goods for imports is made only indirectly. Since the investment is non-inflationary, national expenditure does not exceed national output; therefore, to buy the additional output from the new investment on the home market, there must be a reduction in imports. Such a switched expenditure from imports will offset any increase in imports caused by the investment in the home industry.[2]

It must be emphasized that since inflation is an over-all problem in the economy, its adverse effects on the balance of payments do not depend on any particular distribution of investment. What matters for the avoidance of balance of payments problems is not the composition of the investment, but whether it provides the highest possible social marginal product. It is erroneous to believe that balance of payments problems can only be avoided if the investment is directed toward export or import-competing industries. For, as long as investment is making the greatest possible contribution to an expansion in national output, and is not giving rise to inflation, it will also be aiding the balance of payments. To allocate investment arbitrarily to import-competing or export industries, instead of in accordance with the principle of acquiring the maximum marginal productivity from investment, is to be misled by a narrow 'commodity approach' to balance of payments policy; it fails to recognize the overall contribution of investment to national output and thereby indirectly to the balance of payments.[3]

This passage should awaken acute discomfort in the reader. At first glance it is an insane tilt against common sense, and a dogmatic condemnation of very much economic policy in all countries: surely practical men cannot be *such* fools? At second glance it is an intelli-

[1] *International Trade and Development* (New York, 1963), pp. 76-7; my italics.

[2] Cf. A. E. Kahn, 'Investment Criteria in Development Programs', *Quarterly Journal of Economics*, February, 1951, pp. 42-7; Ragnar Nurkse, 'International Trade Theory and Development Policy' in H. S. Ellis (ed.), *Economic Development for Latin America* (St. Martin's Press, 1961), pp. 259-60 (Meier's footnote).

[3] R. Nurkse, *Problems of Capital Formation in Underdeveloped Countries* (Oxford, 1953), pp. 137-8; 'International Trade Theory and Development Policy', op. cit., pp. 262-3 (Meier's footnote).

gent application of sound theory to the real world; a brilliant addition to—or rather subtraction from—the armory of public policy by the use of rigorous thought. Albeit the rigor would have been improved by omitting the phrase in italics; for Mr. Meier's whole point is, without equivocation, that *only* a movement toward monetary equilibrium improves the b.o.p. An export-creating output, if he is right, will by no means 'directly improve the b.o.p.,' since it will generate greater internal demand via the multiplier, and thus greater imports via the marginal propensity to import (m.p.i.).

Looking aside from this lapse, the present writer has only got as far as a third glance: the thing has no application whatsoever to an STE and relies in part on the instantaneous multiplier. The explanation of this will take us rather far afield; it will shed much light on MEs and leave us between our first and second positions.

4

How, then, does this matter look in an STE? It is still usually[1] true that new output, in Mr. Meier's words, 'regardless of its character . . . allows aggregate supply to keep pace with aggregate demand', but this does not now 'remove pressure on the balance of payments'. That balance is, of course, physically planned. Foreign price movements may hurt it, and so may internal output failure, characteristically that of the harvest. But the trading corporations will not alter their behavior in response to money flows.

It follows that in an STE it matters very much indeed whether the output is export-creating, import-saving, or 'other'. Since the multiplier is no longer 'real', 'other' is now the same as 'irrelevant'— unless, indeed, it be actually import-necessitating or export-consuming—categories that Mr. Meier neglects. In a sense, of course, since everything affects everything, there is no perfectly irrelevant output decision: every use of factors has *some* effect on the balance of trade. Indeed, now that aggregate monetary balance is out of the way and we must look at the physical side of things, we are forced to ask exactly how 'export-creating' is a particular export? Does it use imported raw materials? Does it divert labor from other

---

[1] But in an STE, marginal output often makes a monetary loss, and must be financed by inflationary short-run bank credit (Chapter III, Section 5). However while raising the quantity of money this need not alter aggregate supply *vis-à-vis* aggregate demand. But in the most general possible way, it is not obvious why new output should lead to monetary balance; many theories of the trade-cycle downturn rest upon bunched investment followed by a deflationary flood of new current output. Again new output must often be monetarily neutral, and therefore will upset Mr. Meier's prediction that, if sold on the home market, it will reduce imports.

exports? etc., etc. And so we see that *in an STE trade balance is an input-output matter.* The perfect calculation of all the results of a particular change can only be read off an input-output table, preferably, of course, one adjusted for the possibilities of substitution. What Mr. Meier rejects as the 'narrow commodity approach' is the only possible approach.

Now, no doubt, Mr. Meier would have been the first to admit that he implicitly excluded the STE from his analysis, since money has no influence there. But while the STE is quite different from the ME, the ME—so to speak—is by no means so different from the STE. Input-output considerations still operate, and must be added to the purely monetary analysis he offers, in which all physical outputs are transformable into each other with perfect ease. It seems at first view that the whole theory of international trade, as it has grown up since Keynes, neglects this. Thus in very simple expositions the m.p.i. is held to depend on consumer demand alone: one 'consumes a foreign good' as if there were no value added to it domestically, e.g., by trade. Properly defined, however, the m.p.i. makes ample allowance even for very indirect effects of new consumption on imports, and results calculable only by very sophisticated input-output work are implicit in the concept. Thus if a Briton buys a British bicycle, 10% of the retail value of which is Belgian steel, c.i.f. London, his m.p.i. is 0·1; provided the steel is shipped on Belgian or other foreign bottoms. But if, again, 10% of the value of Belgian steel, c.i.f. London, is British coal, c.i.f. Ostend, and the coal is always shipped on British bottoms, the m.p.i. of the Briton drops to 0·09. All of which, complicated as it sounds, is an oversimplified example of what the m.p.i. really means, even to a simon-pure Keynesian. Of course, the lags are quite long and the magnitudes small, but one cannot complain that the input-output considerations are neglected. The m.p.i. is thus itself a rather different affair from the marginal propensities to consume, to save and to pay taxes. All these represent an ultimate division of his income consciously made by the final consumer; whereas the decision to import as a result of his consumption is scarcely ever taken by himself, but, on technical grounds, by producers.

5

The Keynesian theory of trade balances errs, then, not by wrongly defining the m.p.i., but in other ways. The first is the *damnosa hereditas* of the instantaneous multiplier itself: the lags are not properly allowed for. The unrealism of Mr. Meier's account of the matter may be illustrated thus. In a fully-employed ME there is a marginal coal mine, surplus to domestic requirements but reasonably equipped to produce without much further investment. Faced with a b.o.p. deficit the government decides not to cut back income but to subsidize the reopening of this mine. The sum of £10,000, raised by inflationary finance, is *given* to the enterprise, which effects the necessary initial improvements in three months. Thus relieved of overhead, the mine proceeds to export profitably for £60,000 p.a. The country's m.p.i. is 0·2, the m.p.h. 0·4, and the income velocity of circulation four times a year. Then within twelve months of the government's gift exports rise by $9/12 \times £60,000 = £45,000$, while imports rise by, very roughly, £15,128.[1]

But the omission of time lags is not all. For imports *eventually* to increase as much as exports—which is at the bottom of Mr. Meier's thesis—it would be necessary for the m.p.i. to be the only leak. The existence of saving and taxation makes such a thing quite impossible, so long as we confine ourselves to the multiplier. For imports *instantly* to cancel out the new exports so that there is not even a

---

[1] This figure is arrived at as follows. All payments are assumed, for simplicity, to be made in the middle of the quarter (and imports are, for further simplicity, paid for in advance at that moment). Second- and further-round income is generated only by the m.p.h. No own exports are generated in the *n*th round by imports in the (*n* — 1)th round, as in the British-Belgian example in the text. This last assumption is made not only for simplicity but also because 'generated own exports' are likely to be very small and strongly lagged. Then we get (£ '000):

	Quarter				
	I	II	III	IV	I
Initial expenditure and multiplier effects:					
Income	10	4	1·6	0·64	0·256
Resulting imports . . .	2	0·8	0·32	0·128	0·064
Mining income and multiplier effects:					
Second quarter		15	6	2·4	0·96
Resulting imports . . .		3	1·2	0·48	0·192
Third quarter			15	6	2·4
Resulting imports . . .			3	1·2	0·48
Fourth quarter				15	6
Resulting imports . . .				3	1·2
First quarter, following year . .					15
Resulting imports . . .					3

A year of current operation is still better: extra exports are £60,000; extra imports, £18,064.

useful short-run relief to the b.o.p., the multiplier must be instantaneous. But the multiplier is not and never could be instantaneous. *Therefore, there is such a thing as solving a balance-of-payments problem by physically increasing exports.* Granted all the leaks, the multiplier is so small in an ME and the lags so long that expansions of output in the right direction, even if directly inflationary, cause a net inflow of foreign currency. Common sense is, after all, vindicated. Should there be unemployment the case is far stronger still. And an STE is merely an extreme case in which both multiplier and m.p.i. are zero.

All large and interesting conclusions have qualifications. First, our example comprises very special arithmetical magnitudes. In particular, the initial investment is unusually small and quick. It is clear that a larger and longer initial investment would put the whole procedure out of court as an immediate cure for a b.o.p. crisis. This would be particularly true if we needed to import in order to invest. A quite special significance attaches to the import content of the initial capital expenditure, as opposed to that of the whole venture. The point is platitudinous, though neglected with, so to speak, particular emphasis by Mr. Meier in our quotation. Simply, the lengthy process of installing fixed assets is accompanied by no exports at all. The lag is much longer than that between an imported raw material and an exported finished product. On the other hand many export schemes require hardly any initial expenditure, since the product to be exported or substituted for imports is subject to an artificial output restriction—one thinks of United States grain, oil and coal. It would also be possible to run down stocks of the product, and then to recoup them with current output from the investment project.

Secondly, we have assumed away all consequences unconnected with the multiplier. The new exports would depress the terms of trade; the initial investment would have an accelerator effect; also, probably, untoward speculative consequences. Thirdly, there is a difficulty of commercial policy in the case chosen: our investment was a state gift; hence, we have committed the well-known international crime of export subsidy.

Above all, we have not disproved the essential Meier thesis, which remains perfectly correct and extremely useful: extra output is about as deflationary as it is inflationary; so new investments that serve the home market have, when they begin to yield, no special effect on the b.o.p. It is the corollary that is wrong: it does not follow that neither export-biased improvements improve the b.o.p., nor import-biased ones worsen it.

Thus this passage in one of Meier's authorities is wrong:

The fact that the new production may require foreign raw materials still creates no presumption of a b.o.p. problem, under present assumptions. To the extent that part of the cost of the added goods consists of imported raw materials, the sale of the added output entails a greater diversion of [domestic] purchases from [domestic] goods—whose products *may* equally require imported raw materials— and from imports than [the income of the factors employed in the new production] increases. The net effect remains indeterminate.[1]

On the contrary, even if all substitutes for the new good use precisely as many imports as it does, there only has to be the slightest increase in output, or the slightest degree of inflation for the m.p.i. to come into play and worsen the b.o.p. And even without that, the new raw materials have to be imported *first*; the output that cuts the demand for other imports is sold *later*. It is, therefore, no matter of indifference, but one of urgent national policy, to know whether or not the new output requires more imports than its likely alternatives—and especially initial imports, which Kahn also fails to distinguish.[2]

6

So the first reason why an ME in b.o.p. trouble does not instantly increase its exports might be incorrect theory. But few people pay attention to theory anyway, and this particular piece of theory is particularly little known.

A much more important reason is that an ME *cannot* normally increase its exports to order. Even if a good opportunity presented itself, with a high elasticity of foreign demand and small need for preparatory investment, an ME has by definition no direct way of taking advantage. True, there is little difficulty if enterprise is plentiful enough and factors are mobile enough; if the banks behave 'properly' and prices move quickly enough without creating uncertainty. Exports increase quickly as opportunity offers, though not, indeed, in anticipation of the event. If we are on the gold standard, national price levels diverge enough to increase trade as gold flows; on a flexible exchange system the divergence occurs in the product of national price level and rate of exchange.

---

[1] Kahn, op. cit., pp. 44-5, my italics.
[2] Very similar to the 'Meier thesis' is the thesis that extra savings are smoothly convertible into foreign exchange. Cf. below, Chapter VIII, Section 11.

However, that is all quite unrealistic. None of the preconditions listed in fact, obtains, and few of them could be brought about by a change of government policy, even if the electorate were to vote for it. Clearly a free market suffers badly in a b.o.p. crisis, which it can only in practice correct by deflation and unemployment. Nor do these normally increase exports much: it is simply not the case that deflation releases in the short run many potential exports from the clutches of home demand, or that it lowers prices so as to attract foreign demand. Its function is to choke off the domestic demand for imports. Moreover, the raised rate of interest has whatever restraining effects it has not only on production for the home market, but also on exports.

If, then, we are to use the export weapon, we must have a regulated market. Which leads us back to export subsidies, covert[1] or overt. Now export subsidies are far more unpopular in international trade circles than import taxes. At few places does the advantage of an STE over an ME come out more clearly. For as we show in Chapter IX, it cannot be proved that an STE is subsidizing its exports or dumping. Its accounts are simply not open to inspection and even if they were, prices are so irrational that they would be meaningless.[2] Moreover, in an STE it is not the uncertain and dilatory mechanism of prices and taxes, relying on the profit motive and the elasticity of supply, that generates the new exports. These are brought about simply by the planners' fiat. The requirements for this are political will and administrative competence alone.

The unpopularity of the export subsidy is hard to account for. The import tax is equally arbitrary and discriminatory, equal in the damage done to both the business interest of a particular foreigner and the optimal allocation of resources. Of the two, it is the export subsidy that is more likely to be removed, since it involves the government in direct expense, not revenue; moreover, it is almost alone among b.o.p. correctives in seeking to increase, not decrease, the volume of international trade—two points that should strongly appeal to free traders. It is, of course, a less efficient corrective, since it worsens, where the tariff improves, the terms of trade. But the real reason for the prejudice against it is probably far more foolish

[1] E.g., we can subsidize a firm on the grounds that it is going to settle in a depressed area, but really because it will export; the state's export credit guarantee can rest upon an underestimation of the export risk; bank lending to non-exporters can be curtailed; freight-rates outward toward the frontier can be manipulated; indirect taxes can be remitted . . . but the list is endless.
[2] Note that we do not here speak of an ideal socialist economy.

and metaphysical: a foreign export is seen as a sort of aggression by 'them' on 'us', indeed, an invasion since it 'occurs' on our territory. The weapon of aggression is actually present within our walls, like the Trojan horse. Whereas, if 'they' stop our exports (i.e., their imports) this is something occurring on their territory. We may protest, but sovereignty is sovereignty.

But while the arguments from government revenue, the terms of trade and metaphysics tell us why the export subsidy is little used by practical men, they do not explain the failure of economists to popularize it. I suggest that both orthodox theory and the experience of STEs, as given in Chapter V, make a strong case for the export subsidy.

Imagine in particular a long-term forced investment program—a thing entirely characteristic of nearly all modern MEs. Whatever we promise ourselves, it will in fact be inflationary. This will not matter much if the plan is biased toward exports or import substitutes, for then the inflationary pressure toward an unfavorable b.o.p. will always be matched by a structural pressure toward a favorable one. But if the international division of labor is not to suffer, we must prefer exports to import substitutes.

Are not export subsidies, or export drives in general, a beggar-my-neighbor policy? The short answer is, yes, but so is every single measure taken to correct a b.o.p., except one. When the balance is unfavorable, the foreigner gets more money. To correct the balance is to recapture that money, which is literally to beggar my neighbor. If we correct it by deflation, we take our neighbor's gold, and lower his exports and everybody's income. If we raise short interest rates, our gain is either speculative and temporary or permanent and really effective—but then it must have been due to deflation. If the elasticities are such that an improvement in our terms of trade would be effective (e.g., by tariff, export tax, appreciation of own currency), we take our neighbor's gold, worsen his terms of trade and inflict unemployment.[1] If we simply put a stop to his exports (tariff, quota, exchange control), we have again worsened his terms of trade, inflicted unemployment and taken his gold. If the elasticities are such that it pays us to worsen our terms of trade (e.g., by devaluation), we still take his gold, and cause him a degree of unemployment that easily outweighs what he gains

[1] However, the speculative reaction to currency appreciation as a cure for a b.o.p. deficit would normally be highly negative and overwhelm its intended effects. This particular weapon remains quite academic.

from improved terms of trade. And beyond this particular remedy lies, of course, the export drive which is our subject; it has much the same effect as a devaluation. It follows that even between ACCs the export drive is at least not worse than other b.o.p. correctors. The only one that is manifestly a great improvement upon it is a multilateral expansion of international liquidity. This alone is a purely enrich-my-neighbor-and-enrich-me-too policy, though at bottom, since no country can run an import surplus for ever, it is no real remedy at all. It simply gains time until other remedies can be applied.

Moreover, when we take as our imaginary trading partner not another ACC but an STE and even a UDC, the export drive gains slightly over competing measures. This is simply because both these types of economy are better able to absorb imports, as we see in Chapter XV.

7

We now turn to the relation between imports and input-output. Every Keynesian knows that to cut imports is inflationary; and since with unemployment the multiplier is real as well as monetary the import cut also increases domestic output. But every child knows that an oil blockade diminishes output, and Marshall Aid made Europe boom. Can, then, the child and the Keynesian be reconciled?

Imagine a non-Keynesian ME governed by Say's Law. It is much like an STE. In the one, full employment is automatically brought about by the price mechanism; in the other, consciously but perpetually by the government. In both, a cut in imports diminishes consumption if consumption goods are the ones cut. In an STE the government may or may not decide to restore that cut by rearranging its plan, but it can only make partial restoration, since, if all previous decisions were wise, the new resource allocation is less productive than the old. In our hypothetical ME this kind of readjustment will inevitably come about, with the same ultimate results. If, on the other hand, it is imports of intermediate goods that are cut, and the readjustment cannot be quick (for some technological reason, of course), in any economic system there must be some temporary unemployment and a still more obvious fall in production. This is, of course, technological unemployment, a kind compatible with Say's Law, though scarcely considered by its proponents. The ultimate return to full employment brings about a resource allocation not widely different from the one considered above. In particular it is similar in bringing about a smaller total output.

Thus output falls entirely apart from deflationary unemployment. If, now, we repeal Say's Law the import cut inflates the economy *as well*. The technological unemployment still occurs but it lasts a shorter time. The final allocation of resources is still similar, and still likely to produce a smaller total output. But this time employment may actually exceed its initial level, and it will then depend on the exact change in productivity whether total output has risen or fallen.

At this point we can really validate the charge that the Keynesian analysis neglects input-output, even though our verdict was 'not guilty' in the case of the m.p.i. The monetary or consumer viewpoint of the theory appears to be so partial as to lead to actual error: an error identical with the Keynesian refused to consider technological unemployment. The basic fallacy is that *inputs are as easily substitutable for each other as final outputs*; and *factors of production as mobile between jobs as consumers' spending final goods*. The truth is that enterprises' production-possibility curves mostly have sharp corners, while consumers' indifference curves are smooth and curve gently. Hence the possibilities of friction are greater, and the effectiveness of price changes is smaller, when we leave the market for final goods. And this, indeed, is why input-output in its original, fixed-coefficient form might possibly do as a first approximation to the flow of intermediate goods and ultimate factors of production in the short run. Whereas we can and, indeed, must also consider the consumer as an enterprise, whose consumption and education are inputs, while work and leisure are outputs; and here very plainly the input coefficients are not fixed at all.

8

Keynesian theory holds, broadly, that imports compete imperfectly but adequately with import-substitutes. So an import cut raises costs a little, but this effect is entirely swamped by the monetary one. Money flows in from abroad; incomes rise; therefore output rises. To be precise, employment rises more than output, owing to the increase in costs. But this is fully valid only for two classes of goods. First come consumer goods, to which no value is added in home trade. Individual items in this class—which is, in fact, a null class, since all imports pass through trade channels—would scarcely influence output at all. For all consumer goods affect output only as incentives to work or as providers of physical energy to workers. Save in a famine, a fluctuation in imports of such goods will not have much short-run effect on actual output.[1] The second class is imports of any kind for which there is a *perfect* domestic substitute which is, moreover, in perfectly elastic supply. Then if the imports cease, costs do not rise, and again the change puts no obstacle in the way of production.

9

Now, going to the other extreme, consider an imported fuel, raw material, or machine (P) for which there is in the short run no domestic substitute at all. Then if a b.o.p. crisis be so severe as to hit this good the whole branch of production (Q) upon which it depends must cease; and since most of the cooperating factors are immobile in the short run they will be unemployed. Moreover, it may be that Q goods are irreplaceable and necessary inputs for the output of R. . . . We have here in effect a new 'multiplier', starting with inputs and working its way up toward outputs, in which the successive actions of demand upon demand are replaced by the successive actions of supply upon supply. This 'supply multiplier' might possibly be explosive, in that $R>Q>P$; but the possibilities of substitution are surely in general such as to damp it. Since it is so very irregular and unpredictable we shall not call it any kind of multiplier, but the *bottleneck effect*. The effect is real, with monetary consequences; while the multiplier is monetary, with real consequences. It is also only negative: an 'unbottleneck', or great surplus of a commodity, will give no special thrust toward physical expansion.

The thing is worth elementary symbolical analysis. In the table below we set out the monetary value of domestic expenditure on final goods, intermediate goods, and the ultimate factors of production (land, labor, capital, enterprise) whose payments constitute the national income. For simplicity A, the domestic intermediate good, is made by hand, like D. M is strictly not a good but the foreign exchange component of B and E. E is that nearly impossible thing, an import to which no domestic value is added before sale to the consumer. Z is the national income. Small letters denote fractions

---

[1] It is appropriate to remember Professor Bergson's epigram: 'To Stalin bread was an intermediate and steel a final good' [P. J. D. Wiles, *The Political Economy of Communism*, p. 283]. In the specific case of bread we can, perhaps, speak of a fixed coefficient consumption good: cf. Chapter XVI, Section 9.

of the supply of each input used up by the particular output. We are in a market economy, and the government and the banking system are neutral.

Final Goods	Intermediate Goods	Ultimate Factors of Production
B	kA	mZ
	jM	
		nZ
C	$(1-k)A$	pZ
		qZ
D	$(1-m-n-p-q)\,Z$	
E	$(1-j)M$	

10

(i) Take first the extreme case, that we prohibit the importation of $(1-j)M$. There is no unemployment; indeed, no domestic factors can even be threatened with unemployment. The inflationary gap can be calculated in two ways: either as the diminution of imports $[(1-j)M]$ or as the difference between lowered sales and incomes (E). Since domestic factors have not been set free by the import cut, the excess demand exercises its full effect toward inflation and/or fuller employment.

(ii) Now let us go to the other extreme and prohibit the importation of jM. There is, furthermore, no domestic substitute for the physical object represented by this expenditure. Then all final sales of B cease, and along with them $mZ + nZ$, the incomes generated at home by the production of B. We have, therefore, created an inflationary gap of $B - Z(m+n)$, which $= jM$. I.e., the inflationary gap can be described in the same two ways as before, as either the diminution of imports or the difference between lowered sales and (also lowered) incomes.

A closer analysis, taking stocks into account, makes little difference. Thus if there exist stocks of jM, the import cut does not take effect until either they have been worked off or enterprises decide to hoard the remainder. If there are stocks of B, consumer expenditures on B will continue longer than factor incomes generated by B, and the enterprise will probably hoard the proceeds of the sale from stocks. This adds an element of deflation to the whole

economy, which does not quite cease when B stocks run out or begin
to be hoarded; for the money has been withdrawn, and may take
some time in returning to the stream of active circulation, e.g.,
via the short money market and the banks.

II

But the main thing is that in case (ii) we have also created unemployment $= Z(m+n)(1/w)$, where w is the rate at which factors are
paid. This is a substantial matter, seemingly quite neglected in the
simpler Keynesian expositions, which implicitly treat only the case
E, where there is no domestic value added to the import. If the
factors $Z(m+n)(1/w)$ are mobile they will be absorbed by the rest
of the economy C, D, provided there is enough demand. Now, of
course, the inflationary gap will provide some of this demand. But
enough? Seemingly not so. For we have not now a large unsatisfied demand, B, chasing the available resources $Z(m+n)(1/w)$;
the income of these resources $Z(m+n)$ has been destroyed, and
must be subtracted from B. All we have is the small unsatisfied
demand, already described, and the many unemployed resources.
The import that was cut might have been some quite trivial nut or
bolt, so that the inflationary gap as ordinarily counted is very small.
But the unemployment might be terrific. It is, in fact, *technological
unemployment*, a kind notoriously neglected in the Keynesian system;
moreover—being short term only—it is quite undeniable and needs
none of the long theoretical defense that skeptics demand for long-
term technological unemployment. It is of especial importance for
us here that this phenomenon represents a sacrifice of about as much
income as of production, and so neither its onset nor its cure has a
marked effect on over-all monetary balance. Indeed, this is equally
true of 'Keynesian' unemployment. Serious over-all monetary
imbalance only occurs when prices and outputs cannot respond to
some monetary lead; as to a monetary expansion when there is no
'Keynesian' unemployment. Such a case is described in (iv) below.

Some of the inflationary gap will, of course, leave the country in
increased purchases of the other import E, unless that is also prohibited.

12

(iii) So much in the simplest possible terms. Now in practice the
unemployed will certainly dissave, cease to pay taxes, and begin to
draw on the social services. There is then a very substantial addition

to the inflationary gap if jM be cut, which has no parallel in the case of $(1 - j)M$. It will mitigate, to a quite uncertain degree determined by chance and institutional factors, the unemployment predicted in (ii) above.

(iv) Moreover, it was quite arbitrary to suppose that these factors were mobile. The less mobile they are the more they will spend in the manner just described, and the more the inflationary gap will drive up the prices of whatever *can* be produced, so that rising prices and (if permitted) a secondary increase in imports will coincide with unemployment. This is because that unemployment not only was caused in a non-Keynesian manner, but also cannot be cured in that way. However, the reflationary possibilities of (iii) will, under most institutional set-ups, die away in time, as hoards are spent and the less generous social provisions commonly allotted to the long-term unemployed come into play.

(v) Next, let jM have a domestic substitute. Let it be D (and let D be mobile). We now move D partially into the 'intermediate goods' column. We could, of course, have postulated that D be an intermediate good in all its uses, but the case is stronger and more interesting if it remains basically a consumer good. Now to say that a substitute exists is not to say that it is forever in perfectly elastic supply.[1] In the short run D's price rises owing to diminishing returns, and to the great pressure of demand; for not only is it in demand as an input for B but also more than ever as a final good in its own right, owing to the prevailing inflation. As we see below, there is no special reason to predict that enterprises, in competition with final consumers for some good or service, will outbid them. If, apart from the substitutability of D for jM, input proportions are rather fixed in the B industry, it is quite improbable that enough D will be forthcoming for the cooperant kA ($= mZ$) and nZ all to be re-employed there. If these latter cannot set up a new industry, F, on their own, and are not easily substitutable for the ultimate factors of production employed in the C, D and E industries, they will remain unemployed. Case (v) is very similar to case (iv): the partial substitutability of inputs presumes, of course, their mobility.

13

The reactions of the multiplier and the bottleneck effect with each other are thus very complicated, and I have not succeeded in building

[1] Or even that it is a perfect substitute over the whole isoquant; but let us allow that here.

up a general theory of them. Clearly, however, such a theory would start with a matrix, and certainly many more cases can be illustrated that way. In the matrix shown, oil is an import, all other imports are represented by foreign exchange, all input-output ratios are

FIGURE IV/1

Sold From ＼ Bought By	F	G	H	J	Oil	Exports	Final Consumers
F	／	0	0	a	0	0	b
G	c	／	0	d	0	0	e
H	0	f	／	g	0	0	h
J	i	0	0	／	0	j	0
Oil	k	m	0	0	／	0	n
Other Imports	p	0	0	0	0	／	q
Ultimate Factors	r	s	t	u	v	w	

fixed, letters or crosses denote specific quantities, O denotes nothing. H is an independent sector of the economy, say a primitive agriculture. H can produce under all conditions.

The specialist will note that this matrix is not triangular, nor can it be roughly divided into 'Ghosh blocks'. A triangular matrix that confined imports to the south-west corner would abolish·

imports for final consumption, and over-simplify the analysis. More to the point, it would be unrealistic since we have treated 'other imports' as undifferentiated foreign exchange, not as a particular physical good. This is precisely what a matrix should do if it is to aid the formulation of b.o.p. policy. For the same reason there could be no relevant Ghosh block, since 'other imports' are confined to no block. But the reader may amuse himself by creating such a block: set f and g at o, and subdivide H into, say, crops and livestock.

First let this matrix describe an STE, and let there be a b.o.p. crisis. So the planners cut q. If that is enough, well and good. If not, they must not be so foolish as to cut p, for that is quite as essential as k or m. The next to go should be n. Or they might begin with a mixture of n and q. But if they have to go further they are in a very bad way. If m goes there is no G and, therefore, no c; so no F. It might seem less disastrous to cut k and p, for one is useless without the other and this saves more foreign exchange. But then there is no F; so no a; so no J. And J is our only export (j); so before long there will be no m; m, and with it G, will survive only as long as our foreign exchange reserves survive. Therefore, if n and q are small, and the b.o.p. crisis is big, only H will survive.

The trick, of course, was to assume fixed coefficients. Suppose that oil has, indeed, such coefficients, but that other imports have not. We then have p to play with as well, and the real crisis will be longer in coming. This also gives heightened interest to oil, and to all fixed coefficient imports, in economic warfare (see Chapter XVI, below).

14

Hitherto we have insisted on a rather absolute distinction between intermediate goods, with nearly fixed coefficients, and final goods, which are pretty complete substitutes for each other. This rests not at all upon the assumption of perfect competition among final goods, but upon the fact that consumers will spend their income in one way if not in another, but enterprises cannot hop from industry to industry. While this is always so there remains one case, already hinted at, in which a consumption good has a virtually 'fixed coefficient': a staple good during a bad harvest year in a country without a food surplus. The example does not occur easily to the Western mind, and theory might easily be so phrased as not to allow for it. If in general truth is stranger than fiction, in economics the logical imagination is slave to the empirical facts with which it deals day by day. The possibility of a 'fixed coefficient consumption good' is ever-present to a Communist government. For if labor is an input, then consumption is also an input in its turn, and without his staple food the consumer will not, indeed cannot, produce. It follows at once that staple foods 'should' be an object of economic warfare like oil.

15

Now apply the matrix to an ME, indeed to the 'perfect' form, a free market. Let the b.o.p. crisis arise exogenously, through a bad harvest (necessity to substitute q for h) or a fall in the price of J. Home prices fall relatively to import prices, through either exchange depreciation or deflation. The industries F and G, immediately dependent on imports, are in full competition with the final consumer. Their profit position may be such, indeed, that the consumer beats them to the punch: q, being in inelastic demand, may flourish while k, p, m and n shrink. We may think of the Indian demand for automobiles, as opposed to raw cotton. So far from being abnormal, this case is quite unremarkable. The demand for each import, whether final or intermediate, will shrink according to its elasticity (in a free market, where the only adjustment is via prices, and given perfect elasticity of foreign supply).

More in detail, with fixed coefficients the elasticity of derived demand for an input (E_x) is smaller than that for the output it helps to make (E_y), but not indefinitely so. Thus if home prices are sticky, or home supplies very elastic, the unit domestic value (V) added to an imported input x of price P_x is constant. So P_y, the price of the final good, is always $V + P_x$. In that case[1]

$$\frac{E_y}{E_x} = \frac{V + P_x}{P_x}.$$

It is perfectly clear that another import z, with $V_z \simeq 0$, could be less elastically demanded than x. Therefore, z is successfully competing with x for foreign exchange, and causing unemployment among the resources entering into V_y.

[1] If coefficients are fixed $dq_y/q_y = dq_x/q_x$. If V is constant $\Delta P_y = \Delta P_x$. So $E_y = [(V + P_x) dq_x]/ q_x dp_x$.

If, on the other hand, coefficients are not fixed, there are domestic substitutes for x. E_x rises, and may have any value vis-à-vis E_y. The competition of z for foreign exchange still threatens x, but no longer, or to a lesser extent, the cooperant factors V_y. It would, therefore, be profitless—and beyond my powers—to pursue the more complicated mathematics of this case.

In the short run, then, and returning to our matrix, the continued importation of q at the expense of k, p and m, will cause unemployment. In the medium run, however, equilibrating factors will set in. The ultimate factors of production r and s will accept lower rewards, re-establishing the profitability of F and G, so that they can compete with the final consumers for foreign exchange. If the crisis was due to a bad harvest, and exchange depreciation is permitted, industry J will flourish; the price of a will rise, bringing prosperity to F, and so via c to G.[1]

16

We have thus two extremes. (a) One is quite realistic: the 'perfect STE'. Here there is no m.p.i., enterprises obediently hoard the money they cannot spend on imports, and the only monetary effect of an import cut is that the consumer tries to spend his income somewhere else. But since this is a *perfect* STE, he cannot, in fact, do so, and must hoard his money, too. Then, substitution or no substitution, the input-output effects of the import cut are the only ones, and consumer goods are radically different from producer goods. (b) The other extreme is for illustrative purposes only: an ME where all intermediate goods have perfect substitutes in perfectly elastic supply. The nearest, not very close, approach to such a state of affairs is a large ACC with unemployment, indeed, one of those countries in which modern economists mainly live. The income effect swamps the bottleneck effect, so we never see the latter. It is not even partially manifested through rising costs, since whenever there is a b.o.p. crisis that might bring it on the monetary authorities deflate the whole economy, and this discourages import substitution. Indeed this is my whole objection to deflation: the use of expensive import substitutes is superior. In this case, then, it does not matter at all whether the import cuts hit producer or consumer

---

[1] But with fixed exchanges J will not benefit, except through the release of resources r and s, and in so far as these are mobile. *A fortiori*, if a fall in the price of j had been the prime cause of the crisis J will be spreading contraction, not expansion.

goods: no unemployment is caused to the cooperant factors in the former case, and everything sorts itself out easily. The effects via the foreign-trade multiplier are the only ones, the initial inflationary gap is equal to the extent of the import cut, and the employment multiplier equals the income multiplier. This is the Platonic Idea of an economy analysable in Keynesian terms alone.

In reality, MEs lie between these pure cases, but closer to the latter. (c) Let intermediate goods have rather imperfect substitutes which are in somewhat less than perfectly elastic supply, and let the import demand for them be less elastic than for consumer goods. Then the foreign-trade multiplier is still the main tool for analysing the effects of an import cut, but costs do rise so that the output multiplier, while still positive, falls short of the employment multiplier. (d) Let intermediate goods have only quite imperfect substitutes, inelastically supplied, but let the import demand for them chance to be more elastic than for consumer goods. Then it is inappropriate to speak of an output or employment multiplier, since an import cut reduces output, owing to the bottleneck effect. But there is a positive monetary multiplier, so that inflation accompanies the increase in technological unemployment. Since we are still in an ME the m.p.i. is not zero. Indeed, it will be very high, and further restrictions on imports will be needed.

17

The conflict between the Keynesian multiplier and the bottleneck effect is thus very complicated indeed. I feel able only to offer particular, disconnected, conclusions.

(i) It is more inflationary to restrict the import of finished goods than of intermediate inputs.

(ii) If the latter are restricted, and coefficients are fixed, there will be technological unemployment. If social services and money hoards are small, this unemployment will leave unaffected the inflation brought about by the import cut.

(iii) In intermediate cases it is simply not clear without much calculation *ad hoc* whether the multiplier defeats or is defeated by the bottleneck effect, even in monetary terms. But whatever the change in money income, real income is likely to grow considerably less, or fall considerably more. For in addition to diminishing returns in such output as does expand—a point known well to Keynesians—there is technological unemployment.

(iv) However, this whole input-output analysis, like the Keynesian, concerns the short run and the immediate b.o.p. crisis. Economic growth has other connections with the structure of imports, which are dealt with in Chapter VIII.

(v) But in one respect, long-run considerations are relevant here: in the absence of other kinds of international liquidity an ME and an STE alike need to have large imports of consumer goods, with little domestic value added, in normal times. These are their first cushion against a crisis: such imports are to be viewed as a positive advantage. If a country spends most of its time in crisis and semi-crisis it will lose this cushion for good—as many an STE or UDC can illustrate. The great exception is the politically backward UDC in which a traditional ruling class can still spend foreign exchange at Dior's or hoard it in Zürich. A good case in point is the USSR, which reduced its imports of consumer goods from 20·8% of the whole in 1913 to 4·7% in 1938. This is a dangerously low level, which post-Stalin policy has much exceeded, for whatever reason.[1] In such cases b.o.p. crises become more and more serious, just as if stocks of convertible currency had dwindled.

(vi) Similarly with an export drive. If we encourage the export of intermediate goods that are also used at home we run the risk of unemployment during a b.o.p. crisis. And this applies however 'structurally' rational such exports may be in the long run (Chapter VIII). We should, therefore, concentrate on final goods, or intermediate goods not having a domestic use. Every step in the previous analysis can be duplicated in this way.

(vii) For an STE, which is more or less in the situation (a) above, inflation and deflation have no direct effect on the b.o.p. Where the m.p.i. does not exist the planners have merely to consider the bottleneck effect. And in this connection they are better able to cut consumers' imports. It might, therefore, seem that an STE was in better case, but in practice not so. For substitutability is much enhanced by flexible prices, and much diminished by a cumbrous system of central command. Therefore, cases of short-run fixed proportions are much commoner in an STE than an ME, and if the zero m.p.i. is a help, the bottleneck effect is a hindrance.

(viii) The more advanced the economy the less its nonagricultural sectors, and the more its agriculture, depend on particular imported inputs. For, on the one hand, its industry can the more easily make substitutes for the imports used in industry, construction and trans-

[1] *Narodnoye Khozyaistvo* 1960, p. 747.

port; but, on the other, its agriculture will for the first time be using foreign or non-agricultural inputs. So, on the whole, the bottleneck effect is smaller, but imported fodder, fuel and tractors work the other way.

(ix) An ACC tends, in general, to be in the situation described in Section 16 (c). The simple fact of being advanced has two beneficial effects. First, more substitutes can be made and more can be used (always excepting agriculture; see (viii)). Secondly, the authorities are more competent and in less of a hurry and less subject to optimistic or hasty politicians. They can foresee a crisis, lay in stocks, ease transitions, avoid panic.

(x) *Per contra*, the UDC tends to be in the situation of Section 16 (d). Like the STE it has no cushion of inessential imports. It is also bad at making substitutions, but for different reasons: lack of entrepreneurial initiative, sheer technical incapacity. Again, like the STE, it will be psychologically likely to overdo things. The investment program will enhance both imports and inflation, and import cuts will not be made until too late and in a panic.

(xi) The smaller the country the greater the bottleneck effect.

(xii) The whole input-output analysis of a b.o.p. crisis has more application to extreme than to normal conditions, and most application to economic warfare (Chapter XVI), where the import prohibition is imposed from without, and with a view to exploiting, not mitigating, the bottleneck effect.

CHAPTER V

THE BALANCE-OF-PAYMENTS CRISIS IN THE COMMAND ECONOMY

1   Definitions.
2   Each crisis is particular, in all economies.
3   The main cause in all cases: planners' Micawberism.
4   The faster growth of STEs, in the light of the b.o.p.
5   The braking effect of crises on MEs.
6   The same on STEs.
7   The quantitative effect of micro-economic distortions.
8   The liquidity of foreign debt.
9   The causes of b.o.p. trouble in STEs.
10 The Soviet crisis during the first FYP.
11 The Hungarian crisis of 1954–55.
12 The minor Soviet and Hungarian crises.
13 The Czechoslovak crisis of 1962–63.

I

A BALANCE- of-payments (b.o.p.) crisis in an ME is a moment when net revenue in foreign currency matters more than profitability in all currencies put together. The two are temporarily out of phase, and 'social profit' is more accurately represented by the former. For otherwise there will be grave unemployment, whether of the Keynesian or of the bottleneck variety, or both. Indeed, in a food-importing country there might be actual starvation. In the long run however, as shown in Chapters VIII and XV, there should be and normally is no reason why profit, expressed in home currency and converting all foreign exchange components at the purchasing power parity (p.p.p.), should not govern our foreign economic relations.

This remains true in an STE, provided that the p.p.p. is taken as a shadow rate of exchange (Chapter VII). The fact that it is not merely complicates, without altering, the basic position. Deprived of a rational means of comparing exports, imports and import-substitutes with domestic activity, the government of an STE may adopt 'crisis-like' behavior earlier, or later, than is necessary.

All economic crises in a particular country are in a sense international, in that different international circumstances could have prevented them from beginning, and could alleviate them once begun. But we deal here only with crises that in fact hit the b.o.p., however they originate.

In a crisis, on the dictionary definition of that word, the government must take unusual measures. It depends on the severity of these whether the country merely gets into—or stays in—*b.o.p. trouble* or actually incurs a *b.o.p.-generated setback*. We define these two terms thus. There is b.o.p. trouble when the central bank is bothered about reserves, when the government takes somewhat irrational, short-term measures to restrict imports, when exports and import-substitutes are subsidized and investment is unnaturally concentrated upon their expansion. Very likely some of these distortions were already present: they are simply intensified. There is a b.o.p. setback when the whole economy is throttled down in order to cut the demand for imports, and unemployment is positively desired in order to set resources free for export. In an STE this is simply a matter of the bottleneck effect. Imports are reduced to the extent required, but since some of them are production inputs, production falls in so far as substitutes cannot be found. In an unregulated ME, on the other hand, the marginal propensity to import (m.p.i.) alone operates. Income, and therefore production, are reduced by overall monetary or fiscal policy until imports fall: substitution is not necessarily encouraged. The advantage of this procedure for the ME is that no micro-distortions follow; this method is, therefore, preferred by those who think such distortions are a sin against the Holy Ghost. Thus in 'trouble' we correct by irrational micro-allocation; in 'setback' by unemployment. We almost certainly lose more by the latter, because of the likely orders of magnitude (see Sections 5 and 7, below); and this partially accounts for the quicker growth of STEs.

2

In dedicating a chapter to the comparative lore of b.o.p. crises, I take a risk that might not be at first appreciated. Just as the old trade cycle resisted purely endogenous analysis, so is each crisis the product of particular historical circumstance. Nor is any crisis cured purely according to the textbook; there is always some special measure taken. Thus among MEs we can distinguish two textbook sets of measures, depending mainly on the politics of the government:

(a) setback-inducing—raise bank rate and budget surplus, so as to deflate; (b) trouble-inducing—bring about a trade surplus by the appropriate mixture of taxes and subsidies, interfere with international transfers of money, devalue or even, possibly, appreciate the currency. And we might expect every ME to use (a) or (b) or some mixture, while an STE would use the command mechanisms to achieve results similar to (b).

But in practice in 1961, facing an unusual gold outflow, the United States Government, in addition to some of the above measures, did the following: brought soldiers' families home; cut the duty-free allowance for returning United States tourists; and used diplomatic pressure to lower foreign tariffs on United States goods. It might also have: cut foreign civilian aid; withdrawn its troops from Vietnam; replaced the silver in the currency; reduced the legal gold coverage of the note issue; and sold strategic stocks. These actions were proposed and were quite practicable, but not taken.

A similar mixture of textbook and once-for-all actions has been the British Government's reaction to its numerous post-war b.o.p. crises. The STE, where everything is political, is even less subject to generalization (see Sections 10–13). But not only has every b.o.p. crisis its historic specificity, each is a crisis of the whole economy. This follows instantly from the mere fact that there equilibrium must be general. So small a magnitude as the difference between exports and imports, or so delicate an affair as foreigners' feelings about the currency of an ME, are affected by events in the whole economy, and by no means only in the sectors formally labelled 'imports', 'exports', 'import-substitutes' or 'finance.'

3

How do countries get into these crises? Even politics has its generalizations, and here surely is a reliable one: the Micawberism of politicians and planners is much more important than any other cause, be it harvest failure or some complicated quirk of econometrics. Mere human miscalculation, mere self-deception as to the probabilities, is always present and always enough. This is especially true of the *balance* of payments, which is the small difference between two large and unpredictable quantities. To allow conscious human regulation of the economy is to make it possible to postpone stern measures; but human nature then makes it certain there will be overpostponement and a b.o.p. crisis.

A setback is—or was—the only way out of such a crisis in a quite unregulated ME. But had it been on the gold standard it is most unlikely that it would have got into a serious crisis in the first place. Rather may the gold standard be described, using our terminology, as a perpetual minor setback—employment was always lower, and liquidity higher, than would otherwise have been the case. There are, of course, also a few major, but crisis-free, setbacks, but they were international, so crisis-free. We used to call them the trade cycle. The basic feature of the gold standard was, we can say with hindsight, political: it excluded politicians and put the b.o.p. in the control of an automatism. In so far as central bankers could mitigate the system they yet did not; for they were mere bankers, not planners. They defended their reserves, not the volume of employment or the standard of living.

It is one of the main advantages, and, indeed, *raisons d'être*, of the regulated ME that it can to some extent substitute trouble (i.e., distortions) for setbacks (i.e., unemployment). This is offset, however, by the tendency to run much further into deficit in the first place. For when economic policy becomes a political football, and is taken out of the 'expert' hands of the central bank, we have seen that full employment and rapid growth will be pursued right up to the brink of total loss of gold reserves. This is the typical cause of crisis in both regulated MEs and STEs, i.e., wherever automatism yields to politicians. It is in particular vain to seek endogenous economic cycles any more, or indeed cycles of any kind. There is at most a crisis syndrome that occurs irregularly when the government feels that way. The syndrome appropriate to the STE is described in Section 8. All talk of a 'socialist trade cycle'[1] boils down only to this.

4

The b.o.p. setback is so out of tune with the general system of an STE that one might think it inconceivable, did not history provide a rare example or two: e.g., Czechoslovakia, 1962–63. To b.o.p. trouble, on the other hand, the STE is no stranger at all. Perpetually short of foreign exchange, it resorts to bilateralism, autarky, restrictions on private gold holdings, etc., all the time. But b.o.p. trouble is not serious: it is simply something that keeps bankers awake long

[1] Joseph Goldmann in *Rinascita*, January 16, 1965; idem in *Economics of Planning* (Oslo), winter, 1964; Jozef Pajestka in *Zycie Gospodarcze*, February 28, 1965; Alec Nove, 'Cyclical Fluctuations Under Socialism,' in the forthcoming London symposium, ed. Martin Bronfenbrennes.

hours and distorts the allocation of resources. Since it does not affect the rate of growth, it hardly matters at all.

Thus we may set out four time-series of growth for comparison, in percentage points of national income per head per annum. Each has only a moderate degree of empirical warrant, and is rather to be understood as a schematic *Idealtypus* in Max Weber's sense. The pre-Keynesian ACC, an unregulated ME subject to 'the' trade cycle, grew at about 1.7% per annum, the average of an approximately eight-year periodicity: for instance, 3 4 7 2 − 1 0 0 1. Whether b.o.p. problems were a major cause of the cycle itself we need not here inquire in detail. It suffices that there were few real crises, but the fear of them kept growth below potential even in peak years.

Since the second world war our 'representative' ACC, having switched from a broadly unregulated to a broadly regulated system, has been able to sustain its previous rate in cycle upswings year by year. But it is interrupted by occasional severe b.o.p. crises, which are followed by short, sharp setbacks. These, in turn, permit reflation and exceptional growth, which, however, never completely efface the setback. Such a crisis might happen once every six years, irregularly: 4 4 4 0 6 4 4 0 6 4 4 4. The average rate of growth is 3·5%. Thirdly, however, an ACC might choose, like the United States and the United Kingdom, to provide the world with a reserve currency. It will still benefit by the demise of the trade cycle and by many of the remedies of government intervention. But b.o.p. crises come much more often—say, once in three years— and it must be more careful even in good years: 3 3 0 5 0 5 3 0 5 3 0 5. The average is 2.2%[1]. Fourthly, the STE keeps up a fairly steady 4%, with a mild crisis about every ten years: 4 4 4 4 4 3 6 4 4 4.

The infrequency of Soviet-type crises is of great importance for our argument, and individual crises are little known. We list below, therefore, all Soviet-type peace-time b.o.p. crises known to us, in the countries with which we shall deal.

The general causes are discussed in Section 8, below. As to the frequency of crises, by 1966 these three countries had spent sixty-four peacetime years as STEs. For the rest the definitions are arbitrary: what others may call peak periods of trouble I have called crises. It is upon this slender evidence that I base the assumption of a crisis every ten years. A Soviet-type b.o.p. crisis is evidently

[1] Rates from Simon Kuznets, *Post-War Economic Growth: Four Lectures* (Harvard, 1964). 'Pre-Keynesian': USA throughout, 12 other ACCs in 1880–1914. 'Keynesian': 1951–61, the same 12 ACCs less UK.

so particular and political that it is bold, indeed, to try to build up statistical experience of it.

Date	Country	Proximate Causes
1929–32	USSR	Agricultural production lowered by collectivization and confiscation of seed-grain for military purposes; very heavy machinery imports; bad terms of trade.
1946[b]	USSR	Harvest failure.
1963[b]	USSR	Harvest failure.
1954–55[c]	Hungary	Over investment in unproductive factories; collectivization; accumulation of previous trade debt; concessions to population by Imre Nagy.
1957[b]	Hungary	Concessions to population after revolution.
1962–63[d]	Czechoslovakia	Wasteful dispersal of investment funds by new decentralized planning system; shortfall of agricultural imports from USSR and China; arms imports; excessive foreign aid.

[a] See Section 9.
[b] See Section 11.
[c] See Section 10.
[d] See Section 12.

5

These are, historically and approximately speaking, the actual differences in general growth, and in the severity and frequency of crises. Let us briefly and dogmatically examine how much each kind of economy falls short of its potential by reason of b.o.p. troubles and setbacks.

Whether the pre-Keynesian trade cycle was actually caused by the gold standard and other forms of free trade in money, we need not inquire. But the cycle existed, however chronologically irregular and theoretically inexplicable. And obviously it retarded growth; for while it is true that growth was quick, sometimes very quick, during upswings, it could not make up for the downswings. The occasional very rapid growth was due only to the re-employment of surplus capacity. As to the stock of capacity, no one was going to invest during an upswing enough to make up for the failure to invest during the previous downswing, since he knew another downswing was coming. It is equally plain that free trade in money, whether or not it helped to *cause* the trade cycle, did *involve* a country in it; it made counter-measures impossible. Therefore, the monetary system in that period depressed economic growth. On the other hand there were, to repeat, no crises *sensu stricto*, and this must be accounted a great virtue of the system.[1]

It is very different with the post-war ACC, which grows rather faster and—it should not surprise us—has b.o.p. trouble a great deal of the time. Moreover, this trouble sometimes develops into crises. Clearly growth is irregular now because of these, and not the trade cycle, since there is no trade cycle. These crises hit different countries at different times. But the irregularity affects the volume of investment *per se* by making it more risky. Moreover, there is in all market systems a further element: the liquidity preference not of entrepreneurs but of the monetary authorities themselves. Perpetually in fear of going off gold, of devaluation, of a crisis, the authorities will always be holding their own lending rate somewhat higher than it would otherwise have been, and in other ways discouraging economic activity, especially government activity. They will try to except exports and import-substitutes, but operating as they do on the rate of interest and the quantity of money, they will still hit investment harder than consumption. Therefore, their liquidity preference does not merely make for unemployment but also for a low investment proportion. Constant high unemployment *might* not affect the proportion between investment and consumption, and in that case would probably not retard growth. But it will be retarded by a low proportion, whether that is caused by deflationary public policy or anything else.

It is, therefore, plain that an ME, with its unique tropism toward the b.o.p. setback, is *pro tanto* unfavorable to growth, whatever its other advantages. Take our *Idealtypus* of a West European ACC growing at 3·5% per annum, as illustrated above. Suppose that the perpetual pressure of liquidity preference in good years reduces growth by 0·2% below what it would have been. The further loss due to setbacks in bad years we have already set at 2% every six years, or 0·33% per annum. Thus, in all, the growth lost by a 'typical' ACC owing to its b.o.p. vulnerability is the 4·0% it might achieve minus the 3·5% it does achieve, or 0·5% per annum. This is, indeed, the approximate difference between rates of growth in Western and in Eastern Europe until recently.

The deviations from perfect micro-economic rationality, in which

---

[1] The reference is to the classic gold standard period from 1871 to 1914. Previously, there used, indeed, to be sharp monetary crises, e.g., in London in 1857 and 1866. These usually coincided with b.o.p. trouble.

the modern regulated ME indulges most of the time in order to avoid b.o.p. setbacks, are certainly insignificant compared with those of STEs. Since, as we see below, the latter probably make little difference to growth, we may dismiss the former out of hand, as being beneath our *minimum sensibile*.

6

How much, then, does the STE lose through b.o.p. crises? We have already met the essential fact in Chapters III and IV: there is no 'real' foreign-trade multiplier, only a monetary one. The foreign balance is all planned, and the import and export corporations react not at all to domestic money flows. The marginal propensity to import is zero or, better, an inapplicable concept.

There exists, to be sure, a pale shadow of the m.p.i. among the calculations made when drawing up the plan. This process much more closely resembles a market in an STE than the process of actual production. The latter should be merely a matter of administrative execution; but while we draw up the plan, every output has an import component, and this corresponds vaguely to an m.p.i. in the planners' minds. They may even contemplate curing inflation by means of imports, instead of demanding more abstinence; which would be equivalent to saying that investment and defense have a sort of multiplier effect, and the consumer a proper m.p.i. However, we are here dealing with what happens when the plan goes wrong. We may assume it embodies some prediction of satisfactory balance; even if his includes an aid-financed deficit—as it surely does in the case of Albania (Chapter XIV). We are studying the emergency measures taken when the prediction fails. It is not, of course, logically impossible, but there is in practice no such thing as a planned b.o.p. crisis.

Without multiplier or m.p.i. the crisis is much less likely to be severe. If imports are cut or exports expanded that leads, of course, to inflation, but this does not cause yet more imports. Nor is that all: the government can issue instructions (e.g., to save imports) to each industry or even enterprise individually; so *it has no need to use general weapons, such as the credit restrictions that periodically cripple MEs*, including their non-importing sectors. Indeed, not only are such weapons not needed: they hardly exist and would fit very ill into the institutional model (see Chapter III, Sections 8 and 10). Hence, the government has every temptation to *localize* the b.o.p.

crisis in the particular sectors of export, import and import-substitute where it first appears.

A physical plan is necessarily 'local': particular orders are required to enforce particular changes. In the absence of bottleneck effects, the repercussions of these changes 'vanish', i.e., diminish as they pass from enterprise to enterprise. Stocks are reduced here, quality suffers there, overtime is worked in a third place. Costs rise all round, but there is no other serious effect.[1] Even a bottleneck will not normally perpetuate the repercussions. A bottleneck in commodity A causes a shortage of commodity B. But B is unlikely to be another bottleneck, and the shortage of this second commodity will have only the usual 'vanishing' consequences: stocks and quality reduced, overtime increased. In any case all this holds also of an ME—in which by contrast the m.p.i. also operates and the weapon of localized command is by definition absent.

Between the physical and the monetary there lies the fiscal: more general than the one, more particular than the other. But in the STE this is hardly so. For should the Soviet-type government take any physical measure, a parallel fiscal one must accompany it; and vice versa. Above all, there is no such thing as a general fiscal restraint on investment or consumption, untranslated into particular orders to stop doing this or that. Consequently, all fiscal cuts in an STE are just as localized as physical cuts, for the simple reason that they are two aspects of one cut. In order to reduce investment we must strike individual projects from the budget: it is useless to run a generalized budget surplus and trust the multiplier.

So all measures consist in detailed alterations of the plan at particular points, and in the unfavorable input-output consequences thereof throughout the economy. But these are quite minor compared with the effects of multiplier, accelerator and changed expectation in an ME. The government never takes sweeping general measures that will *also* hit imports, like a general credit restriction in an ME; it just hits imports. If it wishes to maintain investment, and put the whole burden of retrenchment on consumption, it faces only political troubles; the institutions are precisely adapted to this end, whereas in an ME, monetary policy necessarily hits investment most, as we have seen.

7

The unregulated ME, then, suffers a 'setback'—unemployment. The regulated ME tries to substitute 'trouble': various

[1] For the one great exception, the Czechoslovak crisis of 1962–63, see Section 12, below.

micro-distortions. The 'perfect STE' succeeds in just this aim: its sole weapons are such micro-distortions—unless, as we see below, they turn out to be micro-corrections, actual improvements. In the (normal) absence of bottleneck effects and sudden technological unemployment, the 'perfect STE' suffers, as we have seen, far less. The semi-decentralized STE will be dealt with below.

How great, quantitatively, is the loss through micro-distortions? It is, of course, only their *introduction* that lowers the national income. Once such a system has been imposed, the perpetuation of distortions is without effect on growth, and their diminution actually increases it.[1] It is not so much the b.o.p. crisis as the Soviet-type system itself that introduces all these irrationalities. And recent shifts in ideology and planning have greatly reduced them again. But perhaps over and above this historical trend there is a steady accumulation of irrationalities due to successive b.o.p. crises?

We have no statistical measure of irrationality in any economy. But if the universal conviction is true, that Soviet-type irrationality is much smaller than it used to be, a *cumulative* distortion through successive b.o.p. crises has not in fact occurred. Indeed, if there is no cumulation, the distortions are at some time corrected. Then although they diminish growth between successive particular years they do not diminish it over long periods of time. So they are not serious.

Moreover, since an STE is micro-economically distorted in the first place it is not obvious that when it re-allocates resources in response to a b.o.p. crisis it makes things worse. This would have to be true of an optimally arranged, perfectly computing STE. But it is by no means necessary, even perhaps rather improbable, of the STEs we have. As we shall see in Chapter VII, foreign trade has in fact been the greatest of all forces making for micro-rationality in STEs: no doubt this force is strongest when the b.o.p. is most troublesome.

In a b.o.p. crisis, after all, it is the duty of any government to cast about to see what it can do. We normally think of the government of an ME introducing exchange control or raising tariffs—distorting resource allocation. But we must not forget the extreme particularity of each crisis. Such a government will also use the opportunity to suppress any foolish and expensive schemes afoot. The weight of economy measures is more likely to fall on the latter. It is thus not impossible that b.o.p. crises act on the whole to rationalize STEs, so many more foolish schemes.

[1] P. J. D. Wiles, *The Political Economy of Communism*, Chapter XII, Section 24.

But this is an adventitious circumstance. In recommending one or other type of economic institution we should assume the far better managed STEs, even those that are not decentralized, that we already begin to see. The crisis will no longer be an opportunity for such a government to correct gross distortions of its own making, but it will still plainly suffer from the new distortions that its nature compels it to impose in a crisis. These may be quantified by educated guesswork as follows. Let imports be cut by 5%, while exports scarcely respond to encouragement; but let this be enough to correct the deficit. Let all imports have been 30% of the national income, so that this cut represents 1·5% of it. We have then lost 1·5% of the national income in bringing it down to the size of the domestic product; but that would have happened anyhow. Non-traded production, in the absence of bottleneck effects, remains constant. Import substitutes cost 30% more than the imports cut off, so that the cost of the irrationalities introduced is 0·45% of the national income. With an m.p.i. of 0·3 and a free market, we should have had to knock 5% off the national income to produce a similar effect on imports.

As with unemployment in MEs, the government will set about repairing this loss in good b.o.p. years. Further, we have seen reason to set the frequency of crises at once in ten years in STEs. It follows that their influence on long-term growth is negligible.

This is not to say that there are no serious setbacks of any kind to the growth of STEs. Quite the contrary, collectivizations, harvest failures, Great Purges and Great Leaps Forward cause most serious difficulties, and among their *effects* are, of course, b.o.p. crises. But that is another story. Nor again is it maintained that STEs trade rationally apart from crises: nearly every page in this book is witness to the contrary. We are concerned here only with changes in the prevalence of rationality.

Summing up these extremely risky figures, classical STEs lose virtually no growth through b.o.p. crises: normal ACCs lose 0·5% p.a.; ACCs that provide reserve currencies lose 2% p.a. Thus a very substantial part—at least one half—of the whole growth advantage of the STE resides in the particular type of cure it can use for external difficulties, and the rarity with which those difficulties become serious.

Of the modern decentralized form of STE, however, it is far too early to speak. In Yugoslavia[1] and Czechoslovakia there is talk of

---

[1] Which has long been an ME, but one riddled with exchange controls and subsidies.

flexible prices, convertible currency, direct contact between home and foreign enterprises, the use of imports for competition and restraint on the price level. Since decentralization under Communism is synonymous with over-investment, wage-creep and cost inflation it is fair to predict terrible b.o.p. crises, corrected by deflation or re-centralization.

8

In this connection we must note the neglected advantage of the STE in the *structure of its foreign debts and assets*. Now since foreign exchange reserves have been a secret ever since Stalin began to conceal his at the end of the NEP, one essential chapter in this book simply cannot be written. But at least we have this consolation, that if we did know the amount we should still not know whether it was 'adequate'. For what is 'adequate'? Economists are amazingly ignorant of basic facts. Few cases are more unsuspected, more crucial and more disgraceful than our knowledge of a country's foreign *liquidity* position. It is depressing to see the figure for gold and foreign *exchange* in the central bank continually quoted, without any regard to other assets and liabilities, as if it had by itself some meaning. This it has only in moments of extreme crisis, when the other assets have been realized and the liabilities thus reduced to a hard and more or less unalterable core.

For the rest it is in all countries inordinately difficult to tell whether either liquidity or mere foreign exchange reserves are 'adequate'. Even in the most publicity-minded countries the official data give nothing like all the relevant facts, and even if we knew them all they would have to be judged in the light of the specific contingencies for which we think we should provide—a matter of individual judgment, or, as Machlup would have it, prejudice.[1] Moreover the valuation of nearly every asset and liability is a conditional sentence: each has value only in certain specified contingencies, and these latter are intimately related to the former contingencies against which we are providing.

The question 'what is our liquidity position?' can best be answered in the form of a balance sheet of quick assets and liabilities, below.

Even among MEs the proportions of these items vary strikingly. Thus in Cuba in the 1950s A12, D2 and D5 were the key items. D5 was of course sugar stocks. D2 was US dollar notes in strong-boxes

[1] Fritz Machlup in *Banca Nazionale del Lavoro Review*, Sept., 1966. I owe much else in this section to this article.

	Assets	*Liabilities*
A. central bank	1 gold 2 convertible foreign currency 3 inconvertible foreign currency 4 foreign bills and short bonds	11 foreigners' deposits 12 own currency notes outstanding abroad (15 all money held by residents)
B. domestic monetary institutions	1, 2, 3, 4 above	11, 12 and (15) above
C. the treasury	1, 2, 3, 4 above	11, 12 and (15) above, plus: 13 own bills and short bonds held abroad
D. businesses and the public	1, 2, 3, 4 above, plus: 5 stocks of easily exportable commodities 6 trade credit with foreigners 7 stocks of imported commodities of all sorts	11 and 13 above, plus: 14 trade debit with foreigners
E. the government apart from the treasury	as for D	as for D

all over the island, and A12 was peso notes in strong-boxes in Miami.[1] In Britain after the Second World War the key items were A11 and C13, the 'sterling balances'. In France D1 is notoriously crucial.

That all items A and C count towards 'our foreign exchange reserves' is no doubt unquestionable. But items B and D, and especially on the asset side, can only doubtfully be included. Precisely private holdings of French gold are unlikely to emerge spontaneously when the franc weakens, nor can they be easily mobilized by legislation. The trick, of course, is to entice them out when the franc is strong, say by an advantageous security issue, purchasable only for gold. This converts D1 into A1 or C1. Only if the individual gold hoarders themselves have increasing debts abroad will this gold move spontaneously to defend the franc. In all other cases we may expect a perverse movement into private gold, as a hedge against the very evil it causes.

D5 and D7 may also act perversely, since they too are in private hands. The fact that there already exist large stocks of goods in

---

[1] The problem of A12 was solved under Castro by a currency reform in which only residents could exchange their notes. This was politically wise, as all possessors of peso notes in Miami were probably opposed to the régime.

private hands is undoubtedly a consolation to any central bank anxious for its gold; since a sharp rise in interest rates will usually bring these stock out, raising exports and lowering imports. But it is a grave disadvantage that such stock can be independently further accumulated: if devaluation is threatened both will rise, since no foreigner wants to buy D5 and every native wants to stock D7. The country thus switches its portfolio from gold to goods at the precise moment when the central bank, by raising its rate of interest, wants to effect the opposite switch. Trade credit will behave in the same perverse way: natives will run up D6 and foreigners will run down D14.

We may count a Soviet-type enterprise as part of 'businesses and the public', though the name implies a most misleading degree of independence. But still the formality of Khozraschet makes possible the same kind of distinction between D and E as elsewhere. E means in most countries the armed forces and the strategic stockpile. It also includes the U.S. Commodity Credit Corporation's stocks of agricultural products and the Soviet Gosreservy of the same. These items are very large indeed. Simply for instance, the Soviet grain purchases of 1963 were probably for Gosreserv and for honoring the trade treaty with Cuba, not directly for making bread.

The reference to item 15 serves simply to remind us that where currency is convertible, 'money', by whomever issued or in whatever form, might take part in a drain abroad. The item is left in parentheses since by far the larger part of 'money' held by residents is for urgent current needs or against private liabilities to other residents. We can therefore have but the vaguest notion of how much might be scared abroad.

Whatever our judgment as to the wisdom of Soviet-type reserve policy one thing is clear: there is no great mass of convertible short-term debt. Of the whole long list of liabilities that weigh upon an ME, pretty well only D14 and E14 survive in the STE. These have to be 'convertible': usually not at all into gold but into exports. The failure to convert them into exports is just as serious as an ACC's suspension of convertibility into gold; it constitutes a b.o.p. crisis. The important difference, then, is not the thing into which the foreigner's claim must be converted but the volume of his claims. And the reasons why this is small are institutional and psychological.

We discuss the psychological aversion of Communism from foreign borrowing in Chapter XIV, where we note also the exceptions to the rule: the small, poor STEs. But what interests us here is the admirable institutional obstacles, which decentralization threatens to remove. First, obviously, there are no independent firms or municipalities, to borrow abroad in defiance of their government. But mainly this reduces long-term borrowing. The more important hindrance is the banking and monetary system. Since money is inconvertible the banks require no stabilization loans. And above all *there is no short-term money market*, no way in which foreign short-term credit could enter the system. Domestic enterprises get individual advances; in exchange they pledge their IOU, which is not negotiable. Banks other than the central bank receive funds only from the budget; if they receive, as they presumably sometimes do, central bank advances their IOUs are not negotiable either. Lastly foreign-trade enterprises do indeed contract short-term debt to foreigners, and their IOUs are negotiable; but only in foreign centers and in foreign currencies. Moreover this is only trade credit; its volume is carefully limited, and it cannot exceed the real trade deficit. To be sure, the foreign-trade enterprise can receive a central (or foreign-trade) bank advance just like a domestic enterprise; but then the bank pays off the foreigner's loan from its reserves, and substitutes the foreign-trade enterprise's IOU. Indeed wherever there is a clearing agreement, and especially between STEs, this happens in the first place. So here again the amount of short debt arising is strictly bound to the real trade deficit.

Whether STEs have administered it well or ill, the advantages of their system seem immense to the writer. There can be b.o.p. crises only when, and only in so far as, there are trade deficits. These deficits have of course a monetary counterpart, since trade is for money; but that counterpart cannot be increased by speculation, still less can speculation perversely run contrary to the current balance. The foreigner has no influence over internal monetary happenings. Moreover these advantages do not rest on bilateralism nor yet on physical planning. Contrary to common opinion, multilateralism is easily compatible with strict inconvertibility (Chapter X). And physical planning is not of course a necessary condition for the inconvertibility of money: behind the central bank's exchange monopoly and the exchange controls an ME might easily lurk, and often has in fact. There is thus plenty of room for Czechoslovakia to rationalize and decentralize herself without condemning herself to be another Britain.

9

How, then, does the STE get into difficulty? Let us omit 'planners' Micawberism', since that, we have seen, is a constant of human nature. Pride of second place must go to the perpetual, and perpetually underestimated, failure of agricultural production. This is not the place to examine Communist agriculture, so let us simply leave the previous sentence, with each word in it bearing equal emphasis, to stand by itself. It should be added that the moment or moments of collectivization are particularly bad in agriculture, in respect of both production and production estimates.

Planner's tension (see Chapter III, Section 5) is extremely important, in so far as it can be distinguished from general Micawberism. It has results on both the macro- and the micro-economic planes. On the latter there is universal pressure by enterprises for more materials, and, therefore, for imports, which the planners doubtless find it difficult to resist.

More interesting, however, is the excessive factory construction that causes what we may call macro-tension. It is characteristic for STEs, and indeed UDCs, to plan tremendous new industrial outputs without particularly caring whence the inputs will come. Plans for feeding the new factories with raw materials rest on optimistic estimates of harvests, mineral yields, or the terms of trade. That is to say, the Communist exaggerates the willingness of forces outside his control to fall in with his plans. As we see in Chapter XV, this effect means that a small STE may strive for autarky (by putting up factories to produce every mortal thing) and precisely in so doing condemn itself to more foreign trade than ever (since the new factories require imported machinery and raw materials).

Tension of these various kinds takes, as we have seen, the place of inflation (Chapter III). There is much inflation, and it can be cured as usual by running on import surplus. But it does not have to be cured, and it does not in any case necessarily cause an import surplus.

Nor must we, in our excitement at the strangeness of the new landscape, forget all the dull old ways of getting into trouble. MEs are not alone in encountering new tariffs, trade wars, unexpected competition, slumps and all the other ills that naturally afflict foreign trade. From one cause of trouble, however, the STE is quite immune: speculation. Its money is never transferable abroad except by official, and very detailed, plan. The very few words that suffice to describe this advantage may cause it to be underestimated; but it is perhaps the most important of all advantages.

The mere smallness of trade as a proportion to national income is also an advantage. A quite small trade proportion is no guarantee against a serious loss of reserves; but it is a sort of guarantee against bottleneck effects, and, therefore, against the most important result of losing one's reserves. This point is not absolute. Thus, if a small country has a small trade proportion it will almost *ex hypothesi* be importing only essentials, and remain vulnerable. But in a general way the practice of autarky has only the aim of reducing such vulnerability. It is difficult to suppose it will altogether fail in its principal aim: at least the number of semi-bottleneck materials will fall. However, we must question whether autarky is either the aim or the result of Communist policy (Chapter XV); it was more likely only a passing phase.

Finally, trade debt tends to accumulate through small deficits, until it is eventually big enough to worry even Communist creditors. But this common occurrence is not *in pari materia* with our other causes. It is merely the result of their operation in previous years.

10

All b.o.p. crises, as we have seen, are particular. So we shall now examine at more length six particular Soviet-type crises: all the ones known to me to have afflicted the USSR, Hungary and Czechoslovakia during peacetime.

The Soviet-type economy entered history with one of the worst b.o.p. crises it was ever to suffer. The first Soviet FYP saw the following setbacks on the foreign front:

(i) The terms of trade turned against primary exporters in the world slump.

(ii) The plan required a sharp if temporary burst of machinery imports, as shown in Table VIII/4. This was Stalin's 'importing to be autarkic'.

(iii) The new command economy functioned badly all over, but nowhere worse than in foreign trade. In particular, export agencies were afraid to sell at the low prices they found themselves facing.

(iv) Collectivization depressed the supply of exports.

(v) Soviet credit being very bad, foreigners charged exorbitant short-term interest (sometimes included in the invoice price of goods).

(vi) Industry was in no condition to supply new exports.

(vii) There was a foreign anti-dumping campaign, as described in Chapter IX.

Stalin's most notorious reactions were to refuse to abandon his import plan, and to export the traditional Russian foodstuffs at the expense of famine at home. Just because the production of these items had failed, their export did not have to, and here the very collectivization that had partially[1] caused the trouble also presented him with the remedy: the new kolkhoz was a most efficient grain pump.

But Stalin had other cards up his sleeve. The most important was a crash campaign to exploit the timber reserves of North European Russia. It was in this drive that his system of forced labor began. In addition to prisoners, people were rounded up without any criminal charge against them at all and simply sent north. The campaign ran into the anti-dumping charges of competing Western timber enterprises.[2]

Stalin also used his police in more direct ways. They raised foreign exchange—we can only guess how much—by ransacking people's houses or arresting them on suspicion of possessing it. Also if a man had rich relatives living abroad they would sell his exit visa to them.[3]

Military intelligence was also harnessed—to forging dollar notes. In 1928–32, on the initiative of Alfred Tilden of Soviet military intelligence, they passed about $10 million[4] in forged $100 notes, mainly in China. The smaller part passed in Germany and the United States; though of extremely fine workmanship, it attracted immediate suspicion, arrests were made in both countries, and suspicion fell briefly upon a 'counterfeiting gang in Russia'. But Communist spies are brave and silent when caught, and no Western authority could really credit the Soviet Government itself with such a scheme. Forging is not cheap, nor is passing the notes when made.

---

[1] I say 'partially' because it is not enough appreciated that the real famine was in the winter of 1931–32, while collectivization peaked in the winter of 1929–30. The proximate cause of the famine was the Japanese invasion of Manchuria, to which Stalin reacted by confiscating the seed-grain to feed his Far Eastern army.

[2] A. W. Pim and E. Bateson, *Report on Russian Timber Camps* (London, 1931).

[3] One case is described at great length, and others are referred to briefly, by R. O. G. Urch, *The Rabbit King of Russia* (London, 1939). The Rumanians have recently taken up this practice; see the *Sunday Telegraph* (London), June 21, 1964.

[4] This figure, and all other details, are from the celebrated defector from military intelligence, General Walter Krivitsky [*In Stalin's Secret Service* (New York, 1939), Chapter 4]. The other, no less, sensational chapters in this book have been confirmed by subsequent revelations, such as Khrushchev's secret speech (February, 1956). Krivitsky, who wrote in 1938, was clearly as accurate as his memory permitted. He was entrusted with the liquidation of the European end of this particular venture when it went wrong.

They were either passed by honest Communist agents to the under-world at a heavy discount, or by means of a respectable but very expensive local 'front'. It may be that Stalin netted about $5 million in this way.[1]

Another emergency measure, often copied since, was the Torgsin shop (cf. Chapter XIII, Section 16, below). These sold to foreign tourists and diplomats for foreign currency only. Tourism itself was pressed forward—even through the famine of 1932. The Bolsheviks had just become disciplined enough to conceal a famine, and the foreign fellow-travellers blind enough not to see one.[2]

But none of this was enough, and the debt mounted. It did so, partly, in an unusual way. We owe to the thoroughness and perspicacity of S. N. Prokopovich[3] the knowledge that there were serious and systematic differences between export movements (in the trade returns) and payments for exports (in the b.o.p.) until 1934–35. Since the very beginning of the NEP Soviet reserves were so low that the USSR had to borrow on the security of her exports. Since the loans were short, no substantial discrepancy arose until 1931–32, but exports grew most of the time and a substantial stock of unsold goods accumulated abroad. We see from Table V/1, rows (i) and (ii), that in Mr. Shenkman's opinion this stock was worth, at his-torical cost, at least R.260 mn. on October 1, 1931—say R.350 mn. if we include 1921–24, which he omits. He also gives the Soviet debt on the security of exports outstanding at that date as R.187 mn. It is logical that this should be a smaller sum, because there was strong reason for stocking goods abroad. They were left unsold because Soviet traders were afraid to lower their prices; these were fixed for them preliminarily in Moscow—and entered into the trade returns—at levels too high for the world slump.

Then in 1931–32, if my workings be accepted as more complete than Shenkman's, the cash balance must have been −R.493 mn. (Table V/2, row (ii)); whereas the official trade returns for exports (Table V/1) make it about −R.200 mn. So in that year alone we obtain R.293 mn. added to stocks of exports. In 1932–33 the formal

---

[1] He reverted to printing other people's notes, but in a much more legal manner, in East Germany in 1945. Cf. Chapter XVI, Section 31, below. It should be noted that the Soviet government was not the only one to forge valuta at this time. The Hungarian government had done so before it (cf. Lajos Windisch-Graetz, *My Adventures and Misadventures*, Barrie and Rockliffe, 1967).

[2] For a bitter and surely accurate account cf. Eugene Lyons, *Assignment in Utopia* (London, 1937).

[3] *Histoire Economique de l'URSS* (Paris, 1952), pp. 493–8. He quotes in particular D. Mishustin, *Vneshnyaya Torgovlya SSSR*, (Moscow, 1938), pp. 289–90.

TABLE V/1. THE SOVIET BALANCE OF PAYMENTS, 1924-37
(mn. current valuta rubles)

	1924/5[4]	1925/6	1926/7	1927/8	1928/9	1929/30	1930/1	1931[15]	1932[15]	1933[15]	1934[15]	1935	1936	1937[14]
(i) Exports according to trade returns[2]	559	677	780	778	878	1002	890	811	575	496	418	367	311	395
(ii) Estimated true value[1] of exports	530	650	735	743	840	965	836	—	—	—	—	411[5]	343[5]	—
(iii) Exports of precious metals[2]	70	81	49	155	70	9	110	114[13]	93[13]	78[13]	98[13]	12	0	242[13]
(iv) Contraband exports[2]	4	3	5	3	6	8	9	7	4	2	3	2[6]	2[6]	2
(v) Total commodity exports	604	734	789	901	916	982	955	(932)	(672)	(576)	(519)	425	345	639
(vi) Interest[3]	7	5	5	6	6	5	4	4	4	4	4	4[6]	4[6]	2
(vii) Currency remittances[2]	33	33	33	30	30	30	30	25	30	20	20	14[7]	21	2
(viii) Tourism						1[9]	3[9]	3	5	3	6	7	8	5
(ix) Diplomatic representation[3]	10	10	10	10[8]	10[8]	12[8]	13[8]	14	15	16	17	18	18	19
(x) Port expenditures of foreign shipping	6[10]	7[10]	7[10]	9[10]	9[10]	10[10]	9[10]	8	7	6	4	3	0	0
(xi) Income from own shipping (net)[16]	6	6	7	7	8	8	8	8	9	10	11	11	16	16
(xii) Misc. current receipts	—	—	—	—	—	—	—	—	—	—	—	16[12]	4[12]	—
(xiii) Total exports	666	795	851	963	979	1048	1022	(994)	(742)	(635)	(581)	498	397	683
(xiv) Imports according to trade returns[2]	724	756	714	946	836	1068	1044	1105	704	348	232	241 / 196[5]	308 / 306[5]	308
(xv) Imports of precious metals[3]	46	9	15	0	3	1	0	0	0	0	0	0[6]	0[6]	0
(xvi) Commercial and gift parcels[2]	3	9	2	0	0	6	6	4	2	6	2	1[6]	1[6]	1
(xvii) Contraband imports[2]	27	30	35	29	35	35	35	25	15	25	15	10[6]	10[6]	10
(xviii) Total commodity imports	800	804	766	975	874	1110	1085	1134	721	379	249	207	317	319
(xix) Brokerage and commissions[3]	11	12	14	14	16	18	18	18	13	9	6	6[10]	6[10]	6

(xx) Foreign expenses of trade organizations[3]	30	23	30	35	42	50	50	50	35	25	16	16[10]	16[10]	16
(xxi) Other diplomacy, espionage, tourism, remittances and propaganda[3]	8	26	25	21	6	25	30	25	20	15	20	15[11]	15[11]	20
(xxii) Interest[3]	6	9	13	17	25	30	35	40	40	35	30	24	14	1
(xxiii) Foreign labor and technical assistance[3]	3	5	5	10	15	18	38	30	22	16	10	5	5	3
(xxiv) Misc. current expenditures	—	—	—	—	—	—	—	—	—	—	—	0	15	—
(xxv) Total imports	858	879	853	1072	978	1251	1256	1297	851	479	331	273	382	365

Sources unless otherwise stated: E. M. Shenkman in *Weltwirtschaftliches Archiv*, 1932, and Birmingham Bureau of Research on Russian Economic Conditions, *Memo.*, no. 4, 1932; League of Nations, *Balances of Payments* 1936. Mr. Shenkman's data are surprisingly often official; for the rest, he was a refugee from the Finance Department in the Moscow Institute for Economic Research. The league got its data directly from the Soviet Government. I have transposed these data into the old rate of exchange, dividing them by 4·38.

[1] Written down for reasons explained in text.
[2] Various official sources quoted by Mr. Shenkman.
[3] Shenkman's estimates.
[4] These combined years end on October 1 of the latter mentioned.
[5] *Cash earned* in b.o.p. statement. The 'true' value of previous years need not correspond to cash earned within that period of time.
[6] My guess.
[7] These figures are given as net. I have guessed a countervailing import of 0 in each year.
[8] I obtain this whole series until 1930–31 inclusive as a residual: Shenkman gives (vii), (viii), and (ix) together in his table, and (vii) separately in his text. Only his estimate for (vii) seems to rest on official sources. There must be an element of pure residual in his underlying estimate for (vii) and (ix), since although they should be rather stable items they fluctuate widely, being 5 in 1928–29 and 25 in 1930–31. Accepting my own tourism figures, I take diplomatic representation to have been of the general order of 10, and to have risen slowly. This is generally plausible when we consider that foreign powers spent $7 mn. in Germany and $5 mn. in USA (old gold $—the corresponding Soviet figure would be $5 mn.).
[9] The number of tourists increased as follows: 1928 = 100; 1929 = 135; 1930 = 302; 1931 = 492; 1932 = 723; 1934 = 816; 1935 = 1031; 1936 = 1076—A Gorchakov, *Vneshnyaya Torgovlya* 10/1945. I have, therefore, extrapolated backwards from 1935–36. Note that Gorchakov omits 1933.
[10] Extrapolated in proportion to trade turnover.
[11] The net balance of 'diplomatic and other government expenditure' is 13 in 1935 and 1936. Comparing (ix), we get 16+15—18 = 13.
[12] The official figures are 20 and 8. I have deducted my guesses as to interest.
[13] League of Nations, *Money and Banking* 1937–38, p. 13, converting old gold dollars into rubles at R.1·94 = $1. I have preferred the official Soviet figures for 1935 and 1936 to those of the League, which are 29 and 14. The amazing 1937 figure is actually $ (old gold) 118 mn. for the first nine months. I assume that the good harvest of 1937, becoming known in September, kept the twelve-month figure down to 125.
[14] Extrapolated by myself from 1936, except for rows (i), (iii) and (xiv). I have kept the old rate of exchange.
[15] Interpolated by myself except for rows (i) (iii), (xiv) and (viii). I have allowed for the fact that 1932 was a year of famine.
[16] Given officially for 1935–36. Extrapolated by myself from the following series in *Sotsialisticheskoye Stroietel'stvo SSSR* (Moscow, 1936), p. 465, for millions of tons of exports carried by own shipping; 1928 = 9·3; 1932 = 17·2; 1933 = 16·7; 1934 = 16·1; 1935 = 15·9. The corresponding figure for 1924 was about 7·8, if the proportion of exports to imports carried in own ships was as in 1928 (Louis Segal and A. A. Santalov, *Soviet Union Yearbook* [London, 1926], p. 199). I have made a small arbitrary allowance for the fall in freight rates during the slump.

TABLE V/2. SOVIET FINANCING 1924-36
(minus sign means owed by the USSR; mn. current valuta rubles)

	1923/4	1924/5	1925/6	1926/7	1927/8	1928/9	1929/30	1930/31	1931/2	1932/3	1933/4	1934/5	1935/6
(i) Net import and export credits granted[2]		−57	−92	−87	−93	−130	−250	−430	−40[3]			225[5]	15[5]
(ii) Movement in total balance from Table V/1		−192	−84	+2	−109	+1	−203	−234	(−493)[4]	(475)[4]	(475)[4]		
Cumulative balance at end of period:													
(iii) as per (i)[1]	−156	−213	−305	−392	−485	−615	−865	−1295	−1335[3]				
(iv) official[1]						−470			−1400	−450		−139	−86

[1] *Pravda*, January 4, 1934; November 7, 1935; November 25, 1930. All at the rates of exchange obtaining before the great devaluation of 1936–37. Cf. Prokopovich, op. cit., pp. 556–7.
[2] Shenkman in *Weltwirtschaftliches Archiv*, 1932.
[3] July 1, 1932.
[4] The balance required to obtain agreement with row (iv).
[5] Calendar years 1935 and 1936: no agreement with row (iv) attempted.

balance turned positive, and from October, 1932 to October, 1934 may have run at R.400 mn. (Table V/1), whereas about R.950 mn. are required to explain the fall in the cumulative debt (Table V/2). It seems that we can supply the whole gap of R.550 mn. out of stocks of exports: 350 as a result of the accumulation in 1921 to 1931 plus 293 in 1931–32 alone = R.647 mn. But the working is bold and inaccurate, and the prices of realization must have been much lower than those historically recorded. Moreover, a minor mystery remains: if the Soviet external debt was really written off by October, 1936, why the huge gold sales of 1937?

Be that as it may, we observe yet another success of that very successful period, the second FYP. By October, 1932, the USSR's external debt, accumulated since the expropriations of 1917–18, was 1400 mn. current valuta rubles, or about 3% of the net national income at domestic factor cost. It was nearly all paid off by October, 1936 (Table V/2). This was achieved by:

(a) the liquidation of the stocks of exports held abroad described above;

(b) a current visible trade surplus;

(c) a gold-mining drive.

An annual external surplus of less than 1% of the national income is, of course, not much, and is easily accounted for by agricultural recovery alone. Nevertheless, it sheds light on the workings of STEs that this surplus was achieved in the teeth of continued gross inflation, and of a substantial recovery in the standard of living. We can best describe this early b.o.p. crisis by saying that the first FYP was like a civil war, except only that it enlarged productive capacity; while the second FYP was like a post-war recovery.[1]

It seems there were no military aspects to the Soviet b.o.p. at this time. The much-discussed collaboration of the Red Army with the Reichswehr has left no strictly economic documents behind, but it appears that little payment was made either way. The USSR provided the land, Germany the technique, and both parties were satisfied with the results. Domestic arms output rose very rapidly after 1928, and I can find no trace of exports or imports.

II

The Hungarian crisis of 1954–55 was essentially a crisis in

---

[1] U.S. Sovietology is hag-ridden by the 'bench-mark' years 1928 and 1937, to the neglect of economic performance during the NEP and of variations during the next eight years. For serious discrimination among these years cf. Naum Jasny, *The Socialized Agriculture of the USSR* (California, 1949); *Soviet Industrialization 1928–52* (Chicago, 1961).

non-Soviet currencies, owing to debt built up over many previous years. Trade ran—sources differ—approximately as follows:

TABLE V/3. HUNGARIAN COMMODITY TRADE

	With STEs	Visible Balances With Other Countries	Total	Exports[a]	Agricultural Production (Indices, 1938–39	Industrial Production = 100)
		(mn. valuta forints)				
1949	+145[b]	−235	−90	3293	84	128
1950	+445[c]	−295	+150	3857	94	153
1951	+333	−357	−24	4646	112	187
1952	+81	−360	−279	5143	70	219
1953	+629	−558	+71	5849	97	242
1954	+320	−555	−235	6095	92	243
1955	+1123	−565	+558	7055	107	262
1956	—	—	+68	5717	89	237
1957	−2090	−197	−2283	5728	104	276
1958	+216	+402	+618	8024	107	310
1959	−559	+285	−274	9035	112	339
1960	−949	−247	−1196	10,260	100	385

Sources: *Statistical Yearbook 1964* (in English), (Budapest, 1965), p. 181; Peter Kende, *Logique de l'Economie Centralisée* (Paris, 1964), pp. 76, 88, 95. The valuta forint is worth 8·5 US cents.

a Total is approximate. Figures do not agree with previous columns. Cf. P. Kende, op. cit., pp. 94–5, fns. 16 and 17.

b Including Yugoslavia.

c From 1950 on, figures exclude Yugoslavia.

Thus already when Imre Nagy took over as premier in July, 1953 there was a huge backlog of short-term debt with ACCs which favorable trade balances in inconvertible Communist currency did nothing to offset. The principal causes of these debts were excessive factory construction (Section 9), which depended on foreign machinery and raw materials, and, of course, collectivization. As we shall see in Chapter VIII, an STE is supposed to spend its valuta on machinery until it can produce its own. Hungary quite failed in this (see Table V/4).

Thus in the Rakosi era planning was so bad that imports of fuels and raw materials rose quicker than those of machinery. Indeed, in 1955 machinery imports fell below the pre-war proportion. At the same time food and livestock exports dwindled. Hungary was exporting whatever else she could merely in order to import enough current inputs to keep her useless factories turning. The new steel works at Dunapentele (then Sztalinvaros) were alleged to import a greater value of raw materials than the total value of their output.

Moreover, micro-choices in foreign trade were fearfully irrational.

Hungary was the classic example of the under-pricing of imports. Thus in exports, for which, of course, the Ministry of Foreign Trade had to pay the full domestic cost, the ratio of valuta to domestic prices, even in 1955, was about 1 : 3·45.[1] This, then, was about the extent to which the valuta-forint was over-valued. Yet on the import side the ratio was only 1 : 1·66! Trade being roughly balanced in valuta, the Ministry's loss in domestic currency was over 11 md. forints, or some 14% of the national income.

TABLE V/4. STRUCTURE OF HUNGARY'S COMMODITY TRADE
(percentage of total value in valuta forints)

	Exports				Imports			
	1938	1949	1955	1964	1938	1949	1955	1964
Machinery, equipment, tools and precision products . . .	17·2	17·4	29·4	33·8	12·5	17·4	11·4	29·3
Fuels and raw materials	10·2	22·2	28·9	25·9	48·4	76·4	67·6	57·0
Livestock . . .	17·4	6·7	2·9	0[a]	—	0·1	0·1	0[a]
Food, including manufactured food . .	37·3	36·5	27·6	21·1	6·8	3·4	17·5	8·6
Other consumer goods	17·9	17·2	16·2	20·1	32·3	2·7	3·4	5·1

SOURCES: Bela Balassa, *The Hungarian Experience in Economic Planning* (New Haven, 1959), p. 267; *Magyar Statisztikai Evkönyv* (Budapest, 1964).

[a] Figures add to total without this item appearing in the original. Discrepancies here are due to rounding.

But this was not merely an accounting loss on imports. For in order to obtain these imports in ever greater volume, the Hungarian Government had exported prodigally, at unfavorable terms of trade. The process was so manifestly uneconomic that the government has not recently dared to publish a trade volume index, lest the terms of trade be thus revealed. Peter Kende,[2] however, has unearthed the following figures for cotton cloth exports in 1955 (1949 = 100):

Quantity exported: total	224;	to countries outside the bloc	450
Foreign exchange earned:	150		263
Therefore price in valuta forints:	67		58

This was, moreover, not a time of falling world prices for cotton cloth in Europe. Simultaneously the valuta price of agricultural exports fell by 33%, while it remained constant in the world as a whole. However, according to my own calculations, Hungary's overall terms of trade declined by only 18% in 1950–54.[3]

[1] Privately calculated: workings available from the author on request.
[2] Op. cit., p. 99.
[3] Official volume indices seem to have been published for these years alone; cf. U.N. Economic Commission for Europe, *Economic Survey of Europe in 1957*, p. A 66. They are in domestic prices of 1949, and on 1950 = 100 we find export volume at 191, import volume at 167. The official value indices in valuta forints read 158 and 163 respectively.

Imre Nagy made everything worse in this field by his concessions in labor discipline and consumption volume. These had immediate effect, while the slow-down in industrialization and the halt in collectivization did not. When Nagy fell in March, 1955 his Stalinist enemies again took charge, and were at least able to pile up a sizable surplus with STEs. In perhaps no other field was Nagy's stewardship so seriously at fault. Nor is this surprising: the b.o.p. is at the periphery of every politician's vision, and reform through relaxation, taking time before its fruition, is bound to result in external deficit at first. Here, in any case, is his not altogether convincing apologia. It is quoted at length as being virtually the only frank top-level account of such a matter for any STE:

It must be pointed out that, although the economic cooperation and mutual assistance between the socialist countries brought significant results, the activity of CEMA [the Council for Mutual Economic Assistance] from the point of view of industrial production and development was exceptionally limited during the period of the First Five-Year Plan. This also contributed to the rise of inequities in work distribution among the friendly countries. Despite the fact that agreements were made with some of the democratic countries with a view to assigning work in a way that would promote economic production and work distribution, parallel manufacturing, especially in the field of machine industry, had an increasingly detrimental effect on our export opportunities and consequently on our foreign trade balance. Parallel manufacturing affected not only trade among the friendly countries themselves but led to an unhealthy competition among them in the capitalist markets as well. The exaggerated trend toward autarky, which manifested itself in the machine industry in the other friendly countries, too, was most apparent also in the fields of precision instruments and telecommunications. This was a serious blow to our most developed and most favorably producing export industries. Parallel manufacturing and the exaggerated trend toward autarky within the socialist camp not only reduced our opportunities to export within the camp, but also deprived us of chances of importing basic and raw materials. Consequently our foreign trade was shifted more and more toward the capitalist world and increased our indebtedness in this direction.

The foreign trade situation was further aggravated during the second half of 1954, when trade conferences with the Soviet Union and the other friendly countries revealed that in 1955 we would get from them only 50 per cent of what we received in 1954 in the way of essential products and raw materials; the remainder would have to be obtained from the capitalist countries. This also meant that, to compensate for the sudden jump in the need to import from capitalists, we would have to augment our exports to them drastically. But neither our industry nor our foreign trade was prepared for this.

The Council of Ministers, acting on the resolution of the Political Committee, established the volume of foreign trade imports and exports for 1955 in such a way as to release one billion forints more in assets to the socialist camp. Furthermore, it ordained that in 1955 our indebtedness to capitalist countries was not to increase, and we made it our goal to limit the import of material to the quantity set in the 1954 barter agreement (calculated without credit). We planned that the Soviet Union would supply more material and credit than it had supplied in 1954, and would accept more machinery in exchange. However, the outcome of the conferences, concluded in January, 1955, was that the Soviet Union was willing to guarantee us only 50 per cent of the 1954 import volume and only 36 per cent of the items on our want list for 1955. Our export possibilities developed in approximately the same way. At the same time the democratic countries, especially Rumania and Poland, also desired to reduce their export of materials to us as compared to 1954. They were willing to let us have important raw materials only in exchange for goods obtainable exclusively from capitalist countries, or agricultural products that we had not stockpiled and would also have had to purchase from capitalist countries.

Thus the situation that developed between November, 1954, and January, 1955, posed unusually great difficulties for our entire economy. It seriously affected our supply of material and again made it necessary to realign production. The effect of this on foreign trade was to further depress the trade and foreign payment scale to such an extent that only a tremendous increase in credit could remedy it. However, there was no practical possibility of accomplishing this on the world market. Furthermore such a solution ran counter to the government resolutions on this subject. It became apparent that the only way in which we could have provided material for industry, without drastically reducing our production plans and realigning the production of industries requiring large quantities of imported material, would have been by getting from capitalist countries the several billion forints' worth of raw materials and goods that the socialist camp would no longer supply. Even so, some of the import materials, such as metallurgical basic materials, would have been hard to obtain from the West even had foreign exchange been available to us for the purpose.

In general, the increase in our foreign debt, especially our debt to capitalist countries, can be traced back to the foregoing causes. As a result of the harmful economic policy of the First Five-Year Plan, the New Course inherited a heavy burden in this field also. The effects of this were especially noticeable in 1954 and were far from disappearing. They could not have disappeared; on the contrary, owing to the reasons already outlined, they continued to exert a harmful influence. The serious consequences of an erroneous and harmful economic policy that has been pursued for years cannot be eliminated in eighteen months, especially when the government's new corrective economic policy is resisted to a great extent. Not only internal, but much more powerful external forces and factors exerted a harmful influence, especially in the field of foreign trade agreements; this made it all but impossible to overcome the difficulties. Since it is a state secret, I will give no figures and be brief, but it must be pointed out that a considerable part of our foreign debt derives from expenditures and investments for security and defense, which place a heavy load on our foreign trade balance. The June, 1953, resolution pointed out that there were excesses in this field also.

The already difficult position of our foreign trade was further aggravated by an accumulation of unpaid debts in virtually all of the capitalist countries. Payments falling due on expensive short-term foreign credits constantly used up our foreign exchange income, making it impossible to use the exchange to purchase essential import products. Despite the fact that in the given international situation it would have been possible for us to convert our capitalist debts and concentrate them in just a few places, thereby reducing our payment balance, and despite the fact that on several occasions I specifically instructed the leaders of the Ministry of Foreign Trade to do this, our debts were not liquidated. This was primarily because the Political Committee, at the recommendation of Mátyás Rákosi, took the attitude that such a solution would be dangerous and should be resorted to only later and then with extreme caution. In the meantime, other People's Democracies successfully solved similar problems in this way, and lightened their financial obligations in this way.

The unusual slowness and inflexibility of our foreign trade organs added to the difficulties of locating and winning new markets, of financing our exports, and of issuing letters of credit. Our foreign trade was unable to see the opportunities offered us by the semicolonial countries, the Near and Middle East, and South America. The mistaken foreign trade view—which is not entirely attributable to our difficulties—that a deal could be closed only upon immediate payment of exchange added to the problems. It was possible to alter this harmful inflexibility to some extent, but it is still prevalent even today.

In broad outline, these are the causes of our foreign indebtedness. I cannot be held responsible for it, because in the first place it was due to the mistaken economic policy of the First Five-Year Plan, for which, before June, 1953, in the period of individual leadership, Mátyás Rákosi was responsible—Rákosi, who was both the First Secretary of the Party and the Premier. In the second place, our economic policy, including our foreign trade, was directed by the Party, and every new foreign credit action had to be carried out on the basis of Party resolutions. And finally, I cannot be held accountable because, within the Council of Ministers, foreign trade was not under my direction but under the supervision and direction of Ernö Gerö, First Deputy Premier.[1]

A less partial view would have acknowledged Gerö's subsequent success in increasing exports during 1955, but might also have claimed for the New Course of 1953–54 the credit for the 16% increase in agricultural production, 1954–55. No doubt this had much to do with the increased exports under Gerö. The latter's success was in any case only partial, and yielded quickly to the revolution, which also brought on a b.o.p. crisis for reasons too obvious to mention.

12

The Soviet crises of 1946 and 1963 are purely—if anything so complicated can be called pure—agricultural. They need, therefore, no long analysis. Fairly good figures exist for the latter (Table V/5). The figures for retail and wholesale stocks are included merely to

[1] *Imre Nagy on Communism* (New York, 1957), pp. 189–92.

show their irrelevance to the b.o.p. It is, indeed, characteristic[1] of STEs to pile up tremendous unwanted stocks of finished goods, simply because planning is bad, quality low and prices rigid. We can see this happening in 1958–59, which show far bigger stocking-up than subsequent, and indeed than previous, years. It is also, incidentally, characteristic to keep down raw material stocks, for planner's tension exerts a permanent downward pressure on input-output ratios, and the command economy is thought to work best when the enterprise is short of cash and physical reserves, so that it cannot defy the center.

So, presumably, raw material stocks were small as usual after 1959. Meanwhile, stocks of finished goods grew scarcely faster than retail sales. These series reflect in no way the gravity of the b.o.p. crisis. Neither does that for small savings, which gives us some idea of the change in the monetary overhang.

A comment is in order about all five of the crises we have hitherto discussed: not one of them resulted in a setback. In Hungary there was, indeed, a production setback in 1956, but this was caused by revolution, not the crisis of 1954–55. I.e., production increased normally until October. The b.o.p. crisis of 1957 had, as we have seen, the same cause, but was cured by the generous aid of the very countries that had suppressed the revolution. It did not itself diminish production. Of the three Soviet crises under review, only one gives even the appearance of causing a setback: that of 1963, when the national income grew by about 2·5% instead of the usual 5%. But this was due to a harvest failure, and was cause, not effect, of the crisis. The crisis itself was serious, but it is virtually impossible to ascribe the setbacks in production to it. It caused only one such setback: the lack of agricultural inputs affected certain industrial outputs. This technological effect could have been corrected by a still more generous expenditure on imports from gold reserves.

[1] For Hungary, Mr. Portes communicates these astonishing figures:

	Ratio of Stocks to n.m.p.	Increase of Stocks as % of Total Net Investment
1959	1·13	28·0
1960	1·10	27·7
1961	1·15	37·8
1962	1·19	38·2
1963	1·23	36·5
1964	1·26	34·0
1965	1·30	27·0
(UK 1960–64)	(c. 0·52)	(11·0)

The British figures are from the 1965 national income blue blook. 'Stocks' include both finished goods and raw materials in both countries.

TABLE V/5. THE SOVIET ECONOMY, 1958-64
(per cent of previous year, or unit as stated)

	1958	1959	1960	1961	1962	1963	1964
(i) GNP in real terms, as per CIA[1]	108·5	104·2	104·9	106·8	104·3[4]	102·6[4]	107·2
(ii) N.n.i.o. in current rubles	110·6[11]	107·7[10]	106·8[10]	102·5[10]	107·7[10]	102·5[12]	107·6[12]
(iii) Approximate national income deflator[3]	102	103	102	96	103	100	100
(iv) Real growth of (ii), official[2]	—	108	108	107	106	104	109
(v) Net industrial production, CIA[1]	109·1	108·5	106·8	107·1	107·8	106·6	107·2
(vi) Net agricultural production, CIA[1]	110·4	94·9	100·5	108·6	98·8	94·9	112·1
(vii) Net grain export (mn. tons), official[2]	4·32	6·75	6·56	6·80	7·76	3·16	−3·78
(viii) Grain stocks, October (ditto)[9]	21–23	18–20	11–13	5–8	7–10	2–5	—
(ix) Gold sales (mn. valuta R.)[5]	191	232	191	241	195	509	455
(x) Gold reserves end of year (ditto)[5]	about 3000	—	—	—	—	about 2000	—
(xi) Visible exports (mn. valuta rubles)[2]	3868	4897	5005	5398	6331	6550	6910
(xii) Balance (ditto)	−53	331	−61	153	526	−21	−50
(xiii) V.e. to China (ditto)[2]	570	859	735	331	210	170	120
(xiv) Balance (ditto)	−220	−131	−28	−166	−254	−200	−160
(xv) V.e. to other STEs (ditto)[2, 7]	2258	2852	2988	3300	4210	4420	4740
(xvi) Balance (ditto)	107	431	264	345	570	20	40
(xvii) V.e. to UDCs (ditto)[2]	410	440	407	813	890	820	870
(xviii) Balance (ditto)	20	−51	−216	9	360	240	310
(xix) V.e. to ACCs (ditto)[2]	630	746	875	954	1020	1140	1180
(xx) Balance (ditto)	40	82	−81	−35	−150	−140	−410
(xxi) Sugar refined (mn. tons)[2]	7·2	7·8	8·3	10·4	9·7	8·2	10·4

	1958	1959	1960	1961	1962	1963	1964
(xxii) Leather shoes produced (mn. pairs)[2]	356	390	419	443	456	463	475
Cloth output (mn. metres):[2]							
(xxiii) Cotton	5789	6149	6387	6425	6453	6619	6976
(xxiv) Woollen	303	326	342	355	366	370	372
(xxv) Linen	481	527	559	531	516	541	580
(xxvi) Silk	844	800	810	817	947	958	978
(xxvii) Savings-bank deposits[2,6]	108	115	108	107	109	109	112
(xxviii) Retail sales[2,6]	108	106	109	103	108	105	105
(xxix) Retail and wholesale stocks[2,6]	127	116	104	109	108	108	109[8]

[1] In *Current Economic Indicators for the USSR* (U.S.G.P.O. Washington, 1965, 1966).

[2] Statistical yearbooks.

[3] (ii) ÷ (i). This disagrees strongly with the official cost-of-living index, but I am quite confident it is more reliable. Cf. P. Hanson, Oxford Institute of Statistics Bulletin 3/1965.

[4] This used to be a cause célèbre among Sovietologists: cf. P. J. D. Wiles in *Bulletin of the Association for the Study of Soviet-type Economies*, Pennsylvania, winter, 1964; Alec Nove and Stanley Cohn in *Soviet Studies*, July, 1944; November, 1965. In its original press release (*New York Times*, 9 January, 1964) the CIA put growth in 1962 at an absurd 2·2%. But in the 1965 *Indicators* this has gone up to 4·3%, which is quite credible. The CIA never altered their low estimate for 1963, which now commands general assent.

[5] Von Berg in *Ost-Europa Wirtschaft*, I/1963; Keith Bush, *Soviet Gold Production and Reserves Reconsidered*, Radio Liberty, 23 November, 1965.

[6] Mainly from Goldman, *Journal of Political Economy*, August, 1965.

[7] Including Yugoslavia, Albania and Cuba.

[8] Retail only.

[9] Nancy Nimitz, RAND Memorandum RM-4127-PR of November, 1964, p. 58.

[10] Abraham S. Becker, RAND Memorandum RM-4394-PR of June, 1965, p. 14.

[11] Nancy Nimitz, RAND Memorandum RM-3112-PR of June, 1962, p. 16.

[12] N.m.p. alone: *Nar. Khoz.*, 1964, p. 575.

13

If all b.o.p. crises result from and react on events in the whole economy, this was pre-eminently true of the Czechoslovak crisis of 1962–64: which was not merely one of economic performance, but also one of the economic model as a whole. It would even more than usually be a serious distortion not to present the whole situation.[1] The series for sheer economic performance are as follows:

TABLE V/6. MAIN CZECHOSLOVAK INDICES
(per cent of previous year)

	$\frac{1958}{1948}$	1959	1960	1961	1962	1963 plan	1963 actual	1964	1965	(weight in 1962)
National net material product . .	218	106	108	107	101	—	98	101	103	(100)
Private consumption	174	105	110	103	102	—	101	103	105	—
Value added in:										
Industry . .	220	108	109	110	106	101	97	102	106	(66)
Construction .	332	118	109	104	95	94?	85	112	114	(8)
Agriculture and forestry . .	124	88	104	98	83	109·5	114	95	86	(15)
Other material Production .	339	99	101	104	102	—	97	93	102	(11)
Volume of visible trade turnover .	276	118	113	110	106	—	107	108	107	—

These official series are not necessarily exact. It is their relative movements that interest us. Further, to give us a rough sense of the proportions of things, we should note the following magnitudes at current prices in 1956:[2]

national net material product, official reckoning . 143 md. kčs.
GNP at market prices, Western concept . . 162 md. kčs.
'net national income originating' . . . 116 md. kčs.
$1 = 7·06 valuta kčs.
1 valuta kčs = 1·63 domestic kčs.

The Czechoslovak economy, then, behaved admirably up to 1958, and was a great advertisement for Stalinism. It was burdened, indeed, by no reparations or mixed companies, but it was forced to distort its export structure: developing, as we see in Chapter VIII, a monstrous bias towards machinery, and neglecting the shoes, textiles and glass for which it had been famous. This structural change came about because many Western machinery sources

[1] I quote no specific source, having read widely in translations of the press and talked to many Czechoslovak economists and foreigners interested in the subject. All statistical data are from official handbooks unless otherwise stated.

[2] Thad P. Alton et al., Czechoslovak National Income and Product, 1947–8 and 1955–6 (Columbia, 1962), pp. 20, 61, 173, 228. What I have called 'n.n.i.o.' is simply GNP less turnover tax plus subsidies (39 md.) and less depreciation allowances (17 md.); see Chapter XV here, Section 10. The valuta/domestic ratio is my correction of Alton, based on evidence that appeared subsequently.

had been dried up by the embargo, and the USSR imposed upon Czechoslovakia the role of substitute. She did not, however, suffer from this specialization for at least ten years. Internally there was a surplus of rural labor, the classic situation in which Communist methods of resource mobilization, as opposed to allocation, come out best. Agriculture performed disappointingly, of course, but this caused no crisis either of domestic growth or in the b.o.p. In 1958 a spirit of innovation raised its head. For all the talk little was really changed, except in the field of investment. Here, many decisions were decentralized to enterprises and local government. The result was an orgy of 'investment scatter'. All kinds of projects were begun, many of them in the hitherto neglected service trades, and many for the production of goods requiring imported materials. Fixed investment work went far above the value of finished capacity going into operation:

TABLE V/7. INVESTMENT SCATTER IN CZECHOSLOVAKIA
(percent of previous year, or unit as stated)

	1957	1958	1959	1960	1961	1962	1963	1964
Value added in construction	105	108	118	109	104	95	85	108
Volume of machinery and equipment installed .	113	123	117	116	110	98	89	117
Fixed assets in use in the economy as a whole .	105	104	106	106	106	105	105	105
in industry . .		106	118	108	107	107	107	105
in construction .		112	115	115	115	111	108	107
in all sectors of agriculture and forestry .		109	111	109	109	106	105	105
Excess of expenditure over value of capacity brought into use (mn. domestic kčs of 1963)[a] .	−300	3300	200	4200	3900	3800	−500	−1300

[a] This is table 6–2 minus table 6–14 in *Statistická Ročenka 1964*. The coverage of the two tables may not be the same, but the movement of the difference is clearly significant. Investment in 1962 was 44 md. kčs. The figure for 1964 is in kčs of Jan. 1, 1964, and is from *Statistická Ročenka 1966*.

It is extremely striking that investment work could fall for two years in a row, and yet capacity in actual use increase at an undiminished rate. The volume of uncompleted projects must have been stupendous. But even what capacity did enter production had no tendency to help the b.o.p., as we saw above.

Thus was demonstrated a lesson that few seem to have thoroughly digested: it can be disastrous to decentralize a command economy, unless it is done with extreme care, and the remaining controls are firmly exercised. From about 1961 this small but unfortunate measure of decentralization was reversed. But its ill effects had not worn off before a series of unforeseeable exogenous disasters hit the economy:

(i) After its Great Leap Forward the Chinese economy fell flat on its face, and Czechoslovakia had to turn elsewhere for food imports. She did, however, reduce her exports to China accordingly:

TABLE V/8. CZECHOSLOVAKIA'S VISIBLE TRADE
(mn. valuta kčs)

	1948	1953	1955	1957	1958	1959	1960	1961	1962	1963	1964
Balance with STEs	200	595	404	−631	776	691	725	342	707	1944	998
Balance with ACCs	69	119	176	−98	−56	1	−161	−368	−212	43	−316
Balance with UDCs	147	109	308	504	381	206	256	189	394	181	375
Imports from China	—	—	437	482	655	688	672	302	184	209	148
Exports to China	—	—	415	585	786	717	787	245	86	67	67
Total imports	—	—	7579	9985	9772	11,537	13,072	14,570	14,904	15,554	17,488
Total food imports	—	—	2196	2322	2259	2748	2861	2680	2763	3226	3415

(ii) The 1962 harvest failed, as we saw above. This was, of course, the major event. It was complicated by (iii) the previous failure of Soviet grain exports, which forced Czechoslovakia to buy outside the bloc:

TABLE V/9. CZECHOSLOVAK GRAIN IMPORTS
(thousand tons: from the USSR/from elsewhere)

	1959	1960	1961	1962	1963	1964
Wheat	1103/38	987/27	661/343	898/29	1030/335	563/926
Fodder-barley	5/8	52/12	114/0	144/0	130/26	238/158
Maize	16/79	15/245	117/13	230/70	171/118	197/236
Other forage	516/103	492/95	143/69	18/66	18/174	19/273

(iv) We owe to the hostile curiosity of a refugee[1] the suggestion that much of the trouble originated in the military b.o.p. with the USSR. On April 12, 1962, Novotny told the Central Committee: 'We did not know that we should have to buy grain and rolled materials on the capitalist markets', and 'we did not know that the new military technology would be so expensive as to become a

[1] Milos Vanek, *Relations Between Czechoslovakia and the Soviet Union*, cyclostyled document from the Socialist International, 1964.

burden to the whole national economy'. The authority of this speech is enhanced by the fact that it did not come out in the press at the time, but was only published in December. This is normal Communist treatment for particularly important and sensitive subjects.

The Soviet role in arms imports is less easy to show. But the Czechoslovak visible surplus with the USSR is difficult to explain otherwise.[1]

TABLE V/10. A SPECULATION ON CZECHOSLOVAKIA'S MILITARY B.O.P.

1953	1954	1955	1956	1957	1958	1959	1960	1961	1962	1963	1964

balance with the USSR (mn. valuta kčs):

−163 −12 +269 +277 −990 +326 −76 +203 +413 +338 +819 +352

defense and security expenditures in budget (md. domestic kčs):

10·4 9·6 9·3 8·9 8·8 8·8 9·5 10·9 11·3 10·9

It is easiest to agree with Mr. Vanek. No exact correlation should be expected between the annual movements of the two series. The period 1953–59 shows substantial visible balance between the two countries, as might be expected since neither performs many transit services for each other. The immense deficit in 1957 is, of course, the back payment for uranium that was the reward for good Czechoslovak behavior during the Hungarian Revolution in 1956. But thereafter things change. The increased defense allocation of a mere 2 md. domestic kčs in 1960–62 was only 1.2% of the net national income. Since more than a half of this can scarcely have gone on 'the new military technology' it hardly justified Novotny's complaint, if the hardware was produced at home. But the visible surplus with the USSR averaged 4 mn. valuta kčs in 1960–64, or 7% of all exports to the USSR and 2·5% of all exports. This almost must have gone on arms, and new types at that, since Czechoslovakia makes her own small arms. No doubt the USSR was, as usual, a patient creditor, and she surely did not demand conversion. But the mounting debt might very well have alarmed the government.

(v) The last unforeseeable trouble was that the winter of 1962–63 was exceptionally severe, hitting construction and transport.

To these we must add foreseeable troubles, for which it seems that the plans had culpably not made allowance:

(vi) The labor shortage grew acute once the rural surplus had

---

[1] The regular surpluses with Poland and Rumania plainly pay for goods transit, and make up over half of the surplus with other STEs, the remainder being just as plainly aid to Asian STEs.

been used up. But capacity installation went striding ahead, although there was no-one to man it (cf. Section 9). This leads in a general way to inflation and inefficiency, and it also directly worsens the b.o.p., since the new capacity demands imported materials to keep it going, but being undermanned it is an inefficient converter of these materials into exports or import-substitutes. Employment moved as follows ('000):

TABLE V/11. CZECHOSLOVAK EMPLOYMENT ('000)

	1958	1959	1960	1961	1962	1963	1964
Socialist sector (yearly average) .	4572	4682	4829	5000	5152	5233	5351
Total:							
Industry .	2088	2158	2258	2329	2404	2406	2432
Construction .	460	495	501	517	515	498	501
Agriculture and Forestry .	399	398	378	378	390	409	430
Agricultural and other coops., own account (end year) .	1519	1358	1242	1173	1131	1097	1048
Grand total (end year) . .	6069	6030	6098	6194	6265	6323	6392
Population (mid year, mn.) .	13·47	13·57	13·65	13·78	13·86	13·95	14·06

Note that this is not the same problem as 'investment scatter'. That is a discrepancy between investment work and fixed assets brought into use, such as resulted from the 1958 reform; this is a discrepancy between fixed assets and labor.

Thus all the water was squeezed out of agriculture by the end of 1960, and from then on industry and construction showed negligible increases. Nevertheless, the fixed assets at work in these branches increased as rapidly as ever (Table V/7). It may be objected that this was but a very sensible substitution of capital for the newly scarce factor, labor. But it is not likely that that could proceed apace in an economy already technically sophisticated. Note that agriculture, which needed more capital and could have effected such a substitution, got less after 1960.

(vii) There are, of course, always diminishing returns to labor and capital in mining and agriculture. But Czechoslovak sources agree that by the early 'sixties returns were diminishing in these extractive industries more sharply than usual.

(viii) Promises of foreign aid had eventually to be fulfilled. We must take this matter with the general problem of the b.o.p., which is our principal concern. Since invisible turnover with UDCs must be negligible, a good measure of *civilian* aid to UDCs might be the change in the commodity balance. However, the complication arises that in the 'fifties Czechoslovakia was clearly converting large balances with UDCs into dollars, sterling, etc. At that time there was no Czechoslovak aid to UDCs. Nevertheless, it is reasonable to interpret the change in 1962 over 1959–61 as aid. For this see Table V/8. I take these figures to mean that Czechoslovakia regularly runs an invisible deficit with ACCs which until the late 'fifties she paid for out of a visible surplus with both ACCs and UDCs. In 1960–61 her b.o.p. with ACCs turned sharply adverse, but her favorable balance with UDCs was neither so big nor so convertible as in earlier years. In 1962 there fell the treble blow of extra aid deliveries to UDCs of the order of 200 mn. kčs, a further shrinkage of Chinese food deliveries (say 100 mn. kčs), and a 17% drop in the output of agriculture and forestry. This latter might equal about 3000 mn. valuta kčs.[1] Suppose it was urgent to make up one half of the agricultural deficiency. Then with extreme approximation the drain on the gold and foreign exchange reserve was, or would have been without counter-measures, 2 md. valuta kčs in 1962, which was not far short of the total recent average annual importation from ACCs. Yet only the ACCs could make up the losses.

This would appear to be a full list of the *new* things that went wrong *in the early sixties*.[2] If we forget the b.o.p. it seems scarcely to account for so great a catastrophe as that the official growth rate of the national income fell from 7% to 0%. But Communist secrecy about the b.o.p. encourages one to forget it, and this is doubtless one of the reasons why both native and foreign economists have been free with other explanations, such as:

(a) Overcentralization—but the economy was overcentralized and highly successful up to 1958, and the decentralization of that year is one of the undisputed causes of the trouble. Specifically, there would have been far less investment scatter if Stalinist principles had been properly adhered to.

(b) Agricultural failure, and particularly collectivization—but all STEs suffer this, and there was nothing here to differentiate the periods before and after 1961. The severe shortage of young agricultural labor has already been mentioned, of course, under (iv) above.

(c) There was much inflation, but in a command economy this

---

[1] 17% (the decline) × 15% (the weight of agriculture in the national income) × 220 md. (very approximately the national income) ÷ 1·85 (Alton's conversion ratio into valuta kčs).
[2] It is quite untrue that Rumania turned from Czechoslovak to Western machinery. Her total imports from Czechoslovakia shot up, and her imports of machinery in particular ran as follows (mn. kčs): 1961 = 279; 1962 = 341; 1963 = 387. Only one STE other than China bought less Czechoslovak machinery in these years: Poland bought 5 mm. kčs less in 1963 than in 1962.

can only be a symptom, not a cause. Nor does it appear that inflation was much more serious in 1962; there was simply much more talk about it. See Table V/13.

(d) The all-important machinery industry was underspecialized. Indeed, it is alleged to produce 80% of all types of machine in the world. Though it is quite unclear how such a proposition could be affirmed or denied, it is evident that the industry is a small one and bulks large only because the country is small. Economies of scale are neglected. But this is a fault of many years' standing, which dates, indeed, from Stalin's reaction to the United States embargo. It would be good to correct it, just as it would be good to de-collectivize agriculture, but as the proximate cause of a sudden disaster it is a non-starter.

(e) It is also generally urged that Czechoslovakia is an advanced economy unsuited to Stalinist methods. This argument, with its Marxist-seeming historical determinism, is particularly popular among native economists who wish to carry conviction in ruling circles. If it refers to the splendid capacity of Stalinist coercion to mobilize a rural labor surplus it is correct and we have already admitted it. If it refers to the incompatibility of a command econ-omy with a sophisticated level of industrial technique, I can only say that the argument is very plausible and engages my emotions, but it is not persuasive. For why has the still more sophisticated economy of the DDR not suffered worse? Why was the USSR first with the hydrogen bomb and first into space? Why, indeed, is it *un*sophisticated industries like baking and weaving that always lag in STEs? Was Czechoslovak industry *significantly* less sophisti-cated in 1950–58?

(f) A more plausible version of (e) is confined to exports: you can export raw materials to ACCs, like the Russians, without great microflexibility in each exporting enterprise, but you cannot do this with tourism or manufactured products of any kind. Given that ACCs exist and are the only source of new technology and marginal food, and given that we are a manufacturing nation, we must adjust our model. Strong as this argument is, it does rest on the b.o.p. It would also seem a slender base for a total model change. The DDR has for whatever reasons rejected it, and survives.

Be these things as they may, the authorities reacted very strongly in mid-1962, abandoning the third FYP and setting the 1963 plan at the unprecedently low levels that sent a *frisson* through the Communist and Sovietological worlds. This plan had two purposes; first, to abolish investment scatter by concentration on projects already under way. In consequence of this, output and employment fell in construction, while the growth of capacity in use continued, as we saw. In other words, the plan succeeded. Secondly, it tried to correct the b.o.p. But evidently the crisis could not wait simply for structural shifts: to import-substitutes, to new exports, to rationalization of the existing exports. Material imports had to be cut there and then, and this meant diminished building and industrial production:

TABLE V/12. CZECHOSLOVAK IMPORTS
(mn. valuta kčs)

	1959	1960	1961	1962	1963	1964
Total imports of which	11,537	13,072	14,570	14,904	15,554	17,488
I. Machinery, equipment and tools for production	2346	2831	3426	3903	3987	4918
II. Fuels, raw materials and materials	6089	6906	7836	7589	7759	8475
(a) fuels, mineral raw materials and metals	2917	3628	4273	4517	4435	4833
(b) chemicals, fertilizers and raw rubber	890	1178	1286	1106	1204	1322
(c) building materials, blocks and other products	173	112	135	121	107	113
(d) raw materials of vegetable and animal origin (without food-stuffs)	2109	1988	2142	1845	2013	2207
III. Cattle and other animals for breeding purposes	7	9	4	3	2	17
IV. Foodstuffs incl. raw materials	2771	2885	2680	2763	3226	3415
(a) raw materials for the production of foodstuffs	1549	1545	1363	1253	1523	1829
(b) foodstuffs	1222	1340	1317	1510	1703	1586
V. Non-foodstuff goods for consumption	324	441	624	646	589	663

Some of these decisions are certainly surprising. Let us accept that 463 mn. kčs more foodstuffs had to be imported in 1963 than in 1961; then if it was possible to raise total imports by 650 mn. kčs, why was it necessary to cut 'fuels, raw materials and materials' at all? Why press on with the importation of machinery, etc., especially if there was surplus capacity? This, at any rate, is what happened, and the result was that not only investment but also current production fell.

It is for this reason that I have laid far more emphasis on the b.o.p. aspects of the crisis than have Czechoslovak economists. There has to be some powerful reason for reducing the growth of current production to zero, when usable fixed capacity is increasing and the labor force is stable. It is no explanation to say that there has recently been gross waste of investment; the solution for that is simply to correct it, by investing differently. The stoppage of current output was either an act of insane panic—which I do not wish to exclude— or an objective necessity owing to an import bottleneck.

Meanwhile at least one decision in the foreign trade field was wholly rational: tourism was rapidly expanded, and in such a way as to improve the b.o.p. We see in Table XIII/8 that the favorable balance improved from 20,000 'unit tourists' in 1960 to about 1,300,000 in 1964. At $150 a head this is $200 mn., or 8% of imports. Also bilateralism was more strictly enforced than ever (p. 283).

Inflation was, of course, rampant all the time, but nothing indicates that the decentralization of 1958, or the harvest failure of 1962, specially exacerbated it. Personal savings did not shoot up, and state betting, for whatever reason, declined. Wages, as befits a well-disciplined STE, were as level as the grave. But the government did take two deflationary measures. From reducing the cost of living à la Stalin, as it had since the 1953 currency reform, it turned to stability in 1960. This meant, of course, that some prices had to rise—a consequence that caused a lot of comical public heart-searching.[1] Further, hire purchase (instalment credit) was sharply cut in 1961, and other loans (which include building loans) in 1962.

It is difficult to be sure whether or not this is an exception to the rule laid down in our previous chapter: that an STE need not bring about general deflation in order to cure a b.o.p. crisis. Of literal monetary deflation there was, of course, hardly any; but was not the cessation of planned growth, so to speak, of the planners' physical inflation, more general than that required purely and directly by the import problem? It is impossible to say; it may have been. Certainly the choice of imports to cut was very peculiar.

The historical importance of the crisis was very great for the country. It destroyed the authorities' confidence in their model, and emboldened revisionist economists to speak up. This resulted in very great changes towards decentralization and the use of profit, of which it is too early yet to speak. Setting ideological sympathy on one side, I do not hold that these were the changes indicated by the specific crisis, nor that the Stalinist model was responsible for it, except as concerns point (f) above. Responsible are rather the partial decentralization of 1958, bad luck, and the policy errors of the authorities. Regretfully, I share the opinion of such standpat administrators as Otto Cerník,[2] who wanted only 'structural'

---

[1] It will be recalled from Chapter III that rising retail prices are deflationary in an STE.
[2] Cf. New Trends in Czechoslovak Economics, Prague, no. 3.

TABLE V/13. INDICATORS OF INFLATION IN CZECHOSLOVAKIA

	1957	1958	1959	1960	1961	1962	1963	1964
Personal savings, net of withdrawals (mn. kčs):								
In special a/cs for personal automobiles	427	94	46	120	195	532	-198	209
In savings books	3120	2819	2858	2308	2910	2667	2554	3700
Personal loans (mn. kčs):								
General loans paid out, gross	-865	-768	-1261	-1645	-1541	-822	-1072	-2186
(ditto, contracted for)	(-606)	(-501)	(-1486)	(-1480)	(-1039)	(-562)	(-2418)	(-2475)
Hire purchase loans, gross	—	-36[1]	-624	-706	-237	-20	-1705	-1800
State lotteries and pools, sums wagered (ma kčs):	652	985	882	781	455	230	176	—
Tax receipts from individuals (md. kčs)	10·7	11·3	11·3	11·3	11·8	12·5	12·8	13·1
Average monthly wage in socialized sector (kčs)	1255	1282	1309	1349	1382	1391	1390	1430
Cost of living (1953 = 100)[2]	82·5	82·4	80·5	78·8	78·3	79·2	79·7	80·0

There was budgetary balance, with a very small surplus, in every single year.

[1] Hire purchase began on November 20, 1958.
[2] Statistická Ročenka, 1964, p. 390: for an employee's family. Previous series differ slightly.

changes, e.g. in the direction of investment under central control, rather than more radical 'model' changes.

In general it seems that there has been too much high philo- sophizing about the 1962–63 crisis. It is a Marxist prejudice that important and dignified disasters must have important and dignified causes and cures; but there is no logic in this. The most philosophical remark the author can permit himself is that Stalinism is a politico- socio-economic phenomenon; so a pre-condition for the pre-1958 economy, successful or not, was a system of government by lies, terror and secrecy. Such a government might easily make policy errors and not correct them in time; it would be so prone to self- deception, so immune to criticism, that it would only halt at the cliff's edge. And so it was, and so it did, but no British author, writing on the balance of payments, has the right to complacency. A democratic government, with one and a half eyes on the polls and an occasional blink towards the duties, will also gravitate to the cliff's edge.

By 1965 the crisis was over (Table V/6). It was a very successful year apart from the harvest. 1966 was better still, with every pro- ductive sector growing even faster. Yet the new economic system did not come in until January 1967. It is ironical that 1967 should also have been a good year! Thus recent Czechoslovak history throws much light on the importance of trade and government policy, little on that of institutions.

We can hardly close, however, so political a discussion without welcoming the crisis and the dubious analysis to which it gave rise, since so much liberalization and humanization have flowed from them.

CHAPTER VI

EXCHANGE RATES

Only in so far as paper money represents gold, which like all other commodities has value, is it a symbol of value.　　　—MARX

When we are victorious on a worldwide scale, we shall make public lavatories out of gold on the streets of the world's largest cities. . . . Meanwhile we must save the gold in the RSFSR [the predecessor to the Soviet Union], sell it at the highest price, buy goods with it at the lowest price. 'When living among wolves, howl like the wolves.'
　　　　　　—LENIN, *The Importance of Gold Now and After
　　　　　　　the Victory of Socialism*, 1921

1　The original Soviet clamber on to gold.
2　The treasury and the note issue.
3　Are Soviet-type currencies backed by gold?
4　The independence of internal inflation.
5　The valuta ruble and the *Preisausgleich*.
6　The historical course of the Soviet *Preisausgleich*.
7　Foreign trade rationality and the *Preisausgleich*.
8　The administrative consequences of the *Preisausgleich*.
9　Western parallels to the *Preisausgleich*.
10　Non-commercial rates.
11　The fair clearing of balances is not an easy matter.
12　A disorderly cross-rate: the Sino-Soviet quarrel.
13　The statistical effects of (12).
14　The Soviet-type devaluation.
15　Soviet-type convertibility?
16　Statistical measurement and purchasing power parities.

I

THIS chapter deals with the monetary, administrative, and statistical aspects of the rate of exchange. For its role in resource allocation, see Chapter VII. The problems are treated roughly in the historical order of their appearance.

The first question is, how are Soviet-type currencies related to gold?[1] During the civil and Polish wars, the Soviet government

[1] I am indebted at many points to Mr. Altman, in *Optima*, September, 1961.

deliberately and proudly debauched the currency.[1] With the NEP came a complete change of heart, and a currency reform.[2] No Communist government has since that day willingly engaged in inflation. Indeed it is a point of honor to have falling or stable retail prices. So important is this to an STE that price flexibility is sacrificed to it, and the very model itself shaped accordingly. During the NEP, in particular, the currency was required to provide not merely a stable unit of account for shoppers and wage-earners, but also for inter-enterprise transfer and even for international trade. Even though state ownership remained wide-spread, foreign trade was a state monopoly, and many powers of the command economy were held in reserve, money was required to be active from top to bottom. Furthermore, this was long before Keynes' *General Theory*, and even longer before the consequences of that theory were drawn for international economics. Again, Marx had strongly backed convertibility under capitalism, and the NEP was nearly capitalism. Moreover, a gold-backed currency was required to re-establish the faith of an unsophisticated population in the stability of prices. Then, too, the USSR is one of the worlds' largest miners of gold.

2

It need not surprise us, then, that along with a stuffy Gladstonian attitude to budget-balancing, there grew up in the USSR a rigid gold-standard philosophy of international money. The gold[3] cover of the new ten-ruble *bank* notes (*chervontsi*) was fixed at 25% on October 11, 1922, and so far as is known this has never been changed. When Keynes visited the USSR in 1925, the Gosbank authorities were particularly keen for him to see their gold. However, the Ministry of Finance simultaneously pursued its own policy, covering its continuing deficit with its own treasury notes (*znaki*). These circulated at an enormous discount. On February 5, 1924, the old, inflated, *treasury* notes were exchanged for new ones at 50,000 to 1, and the new issue tied to the *chervonets* at the rate of ten new ruble notes for one *chervonets*. There was no gold clause restricting this

---

[1] There was some resistance by a few leaders; see E. H. Carr, *The Bolshevik Revolution, 1917-23* (New York, 1952), Chapter XVII.

[2] Cf. L. I. Frei, *Mezhdunarodnye Raschety i Organizovanie Vneshnei Torgovli Sotsialisticheskikh Stran* (Moscow, 1960), pp. 7–12, 101–2; A. M. Smirnov, *Mezhdunarodnye Valyutnye i Kreditnye Otnoshenia SSSR* (Moscow, 1960), Chapter I.

[3] Strictly speaking, gold, precious metals, and stable foreign currency.

new issue, however, for the intention was that the Ministry of Finance should balance its budget. In 1924 it did not do so, and continued to issue its *znaki* directly to the public. In 1925, however, and for all subsequent peace-time years, the budget has balanced. All new *znaki* (which cover the smaller denominations) are issued by the Ministry outside the budget to Gosbank alone, and Gosbank issues them to the public in such proportion to its own *chervontsi* as convenience dictates. As we saw in Chapter III, the budget is not normally a source of inflation, but the bank is. Although they nominally still originate in the treasury, the *znaki* only emerge to inflate the economy in the same way as do *chervontsi*—by excessive enterprise borrowing.

3

The reforms of 1924 thus still left the ruble formally tied to gold, but only so long as the budget was balanced and Gosbank did not cheat by issuing treasury notes in excess of the 'dictates of public convenience'. However, to keep a 25% gold-*chervonets* ratio is one thing, and to make the *chervonets* convertible is another. What Gosbank doubtless mainly did was collect gold from state mines and state foreign trade, and observe the ratio. Convertibility means that a large number of private people are allowed to present the note and take away the gold. There was very little of this ever, since even in the depths of the NEP little foreign trade was private, and the government mostly dealt in foreign exchange directly. The need to convert was primarily connected with tourism and emigration, and these, too, were closely controlled. Nevertheless, the all-important *foreign-exchange monopoly of Gosbank* had already been relaxed on February 15, 1923: even private people were allowed to make deals in gold and foreign exchange. And, in fact, in 1924–26, the *chervonets* was quoted in foreign markets around gold par, and kept there by Gosbank, which intervened to buy it up.[1] But on July 9, 1926, the export of Soviet notes and checks was forbidden, and the little gold-standard episode was at an end. The foreign-exchange monopoly of the Gosbank was not formally restored until much later, but that is a matter for lawyers.

It would appear, then, that the very frequent Soviet claims of gold backing for the ruble are mere propaganda. Since 1926, they

[1] The whole episode is reminiscent of Count Witte's interventions in the Berlin market in favor of the inconvertible ruble, and his final clamber on to the gold standard in 1897.

can only have meant that the 25% rule has been kept, solipsistically, by the Gosbank. But the tremendous devaluations of 1936 and 1961 (see Table VI/1, below) show that the note issue has increased by leaps and bounds. Evidently, the currency reform of 1947, which reduced the volume of notes but did little else, was not enough to stem the tide. It is inconceivable that gold stocks could have increased fast enough for the rule to be observed just before each of these events. It is also extremely suspicious that Stalin should have suppressed the figures for gold production, gold stocks and the note circulation all at the same time (1937).

Moreover, if we read the better authorities carefully, they make no such claim. Both Frei[1] and Smirnov[2] mention the same three laws as being 'basic' (*osnovnyi*) for this subject: January 7, 1937, and October 25, 1948, on the foreign-exchange monopoly of Gosbank, and March 1, 1950, on the gold *base* of the ruble. Frei is explicit that the 1950 law makes it official that the ruble is to be reckoned as a certain weight of gold, not, as previously, a certain number of dollars. This sensible provision is to avoid inconvenience when the dollar is devalued. But a gold base for calculation is worlds away from a gold *backing*, let alone convertibility. The law of October 11, 1922, establishing a gold backing, is not mentioned. It is evidently a dead letter, but no-one wishes to say so.

Stalin went a long way when he admitted in January, 1933 that the ruble would be maintained

not only by gold supplies. The steadiness of the Soviet ruble is guaranteed above all by the vast quantity of goods in the hands of the government, put into circulation at steady prices.[3]

However after the appreciation of 1950 there was some quite specific talk of gold backing again:

Bank notes are issued by Gosbank and guaranteed by not less than 25% gold and other precious metals.[4]

Even after the devaluation of January, 1961 we read:

The difference between them [bank and treasury notes] is that bank notes are guaranteed by 25% of precious metals and steady foreign exchange and by 75% of bank assets, while treasury notes are backed by the property of the government.[5]

[1] Op. cit., pp. 104–7.
[2] Op. cit., pp. 55–65.
[3] Quoted here from N. N. Rovinski, *Finansovoye Pravo* (Moscow, 1946), p. 303. I owe many of these references to my pupil Mrs. Winton.
[4] V. Batyrev, *Organizatsia i Planirovanie Denezhnogo Obrashchenia v S.S.S.R.* (Moscow, 1952), p. 13.
[5] V. P. D'yachenko, *Finansovo-Kreditni Slovar'* (Moscow, 1961), p. 369. Compare a virtually identical statement in V. V. Lavrov, *Finansy i Kredit S.S.S.R.* (Moscow, 1964), p. 380.

The simplest explanation of this paradox is to be preferred. The Soviet authorities were not lying because they do not have to. They govern the volume of bank notes by the 25% rule, both before and after devaluations and currency reforms; and make up the difference with treasury notes, for which the sky is the legal limit.

In no other STE is the official claim made that the currency is 'gold backed'.[1] It would appear that very few serious authors in other STEs ever do claim gold backing for their currency. An exception is Kohlmey, who says that:

Like every commodity-producing system, the socialist one has a general money-commodity. This is gold. *Socialist currencies are based on gold.* . . . Independently of the problem of currency cover, that does not immediately belong in this context, every currency unit, including those of socialist economies, has a gold content; it has some [*irgendeine*] relation to gold, which can be direct or indirect, official or unofficial, fixed or fluctuating. The issued 'bank notes' represent a certain sum of gold. *Their value is determined by the value of the gold quantum that they represent.* They are value-tokens.

Atlas says rightly of the Soviet ruble: 'If we deny the significance of the gold content of Soviet money for its functioning as a measure of value, we deny that Soviet money really is money.'[2]

The second italicization is mine, not the author's. It draws attention to the only directly untrue sentence in the whole passage. For domestic values are determined in no such way. It is only the valuta ruble (see Section 5) that has a link to gold; it does, indeed, *represent* a gold quantum, but is not convertible into it. However, it is clear that Professor Kohlmey's purpose here is mainly liturgical. He is honest enough to exclude gold cover *totidem verbis*, and convertibility by implication. Another exception is more serious: the Soviet official textbook itself:

Of course, only a monetary commodity which itself has a value can have the function of a measure of value—such as gold. In the Soviet Union and *the other countries of the socialist camp*, gold plays the part of universal *equivalent. Soviet* currency has a gold *content*, being tokens of gold. In socialist society, money can only fulfill the functions of a measure of the value of commodities by virtue of its connection with gold. . . . Soviet money retains the historically derived connection with gold.[3]

Note the implied distinction between USSR and other STEs.

[1] For China in particular cf. *Chinese Youth Daily*, January 6, 1962: 'The reserve of this Jen Min Pi of our country consists of goods. It has no fixed gold value.' For an earlier statement to the same effect cf. *Research in Economics*, 4/1957. (Source used: *China News Analysis*, Hong Kong, no. 409.)

[2] Günther Kohlmey, *Der Demokratische Weltmarkt* (East Berlin, 1956), pp. 252–3. The quotation in the second paragraph is from S. Atlas in *Neue Welt*, 15–16/1953.

[3] *Politicheskaya Ekonomia*, 1955 ed., p. 470, my italics.

This is very similar, in its qualified honesty, to Kohlmey, who also draws attention (in a passage not quoted here) to the historical connection of gold with Soviet-type money.

Kohlmey is attacked as 'certainly wrong' by Stefan Varga in these terms:

The gold content of socialist money is a declaration [. . . without . . .] the slightest influence on the p.p.p. [purchasing power parity] of socialist currencies among themselves or *vis-à-vis* capitalist countries. . . . The foreign trade monopoly of the socialist state makes it possible to bridge the gap between domestic and foreign prices by a system of subsidies and of foreign payment obligations is settled in gold, which then really fulfills the function of 'world' money and something like a 'treasure' function.[1]

It is, of course, good for an STE to have a gold reserve, and Varga is right to insist on the settlement function of gold. But in general he is wrong to say that 'foreign payments obligations [are] settled in gold', particularly between STEs; they are mostly settled in goods. However gold is often used in settlement with MEs, though between STEs it seems only to be lent, and thus to figure in formal acts of short-term aid. To this extent Soviet-type currencies enjoy *administrative convertibility*. To be precise, however, only the valuta form of the currency (see Section 5, below) is thus privileged. Again, one *might* suspend convertibility but still, by administrative means, keep the quantity of notes at a proportion to the gold reserve. And this may have happened during the NEP. But in an STE, it is the foreign-trade plan that is adjusted to the gold reserve, while the quantity of notes is adjusted to the supply of consumer goods, the wage bill, and the presumed liquidity preference of the consuming population. This is very rational in view of the institutional set-up.

For the rest, a gold-backed currency means a currency a foreigner can hold and turn into gold, on at least some fairly common occasions. It does not merely mean one the quantity of which is administratively regulated according to the gold reserve, let alone according to other, and independent, criteria. The ruble is, therefore, not 'gold backed' in any usual, or, indeed, in any sensible, meaning of the phrase.

4

Indeed, it would be irresponsibly to waste one of the most precious advantages of the STE if the quantity of notes were linked

[1] Stefan Varga, 'Money under Socialism', in *International Economic Papers* no. 8, p. 216. Note, however, that Varga describes himself as 'a non-Marxist in a country struggling to establish socialism, who wants to do justice to the achievements of Marxism'. He was then Professor of Economics at Budapest; so, all in all, he cannot be taken as official or orthodox.

to the gold reserve, whether by administrative procedures or by imposing a gold-standard automatism on the central bank. For either case would mean deflation every time there was an unfavorable current balance; and immunity to this disease is one of the main reasons for Soviet-type growth (see Chapter III). By all means prevent inflation, but do not unnecessarily oblige yourself actually to deflate.

Moreover, if the reader will hark back to the process of inflation by bank credit described in Chapter III, he will be reminded that bank credits to loss-making enterprises enable them to generate new personal income, and thus necessitate the issue of more notes (since people are nearly always paid in notes alone). In this way, the supposed 'tail' of credit wags the 'dog' of currency. Now if it were really true that the currency were tied to gold, credit would ultimately also be tied to it, since bank loans would not be allowed to generate personal incomes beyond the point where the fixed volume of currency could finance them. Yet they are, in fact, permitted to go beyond this point.

5

So much, then, for the shift from gold backing to gold base in the USSR. What eventually did happen under Stalin was that the rise in prices rendered the old rate of exchange 'obsolete'. Note that we have not written 'untenable'; there was nothing to stop a subsidy to exports and a special tax on imports, and this is, indeed, what occurred. But this is an understatement. A Soviet-type currency differs essentially from an ME's currency under exchange control, in that it is scarcely ever exchanged at all. Under exchange control the importer is eventually permitted to buy his ration of foreign exchange, and handle it himself: his pound becomes 2·4 dollars. The balancing of all Britain's dollar earnings against all her dollar expenditures is the task of the central bank, which uses this or that indirect restraint on the independent principals. It has simply added exchange control to its previous, mainly monetary, weapons. In an STE, on the other hand, the importer's ruble never becomes 1·1 dollars: the Ministry of Foreign Trade (not the central bank) spends the dollars it has earned by exports on his behalf, and directly sees to it that dollar earnings and outgoes balance. The 'importer' is the mere recipient, according to plan, of a foreign good from the Ministry. He pays the latter an arbitrary transfer price in rubles, which may or may not balance the rubles that the Ministry has to spend on acquiring exports.

The Ministry's essential balance, then, is the one in valuta. It never exchanges valuta for domestic currency, but, on the contrary, balances also its ruble outgoes and earnings. Characteristically this balance is in deficit, since imports are underpriced; and the Ministry of Finance simply makes up the difference. Since all Soviet-type prices are irrational, no-one is deeply concerned at this difference; the main thing is that we managed to sell our exports, and so buy some imports.

Thus it is misleading, or at least it does violence to the Soviet-type vocabulary and cast of mind, to say that when the official rate of exchange stands above the purchasing power par (p.p.p.)—and it usually does—exports are subsidized and imports taxed. The foreign trade monopoly keeps the valuta balance and the domestic balance separate. It pays exporters out of the proceeds of import sales, and requires only such net subsidy as shall equate these.

Nevertheless, the gross subsidy (exports in home prices minus exports in foreign prices multiplied by the rate of exchange) is also a concept that concerned the STE, even at the height of Stalinist irrationality. So also, less urgently, did the gross tax on imports.[1] As a matter of fiscal procedure the budget seems to have always carried the gross figures, as a tax and a subsidy along with other taxes and subsidies. It may, however, and probably does in Poland, enter only the net subsidy to each separate foreign-trade enterprise.[2] This whole complex of arrangements we call, with acknowledgments to the DDR, the *Preisausgleich*.[3]

Now since the net subsidy is likely to be small the government may prefer the prestige due to retaining the old rate of exchange. Only those current transactions will truly take place at the 'obsolete' rate which the *Preisausgleich* happens not to cover. These, historically, have been small invisible items like tourism and diplomacy (not freight charges). In this way there arises the distinction between the 'foreign-exchange ruble' (which we shall call the valuta ruble)[4] and the domestic ruble. The former is even more of a mere unit of account than the domestic wholesale ruble. Its principal functions are to translate the prices of exports and imports, settled in capitalist currencies, into a single convenient unit with a patriotic name; and

---

[1] Which was over and above the turnover tax.

[2] I say this because the zloty is very grossly overvalued, and the known subsidies in the budget are quite insufficient to cover the difference.

[3] Meaning price equalization. The Polish terminology is significantly different, and captures better the spirit of the thing as I have understood it above: 'różnice budżetowe', or budgetary differences.

[4] Russian invalyutny, Polish dewizowy, German devisen-.

to enable similar prices to be attached to goods traded with other STEs. It is the valuta ruble that has the official rate of exchange but virtually no independent existence, except (before April, 1957) for invisible transactions. The domestic ruble, even the wholesale ruble, has a more important role, but is only tenuously linked to the rate of exchange by the *Preisausgleich*.

6

Doubtless for reasons of prestige, Stalin always refused to operate multiple rates at the central bank.[1] The *Preisausgleich* was a more flexible instrument, i.e., led to greater irrationalities, than any system of multiple rates. However, the bare existence of a *Preisausgleich*, discussed so openly in the satellites, has never been admitted in the USSR, and this, too, was doubtless on grounds of prestige. The very word *invalyutny* has only recently reached public print in the USSR.[2] The ruble was certainly overvalued in 1926–27, but may not have, in fact, required a *Preisausgleich*.[3] However, by 1929 there must have been some kind of export subsidy.[4] Factory and wholesale prices did not, in fact, increase very rapidly in the early 1930s,[5] since in STEs they have little function and are 'passive' (see Chapter II). However, world prices, especially of Soviet exports, fell sharply, and we are entitled to infer that export subsidies, if not import taxes, increased. In view of the violent campaign against Soviet 'dumping' (see Chapter IX, Section 6) it can scarcely surprise us that its existence was concealed. Anyhow, the big devaluation of 1936 must have taken care of even a rather large *Preisausgleich*.

[1] *Which* rate would have been 'backed by gold'?! But note that there is nothing impracticable about backing them all by gold, so long as the central bank prohibits the conversion of one kind of ruble into another.

[2] But a very knowledgeable defector was already using it in 1932: E. M. Shenkman in Birmingham Bureau of Research on Russian Economic Conditions, *Memorandum*, no. 4.

[3] Paul Douglas estimates that in 1926 the ruble was overvalued by 10% in respect to the cost of living, 27% in respect to its wholesale purchasing power. The legal foreign currency markets at that time quoted a 25–33% discount (Stuart Chase *et al.* [ed.], *Soviet Russia in the Second Decade* [New York, 1928], pp. 240–1). However, exports were mostly primary products, the internal prices of which had not risen anything like as rapidly as those of manufactures; and these were very likely sold without subsidy. Evgeni Preobrazhensky (*The New Economics* [originally Moscow, 1926], trans. Brian Pearce [Oxford, 1965], p. 30) puts the disparity in prices of manufactures at 100%, but he was not a precise statistician. Manufactures, being import-competitive, simply owed their high prices to tariffs.

[4] Franklyn Holzman in *Comparisons of the U.S. and Soviet Economies*, Joint Economic Committee, 86th Cong., 1st Sess. (1959), p. 429.

[5] In 1928–37, when the turnover tax was first imposed, retail prices rose much faster, but that is irrelevant to international trade, except tourism. The wholesale prices of intermediate goods doubled in this period, while those of machines scarcely changed (A. Bergson and L. Turgeon in *Journal of Political Economy*, August, 1956; Richard Moorsteen, *Prices and Production of Machinery in the Soviet Union* [Harvard, 1962], p. 72).

Inflation continuing, retail prices shot up again until the currency reform of December, 1947, but wholesale prices remained stickily behind as usual, rising by about 30%. Since foreign prices rose still more over the war, it is doubtful that any large *Preisausgleich* resulted. The currency reform, being directed only at idle cash, affected hardly any state prices, whether wholesale or retail, but only those on the kolkhoz market. So the disparity between retail and wholesale prices remained, and the latter were finally raised by between two and two-and-a-half times in January, 1949. It is from that date that the *Preisausgleich* must have become serious again. So great a rise in prices urgently demanded a devaluation of the ruble, but in 1950 everything was incontinently reversed. Machinery prices were reduced by about one-third, and intermediate good prices by about 15%. Simultaneously the ruble was *appreciated* by 32%! Thus if the rate was at approximate wholesale p.p.p. in 1948, it hopelessly overvalued the ruble by the end of 1950.[1] Subsequent falls in wholesale prices must, however, have diminished the *Preisausgleich*, until the devaluation of 1961 again—presumably— wiped it out.

It is generally reckoned that the 1961 devaluation restored the ruble to wholesale purchasing power parity with the dollar; but the turnover tax and the great profits levied on consumer goods make it unfair as a tourist rate, i.e., as a retail p.p.p. (see Section 10, below). This must have been the first time since 1913 that things were so rational.[2] Table VI/1 presents the general history of the ruble, exclud-

[1] Sources for wholesale prices as before. The reversal of policy is beyond doubt due to the arrest of the great Soviet planner and protagonist of the 'law of value', N. A. Voznesensky, in March, 1949. *cf*. Chapter XII, Section 5.

[2] The CIA conjecture that the planned Preisausgleich for 1960 is implied in the following figures, all in milliards of new rubles. The finance minister gave originally planned revenues of 77·30 and expenditures of 74·58. But after the devaluation he said the plan had been for 75·21 and 72·63 respectively. This implies a special import tax of 2·09 and a special export subsidy of 1·95, wiped out by the devaluation. The trade plan for 1960 probably ran at 2·1 for imports, 2·3 for exports (in md. valuta rubles).—Sources: CIA, *The Soviet Budget for 1961* (Washington, 1962); Garbuzov in *Pravda*, December 21, 1960; Garbuzov in *Planovoe Khozyaistvo* 12/1959.

Professor Nove calculates the export Preisausgleich in 1955 and 1956 as follows (mn. old rubles):

	1955	1956
budgetary allocation to all trade . . .	10,734	12,202
,, ,, ,, internal trade . .	800	1,100
∴ Preisausgleich	9,934	11,102
exports in valuta rubles	13,694	14,446

—*Finansy i Sotsialisticheskoye Stroitel'stvo* (Moscow, 1958), p. 347; Zverev in *Planovoe Khozyaistvo* 3/1957.

All four figures must be taken as minimal estimates for the Preisausgleich, since it is not excluded that individual foreign trade enterprises subsidize some of their exports out of the profits on imports, without the sum passing through the central budget.

ing the new non-commercial rate (Table VI/2) and the curious history of the yuan-ruble rate (Section 12).

TABLE VI/1. RUBLE EXCHANGE RATES AND PURCHASING POWER, SELECTED DATES, 1913–61

	Rubles to the Dollar (Official)	Grams of Gold to the Ruble	Grams of Gold to the Dollar	National Income Deflator USSR[a]	USA[b]
1913	1·94[c]	0·774234[d]	1·50463[c]	c. 44[e]	63
From April 1, 1924 .	1·94[f]	0·774234[d]	1·50463[c]	c. 90[e]	99
July 9, 1926 . .	(Export prohibition on ruble notes)				
1928	1·94[c]	0·774234[d]	1·50463[c]	100	100
1933	(1·57)[g]	0·774234[d]	1·50463[c]	c. 150[h]	75
1934	(1·16)[g]	0·774234[d]	0·888671[c]	—	80
1935	(1·15)[g]	0·774234[d]	0·888671[c]	—	79
From April 1, 1936 .	5·03[c]	0·17685[d]	0·888671[c]	—	82
October 28, 1936–June 30, 1937[i]	—	0·187425[d]	0·888671[c]	—	—
From July 19, 1937 .	5·30[c]	0·16767[d]	0·888671[c]	345/583[j]	83
December, 1947 .	.(Currency reform: Drastic reduction in quantity of money, but no change in official prices or exchange rate)				
March 1950 . .	4·00[c]	0·22217[c]	0·888671[c]	820/1380[j]	152
April 1, 1957 .	.(Beginning of noncommercial rates; see Table VI/2)				
January 1, 1961 (old rubles)[k]	9·00[c]	0·0987412[c]	0·888671[c]	c.918/1546[j]	196

(From January 1, 1961, divide by ten in all domestic transactions; it follows that the new rate is strictly 0·9 new rubles to the dollar.)

[a] From sources in P. J. D. Wiles in *Analyse et Prevision* (Paris), September 1966. For 1961, I have chained the results in Table V/2 to those in *Analyse et Prevision*.
[b] *Historical Statistics of the United States* (Washington, D.C., 1960), p. 139. The deflators for 1936 (ninth row) and 1937 (eleventh row) are for the calendar year.
[c] *Narodnoye Khozyaistvo SSSR 1960* (Moscow, 1961), p. 747.
[d] S. N. Prokopovicz, *Histoire Economique de l'URSS* (Paris, 1952), pp. 554–7.
[e] Cost of urban living.
[f] From July, 1923, to April, 1924, the ruble fluctuated at a lower rate of two or more to the dollar. Cf. Louis Segal and A. A. Santalov, *Soviet Union Yearbook 1926* (London, 1926), p. 379.
[g] These are the average dollar-ruble rates during the devaluation of the dollar, which began in August, 1933, and finished on January 31, 1934. Despite the language in *Narodnoye Khozyaistvo SSSR 1960*, p. 747, they are not used for statistical conversion purposes. Such conversion is always based on the ruble-gold rate.
[h] Very approximate. State food-shop prices had doubled by 1932 (S. N. Prokopovicz, *Russlands Volkswirtschaft under den Sowjets* [Zurich, 1944], p. 306). Free market prices had risen more; wholesale prices, hardly at all.
[i] There seems to have been no official rate from June 30 to July 19.
[j] Weights for first figure in pair are from 1937; for second, from 1928.
[k] Note the connection between the new currency reform and the devaluation. In order to conceal the more than twofold devaluation from the ignorant, a very mild, indeed, purely nominal, currency reform was imposed at the same time.

Thus the Soviet national income deflator has risen about nine times as fast as the American, while the ruble has been devalued only 4·6 times vis-à-vis the dollar. The difference is largely due to the fact that the 1961 devaluation aimed at a wholesale purchasing power parity, and neglected perforce the turnover tax imposed since 1928, which bulks largely in the national income deflator. But the gross inaccuracy of all price indices must also be borne in mind.

7

In practice, the *Preisausgleich* is far more complicated than a simple proportional subsidy to all exports, exactly balanced by a special proportional tax (over and above all turnover taxes and tariffs) on all imports. The complications are best studied in their most perverse case: East Germany,[1] which subsidizes not only her exports but also her imports. The fact emerges from a stolen document, quoted by Klinkmüller,[2] which gives a detailed breakdown for July–December, 1951.

Thinking too much in Western terms, one ordinarily says to oneself: the Deutschemark (Ost), or the ruble, is overvalued *vis-à-vis* the pound or dollar; its official rate of exchange is more favorable to it than the wholesale purchasing power parity. So if a balance of trade is to be maintained in terms of pounds or dollars, exports must be subsidized in order to sell enough of them, and imports taxed in order to keep them down. But this is not necessarily true even of an ME. If any ME is lucky enough to have a very inelastic demand for imports and faces a very inelastic demand for its exports, by overvaluing its currency it will simply improve its terms of trade without worsening its balance of trade. It has no need, arising directly from its payments position, to subsidize exports or tax imports.

The thing is even less true of an STE. Suppose the DM(O) is in general overvalued, but individual price relatives neither correspond to those of the world market nor govern relative outputs. Then it might happen, for instance, that the DDR only imports 'growth' commodities, the use of which she wishes to encourage. Import substitutes in these lines are subsidized, and imports also are priced cheap domestically, the quantity bought being kept in order by administrative fiat. This low domestic price of imports might be obtained simply by converting directly at the overvalued official rate of exchange, or it might even be necessary further to subsidize, since the desired price is very low. And this seems to have been the DDR's case.

Similarly, on the other side, the prices of exports might be exceptionally low already, so that it was necessary to tax them in order to equate world price to the domestic price times the official rate of exchange in the books. This, however, is not the DDR's case: here she behaves like a normal STE, and has to subsidize her exports.

We can make no certain deduction, then, from the general excess of domestic prices over foreign prices at the official rate of exchange. If not very great, it may yield in importance to the relations between

---

[1] The following eleven paragraphs are taken, with corrections, from my review of *Die Gegenwärtige Aussenhandelsverflechtung der Sowjetischen Besatzungszone Deutschlands* (Berlin, 1959), by Erich Klinkmüller, in *Soviet Studies* (January, 1961).

[2] Ibid., p. 100.

the foreign and domestic prices of each particular traded good, for these may differ significantly and systematically from the average. The micro-economic independence of East German prices from world prices has, in fact, so great an influence that it swamps the macro-economic inflation of its currency in relation to its rate of exchange.

Some may be helped by algebra. Let the DDR import one good, m, and export one good, x. Let r be the rate of exchange and all other symbols be prices. Let trade be in balance. Then we get:

Currency, etc.	Imports		Exports
Trade at world prices	im	$=$	ex
Trade in valuta DM(O)	rim	$=$	rex
Trade at internally realized prices	Im		Ex
Conversion factors	$\dfrac{I}{i}$		$\dfrac{E}{e}$
Import levy	$Im - rim$		
Export subsidy			$Ex - rex$

Now let us introduce k and K, the deviations from the official rate of exchange, such that $I = kri$, $E = Kre$. Then in an uncomplicated, 'rational', economy, $rim = Im$, $rex = Ex$, $I/i = E/e = r$, $k = K = 1$. If the economy remains rational in all respects but the overvaluation of its currency, $Im - rim = Ex - rex > 0$, $k = K > 1$; i.e., relative domestic prices still correspond to relative world prices, and the import levy (entailing $k > 1$) and export subsidy (entailing $K > 1$) run at the same percentage on all goods. If the economy is irrational but its currency is not in general overvalued much (the East German case), $k \neq K$, but both are near to 1. This is the 'irrationality condition': it means that domestic price relations of traded goods do not correspond to world price relations, which are, of course, the opportunity costs facing all nations.[1] Prices no longer govern exports and imports, so bear no special relation to them. Then $Im - rim \neq Ex - rex$, and the budget will show a net profit or loss on foreign trade, even though trade is still in valuta balance, since the levy no longer offsets the subsidy.[2] Indeed, rim may easily $> Im$, or there will be an import subsidy along with the export subsidy, since $k < 1$. This is precisely the DDR's case. There might also be an export levy, since $K < 1$; a condition the DDR happens not to exemplify. For example, the stolen document of July–December, 1951, gives the following figures (millions of East

---

[1] On the notion that world prices are every nation's opportunity cost, cf. Chapter VII.
[2] Cf. the Hungarian case in Chapter V, Section 10.

German marks): $rim = 1251 \cdot 9$, $Im = 879 \cdot 6$, $Ex = 1932 \cdot 9$, $rex = 1506 \cdot 0$. Now, express world prices in valuta rubles, and bear in mind that the official rate of exchange is 1 ruble = $0 \cdot 833$ DM(O). $Kr = E/e = 1 \cdot 07$; $r = 0 \cdot 833$, $kr = I/i = 0 \cdot 585$.

If we took the prices of traded goods alone we should not wish to say that the DM(O) was overvalued in general. The degree of overvaluation is simply a weighted average of k and K. It might in this case be either side of 1, whereas in the USSR it used greatly to exceed 1, which, indeed, it still does in Poland. But the DM(O) will be found to be, in fact, 'overvalued' when we take into account purely domestic goods. This is, of course, a purely statistical over-valuation, in terms of general purchasing power parities, useful for standard-of-living comparisons but not necessarily influencing international trade.

In the USSR the general degree of overvaluation, as measured by including non-traded goods, was until 1961 so great that an import subsidy ($k < 1$) was very improbable. Note that it was not impossible; it is only unlikely that chance will give us $k < 1$ if the currency is in general overvalued. Even if the USSR imported goods that were relatively cheap at home, she had still to tax her import corporations.

The more K or k exceeds 1, the greater the export subsidy or import levy; the more they fall short of it, the greater the export levy or import subsidy. The true measure of irrationality is, as we have seen, not that k or $K \neq 1$ but that they are unequal, i.e., the failure of relative home prices to correspond to relative world prices. We can, that is to say, overvalue our currency and then correct it by an across-the-board levy-subsidy so that micro-economic ration-ality is quite unaffected.

East German prices must have been very highly irrational, since there are such astonishing differences between the so-called export and import conversion factors in the same branches of production. These factors are, in our terminology, simply $kr = I/i$ for imports and $Kr = E/e$ for exports. The stolen document of 1951 gives such factors by branches, including such comparatively homogeneous ones as 'textiles' and 'paper and printing', which yielded both exports and imports. Textile imports had to be heavily subsidized (conversion factor $0 \cdot 43$, or $k = 0 \cdot 516$), but so did textile exports (conversion factor $1 \cdot 85$, or $K = 2 \cdot 225$!). In paper and printing the import conversion factor was the lowest of all ($0 \cdot 29$), while for exports it was $0 \cdot 96$. Thus, fairly close substitutes were selling at

half and at double world prices. We can see the same phenomenon
in Poland, where the zloty is far more overvalued, so that fairly
close substitutes sell, say, at double and at eight times world
prices.

8

Clearly the *Preisausgleich* is in all circumstances a bad thing, and
should be abolished. Yet in whose interest is it to do so, and what
actions are needed? It is an interesting fact that the treasury is little
concerned, and in particular will not be helped by devaluation. For
the net sum of the import and export *Preisausgleiche*, which is what
the treasury gains, is unaffected by the rate of exchange if imports
balance exports in foreign currency:[1]

$$Im - rim - Ex + rex = Im - Ex - r(im - ex),$$

where r drops out if $im = ex$. Thus the effect of a devaluation on
budgetary balance is minimal.[2]

Of course, too, in the 'perfectly rational' case described above,
where $k = K = 1$ it does not matter what the foreign balance is,
since there is no *Preisausgleich* at all. The treasury's interest, then, is
not to rationalize and equilibrate the economy but to bring in
revenue. I.e. it wants a valuta deficit $(im - ex < o)$, coupled with a
domestic surplus $(Im - Ex > o)$, such that $k > K$. Its influence cannot
be good.

If in a command economy the treasury is still anxious to minimize
outgo, the central bank has no special concern. It is, in any case,
almost wholly unaffected by both the level of the rate of exchange
and the mere existence of the *Preisausgleich*, let alone its net sum.
Its function here is to administer the foreign-exchange plan, and the
domestic currency equivalents scarcely concern it. An exception has
been the DDR since January 1, 1959.[3] From that date, the Deutsche
Notenbank received from importers and paid to exporters its own
Preisausgleich (PAG I), which was the difference between the official
rate of exchange, $1 = DM2.20, and the officially calculated pur-

---

[1] With acknowledgments to F. L. Pryor, *The Communist Foreign Trade System* (London, 1963), p. 102.
[2] Edward Ames (in *Review of Economics and Statistics*, 1953) concludes that devaluation does matter, but I cannot follow his reasoning. One flaw in it, certainly, is to put valuta and domestic currency in the same balance sheet.
[3] Pryor, op. cit., pp. 104–5.

chasing power par, $1 = DM 4.20.[1] In other words, the bank carried through a thinly disguised devaluation. The old *Preis-ausgleich* through the treasury, now called PAG II, remained, only the gross sums paid in and out were smaller.

This split of the *Preisausgleiche* fits very well into our previous analysis. There are, in fact, normally two elements. PAG I is due to general overvaluation, which is more honestly countered by a devaluation but should in any case be the bank's business. PAG II is due to micro-economic irrationality, and is really only a special part of the variable turnover tax. If the consumer buys a foreign consumer good, there is, just as at home, no predictable relation between cost and price, owing to the prevailing irrationality, and the difference is made up in each case by a variable tax. The principle is extended to the producer buying a foreign producer good. Similarly, the foreigner, buying at a price agreed upon in some foreign currency or in the valuta version of the exporter's currency, is like a final consumer; only in this inverted case he gets a subsidy on the same principle. It is, then, PAG II that is really important. PAG I is merely a prestige element, a way of avoiding devaluation.[2]

Thus, the *Preisausgleich* does not really cost anything except in irrationality, a cost borne by the whole economy. It is, however, also an administrative burden. PAG I in the DDR is doubtless a mere book-keeping transaction in the central bank. But for the rest the *Preisausgleich* is a full normal fiscal transaction, the profit on imports flowing into the treasury as a tax and the loss on exports flowing out as a subsidy. The foreign-trade enterprise is not normally allowed to set off the one against another. This is surprising, but some such enterprises either only export or only import. Doubtless, too, it is in part because of the general extremity of fiscal centralization in an STE. Thus, however small the net cost to the treasury, the gross flow of funds through it can be very big. Our formulae above do not refer to the gross flow, which is

$$Im - rim + Ex - rex = Im + Ex - r(im + ex).$$

This is obviously a function of trade turnover and of the rate of exchange. A devaluation does, very notably, reduce the gross flow.

[1] This rate presumably applies to products before turnover tax. See Section 10, below. From 1965 onwards the statistical yearbooks give foreign trade turnover in 'Devisenmark' at this new rate, although they nowhere explain what they have done. Previous yearbooks used the valuta *ruble* at its current rate.

[2] In 1959 Poland did much the same. The old valuta rate of 4 zl. = $1 remains in the statistics, but the Bank reckons imports and exports at 24 zl. = $1 (H. Machowski in *Konjunkturpolitik*, West Berlin, 5–6/1966).

9

For the use of the *Preisausgleich* as a micro-economic trade criterion see Chapter VII. For the rest there is an obvious parallel to the *Preisausgleich* in the tariffs and export subsidies of MEs. However, the motivation of these is different: the state protects or encourages particular industries at their urging, whereas in an STE the state is making financially possible the exports or imports upon which it has itself decided. Also the formal financial arrangements are very different, as we have seen. The multiple-currency practices of Latin America differ still more, since they use the central bank. Even the DDR's PAGI is not a multiple-currency practice, but a concealed devaluation.

The most interesting comparison is with Western exchange control systems. An STE permits 'resident convertibility' only to tourists and others about to go abroad. The right is, of course, very restricted, but it is formally identical to the right of an intending tourist in an ME with exchange control. The importer in such an ME is, as we have seen, very different from the Soviet-type ministry of foreign trade. The latter's formal position seems to be unique. The position of the two central banks, on the other hand, is more similar than might appear. The Soviet-type bank does not regulate domestic inflation and deflation in the same way (Chapter III), so is not called upon to operate in foreign currency *for that reason*. But it can still operate, and does so, in much the same way. If the Gosbank can operate through branches in London and Beirut (the Moscow Narodny Bank), there is nothing to stop it setting up a short-term money market in valuta rubles in Moscow. The valuta ruble would then cease to be an abstraction, and take on reality as an international currency backed (!) by gold, much like dollar account sterling in the early 'fifties. The domestic ruble would be, of course, far more insulated from the valuta ruble than was resident from dollar account sterling; but that would be a clear advantage on the Soviet side.

10

As we have seen, invisibles, other than merchandise freight, are more difficult to plan. Diplomats, experts, sportsmen, visiting lecturers and entertainers, foreign students, tourists, etc., simply arrive in one's country and want to buy things. They are not native foreign-trade enterprises, so it is impossible secretly to admit them to the delights of the local PAG. The old system—which I experienced in Moscow in 1952—was simply to charge them the official rate of exchange. In the long run, however, this made civilized intercourse between East and West impossible, since it led to absolutely prohibitive costs.[1] It was also very unfair, though not so astronomically unfair, between one STE and another. The ice cracked, but did not break, when on August 15, 1956, the USSR gave a 'tourist allowance' to visitors from capitalist countries of R.25 per diem. Increased frankness and rationality, plus a genuine desire to take in tourists, forced multiple rates, i.e., a special tourist rate, on most STEs on April 1, 1957. These are now quite openly published. The principle of such 'non-commercial' rates, utterly different from that of the 'commercial' or official rates, is simply that they are retail purchasing power parities. Between STEs there is a fair correspondence of non-commercial and official rates, except that the official rate of the zloty is a gross overvaluation. For some reason this currency has never been devalued. Table VI/2 gives the usual inter-STE table from the Polish point of view. The cross-rates harmonize with the rates published by other STEs.

Similar non-commercial rates are also given for invisible trade with non-Communist countries. These are quite as fair, indeed often—with an eye on tourists—very generous. In Table VI/2 rates for currencies of non-Communist countries other than the dollar are not given, since they are all obtainable simply by using the official dollar rate of exchange with that currency. I.e., although the relation between commercial and non-commercial rates has been differentiated for every Soviet-type currency, there has been no attempt to hit exact purchasing power parities in the other cases. A standard multiplier of 6 has been used instead. Such rates should persist even if the official rates were sensible. For the STE's peculiarly heavy indirect taxes, all concentrated on goods sold at retail, make for a wider gap between wholesale and retail prices than in non-Communist countries, so that there cannot be a single p.p.p. A notable case is the ruble, for which no non-commercial rate has been offered to visitors from capitalist countries since the official rate was devalued on January 1, 1961. The new ruble-dollar rate was chosen as a weighted average of retail prices, services at factor cost, and

[1] And, in Poland in 1957, to the amusing situation that a private person could *import* certain services like international air fares and telephone calls at the obsolete rate. But this was due to the special circumstances of the Polish Thaw. The USSR permitted no outgoing tourists, so all such windfalls accrued to public bodies, except for diplomats' families.

investment costs.[1] This automatically makes it unattractive to capitalist tourists. In addition, *more Sovietico*, each sectoral p.p.p. has been somewhat exaggerated by a failure adequately to account for the better quality of things in the USA. But the USSR continues to offer special non-commercial rates to STEs.

TABLE VI/2. THE VARIOUS EXCHANGE RATES FOR THE ZLOTY, 1963
(number of zlotys per 100 foreign units)

			Noncommercial[a]		*(Units per*	*(Shaefer*
			Before	*After*	*$1 at*	*Ratios*[c]
		Official	*April 1, 1963*		*Official Rate)*	*1964–5)*
Albania	leks	8	14·96	18·23	(50)	(5·1)
Bulgaria	levs	59[d]	1719·80	1956·63	(6·74)	(2·0)
China	yuans	200	897·75	1183·08	(2)	(2·0)
CSSR	crowns	55	128·99	158·15	(7·26)	(4·1)
DDR	marks	180	391·96	476·93	(2·22)	(2·3)
Hungary	forints	34	106·87	116·40	(11·76)	(3·4)
N. Korea	vons	332	871·00	1059·84	(1·206)	(3·7)
Mongolia	tugriks	100	329·17	335·11	(4)	(3·2)
Rumania	lei	67	154·25	183·87	(5·88)	(4·3)
N. Vietnam	dongs	138	486·00	794·88	(2·90)	(2·0)
USSR	rubles	444	1496·25	1526·17	(0.909)	(3·4)
USA	dollars	400	2400·00	2400·00[b]	—	—
(Poland)					(4)	(11·9)

SOURCE: *Polish Economic Survey*, 11/1963; op. cit., p. 241; *Izvestia*, April 5, 1961.
[a] Strictly, the rate at which the central bank will sell zlotys for foreign currency. It sells foreign currency at a rate about 0·6% higher.
[b] The rate for emigrants' remittances is 7200 zlotys (see Chapter XIII, Section 13). My own estimate of a consumer's purchasing power parity, computed by Fisher's 'ideal' index formula, is 1300 zlotys (see Chapter XV, Section 7).
[c] Cf. Section 11 below.
[d] From January 1, 1962: 342.

II

So far we have dealt with problems that face a single STE merely because it is one. We now turn to the problems that beset groups of STEs. The first of these is, in what unit of account shall they conduct their mutual business?

As far as normal trade in visibles is concerned, the answer is plainly that the name and purchasing power of the unit have only psychological importance. It could be a dollar, a ruble, a lek, or a cowrie shell: its sole function is to be accounting money, translating the agreed barter transactions into symbols suitable for clearing accounts. Until January, 1950, the dollar was the commonest unit

[1] I. P. Aizenberg, *Valyutnaya Sistema SSSR* (Moscow, 1962), pp. 143–4.

of account, but the Swiss franc and other units were also used. In that month the ruble was appreciated and became standard, and accounts expressed in other currencies were gradually closed out. This was, of course, the valuta ruble, that almost fictional unit equal to twenty-five US cents; but at that time the very word *invalyutny* was unspoken, since to utter it would imply the existence of the *Preisausgleich* and of a disparity between the exchange rate and the p.p.p. But, to repeat, it hardly mattered what the unit was, and the step was psychological.

The reason the USSR gave for the change was that dollar prices kept rising while ruble prices had been falling (and, indeed, they had, since the currency reform of December, 1947): therefore, the ruble was a better basis. In fact, however, all bases were equally good provided that relative prices corresponded to world prices, i.e., dollar prices!—a correspondence that the propaganda played down for a number of years.

The situation was, and is, slightly complicated by the balances that, planned or unplanned, arise in the visible trade-clearing accounts at the end of the agreed period. Mostly, as we shall see in Chapter X, equal deliveries are planned and balances arise from underfulfillment, or greater underfulfillment, on one side. The normal way to clear the balance, therefore, is to deliver more during the next period.

Even triangular clearance between STEs is possible without much concern over the unit of account, if all the underlying barter prices are the same. Thus let A underfulfill its deliveries to B, and B to C, and C to A, each to the same number of units of account, and consider the position of B when she is asked to accept a general cancellation of debts. Her favorable balance with A has the same purchasing power over A exports as her unfavorable balance with C over her own. To forgive the one and be forgiven the other is to set off her own exports and imports at the very barter rates that she has been using in trade with A. If the amounts are small, so that marginal transformation ratios alone apply and consumer's or producer's surpluses are small, B gains in administrative convenience and loses nothing in economics.

The choice of unit of account matters, then, only when balances are consolidated from accounts that have used different barter relationships. As we shall see in Chapter X, the recent growth in multilateral visible trade has, indeed, raised such questions: are prices in each bilateral channel in fact sufficiently similar for no STE to gain or lose adventitiously by the convertibility of balances? But the question was already actual in the period of strictest bilateralism, simply because invisible trade between STEs was conducted at the official rate, and the bills for it had to be settled somehow. It would be wrong, for instance, to clear against each other sums of diplomatic expenses accumulated under the pre-1957 system at the official rates of exchange in Warsaw and Moscow; for, as still is the case, the zloty is greatly overvalued at retail *vis-à-vis* the ruble, and this gives Poland an unfair advantage. It would also be wrong to clear the balances of such a clearing against those arising from visible trade, for the valuta ruble had a hugely greater purchasing power than the retail ruble. Note, too, the extra complication in the non-commercial case: Soviet imports (the expenditures in Warsaw) use a different unit of account from Soviet exports (the sales in Moscow). I have not been able to discover how, in fact, they were settled.

However, in April–May, 1957, uniform 'non-commercial' rates were introduced, as explained above. These obviously made it fair to balance invisible exports against invisible imports, but they did not necessarily make it fair to cancel the balances in this trade against visible balances. Thus although now old R.1 = zl.1·5 (i.e., the non-commercial rate correctly expressed the p.p.p.), the currencies were still at one-to-one officially, i.e., for visible trade, and, moreover, had quite different purchasing powers over visible exports. Hence arose the little-known 'Shaefer ratios'[1] (Table VI/2), whereby for instance the non-commercial forint is divided, by international agreement, to make it into a clearable valuta forint.

12

In a system without arbitrage there is nothing to stop *disorderly cross-rates* from arising, except the official determination not to have them. The non-commercial rates, which as we have seen have genuine meaning, seem to have always yielded orderly cross-rates, and the same is, of course, true of cross-rates with capitalist currencies. But in that clash of mighty opposites, the official rates for the ruble and the yuan,[2] official determination has been to make trouble.

---

[1] Owing to the ingenuity of H. Shaefer, Radio Free Europe circular, January 23, 1968.

[2] I am indebted for references and ideas to Kang Chao and Feng-hwa Mah in *China Quarterly*, January–March, 1964, and to Mr. Chao in *China Quarterly*, July–September, 1964. Their actual reasoning, however, is faulty in many places, and I have substituted my own. Cf. also Alexander Eckstein, *Communist China's Economic Growth and Foreign Trade* (New York, 1965), Appendix C.

It is, indeed, doubtful, through the veil of secrecy, whether the USSR and China ever agreed on an official rate until 1962. The basic data are in Table VI/4.

How can this muddle be explained? It looks as if there had been no disorderly cross-rate at the moment that the Chinese brought their inflation to a halt, and the USSR had accepted the ruble-yuan rate resulting from the dollar-yuan rate at that moment of time. Subsequently, however, by market manipulations in Hong Kong, or by mere central fiat, the Bank of China reduced the dollar-yuan rate by 40% and expected Gosbank to adjust the ruble rate. Gosbank seems to have refused, and to have refrained only from publishing the original official rate. That it even existed we only learn from Aizenberg's book written in 1962 during the Sino-Soviet schism. Aizenberg simply gives the $1R = 1Y$ rate along with very many other official rates, including capitalist currencies, in a table; as if it had been valid for a long time. Meanwhile, the Bank of China also refrained from publishing any official rate.

Why did the USSR refuse to adjust the rate to the new realities of the situation? Without evidence, one can only guess: because the ruble could not be allowed to be worth less than one unit of another Communist currency.[1] Besides, in this instance the appreciation of the yuan vis-à-vis the dollar could be written off as mere financial manipulation: the rate was not a free market one, tending towards the p.p.p.

The Chinese, on the other hand, had every reason to stick to their guns. The ruble, grossly overvalued in any case, had just been further overvalued by the ludicrous 'reform' of March 1, 1950. Meanwhile, the yuan was being fixed at an appropriate p.p.p. with the dollar. Undervalued at 3·9, it was brought up to 2·35, a very fair p.p.p. according to all authorities,[2] as Table VI/3 shows (1952 prices). The geometrical mean of the two GNP deflators is 1·8. Since 1952, Chinese prices rose less rapidly than American,[3] so probably the official rate of 2·35 also undervalued the yuan by 1957. However, in fact, there was a Preisausgleich in trade with the West in that year.[4] A peculiar choice of goods in which to trade, coupled

---

[1] Except the DM(O) which had to have a prestige valuation vis-à-vis the DM(W).

[2] Even, in a sense, according to the Russians! For the new ruble-dollar rate of 0·9 is claimed to be a wholesale p.p.p. Allowance for the turnover tax, and consultation with tourists suggests a retail p.p.p. of 1·3. But the Russians have themselves agreed that the yuan-ruble retail p.p.p. is 1·667. This yields a yuan-dollar p.p.p. of 2·17.

[3] Cf. Hollister, op. cit., Tables 1 and 14.

[4] Audrey Donnithorne, China's Economic System (London, 1967), Chapter 12; Eckstein, op. cit. 1965, Appendix C.

with the extremely wide spread of individual price ratios, makes this perfectly possible.

Be this as it may, in late 1957 discussion arose as to the 'internal conversion rate' in China. This was the rate used for setting import prices on the basis of foreign delivery prices; it was 0·95 yuan to 1 ruble, and has been constant since April 19, 1950.[1] It will be observed that since Aizenberg continues his 1-to-1 rate until the

TABLE VI/3. YUAN-DOLLAR P.P.P.s

By sector of origin	Chinese Weights	US Weights
Industrial producers' goods[a]	3·31	
Industrial consumers' goods[a]	3·01	
Agricultural delivery prices	$\left\{ \begin{matrix} 1·06^a \\ 0·942^b \end{matrix} \right\}$	1·361[b]
Machinery and equipment[c]	5·10	5·10
Military and other wages[c]	0·29	0·29
Construction[c]	1·54	1·85
By end-use[c]		
Consumption	0·94	3·45
Government purchases	0·61	3·03
Investment	2·00	3·61
GNP	0·95	3·38

[a] Wu Yuan-li et al., The Economic Potential of Communist China (Stanford Research Institute, Menlo Park, Calif.), June, 1963, vol. I, p. 353. Cf. their Table 81.
[b] Alexander Eckstein, The National Income of Communist China (N.Y., 1961), p. 186.
[c] William W. Hollister, China's Gross National Product (M.I.T., 1958), pp. 142–7.

devaluation of the ruble on January 1, 1961. Up to this date Izvestia, in its pro forma reports of the official rates for foreign currencies on about the third of each month, gave no rate for the yuan, or for that matter the von and the dong. Neither did it in January, February and March of 1961, after the ruble was devalued. But it did eventually come out with the rates shown in Table VI/2, on April 5. Meanwhile, the Chinese seem to have accepted the new Soviet rate, and all is at last orderly, as is shown in the last line of Table VI/4.

But the Soviet-type official rate lays itself wide open to just such unilateral actions, based on international prestige or malice. For what other purpose can the official rate have than to be the football of such emotions? Since the non-commercial rates came into operation the official rate has had no effect on invisible payments. Had not such a non-commercial rate been established at the very same moment as the Chinese raised their official rate, the USSR would have had most serious grounds for complaint; for diplomats and

[1] Mah and Chao, op. cit., pp. 194–5.

TABLE VI/4. THE YUAN VERSUS THE RUBLE

(All in new yuan: 1 new yuan = 10,000 old yuan. Conversion on March 1, 1955)

	Official			Yuan to 1 Dollar			Yuan to 1 Ruble		Free Market in Hong Kong, Yuan to 1 Dollar
	Yuan to 1 Ruble (Soviet)	(Chinese)	Rubles to 1 Dollar	Market, Semi-official	'Reference'	Cross-rates	P.P.P.	'Non-Commercial'	
April 19, 1950 (beginning of deflationary measures in China)	1·0[6]	?		3·9		0·975			
April, 1950–December, 1952 (fluctuations)	1·0[6]	?		4·2–2·2[7]		1·05–0·55			
December, 1952–January, 1954 (pegged)	1·0[6]	?	4·0	2·46[7]		0·615	Chinese exports[8] to the USSR = 13.45 / Chinese imports from the USSR = 0·85[8]		
January, 1954–July 1, 1957	1·0[6]	?	4·0	2·35[7]		0·5875			
July 1, 1957–July 1, 1959	1·0[6]	?	4·0	2·35[9]	2·617[7,9]	0·5875/0·654			
July 1, 1959–January 1, 1961	1·0[6]	0·5[5]	4·0	2·35[9]	2·617[9]	0·5875/0·654		0·167[1]	
January 1, 1961–April, 1963	2·22	2·22[10]	0·9	2·35[9]	2·617[9]	2·611/2·906		1·667[10]/1·29[11]	11·45[3]

The underlining shows in each case the primary element that has changed. There may be consequential changes along the same line.

Since virtually every item in this table is controversial we must give every source:

[1] Feng-hwa Mah and Kang Chao in *China Quarterly*, January–March, 1964, pp. 196–7. As we have seen, the East European STEs and USSR established their non-commerical rates in April, 1957. For China the earliest record appears to be for July, 1959. But M. A. Klochko, *Soviet Scientist in China* (Praeger, 1964), p. 162, says that Soviet economists were using approximately this rate in early 1958.

[2] I.e., on the devaluation of the ruble. Note that since the previous non-commerical rate was right, it was reduced at the same rate as internal prices: by the full 10 times instead of merely 4.5 times.

[3] In May, 1961: E. Szczepanik (ed.), *Economic and Social Problems of the Far East* (Hong Kong, 1963), pp. 80, 175.

[4] Mah and Chao, op. cit., p. 194.

[5] This is the Bank of China quotation for 1 July, 1959 (ibid., p. 196). There seems to have never been an official quotation before (ibid., passim, esp. p. 195). But the *Statistisches Jahrbuch der DDR. 1956*, p. 535, gives a rate of 100 Y = 11·12 DM(O), and therefore = R200, as valid from December 1, 1955; at least one Chinese source used it as early as May, 1957 (Eckstein, op. cit. 1965, Appendix C); and Klochko, loc. cit., referring to early 1958, simply calls it the official rate.

[6] I. P. Aizenberg, *Valyutnaya Sistema SSSR* (Moscow, 1962), p. 149. It is not known at what date this began.

[7] Kang Chao in *China Quarterly*, July–September, 1964, p. 49.

[8] Mah and Chao, op. cit., pp. 200–3. The wholesale or retail prices of 126 imports and 58 exports. Chinese prices for 1950, Soviet price for 1950, weights from Sino-Soviet trade in 1955.

[9] The 'reference' rate is described as not being an official exchange rate but a conversion rate 'computed from relevant data for general reference only' (*Chi-hua Ching-chi*, December, 1957, p. 29).

[10] *China Youth Daily*, 6 January, 1962 (Cf. *China News Analysis*, Hong Kong, no. 409).

[11] Chinese People's Bank, *Handbook of the Currencies of All Nations* (Peking, 1963).

technicians would have had to pay more rubles for their expenses. On the commercial side, all prices are agreed in hard bargaining, and visible trade approximates to barter at world prices. When clearing balances arise they can always be cleared by physical deliveries at the agreed prices—indeed, it was the failure to fulfill the plan for such deliveries that caused the balances. The balance is only rarely convertible, and then on terms acceptable to the debtor; such terms need include no reference to the official rate.

Thus when the official rate ceased to govern invisibles it ceased to have any but statistical and propaganda functions: *no exchanges need ever take place at it.*[1] The Chinese can call it one number and the Russians can call it another. Neither number need correspond to the commercial rate or the dollar cross-rate—and neither does.

13

As concerns trade statistics, we cannot tell how the Chinese adjusted themselves to their 'appreciation' of the yuan, since 1959 is also the date of their general statistical black-out. Previously, however, they seem to have used different statistical conversion rates for trade with various areas, and perhaps also for international finance. This is shown by Table VI/5.

For Sino-Soviet trade, the Chinese used a rate of about 1 to 1. Whether this was the Gosbank's official rate of 1·0 or their own unofficial internal conversion rate of 0·95, our data are too imprecise to determine. We have no means of knowing how trade with other STEs was valued, but may presume that the yuan–zloty, etc., rates for this purpose were consonant with the yuan–ruble rate and the official ruble–zloty, etc., rates. As for non-Communist countries, it would appear that they used their official yuan–dollar rate and the various published rates for sterling, etc., which in fact yield orderly dollar–sterling, etc., cross-rates.[2]

The reader should bear in mind the demonstrations of Messrs. Morgenstern and Allen[3] that one country's trade returns are not easily reconciled with another's. There is certainly something

---

[1] Indeed, there is an even more absurd possibility. In the absence of an agreed non-commercial rate the Chinese could charge Soviet diplomats 2R to the Y, and the Russians could charge Chinese diplomats 1R to the Y. The yuan balances would be hoarded in Moscow, and the ruble balances in Peking, without any agreement as to their disposition.

[2] Though even here there are unexplained oddities. Thus the yuan–£ rate quoted in section 13 below is incompatible with any known yuan–$ rate.

[3] Oscar Morgenstern, *On the Accuracy of Economic Observations* (Princeton, N.J., 1963), Chapter 9, and Robert L. Allen, *Soviet Economic Warfare* (Washington, D.C., 1960), pp. 268–91.

deeply untrustworthy about Sino-Soviet trade in 1950, when each side reported a large trade surplus. But that was the confused year of economic take-over in China, when, doubtless, anything went. The three peaceful years 1954–56 make convincing reading.

TABLE VI/5. SINO-SOVIET TRADE, 1950–56
(mn. old rubles or new yuans)

	China's Total Foreign Trade[a] (Yuans)	Sino-Soviet Trade Yuans	Rubles[b]	Trade with Non-Communist Countries Yuans	Dollars	Implied Statistical Conversion Rates Yuans per Ruble	Yuans per Dollar
1950							
Total	4150						
Imports	—	392[c]	1553	—	—	0·25	—
Exports	—	576[c]	765	—	—	0·75	—
1953	8090	—	—	1980[g]	632[h]	—	3·14
1954	8470	c. 4840[d]	5351	1697[g]	590[h]	0·90	2·88
1955	10,980	5145[e]	5567	—	—	0·92	—
1956	10,870	5760[f]	5989	2717[g]	945[h]	0·96	2·89

SOURCE: Except as noted, I take most of these data from Kang Chao in *China Quarterly*, July–September, 1964, p. 60. I have excluded years in which Messrs. Chao and Li (see note g, below) have been forced to use less reliable Formosan sources.

[a] State Statistical Bureau, *Ten Great Years* (Peking, 1960), p. 175. There is no official breakdown by countries.

[b] *Vneshnyaya Torgovlya SSSR* (Moscow, various dates).

[c] These figures represent 19·84% of imports and 26·58% of exports (*Jen Min Jih Pao*, September 29, 1951); these were 47·77% and 52·23% of trade turnover, respectively (*Ta Kung Pao*, October 17, 1951).

[d] About five times as much as in 1950 (*Jen Min Jih Pao*, April 30, 1955).

[e] This is 5·31 times as much as in 1950: *Essays on Foreign Trade* (Peking, 1957), III, 39.

[f] This is 53% of turnover (*Jen Min Jih Pao*, April 27, 1957).

[g] These are 24·51%, 20% and 25%, respectively, of all trade, Choh-ming Li, *Economic Development of Communist China* (Berkeley, 1959), p. 186.

[h] United Nations, *Yearbook of International Trade Statistics* (New York, 1961), Table B. As 'China Mainland' is lumped together in this table with Mongolia, North Vietnam and North Korea, I have deducted 5% of the totals given there. The logic is that these three countries have about the same standard of living, and 3·5% of the population. Being so small, they must do more than their *per capita* share of trade.

It follows that if Sino-Soviet trade is valued in dollars at the ruble-dollar official rate, or in yuan at the cross-rate, its weight in total Chinese trade diminishes.[1] On this, see Chapter XV.

Could China be 'the only one in step?' Is it even logically conceivable that all the official yuan rates should have been in some sense correct, and that all the world's other rates should be disorderly cross-rates? Our answer to this question must be no. Only rates that roughly correspond with p.p.p.s are 'in some sense correct', or at least those that diverge from p.p.p.s everywhere to the same extent. We could, for instance, revalue the whole trade of the world in

[1] I owe this observation to Chao, op. cit.

valuta rubles without serious loss: they are worth in all circumstances a constant multiple of the dollar. But the yuan is, in trade with non-STEs, one multiple of the dollar (or for that matter valuta ruble), and at a rate approximating to its p.p.p.; but in trade with STEs it is another multiple, at a rate that does not correspond with its p.p.p.

As to the possibility that China uses yet another ruble-yuan rate, perhaps the dollar cross-rate, for taking Soviet loans into the budget, the question is so complicated and doubtful that it must be largely omitted. One thing is certain: the definitive Chinese statement of the total borrowed in 1950–57 (Y.5294 mn.) coincides with the definitive Soviet statement[1] (R.1816 mn.) if we use the yuan-dollar 'reference' rate of 2·617 (cf. Table VI/4). The Chinese figure reduces to $2023 mn., and the Soviet figure (at the new rate of exchange, of course) to $2018 mn.

That China should reject the USSR's official rate, we have seen to be entirely reasonable. But it seems that she very seldom used her own 'official' rate of R.2 = Y.1, but used the Soviet rate, or the very similar import conversion rate of R.0·95 = Y.1, for the statistical valuation of her trade with the USSR, and probably Eastern Europe. Here, of course, it was a mere *numéraire*, and the concession to Soviet pride was minimal. For serious purposes, where the purchasing power of the currency handled was an important issue, and at least since 1957, China has set her own valuation on the ruble. Thus in 1957 she valued her borrowing at the Y.2·617 = $1 'reference rate' multiplied by the official $ ≠ R. rate. We simply do not know how she treated current non-commercial expenditures up to 1959, when the agreed non-commercial rate was introduced. Presumably from then, but certainly from 1962 (see the quotation below), she used this rate to value borrowings also. Since no trade statistics have been published since 1958, we do not know how China valued trade with the USSR in 1959–62. But we do know that in 1962 there was, as earlier, a special rate more agreeable to the Russians. It was, indeed, the officially published Soviet rate.

The official Chinese view in 1962 was given in reply to a reader's question by the *Chinese Youth Daily* of January 6 as follows:

---

[1] By Li Hsien-nien, in his budget report of June 29, 1957; and by M. A. Suslov on February 13, 1964. For both statements cf. Chao, op. cit. footnote on pp. 58–9. Eckstein, loc. cit., converts all credits at Y.1 = R.1 = $0·25. He thus much understates the dollar amount implied by Li at $1325 mn., which he fails to match with Suslov's figure. So low a total would indeed be difficult to reconcile with Chou En-lai's $1560 mn., which was the interest and principal outstanding some time in 1964, apparently to the USSR alone. It is interesting that Chou gave this figure in rubles (1406 mn.) not yuan.

Exchange of currency with capitalist countries is based on mutual comparison of prices with consideration of the value of currency on the international market. For example, at present the purchasing price of the English pound is 6·859 yuan and selling price 6·927 yuan. Between socialist countries there is a unified rule about exchange of currency and this is based on the comparison of 47 kinds of commodities like rice, flour, etc. At present 100 Russian rubles equal 166·67 yuan. This official price is applied to items other than import and export trade, like foreign investment, diplomatic representations, travel expenses, home remittances, etc., all non-commercial exchange. In trade an official price exists only between our JMP and the Soviet Russian ruble. This at present is 100 Soviet trade rubles for 222·22 JMP.[1]

14

Only now, fortified by all this information, can we study the *consequences of a Soviet-type devaluation*. Beginning with the official rate, it has clearly no effect at all on the current visible trade for which it is the accounting unit. Since all prices are merely 'world' prices converted at the current rate of exchange, the *numéraire* has changed, and that is all. Internally, of course, the *Preisausgleich* is affected; but to a quite unimportant extent, as we saw in Section 7. Therefore devaluation is not inflationary. But foreign balances and debts, whether they are settled in goods, in gold or in foreign currency, are partially repudiated by any devaluation of the currency in which they are expressed. This is a necessary accounting consequence of devaluation the world over. The only Soviet-type currency with important balances is, of course, the ruble itself. The devaluation of January 1, 1961, was so conducted as to preserve the real value of all such balances, all sources say. None explains what this means, but the only possibility is that the gold value of all debts and credits was kept constant, and the ruble value reduced at the rate of 0·225 new rubles for every old one. No doubt, the Soviet sources are reticent because a direct admission would make too obvious the fact of devaluation, which they try to conceal. Be that as it may, the Soviet devaluation was in this vital respect a huge improvement on Western ones. It is ironical that this commercial honesty, unprecedented among ACCs when *they* devalue, has not been more highly praised.

There is a substantial difference here between devaluation in an STE and in an ME. Devaluation is tolerated among MEs, even though it is debt repudiation, because most international debt is private, especially if we include short-term trade debt. Even the

[1] Cf. *China News Analysis*, Hong Kong, no. 409.

public debt has often been contracted by local or specialized authorities quite independent of the government. So when that government devalues it is an act of God for which the contracting parties on its territory are in no way responsible. But an STE is a totalitarian state, and its political philosophy prohibits such distinctions. It is true that Communist states reserve the right to repudiate contracts made with foreigners by their officials if these latter are acting *ultra vires*; and regularly publish the names of officials for the time being entitled to make contracts. But this leaves us a long way short of the situation where one department of state gaily devalues the currency while another calmly tells the foreigner it now owes him less money and is not responsible and cannot be sued. The STE is thus inhibited, though not prevented, from a kind of repudiation that custom has sanctioned among MEs. The author is stuffy enough to consider this an advantage of the former system.

15

The new trend in Eastern Europe is to emphasize the disadvantages at micro-level of this whole system. They are indeed manifold, as we shall see. But the revisionists, young, eager and brave, are too inexperienced with a market economy to understand that it also has its pathology. Crudely and even unconsciously, Stalinism offered certain tremendous macro-benefits, outlined in previous chapters. The writer, whose formative years as an economist were spent under the oppression of the British b.o.p. problem, has been thought obsessively hostile to convertibility by economists native to other ACCs. It has been a great morale-sustainer to meet economists from UDCs with a very similar background, but it is distressing now to see in Yugoslavia and perhaps also Czechoslovakia a *drive towards convertibility*[1] which can only be called ignorant and uncritical. It is due to a dogmatism of automaticity and decentralization which is only a little better than the previous unargued faith in centralization.

Convertibility is an illegitimate extrapolation from the demand that home and foreign *price-relatives* be equal, which as we see in the next chapter is the essence of rationality. Yugoslav *prices* are to be equalized, not by planning or controls, but by actual uncontrolled importation. It is, moreover, thought that the pro-

---

[1] Enshrined, for instance, in the fifth Conclusion of the League Plenum of February–March 1965. Convertibility is to be achieved 'as soon as possible' (*Borba*, March 13, 1966).

blems of making the dinar convertible are merely transitional: finally get the prices equal, suppress the subsidized enterprises, raise general efficiency a little, and then you can sit back. In the process we must of course abolish the government's valuta monopoly: an enterprise may hold the valuta it earns by exporting—or acquires otherwise—in any Yugoslav bank, not merely the central bank.[1] Indeed it may soon be allowed to hold it in a foreign bank. And from this latter concession it is but a step to that complicated interchange of short-term assets and liabilities with foreign countries that so much exacerbates the problems of an ME (Chapter V, Section 8).

Now it is true that convertibility gives the exporter direct access[2] to valuta, and thus enormously encourages exports. It is even true that imports rationalize home prices—an obsession in Yugoslav economics today; and this, like all other rationalizations, constitutes growth—once for all and of a sort. But Yugoslavia is a small ME, so monopolies are natural. A small ME must either live with monopolistic irrationalities or import enormous and unpredictable amounts.

Moreover, Yugoslavia still has a Communist government, i.e. one hellbent on development. Again, her workers' councils are not exactly a deflationary institution, likely to repress wage-creep.[3] One way and another she has already demonstrated a propensity to price-rises and devaluations unique in Europe. Such a country, it is obvious, cannot combine growth or full employment with stable money *ever*: it is not a transitional problem that she faces. Either her present (1967) deflationary stagnation is merely the first of a long British-type series, or she must abandon all pretense at convertibility.

It was said above that the Stalinist cure for these troubles was crude and only semi-conscious. By this I mean that the state's valuta monopoly, existing during the NEP, preceded the command economy. So the latter is not necessary for inconvertibility, and the arguments for the two institutions are quite different. Nor is Stalinism based on an adequate understanding of the issues involved. For it sees the state's valuta monopoly as a mainly political necessity and denies to even an isolated market economy any virtue at all.

---

[1] Yugoslavia has established the two-tier banking system characteristic of ACCs.

[2] The Yugoslav exporter must still sell over half of his foreign exchange to a bank.

[3] Or, to coin an appropriate Titoist term, income-creep. For there is now nothing called a wage in Yugoslavia: the workers are masters of the enterprise, and its gross income is their gross income, which they appropriate as they think best, subject to certain taxes and controls.

But one argument in mitigation of Stalinism is also a defense of the valuta monopoly: a little irrationality is a trivial price to pay if we want to abolish stagnation or unemployment, since it wastes so much less of the national income.[1]

We have referred above, of course, to 'resident convertibility' alone. The much less serious matter of 'non-resident convertibility' is entirely compatible with strict control over leaks of money across the border. It means little more than that, say, USSR should pay for all her exports in gold or dollars: a very expensive change but not one affecting her institutions (cf. Chapter X). Again we have implied that a central government practicing currency convertibility has no foreign trade monopoly. Such a monopoly nevertheless is institutionally compatible with free convertibility, as the NEP illustrates (Section 1); but turns it into a nugatory matter, since apart from exports and imports so few people need valuta.

16

Since in this book we do not enter into the general theory of measurement, nor even into the particular problems of international comparison, it is enough to repeat that price relatives in STEs differ systematically from those in other economies, owing to the high turnover tax that intervenes between wholesale and retail prices. It may, then, be not altogether misleading to speak of 'the' purchasing power parity between the pound and the dollar: so long as we take both Paasche and Laspeyres weights, and generally obey the rules of the game, we shall not go far wrong. But there are at least two distinct purchasing power parities between the pound and the ruble: that for wholesale, factory and procurement prices and that for retail prices. This is not quite the same thing as investment or intermediate versus consumption goods, since investment or intermediate goods like bricks and nails sold to private people also attract a turnover tax. This qualification is only important, however, in Poland, with its private peasantry. But the Polish and Soviet tax structures are very similar, so that one can again speak of 'the' purchasing power parity between the zloty and the ruble.

On top of this tax difficulty comes the usual hedonic difficulty: STEs simply do not sell as many kinds of product as ACCs, even as

[1] Cf. Chapter V, Section 7, and my *Political Economy of Communism*, Chapter 11.

some UDCs. This point I have exhaustively examined elsewhere.[1]

But there is one very important simplifier. Since all prices in Communist visible foreign trade are world prices, or nearly so (see Chapter X), all volume figures for visible trade in Communist currency can be immediately translated into the currency of MEs at the official rate of exchange. Whatever meaning such figures have in the one currency they have in the other. Indeed, the thing is easier than in the case of a Latin American country, since no allowance is necessary for multiple rates. Nearly all Communist figures of foreign trade are, in fact, published in this pre-*Preisausgleich*, or valuta, form.

[1] In 'Soviet Planning', *Essays in Honour of Naum Jasny* (Oxford, 1964), pp. 77–115. On general problems of measurement in STEs cf. P. J. D. Wiles, *The Political Economy of Communism*, Chapter 12.

CHAPTER VII

MICRO-RATIONALITY AND FOREIGN TRADE CRITERIA

I

A CRITERION is something that influences planners' choices; a command is a flat specific order the planners give to an enterprise; an indicator is a general operation order that they set an enterprise (e.g., 'maximize gross output in money terms at the prices we have set'); an activator is an economic motive (e.g., desire for money or prestige, fear of punishment, altruism). In an ME, private profit is criterion, indicator and activator rolled into one. In an STE, profit might be any one of these but not the others; or, indeed, it might play no role at all. The individual worker's or manager's desire for money is not to be confused with enterprise profit; his plan-fulfillment bonus may, owing to the way the plan is set up, only be obtainable by actions that reduce such profit.

At the macro-economic level planners all over the world use non-profit criteria: growth, full employment, autarky, strategic strength, social equality, preference for backward areas, etc., etc.

Most of these can be interpreted as variations on the criterion of social profit or macro-profit; but that is to say little more than that they represent concrete interpretations of that extremely vague phrase, the greatest good of the greatest number. So to assert that 'macro-criteria are non-profit criteria' is to utter a concealed definition of macro-profit.

We may leave such semantic issues aside, since our concern here is with micro-criteria. Now it is only in an STE that the planner can have a micro-criterion, since in all other economies micro-choice is left to the enterprise. The planner in an STE might use profit as a micro-criterion, but equally well he might not. There is no shortage of alternatives. The next chapter is mainly a list of them. This chapter is about profit.

First, we must make clear the role of 'world' prices. For an exact definition of this concept the reader is referred to Chapter IX. We simply assume here that this very difficult question can be approximately settled, i.e., that there is such a thing as the world price of Polish coal of such and such quality, c.i.f. Minsk or Copenhagen. We shall see in Chapter IX that such prices, though not always current ones, are, in fact, used between STEs; and, of course, the current ones have to be used between MEs and STEs.

2

Prices by themselves are not criteria, but simply agreed charges. They become criteria only as the planners adapt to them in some way the quantities exchanged. Even in this case they must be distinguished from profits. That is, one may easily maximize price, or total sales, rather than profit; and if domestic prices are very irrational and foreign exchange very short, total sales is both a reasonable and a probable criterion.[1] But if quantity is not adapted in any way, prices are income distributors alone: the sale and purchase of a given quantity of a good enriches or impoverishes, say, the seller according as the price is high or low. That a price should have this function alone, and not simultaneously that of a resource allocator, is a possibility pretty much confined to STEs. Wholesale prices within the nationalized sector have not even so much function, since if prices are too low for an enterprise to meet the standard wages it gets a subsidy.[2] But the prices paid for the compulsory

---

[1] Compare our remarks on the b.o.p. crisis, Chapter V, Section 1; also Section 9, below.
[2] But low enterprise profits do lead to a low 'enterprise fund', which does restrict fringe benefits.

deliveries of kolkhozy have exactly the role named. They do not affect the quantity delivered, but only the distribution of income between the state and the kolkhoz. We may compare two somewhat similar cases in an ME: where demand or supply, or both, are very inelastic, or where there is price discrimination against intramarginal sellers or buyers.

Now the prices paid on trade between STEs are not quite so passive as those paid on kolkhoz compulsory deliveries; for there is no supranational power telling the traders what to do. In the bilateral bargaining that goes on, the formal sources do not tell us how much haggling there is over exact prices—for 'world price' is, of course, a very vague concept with plenty of margin for disagreement. Above all, they do not tell us how much either party during such haggling varies his quantitative offer to sell or buy. Similarly, they give us little idea of how much STEs react to price changes when they trade with MEs. We, therefore, are not told the extent to which prices are criteria of STE trade.

3

The writer, nevertheless, makes bold to put forward his personal *a priori* view. He suspects that an STE behaves far more like an ordinary enterprise than it cares to admit, for the very simple reason that it is a sovereign body in a market. The theories in the books, and especially the sophisticated new theories of the younger Communist economists, are all normative and based in no degree whatsoever upon the empirical questioning of trade negotiators. If the actual conduct of Communist enterprise managers *vis-à-vis* the central plan is too hot a potato, and its empirical study has to be left to Westerners, the behavior of the STE on the world market is a still hotter potato. For embarrassing and un-Marxist as both studies are, only the second is likely to involve the prestige of the whole state, and to have diplomatic repercussions.

This applies, of course, very particularly to inter-STE trade. Much informal literary evidence backs up the view that among themselves STEs maximize (or, if they are importers, minimize) prices. The Slánský and Kostoff[1] trials contained admission of such price-maximizing behavior directed against the USSR by Czechoslovak

[1] *The Trial of Traicho Kostov and his Group*, Ministry of Justice (Sofia, 1949), pp. 192–5, 228–33, 241; *Prozess gegen die Leitung des Staatsfeindlichen Verschwörerzentrums mit Rudolf Slánský an der Spitze*, Ministry of Justice (Prague, 1953), pp. 394–5, 434–5, 442–4. There are short extracts in F. L. Pryor, *The Communist Foreign Trade System* (London, 1963), pp. 136–8.

and Bulgarian negotiators. Inter-satellite trade, according to the same sources, was a less inhibited free-for-all. But however plausible, these oft-quoted admissions were extracted by the security police under torture, and cannot rank as first-class evidence. Other evidence comes from refugees and dissident Communists, so should be more reliable. It is, for instance, abundantly clear that Yugoslavia, while still an STE, maximized her prices *vis-à-vis* the USSR, and even tampered with the ideology in order to do so (Chapter I). As to the USSR itself, the literature speaks of little else but her maximizing behavior.

4

But if STEs are aggressive 'marketers', the principles of their behavior may still differ, and they may not be maximizing the same things as capitalists. Thus, as is only to be expected in a command economy, the export and import plans grow out of an *a priori* overall quantitative plan, and are themselves at first quantitative. *In inter-STE trade the quantities are negotiated before the prices.*[1] That is, physical availabilities are sought out by individual foreign trade enterprises, and then the trade delegations meet to consolidate these items and settle the prices. The prices are maximized or minimized 'rationally', but the quantities are set anyhow. It is extremely doubtful if the negotiators know which quantities are best for their countries. It is clear that STEs approach MEs in the same way: with *a priori* quantities in their heads, almost irrespective of price. Naturally, the negotiator will do his best over the price in each case, but his supply or demand curve is in the short run far more inelastic than would be a capitalist's. He might switch between one ME and another, for instance—if his particular foreign-trade enterprise dealt with more than one; and he might shade qualities and delivery dates. But essentially the moment comes when he is stuck with his quantity plan and cannot adapt it to the price. All the other capitalist levers he can use: deceit, threats for the future, special pleading, appeal to sentiment, etc., etc. The main lever he cannot; he has to buy or sell so much. *The basic foreign trade criterion is, or was, the method of balances and the plan.* This is particularly true, as we shall see, on the import side.

It is not to be supposed that prices are never settled separately from quantities in MEs. In civil engineering, in commercial research

---

[1] F. L. Pryor, op. cit., p. 135. Cf. the Soviet-German agreement quoted in Chapter IX here, and the sources quoted in the previous section.

and in the manufacture of prototypes, just this happens, because cost cannot be foretold. But in each case the buyer does his best to limit the final price by the contract in which he undertakes to buy the good, and to intervene in the process of costing. Among STEs the matter is not one of prototypes alone, nor of the uncertainty of costs. The object is not to ensure *ex post facto* a price that gives a fair profit. It is to get the essentials (the decisions on physical quantities) over as punctually as possible so that planning and production may go on, and to leave the 'mere' financial reckoning to a later bargain.

Thus the fact that world market prices, or something approaching them, or, indeed, any prices whatsoever are paid tells us little about the criteria of trade; it depends how quantities are adjusted to these prices, if, indeed, they are adjusted to them at all. We have just seen that until the most recent times prices were hardly criteria at all, but tended to be only income distributors, i.e., determinants of the terms of trade. It would follow that if the physical trade plan between two STEs were not altered in any way the price settlement would simply determine in whose favor the trade balance worked out.

In STE-ME trade, on the other hand, the quantity has always been used as a bargaining factor to influence the price. Bound as he still is by an *a priori* quantitative plan, the STE's representative at least does not have to reveal it. Moreover, he cannot settle price and quantity separately. So he cannot but affect the price, though less than would a bargainer unbound by a plan.

5

We may now turn to the criteria themselves. Rejecting narrow nationalism, 'optimum tariffs', etc., I take the correct criterion to be the application of Lerner's Rule, marginal cost = price, to international trade. In this way humanity achieves the best micro-allocation. The relevant marginal cost is that ruling inside the country in its own money; the domestic price and the world price are the same at the current rate of exchange. Output is adjusted to make m.c. = price. As far as any particular enterprise goes, foreign trade is subjected to exactly the same rules as internal trade, yet the international division of labor is simultaneously optimized in accordance with the law of comparative cost. The proof of this is exceedingly simple:

Let C be marginal cost in money terms, 1, 2 and 3 be products,

A and B two countries, and P the price; let all money be converted at the same rate of exchange, and let all products be in worldwide perfect competition. Then if $C = P$ as a general rule in each country, in particular

$$C_{1a} = C_{1b} = P_1$$

if product 1 is produced in equilibrium in both countries. If furthermore

$$C_{2a} > C_{2b} = P_2 \qquad . \qquad . \qquad . \qquad . \qquad . \qquad . \qquad (1)$$

and

$$P_3 = C_{3a} < C_{3b} \qquad . \qquad . \qquad . \qquad . \qquad . \qquad . \qquad (2)$$

and marginal cost increases with output, A will produce less of 2 and B less of 3 until equality restores equilibrium. If marginal cost falls, there is complete specialization, A producing no 2 and B no 3. Now let A be more productive throughout, i.e., there are embodied in each C_a higher factor-prices and smaller factor-quantities than in each C_b. Let there be perfect competition in all factor markets, broken, however, by the international boundary.[1] Let F be the marginal 'dose' of factors, however composed, converted into physical units of one standard factor at the ruling factor prices. Then:

$$F_{1a} < F_{1b}, \; F_{2a} < F_{2a}, \; F_{3a} < F_{3b}.$$

But also, from (1) and (2):

$$\frac{C_{2a}}{C_{3a}} > \frac{C_{2b}}{C_{3b}}, \quad \text{or} \quad \frac{F_{2a}}{F_{3a}} > \frac{F_{2b}}{F_{3b}}.$$

So B makes 2, even though she must use more factors than A would have had to; and equilibrium without complete specialization in 2 and 3, or

$$P_2 = C_{2a} = C_{2b}, \; P_3 = C_{3a} = C_{3b} \qquad . \qquad . \qquad . \qquad . \qquad (3)$$

entails

$$\frac{F_{2a}}{F_{3a}} = \frac{F_{2b}}{F_{3b}} \qquad . \qquad . \qquad . \qquad . \qquad . \qquad . \qquad (4)$$

Equation (3) is Lerner's Rule, or marginal cost = price; (4) is the law of comparative costs.[2]

6

Now Lerner's Rule is a fine theoretical criterion, but it has not to my knowledge been proposed for the conduct of STEs in the world

---

[1] If, more realistically, we assume that capital flows freely across the boundary the following argument is unaffected.

[2] Relative factor price equalization is, of course, irrelevant, and need not concern us here.

market (except possibly in Hungary recently). It would, after all, mean a wilful refusal to maximize the state's profits by pushing its exports beyond the point at which marginal cost = marginal revenue. A group of Communist governments, converted to marginalist welfare economics, might possibly arrange their inter-trade on such principles out of proletarian brotherhood; but they would surely continue to maximize their profits *vis-à-vis* capitalist countries. For this the STE, with its power to convert each export industry into a monopoly, is very well situated. In much the same spirit the United States monopoly law permits enterprises to form monopolies in foreign trade. However, we must first await the conversion of Communist economics to marginalism.

The mere maximization of profit in home currency, however, has been proposed. This, of course, implies better terms of trade unless the trading partner retaliates by adopting the same criterion. But an ME, which is by nature not a monopolist of its own exports or monopsonist of its imports, has at least some difficulty in acting this way. The competing traders of an ME are much more likely to bring marginal cost close to price than the non-competing traders of an STE.

7

Newcomers to Sovietology may still find it difficult to believe that neither Lerner's Rule nor profit itself plays, or until recently played, any role. At the risk of wearisome iteration, I include one such quotation from a respectable source:

Foreign-trade enterprises buy and sell goods in the USSR at domestic prices, and changes in foreign prices or the ruble exchange rate are not reflected in their accounts with production enterprises. In sales or purchases abroad Soviet organizations proceed from the degree to which the sale or purchase of this or that good contributes to the development of our productive forces, the building of socialism, or the satisfaction of the needs of the population, and not from the profitability of this or that foreign-trade operation. This consideration has secondary significance in the drawing up of plans for export and import.[1]

Mr. Frei's statement must stand for the old view. The more rational Communism of today discusses profit as a criterion very openly, and there can be no doubt that it influences foreign-trade plans. Thus, a Hungarian document says:

[1] L. I. Frei, *Mezhdunarodnye Raschety i Organizovania Vneshnei Torgovli Sotsialisticheskikh Stran* (Moscow, 1960), p. 108.

The index of foreign currency production shows how many forints should be allocated to obtain $1 of exports or to save $1 of imports. The aim is, of course, to produce $1 value at the lowest forint cost possible. With a view to foreign trade, in the people's economy the production of commodities at an indicator rate of 45 forints = $1 can be considered as economical, and calculations of the economy of investments are computed on the basis of this principle.[1]

At internal prices, Dr. Madas shows that 27·4 forints = $1 of timber. But this might only mean that Hungary should raise its internal price; the loss on timber might be so great that even at 45 forints it was not wiped out. However, this is not so: the internal prices, he says, do at least cover prime cost, and the great difference between the two rates of exchange indicates a profit at the higher one. Dr. Madas then reckons the output of 1 hectare under poplar at dollar prices, multiplies by 45 and compares this with the forint cost. He duly finds a very big profit. If his treatment of capital cost is unclear to me, the whole procedure is simple enough in principle.

There has indeed been an infinite and rather boring proliferation of these criteria. The differences between them are not very remarkable. Some take a raw material valued at 'world market price' and concern themselves only with value added; some consider the gross price of the product. Some use price relatives, some absolute prices, etc. etc. Mr. Antonio Costa[2] provides an exhaustive list of them, so we shall confine ourselves here to a general observation: the Soviet-type angle of vision is quite different from that of Western economics, but the result is the same. For what has been carried over from the previous 'material balance' period is the concern with trade as exchange, with exports as a direct means of getting imports, with the terms of trade as an almost micro-economic question, not the profitability of exports *per se* or imports *per se*.

This distinction is now embodied in the language of Soviet-type economics. The apparent desirability of trading a particular good is its Rentabilität or rentabl'nost', roughly our private profit; the true desirability is its Nutzeffekt or effetivnost', roughly our social profit. Different authors define these words differently, but the terms-of-trade aspect always figures in the second, often not in the first.

Thus Mr. Costa's basic Nutzeffekt is C_i/C_e, where C_i is the cost of the import substitute that we do not have to produce if instead we export at cost C_e; and all prices are in home currency. This

---

[1] A. Madas, *The Economics of Poplar Cultivation* (undated document, shown to me by my colleague, Mr. Dag Bakker-Jarness, in March, 1964).

[2] In his *Economia Internazionale Socialista* (forthcoming), Chapter 4.

formula is of course meaningless without the terms of trade, and the optimal point of exportation and importation is where the Nutz-effekt is the same as the terms of trade. Thus if country A in our Section 5 be Mr. Costa's exporter, his symbols can be translated at once into ours. The optimum is when:

$$\frac{C_i}{C_e} = \frac{C_{2a}}{C_{3a}} = \frac{P_2}{P_3}$$

where the last term is the terms of trade under perfect competition. Imperfections merely complicate the issue, in well-known ways that we need not pursue.

Note how Ricardian this whole attitude is. Just like Ricardo, the Communist asks, why should a *country* trade at all? The Westerner asks why an *enterprise* trades. But the ultimate optimum is the same, as we saw in Section 5, owing to the basic consilience of private and public profit when prices are rational. The reason for this pre-occupation with the 'micro-terms of trade' is that *neither the Ricardian nor the Soviet-type theory embodies a rate of exchange.* An 'appropriate' rate, we see in Chapter XV, is the wholesale purchasing power par (p.p.p.), which makes it safe for us to compare exports (imports) with foreign (home) money, and maximize profits accordingly. But since its currency is normally overvalued, an STE cannot simply maximize profits, say, on imports, since this would lead to a grave excess of imports, nearly all of which are profitable, over exports, nearly all of which need subsidizing. With a wrong rate of exchange profit maximization leads to absurd trade imbalances. In such a case we need the more complex Nutzeffekt-type formula, which short-circuits the rate of exchange: C might be in rubles and P in dollars.

8

Now assume that the rate of exchange is indeed the wholesale p.p.p. Then both Lerner's Rule and the maximization of profit depend on the *Preisausgleich* (Chapter VI); indeed, they are the same thing as policies with respect to it. For the money collected (usually on imports) and the money given out (usually on exports) are simply another form of indirect tax, and in an STE indirect tax is just another word for profit (or, in the case of subsidy, loss). If, then, the regular turnover tax[1] and the profit rate as formally defined are

---

[1] In institutional fact, it is unlikely that there will be any turnover tax on exports themselves though there is usually some tax on the materials embodied in them. See Section 11.

both kept at constant per-unit rates, the state maximizes its profit by adjusting the *Preisausgleich* so as to maximize the sum of all three. This is easiest seen diagrammatically:

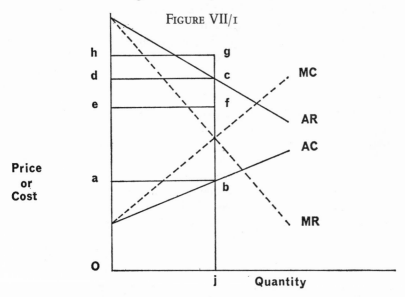

FIGURE VII/1

The most profitable output of the export is *Oj*, at price *jc*. If average turnover tax and formal profit together are *fb*, the correct rate of *Preisausgleich* is *fc*. If they are *gb*, the correct rate is —*gc*. The object is in each case to obtain for the state and the enterprise *abcd*, the maximum total profit. Note that the *Preisausgleich* alone is not being maximized, nor anything like it. Thus, if average turnover tax plus profit = *gb* it is easy, by producing little enough, to obtain a positive average and total *Preisausgleich*—but only at the expense of the state's total profit. In the case of an import, the same diagram will serve: *AC* becomes the price the foreign-trade enterprise must pay the foreigner, *AR* the price it realizes at home.

The *Preisausgleich* or Nutzeffekt in their simple form cannot be used as criteria even yet. For first we need 'tax-and-subsidy-clean' prices in the sense of Section 11, and secondly we must take account of capital and land. Even then we must be sure that profit rates are everywhere equal. Only then should we instruct enterprises to maximize the export and minimize the import *Preisausgleich*—subject of course to an overall trade balance constraint. But even the unimproved *Preisausgleich* was a more rational criterion than the method of balances. Knowing perfection, we must never hastily reject the merely practicable, for it is likely to be in favor of the frankly bad.

It is in particular correct to use, as in Hungary, the Preisausgleich as an incentive for foreign-trade enterprises. For here it is not a question of what to export or import, but of when and to whom.[1] The rationality of trade in goods once produced is not dependent on the considerations listed above.

9

Next we must dispose of a problem of some perplexity: the role of indirect taxes in deciding what to export and at what price. If these are levied equally on all goods, both raw and finished, say by a tax on value added, they do not disturb the relativities of prices and are hardly interesting. But no existing system of indirect taxes has this property. We are particularly concerned with the tax structure characteristic of STEs, in which capital goods, raw materials, and semi-fabricates bear little tax, and the final stage of production[2] of goods sold to the population a very great one. In the absence of a high income tax, this stage of production yields the government most of its revenue. Should, then, the foreigner be charged this tax when such goods are exported? or, indeed, a good part of it when semi-fabricated components of such goods are exported? More frivolously, is the tax-free airport shop, characteristic of ACCs, economically desirable for the country on whose soil it stands?

First, a strictly irrelevant observation, but a very important one that is often neglected. In the short run, and especially at moments of b.o.p. crisis, as we have seen in Chapter V, foreign currency in the central bank may be of far greater value to a country than domestic currency in the treasury. For a shortage of the latter only means a little more domestic inflation, financed by treasury bills, 'ways and means' advances or what not; while the former means devaluation, foreign borrowing on humiliating, perhaps political, conditions, the disposal of strategic stocks at a loss, unemployment and other very serious setbacks. *Mutatis mutandis* this applies as well to STEs as to MEs. But in the long run, and where prices and rates of exchange are rational, all units of money are of equal marginal value. In particular, marginal government expenditure on home goods is of equal value to

[1] Alan Brown in the forthcoming University of Southern California symposium, ed. Alan Brown.

[2] As it happens, the formal incidence is not on the store but on the factory. We shall refer to such goods here as 'consumer goods' for short, though the category includes also, for instance, building materials sold to the population for private construction.

society with marginal private expenditure on imports. This also applies in full measure to the STE. There is, therefore, in general no call for the government to sacrifice its own income (indirect taxes) for the sake of exporters' income (foreign exchange). Incidentally, it is a fine thing to tax the foreigner, but it is equally fine to have him shaken down by our exporters and then to tax them. The only important difference is psychological.

So when we are dealing with foreigners the enterprise should maximize its profits; this is the country's interest. Now since a private enterprise counts its profits net of indirect tax, it will reckon only its own cost into its profits, and will sell at home or abroad according to where marginal revenue net of tax is greater. Is its neglect of indirect tax right or wrong from its country's point of view? We may answer the question most simply by considering the opposite case of the STE. For the government of an STE, with its foreign-trade and foreign-exchange monopolies, is in some sense an enterprise; moreover, its indirect taxes are a form of profit to it. The temptation is then strong to conclude that the government should behave as a discriminating monopolist and charge such prices in the separate home and foreign markets as seem to it best. It will then so distribute goods between export and home use, and so price them, that the marginal tax-plus-profit-yield is everywhere the same. Note, not so that the marginal yield is everywhere zero, which is the equivalent of the condition of maximum profit for an enterprise. For in the case of a government, even a Communist government, we do not require to maximize tax revenue, but only to raise a determinate sum in the best possible way.

10

It is evident that a perfectly rational central plan would tax all goods equally (except where consumers' irrationality has to be countered), and would include exports and imports in this principle. This is as much as to say, it would use a uniform value-added tax. But we have ruled this out *a priori*, since we are discussing the specific, traditional Soviet-type structure of indirect taxes. Our question is, could this structure also yield rational foreign trade?

We can see that it is so once we have shaken off the enterprise analogy, which has no validity in this context. For not only is the Soviet-type government, like all others, uninterested in maximizing tax revenues, it is also uninterested in foreign currency as such. It earns foreign currency only to spend it; moreover, on quite specific imports, which were the only purpose of its exports and *some of which again it taxes and some it does not*, applying as usual its traditional tax structure. If, for instance, final consumer goods are exported at factor cost against an equivalent import of final consumer goods, tax yields do not change much. All that happens is, presumably, that more wanted goods replace less wanted goods, so that taxes may be raised somewhat. Similarly, if investment and intermediate goods are exchanged against each other in that category, the fiscal position is more or less unchanged. Note that this is another case for Nutzeffekt-type thinking.

II

In general a tax is not normally an opportunity cost to a government. Since it is not maximizing tax yields it can always substitute one tax for another. Administrative and psychological considerations retard but do not seriously prevent such substitutions. Nothing is an opportunity cost that a stroke of the pen can make good.

If, however, 'short period' be defined as the period within which taxes are not changed, it is plain that both STEs and MEs lose by the exportation at factor cost of highly taxed goods, unless it should happen to be balanced by the equal importation of similar goods. As we shall see in Chapter X, one of the various forms that the Communist passion for bilateralism takes is precisely 'structural' bilateralism: the exchange of capital goods only against other capital goods, etc. This in general quite irrational criterion has at least this much to support it, that in the case of consumer goods in the final stage of production immense tax revenues stand to be lost or gained in foreign trade unless it is observed. This is as much as to say, the Soviet-type tax structure hitches tax yields to the volume of consumption, and an exportation of consumer goods against imported investment goods is merely one of many ways by which consumption, and therefore tax yields, can be diminished.

In the longer run, however, taxes are very malleable, especially in STEs. If, then, factor-cost criteria are adopted as a base, tax losses can always be made good by new decrees, without 'structural bilateralism'. Taxes being, as we have seen, not true opportunity costs, a fiscal loss through the export of consumer goods need not be taken seriously. The true opportunity costs are the factor costs of goods, and foreign trade criteria should be based on these.

Therefore, the Soviet-type indirect tax structure, weighing almost exclusively on the last stage of production, is quite compatible with rational foreign trade. The STE need not, of course, inquire whether world prices correspond on the whole to factor costs in other countries, or are formed on the basis of some indirect tax-*cum*-subsidy system similar to, or different from, its own. It has only to compare its own factor costs with the prices outside.

But 'only' is a large word: it is not easy to know your own factor costs. Specifically in USSR, where there is hardly any turnover tax on intermediate goods, an export will not be composed of materials that themselves embody the tax. I.e., the price system automatically yields us the tax-free factor cost—or would do so if land and capital were charged for! But in other STEs the turnover tax is by no means confined to goods for final consumption; thus in the DDR as much as 25% of it comes from intermediate goods. The extraction of such taxes, so as to form 'shadow factor costs' for the purposes of foreign trade, is a major industry in Poland, using very sophisticated means. No wonder, then, that a uniform value-added is such a popular idea in Eastern Europe.

This analysis does not prejudge the macro-policy a country should pursue. For instance, it might seem good to improve a country's terms of trade at the expense of its volume by a general export tax. All we have proved is that such a tax need have no detailed relation to internal taxes, but should be levied directly on factor cost, in such proportions as the relevant elasticities indicate. Clearly, a general import tax or a number of other measures would have the same effect; and they too need not be related to the internal tax structure.

12

One of the very greatest problems for an STE is to settle the *domestic prices of imports*. This is more difficult than wringing the tax water out of domestic factor costs, in order to establish an export price. For at least these costs are based on a solid, or fairly solid, reckoning of wages, depreciation, etc. (and, nowadays, even interest). But the import may well be incomparable with anything produced at home. This situation is easily solved in an ME by a method here excluded in principle: the trial and error of supply and demand. The STE's pricing troubles are not over even if the good has a domestic substitute. For suppose, first, that it is an intermediate good; then the price of this substitute is arbitrary, and the planners are well aware of this. Moreover, the price they set on the import will not affect its sales, since its recipient will have been commanded to buy it. If, on the other hand, the import is a consumer good with a close domestic substitute, while the existing retail price is clearly about correct, now the turnover tax may be of any size. So the price at which the good is transferred from the foreign-trade enterprise to the store is now arbitrary.

Devoted as they are to price stability, but vulnerable as they are to inflation, STEs have a strong tendency to freeze import prices alone, these being the only ones independent of costs. The classic case is Hungary, where domestic prices of imports lagged so far behind, and the volume of trade was so important, that in the late 'fifties the government's net loss in the *Preisausgleich* amounted to 7% of the n.m.p.![1]

We shall see below, in Chapter XV, that imports are anyway much more irrational than exports, even to the extent that Polish planners almost confine their attempts at rationality to optimizing the export mix alone. Indeed, the *macro*-economic volume of Polish imports is highly suspect—which illustrates the important but unpopular point that rationality in small things is sometimes a pre-condition for rationality in big ones. The basic reason for this asymmetry is that there is no agreed way to price imports.

13

The preceding sections should have seemed irritating and superficial because they neglect general equilibrium. It has been implicit all the time that the foreign-trade enterprises are allotted so much to buy exportable goods, earn foreign currency, and import; that their activities can be rational in a vacuum. But, in fact, we need to know whether the costs they pay for exports and the prices they charge for imports are rational having regard to the economy as a whole, and whether, above all, the non-trading sector adapts itself rationally to the activities of foreign-trade enterprises.

The answer is, of course, that it does not, being neither perfectly computative nor perfectly competitive. Nevertheless, the problem of micro-rationality in foreign trade has had an immense effect on Communist thinking and behavior as a whole. This should not surprise us. For first, as we have already seen, prices in foreign trade cannot anyhow be planned. When trading with an ME, the STE

[1] Bela Balassa, *The Hungarian Experience in Economic Planning* (New Haven, 1959), pp. 214, 274–5. Mr. Balassa's explanation of this phenomenon, however, is surely wrong.

has no alternative but to bargain like any other enterprise. When trading with another STE it certainly bargains fiercely, though perhaps not quite like an enterprise (see Section 3, above). Unlike most other prices with which the Communist economist has to deal, foreign-trade prices are 'active', at least as income distributors, and to some extent also as resource allocators. They matter, and one tends to think harder about things that matter.

The second reason why foreign trade has so much influence on economic thinking is that most STEs, and specifically the most civilized ones with the best economists, are small. We face here our first case of the great difference between small and large countries. Like economists in small MEs, Polish and Hungarian economists tend to think of their price structure as an import. It is particularly striking that the first serious set of rational shadow prices in Poland was worked out in the Ministry of Foreign Trade, and then borrowed by the Planning Commission. Again, the first practical application of computers to Polish planning will be in foreign trade. In the USSR, on the other hand, where rationalization has not in practice gone so far anyhow, one may comb the voluminous literature on it for references to foreign trade.

A third reason for the greater rationality of foreign trade is that many—but by no means all—of the measures it requires are institutionally and ideologically indifferent. To obtain a more rational flow of resources at home, the government must establish new enterprises; therefore make new location decisions and persuade local Party bosses; retrain labor; reform the turnover tax; clap a charge on long-term capital . . . the list is endless. To obtain a more rational flow from abroad it needs only to give different instructions, of the same old kind, to its foreign-trade enterprises alone. Nay more, there is an immense problem of where and when to sell *exports already produced*, or buy imports already requisitioned; and it is in this comparatively modest field that rationalization began in Poland. From this, of course, one must proceed to the planning of new exports and, therefore, of the whole economy.[1]

So Communist reformers base domestic price reforms on foreign prices. Anxious to make the use of the *Preisausgleich* sensible, they see that rationality in foreign trade will not be achieved by rational foreign-trade prices alone. So they demand the reform of domestic costs, and—if they are logical—the adaptation of production to these new costs. The consequences of this, which we now see before our

---

[1] For the institutional side of this cf. Chapter IX, below.

eyes in every small STE, are too large and too general to be dealt with in a work on foreign trade.

14

All countries place various restraints upon the free play of micro-rationality in the name of some macro-policy or other. In this way the macro-quantities cannot simply emerge, as the chance products of small decisions. But STEs do this in very much greater detail, employing all sorts of macro-criteria unknown to Western economics. We examine these criteria mainly in the next chapter—and find them wanting. For the moment, however, let us accept them as given and inquire how, this being the case, the maximum of micro-rationality can be preserved.

The principal such restraint is due to the Cold War, and by no means only to the policy of STEs: the preference barrier between the 'two world markets', as the Communists like to say. Were the barrier absolute there would be two separate sets of scarcity conditions, demanding two separate sets of prices. The one set would be determined by the free, or in practice not so free, play of the market. And the other? Perhaps one day by supranational perfect computation—but that is for the moment entirely a pipe-dream (see Chapter XI). Perhaps by an agreement to imitate the prices of MEs—certainly an innocuous solution politically, since it seems so fair, but just as certainly irrational. Perhaps by an inter-STE market as perfect as it could be made—but it could not be other than extremely oligopolistic, and the bargaining would surely lead to the most appalling political quarrels. Or perhaps, and most probably, by muddling through.

Now, in fact, the barrier between the two world markets is fairly porous, and about 3% of world trade takes place across it. The briefest glance at the trade statistics of STEs other than the USSR (see Table IX/2, below) tells us that they would on commercial grounds wish to trade more with MEs. There is no doubt at all of the 'preference', but how should prices be settled when there is a rather strangulated connection between the two world markets?

A simple device for combining this 'strangulation' with micro-rationality is to take the word 'preference' literally, and put a proportional tax on all exports to, or imports from, MEs. Then capitalist buyers and sellers will continue to exercise an influence at the margin, and *relative* prices will continue to be the same in the two markets. However, this is not the device used. Rather are contacts with MEs reduced by arbitrary physical planning, i.e., by imperfectly computed quotas: and this is true on both sides of the fence. Indeed, most notably, the United States strategic embargo is not a differential export tax but a list of specific prohibitions. Yet, clearly, there is *some* price for a 'strategic'[1] good that, could it be screwed out of the Russians, would better achieve United States strategic policy than a flat prohibition. For that policy is, after all, to weaken the USSR relatively to the USA.

On the side of the STE, the failure to impose an across-the-board preference is perhaps still more foolish. STEs do indeed produce 'strategic' goods, but hardly any that the NATO powers would wish to buy; and such as they are, they are indeed embargoed.[2] But for the most part they wish to keep trade down simply to avoid economic dependence. The correct policy would then be to have a few explicit preferences; for consumer goods, for machinery, for agricultural materials, etc. Then, as in the case of some non-Communist monetary quotas, the foreign-trade enterprise would use the money that the quota allocates in accordance with the prices on the market. Instead of this, however, imperfect computation reaches right down into the details.

Inter-STE prices, then, resemble world prices not at all because goods move to make them so, but because administrators choose to impose the resemblance, for the reasons of fairness, psychology, ease of decision, etc., already discussed.

The other common restraints upon micro-rationality are themselves far less rational: they deal with commodity structure, described in Chapter VIII, below. However, once accepted as aims of policy they could and should be treated in the same way as the restraint upon STE-ACC trade: by 'preferences', i.e., differential tariffs, set this time according to commodity instead of country of origin or destination. But, in fact, here again it is arbitrary physical planning that fundamentally decides, right into details, what the preference for a particular commodity structure shall be.

A particularly awkward criterion to combine with micro-rationality is *bilateralism*. The fundamental trick is to set for each pair of countries a separate uniform tariff or rate of exchange that brings trade into reciprocity (Chapter X), or that achieves such and such an agreed balance of trade, so that within the restraint of bilateralism

---

[1] For a definition of this curious word, and the advantages of trade with the enemy, see Chapter XVI.   [2] Cf. Chapter XVII, Section 3.

as much micro-rationality between commodities is retained as possible. The marriage of these two desiderata has hitherto been the life-work of the Swedish mathematical economist Tom Kronsjö, and of his Polish counterpart Witold Trzeciakowski.[1] A very high degree of sophistication has been reached, with actual practical effects on Polish foreign trade. But the enterprise still seems to me to be a questionable investment of skill. Bilateralism is quite irrational, *and also unnecessary among STEs* (cf. Chapter X). For whatever reason, the rates of exchange actually developed—a different one, as we have seen, for each market—quite certainly overstate the profitability of exporting (cf. Chapter XV). The 'curse of aggregation', that defeats other exercises in current planning by computer, limits this one too.

Very appropriately, these planners begin with the distribution of goods already produced and included in the export and import plans. They hardly reach back yet into the sphere of production. But basically, bilateralism is still simply 'achieved' in most cases. It is probable that Dr. Trzeciakowski's development of 'tax-and-subsidy-clean' prices (Section 10, above) has been a much greater improvement.

15

So much for strict micro-rationality, and the criteria that it demands. The next three chapters discuss the very different macro-criteria that there really are. Since most of them are wrong, they produce an atmosphere hardly conducive to rationality at any level. But it must be borne in mind throughout that there was always some micro-rationality, and that now there is more and more. This has, in turn, reacted upon the larger policies that now fall to be discussed. It is not merely a matter of intellectual questioning; it is also that micro-rationality is itself an important determinant of what macro-policy shall be. For instance, once we begin seriously to discuss the cost of particular machines, just how much extra money are we going to spend, project by project, in loyalty to the ancient Communist macro-criterion of autarky in machine-building? The answer is clearly, less than before.

---

[1] Cf. Kronsjö, *Economics of Planning* (Oslo), 1/1963, and *Iterative, Price and Quantity Determination for Short-Run and Foreign Trade Planning* (Cairo, 1964); Trzeciakowski, *Theoretical and Practical Methods of Optimization of Foreign Trade in a Centrally Planned Economy* (Warsaw, Central School of Planning and Statistics, 1964). Dr. Csikos-Nagy tells me that Hungary also intends a different shadow exchange rate with each country or convertible currency area.

CHAPTER VIII

TRADE 'STRUCTURE' AND LONG-TERM POLICY

This realm hath three commodities, wool, tin and lead,
Which being wrought within the realm each man would get his bread.

> —an early English commercial theorist,
> quoted by G. N. Clark, *The Wealth
> of England from 1496 to 1760* (London,
> 1946), p. 49.

On a schematic view we import from the Eastern bloc, principally
USSR and Poland as we have seen, large quantities of special raw
materials and intermediate products which are, to an extent, of the
greatest importance for our economy, while our export to the Eastern
bloc consists mainly of fabricated industrial goods (but note among
others, logs, copper and cellulose). This means that from the purely
employment point of view the Eastern-bloc trade balance is generally
positive on our side.

> —Finnish professor, latter half of twen-
> tieth century (Ilmari Hustich, in
> *Ekonomiska Samfundets Tidskrift* [Hel-
> sinki], 1/1963, pp. 5–6).

Not one step back! Our oil is a national patrimony.

> —Electoral propaganda for López Mateos,
> observed in Mexico City, 1958.

If the economically backward pre-revolutionary Russia exported to
foreign countries mostly such goods as grain, timber, fur and other raw
materials, today the decisive categories of export of the RSFSR are the
products of machine-building, instrument-building, the petroleum
industry, metallurgy and many kinds of valuable raw material.

> —Any Soviet economist, taken practically
> at random; e.g., L. Baulin, *Vneshnyaya
> Torgovlya*, 5/1962, p. 7.

Economic equality could only be attained in a world with a new division
of labor. This, however, must not be one in which the underdeveloped
countries perform the technologically 'inferior' activities and the advanced countries the technologically 'superior' ones, for this would
inevitably lead to economic monopoly, domination and exploitation.

> —Yugoslav economist Janez Stanovik in
> *Naša Stvarnost* (Belgrade), March, 1961.

... There is no doubt that while assessing the prospects, especially the
more distant ones—of the development of trade exchange between

Poland and the German Federal Republic, the problem of the EEC comes to the foreground. Elimination of the consequences of the discriminatory trade policies of the Common Market 'Six' is the decisive element in the successful development of trade cooperation between Poland and the German Federal Republic. We would like to point out, however, a second aspect among various others, which is the necessity to transform the goods structure of our exports to the German Federal Republic. Table 2 demonstrates the existing proportions and... disproportions.

THE GOODS STRUCTURE OF POLISH EXPORTS AND G.F.R. IMPORTS IN PERCENTAGES

	Polish Exports, 1962		Total Imports of G.F.R.
	Total	To G.F.R.	1959
Machines and equipment .	30·0	—	
Industrial products . .	11·8	4·0	$\left\{ 30·8 \right.$
Raw materials and materials .	39·0	46·0	39·2
Agricultural products .	19·2	50·0	30·0

If we compare the structure of goods of the total Polish exports and the total imports of the German Federal Republic, we notice a far-reaching coincidence which proves the complementary character of the economies of Poland and the German Federal Republic. From this it follows that there are wide possibilities of developing trade exchange. Yet, if we compare the structure of our exports to the German Federal Republic with the structure of imports of that country, we see that the share of machines, equipment and industrial products in our exports to the German Federal Republic is of no proportion either to our possibilities nor to the needs of the German Federal Republic. Since Poland is becoming an ever more industrialized country, this change should be reflected in our trade turnover with the German Federal Republic.

—S. Albinowski in *Zycie Gospodarcze* (Warsaw), 23/1963. This article was thought important enough to reprint in *Polish Perspectives*, 13/1963.

1   A little garland of fallacies.
2   Technological snobbery—
3   and non-equivalent exchange.
4   The fallacy of 'capturing value added' (thesis A).
5   The 'depletion neurosis' (thesis A).
6   The Prebisch doctrine.
7   Thesis (B): maximize employment-intensity in foreign trade.
8   Thesis (C): maximize capital-intensity in foreign trade.
9   The Western lore of relative factor-endowment and factor-price equalization.
10 Is it frivolous to import consumer goods (thesis D)?
11 Savings can easily be turned into foreign exchange.

12 It is not *a priori* virtuous to make your own machinery (thesis E): the 'appropriate' rate of exchange should guide you.
13 Is it exploitative to have to import finished goods (thesis D again)?
14 Industry versus agriculture (thesis F).
15 Statistical illustrations.
16 Sophistication and novelty (thesis G).
17 Diversification (thesis H).
18 Diversification and small countries.
19 How seriously is 'structure' actually taken?
20 Rumania, the 'metal-eater'.
21 'Structure' should not be even a secondary aim of policy.
22 Growth and 'structure'.

I

SHOULD a country, in defiance of the price mechanism, the optimum international division of labor and its own factor endowment:

A. Export its raw materials only after it has fabricated them further at home? and, vice versa, import things as little fabricated as possible, in order to do more of the fabrication at home?

B. Export only labor-intensive products?

C. Export only capital-intensive products?

D. Import only raw materials and investment goods?

E. Build up its own machinery industry, so as to avoid importing machines?

F. Export only industrial as opposed to agricultural goods?—this is not quite the same as A, for mining[1] now changes sides, and the arguments used are different.

G. Export only new, or 'sophisticated', goods?

H. In a general way diversify its exports, without paying attention to theses A–G?

'Structure', then, means the composition of one's imports and exports analysed into the above or similar categories. Many of these categories figure prominently in Communist statistical handbooks. Ideas of these kinds circulate in all countries, and some of them have done so for hundreds of years, as the preceding quotations show. They are beneath the intellectual notice of the best Western textbooks, yet they govern commercial policy. One of them, A, can bring crowds into the streets all over Latin America. Marxists, or

---

[1] In Communist parlance mining, along with 'manufacturing', goes to form 'industry'.

Communists, seem to subscribe to all of them except B and possibly H. The Marxist attachment to these beliefs was one of the main causes of the Tito-Stalin split (see Chapter I, Section 6), and is the main cause of Rumania's present independence. These doctrines, then, have the same power to move men to action as had once free trade.

2

So far as I can see, only H has any intellectual content. Indeed, H should be a main guiding principle in any country. For the rest, all the arguments are fallacious, and the explanation must chiefly be sought in men's passions. The most common passion here, which explains most of the above fallacies, is *technological snobbery*. For all politicians, journalists, engineers, Communists and inhabitants of UDCs are little boys at heart. They like to gawk at the very latest thing, and when it is done by one of their own countrymen their hearts flutter with patriotic pride. They are, indeed, similar to young economists, who would rather answer a silly question with mathematics than an important question with common sense. Just as a British youth will ride ten yards on a 'ton-up' motorcycle, or an American take the elevator rather than climb one flight, so the rulers of our destinies are victims of the notion that the most modern way of producing the most fashionable product is the best way to employ our resources. But economists, even perhaps young economists, know better: the best thing to do with your resources is to maximize your profits.

They know it, but they too seldom say it. It shows a poor grasp indeed of the 'way the world works' that technological snobbery barely rates a mention in works of economics. Rationality, we seem continually to forget, is either a convenient methodological assumption or a normative recommendation; it is not a factual description. A partial but still honorable exception are Klinkmüller and Ruban— not surprisingly, sovietological economists—who point to the change in Soviet attitudes on this matter. Stalin, they point out, formulated the 'fundamental economic law of socialism' thus in 1952: 'The *maximal* satisfaction of the constantly growing material and cultural needs of the whole society through the unbroken growth and continual perfection of socialist production on the basis of the *most highly developed* techniques.'[1] But the third edition of the

---

[1] Josef Stalin, *Economic Problems of Socialism in the USSR* (Moscow, 1952), pp. 48–9. My italics. Original Russian here translated from German.

Political Economy textbook (1957) says: 'The continual expansion and perfection of production on the basis of *advanced* techniques, with the aim of satisfying *as completely as possible* the growing needs of society, systematically raising welfare and developing all members of society all round.'[1]

Despite this shift, technological snobbery remains very dominant among Communists. It operates with particular strength in foreign trade, and by no means alone among Communists. We all want to put a better face on our economy when it is turned toward the foreigner than when it is turned inward. Our exports and imports are our front parlor, where we keep the structural aspidistra flying; meanwhile, we live in the kitchen. Foreign trade serves the same façade purposes as the modernity of airport reception rooms (why not 'bus stations?) and the cleanliness of streets in the government quarter (why not in the slums?).

The case of structure snobbery is rather similar to that of forced investment. It pays to force the overall volume of investment; but almost nothing is gained and something is usually lost by discarding orthodox, perfectly competitive, micro-criteria in allocating the funds thus squeezed from an unwilling population.[2] So in international economics: it may in certain circumstances be good to concentrate on labor-intensive products generally, but exports are not a particularly good or particularly bad field for this (see Section 7, below); autarky may be good, but autarky in consumer goods has no special charm (see Section 10 below). In general, the student of planning finds innumerable good cases for violating the rules of the market place. But one does not justify another; there is even a curious lack of connection between them. Each must be argued separately.

3

In the Communist case, all these theses are given a special twist by the labor theory of value. But just what this twist is, is not immediately obvious. We have dealt with traditional Marxist attitudes to this in Chapter I: the doctrine of nonequivalent exchange strongly favors all our fallacies except B. However, it is a striking indication of the uselessness of the labor theory that more

[1] Erich Klinkmüller and Maria Ruban, *Die Wirtschaftliche Zusammenarbeit der Ostblockstaaten*, Berlin 1960, p. 48.
[2] As I hope to have shown, even if *contra mundum*, in P. J. D. Wiles, *The Political Economy of Communism*, Chapters 14–16.

modern Marxist arguments for these theses, except C, do not rest
upon it so much as upon considerations of 'structure snobbery'
almost indistinguishable from those urged in Latin America—or
Britain.

4

Take, first, thesis A. We extract from the soil, we fabricate, we
assemble, we retail (wholesaling intervenes at every stage). Strictly
interpreted, the thesis is that it is better to invest in the fabrication
of the raw materials that we already 'extract', and export them
fabricated, or to invest in making at home the finished goods we at
present import and only 'assemble' here, than to invest in other
things. In other words, here we have our extracted raw material:
should we add value to it, or should we add value to something else?
The doctrine is best analysed by breaking down 'value added' into a
supply and a demand concept: cost added and revenue added.
Further, let each concept be marginal: m.c.a. (marginal cost added)
and m.r.a. (marginal revenue added). Then equilibrium lies in their
equalization. Is there some reason to suppose that the addition of
value to our native raw material yields greater m.r.a. or smaller
m.c.a. than the addition of value to an imported raw material, or
the development and extraction of another native raw material, or
the creation of value in some service trade?

The question has only to be so put for us to see that whatever
advantages may lie in the further fabrication of what we already
have, they are all included in private profit. Thus, for instance, such
an industry will have lower transport costs than others; or it can
assume some technical knowledge in its labor force, since much of
the information required to extract the material is also useful in
working it up. These economies may be in some sense 'external',
but they are certainly caught by the price mechanism. They are
simply the old-fashioned economies of vertical integration. There
is, therefore, no need for an artificial bias toward such projects.[1]

5

But this is not the end of thesis A. How about the *patrimonio
nacional*? The sucking away of our lifeblood, of the very ground on

[1] Only one qualification is necessary: if we get into the habit of exporting raw materials
that we also use at home, we shall suffer unemployment during a b.o.p. crisis. For we shall
then be tempted to export more than usual. Cf. Chapter IV, Section 17.

which we stand, by the *explotadores norte-americanos*? In so far as
this is a general bias against foreign equity investment it has on
political and social grounds my reluctant but definite support. That,
however, does not concern us: is not the state or even a native
private investor, in exporting unworked minerals, running down
the national patrimony? Note that the objection only applies to
minerals, i.e., to irreplaceable gifts of nature. And hereby the
objection supplies its own answer: there is *some* price at which any
enterprise or nation should be happy to sell its minerals. The
passions aroused by this subject in Latin America are perfectly
inappropriate. Let the government estimate reserves, future demand
and cost; let it assign to itself a futurity discount; and it will arrive
easily at a minimum royalty or tax below which it considers the
nation's interests prejudiced. External economies mostly favor
immediate exploitation, because there is so great a need for any
profitable enterprise that can bring in techniques, train labor, give
people taxable incomes, etc. I.e., the royalties could well meet
competition from other mines by falling *below* their level in an
ACC. Moreover, the fact that the mineral is going abroad is actually
good, not bad: it helps—as does the royalty—to balance our external
accounts.

The 'depletion neurosis', then, is absurd. The international rent
our extractive industries can earn is a vital national asset, on which
it would be criminal to sit. It is enormously more profitable to
invest labor and capital in such industries than in the further stages
of fabrication, which normally yield no rent. Deliberately to favor
fabrication over extraction is to return Mother Nature's gifts un-
opened. It is a great deal sillier than an arbitrary preference for one
sort of fabrication over another.

In other countries, especially ACCs and STEs, feelings on this
point are much less acute, but do from time to time issue in some
scare or other. When reserves are underestimated—as they usually
are[1]—it appears inconceivable to the untrained mind that any price
could compensate the nation for the export of its mineral. Stalin
seems to have been the victim of this fallacy in regard to Soviet oil,
and United States history is full of such cases.

We may sum up Sections 4 and 5 by returning to the Finnish
quotation at the head of this chapter. Would it pay the USSR to
fabricate her raw materials still more and *then* sell them to, say,
Finland, and would Finland suffer thereby? The answer is simply,

[1] Cf. Fritz Baade, *Der Wettlauf zum Jahre* 2000 (Oldenburg, 1963), Chapter VII.

the USSR would gain if this was the most profitable thing to do with her factors of production, and Finland would lose if the particular stage of fabrication she was thus done out of was the most profitable way in which she could employ those factors; if not, not. There is an *a priori* argument here, but it fights for raw materials. It is that since hitherto rents have not been charged in the Soviet pricing system it would probably pay the USSR to develop still more any raw materials in Karelia or the Leningrad *oblast'* that the Finns want, for she has here a rent of site *vis-à-vis* all competitors c.i.f. Helsinki.

6

To opposing this rigid application of static 'welfare' theory Raúl Prebisch[1] has given his name and his life's work. His case is so serious as to need a section to itself. It consists of two arguments: that from the 'technology trap' and that from the terms of trade. Taking the former first, it is in general the case that technical progress—i.e. the lowering of average real cost—has recently been slowest in building and some services (e.g., education); though not always in agriculture, still less in mining, to which the argument is often carelessly extended. *If this should continue to be so*, a nation has, indeed, an advantage in getting into the fabrication of its own raw materials. But this is only because such fabrication is a part of manufacturing industry in general; it is no more likely to enjoy technical progress than any other part—nor, indeed, than mining.

Moreover, we have no means at all of knowing where there will be technical progress in the distant future. As to the immediate future, our knowledge of new *inventions* rests upon what scientists say they are trying to discover, which is not necessarily what they will discover. But we can at least make a prediction about *development and application*: it will continue to be very slow in peasant agricultures. To this extent at least there really is a 'technology trap'. In the past, on the other hand, in eighteenth-century Britain, or in Malaya at the turn of this century, agriculture was precisely the great field of technical progress. The faster progress in other sectors is merely a generalization.[2] We have no grounds at all, therefore,

[1] E.g., *American Economic Review*, May, 1959.

[2] Which does not hold, for instance, for the USA in recent years. I extract the following figures for 1939–58 from the United States Dept. of Agriculture, Stat. Bull. 233, *Changes in Farm Production and Efficiency* (Washington, D.C., 1964), and from Edward F. Denison, *The Sources of Economic Growth* (New York, 1962), p. 146: GNP outgrew over-all input in real terms by 27%, while the corresponding net figure in agriculture was 43%.

for believing that mining or large-scale agriculture are a 'technology trap', and it would be quite arbitrary to base investment policy upon such an unfounded prediction.

Nor, secondly, is it manufacturing but—so far as we can foresee!— services that face the greatest future expansions of demand; and demand is almost as important as technology in determining factor incomes. This brings us to the terms of trade, which many still forget. Indeed, it seems that Western growth economists—and Marxist economists—are continuing to use the argument from differential productivity growth in its simple form long after the theorists have shown it to be treacherous.[1] Briefly, in a state of free world trade, there is only one price relation between agriculture and industry, whether at present or in the future, whether 'statically' now or 'dynamically' in ten years' time. That country invests and trades most wisely which over the average of all periods so uses its factors of production as to make the best of this price relation. The benefits of increasing returns and technical progress have to be exported in competitive conditions: no industrialized country can hog them. The loss of decreasing returns must similarly be exported: no agricultural country is called upon to bear the burden alone.

The matter is really one of shocking simplicity: you cannot evaluate a transaction on the basis of supply conditions alone—those of demand also apply, and the price is vital. Yet the argument we are discussing does treat supply alone. It is also empirically refuted, not only by all Australasian history, but more relevantly by the Czechoslovak and Soviet b.o.p. crises of 1963 (see Chapter V), a major trouble here being over-reliance on manufactured exports.

So, apart from predicting technical progress, it must be further assumed that the product terms of trade will not so move as to wipe out the advantage of concentrating on manufactures. Strictly, of course, we are interested not in the product but in the single factor terms of trade; not in how many imports our exports will fetch but in how many imports an hour of our labor will fetch. When we allow thus for the growth of our own productivity we can see that however much market movements are likely to rob us of an improvement in our product terms of trade, we shall probably still retain some benefit in the factor terms. For it is only between

[1] The connection between national productivity growth and the terms of trade has become a major branch of theory. The first specialized work is J. R. Hicks, *Essays in World Economics* (Oxford, UK, 1959). A useful more modern one is B. Södersten, *A Study of Economic Growth and International Trade* (Stockholm, 1964); cf. especially Chapter VI therein, for the 'Prebisch' complex of arguments.

nations that there can be any permanent advantage in being employed by a progressive industry. This is because only between nations are the factor flows missing that help to bring incomes into line again, when progress has occurred in one industry but not another. Product prices, as we have seen, continue to move, but this may not be enough by itself.

It is commonly predicted, by Mr. Prebisch and to some extent by Marxists, that the product terms of trade will perpetually move against raw materials because they are very competitively supplied, in such a manner that no producer can control the price but, on the contrary, all improvements in efficiency lead to lower prices; while manufactures are supplied by oligopolists or monopolistic competitors who are continually forced to raise their prices by union pressure, so that improvements in efficiency accrue, if not to the employer, then at least to his workers. The argument is in itself very persuasive, but for whatever reason is wholly unreflected by reality. The product terms of trade of UDCs with ACCs[1] stand in 1964, even on an orthodox reckoning, above those of 1938 and not much below those of 1928; they have fallen only from the obviously abnormal Korean War peak of the early 'fifties.

Now it so happens that raw material price indices are those least subject to 'hedonic' distortion. Quality and variety do not increase year by year in ways unperceived by orthodox statisticians. Manufactures, on the other hand, and in particular machines, are among the things most liable to such distortion. It is very certain that a price index of UDC imports grossly exaggerates the increase in prices paid for truly comparable articles.[2] The *hedonic product terms of trade* have therefore moved greatly in favor of raw materials, and so somewhat in favor of UDCs.

So what are the practical consequences for policy? We have learned that a country that correctly anticipates the combined future of technique and the product terms of trade will gain, and that *in the recent past* those that specialized in agriculture have suffered— through the technology trap but not through the terms of trade. Those, moreover, possessed of a peasant agriculture *will* continue to suffer technologically. In other words, we have learned very little.

[1] Which is, of course, by no means the same as those between raw materials and manufactures. I am indebted here to Theodore Morgan (in *Economic Development and Cultural Change*, October, 1959), who also warns against neglect of transport costs. A fall in these costs could improve the United Kingdom's terms of trade with Ghana c.i.f. London, but simultaneously improve Ghana's terms with the United Kingdom, c.i.f. Accra.

[2] For the hedonic problem cf. Wiles, op. cit., Chapter 12, and especially the sources mentioned on page 243.

7

If the fundamental thought of thesis A is the capture of a particular line of employment from the foreigner, that of B is the maximization of employment by all means and so, in particular, by influencing the structure of trade. Suppose, indeed, that we were to maximize employment, not income? This seems an obvious policy for a UDC more interested in immediate welfare than growth, but what exactly does it mean? Granted perfect competition, some small degree of substitutability and Say's Law, the supply of labor and other factors will always bring wage rates and other factor prices into such a relationship that both will be fully employed; i.e., to maximize income is the same as to maximize employment, whether of labor or of capital.[1] Take away Say's Law, and we get merely the likelihood that *both* factors will be unemployed; the proportions in which they continue to be used will no doubt differ from those of full-employment use, but not in any predictable or interesting way.

But it is extremely common in UDCs for labor to be immobile and/or overpaid. Again substitution is often impossible, or technological snobbery rampant. In all these cases labor suffers structural unemployment which can indeed be cured by subsidizing labor-intensive industries. It follows that an artificially labor-intensive foreign-trade structure[2] might be a good thing—but no more than a bias toward labor-intensity elsewhere. There is, as usual in this context, no reason to set foreign trade apart from internal exchanges.

8

Thesis B, alone of all those enumerated, is not popular among Communists. It is the only one that offends against their structure snobbery. Of thesis C the reverse must, therefore, be said. Yet it has, of course, no more rational grounds than its opposite. If foreign trade is in no sense a specially good repository for labor-intensive goods, neither is it for capital-intensive ones. In addition, however, there is no good argument of any kind for a bias toward capital-intensity in any *part* of the economy.[3] Such a thing is mere waste: to use too much capital in one place is, of course, to use too little in another, and both are equally wasteful. As to the whole economy,

[1] Taking capital to mean the existing physical capacity bequeathed to us by past abstinence.
[2] Note that this would include preferential imports of things for which the domestic substitute is labor-*ex*tensive; i.e., we shuffle off on to the foreigner the making of goods which would not cost us much labor to make.
[3] Wiles, op. cit., Chapters XIV–XVI.

that will become capital-intensive only at the rate at which capital is accumulated. Thesis C, therefore, may be dismissed as a piece of very pure structure snobbery.

9

Before leaving these two theses we should also observe their relation to the ordinary Western lore of relative factor-endowment, factor-intensity, factor-price equalization, etc.[1] Our concern here is different from the general preoccupation of this literature: how will factor endowment affect trade under *laissez-faire*? We ask how, if at all, a planned economy *should* influence the factor-intensity of trade.

The Western literature is particularly concerned with the effect of international trade upon income distribution. There is, of course, the simple, short-run effect of shifts in trade upon particular industries: income is redistributed 'vertically' from the land, labor and capital employed in this industry to that employed in another. But this literature directs our attention to the longer-run and more complicated 'horizontal' shifts of income. For instance, we export more grain and import more cloth, switching domestic inputs from cloth to grain. Land becomes scarcer in a general way throughout the economy, and labor more plentiful. The more perfect the factor markets and the longer the run, the more this effect outweighs the initial impact on specific cloth producers and grain producers of all categories.

It is not clear to me that this kind of problem has been worth the intellectual effort expended on it, even within the context of an ME. For, first, it is the short-run income redistribution that stirs men's passions and provokes legislation. Secondly, all states are now welfare states. There are everywhere unemployment insurance, subsidies, progressive income taxes, retraining grants, etc., etc. These blunt both the short- and the long-run effects. Thirdly, the long-run effect is rather neutral as to capital, since in ACCs agriculture and industry are of roughly equal capital-intensity. Historically, the big redistributions have always been between land and labor.

[1] The factor-price equalization theorem is briefly and elegantly demonstrated by Jaroslav Vanek, *International Trade: Theory and Economic Policy* (Urbana, Ill., 1962), pp. 208–11. Factor-intensity reversal, which Vanek thinks unimportant, is exhaustively discussed in theory and practice by B. S. Minhas, *An International Comparison of Factor Costs and Factor Use* (Amsterdam, 1963). For a more general treatment of the whole subject, cf. Richard E. Caves, *Trade and Economic Structure* (Cambridge, Mass., 1960). For human skill, or intellectual investment in human beings, as part of the factor endowment, cf. Peter Kenen in *Journal of Political Economy*, Oct. 1965.

So as agriculture diminishes in relative weight the whole question diminishes in importance. It probably still matters in UDCs, where agriculture still has great relative weight and is not as capital-intensive as industry.

When we come to the STE, it is enough to point out that there is only one kind of factor income: wages. Whether the state charges interest and rent or no, changes in the land- and capital-intensity of the country's over-all output have no effect whatsoever on the distribution of income. And with this the whole question loses whatever importance it may have had.

Moreover, apart from theses B and C we use the word 'structure' much more broadly, to cover many things not related to factor-intensity. If the choice between agriculture and industry is always somehow related to this question, that between consumption and investment goods, for instance, shows no clear connection. For many capital goods are tailor-made, thus embodying an unusual amount of labor. To support thesis B or C is not, then, to take any general line about the other theses.

10

Thesis D, the conviction that one should never import consumer goods, took a central place in Preobrazhenski's alternative policy for development during the NEP: not only were the peasants to be exploited by taxation, but also there were to be no more imports competitive with domestic industry. On the contrary, all foreign exchange was to be used to purchase raw materials and investment goods, i.e., 'A' not 'B' goods.[1] The Preobrazhenski line became the Trotsky line, and advocacy of a command economy was added to it.[2] Stalin took it over when he liquidated them both, adding the collectivization of agriculture; and since then it has been part of Communist orthodoxy everywhere that foreign exchange is essentially an investment resource. Most UDCs behave in the same way, and even the ACCs of Western Europe followed Preo-brazhenski in the dark days of 1946–50.

Our general criticism must be the same as before: once the macro-economic proportions are fixed for the economy as a whole we must behave as micro-rationally as possible, importing and

---

[1] Wiles, op. cit., Chapter XIV.
[2] Alexander Erlich, *The Soviet Industrialization Controversy* (Cambridge, Mass., 1960); Evgeni Preobrazhenski, *The New Economics* (originally Moscow, 1926), trans. Brian Pearce (Oxford, 1965).

exporting whatever is best. For instance, a large investment pro-gram is perfectly compatible with exporting machinery and import-ing textiles. There have to be *some* textiles; so if our comparative-cost position gives us an advantage in machinery, that is our cheapest way of acquiring them. Nevertheless, in a UDC (but not in an STE) there is one mitigating factor for thesis D. This is that foreign trade is administratively so much easier to control. If we use exchange control to force the holders of foreign money to import only machinery we are already some way toward achieving our investment program. This policy may well be more effective than, say, cheap money. But it is, by itself, a short-run policy only. For in the end, domestic resources will, if not separately prevented, flow into consumption goods, even if substitution is not easy and the flow is slow. Again, exporters will be discouraged, since we have rendered the proceeds of exporting less attractive. But this too will take some time to show itself. In any case, an STE has no such administrative problem and, therefore, no excuse for confusing im-ports with investment.

The notion that it is frivolous to spend foreign exchange on consumer goods is ludicrous. It is to some extent frivolous to spend *money* on consumer goods, but in the long run foreign exchange, too, is 'only money'. Indeed, there is, as we saw in Chapter IV, a risk in not importing consumer goods. For without that cushion we shall be forced in a b.o.p. crisis to stop importing producer goods instead, and so bring the bottleneck effect into play.

II

Behind my objections to thesis D there is a general proposition: *Savings are in the long run convertible into foreign currency at the 'appro-priate' rate of exchange.* I.e., the resources they set free become extra exports, and the savings themselves can then be spent on extra imports. It is true that this change will depress the terms of trade, but there is no *a priori* reason to think that this will be more expensive than the increasing supply price of domestic investment goods, should these savings have been spent at home.

This point is not simple or obvious. In the short run, it is even simply false. There is, first, a basic difference between nineteenth- and twentieth-century conditions. In the earlier period, all decisions were supposed to be, and most were, taken by firms small in relation to a large world market, and small even in relation to their country's central bank. The enterprise saved domestic money, or borrowed someone else's savings, and then if it wanted to, simply carried it to the bank and converted it into foreign exchange. With this it could, in turn, buy a foreign machine. However many rupees were saved, just so many pounds, at the current rate of exchange, were made available to the investor. If all investors' tastes changed together, from home to foreign machinery, there was, of course, a run on the reserves; and so too if the taste of the population as a whole changed from consumption (based on domestic goods) to saving and investment (based on imports). But such marked shifts in taste were seldom sudden or big.

The government of a modern ME, planning to increase the importation of capital goods, faces a more serious problem. Its decision is big enough relatively to the whole to be subjected to the full macro-economic treatment. First and foremost, its proposed annual imports of machinery will almost certainly be of the same order of magnitude as its foreign-exchange reserves. Secondly, the 'convertibility of savings into foreign exchange' now acquires a more sophisticated meaning: new saving must either cut import spending or release resources for export. The ensuing steps in our illustration require algebraical treatment.

Let the government decide to increase investment by A. The import content of A is kA, the marginal propensity to save is s and the m.p.i. is i. Let the budget be balanced (or equally unbalanced) before and after the decision. Then taxes rise by A, and private saving falls by sA, and private importation by iA. So in the short run, imports rise by $(k - i)A$. However, there is now a multiplier effect, since $(s + i - k)A$ has been injected into the income stream. At this point, we must think in actual numbers. Suppose, as is characteristic for UDCs, all machinery is foreign and all construction domestic. Then k is about 0·5, while s might be 0·05 and i, 0·4. Then $k - i$ is positive, though not great, while $s + i - k$ is about zero. Existing exports, therefore, will be largely unaffected by new claims on home production. Much can be achieved by a careful planning to keep k down, and much—as we saw in Chapter IV— by export-biased investment. But it is clear already that even without much conscious policy mere budgetary balance will provide most of the foreign exchange required for an increase in investment. In the longer run, cuts in private imports, or in imports of consumer goods, are merely two among a whole range of measures for relieving pressure on the b.o.p.

12

The proposition that saving is convertible into foreign exchange has two important corollaries. The first we have met already: there is no point in artificially restricting imports of consumption goods; it is enough—if administratively possible—to restrict consumption, and let this division between imports and home output take care of itself. The second corollary is an argument against thesis E: there is no point in artificially restricting imports of investment goods either, and building up an expensive domestic engineering industry. For this is to waste scarce savings that could have been better spent on imported machinery. Thesis E has, once this is admitted, only strategic arguments in its favor, and so may be dismissed here in short order.

What is this 'appropriate' rate of exchange, however? Clearly, it must express the opportunity cost of sending consumption funds— or investment funds—abroad. In other words, it is micro-economically appropriate, and as is shown in Chapter XV, the only such rate conceivable is the wholesale purchasing power par. At this rate every specific article of a given quality has the same price in home currency, wherever it is produced; or if not, it becomes right and profitable to export or import it. In an ME such a rate might easily be macro-economically inappropriate, on this or that Keynesian ground. It is the task of macro-economic policy to correct such a situation, so that the international division of labor may proceed to just the right point. The specific corrective measures required do not concern a study of STEs; it is one of the advantages of the STE that it is immune to Keynesian macro-economics. For it the 'appropriate' rate is beyond question the wholesale p.p.p., for as is shown in Chapter XV, this is also the point where, with reasonably flexible internal prices, over-all external trade is in balance.

13

There is another, more lowbrow, version of thesis E: we are exploited if we import too many *finished* goods; it is non-exploitative to import raw materials, semifabricates, and finished goods in proportion to their domestic output. Strictly, this is an argument against machinery imports, but perhaps an exception can be made for them on developmental grounds; so the doctrine boils down to the same old hostility against importing consumer goods.

Something like this is very much in the air. To my knowledge only Popović is explicit.[1] He tries to prove the point directly from the labor theory of value. The exporter of finished products, he says, necessarily exploits his opposite number, the exporter of raw materials, if the exchange takes place at market prices. Considering how much of his book rests upon this doctrine, it is astounding to find it proven in exactly three paragraphs (page 34). These bring up just one example:

Value added in iron-ore mining per worker (Yugoslavia)	113,960 dinar
Value added in steel rolling per worker (Yugoslavia) .	242,250 dinar
Mining/milling productivity ratio (Yugoslavia) .	1/1·98

Then, continues the author, let productivity in Hungarian steel mills be 50% greater. Then to exchange Yugoslav ore for Hungarian steel is to exchange nearly three labor-days for one, whereas if commodity trade were structurally random Yugoslavia would be exchanging $1\frac{1}{2}$ for 1. Moreover, things are really even worse than that, because beyond rolled steel again there are finished products, which Yugoslavia must also import, and where the ratio is still less unfavorable—a point he does not bother even to illustrate statistically.

Upon the slender statistical foundation of this single case rests the whole of Popović's structure theory. How slender it is, we see when we learn that his conception of value added in steel rolling is gross revenue minus ingot cost alone: neither depreciation[2] nor fuel is mentioned. There is, in fact, nothing in Marx to give theoretical backing to such talk, and since the main element in value added is always wages, we should be deeply suspicious of so big a difference between steel and iron ore. Indeed theory tells us that the opposite difference is just as likely. Yet, to repeat, such complaints had big significance for the Tito–Stalin split. Irrational economic doctrines are worth much more examination by professionals than they ordinarily get.

14

Or perhaps (thesis F) we should export only industrial goods? I.e., discriminate against agriculture? It is, in general, true that a small directly agricultural labor force characterizes an advanced economy. Note the careful phrasing: nothing is implied as to

---

[1] Milentije Popović, *Über die Wirtschaftlichen Beziehungen zwischen Sozialistischen Staaten* (Mainz, 1950).

[2] Proper Marxists reckon, very correctly, in terms of net income. They eschew the sophisticated Western error that depreciation does not count (Wiles, op. cit., pp. 307–11).

agricultural gross output or inputs into agriculture from transport, manufacturing, construction, and services. What, after all, is 'employment in agriculture'? It means, perhaps, working in direct contact with soil, living plants, and livestock, e.g., in modern circumstances, driving a tractor, heating a greenhouse, or spreading the shavings to make a deep litter. It hardly means cementing a tractor yard, mending a greenhouse pane, or grading eggs. I.e., more and more things are being done near farms, even on farms or by farmers, which we cannot call 'agriculture'. As the tasks connected with 'fiber- and food-making' multiply and differentiate, the proportion of them called 'agricultural' shrinks. Also, the productivity of labor directly employed in those latter tasks rises with the application of capital and technique. No wonder, then, that 'agricultural' employment declines as time passes:[1] expenditure on finished food and fiber hardly does.

It is perhaps the commonest and most fatal of all 'structural' fallacies to infer from this decline in direct employment that the growth of food and fiber *output* should be restrained in any way. Yet in the USSR under Stalin, in Argentina under Peron, in Cuba under Castro,[2] and in China under Mao (1958) precisely such policy decisions were made, with disastrous effects internally and on the balance of payments. Clearly, an output pattern that is rationally adapted to present factor endowments and markets must remain the same until those latter have changed or been changed.

Plainly, too, in our overpopulated world there must be priority for agriculture. This priority is, indeed, compatible with the view that the most natural division of labor would be an exchange of simple labor-intensive manufactures from the UDCs for the land-intensive food products of North America. It is an anomaly that North America should export industrial products, except a few that are so skill- and capital-intensive that Europe cannot make them; and in the same way it is an anomaly that UDCs should export food. But this quirk of economic history is deeply

[1] E.g., in the United States between 1929 and 1957 income originating in agriculture, forestry and fishing fell from 9·3% to 4·5% of the national income, while expenditure on processed food and fiber rose from 35% to 38% of all consumer expenditure. 'Processed food and fiber' means food, beverages, tobacco and clothing as bought by final consumers. If allowance is made for the rise of artificial fiber and federal taxation the percentage of expenditure remains constant at 35 (*Historical Statistics of the United States* [Washington, D.C., 1960], pp. 140, 178, 414–15, 733). It follows that we must be specially careful in comparing the percentage of the labor force that is agricultural in an advanced and a backward country, e.g., the United States and the USSR. Cf. Ya. Yoffe in *Planovoe Khozyaistvo*, 3/1960.

[2] The area under sugar-cane was reduced for no other reason than that it seemed to be a symbol of colonialism (Che Guevara in *Revolución* [Havana], August 24, 1963).

rooted in 'things as they are', and it will not be the business of one decade to correct it. Nor does it provide an excuse for neglecting agriculture anywhere in the world. Such few UDCs as do have an agricultural export should plainly cherish it like the apple of their eye.

15

Theses A, D, E and F may be illustrated empirically. The structure of Soviet visible trade behaved, according to the careful compilation of Franklyn Holzman, as shown in Tables VIII/1 and VIII/2. We may compare the United States figures in Table VIII/3.

Thus on theses A, D, E and F the USSR should import noticeably fewer finished goods than in 1913, and be a net exporter of machinery. But, in fact, she buys more machinery than she sells, and—if we correct for coke and coal—has added a mere 11% to the finished goods sub-total in forty-seven years. This is all admitted by Rubinshtein and Baksht,[1] who add, however, that with Czechoslovakia and the DDR bulking so large in Soviet trade, mere socialist brotherhood dictates that the USSR must export the raw materials they need and import the finished goods they make. In other words, geography and trade preference—the latter even if politically determined—must influence structure. But the argument is quite invalid, since about 40% of Soviet machinery imports comes from other countries, and could be cut if too much were being imported in total. Nay, more, the USSR positively forced Czechoslovakia into this specialization in the early 'fifties, as we see in Table VIII/5.

On the export side, the structural 'improvement' over 1913 is in great part due to agricultural failure: had grain exports alone held up at their 1909–13 average of 10·9 mn.[2] tons they would have added R.1625 mn.[3] to the finished goods category in 1958, or 9·4% of all exports.

Turning to thesis F, it is indeed obvious that agricultural exports, finished and unfinished, have collapsed; so the products of manufacturing and mining have had to take their place. If this is desirable, collectivization certainly achieved it! But it was, of course, a catastrophe.

On theses B and C our data provide no evidence. It might be

[1] In *Vneshnyaya Torgovlya*, 4/1962.
[2] United States Dept. of Agriculture, *Survey of Soviet Russian Agriculture* (Washington, D.C., 1951), pp. 178–9.
[3] *Vneshnyaya Torgovlya SSSR 1958*, p. 22.

TABLE VIII/1. COMMODITY STRUCTURE OF USSR VISIBLE EXPORTS (INCLUDING RE-EXPORTS), 1913–58
(percentage of total)

	1913	1928	1929	1930	1931	1932	1933	1934	1938	1950	1955	1958
Machinery and equipment	0·3	0·1	0·3	0·2	0·6	0·8	0·9	1·3	2·5	11·8	17·5	18·5
Fuels and raw materials	42·8	63·1	—	—	—	—	—	—	57·7	64·4	67·9	65·9
Coal	0·1	0·6	1·4	1·7	1·8	2·3	2·3	2·6	1·4	0·6	1·9	3·7
Oil and oil products	3·3	13·5	14·9	15·1	14·2	18·6	15·3	14·2	7·9	2·4	6·7	10·0
Ferrous and nonferrous metals and products[a]	0·6	0·8	0·7	0·7	0·7	1·0	1·2	1·6	1·6	8·5	12·6	16·1
Lumber, sawn	6·3	6·8	16·5	16·4	14·0	14·0	15·5	21·4	14·1	1·6	2·8	3·2
Other wood products	4·5	5·1							6·0	0·8	1·2	1·4
Cotton	—	—	0·3	0·7	2·2	1·0	0·0	0·6	1·9	9·7	8·7	5·6
Flax thread[b]	6·2	3·1	5·3	3·0	2·2	3·7	4·1	5·0	1·7	0·2	0·1	0·2
Pelts and raw fur	0·4	15·1	11·5	7·4	6·9	7·3	7·8	7·7	9·4	2·3	1·1	0·8
Grain	33·3	3·3	1·1	19·4	18·5	9·6	8·2	4·5	21·3	12·1	8·3	8·3
Consumers' goods	23·6	33·5	30·5	23·0	27·0	29·0	26·0	27·0	16·0	11·7	6·3	7·3
Meat and milk products[c]	12·0	13·1	6·9	1·5	1·1	3·2	2·5	2·6	0·3	3·5	0·4	1·0
Sugar	1·8	4·3	3·8	2·6	4·2	2·2	1·1	1·1	2·5	0·9	0·7	0·6
Cloth[d]	3·0	6·5	4·7	4·5	7·5	8·7	6·0	5·5	4·8	2·0	1·2	1·3
Finished goods	36·0								40·8		61·8	60·4
Raw materials	64·0								59·2		38·2	39·6

a For 1929–34, only ferrous metals.
b For 1929–34, category is 'flax, tow, and swing tow'.
c For 1929–34, category includes butter, bacon and eggs.
d For 1929–34, category includes only cotton cloth.

TABLE VIII/2. COMMODITY STRUCTURE OF USSR VISIBLE IMPORTS, 1913–58
(percentage of total)

	1913	1928	1929	1930	1931	1932	1933	1934	1938	1950	1955	1958
Machinery and equipment	15·9	23·9	29·9	46·9	53·5	55·2	42·4	24·4	34·5	21·5	30·2	24·5
Electrical equipment	1·9	5·1	3·9	4·6	4·9	9·3	5·6	3·6	4·2	—	0·7	0·7
Transportation equipment	—	—	7·4	11·3	12·9	3·3	3·9	2·4			12·5	9·8
Fuels and raw materials	63·4	67·8	—	—	—	—	—	—	60·7	63·3	51·5	51·6
Coal	5·5	0·1	...	...	...	...	...	...	...	6·0	3·9	1·4
Petroleum and products	0·4	0·0	...	...	...	...	...	...	1·2	5·2	4·0	3·1
Ores and concentrates	0·1	0·0	0·8	1·0	1·5	0·9	0·7	1·3	2·6	5·8	8·2	9·3
Ferrous metals and products	4·3	7·8	8·2	13·3	20·6	17·9	22·7	18·6	7·7	7·2	2·3	4·2
Nonferrous metals and products	3·9	6·3	6·9	5·2	4·6	4·6	6·8	9·2	18·1		4·3	3·1
Natural rubber	2·9	2·5	1·3	1·3	1·2	1·1	1·8	7·1	3·5	3·1	0·9	3·5
Raw cotton	8·3	16·3	13·3	5·3	3·7	2·5	2·8	2·8	1·8	2·8	0·7	3·1
Other textile raw materials	10·0	10·3	8·1	4·3	3·0	3·6	6·4	5·3	7·9	5·0	4·8	4·0
Hides, skins, leather	3·4	5·6	5·3	2·5	2·0	1·5	2·0	3·2	2·4	—	0·9	1·1
Peanuts, soybeans, etc.	0·1	...	...	...	...	...	...	...	0·1	3·7	3·3	1·5
Consumers' goods	20·7	8·3	...	—	—	—	—	—	4·8	15·2	18·3	23·9
Tea	4·5	3·9	3·3	1·9	1·1	1·1	1·6	2·8	—	—	0·3	0·8
Meat and milk	0·7	...	...	...	...	...	...	...	0·3	2·3	4·2	2·6
Cloth	2·7	0·1	...	...	...	...	...	...	0·4	3·9	2·9	3·0
Sugar	0·0	0·1	...	...	...	...	...	...	—	3·1	2·8	0·8
Fruits and Vegetables	2·8	1·8	—	—	—	—	—	—	1·9	0·5	1·4	2·4
Finished goods	56·3								50·4		65·0	63·7
Raw materials	43·7								49·6		35·0	36·3

NOTE: The dash (—) indicates that data are not available; may be negligible. The symbol (...) indicates that quantities are negligible.

SOURCE: This table and Table VIII/2 have been lifted almost bodily from Franklyn Holzman, 'Foreign Trade', Economic Trends in the Soviet Union, ed. Abram Bergson and Simon Kuznets (Cambridge, Mass., 1963), Tables VII/4 and VII/9. Holzman relies heavily on official Soviet classifications, and continuity of definition year by year is not assured.

The 'finished goods' and 'raw materials' data are from Narodnoye Khozyaistvo SSSR 1960 (Moscow, 1961), p. 747, and Vneshnyaya Torgovlya SSSR 1958 (Moscow, 1958), p. 11. The Soviet definition rather oddly places coal and coke, along with products of oil refining, in the finished goods category. Approximately to correct for this, we should transfer the following percentages from 'finished' to 'raw': 1938, exports 1%; 1955, exports 4%, imports 4%; 1960, exports 4%, imports 2%.

TABLE VIII/3. STRUCTURE OF UNITED STATES VISIBLE FOREIGN TRADE, 1820–1960
(percentage of total)

| | EXPORTS | | | | | IMPORTS | | | | |
	Crude Materials	Crude Foodstuffs	Manufactured Foodstuffs	Semi-Manufactures	Finished Manufactures	Crude Materials	Crude Foodstuffs	Manufactured Foodstuffs	Semi-Manufactures	Finished Manufactures
1820	61	4	19	10	6	6	11	20	7	56
1860	69	4	12	4	11	11	13	17	10	49
1870	57	11	13	4	15	13	12	22	13	40
1890	36	16	27	5	16	23	16	17	15	29
1910	34	6	15	16	29	37	9	12	18	24
1920	23	11	14	12	40	34	11	23	15	17
1929[a]	22	5	10	14	49	35	12	10	20	23
1939[a]	17	4	7	19	53	33	13	14	21	19
1950	19	7	6	11	57	28	20	10	25	17
1960	13	8	5	17	56	21	12	11	21	36

SOURCE: *Historical Statistics of the United States* (Washington, D.C., 1960), pp. 544–5; *Statistical Abstract of the United States* (Washington, D.C., 1964), p. 873.
[a] I have chosen these two years as less disturbed by slump and war.

guessed that machinery, on which such emphasis is laid, is rather labor-intensive; and Soviet agriculture certainly is. But while one has grown, the other has diminished, so it is difficult to know whether, compared with the Soviet economy as a whole, exports and imports are more labor- or capital-intensive, or whether they ever were, or how the relation has changed.

Messrs. Rubinshtein and Baksht add, not altogether unreasonably, that if ACCs have a 'more advanced' structure than the USSR, that is due to imperialism: their traders use political influence and economic bargaining power[1] to maintain the old colonialist trade structure. However, it is not *a priori* evident that that structure is unfavorable to the ex-colonies, as Marxists assume; see Chapter I, Section 9. Moreover, ACCs mainly trade with each other.

A striking proof of the falsity of theses A, D, E and F is that at the very moment of greatest Soviet industrialization the trade structure moved in most respects 'backward'. The products of agriculture and forestry were exported and machines were imported in greater proportion and indeed in greater volume than ever since the Revolution:

TABLE VIII/4. THE EFFECT OF THE FIRST FYP ON SOVIET TRADE STRUCTURE

(per cent of total visible exports or imports)

	1925–26, 1926–27	1927–28, 1929	1930, 1931	1937, 1938
Exports:				
Agricultural raw materials .	35·0	15·0	23·0	21·5
Slightly processed agricultural materials[a] .	11·0	11·5	10·0	5·5
Other raw materials[b] . .	24·5	31·5	26·5	40·0
Other . .	29·5	52·0	40·5	33·0
Imports:				
Machinery, equipment, metals .	30·5	30·0	60·5	56·5
Other . .	69·5	70·0	39·5	43·5

Volume index:	1925	1926	1927	1928	1929	1930	1931	1937	1938
Exports . .	76	90	93	100	107	129	101	49	38
Imports . .	87	72	80	100	93	111	116	32	34

SOURCE: A. Baykov, *Soviet Foreign Trade* (Princeton, N.J., 1946), Tables I, IV, V, VI.
[a] Sugar, oil-cake, tinned fish, tobacco, 'Bladders, casings and sausage-skins', caviar, vegetable oils, glycerine.
[b] Wood, fur, coal, ore, asbestos, fertilizer.

[1] Not to mention GATT and IMF, I would add.

To the Western mind this is obvious: an industrializing country *should* behave like this, and Stalin was very rational. But Soviet historians like to hurry over this aspect of the first five-year plan, and on to the second, when the trade structure became more 'respectable' again, even if only very slightly. Broadly speaking, then, the Soviet trade structure has behaved 'improperly'.

One Communist country at least is under no comradely necessity to import from Czechoslovakia: Czechoslovakia. A model of orthodoxy in so many other matters, so it has also been in its trade structure (Table VIII/5). It has clearly been *forced* to specialize in machinery exports: there was no such specialization in 1936. Indeed right up to 1950 the process would have been natural. For in 1945–48 Bohemia was one of the few undestroyed industrial centers between the Rhine and the Volga, and moreover it had benefited from wartime German investment. So Czechoslovakia would have quite rationally turned to making almost anything her neighbors really wanted, being in a better position to make everything than any other supplier. As to the prolongation of this trend after 1950, it is not certain that Stalin rather than Gottwald took the necessary decisions, for they typify a certain kind of Communist megalomania. They give the background for the b.o.p. crisis of 1963 (see Chapter V, above). The figures also show the exhaustion of the Czechoslovak mines, which has doubtless been inevitable; the habitual Communist failure in agriculture; and a curious reversion to type in the matter of manufactured consumer goods.

The Bulgarian frontier changes (in 1941) were very small, and the statistics contain very full figures on 'structure' (Table VIII/6). Thus Bulgaria too has played the game of structure more according to Marxist rules than the USSR. Yet she has now apparently settled down with a structure that is still far from Marxist respectability, and was, indeed, recently commended by a Soviet author for so doing.[1] This is in connection with the recent drive for a better division of labor among STEs: Bulgaria will continue to sell food and buy machinery, thus differentiating the rate of installation of plant from the rate of its domestic production.[2]

With Poland, of course, pre-war comparisons are meaningless. It suffices to say that on the import side there was no exciting structural change from 1955 to 1960. On the export side, coal and coke, 51% of all visible exports in 1955, fell by one quarter in

---

[1] S. Stepanov, *Vneshnyaya Torgovlya*, 1/1962.
[2] Cf. Wiles, op. cit., pp. 296–7.

TABLE VIII/5. CZECHOSLOVAK TRADE STRUCTURE, SELECTED YEARS, 1936-60
(percentages of total visible exports or imports)

	1936 Exports	1936 Imports	1948 Exports	1948 Imports	1950 Exports	1950 Imports	1955 Exports	1955 Imports	1960 Exports	1960 Imports
Machines	6	8	20·3	7·2	26	11	43·5	13·3	45·1	21·7
Fuel, minerals, metals	28	20	23·0	20·1			28·6	24·2	19·7	27·7
Chemical materials, fertilizers, rubber	4	8	5·5	8·7	⎱ 35	⎱ 61	2·9	8·5	2·8	9·2
Building materials and other industrial materials	0	0	5·1	0·5	⎰	⎰	2·1	0·9	1·5	0·9
Materials of agricultural origin	28	30	9·9	27·2	⎱ 13	⎱ 26	5·7	20·0	5·2	15·2
Livestock	0	4	0·0	0·2			0·0	0·0	0·1	0·1
Materials for food	6	11	1·7	19·5	⎰	⎰	2·8	16·0	1·8	11·0
Finished foodstuffs	6	13	3·8	13·9			3·3	13·0	3·4	10·9
Inedible consumer goods	20	3	30·7	2·7	25	2	11·1	4·1	20·4	3·3
(Omitted)	(2)	(3)								

SOURCE: *Annuaire Statistique de la République Tchécoslovaque* (Prague, 1938), pp. 136–7; *Statistická Ročenka ČSSR* (Prague, 1961), pp. 374–5, xix. The 1936 figures have been analysed by me and are approximate. The 1950 figures were read off a rather ill-printed graph. The 1948 figures are from *Facts on Czechoslovak Foreign Trade*, Chamber of Commerce of Czechoslovakia, 1963, pp. 81, 84.

TABLE VIII/6. BULGARIAN TRADE STRUCTURE, SELECTED YEARS, 1939–60
(percentages of total visible exports or imports)

	1939		1955		1958		1959		1960	
	Exports	Imports	Exports	Imports	Exports	Imports	Exports	Imports	Exports	Imports
'Tools of labor'	0·0	31·0	2·5	50·8	7·9	33·3	12·1	37·2	13·2	39·9
'Materials of labor':										
From agriculture and forestry	68·4	26·5	35·0	13·1	24·7	15·4	26·4	16·2	26·3	15·0
From mining, metallurgy, and oil	0·2	23·1	23·9	30·7	17·0	37·2	13·3	34·1	11·1	32·4
'Objects of consumption':										
From agriculture	31·4	9·0	38·3	1·7	49·2	8·3	47·4	6·8	48·0	7·6
From industry	0·0	10·4	0·3	3·7	1·2	5·8	0·8	5·7	1·4	5·1

SOURCE: *Statisticheski Godishnik* (Sofia), December, 1961, p. 303.

relative volume to account for only 26% in 1960. It need not then surprise us that all other exports, including food and minerals, improved their 'structural' position.[1]

Generalizing, it would seem that since about 1955 deliberate structural distortion ceased in European Communist foreign trade; the countries settled down with their then structures. The only exception is Hungary, which was going through a crisis at that time and has since effected an improvement in her structure that we shall not depreciate with quotation marks (Table V/4).

16

Now take thesis G: we must specialize in what is new or sophisticated. Even though the weight of a country's exports lies in manufactured goods it can still be in important senses a primitive country. It may, for instance, only be able to sell its manufactures to other primitive countries. Thus, the average advanced STE, with its strong specialization in manufactures and specifically machinery, is found on examination still incapable of selling sophisticated goods to ACCs. Trading in this direction, it has to rely upon its natural resources. The weight of its manufacturing exports goes to protected markets: either other STEs or non-Communist UDCs taking its bilateral aid, anxious for the stability of bilateral agreements, afraid of Western imperialism, or whatever it may be.

A good illustration of this is the USSR itself. Table VIII/7 gives the combined figures for 1960–61.

TABLE VIII/7. SOVIET VISIBLE TRADE STRUCTURE BY AREAS

	(i) Soviet Visible Exports to ACCs[2]	(ii) Whole World	(iii) (i) As % of (ii)
All goods—mn. R. .	1645·0	10403·9	16·3
Machines—mn. R. .	31·6	1895·3	1·4
Petroleum products (excl. crude)— mn. tons .	125·8	332·2	47·7
Rolled iron and steel—thou. tons .	1432	57462	2·6
Steel pipes—thou. tons .	4·6	435·4	1·0
Cotton textiles—mn. metres .	174	3924	4·5
Refrigerators—thou. .	0	39·8	0
TV sets—thou. .	0	182·3	0
Watches—thou. .	57·5	8786·0	0·7

[1] *Rocznik Statystyczny 1961* (Warsaw, 1961), pp. 208, 269, 272.

[2] W. Europe except Yugoslavia, Finland, Iceland (excluded because of their political bias towards Soviet exports); USA, Canada, Mexico, Argentina, Uruguay, Japan; Australia, N.Z. Source for whole table: *Vneshnyaya Torgovlya SSSR 1961* (Moscow, 1962), Table VIII.

Thus, the USSR finds it difficult to sell sophisticated products to ACCs except when she works up one of her major natural resources (crude oil). Yet, taken over-all, her export structure is hardly 'primitive'.

Even with Finland, a country not very advanced and much under its influence, trade figures show the USSR to be a comparatively 'primitive' country.[1] This is because Finnish machinery and consumer good standards are Scandinavian.

A still more sophisticated way of being primitive is the British. It is not that Britain fails to sell manufactures to other ACCs, but that the particular manufactures are not of the most sophisticated sort. Thus in 1961 Britain had both a lower trade turnover and a lower favorable balance than her main competitors in the newest categories of manufacture, where novelty may be taken as good evidence of sophistication (Table VIII/8). In this table row 5 eliminates the effects of size.[2] It shows that the United States, the most sophisticated country, has an actual deficit in the least sophisticated articles, while the United Kingdom has a sizable surplus in them and a significantly smaller surplus in the most sophisticated articles.

Britain is thus part-way over to the position of a real UDC, which characteristically exports cheap textiles and imports food in order to keep its teeming population alive. She has fallen into a more sophisticated version of the same 'technology trap', and unlike the USSR has not the protected markets through which she can get out of it.[3]

All of which makes gloomy reading, but the way out is not, of course, directly to force nor even to subsidize exports of the new goods. Indeed, in two notorious cases, precisely that has been done, with government money: jet aircraft and atomic power stations. Both of these have been prestigious money-losers. For Britain's present adjustment must be presumed to be the one most immediately profitable in view of her factor endowment, and such changes would be a waste of that endowment. The solution is to improve the endowment; i.e., to push technology forward in a general way,

[1] Hustich, op. cit.

[2] Size is taken to be, not population or real national income or even total trade, but total turnover in manufacturing trade (Turnover, row 4). The logic of this is that some countries are naturally more autarkic than others (which excludes the first two standardizers), and that natural resources are irrelevant to our argument (which excludes the third).

[3] Except, of course, by breaking the CoCom embargo, and selling to STEs. The failure to sell elsewhere no doubt partially explains this action. Incidentally, the British failure to export new goods is not a new thing. Alfred Marshall drew attention to it in 1903: 'Memorandum on the Fiscal Policy of International Trade', in *Official Papers of Alfred Marshall* (London, 1926), paras. 59–70.

and see what happens. Even so, however, we must bear in mind that *some* country should be making the row 3 goods; if foreign enterprise is lacking in these fields then even a more technically advanced Britain should continue to specialize in them. In just the

TABLE VIII/8. BRITISH TRADE IN MANUFACTURES, 1961 (md. $)

	UK	USA	West Germany
1. The 15 most rapidly growing product-groups:			
Exports	2·4	4·3	3·9
Imports	1·1	0·9	1·1
Turnover . . .	3·5	5·2	5·0
Balances	1·3	3·3	2·8
2. Other engineering and chemicals, chemical products:			
Exports	3·3	5·1	3·8
Imports	0·5	1·4	0·7
Turnover . . .	3·8	6·5	4·5
Balances	2·7	3·8	3·0
3. Other manufactures:			
Exports	3·3	3·9	3·7
Imports	2·3	5·1	3·3
Turnover . . .	5·6	9·0	7·0
Balances	1·0	−1·2	0·4
4. All manufactures:			
Exports	9·0	13·3	11·3
Imports	4·0	7·4	5·1
Turnover . . .	13·0	20·7	16·4
Balances	5·0	5·9	6·2
5. The four balances standardized:			
1	1·3	2·1	2·2
2	2·7	2·4	2·4
3	1·0	−0·8	0·3
4	5·0	3·7	4·9

SOURCE: T. Barna in *The Times* (London), August 12, 1963. Row 5 and the turnover figures are my own work. Figures may not add because of rounding. Row 1 products are all engineering or chemical, and had been growing faster than all other groups in trade among MEs.

same way the Finno-Soviet trade pattern, and the pattern of trade between the USSR and the main ACCs, and the patterns of over-populated UDCs, are all 'the best trade-patterns we've got'.

17

That leaves us with H, the forced diversification of our exports. Should we pursue this, then, for its own sake and in a manner neutral to labor- versus capital-intensity, the fabrication of our own raw materials, and all the rest? This of all our theses seems to be the only rational one. For there is a genuine divergence of private and social profit here, due to the foreign-trade multiplier. This is the same as to say, 'due to the local action of the multiplier', a phrase often used in location economics. For the important thing in each case is the concentration of multiplier effects within a small territory. The argument goes as follows: let pre-1959 Cuba earn $1/3$ of her national income Y from sugar exports S, and let $\Delta Y/\Delta S = 2 \cdot 5$. For realism, this need not be the formal foreign-trade multiplier, but the expected total effect on national income after monetary and fiscal policy have been adjusted to the b.o.p. deficit that inevitably follows a decline in sugar earnings. Let Y be originally 9, and another $(1/5)Y$ originate in manufactures M, which supply only the domestic market. Let the marginal propensity to consume manufactures be $1/3$. So $S = 3$, $M = 1 \cdot 8$. Then if $\Delta S = -1 \cdot 0$, $\Delta Y = -2 \cdot 5$, $\Delta S/S = -0 \cdot 33$, $\Delta M/M = -0 \cdot 46$. A decline like one third is unpleasant, but if in boom times there is no surplus capacity it may mean no more than that the sugar trade has fallen to the break-even point. But a decline like one half—which occurs in manufacturing—means bankruptcy. Therefore, it is much less risky for an individual to invest in sugar, even though the economy has a high over-all rate of risk precisely because it has specialized in sugar.[1]

Another, simpler, divergence of private and social profit occurs if the country's central bank has small reserves. These are endangered by specialization in foreign trade. Without cost to itself, the individual firm imposes on the country the necessity to carry higher reserves.

But if the need to diversify against the promptings of the free market must receive the blessing of the most classically minded economist, we must yet insist that it does not necessarily point toward manufacturing industry, still less, of course, toward capital- or labor-intensity. We preach diversification to agricultural countries more, because they have not practiced it, indeed, mostly have been quite unable to afford it. But a mere diversification of their agriculture would be enough. On the other hand, we do not preach to industrial countries because industry is naturally diverse. Moreover, such countries mostly give agricultural subsidies, and so

[1] With acknowledgments to International Bank for Reconstruction and Development, *Report on Cuba* (Baltimore, Md., 1951), pp. 524–6. A similar analysis could clearly be applied to the accelerator.

practice diversity in this way, too; how wisely, we can see from the exceptions of the USSR and Czechoslovakia, which have permitted their agriculture to slip (see Chapter V, above).

18

Artificial diversification is clearly most incumbent on small countries. Yet one can diversify far too much, and this was a grave fault of Stalin's policy for his satellites, with the possible exceptions of the DDR and Czechoslovakia. Had he lived long enough to produce nine little USSRs, the economies of scale would have been criminally underexploited (see Chapter XII, below). He did not do this, to be sure, in the sacred name of diversification, which is not a Marxist dogma, but in that of industrialization, and most particularly because of his adherence to thesis F. There is in the Marxist imagination only one perfect society, and each quite small area must reproduce it.

For structure presents in many ways another 'small-country problem'. In a free market a small country develops as is most profitable, and that is in all but macro-economic respects the fastest way to develop.[1] It may turn out with an impeccably Marxist internal and external structure like Belgium, or fairly creditable ones like Holland and Denmark, which are suitably industrialized and urbanized as a whole but export rather a lot of food for Marxist tastes. But it may turn out altogether queer, like Norway with its shipping, and it may turn out downright heretical, like the horrendous case of New Zealand, which contradicts nearly everything everybody says about industrialization.

When we consider structure, a small country is often just an area of some larger unit; and the Marxist's structural vision of the future is not obviously wrong in all respects (I can put it no higher) for large units, in particular for the world. But the fact is that Marxist location theory forbids even areas in a country to specialize much; at least, they must all develop industry, even heavy industry.[2] So Bulgaria cannot shrug off the problem on the ground that she is just New Zealand to the USSR's Britain, for the USSR should have no purely agricultural provinces even within her boundaries. Nor would Bulgaria's Party leaders in any case be inclined to take such a position, any more than an *oblast'* committee secretary in the

[1] Wiles, *The Political Economy of Communism*, Chapters 14–16.
[2] Ibid., Chapter 9.

USSR. For these minor Party leaders are also Marxists, and it belongs to their *amour propre* to industrialize the area they have in charge.

19

Yet as a micro-criterion for the day-to-day choice of goods to sell and buy, 'structure' surely has not played a big part in *Soviet* foreign trade. For the USSR has industrialized in an orthodox Marxist way, but has hardly undergone the orthodox change of trade structure, although a proportionally trivial effort, on the scale of the national income, could have achieved a great change in trade. Thus let industry provide one-half of a country's national income and also of its exports, but let exports be only 4% of national income—a situation characteristic of the USSR. Then it suffices that industry grow by 2%, and that we find foreign markets for this instead of other exports, to bump up industry's share from a half to three-quarters.

Thus in a general way Soviet trade structure seems to be more something for ideologists and economists to talk about, whether boastfully or in self-deprecation, than for planners to manipulate. But not so with the smaller European STEs. Our chapter begins with a highly official Polish declaration of intent to make 'structural' trouble with West Germany. The Yugoslav quarrel with the USSR (1948) was in part about structure, and the Rumanian (1963) wholly so. Of course, behind the structure of trade lies that of the economy as a whole, and the main argument on both occasions was about the latter. But the USSR is at least not supposed to intervene in her satellites' long-term domestic planning. Even at the height of Stalinism, let alone today, it is easier for her to argue about what she shall export to and import from the erring satellite.

Such arguments present the difficulty, how shall two countries with the same structure-snobbery trade with each other? Curious cases do occur. In 1946–50, West European countries, hostile to importing consumer goods (thesis E), nevertheless continued to make each their own traditional, most luxurious and prestigious consumer goods, as the strongest parts of their separate export drives. So lace was traded reluctantly against champagne, or pushed upon the unwilling buyer of coal as a condition of sale. Among the Comecon countries of today we see (Section 15, above) that 'socialist brotherhood' has—or is alleged to have—to be brought into play to make the USSR accept the machinery of the DDR and Czechoslovakia, which, as the senior Communist country, she should be making for herself. Clearly, countries without these prejudices make easier trading partners.

A compromise, enabling each country to satisfy the same snobbery and yet trade, is what we may call 'microspecialization'. Let each STE specialize in a particular kind of machinery for export, or agree to import and export particular kinds of consumer good. The USSR proposed something like this to Rumania in 1962, which, however, has insisted on developing her 'A' industry all round.[1] This solution implies a balance not only in imports and exports but also in particular subcategories, a restraint as damaging to the expansion of the total as is bilateralism between countries. Indeed, both restraints tend to be applied together.

20

But, however silly the Soviet proposal was, it at least aimed at having trade. The Rumanian counterproposal was a lot sillier. It was quite simply that Rumania should aim at 'all-round development', which in a small country is nothing better than autarky. Rumania, in fact, aimed at a particular *domestic* structure, and was indifferent to her foreign-trade structure, indeed, to foreign trade. This whole episode seems, indeed, to have been a classic instance of technological or structural chauvinism. Mr. John Scott gives us its authentic flavor:

'Why,' I asked them, 'do you [as Rumanians] want a steel mill? You have the best oilfields in Europe. Why don't you put your money into petro-chemical industries, and make yourselves the best in the world in that field, rather than spend maybe $2 billion on three steel mills when you have no good ore and not enough coking coal?'
The directors lashed back: 'You talk like a Russian.'[2]

The Rumanians resemble in this respect Khrushchev's domestic Stalinist enemies, the 'metal-eaters'. Like so many technological chauvinists, they are technologically behind the times. Steel, Stalin's eponymous metal, was a fine object for this type of emotion in the 'thirties and 'forties. It figured largely in the plans of UDCs (and Greece and Norway) as late as the 'fifties. But in the 'sixties precisely petrochemicals would be a more natural fetish. 'Metal-eating' might

[1] J. F. Brown, in *Survey*, October, 1963.
[2] In *Eastern Europe* (Munich, January, 1965).

almost be regarded as a distinct structural fallacy on its own. It is certainly the best possible illustration of this chapter's central theme: foreign-trade planning is a matter of emotions.

21

These emotions, moreover, are virtually indefensible. It is difficult to conceive of any *coherent* value system which would justify any one of the theses we have condemned. Admittedly, the economist's business is to draw the technical consequences only of other people's value judgments—and no economist is more conscious of this limitation than those our unfortunate colleagues who live in totalitarian countries. But it is surely our duty to probe a little beneath the surface of our 'clients'' instructions—just as would a conscientious lawyer. *Why* did the late Mr. Gheorgiu-Dej want more steel? Or if labor-intensity is humiliating, is not unemployment in our client's view intolerable? Has he really thought out his 'instructions' to us?

In the light of such considerations, I assert that, except for diversification in small countries, 'structure' per se *ought not to be an object of economic policy*. There are primary aims of policy like sheer armed might, economic warfare, civilian welfare, and full employment, and secondary aims such as forced investment, more perfect competition, inflation, sound money, autarky, a greater international division of labor—whichever we think will serve our primary purposes. A defined 'structure', whether of the economy as a whole or of foreign trade in particular, is not even a secondary aim. It should simply be the result of pursuing these other aims. Thus, if we want reliably full employment we must diversify our exports; if we want more perfect competition or sound money we must have free trade, and this means simply accepting whatever foreign-trade structure heaven sends; if we want sheer armed might we must trade in nothing very much and preferably manufactured consumer goods at that; in order to wage economic warfare we need a very flexible structure, autarkic if we are attacked, specialized if we are attacking, etc., etc.

22

Most important of all, however, what kind of structure do we want for the growth of the whole economy? The answer is, whatever appears *ex post* to have happened to suit it. Thus, it is very true that advanced economies are capital-intensive. But we certainly do not want a structural bias in favor of capital intensity in particular industries; rather a general use of capital in the best proportions everywhere, considering its present scarcity.[1] And exports have no special claim.

There is scarcely such a thing as a primitive economic structure; there is only the structure appropriate to a primitive technology. As techniques improve the structure is indeed likely to shift away from direct agricultural employment, and certainly from labor-intensity; but toward what products, only the then constellation of world trade and technology can tell us. It may pay us to specialize in particular agricultural or consumer good exports, even if only to import and install more capital goods at home. It will certainly pay us for a long time to persist in moderately labor-intensive techniques. When we finally become fully developed we must remember that there are sophisticated ways of producing simple things: the sophistication lies in the techniques used, not the products chosen, and the uneven international endowment of 'land' should receive as much consideration as ever.

[1] Wiles, op. cit., Chapters 14–16.

CHAPTER IX

SETTLING THE TERMS OF TRADE[1]

A: I am trying to sell my dog.
B: How much do you want for it?
A: 4000 zlotys.
B: What, for that mongrel? Are you out of your mind? It isn't worth 100.
A: You wait, I'll get my price.
Later
B: Hello, where's your dog?
A: I sold it, and for 4000.
B: Don't be absurd.
A: Oh yes I did. You see there was this man with two 2000 zloty cats. . . .

> —I have heard this story now in Jewish circles in New York and in Warsaw, and like to think it is of nineteenth-century Polish-Jewish origin.

[1] I am very grateful to Mr. Paul Marer for correcting a number of errors.

I

In international economics, as we have seen, the STE is a large enterprise as well as a country, while the ME is only a country. In an ME, the state 'intervenes'; in an STE, state and economy are one. One could say that there is no trade between MEs, only between enterprises within MEs. All this is particularly evident in trade between an STE and an ME, the purest form of which occurs when the STE is small and the ME big. The STE in this case is or ought to be merely a large enterprise among others, nor, indeed, always among the largest: Albania could never make such a splash in the British b.o.p. as the United States Ford company, with its $367 mn. stock purchase.[1]

Much follows from this simple proposition. First, it is not in the least obvious why a small STE and a large ME annually negotiate a trade protocol. Consider, first, the ME. The strategic export ban, if any, can be enforced in a dozen other ways. Tariffs are, of course, levied on imports as they enter in any case. Exchange control is not normally negotiated at annual intervals; if that is desirable, the ME needs also an annual protocol with other MEs. And needless to say, the exact bill of goods in the protocol cannot be guaranteed by the state presiding over the ME, since it is not an importer or exporter; yet it is the state that signs the protocol. All this looks suspiciously like 'epiphenomenal planning'.[2]

Perhaps the STE needs to negotiate such a protocol? The answer is, certainly not. The USSR never did so before the war, until the growing bilateralism of MEs forced it upon her (see Chapter X, Section 14). After all, how could any enterprise benefit from revealing its plans?

Moreover, although the protocol is, of course, by its nature bilaterally negotiated, it does not have to provide for 'reciprocity' i.e., an equivalence of payments and receipts on current account (se Chapter X, Section 1). A positive or negative balance is ofte: agreed on in the protocol, and if the ME is big and the STE sma this balance should be of no greater interest to the ME than i prospective balance with any other small country.

[1] In December, 1960, of stock in British Ford. I assume above that Albania is acting on own behalf, not China's.
[2] P. J. D. Wiles, *The Political Economy of Communism*, pp. 73–6.

We have here a genuine mystery, which talk with many trade officials of MEs and STEs has not cleared up for me. It would appear as if exchange control, originally introduced by certain ACCs in the mid-1930s, rendered some kind of discussion necessary between one country and another, at irregular intervals; and that the extension of this practice to an annually negotiated protocol is due to STEs, which need them between each other and so have simply extended the practice by force of habit, even though it is to their disadvantage. Certain it is that the government of an ME exercises all sorts of improper pressures on its own economy during such discussions: protecting this industry and encouraging the exports of that, in a manner entirely contrary to the rules of the free-trade game. Yet these rules ought to apply to such a case. For they are really there to protect countries against themselves, and their violation causes resources to be misallocated within the negotiating ME.

The undoubted fact that resources are also misallocated within the STE is neither here nor there, from the point of view of its trading partner. We should not ask why supply and demand are as they are in the world market; unless we suspect some grave instability we should simply accept them, and adapt ourselves accordingly. If some of this environment is due to STEs, that makes no difference. Even when we know they are acting quite irrationally, that is their affair. There is, then, no *a priori* case for treating Albania differently from the Ford Motor Company.

2

The one case for an annual protocol is that of trade between a small ME and a large STE. But then, small countries have quite generally to be careful and think twice before they approach large ones, and relative size seems to matter as much as the economic model of either trading partner. We are thus driven to discuss small and large countries as such.

In the theory of comparative costs the position of the small country is quite simple: it stands to gain more than the large one from the international division of labor. That is to say, autarky hits it harder, since it can provide neither the factors nor the markets needed to enjoy the economies of scale. A hypothetical movement from autarky to free trade would disturb its structure more than that of a large country; and the degree of disturbance is a good measure of the long-term gains from trade.

For the rest, however, we are uninterested in the size of countries under free trade. Once a country is fully integrated into the world market its size no longer matters. A very large firm can settle anywhere; if it happens to settle in a small country it enjoys the economies of scale through international trade; if in a large one, through domestic trade. The matter is one of indifference, and the firm will settle in accordance with the principles of location economics, not international economics. Of course, it may well have to draw its capital from some foreign source, but that is in no way unrealistic, nor normally undesirable (see Chapter XIV, Section 2). Most of these points are empirically well illustrated by Swiss chemicals and Swedish office machinery. Similarly, free trade in money spreads unemployment and full employment almost indifferently among countries that trade freely in goods. The monetary and trade connections are nearly as intimate between a small country and 'abroad' as, *ceteris paribus*,[1] between a region and the rest of a large country; therefore, multiplier and speculative effects are only in a minor degree concentrated within the boundaries of the country where they arise.

Only perhaps in one semi-economic way is size of country interesting under free trade. This is what the Americans used to call the 'problem of the overmighty subject'. The threat posed by John D. Rockefeller to the United States federal government was as nothing to that posed by United Fruit to Nicaragua. A large capitalist firm may have a turnover about as big as the national incomes of some of the small, backward countries with which it deals. Even quite advanced countries, with rather incorruptible governments, like Ireland and Norway, can face serious b.o.p. problems if they quarrel, say, over taxation, with large foreign firms. It is much as if such a firm were to have an argument with a county council or one of the less populous states of the United States. But this subject is outside our field.

3

However, the moment the state intervenes, this is all changed. A small country cannot manipulate its terms of trade so well, since it is much less likely to be in a monopolistic position. It is less free

---

[1] I say *ceteris paribus* because one can very easily conceive of a region that is more isolated by geography and underdevelopment than any country. Our interest here is in the effects purely attributable to being a separate country.

to expand the domestic money supply, since its marginal propensity to import is in all probability greater. It can hardly wage economic war. In any international negotiation, say, about tariff reductions or the formation of customs unions, its bargaining power is small. On the other side, if it runs a persistent surplus on current account it will not be deflating the world; and its various other 'misdemeanors' may also be overlooked.

In a word, in the nineteenth century *firms* adapted themselves to a rather perfect world market, and there was no problem of *country* size. In the twentieth, countries and firms must both adapt themselves, and country size is as important as firm size.

Revenant à nos moutons, take first a small ME and a large STE. It matters a great deal how big are the STE's purchases and sales in relation to the ME's economy, while the converse is hardly important; only rarely is a single corporation in an ME of vital importance to an STE. Thus, if Albania does business in the United States, the event is less important to the United States than a decision by one of dozens of domestic and foreign corporations. But if the USSR does business in Sweden, it raises problems of 'structure' and the foreign-trade multiplier, not to mention the prices of particular goods. Indeed, it is much the same when any large decision is taken *inside* a small ME: the larger the one and the smaller the other the more macro-economic and political the matter is, i.e., the more external economies there are.

So it is rational for both the industry concerned and the government in, say, Sweden to consider all the external economies and diseconomies of a purchase or sale by, say, the USSR, and control it accordingly. We may consider the USSR's effect on Sweden under the following purely economic headings:

(i) the risks entailed by a specialized country-wise distribution of Swedish purchases and sales;

(ii) the risks entailed by a specialized commodity structure of Swedish purchases and sales;

(iii) multiplier effects;

(iv) vulnerability to economic war;

(v) oligopoly-oligopsony effects on Swedish prices.

The micro-economic effects (v) are best considered when we turn from the ME's government to the reactions of its individual firms.

Considerations (i) and (ii)—country-wise and commodity-wise specialization—influence the Swedish government at all times in one direction only: restriction. There are scarcely any advantages in such specialization. Even the economies of scale gained by Swedish industry are negligible compared with the risk of a switch in trade; indeed, it requires new investment to attain such economies, and this puts the industry in a very exploitable position. On such grounds, the Swedish Government intervened in 1940 to prevent an enormous Soviet order for railway wagon wheels,[1] which would have totally occupied and, indeed, transformed this branch of its engineering industry.

Not all the dangers of over-specialization are perceptible to, or even borne by, the enterprises concerned. If, for instance, the foreign-trade multiplier is high, and home manufactures have a high income-elasticity of demand, the deleterious effects of over-specialization are quite devastating, and yet private profit leads investors to increase it. This is the Cuban case described in Chapter VIII. For the most part, the other dangers of specialization are visible to the enterprises concerned, and the government of the small ME need not worry about them.

We have already illustrated consideration (iii)—the multiplier effects against which precautions should be taken. But in given circumstances these effects can be positive, and sharply expanded trade with an STE can be highly desirable. Diplomacy can often turn on such trade as with a tap, calling in the noncyclical Soviet-type market to balance a downswing in the capitalist world. The great case of this is the Swedish loan to the USSR in 1946 (Chapter XVIII, Section 14). In common with nearly every economist in the world, and relying on an oversimplified Keynesian analysis, the Swedish Government expected a United States slump in 1947. Almost alone among governments, however, it had the wisdom to take avoiding action, negotiating a very large loan to ensure un-requited exports to the USSR instead. The whole scheme turned, as such schemes will, to dust and ashes: econometrics turned out to be unable as yet (can it now?) to predict the United States economy, and the USSR for some reason failed to use up the loan (see Chapter XIV, Section 9). But on the information available to a normally intelligent man in 1946, it was a wise move.

4

Our fourth heading for the precautions a small ME should take

---

[1] Some have it that the producers themselves refused the orders. Cf. also L. I. Frei, *Mezh-dunarodnye Raschety i Organizovanié Vneshnei Torgovli Sotsialisticheskikh Stran* (Moscow, 1960), p. 211. One wonders, however, whether Nazi influence did not play a part.

is vulnerability to economic war. As we shall see in Chapter XVI, the more a small country trades with a large one the more it exposes itself to every weapon of economic war. The precise economic model of the larger country has been, historically, rather unimportant.

Thus the exploitation of Finland by the USSR is described in Chapter XVII. But this case arose out of defeat in war, and excessive reparations. Cuba is, or was, much more dependent on the United States, and yet the influence of politics was no greater here, and the United States is not an STE. In part this more devastating result was due to the pure geographical chance of propinquity and climate. It is true, also, that there is no *command* mechanism in an ACC that could so divert its foreign trade and investment as to overspecialize another country—which is what the USSR did to Finland. But trade preferences and diplomatic protection for investments can work results just as striking. Indeed, the machinery of imperialism need not be brought into play at all. The market alone brought Denmark, through her bacon, into a parlous dependence on Britain; geography alone places Holland at the mercy of German transit trade and, therefore, of German transport planners seeking to find new employment for Hamburg and Bremen.

5

The small ME, then, must take special precautions with regard to all large countries, however organized. The small STE, on the other hand, takes such precautions automatically, since it plans every detail of its foreign trade, and the enterprise-state distinction is unimportant. Thus in matters of undue specialization, etc., it is the master of its own fate, and can automatically enforce its judgment even against the largest ME or STE—unless subjected to diplomatic pressure or economic warfare. Nor are there any multiplier or other monetary problems, with whomever it trades. The marginal propensity to import being zero (see Chapter III), it is as well placed to have an independent domestic inflation as the largest STE, and better placed than a large ME. But inflation and deflation can never be induced from without, since there is no multiplier and a speculative influx of money is impossible. As to the international division of labor, in so far as an STE wishes to or can exploit it, a small one is likely to benefit more, for the same reason as any small country. But the small STE's main problem is quite simply that, since a

Communist country *is* a large enterprise, *all trade is a matter of bargaining between states* and, therefore, between unequals. The Soviet foreign trade system positively invites large states to exploit small ones and wage economic warfare against them, since it is quite straightforwardly an oligopoly. After all, I.C.I. and G.E.C. do not hesitate to throw their weight about when they meet small firms; it is the logic of profit maximization that tells them to do so. The ideology of Communism, with its absolute insistence on the equality of all men and nations, is indeed strong enough to counteract the desire for profit when Communist states trade, but nationalism is stronger again than Communism, and pulls the other way.

6

In particular the STE is tempted to *dump*. The great case of this is timber in the early 1930s. Timber merchants did campaign against Soviet timber exports, threatening importers with the indirect boycott.[1] The charge of dumping, in so far as applicable to an STE, was justified. But even so, the agitation drew much of its strength from politics: the entirely justified complaint that the Soviet wood had been cut by forced labor.[2] Without this element, it is very doubtful if the campaign would have lasted. To judge its effectiveness would, of course, require a major research effort.

In those early days it was still possible to speak of Soviet dumping as sale below Soviet domestic costs converted at the official rate of exchange. The increasing irrationality of Soviet-type wholesale prices, the omission of interest and rent, and the ludicrous stability of exchange rates in the face of inflation, have long since rendered such simplicities out of date. But just what complexities can replace them?

There is, certainly, such a thing as selling below domestic cost in an STE. When the rationalizing procedures discussed in Chapter VII have been gone through, and all factors of production are duly priced, the tax water has been wrung out and the correct shadow rate of exchange applied, we can demonstrate that there is, or is not, 'shadow dumping'. But nobody seems to be interested. We only cry 'Soviet dumping' when Soviet exports perceptibly lower world prices. In just the same way we do not bother if a capitalist competitor sells at or above our own going price, whatever his costs.

Dumping, meaning sale below domestic cost, is an *argument*

---

[1] I.e., we shall make your customers boycott you by threatening to boycott them.
[2] A. W. Pim and E. Bateson, *Report on Russian Timber Camps* (London, 1931). For Soviet-type dumping generally cf. J. Wilczynski in *Journal of Political Economy*, June 1966.

people use, like 'cheap labor'. The analysis of Soviet costs is the merest rationalization; what matters is the effect on price. And rightly so, for the world economy, as we have had occasion to observe before, is as it is. Queer foreigners have queer supply curves, and these are among the things that determine world prices. If they choose to supply at below cost—we may skate over the question of marginal versus average cost here—that is their affair. *Caveat venditor,* and anyway it improves our terms of trade. All that we may fairly demand is stability, so that we may adapt ourselves according to our own comparative *costs* to the comparative *prices* that the world market sets. What most irks people about dumping is that it stops and starts; selling above cost is more predictable.

Now Soviet-type dumping *is* reasonably predictable. For whatever irrational reasons an STE decides to export a particular thing, it does on the whole continue to do so. It does appear[1] that Soviet-type trade, particularly exports, is more unstable than that of ACCs, and no doubt the neglect of costs is important here. But other causes, such as planner's tension, probably matter more, for the trade of UDCs is still less stable, and in these market economies costs do count.

Except in sudden depressions, when we sell things *already* produced below the cost they *had,* dumping is irrational. Much of this book is a sermon against Soviet-type 'shadow-dumping', i.e. the deliberate production of something in order to sell it below the true shadow cost. Nothing in this section excuses such trade from the point of view of the exporting STE. We criticize only the view of the outside world, which we shall understand better when we bear in mind its institutional basis in capitalism. An ACC fears imports and desires exports, while an STE does just the opposite (Chapter XV). Again international trade is not between ACCs but between enterprises in them. As far as the country is concerned, dumping improves its terms of trade and is not an unmixed curse. It is the separate, sovereign enterprise, an institution unknown to STEs, that complains—and then only if its product competes with imports.

<h2 style="text-align:center">7</h2>

It is rather notorious that STEs do not throw their weight about in world markets. The only case apart from Soviet timber that

[1] From unfinished statistical enquiries by the writer. Stability is defined as the percentage variation year by year.

comes to mind is the nasty break in the price of tin in September 1958, due to large Soviet sales, which attracted much unfavorable comment. But for whom was the break nasty? Evidently not for those notorious importers of tin, the NATO powers, but for Malaya, shortly to become independent. After the first flurry the Western press could find no better explanation of this event than a Soviet error, both political and economic; and surely they were right.[1] There are those to whom all history is a conspiracy, and most of its protagonists rational, and these either black or white. The facts are otherwise. In the strictly economic sense, STEs are fair traders, not bad to do business with if their slowness be excused. Knowledgeable traders known to me—who are, in the absence of very lengthy researches, my only source—think that they exploit neither monopoly nor monopsony power exceptionally. We shall meet the same rather surprising results in Chapter XVII: despite all their superior opportunities for waging economic war STEs do not do it so very often or so very well—except against each other. The whole notion of tricky behavior in the market place is strange to a Communist: his economic misbehavior normally has political roots. I hazard a guess (in Chapter XVII, Section 13) why within the bloc economic warfare is the rule, outside it open warfare.

Generalizing, the *economic* dangers of being small turn out to be the dangers of being a small ME. The protective institutions and cautious planning which we have seen to be necessary are automatically present in a small STE. It is political, not economic, independence that the small STE has historically lacked. The dependence of the satellites on the USSR has been paradoxically very great, while their economic model and autarkic doctrine gave them every opportunity to avoid it. But this was due to the Red Army and the Soviet 'advisers', or the political dependence of very unpopular regimes on outside support.

8

So much for size and the terms of trade. Next, *tariffs* exist but are quite unimportant. We saw in Chapter VII that profit was never under Stalin, and today is only seldom, a criterion. So long as this is so, tariffs have almost no effect on purchases. But even if profit is

---

[1] The USSR had imported unusually large quantities from China in 1957 and 1958, evidently in an agreed attempt to settle the Chinese debt. For want of domestic use she had to re-export (Robert L. Allen, *Soviet Economic Warfare* [Washington, D.C., 1960], p. 238; *New York Times*, October 2, 1964; Sidney Dell, Trade Blocs and Common Markets [London, 1963], pp. 247–251).

a criterion it all belongs to the state, anyway, and the state is or should be quite indifferent as to the name under which profit accrues. That is to say, the *Preisausgleich* always contains an element not due to mere general overvaluation; so if we care to call some part of that element a tariff we are merely playing with words.

There is one exception to this rule. The formal incidence of the tariff is on the foreign-trade enterprise, as in any economy. Suppose now that the tariff is differentiated, so that some MEs have a preference, and the enterprise is told to spend its foreign exchange in, say, a geographical area containing both preferred and deferred MEs. Suppose, further, that the *Preisausgleich* is fixed as a rate per article, and not on the 'method of differences' (Chapter II, Section 1, above); that the importers share in the profits on what they import; and that the final price of the import is subject to some restraint, whether by central government or by final buyer. Then—and only then!—is the preference a meaningful incentive: the foreign-trade enterprise is induced to buy in the preferred market. A tariff by itself, i.e., a preference for home over foreign goods, is, of course, in no case an incentive, but merely a waste of everybody's time. For the foreign-trade enterprise gets a sum in valuta to spend and must spend it. There is no protective effect.

All this is a formidable list of preconditions, probably never fulfilled. As far as state trading goes, I am convinced that STEs retain tariffs purely as a bargaining counter or propaganda device. They are better able to exact most-favored-nation (MFN) treatment from MEs, in which tariffs do have meaning, if they themselves have tariffs they can raise and lower.[1] If the government of the ME is sufficiently naif, it will actually believe the Communist tariff will affect its exports and make meaningful concessions in order to avoid meaningless reprisals.

This is not at all to say that an STE can make no meaningful reprisals against an ME that refuses it MFN treatment. Quite the contrary, it has the very excellent weapon of not including the offending country in its trade plan. This leads us on to discrimination by quantity, which we discuss below. But STEs, while they proclaim most officially their intention to trade mainly with each

[1] The United Nations' ECE suggests that all the preconditions for active and meaningful preferences existed in Hungary and the USSR, when they introduced their new tariffs in 1961 (*Economic Bulletin for Europe*, XIV/1, pp. 52–4). They quote no evidence in favor of this supposition in the USSR, but some in Hungary (footnote, p. 53). On pp. 57–8 they admit that even this evidence amounts to very little. For a much more sensible approach to the problem of making Soviet-type MFN promises honest, cf. Franklyn Holzman in (ed.) Henry Rosovsky, *Industrialization in Two Systems* (New York, 1966), pp. 263–5.

other,[1] nevertheless do not threaten quantitative discrimination when engaged in tariff discussions. Thus, instead of insisting on the effective reprisals they will, in fact, take, they press MEs to give them lower tariffs by threatening bogus reprisals.

This state of affairs is so strange it needs documentation. The Hungarian Government had this comment on its new tariff in 1961:

We have to put on record well in advance that protectionist defence of production is *not* among the purposes of this tariff reform. There is for this no need whatsoever in a socialist planned economy. We buy the commodities which we need according to our national economic plans. Another matter is from where we cover our requirements. Obviously, from countries where Hungarian commodity exports are favorably received from the point of view of commercial policy and where no doubts can arise concerning the economic efficiency of our exports . . .

. . . .

We do not aim with this tariff either at protectionism or at discrimination in any relation. We are therefore ready to start customs negotiations with any interested country strictly on the basis of mutual advantage, and even concerning the minimum tariff. This means that we do not refuse reduction either of the maximum or of the minimum tariff—concerning the former through negotiations with countries which continue to withhold unlimited and unconditioned most-favoured-nation treatment, and concerning the latter through negotiation with countries which do assure this treatment. Naturally, in the latter case, the reduced contractual tariff will have to be applied to commodities originating from all those countries which claim its application on the ground of mutual unlimited and unrestricted most-favoured-nation treatment.[2]

The Soviet Government was a great deal more frank. Its new tariff (also 1961) was

. . . an instrument of commercial policy in defence of the most-favoured-nation principle. It stated that the Soviet Union 'is obliged to add this instrument to the ones that are available as a result of the Soviet state monopoly of foreign trade and the planned development of the national economy in order to counteract discrimination against its foreign trade in those countries which disregard the principles of equality and reciprocal advantage in their relations with the Soviet Union.[3]

On January 1, 1965, the USSR made the purely propaganda move of abolishing tariffs on all imports from UDCs.[4]

9

The real impact of tariffs is on private gifts from abroad. It is very general for the inhabitants of STEs to have rich relatives

---

[1] F. L. Pryor, *The Communist Foreign Trade System* (London, 1963), pp. 163-4, and Section 17, below.
[2] ECE, op. cit., pp. 53, 56, 57.
[3] Ibid., p. 53. [4] *New York Times*, February 5, 1965.

in ACCs, even (in the case of China) UDCs. The country's income from these emigrants' remittances in kind is very great (see Chapter XIII), and the state likes to take its cut. Here is the history of such tariffs in one STE alone.[1]

In Poland, gift parcels came in free of charge throughout Stalin's life. The first, very high, tariffs were imposed on December 23, 1953. On a list of common goods the tariff was at a fixed rate per unit of weight. Other goods needed a special import license, and the tariff was 40% to 75% of the price of the good in state trade— i.e., the state demanded the turnover tax it would have received had the good been produced at home. These tariffs forced the goods into the black market, where people sold them in order to pay the tariff. On September 1, 1956, i.e., during the Thaw but just before Gomułka's return to power, the tariff was considerably lowered, and made longer and more sophisticated. On May 23, 1957, many items of food were freed altogether and other tariffs were lowered again (cf. Chapter XIII, Section 13).

The Polish State also levies export taxes on private parcels sent abroad. This is a prewar custom that has been carried straight through.[2] It takes us right back to the medieval 'principle of provision' (Chapter XV, below).

Both kinds of tax matter, of course, because they are not mere re-arrangements within the State's fiscal system. They hit an independently acting economic subject, the consumer.[3]

10

We turn to *discrimination*. This is a little less easy to define than might be thought.[4] But STE-ME trade brings up innumerable mutual charges of it, and the matter is worth long treatment. We shall here distinguish commercial and non-commercial discrimination. The second in turn splits into macro- and micro-discrimination, and the latter again differs in perfect and imperfect markets. Only when the definitions are securely established shall we turn to the data.

[1] Curt Poralla, *Die Reformen des Polnischen Binnen- und Aussen-handels vor und nach dem Oktoberumbruch*, 1956 (West Berlin, 1958), pp. 57–61.

[2] Ibid., pp. 61–2.

[3] Similar data for the impact of Chinese tariffs on the overseas Chinese are given by Yu Chang in Ch'iao-Wu Pao, February 1, 1964 = ECMM 413.

[4] Not too much seems to have been written on the definition. There is a good passage in James E. Meade, *The Balance of Payments* (Oxford, U.K., 1951), pp. 378–83.

Our instant image of non-commercial discrimination is of a buyer (or seller), being approached by two sellers (or buyers) and choosing the one who offers the higher (or lower) price because he is a Jew or a Communist or a white man or an Old Marlburian. This simple definition by means of price differences will only do for micro-discrimination in a perfect market. In such a case the price is known to everybody and is all anyone has to consider.

Imperfect competition changes this simple picture in two ways. First, everything becomes more difficult. We can no longer be sure that all the relevant knowledge was available to the transactor accused of discrimination; and even if he had it all his judgment might quite honestly differ from ours as to the purely commercial advantages of either deal. So to refuse to buy at the lower (sell at the higher) price might or might not be non-commercial discrimination. Secondly, to expand our knowledge or perfect our judgment itself costs time and money; it is not properly discriminatory to stop 'search behavior' at some point in the game and settle for the connections that propinquity, habit or chance have already formed. Only if our *motive* for ceasing to search is non-economic are we discriminating. In imperfect competition, then, the concept becomes a legal one: we must look for *mens rea*, the guilty intention. Hence the extraordinary difficulties with 'fair employment' in the United States.

So far we have seen that if relative prices are such that on commercial grounds widely defined we prefer customer A, then there is discrimination if we have *any dealings at all* with B. If considerations of goodwill, risk, etc., are already allowed for in the 'commercial grounds widely defined', and we still choose B, even a small part of the time, then we are discriminating on those few occasions. Suppose, however, that the relative prices of A and B leave us commercially indifferent; what purchasing policy would be *non*-discriminatory? The answer seems to be, a random one: in the long run, our purchases from A and from B must be in proportion to the quantities each offers us. And this is not necessarily in the same proportion as the quantities each supplies to the whole market, especially in imperfect competition. For there are many reasons why A might press his supplies on us more than B; but whatever the reason, even if it be non-commercial discrimination on A's part, we are non-discriminatory only if we take his offers at face value for our part. 'First come first served' is, then, a good non-discriminatory principle.

II

Discrimination, that is to say, is a matter of both price and quantity, and its absence is a Nirvana difficult to attain. It is commonly believed that it is still more difficult if we begin, as STEs do, from the quantitative end, and set the prices afterward; but this is not so in the case of global quantitative controls. This may seem a surprising claim, global quotas being so unpopular. Authorities normally quote the case of France in the middle 1930s, with the global quotas on livestock imports. There was a wild race to fulfill them every year, which was won by the exporters of neighboring countries, who filled most of the quota in the first month. Anything was considered to be better than that; so the quotas were then divided up among exporting countries on the basis of historical performance—which may be psychologically acceptable but clearly is discriminatory and also leads to resource misallocations.[1]

Further thought shows that while the global quota may have been inconvenient, it was not discriminatory. The discrimination arose from an imperfection in the market. Nothing prevented more distant suppliers from underbidding if they so chose—unless it was ignorance or inefficient communications. If they had underbid enough they would have stopped the flow of supplies from neighboring countries. No doubt they did not do so for a very rational reason: they were the marginal suppliers, and it was rational for those nearer at hand to monopolize the French market now that it had shrunk. There is, then, nothing seriously discriminatory about a global quota in a competitive market. Indeed, it has been seriously proposed in GATT that Poland, an 'associated' power,[2] should use global quotas. This is, indeed, the only way in which an STE could fulfil the spirit of GATT. The letter she could naturally not fulfil, since the Agreement is drawn up for MEs. Note the global quotas would render bilateralism all but impossible. However, we see in Chapter X that STEs have no need of, and often, in fact, do not practice, bilateralism vis-à-vis MEs.

Suppose, however, we agree for whatever reason to reject the global quota: could we administer detailed quotas to particular suppliers without discrimination? To auction the quotas (or the

---

[1] P. T. Ellsworth, The International Economy (New York, 1950), pp. 652–3.

[2] Under the declaration of November 9, 1959. Czechoslovakia is the only Soviet-type member of GATT, having joined before the 1948 coup and never formally withdrawn. By the declaration of September 27, 1951, the USA and Czechoslovakia released each other from their mutual obligations under the Agreement. The same state of affairs holds de facto between Czechoslovakia and all other members.

currency allocations) is to resort to rationing by price alone, i.e., to an effectively global quota, and to shirk the problem. To distribute them at random *a priori* (i.e., before the price is fixed) is to make presents to marginal suppliers, and even to non-suppliers, of quotas they cannot fill. These people will then resell these quotas, a thing highly desirable for the better reallocation of resources. But to give them such a windfall in the first place is clearly discriminatory.

There seems to be no other meaning to non-discrimination than *random choice among trading partners to whom their prices have made one commercially indifferent*; and, of course, the non-random exclusion of any partner whose price is wrong. It follows that a non-discriminatory quota allocation would have to resemble such a choice, and could only be achieved by much detailed computation. The planner first establishes the total foreign supply, and he must also know all about each foreigner's supply curve. He works out the shadow price likely to call forth the given overall supply and the amounts each foreigner will offer at that price. These amounts are 'non-discriminatory' quotas. This is, of course, a quite impracticable procedure in the present state of human knowledge. So the more STEs rely on arbitrary physical calculation in their inter-trade, and the less they rely on prices, the more discriminatory they are likely to be. Innumerable such problems are thrown up inside an ME by licensing and rationing, and inside an STE by the 'distribution' problem.[1]

12

Now discrimination is said to be hard to detect, even to define, in Soviet-type foreign trade. Yet in one very important sense this is not so at all. If two capitalist enterprises and another STE enter the market together as, say, sellers, and the buying STE chooses any trading partner but the one that offers the lowest price, it has discriminated. The case is not conceptually different from any other, since all the normal ingredients of a market are present. Moreover, this buyer is as justified as any other in replying that price is not all: there are goodwill, delivery date, post-purchase service, etc., etc., to consider as well. This is but a particular consequence of the basic fact that in international trade the STE behaves like an enterprise. It does not matter if some physical allocation of purchases between sellers *motivated* the discrimination, instead of, say, a preferential tariff. The result is the same, and the *evidence* for discrimination is the same. Neither does it matter if foreign-trade prices do not correspond to internal prices; we have only to ask, are they the same for all trading partners?

Thus, the secretiveness of the STE's *government* might indeed succeed in concealing discrimination. The economic processes of an open society on the other hand are wide open to inspection. But there is nothing in the present model of the STE that makes us want to redefine the concept, and the required evidence is of the usual kind. However, there is a change of model, much discussed as a long-term possibility, which would very greatly facilitate concealment: STEs might trade with each other by barter, not money, whether bilaterally or on the basis of an international physical plan. How then could we tell whether they were turning down a better deal with an ME? How could they tell themselves? Two great masses of goods are bilaterally bartered: which good has which price, when an infinite number of prices could be so arranged as to make a balance? The answer appears to be that an outsider could only prove the existence of discrimination if he knew all the parameters fed into the computer—if there were any computers or parameters, and if the whole inter-STE bargain had not been arbitrary. He could then show whether the relative prices between goods implied by the parameters did or did not correspond to relative prices on world markets, and also whether there was any general preference parameter. We are clearly an infinite distance from being able to prove discrimination in cases of pure barter. There were a few such cases immediately after World War II, and should international Full Communism ever break out before nation-states have been abolished there will be many.

It follows that a child could convict the United States of applying a 'strategic' embargo, should the United States Government deny it; but similarly, given the same data, a child could convict the USSR of having once put an embargo on the export of manganese. All we need to know is that manganese was exported to another STE, but never to an ME, even though it bid the same price. If, furthermore, the manganese was never even offered to an ME, we have a proof of discrimination that even the practice of pure barter cannot shake. For there must be some finite price at which the barterer would prefer, on purely commercial grounds, to deal for money with a third party. If the market is somewhat imperfect, the barterer cannot reply that he knew the price anyway; so at least the refusal even to negotiate is certainly discrimination.

13

Now STEs do, in fact, discriminate, but on a very special system of their own. Since their prices never quite correspond to those on world markets (Section 20), there is undoubted micro-discrimination. The CMEA has usually been a high-price area; i.e., STEs price against MEs and in favor of each other as buyers. Which is as much as to say, they discriminate against each other and in favor of MEs as sellers!—a corollary seldom perceived. There is no question of the expense of 'search behavior'; they are perfectly aware of what they are doing. But the prevailing bilateralism makes this process mutual. So there is not necessarily any *macro*-discrimination in the terms or direction of trade. A high price of exports is met by a high price of imports. The temptation to export a lot to the partner offering high prices is offset by the cost of having to import as much from him, at equally high prices. The resulting distortion, if any, in a country's general terms and direction of trade is what we call macro-discrimination against the rest of the world. The STE, not maximizing its profits at any point, may be macro-discriminating in the terms of trade but not the direction, or the direction but not the terms, or both, or neither.

We may quote an unimpeachable source, Mr. Gomułka himself:

If, under the method of firm prices applied in trade between our countries for periods of one or two years, coal prices in trade with the USSR were somewhat lower than coal prices on other markets, then correspondingly the prices of some goods delivered to Poland by the Soviet Union were lower than prices on the world market. This concerns, for example, iron ores, textiles, ships (the difference in the price of iron ore even amounted to several dollars [per ton] compared to the price of ores of the same quality on other markets). For equilibrating the price deviation on coal other Polish goods were sold to the Soviet Union at prices higher than the prices on world markets (the price of wool cloth, exported to the Soviet Union in the amount of approximately 5,000,000 meters, was higher by 5–6 rubles a meter in comparison with the prices at which we could sell this cloth on markets). This means that the basic agreement reached by the Ministries of Foreign Trade was based on the level of world prices. If both sides agreed to some deviations for particular goods, the principle in settling accounts was the following: The sum of the deviations above and below must be mutually equal so that neither side would suffer loss.[1]

[1] *Kommunist* (Moscow), 1/1957, p. 106.

The mechanics of the process are not at all like those of a preference system among MEs. The first reason for this is that there is now no important distinction between the enterprise and the state: price formation and tax levying are one process, not two. The tariff is now, as we have seen, a mere alias for the *Preisausgleich* or turnover tax or profit tax. The enterprise buys or sells where it is told, and pays the taxes it is told, under this name or that. An STE wishing to give a price preference would simply pay a higher, or charge a lower, price. The name of its internal fiscal rearrangement is trivial. Thus the recent Soviet abolition of tariffs on imports from UDCs by itself means nothing: in the absence of free price formation the question is, what will it, in fact, do about its prices and quantities?

In an ME as well, a preference only lowers a tariff; it does not directly attack the price at which trade takes place. But the supply price does rise to the extent that the elasticities of demand and supply enable the supplier to acquire some of the gain from the lower tariff. Moreover, if the supplier is also an ME supply will, in fact, be diverted, whereas between STEs higher foreign supply prices— if any!—have no predictable effect. This might be expected in the case of the mutual preference characteristic between one STE and another, discussed above, which leaves the terms of trade unaltered. But where trade takes place according to arbitrary quantitative plans, even a one-sided preference may have no effect on amounts bought and sold. Consequently, we must distinguish price preferences from quantity preferences. In a free market they are the same thing, since if we change prices by $x\%$ that will change quantities by $y\%$, while if we change quantities[1] by $y\%$ that in its turn will change prices by $x\%$. On the whole and in the long run these are but two routes to one destination, a single possible combination of price and quantity. But two STEs can agree to set *any* combination of price and quantity. Price is or may be a mere income-distributor (see Chapter VII, Section 2). Prices could be set on a rigorous hour-by-hour identity to those reigning between MEs, say, because it seemed the fairest thing to do; yet there could be the most tremendous quantitative discrimination in favor of other STEs. And this, roughly speaking, is what has happened historically.

[1] To 'change quantities' is to enforce a quota. I assume that the government imposing the quota acts rationally, so as to give itself the benefit of the effect on prices. For an import quota drives up domestic prices, and if there is no monopsony or government regulation the foreign supplier may actually benefit.

14

From the quantitative preference and the price preference we move to the terms of trade preference. The essential concept here is the *relative* terms of trade.[1] Thus let Bulgaria export attar of roses (A), and the USSR timber (T). And let the rest of the world also both export and import these commodities (a, t). Bulgaria imports T and t; the USSR A and a. Then Bulgaria's terms of trade with the USSR and the rest respectively are:

$$\frac{A_u}{T_b}, \frac{A_r}{t_b},$$

where the subscripts denote country of destination, and her relative terms of trade with the USSR and the rest of the world are

$$\frac{A_u}{T_b} \bigg/ \frac{A_r}{t_b} = \frac{A_u}{A_r} \cdot \frac{t_b}{T_b} \qquad . \qquad . \qquad . \qquad . \qquad . \qquad (1)$$

Similarly the USSR's relative terms of trade with Bulgaria and the rest of the world are

$$\frac{T_b}{T_r} \cdot \frac{a_u}{A_u} \qquad . \qquad . \qquad . \qquad . \qquad . \qquad . \qquad (2)$$

Now where bilateralism rules, or in customs unions and mutual preference areas, discrimination in respect of the terms of trade is the very meaning of 'unfairness' or 'exploitation'. It tells us nothing that the USSR charges other STEs more than the rest of the world for its exports. In a multilateral situation this would indeed mean something, for the USSR would not be obliged to import from other STEs, and might well choose to do so only at world prices. But bilateralism does so oblige her, and we cannot speak of unfairness until we know what prices she pays.[2] Note that this use of the word exploitation fits with the definition we laid down in Chapter I: the effect not of mere market forces but of political force, either alone or in combination with the market. For the condition that the satellite must trade with the USSR, and may not simply avoid the prices charged, is essential to the whole result; and it is political.

Now could Bulgaria and the USSR simultaneously give each other a terms-of-trade preference? Seemingly not, since if I pay 4000

[1] It seems to have been invented by Pryor (op. cit., pp. 145–6).

[2] It is the great merit of Franklyn Holzman to have discovered this (in *Review of Economics and Statistics*, Summer, 1962); though he does not really exploit his discovery, turning instead to a more doubtful thesis (below, Section 24).

zlotys for your dog and you pay 2000 zlotys each for my two cats, how could both of us benefit? Yet it is, in a Pickwickian sense, possible. Thus we might write for Bulgaria and the USSR successively:

$$\frac{A_u}{T_b} = \frac{6}{20} > \frac{A_r}{t_b} = \frac{5}{21} \; ; \; \frac{T_b}{A_u} = \frac{20}{6} > \frac{T_r}{a_u} = \frac{19}{7} \; .$$

This implies, however, very queer behavior by the rest of the world, since it has for some reason quite different terms of trade with the USSR from what it has with Bulgaria, and possibly from what it has with itself. Indeed, if the rest of the world is a perfect market we have posited a flat contradiction:

$$\frac{A_u}{T_b} > \frac{A_r}{t_b} = \frac{a_r}{t_r} \; ; \; \frac{T_b}{A_u} > \frac{T_r}{a_u} = \frac{t_r}{a_r} \qquad \cdot \qquad \cdot \qquad \cdot \qquad (3)$$

I.e., $\frac{A_r}{t_b}$ now $= \frac{a_u}{T_r}$, but $\frac{5}{21} \neq \frac{7}{19}$.

Only, then, if the world buys attar of roses from Bulgaria for 5 and sells it to the USSR for 7, buys timber from the USSR at 19 and sells it to Bulgaria at 21, i.e., engages in discrimination, can the two countries conspire to offer each other better terms of trade; and they do so only because they pass up very profitable trade with each other, and give opportunities for arbitrage to the rest of the world. Moreover, even then a contradiction remains if we insist that prices be consistently higher inside the bloc. In the above example $A_u > A_r$, $T_b > T_r$: i.e., both STEs overcharged each other for their exports. But $T_b < t_b$, $A_u < a_u$: i.e., the outside world was charging still higher prices.

It was not an oversimplification to assume in the above reasoning only two commodities. A and T could, of course, stand also for two sets of commodities, but no third set is admissible. Thus, if the USSR sells wheat in the rest of the world, but not to Bulgaria, no case can be made out for discrimination or its absence. If they both sell wheat we are talking about competition, a quite different subject.

It follows from the equations (3) above that if the world market is reasonably perfect, or randomly imperfect, Bulgaria's relative terms of trade with the USSR are simply the reciprocal of the USSR's with Bulgaria:

$$\frac{A_u\,t_b}{A_r\,T_b} = \frac{A_u\,t_r}{a_r\,T_b} = \frac{1}{\dfrac{a_r\,T_b}{A_u\,t_r}} = \frac{1}{\dfrac{T_b\,a_u}{T_r\,A_u}} \qquad . \qquad . \qquad . \qquad . \qquad (4)$$

In other words, one country must normally be exploiting the other. Exploitation cannot sensibly be mutual, but it can be altogether absent if all these expressions $= 1$.

In the same notation a couple of mutual price preferences, granted to the partner's exports, would be:

$$\frac{A_u}{A_r} > 1 ; \frac{T_b}{T_r} > 1 \qquad . \qquad . \qquad . \qquad . \qquad . \qquad . \qquad (5)$$

The condition of equal price preference leads to:

$$\frac{A_u}{T_b} = \frac{A_r}{T_r} .$$

But if this condition holds then in a perfect world market:

$$\frac{A_u}{T_b} = \frac{a_r}{t_r} .$$

From this it follows that the middle terms in (4) $= 1$. So Bulgaria's terms of trade advantage in dealing with the USSR is zero, and vice versa; i.e., the left-hand side in (4) $= 1 =$ the right-hand side.

In practice most people use formula (1), easily available in Bulgaria's statistics, for her relative terms of trade. Cf. Section 23 below. We require, however:

(i) That A_u and A_r, T_b and T_r, be in demonstrable truth products of exactly the same quality. This is the principal stumbling block, since STEs usually export better quality to ACCs than they use at home or sell to UDCs and other STEs.[1]

(ii) Enough commodities to insure that the imperfections of the world market, indeed, exercise a random effect.

(iii) That the imperfections of the world market be, indeed, random with respect to the problem. But STEs are not such regular customers with MEs as are other MEs, and it is they, not MEs, that mostly make the sudden and unexpected offers to trade in the ME-STE market, which is rather marginal for both parties. So STEs probably do not enjoy discounts for quantity and goodwill when they buy, but have to offer discounts when they sell. This

---

[1] This is the 'quality hierarchy' discussed in Chapter XVIII, Section 15.

seems to me true but unimportant. But it is emphasized by Paul Marer,[1] and Laszlo Zsoldos (below). Marer takes, not STE/ACC, but inter-ACC prices as his basis of comparison:

$$\left(\frac{A_u}{a_x}\cdot\frac{t_x}{T_b}, \text{ where } x \text{ means inter-ACC}\right).$$

He is thereby asking a different question: what would it have been like for Bulgaria if she had not been in the CMEA at all?—and not could Bulgaria here and now be better treated? Of course in perfect competition $r = x$.

15

So far, we have dealt with non-commercial discrimination, i.e., the use of political power or at least the yielding to political passions. In addition, however, one can, as a monopolist or monopsonist, simply discriminate for money. Obviously, enterprises do both. Less obviously, but equally clearly, the government of an ME might manipulate preferences and exchange controls so as to improve its terms of trade ('commercial') rather than so as to tighten the bonds of empire or unite Europe ('non-commercial'). A fortiori an STE, which is both state and enterprise, can and does discriminate commercially. Of course, commercial discrimination by any state remains an act of state, and will therefore have political consequences however simon-pure the greed for money in which the act originated.

Item (iii) above is a typical case of commercial discrimination. As far as we are concerned here, its only role is to disturb statistical comparability.

16

Turning now to the facts, apart from the numerous inter-STE economic wars (see Chapter XVII), the grossest and most permanent discrimination is the quantitative one against MEs. Or is it against STEs by ACCs? Certainly, when the United States embargo began in late 1947, STE-ME trade was much higher than it was to be again for many a year. The Communists excused their retreat into the inter-STE 'preference' system by saying that trade with ACCs had become worthless. That is, they could no longer buy what they wanted, not even from neutral ACCs, for these in turn were inhibited by the United States provision that it would embargo them

[1] In his forthcoming Foreign Trade Prices in the Comecon, Chapter 9.

if they sold strategic goods.[1] But this cannot possibly have been the whole explanation. STEs could still buy innumerable 'non-strategic'[2] manufactured goods in all ACCs, which they badly needed; and their consumers were also starved of the tropical products of UDCs (Chapter XIV, Section 21). In Table IX/1, I show the fate of certain Communist imports in those years.

TABLE IX/1. IMPORTS FROM THE 'WEST' BY THE 'EAST', SELECTED YEARS, 1938–50
($ mn.)

	Total	Food, Beverages, and Tobacco	Textiles (and manufactures thereof)	Metals	Machinery, Instruments, Vehicles	Unspecified and Other
The 'East' Generally						
1938B	1137·1	72·4	120·6	234·1	282·1	136·5
1947A	782·0	177·0	81·0	90·0	224·0	178·0
1948A	857·0	170·0	101·0	141·0	218·0	176·0
1948B	670·0	62·4	22·0	74·4	199·9	72·7
1949B	819·9	61·8	33·3	107·0	281·1	116·8
1950B	712·4	29·6	35·5	105·5	316·1	73·6
Yugoslavia						
1938	137·7	5·8	39·6	15·2	37·4	15·9
1948	80·6	3·3	17·1	10·2	25·8	8·7
1949	103·6	1·1	20·0	15·3	31·2	15·6
1950	127·7	1·3	10·9	26·9	40·7	21·9

NOTE: Figures are derived from West European trade statistics. 'West' means Belgium–Luxemburg, Denmark, Finland, France, Western Germany, Italy, Netherlands, Norway, Sweden, Switzerland, the United Kingdom (series A includes Iceland, Portugal, Austria; and omits French zone of Germany, Finland). 'East' means Czechoslovakia, Poland, Hungary, Rumania, Bulgaria, the USSR (series A includes Finland, Yugoslavia; and omits war reparations from Finland). Figures for 1938, 1947, 1948 are in 1948 prices. Figures for 1949, 1950 are in January–September, 1949, prices. The 1947 statistics are much less reliable; the ECE only gave them in one publication. They also used a different commodity classification.

SOURCE: United Nations, Economic Commission for Europe, *Economic Bulletin for Europe*, II/1951, Table C; ibid., II/1949, Table 1, p. 27.

The drop in the total shown in the table is not so very great; and the continued growth in metals and machinery is particularly impressive. It appears to give the lie to the Communist claim that the United States embargo seriously reduced the area of worthwhile trade. Rather was it food, and other 'non-strategic' commodity classifications not here reproduced, that declined. In other words, Stalin did not *wish* to import, or possibly had not the exports to

[1] United Nations, Third Session of the General Assembly, Part I, *Second Committee on Economic and Financial Questions, Summary Record* (New York), September–November, 1948, *passim*.
[2] I.e., as defined by the United States authorities. For my skepticism that any good is non-strategic, cf. Chapter XVI, Sections 9–11.

offer; and succeeded despite the embargo in concentrating his purchases on the metallic objects dear to him.

17

Besides, consider what happens when a small STE, not at gross enmity with the USSR and subjected to no economic warfare by her, gains a measure of political independence:

TABLE IX/2. PERCENTAGE OF VISIBLE TRADE WITH OTHER STEs, EXCLUDING CUBA, 1938 AND 1946–64

	Poland			Rumania			USSR
	Exports	Total	Imports	Exports	Total	Imports	Total
1938		(7)ᵃ 13			25		13
1946		(56)			—		
1947		(39)			88		
1948		(34) 41			71		
1949		(43)			82		
1950	56·9		61·1		84		81
1951		57			80		
1952		66			85		
1953		70			84		
1954		70			80		
1955	62·5		64·5				78
1956	58·1		65·4				
1957	57·5		60·7				
1958	55·4		55·4	75		78·5	72
1959	57·8		63·2	78·5		80	75
1960	59·5		61·9	72		72	68
1961	59·3		58·6	68		66	57
1962	59·6		63·0	67		66	61
1963	62·0		66·1	63·5		63·5	60
1964	63·7		62·6	63		63·5	60

SOURCE: *Rocznik Statystyczny 1961* (Warsaw, 1961); ibid., *1963* (Warsaw, 1963); *Anuarul Statistic al Republica Populara Romina* (Bucharest, 1961): Pryor, op. cit., pp. 165, 279. Figures in parentheses are from 'P.W.' (Peter Wiles) in *World Today* (London), January 1954, and exclude the DDR.

ᵃ For 1937, not 1938.

This table shows Poland turning sharply away from the bloc in 1955 (an unexpected date), and more gently again in 1956. Rumania's sharp turn in 1960 coincides more logically with her 'Declaration of Independence'. The table also shows a staggering concentration on the bloc in the early 1950s compared with 1938, a phenomenon equally apparent in the other Comecon countries.[1] This concentration cannot but have been due to a strong 'preference'. Note also the little-known 'dip' in 1948, when the satellites reached out Westward; this was doubtless due in part merely to the economic recovery of Western Europe. However, it is also possible that Stalin entertained different ideas about the ideal level of East-West trade until the Tito schism of mid-1948.

It is surprising that for all the publicity and bitterness of her break with CMEA, Rumania has a higher percentage of trade with STEs than Poland. Indeed, she has drawn attention to this point.[2] But if we threw in Poland's enormous invisibles, her export percentage would rise to about 66. In 1964 Poland planned to increase the participation of STEs as follows (%):

	1965	1970
Commodity exports	72·8	77·3
Commodity imports	66·2	73·8

Our source is the head of the planning commission.[3] Note that the plan is to raise the rate back above the peak of the mid-fifties.

I have been repeatedly told, in private, in all sincerity, by Poles intimately connected with foreign trade that there is no formal limit, published or unpublished, on trade with MEs. This is, as the above quotation shows, simply untrue, and even without Jędrychowski's statement it would be flatly unbelievable. Here, then, is an unsolved mystery: how or why could such a confusion arise in their minds? For there is nothing disgraceful about a quantitative preference; it is in no way more evil than a price preference. Is it that the quantitative preference is a hated legacy of Stalinism? Does its denial help Poland to get MFN treatment and other favors in the West? Is it a top secret matter, handled at Politburo level, and only made public by mistake, in the context of a diplomatic quarrel with Rumania? Would a Polish official who didn't read *Lumea* not know about it? Are geographical percentages only planned in the sense that trade with each country is planned ahead,[4]

[1] 'P.W.' in *World Today*, January, 1954; Pryor, loc. cit. The 'deconcentration' from 1947 to 1948 and the 'reconcentration' from 1948 to 1949 seem also to be universal, but statistical evidence for other countries is less good.

[2] I. Petrescu on Radio Bucharest, June 6, 1964. Cf. *Ost-Probleme*, Bonn, July 24, 1964.

[3] Stefan Jędrychowski in *Lumea*, Bucharest, November, 1964. Cf. Paul Wohl in *Christian Science Monitor*, April 12, 1965.

[4] Thus V. Ladygin and Yu. Shirayev (*Voprosy Ekonomiki* 5/1966) give long-term Soviet trade targets with various countries, from which a percentage distribution follows by arithmetic.

so that the distribution is, so to speak, 'planned ex-post'? Whatever the explanation, this present account of the matter is clearly incomplete.

18

As to discrimination by prices, the facts are very complicated. Basically, world prices are used between STEs not as criteria (see Chapter VIII) but because it seems fair to do so and governments find them easy to agree on. They are thus for the most part mere income distributors, but that does not prevent them from being discriminatory.

In imperfect competition the world price is so difficult to ascertain as to be, in fact, a perfectly arbitrary quantity. Owing to Pryor's adventurous researches in East Berlin we have the text of the Soviet-East German agreement on what 'world prices' shall mean in 1958.

1. Prices are to be set on the basis of the average 1957 world market price on the chief market of the good in question, taking into account transportation costs.

2. Speculative and discriminating factors are to be eliminated in the setting of the price.

3. The 'chief market' means the leading market for the good in question. In choosing the chief market for the good, one must take into account the economic and geographic factors of the good in question to the partner countries.

In choosing the chief market for the calculation of the basic price, one must start from the standpoint of the buyer, taking into consideration the interests of the seller. One must take into account on which chief markets the buyer, for purely economic considerations, would conduct his transaction if he were not able to buy the goods from his Socialistic partner.

6. The contract prices in trade of the Socialist nations with Capitalist nations may be used as a basis price in the case where it concerns a good which the Socialist nations sell or buy on the Capitalist world market in considerable amounts.

7. If no documentation from 1957 is available, the price is to be determined on the basis of documents from an earlier period, taking into account recognized price indices and/or other means of adjustment agreed upon by the partners.

For special equipment where no documentation can be offered, the basis price is to be calculated by comparison of prices on the chief markets of similar products.

For agricultural products with special seasonal character, the basis price is to be calculated for the season.

9. Prices for re-exports are to be set on the basis of actual buying prices previously agreed upon, including the transport cost and a 1% commission.

10. When subsequent quality changes are made, prices are also to be correspondingly changed.

11. With the closing of the [yearly] contract, as many final prices as possible should be set. Only in exceptional cases are provisional prices to be permitted, which should correspond to the average world market prices. Final prices must be set three months or, in the case of complete factory units, six months after signing of the yearly contract.[1]

Note the last sentence in clause 3, implying strongly that world prices are seen as the prices of marginal supplies. Note also the unlimited vagueness inherent in clauses 1 and 2. *How* should transportation costs be 'taken into account'? *What* is a 'speculative' factor? Clauses 7 and 10 are also exceedingly vague. Note also the clear implication of clause 11 that prices, being settled after the quantitative contract, are not criteria for action. Yet all in all this is a fair and sober document, dealing as best it can with the immense problems involved.

19

The immensity of these problems cannot be overestimated. World markets are more imperfect, indeed, downright capricious, than the inexperienced imagine. It is one of the main errors of the academic mind to accept documents and principles at their face value. Quite apart from the probable instances of Soviet price exploitation of the satellites in the early years (below), and the unexplained variations in the terms of inter-STE trade, shown in Tables IX/3–IX/6, we have to consider whether STEs use world prices even in capitalist markets! There are, for instance, major politically-motivated deals, like the swap of Chinese rice with Ceylonese rubber in 1953. Ceylon was the only country willing to break the United States embargo; so she got a very high price for her rubber and still better terms of trade when we consider how little she paid for her rice.[2]

Then, too, the mere irregularity, instability and arbitrariness of Soviet-type procedures make for very queer pricing. Thus, in 1950, Czechoslovakia was selling the Tudor car at 98,000 crowns in Poland (approximate cost price), in Holland and Pakistan at 38,000 crowns, and in the other countries intermediately.[3] In 1954 the Greek State monopoly requested offers of matches. Thirteen bids

---

[1] Pryor, op. cit., pp. 235–6.

[2] R. F. Mikesell and J. N. Behrman, *Financing Free World Trade with the Sino-Soviet Bloc* (Princeton, 1958), pp. 90–91.

[3] And at 250,000 crowns on the domestic market, but that included turnover tax (Margaret Dewar, *Soviet Trade with Eastern Europe, 1945–9* [London, 1951], p. 8).

came in, ranging from $17·22 a case (Czechoslovakia) to $58·94 (United Kingdom). The regular Swedish supplier bid $43·00, and later cut it to $35·00. Czechoslovakia further sweetened her bid by offering to spend much of the proceeds on Greek wine. But she was beaten in the end by the USSR, which, beginning at $21·50, finally underbid her, and agreed to buy Greek bay leaves.[1] We may justly suspect that international markets are almost as imperfect where no STEs are involved at all.

On top of mere irregularities, bilateralism destabilizes prices. In particular, if a country runs up an inconvertible balance unexpectedly it may well pay high prices simply to work it off. Thus Italy paid the USSR a premium of 17% over the United States price on wheat in April, 1953, simply to work off her balance.[2] Note, too, the 'marginal bilateralism' (Chapter X, Section 19, below) practiced by both Czechoslovakia and the USSR above, in the Greek match example. That is, by trying to match extra deliveries with extra purchases these countries were offering real terms of trade even more favorable than their mere delivery prices indicated. It seems a certain generalization that when an STE is determined to earn some foreign exchange it will export regardless of cost and reason. For further evidence on this compare Chapter XV, Section 7, on the general export policy of Poland.

20

So are inter-STE prices *fair*? Complaints pour out in a steady stream from non-Soviet refugees. Yet the matter is not clear, even when we know what the world price actually is. As early as 1948 world prices were used between the USSR and the DDR, according to a Soviet administrator there, now a refugee.[3] He says:

Until the end of 1948 the price level for goods supplied by Germany to the Soviet Union was set by the [Soviet] Ministry of Foreign Trade. After 1948 prices for such goods were established by agreement between the Ministry of Foreign Trade and the Administration.[4] The usual practice was for the Ministry to send a fully

---

[1] Mikesell and Behrman, op. cit., p. 73.

[2] Ibid., pp. 70–71. Each of these stories, which United States authors so much delight to tell, needs careful checking. If, in the general dollar shortage of those days, with the lira overvalued by *Italian* exchange control, dollar commodities were worth more to Italy than their prices might indicate, the Soviet deal would still have been good business for Italy. This story is not, then, as told here, a cautionary one against trading with the Communists. It is merely an illustration of how bilateralism destabilizes prices.

[3] Vlas Leskov in ed. Robert Slusser, *Soviet Economic Policy in Post-War Germany*, Research Program on the USSR (New York, 1953), p. 72.

[4] Sc. the Foreign Trade Administration of the Soviet Military Government.—P.J.D.W.

prepared price schedule to the Administration which either accepted the proposed prices without discussion or, in cases where they were definitely too low, submitted their reasons for regarding the proposed prices as incorrect. In these discussions the Administration had the full support of the Planning Administration.[1] In most cases, both those involving goods manufactured in Germany and those involving goods sent to Germany from the Soviet Union, the prices set were in general accord with the current price of similar products on the world market. The greatest discrepancies occurred in the case of prefabricated houses, for which the fixed price was as much as 15% below the current price on the world market, and certain types of textiles, for which it was from 5 to 10% below this level. It was chiefly with regard to the prices set for these goods that the Germans lodged their ineffectual protests.

We may comment that if the DDR was so little exploited in this way while under Soviet military government, few satellites can ever have been. On the other hand, our source is a Soviet refugee, so by no means to be trusted on so emotional a matter.

Secondly, the Yugoslavs complained vehemently in 1948; yet, as we saw in Chapter I, when they published their prices they seemed indeed to be world prices. Many of the complaints are undoubtedly due to intellectual misunderstanding. Thus the Yugoslav complaint, when we examined Mr. Popović's version of it, turned out to be precisely that world prices were applied, instead of ones more favorable to his country. When the Poles complain about their coal, sold at $1·25 a ton to the USSR for many years when the world price was about $14, they forget the origin of this arrangement: it had nothing to do with world prices or discriminatory prices but was part of a Polish-Soviet settlement *in re* German property and reparations. The settlement itself was very unjust, but that is another matter.

Above all, the average refugee dealt with only one small aspect of trade, never with the terms of trade. A minor official buying timber in, say, Czechoslovakia, is conscious that he could have paid lower prices in Sweden than in the USSR; but he forgets that Soviet import prices are equally high and thus distorted in his country's favor. Indeed, he may well not even know. The same applies to the Western researcher: staggered to find actual published figures officially demonstrating that the USSR overcharges for her exports, he forgets to ask whether perhaps she also overpays for her imports. It is depressing to see the figures for discrimination in Soviet export prices quoted and re-quoted in anti-Soviet propaganda, as if they proved something by themselves. Then again, prices in trade

[1] Sc. of the Soviet Military Government.—P.J.D.W.

between STEs tend to be based on past world prices, often last year's; and an official will surely complain if his country's terms of trade with MEs have improved in the meantime (if he is senior enough to know about the terms of trade).
There is, then, nothing unfair about the principles of inter-STE price setting. The practical details are another matter. An American protectionist is said to have said: 'I don't care who writes the tariff; just let me write the specifications.' We may fairly suspect the USSR of every sort of detailed chicanery at least up to 1956. The agreement quoted above certainly leaves room for it, and one is inclined to believe that there cannot have been so much smoke without a little fire.

21

First, in addition to unconvincing there is also convincing literary evidence for unfair Soviet pricing. The mere fact that satellite pricing policy was chosen by Stalin as one of the charges in the Kostov (1949) and Slánský (1952) trials speaks volumes. These very senior Communist leaders, one Bulgarian and the other Czecho-slovak, were accused of Titoism, and in their show trials many 'crimes', plausible and implausible together, were admitted. It is beyond doubt that torture was used; so no admission has to be true. But for what it is worth both Czechoslovak and Bulgarian officials admitted to unfair trading practices against the USSR. Prices above the 'world' level were asked for exports and prices below it offered for imports. Commercial secrecy was maintained *vis-à-vis* Soviet negotiators(!). The quantity of exports offered was kept low in order to prolong negotiations.[1] 'Structural bilateralism' (cf. Chapter X, Section 19) was enforced, so that the USSR had to accept goods she did not want.[2]
If these admissions were true—and they ring true—they tell us nothing directly about Soviet practices. But they do tell us about inter-STE trading, and it is to be presumed that the USSR used, many times over and with better success, the tricks her satellites used.

[1] But the quantity of exports was not mentioned in the same breath as prices, and it is not said that the offer was kept low in order to raise prices! I.e., the witness (Boris Khristov) confirms my statement that prices are negotiated subsequently.

[2] *The Trial of Traicho Kostov and his Group*, Ministry of Justice (Sofia, 1949), pp. 192–5, 228–9, 232–3, 241; *Prozess gegen die Leitung des Staatsfeindlichen Verschwörerzentrums mit Rudolf Slánský an der Spitze*, Ministry of Justice (Prague, 1953), pp. 394–5, 434–4, 442–4.

Continuing with the literary evidence, it was not until 1956 that an official study of prices was made in the DDR. It was so secret that only the Minister of Trade, the chairman of the State Planning Commission, and Ulbricht himself saw it. Moreover, every East German price agreement with other satellites was automatically and officially made known to the Soviet Embassy in Berlin, at least until 1956.[1]

It was also in 1956 that Gomułka negotiated the end of the cheap coal exports to the USSR—an event not logically part of our subject here, as we have seen, but psychologically very much so.

A later instance concerns also the DDR. On December 3, 1965, Erich Apel, chairman of the planning commission, killed himself in East Berlin after prolonged trade negotiations with the USSR. The 1966–70 trade agreement was signed in that city the same day. One would know better what to think about this if there were a few documents, or even one good leak.[2] But an unsigned article, 'Special to the New York Times' of September 11, 1966, confirms the commonsense view that Apel died for his country's terms of trade:

... East Germany is committed to buy large amounts of raw materials from the Soviet Union at prices well above world market prices. And the Russians have demanded at least part payment in hard currency, of which East Germany is as short as other countries of Eastern Europe. ...

East German exports to the Soviet Union—mainly machinery, factory equipment and finished goods—are said to be assessed at lower than world market prices.

The Russians were reported to have told East Germany and other countries of Eastern Europe that they must demand extra-high prices to offset the Soviet Union's immense armaments burden for the Communist-bloc alliance. Another argument used by the Russians was that the standard of living in East Germany, a highly industrialized country, already was higher than that in the Soviet Union.

Mr. Ulbricht was said to have countered by pointing out that his country was involved in a political and economic confrontation with prosperous West Germany.

It is interesting that the DDR won all the same a victory in these negotiations: the Soviet share in her trade turnover, already falling in 1965, is planned to fall further. This is connected with the insistence of the rising technocracy on more trade with the West, which they see as the essence of the 'Neues Oekonomisches System'. Here are the figures in milliards of valuta-marks:

[1] According to Fritz Schenk, in Pryor, op. cit., pp. 138, 152. No known action was taken on the price study.
[2] The German Social Democratic Party claims to have Apel's diaries, but repeated inquiries in rather well connected circles in Bonn have failed to produce them for me. They have never been published even in summary form.

	Total turn-over	Turnover with USSR
1964	21·2	10·9
1965	22·4	10·6
1966–70 as per agreement		60
1970, as planned in 1965	32·2	x

SOURCE: scattered figures in *SBZ-Archiv*, Bonn, 3/1966 and 21/1966.

The missing figure x could hardly exceed 13·5: a point that commentators on the Apel case seem to have missed.

On the other hand, Imre Nagy, in a frank, comprehensive and secret state paper, has a long passage on Hungary's foreign trade that fails to mention prices.[1] Writing in disgrace in 1955, he may well not have dared to mention the matter, but an equally probable explanation is that he knew the prices were fair and had little complaint.

Again, Mr. Seweryn Bialer tells me that in 1954, when he was under consideration as a potential vice-minister of foreign trade, the Polish central statistical office showed him some figures for Poland's relative terms of trade with the USSR and Western Europe. The figures were, of course, top secret. They were not as bad as he, previously an outsider in these matters, had feared. He thinks that formally prices were fair but, for instance, Polish customers never dared to demand penalties for faulty quality, late delivery, etc., whereas Soviet customers did.[2]

It is similarly of interest that in his own two works Mr. Schenk, who was a real insider in the East German economy in a way that Mr. Bialer was not in the Polish, does not mention foreign-trade prices. Such knowledge that Mr. Schenk has of the subject was published by Mr. Pryor, who 'debriefed' him.

22

We may guess that *probably the most exploitative part of the Soviet-satellite relationship was the quantitative, not the price, preference.* I.e., the quantities the satellites supplied were greater than what under perfect competition would have been the case, but under the accepted procedures of inter-STE negotiation they had to agree to

[1] *Imre Nagy on Communism* (New York, 1957), Chapter 15.
[2] Interview with Seweryn Bialer, March, 1965.

be compensated at world prices appropriate to smaller quantities.

We may illustrate as follows: a Soviet satellite has a perfectly rational resource allocation, and is forced to supply an excessive amount of an export to the USSR 'at world prices'. It would have supplied willingly at the initially existing price to:

home use	rest of world	USSR	Total
60	35	5	100

But it is forced to supply 20 to the USSR. Now if there is perfect competition the satellite has no control over price, which remains at its old level. So it adjusts total supply thus:

55	30	20	105

and finds itself supplying more than it would have wished in total, throttling back home demand, not earning enough to finance the imports it wants from the rest of the world, and getting no special price out of the USSR. With imperfect competition, on the other hand, the large Soviet demand raises the world price of the article somewhat, and the satellite reacts differently, perhaps thus:

52	34	20	106

Moreover, the USSR too pays the higher price,[1] since its trade is based on world prices. In this second case—doubtless an unlikely one in Eastern Europe—the satellite's valuta earnings from the rest of the world probably rise, and the USSR at least partially recompenses her for her increased exports. But home use still falls, and factors are still diverted into the industry that would *ex hypothesi* have been put to better use elsewhere.

In neither case does the USSR pay the price that would have induced such a supply to it in a free market. Since clearly there is such a price, we cannot in strictness oppose price- to quantity-exploitation. We can only say that the thing is *felt* as exploitation through excessive quantitative demands, and the prices are felt to be on the whole fair, though they are not. Even so, however, strict proof of exploitation would require that Soviet exports were not similarly supplied. But it is beyond doubt that the USSR granted the same kind of preference, and thus also forwent profitable opportunities, on either the domestic or the capitalist market.[2] Politically, then, there is no doubt whose power brought about this

---

[1] Strictly, she pays it only in the second round, after her excessive demands have had their effect on the world price.

[2] Cf. Bogomolov's argument in Section 24.

state of affairs. But economically it remains in doubt who made the greater sacrifice.

Any monopsonist, be it noted, who contracts for a large supply at current prices, engages in similar exploitation. Our analysis assumes that the initial equilibrium position allowed for all economies of scale.

The pricing of invisibles is also in a sense discriminatory, but the matter is rather unimportant (see Chapter XIII, Section 5).

23

However, when we get down to the statistical evidence we find ourselves in the usual morass, where we all try at first to stand in the position we prefer, and all eventually sink. The figures all come from sources which give both quantity and value of particular products traded in particular directions. The prices are obtained by division. They are, therefore, average annual prices franco-frontier. Of 'quantitative' exploitation there is naturally no evidence whatever: the data are far too imprecise.

TABLE IX/3. CERTAIN STEs' RELATIVE TERMS OF TRADE WITH THE CMEA AND WESTERN EUROPE, 1952–59

	1952	1953	1954	1955	1956	1957	1958	1959
USSR (a) E_c/E_m	—	—	—	117	112	106	114	—
(b) I_c/I_m	—	—	—	99	86	82	92	—
(c) Relative terms of trade = (a)/(b)	—	—	—	118	130	129	124	—
Bulgaria (a)	60	74	104	115	123	—	126	129
(b)	63	89	107	93	80	—	88	109
(c)	95	83	97	123	154	—	143	118
Bulgaria without tobacco (a)	86	118	131	119	127	—	147	148
(c)	136	133	122	128	159	—	167	136
Hungary (a)	113	123	123	114	168	118	134	—
(b)	107	90	138	96	86	93	105	—
(c)	106	137	89	119	195	127	128	—
Hungary without cokes (b)	107	118	150	111	—	—	—	—
(c)	106	104	82	103	—	—	—	—
Poland (a)	—	—	—	—	—	—	132	—
(b)	—	—	—	—	—	—	83	—
(c)	—	—	—	—	—	—	159	—
Poland without hard coal (a)	—	—	—	—	—	—	121	—
(c)	—	—	—	—	—	—	146	—

SOURCE: Pryor, op. cit., 2nd ed. pp. 272–5. All prices are weighted by the quantities traded with the CMEA. 'm' means nearby MEs, 'c' means Communist countries, 'E' export prices and 'I' import prices.

First, comparing STEs with MEs generally, we are tempted to infer from Pryor that all STEs exploit each other (Table IX/3)!

Our confidence is not enhanced when we find Zsoldos getting similarly favorable terms of trade for Hungary, but with very different individual figures:

TABLE IX/4. HUNGARY'S RELATIVE TERMS OF TRADE WITH ALL STEs AND ALL MEs, 1950–58

	1950	1951	1952	1953	1954	1955	1956	1957	1958
(a)	131	98	121	126	126	123	135	138	144
(b)	79	50	78	78	81	81	82	62	93
(c)	166	196	155	161	154	152	163	220	155

Zsoldos' work is particularly careful and fully explained.[1] He confines himself, however, to the same goods throughout (six exports and seven imports), whereas Pryor varies the number every year.

[1] It is a great pity that Mr. Zsoldos refuses to accept the plain sense of his own finding. He proceeds as follows (Laszlo Zsoldos, *The Economic Integration of Hungary into the Soviet Bloc* [Athens, Ohio, 1963], p. 70):

Mendershausen (in *Review of Economics and Statistics*, May, 1959) concluded that the 'Soviet foreign trade data show evidence of discrimination at the expense of the smaller Communist countries in Europe from 1955 to 1957'. This was further reinforced by his findings in ibid., May, 1960, according to which increased differentiation in 1958 between Soviet export prices to Free Europe and the satellites, at the latter's expense prevailed. There seems to be a conflict between the findings of Mendershausen and the information implied by the data in this study. However, the conflict is probably more apparent than real. The data in the study merely suggest that Hungary sold at higher prices to the Bloc than to the West, and conversely, bought at higher prices from the West than from the Bloc. This finding does not, in and of itself, constitute a conflict with the Mendershausen conclusions; on the contrary, with the help of his findings it is possible to argue that the West as well as the Soviets may be engaged in price discrimination against Hungary. For example,

[and here I substitute, from Section 14, my symbols for his—P.J.D.W.]

Let $P \equiv$ world market price

(1) Mendershausen found that	$T_r < T_b$;
(2) In this study it was found that	$T_b < t_b$.
Assuming that	$T_r = P,$
it follows that if	$P < T_{bt}$ and $T_b < t_b$,
then it must be true that	$P < T_b < t_b$

That is, Hungary buys above world market prices in the Bloc as well as in the West, but buys at a still higher price in the West than in the Bloc. The converse is true if Mendershausen's results respecting Soviet purchase prices and the findings of this study respecting Hungarian selling prices are submitted to the same type of reasoning. That is, Hungary sells below world market prices to the Bloc and at still lower prices to the West. . . . Most of Hungarian trade with the West is broken up into bilateral segments, and much of it is occasional and infrequent. Thus, in the absence of regular and frequent transactions in a single market, it is quite possible that Hungary's Western trading partners discriminate against her, in regard to certain items bought from and sold to the West.

The assumptions that Hungary suffers in the world market, and the USSR does not ($T_r = P$), are arbitrary but not implausible. What is difficult to understand is how 'the Soviets may be engaged in price discrimination against Hungary' when they are expressly said to buy from her at higher, and sell to her at lower, prices than the West!

Zsoldos' series is *a priori* more plausible than Pryor's. They both show a peak in 1951—any small country might expect such an event, largely by chance, during the Korean boom. But a peak in 1957 is far easier to explain than one in 1956, for in 1957 other STEs notoriously rallied round to put Communist Hungary back in business after the revolution. Marer (ibid.), using many more commodities and paying less attention to quality, finds favorable Hungarian terms of trade with the USSR in 1955–7, unfavorable in 1958–64.

More generally, all is not lost if we presume that the two countries absent from Table IX/3, Czechoslovakia and the DDR, were being exploited by all the rest. It looks as if this was in fact so. From Holzman's working, the following figures can be deduced:

TABLE IX/5. BULGARIA'S RELATIVE TERMS OF TRADE WITH CERTAIN STEs ON THE BASIS OF WESTERN EUROPE, 1958 AND 1959 (per cent)

		E_c/E_m		I_c/I_m		E_cI_m/E_mI_c	
		1958	1959	1958	1959	1958	1959
USSR	.	125	125	93 (58)	110 (73)	134	114
Czechoslovakia	.	154	147	93 (69)	107 (78)	166	137
DDR	.	156	149	68 (57)	89 (67)	229	167
Hungary	.	100	112	(78)	(106)	?101	?78
Poland	.	159	152	(87)	(114)	?143	?99

SOURCE: Franklyn Holzman in *Soviet Studies*, July 1965, Table 3. The weighting system for the price indices is not revealed.

Since Bulgaria exports simple and imports complicated goods, quality is a very big factor in her import statistics. The figures in parentheses are for a larger number of import categories, including some very heterogeneous ones. The workings of the 'quality hierarchy'[1] come out very plainly with the elimination of these heterogeneous categories (cotton textiles, consumers' and producers' durables): quality for quality, STEs offer Bulgaria not enormous but quite modest discounts.

Pryor also presents[2] similar figures for trade within the bloc. In Table IX/6 the satellite's relative terms of trade are $\dfrac{E_u}{E_s} \times \dfrac{I_s}{I_u}$, where u is USSR and s is other satellites; i.e., a result under 100 shows that it would have been better to switch trade to other satellites. Marer

---

[1] The tendency of STEs to reserve their best quality for exports to ACCs. Cf. Chapter XVIII, Section 15. The queried figures for Hungary and Poland are derived by me. I wrote up the figures in parentheses by 30% in 1958 and 35% in 1959—the average write-ups for Czechoslovakia and the DDR.

[2] Op. cit., p. 150; his own working this time.

TABLE IX/6. SOME RELATIVE TERMS OF TRADE WITH THE USSR AND OTHER
SATELLITES, 1952–59
(per cent)

	1952	1953	1954	1955	1956	1957	1958	1959
BULGARIA								
Whole sample .	98	85	87	76	72	—	85	84
Sample without tobacco	90	96	90	85	92	—	96	97
HUNGARY								
Whole sample .	82	95	91	97	123	131	123	—
Sample without bauxite	100	105	87	101	—	—	—	—
Sample without cokes .	—	—	—	—	116	128	125	—
POLAND								
Whole sample .	—	—	—	—	—	—	102	—
Sample without coal .	—	—	—	—	—	—	105	—

(ibid.), comparing Hungary's Polish and Soviet trade, finds the former more favorable in 1958–64, the latter in 1955–7.

Clearly, this kind of analysis could be indefinitely prolonged. But enough has come out already to show the possibilities. Bulgaria has or had bad relative terms of trade with Western Europe and superlative ones with Czechoslovakia and the DDR. If her relation with the USSR lay in between, was she being exploited?—bearing in mind that the volumes of the first two trade turnovers were about equal and that the third was over twice as big. Exploitation here is a relative term; its use depends on our reference point. My own inclination is to take the West European terms of trade as the fixed datum, unalterable by Soviet-type action, and say that most European STEs favor Bulgaria, where 'favor' is the opposite of 'exploit'. Moreover, the USSR favors by means of a large turnover and a small unit advantage, and Czechoslovakia and the DDR by smaller turnovers and a larger unit advantage.

I am tempted to conclude, then, that *these latter two countries are exploited by all the others.* With our political pre-occupation, we have wrongly concentrated on the Soviet relative terms of trade: USSR is no longer the interesting case. I have put this view confidentially to East Europeans who ought to know. Some very convincingly denied all knowledge; two—both well-informed Party members, one not concerned, the other very much concerned, with trade— flatly confirmed it, none denied it. If my view is right, a Prebisch-Popović[1] type of aid through trade is practiced, not commodity by commodity but country by country; and it is this principle that governs the deviations from world prices within the CMEA.

[1] Cf. Chapter I, Section 6.

Compare the rumors about Apel, above. No wonder, too, that precisely these two rich countries do not publish such figures!

24

Holzman[1] further presents a most ingenious argument for mistrusting all mere terms of trade. In a preference area, he says, the task falls on particular members to produce the things in which no member country has a good comparative cost position *vis-à-vis* the rest of the world. The other members may not consider it fair to saddle that member with the whole loss. They will, therefore, agree to exceptionally high prices for these things. I may comment that the argument will probably not apply to blocs of MEs, for they will continue to import precisely such things, instead of restricting all imports by about the same percentage. But in the CMEA we cannot rely on such rationality; so Holzman could easily have been right were it not for the notorious fact that until very recently neither the ideology encouraged nor the price system permitted cost considerations to weigh heavily upon exporters. He presents no evidence for his own view,[2] though there was already an immense Communist literature on pricing in the CMEA, which must surely have mentioned this point were it true. I am inclined to give it very little weight. For the country with the obvious claim for such compensation is Czechoslovakia, which specialized in machinery at a great national loss. But we have reason to suspect she was precisely the most, not the least, 'exploited'.

However, Holzman was prophetic: since about 1963 arguments based upon cost have indeed been used in inter-STE negotiations, and even in Communist learned journals. Many of these arguments are, even now, on a very low intellectual level, and crudely dictated by national interest. I am most familiar with Soviet arguments for raising the prices of raw materials. USSR is a net exporter of raw materials to the CMEA, so her spokesman O. Bogomolov has pointed to the high capital cost for opening new mines and claimed that 'world' prices do not make enough allowance for this in her case.[3] Thus arises the reasonable Soviet demand that the prospective buyer provide the capital, which now the Czechoslovaks have done. Certainly if Czechoslovakia does not provide the capital she should

---

[1] Op. cit.
[2] Cf. ibid., footnote 12.
[3] In *Mirovaya Ekonomika i Mezhdunarodniye Otnosheniya*, May 1966, and other places. Earlier argumentation of this type in *Ekonomicheskaya Gazeta*, November 16, 1963. Cf. also Imre Vajda on the export price of Hungarian aluminum, in *Aussenhandel*, 22/1958.

pay a higher price. But Mr. Bogomolov's concern with capital costs—a newly permitted topic of discussion—leads him effectually to deny the *labor* theory of value! Moreover when it comes to agriculture he turns right round and says it is unfairly labor intensive, so Soviet export prices should be raised on *that* account.

Another spokesman, K. Popov, has it that finished good prices embody a profit mark-up at each stage of fabrication—so somehow raw material prices are too low.[1] This seems at least to be good Marxism, though hardly good economics. For the profit margin is surplus value and represents no true cost, but at each vertical stage in manufacture a similar percentage margin is charged on the total costs to that enterprise. So—the author seems implicitly to argue— the percentage is also charged on the previous percentages, and the margin is compounded.[2] Yet other Soviet spokesmen[3] argue simply on the basis of present average total costs; i.e. they take the present resource allocation as given. And granted the CMEA's present quantitative preferences they are quite right. Both Popov and they are careful to ask for 'tax-clean' wholesale prices as basis for inter-national trade, in the sense of Chapter VII.

On a higher ideological plane, all these authors claim that *if there are two world markets there ought to be two sets of world prices.* Stalin had left this entirely vague when he invented 'two world markets'. Indeed, as we saw in Chapter I, he seems to have intended the use of world prices; and probably thought that the second world market was defined by the existence of quantitative preferences, a concept he understood better than prices. Kohlmey[4] maintains that the idea of two sets of world prices was first mooted by Gertrud Gräbig.[5] But Kaigl was already attacking the view in 1958,[6] and indeed it is

---

[1] In *Vneshnyaya Torgovlya*, 11/1966, p. 21.

[2] In strict terms of *Kapital*, Book I, surplus value is always the same proportion of value added at each stage, so is unrelated to the value of bought-in materials and equipment; so there is no such compounding. The Marxologist will note, therefore, that I assume above 'Book III prices', in which profit is a constant percentage of total capital everywhere. In non-Marxist reality, however, either margins reflect the cost of capital at each stage, and so compounding them is not exploitative, or because of increasing monopoly power they increase as we move up the chain of manufacture. Popov then becomes identical with Prebisch.

[3] Y. Zhukov and Yu. Olsevich in *Voprosy Ekonomiki*, March 1967, esp. p. 75. A. Alekseyev, in *Vneshnyaya Torgovlya* 9/1967, even wants to revalue the ruble and base valuta prices on domestic prices.

[4] Günther Kohlmey, 'Karl Marx' Theorie von den Internationalen Werten', in *Jahrbuch des Instituts für Wirtschaftswissenschaften*, Band 5, Akademie-Verlag, Berlin 1962, pp. 41–3.

[5] In her *Internationale Arbeitsteilung . . .*, Berlin 1960, pp. 86–8.

[6] In *Wirtschaftswissenschaftliche Informationen*, 10–11/1958, p. 53. The great Czechoslovak expert Cerniansky explicitly demanded one world value and two world markets in 1958 (*Aussenhandel*, 1958, p. 153).

implicit in Imre Vajda's article of that year (op. cit.). For that matter it was quite explicit in Popović as far back as 1950.[1] Popović, as we saw, wanted income-equalizing prices; but Vajda, Bogomolov, etc., want prices that cover rationally calculated costs under the condition of a quantitative preference. No doubt other principles could and will be suggested for diverging from the world norm. Possibly, even, the cost principle is driving out the income-equalizing principle.

Truly when the theory of value becomes a matter for diplomats and national spokesmen we may expect strange economics. The Western economist may recall that France used to urge more indirect taxes on her Common Market partners, because her own bias towards such taxes raised export prices and made trade difficult. To the reply that the rate of exchange automatically took differences of tax structure into account French diplomats turned the deaf ear of the untrained mind. But, let it be repeated, foreign trade *is* diplomacy, and such arguments *do* matter.

In asking their partners to overpay them, these Soviet spokesmen are essentially using Holtzman's arguments.[2] In any preferential group, he says, relative prices will differ from what they are outside. This is simply the result of supply and demand; no-one is exploiting anyone; prices *should* differ. This is hardly so. The country suffering the relative price disadvantage should be free to sell precisely its cheapest exports and buy precisely its dearest imports outside the group. If it is not free to do so it is exploited. If its freedom to do so would mean too much exterior trade by the rules of the group, its very membership of the group is exploitative. Indeed, Holzman proceeds effectively to admit this. If the USSR were to admit this too, she would release her partners from the purchase of her raw materials and herself from the production of them. Both sides, of course, are being exploited, unless the price is extremely low or high.

25

The *Sino-Soviet terms of trade* are of special political importance, and—by coincidence—theoretical interest. Our normal definition of the terms of trade obscures the role of transport costs: what one country loses another may not gain. This is simplest understood by

[1] Cf. Chapter I, Section 6.

[2] In *Hinter dem Eisernen Vorhang*, Munich, 7–8/1962. In the same issue Aleksander Kutt presents further statistics on the USSR's relative terms of trade.

supposing the transport to be provided by a third country, C. Then A is interested in the price she gets f.o.b. factory, and B in the price she pays c.i.f. wholesaler—if the A factory and the B wholesaler are the last and first residents, respectively, of the two countries to be concerned. If in such a case transport costs rise, both A's and B's true terms of trade deteriorate simultaneously; but if A or B provides the transport that country's true terms of trade improve. The movement of their apparent terms of trade depends, of course, on how the statistics are collected.

Intertemporally, such complications are unlikely to disturb us much; the extent to which a country provides international transport is unlikely to vary greatly at least over a few years. But interspatially transport cost is likely to be very disturbing. Thus Mr. Mah[1] points out that Soviet exports to China (being mostly made in European USSR[2]) must bear very heavy *Soviet* transport costs to the border. But since Soviet foreign-trade statistics give f.o.b. frontier values, this makes the goods dearer than similar ones sold to, say, France. The difference is a genuine Soviet service, which rightly earns yuan and rightly enters the b.o.p. as an export; it is unfair to infer that the USSR is exploiting China. Indeed, transport may be so expensive that her f.o.b. factory prices are lower than when she sells to France. But it *is* fair to infer that China is being exploited by, or has deliberately made a bad deal with, the USSR! —that is, if she could have bought the same goods cheaply somewhere else. Chinese exports to the USSR, on the other hand, will embody a much smaller transport cost when they reach the frontier. So if China charges the USSR and France equal prices f.o.b. farm, she will not appear, from statistics collected f.o.b. frontier, to be greatly overcharging the former. Incidentally, in the absence of Chinese statistics we must compare prices at the Sino-Soviet border, taken from Soviet statistics, with Hong Kong prices.

So our previous analysis must be complicated in order to make meaningful statements about the Sino-Soviet terms of trade. Let I now be the price of Chinese imports c.i.f. frontier and T_i be their

[1] Feng-hwa Mah in *China Quarterly*, January–March, 1964.

[2] As a matter of fact, Mr. Mah tacitly assumes this point, which is crucial to his argument. If most Soviet exports to China were made in the Far East, transport costs would not be disturbing. However, 95–98% of Soviet exports to China went by rail in 1956 [M. I. Sladkovski, *Ocherki Ekonomicheskikh Otnoshenii SSSR si Kitaem* (Moscow, 1957), p. 350], and most of them crossed the border in Central Asia, which they would hardly have done had they been made in Vladivostok. Cf. *New York Times*, February 14, 1965, where Mr. Shabad reports on the foundation of a specialized Far Eastern Trading Agency, and of a *new* decision to orient the Siberian economy toward Japan, owing to transport costs.

·transport cost to their point of destination. Let E be the price of Chinese exports f.o.b. factory, and T_e their transport cost from factory to frontier. Let u be the USSR and w be western Europe. Then Mr. Mah arrives at these relative Chinese terms of trade in 1955–59:[1]

$$\frac{I_w}{I_u} = 0\cdot7; \quad \frac{E_u + T_{eu}}{E_w + T_{ew}} = 1\cdot0$$

In Soviet-type trade it is, so far as I know, invariable for each country to pay all costs up to, or in from, its own frontier. Ordinarily the ocean freight on exports would be paid by the Western buyer, and that on imports by China, but these are Hong Kong prices, so we are comparing two land frontiers. Now since China exports raw materials she sends Sinkiang products to the USSR, seaboard products to Hong Kong. So her export comparison might well be unity, as shown. But she imports machinery, which she must install in her industrial centers, which are nearer to Hong Kong. So $T_{iu} > T_{iw}$, and

$$\frac{I_w + T_{iw}}{I_u + T_{iu}} < 0\cdot7 .$$

Then China should trade with the USSR when:

$$\frac{I_w + T_{iw}}{I_u + T_{iw}} \cdot \frac{E_u + T_{eu}}{E_w + T_{ew}} > 1.$$

But this condition does not hold.

But this does not prove that what China loses the USSR gains. The transport cost factor is even more important in the USSR. In his Table 3 Mr. Mah shows, though this time only in terms of 'higher' and 'lower' prices, not by actual figures, that:

$$\frac{e_c + t_{ec}}{e_w + t_{ew}} > 1, \quad \frac{i_w}{i_c} > 1,$$

where e and i are Soviet exports and imports, c is China and t is Soviet transport costs. Thus, the apparent relative Soviet terms of trade are highly favorable with China as opposed to western Europe. But the true criterion for Soviet trade with China is:

$$\frac{i_w + t_{iw}}{i_c + t_{ic}} \cdot \frac{e_c + t_{ec}}{e_w + t_{ew}} > 1.$$

[1] Op. cit., Table 4, taking the more homogeneous commodities only. There are about 11 imports and about 19 exports. I have averaged the five years. Mr. Mah uses the same techniques as in the previous sections here, and his data are subject to the same kind of doubt.

where t_{ic} enormously exceeds t_{iw}. It is instantly evident that also this latest expression may < 1, and that the USSR also may be making great sacrifices in order to trade with China. In all probability neither party is exploiting the other, but geography, or rather geopolitics, is exploiting both.

CHAPTER X

BILATERALISM, MULTILATERALISM, AND INTERNATIONAL FINANCE

I

WHAT do we mean when we say that trade is bilateral? We do not mean that goods balance goods in individual years. Even if services are included we still do not mean anything like that. We mean that currency balances are inconvertible, so that in the end the debt piled up is either forgiven, or changed into long-term securities, or liquidated in goods and services. Bilateralism is thus essentially concerned with inconvertible currency, and only accidentally with the long-term pattern of trade; scarcely at all with trade in a given year. The way to find out whether a country trades bilaterally is to ask its central bank. We discuss in the Appendix the extent to which *annual* statistics for *visible* trade, which are all the statistical evidence we have, can be taken as evidence. Bilateralism is an *ex ante* concept describing a policy or a central banking arrangement. Trade statistics are *ex post*, and describe the interaction of commercial policy with many other things. We shall refer to the equality of (visible and invisible) exports and imports between two countries as '*reciprocity*'.

Thus in a general way it is obvious that since there were until 1963 hardly any triangular or multiangular clearings in the Soviet bloc,[1] inter-STE trade was almost perfectly bilateral. If statistical 'evidence' contradicts that, we have, happily, ample grounds for denying a close connection between bilateralism and reciprocity, or, indeed, between reciprocity and annual trade statistics. So there is no need to agonize.

Although we cannot in the long run have much 'irreciprocity' without multilateralism, even the most perfectly multilateral financial system need not result in much 'irreciprocity'. On the contrary, there is good *a priori* ground to expect the opposite. For if the products of nature are many, those of human artifice are literally innumerable. If all countries in the world were (*a*) of greater than minimal size, and (*b*) reasonably well developed, and (*c*) not bound by preferences, and (*d*) not too numerous, the law of large numbers would ensure that each wanted to trade with the other to about the same extent. Trade could be as free as the wind, and international financing as multilateral as a fly's eye; but *ex post* there would be approximate reciprocal balance everywhere. It is not desirable; it is just how things would turn out. This is the doctrine of 'random reciprocity'. In general, *reciprocity can rule in a multilateral system, but irreciprocity cannot last long in a bilateral system.* If there is to be irreciprocity, balances must be convertible, if only to a planned extent.

The interesting and disputable factors in 'random reciprocity' are (*c*) and (*d*). So, first, consider preferences. For the most part these are mutual, have formally the same height between the partners, and are genuinely meant to confer the same 'advantage' to each. But they are not scientifically designed to succeed in this aim, and very often the elasticities are such that a preference of the same

[1] The few exceptions were of negligible dimensions [F. L. Pryor, *The Communist Foreign Trade System* (London, 1963), pp. 193–7].

formal height diverts a lot of A's trade to B, but not much of B's to A.[1]

2

But, in fact, preferential systems such as the Sterling Area[2] and the Common Market,[3] are associated with an unusually reciprocal trade pattern. This is doubtless because (d) they reduce the number of serious trade partners. Now plainly in the case of only two partners there must be perfect reciprocity[4] owing to the mere arithmetic of the case. But small numbers have somewhat the same effect, since they lead to large market shares, which in turn implies greater diversity in the choice of goods and services traded. Thus if A trades mainly with B, C and D, and they each take 30% of A's trade, they will quite likely buy from him and sell to him many products; and this in turn reduces the prime cause of irreciprocity, which is not financial multilateralism but commodity specialization.

For clearly, if each country were to trade in very few commodities, there would be no 'random reciprocity', for the trade relations between countries would no longer be random. And this kind of specialization characterizes not only the trade of countries that do little trade with each other (e.g., those excluded by preference systems, above), but above all the exports of UDCs. These countries depend upon nature, not artifice, for their outputs. Hence the geographical distribution of their exports is most irregular. But even the poorest of us need innumerable things; so UDC imports would probably not be geographically specialized were it not for preferences, legal or habitual. In any case, the geographical specialization of imports may differ from that of exports; and specialization in one direction only is enough to establish irreciprocity.

We should, therefore, not be surprised that Mr. Pryor finds that west European countries are and long have been in a state of fair reciprocal balance with each other—though not, of course, with other countries, nearly all of which down to this day export pre-

---

[1] E.g., the British preference on Empire wheat caused Britain, in the late 1930s, to import only Canadian and other Empire wheat. But Canada's counter-preference did not reserve her market for British machinery. On the other hand, since Canadian wheat was also sold elsewhere, wheat remained everywhere available at the world price. But the price of British machinery in Canada was indeed lower than it would otherwise have been.

[2] M. Michaely in *American Economic Review*, September, 1962, p. 697.

[3] Pryor, op. cit., pp. 191, 286-7.

[4] Cuba before Communism is a good illustration: her preferences with the United States almost confined her exports and imports to that single partner.

dominantly some natural product. This, then, is the perfect example of random reciprocity.

3

Mr. Pryor has an index of irreciprocity, which we shall call J. It is the trade balance, without regard to sign, divided by the trade turnover.

$$J_{kj} = \frac{\sum_1^k |E_{ij} - I_{ij}|}{\sum_1^k (E_{ij} + I_{ij})}.$$

Thus where j is the country concerned and i any other country, E_{ij} means j's exports to i, and $1 \ldots k$ are all the countries considered. He finds that the (? unweighted) average of J's for the intertrade of the six countries now in the Common Market[1] was 0·15 in 1953–57 and then dropped, after the Treaty of Rome, to 0·10 in 1958–60; while for Bulgaria, Czechoslovakia, the DDR, Hungary, Poland and Rumania it has consistently been about 0·10 since 1948.

It is undeniably impressive that the Six were all along nearly as reciprocal as eastern Europe, and that recently, perhaps because of the Common Market, they have been just as reciprocal. But there are severe defects in Mr. Pryor's formula, which we discuss in the Appendix; whence it emerges that true reciprocity is much greater in eastern Europe. Moreover, when we move from the little inbred group k to all the n countries in the world we get a far different picture. Italy and France are, after Japan, the most irreciprocal of all ACCs, while the STEs are without exception the most reciprocal of all countries. This is shown by Mr. Michaely, who presents sixty-five countries in descending order of J_{nj}. Of these I reproduce a sample on page 258.

Thus, on the world scene, STEs are strikingly more reciprocal than all other countries. But even so we must be careful when we attribute this to particular causes. We know that policy is highly bilateral, but high degrees of reciprocity might well have arisen spontaneously. Thus suppose simply that the European STEs were MEs which had decided to industrialize rapidly, and preserve 'rational' import and export policies except for two things: they would give each other heavy preferences and they would eschew

---

[1] Including Luxemburg in Belgium. Pryor, of course, speaks of 'multilaterality', not 'irreciprocity'.

TABLE X/1. SOME IRRECIPROCITY INDICES, 1938 AND 1954, 1958

Rank Order		J_{nj} in 1938	Average of J_{nj} in 1954 and in 1958
1	Netherlands Antilles	—	0·77
5	Indonesia	0·31	0·45
12	Japan	0·35	0·37
23	India	0·24	0·29
24	Argentina	0·28	0·29
29	Italy	0·29	0·26
30	France	0·25	0·26
32	Yugoslavia[1]	0·14	0·25
39	Netherlands	0·27	0·22
44	Brazil	0·26	0·21
47a	Germany	0·27	—
47b	West Germany	—	0·20
51	Belgium-Luxemburg	0·20	0·19
52	Finland	0·31	0·19
53	UK	0·22	0·19
57	Canada	0·36	0·17
58	United States	0·28	0·17
59	Cuba	0·13	0·16
60	Mexico	0·21	0·13
61	USSR	0·31	0·13
62	Hungary	0·19	0·12
63	Poland	0·40	0·10
64	Czechoslovakia	0·16	0·07
65	Bulgaria	0·12	0·06
Unweighted average, 1–65		0·29	0·275
Unweighted average, 61–5		—	0·095

[1] In 1948, i.e., the year broken in two by the Tito-Stalin split, 0·17.

SOURCE: M. Michaely in *American Economic Review*, September, 1962.

tropical products. They would then have traded largely with each other, as they do now, and they would presumably have been as reciprocal among each other as Mr. Pryor has shown the Six to be. Therefore, East European J_{nj}s would have been little higher than at present, although their financial relations would have been utterly different.

There is, as we show in the Appendix, a minimum below which J can hardly fall. The phenomenon has nothing whatsoever to do with multilateralism or even with reciprocity *proprement dit*, but is the product of chance fluctuations and the formula chosen for the index. Moreover, a low J is very bad evidence indeed that finance is not multilateral. Let us remember that both the Common Market and the Sterling Area countries have $J_{kk} < J_{nk}$, where k is the smaller group. Yet it is precisely within these areas that financing is most multilateral. On the other side, if J is consistently high there must either be multilateral financing or large invisibles or a constant flow of aid; that much at least is certain.

4

It is only possible, given the sources, to be sure that an STE trades irreciprocally if its visible trade shows the same balance over a long period, and aid and invisibles are known not to complicate the picture unduly. Table X/2 gives the Soviet visible trade that is so consistently irreciprocal as probably also to be multilateral.

TABLE X/2. PROBABLY MULTILATERAL SOVIET VISIBLE TRADE, 1955–61
(mn. old current valuta rubles; E = exports, B = balance)

	1955		1956		1957		1958		1959		1960		1961	
	E	B	E	B	E	B	E	B	E	B	E	B	E	B
UK .	677	+392	593	+295	705	+256	582	+291	663	+300	785	+337	1075	+395
France .	239	+95	279	+77	268	+78	348	+26	351	−51	—		—	
USA .	95	+93	109	+90	64	+23	104	+85	103	+32	99	−141	97	−105
Holland .	131	−2	167	+128	181	+100	228	+157	267	+215	196	+72	188	+111
Finland .	425	−87	459	−126	602	−59	469	−80	578	+9	600	+20	547	−36
Austria .	55	−87	44	−215	72	−200	89	−165	159	−167	194	−128	181	−81
Canada .	8	−3	9	−90	17	−19	9	−92	16	−44	21	−19	19	−164
NZ .	0·1	−16	0	−34	0·1	−32	0·2	−22	0	1	0	−36	0	−35
Australia .	5	−22	a	a	a	a	a	a	a		2	−137	3	−113
S. Africa .	0	−38	2	−49	1	−106	1	−46	1	−24	0	0	0	0
Uruguay .	1	−39	11	−38	1	−72	22	−77	37	−24	5	0	2	−14
Malaya .	0	−87	1	−335	2	−193	0	−472	4	−503	8	−438	8	−670
Ghana .	0	−46	0	−33	0	−76	0	−11	0	−33	22	−63	62	+35
Burma .	1	−66	17	−32	26	−10	10	+10	6	−10	7	−13	16	+6
Indonesia	0	−15	1	−51	22	−57	109	+63	63	+19	65	−61	125	−10
Cuba .	0	−143	0	−59	0	−188	0	−62	0	−30	b	b	b	b

[a] No trade, owing to Petrov crisis (see Chapter XVII).
[b] Cuba went Communist about January, 1960; subsequent years fairly reciprocal.

We see that favorable balances are built up in the four great financial and imperial centers of Amsterdam, Paris, London and New York. They are used to buy raw materials[1] from countries that are so firmly attached to Western industry that Soviet manufacturers could not obtain an *entrée*, whether owing to preferences or to inferior quality. As the country obtains its political freedom, or attracts Soviet diplomatic interest, or goes Communist, direct Soviet exports appear (Ghana, Uruguay, Burma, Indonesia, Cuba)—and sometimes

[1] In the Finnish case, manufactures, but Finnish triangular trade is paid for in another way; see Section 8. The Austrian raw material is oil. The Soviet attachment to this oil, which has recently much diminished, arises from the fact that Zistersdorf was once a mixed company, under the Soviet occupation.

disappear again (Burma, Uruguay) when the aid that finances them ceases, or they are found to be unsatisfactory.

In its original form, about 1955, this trade was typically triangular: raw materials from the USSR to ACC, manufactures from ACC to UDC, raw materials from UDC to the USSR. That, of course, was 'natural'. But from 1955 to 1961 exports to these countries (plus Uruguay, Argentina and Mexico, which are in many respects similar) rose by 270%, while all exports rose by 80%. These attempts at reciprocity must, ceteris paribus, have severely hurt the USSR's terms of trade. For the UDCs tend only to accept Soviet manufactures at a discount, or as part of a bilateral aid package.

The extent of bilateralism may also be gauged by the number of treaties signed. Table X/3 gives a view of their importance.

TABLE X/3. BILATERAL AND MULTILATERAL VISIBLE STE TRADE, 1955
(dollars of total trade in millions; parenthetic figures give percentage of trade with countries where some kind of bilateral agreement was in force)

	United States and Canada	Latin America	Non-Communist Europe	Middle East	South Asia and Far East	Total[a]
USSR'S						
Exports to	18 (0)	32 (100)	537 (59)	34 (99)	10 (92)	633 (62)
Imports from	3 (0)	71 (48)	425 (71)	23 (100)	23 (98)	579 (66)
China's						
Exports to	3 (0)	2 (1)	132 (3)	14 (1)	323 (36)	502 (24)
Imports from	1 (0)	5 (3)	111 (11)	26 (95)	160 (57)	310 (42)
European STEs'						
Exports to	52 (0)	102 (91)	960 (94)	61 (77)	53 (91)	1262 (84)
Imports from	15 (0)	101 (97)	840 (94)	70 (98)	67 (75)	1139 (89)

SOURCE: R. F. Mikesell and J. N. Behrman, Financing Free World Trade with the Sino-Soviet Bloc (Princeton, N.J., 1958), pp. 13, 14.
[a] Including Africa and Oceania.

Many bilateral agreements do not cover all trade between the contracting parties. Indeed, they sometimes cover only a very small part. Moreover, many are very loose. These percentages, then, simply give maxima for the trade that was strictly bilateral. The real proportion was a good deal smaller.

This section teaches a lesson that is not clearly drawn by all students. To an STE trading with MEs, bilateralism and reciprocity offer no advantage. So long as its partners' currencies are convertible, it can pile up a balance here and spend it there with less planning and less administrative difficulty than are required to avoid such balances.

5

The connection between reciprocity and bilateralism becomes still more tenuous when we remember the existence of *re-exports*. The Western world, and therefore our economic theory, is only accustomed to what we may call 'natural re-exports': a big *entrepôt* like London buys and sells raw materials and semifabricates.[1] In STEs there is less of this kind of re-export, owing to the ideological hostility to wholesalers and 'speculation'. But certain countries do specialize in the purchase of particular Western goods, which are then redistributed around the bloc; e.g., Rumania used to be a large importer of drugs, some of which she resold. There is, however, a new phenomenon, the 'financing re-export', which works thus: *A* wants convertible currency more than anything *B* can sell for her domestic use, where *B* is any kind of country with an inconvertible currency. So *A* buys one of *B*'s principal exports, normally a raw material, in excess of domestic use, and resells it. Thus *A/B* trade is both bilateral and reciprocal; yet *A* acquires the convertible currency she wants. For instance, Poland resells Soviet oil, the USSR resells Egyptian cotton and Chinese tin, and many STEs resell Cuban sugar. The thing is almost the same as the 'commodity shunting' whereby merchants tried to evade the inconvertibility of sterling in the 1950s.

Thus normal multilateralism rests upon the re-export of currency; the gold standard rests upon the re-export of that particular currency, or good, gold; and 'financing re-exports' are re-exports of other goods. The more perfect and stable the market for these goods the smaller the distinction. I.e., *Soviet-type re-exports are a kind of multilateralism.* Not every good bought by a UDC or another STE reflects a policy of trade reciprocity: some goods are hard-currency substitutes. The magnitudes can be illustrated from the Soviet case. (See Table X/4, page 262.)

It is evident that despite all rumor, financing re-exports of cotton must be trivial. The export volume has not kept pace with the import volume, and scarcely exceeds its 'natural', or 'pre-Shepilov', level;[2] and the growth of the amount of raw material available for

---

[1] There is a statistical difficulty here. If the United Kingdom resident acts as a principal, what he buys is an import and what he sells is an export, both in the navigation returns and in the b.o.p. account. If he is only an agent he renders a service to a foreigner, and his income is an invisible export in the b.o.p. account; but the navigation returns still show an import and an export. Cf. R. G. D. Allen and J. E. Ely, *International Trade Statistics* (New York, 1953).

[2] The reference is to D. N. Shepilov's epoch-making visit to Nasser in 1956.

TABLE X/4. SOME SOVIET RE-EXPORTS, 1955–62
(thousands of tons)

	1955	1956	1957	1958	1959	1960	1961	1962
Cotton fiber								
Imports								
Total . . .	20	51	109	142	190	193	142	150
From rest of world .	10	13	27	45	100	84	57	82
From the UAR . .	10	38	82	97	90	109	92	68
Exports . . .	337	310	319	311	344	391	383	344
Domestic output . .	1488	1348	1430	1460	1467	1546	1532	1492
Available for processing[1] .	1171	1089	1220	1291	1313	1348	1291	1298
Cotton textiles								
manufactured (thou. sq.								
meters) . . .	5905	5457	5588	5790	6150	6388	6453	6619
Sugar, raw and refined								
Imports								
Total . . .	933	336	645	379	318	1697	3577	2466
From Cuba . .	441	214	351	198	133	1468	3345	2233
From rest of world .	492	122	294	181	185	229	232	233
Exports . . .	210	174	191	200	197	243	414	792
Sugar beets in 'factory state'								
domestic output . .	31,000	32,500	39,700	54,400	43,900	57,700	50,900	47,400
Granulated and refined sugar								
manufactured . .	4704	5945	6029	7199	7832	8278	10,382	9734

SOURCE: *Vneshnyaya Torgovlya SSSR* (Moscow) and *Narodnoe Khozyaistvo SSSR* (Moscow), various editions. Note that stock changes are neglected.

[1] The price difference is not very great, so it is fair simply to add the tonnages.

manufacture is not wildly out of line with the growth of manufacturing output.

Imports of sugar, however, have increased along with the domestic raw material; even imports from the rest of the world have risen along with those from Cuba. Some of the new exports, then, can only be 'financing re-exports' on a large scale. These are made at a loss: thus in 1961, refined sugar was imported at R. 108 per ton, and exported at R. 80.[1] Nevertheless, as a way of getting hard currency this may not have been worse than selling one's best-quality machinery at a discount. If 'financing re-exports' amounted to 200,000 tons they brought in R. 160 mn., or enough to buy 3% of the USSR's visible imports. Compare also the Soviet re-exports of Chinese tin (Chapter IX, Section 6).

The B country that provides A with the re-exportable commodity naturally suffers from any depression of the world price that 'financing re-exports' bring about. But not so if the A merchants sell as skilfully as the B merchants would have, and if these amounts would have been exported anyway. In such a case, however, why should they both have gone to all that trouble? Why should not B simply sell and hand over the currency? The answer must lie, not in a

[1] Poland did the same in 1963; J. Wilczynski, *Journal of Political Economy*, June 1966.

market imperfection as ordinarily understood, but in an irrationality of behavior. It might be that B's devotion to inconvertibility was absolute to the point of absurdity: she had rather someone else converted her commodity into money. Or both parties might be irrationally devoted to reciprocity. Or A might be cheating: when B sold A that part of the commodity she hoped to remove a burdensome surplus from the world market and raise the price of the rest. More rationally, in an imperfect market A merchants might genuinely have better conditions of sale than those of B—in which case this would be a 'natural' re-export. Thus in the actual case of Cuban sugar the ultimate buyer was blockading B but not A.

6

Let us now sum up on bilateralism and reciprocity. Not all exchange control is relevant to our theme. *Resident* inconvertibility can leave relations with foreign countries very multilateral. A and B have bilateral arrangements when A traders must spend their balances of B currency on B goods. Thus the essential aim is to bring about reciprocity. But the latter will not appear if (i) A is transferring capital to B, or (ii) there is administrative convertibility at long intervals, in which A always has a positive balance, which B clears with hard currency. Moreover A and B can trade reciprocally, but not bilaterally, when (a) there is 'random reciprocity' or (b) A is ill placed to trade with any other country.

Finally, before we leave reciprocity, is it wasteful or irrational? The answer is clearly no, if it is random and natural. As we have just seen, the European STEs would probably in any case be rather reciprocal in this way. It is also very easy to overestimate the wastes of planned reciprocity, brought about by bilateralism. The normal proof of this proposition refers only to MEs, and runs as follows. Suppose five countries of equal size, trading as follows (see Figure X/1, page 264): the figures are arbitrary, but are designed to show a fair degree of random reciprocity in places. J_{kk} is 0·15 for each country; and when we reflect that these figures are supposed to show permanent or stable trade, and are exempt from the chance annual fluctuations that do so much to increase J, we can be assured that this is about the true world average (cf. Table X/1 and the Appendix).

Now let a world liquidity crisis threaten, but be staved off by exchange controls, which in turn bring on bilateralism and recipro-

FIGURE X/1

Exports to / Imports from	A	B	C	D	E
A	X	8	6	4	6
B	4	X	8	6	6
C	6	4	X	6	8
D	8	6	6	X	4
E	6	6	4	8	X

city. Since no slump develops *ex hypothesi*, national incomes are constant in money terms and the already reciprocal trade flows unaffected. The partner with the favorable trading balance in each pair is not absolutely deaf to the appeal to increase imports, so each 4 creeps up to 4·5. But—and this is the main thing—each 8 collapses to 4·5. Thus each country's total exports fall by 3, or 12·5%. The 3 resources are—*ex hypothesi* again—diverted to less efficient home uses. Then the loss to national income is whatever rise in costs that diversion may be guessed to bring about. Suppose that costs, due to diminishing returns and more monopolistic inefficiency, rise on average by 20%, and that exports were 24% of the national income. Then the loss in real national income is 0·6%. If the only alternative is continued multilateralism and a descent into unemployment, bilateralism is obviously better. The loss, of course, is not due to the bilateralism itself, but to the reciprocity that results.

If these five countries were STEs they would lose the same amount through reciprocity, but in this case the loss is permanent since the policy is permanent. Although crises occur, as we saw in

Chapter V, they are not the result of liquidity preference, nor are they cured by a plunge into bilateralism and reciprocity since these are already fully present. The question then poses itself, why do STEs trade in this manner? The most illuminating way to answer this is to list together all the reasons why any kind of economy might do so. It will be seen that there are quite as many convincing arguments for bilateralism among MEs. *In particular there seems to be no rational reason for an STE to wish to trade bilaterally with an ME, while an ME might well wish to do so with an STE.*

7

Why should any country wish to trade either bilaterally or reciprocally or both with any other? We confine ourselves in this section to the relations of MEs with each other, or with STEs. But we notice in passing that many of these motives for bilateralism also sway STEs, quite apart from any motives peculiar to them (discussed in the next section).

(i) The first great reason is the preservation of full employment, as set out in Section 6. This obviously does not apply to STEs.

(ii) Then—if it is a distinct reason—there is the sheer chronic shortage of foreign exchange. This does very much apply to STEs, especially for dealings outside the bloc. Now inter-STE balances are in principle never settled in convertible currency, but that principle itself may well be inspired by the chronic shortage. It is hard to imagine reciprocity, at least in its stricter forms, surviving the acquisition of large reserves: compare Section 8, below. As things are, however, small reserves mean inconvertible balances; and no country wants to waste its exports earning such a balance if its own reserves are small too.

(iii) An imperial power *A* will always want bilateral relations with its political dependency *B*, since it owns the bank that keeps the accounts, and the power conferred by bilateralism to grant or deny convertibility is a sharp political weapon. But this does not tell us much about reciprocity. Indeed, *A* may regard *B*'s exports as a valuable counter in world trade (e.g., Malayan rubber), and rather encourage *B* to be irreciprocal. This would be rational also if *A* and *B* were STEs. Soviet re-exports of Cuban sugar are quite possibly an example.

(iv) A creditor country, *A*, might wish to impound the proceeds of *B*'s exports to her, where *B* is a defaulting or shaky debtor, in order to be sure of debt service. This is Smirnov's 'one-sided clearing'.[1] If B naturally runs a favorable balance with A she will be permitted to go on doing so, and, presumably, to convert whatever is left out of the balance. Thus there is no tendency toward reciprocity. If it is A that normally has the favorable balance, she will reduce her exports toward the level of reciprocity. This applies whether we are dealing with MEs or STEs.

(v) Two MEs, C and D, each nervous for their own exchange rates, separately introduce exchange control. They then agree mutually to permit more trade. If C naturally exported more to D, it is a matter of bargaining whether the bilateral agreement reduces the balance at all. It would pay C merely to freeze it at its present size, but D is likely to have the better of the argument and to move the trade pattern toward reciprocity. This is because in an ME exports are unequivocally preferred to imports (Chapter XV, Section 13); so D has the whip hand, since she can cut C's exports by more than C can cut hers.[2]

(vi) A single ME, in the situation of case (v), can impose bilateralism and, if necessary, reciprocity on an STE.

(vii) A small ME may have to impose bilateral restraints upon a large STE, simply because its large purchases can upset markets or even industrial structure. Thus Sweden's balance of payments, and the balance of her engineering industry, were threatened in 1940 by an innocent Soviet attempt to purchase railway wagon wheels. This case is discussed in Chapter IX, Section 3; Sweden, in fact, refused the deal. The Finnish economy has, in fact, been distorted in exactly this way, precisely because Finland was in no political position to talk back. And it is for this very reason that Finland, alone of countries, has enjoyed a multilateral arrangement with pairs of STEs.

(viii) Any ME trading with an STE may fear for the convertibility of its export earnings. Bilateralism gives it a counterweapon, in that now the STE's earnings are also inconvertible.

(ix) In a b.o.p. crisis an ME may impose bilateralism from a mixture of motives (i), (ii), (v) and (vi). But it has a further motive worth separately distinguishing: the forcing of its own exports.

---

[1] A. M. Smirnov, *Mezhdunarodnye Valyutnye i Kreditnye Otnoshenia SSSR* (Moscow, 1960), p. 161. Contrast the solution imposed upon China by Western creditors in 1854: a customs service on Chinese soil, manned by citizens of the creditor nations, and amortizing the Western debt out of the revenues.

[2] But if C provides a single bottleneck good to D, and D none such to C, and it comes to an all-out economic war about the level of trade, C may win.

8

Now why do STEs specially incline towards bilateralism and reciprocity? Many of their motives are the same as for MEs, and have been listed above: (ii), (iii), (iv) and (ix). We return to STE–ME trade in Section 14. Here we deal with inter-STE trade, and we neglect *ex post*, or unplanned, balances. It will always happen in the course of a year that trade planned to be reciprocal throws up a balance, owing to under- or over-fulfillment on someone's part. The multilateral treatment of such small balances is dealt with in Section 16, below. Our concern here is with the much more important question of *ex ante*, or planned, balances.

(*a*) STEs can adopt both bilateralism and reciprocity among themselves, or in trade with MEs, out of sheer intellectual error. Such error might only be obsessive tidiness of mind: bilateralism *looks* neater. Or it might be a Mercantilist preoccupation with the balance of trade.

(*b*) STEs must find, in trade among themselves, that these policies genuinely simplify the intellectual and administrative task of international planning. Thus if the number of countries is n, and planned irreciprocity is permitted in conditions of great international illiquidity, there must be a multilateral planning of balances. The central authority or conference has to coordinate $[n(n - 1)]/2$ balances, or twenty-eight within CMEA. Specifically, it must ensure that the $(n - 1)$ balances of each of the n countries add up to zero. Reciprocity, then, is a simplifier, since it reduces the number of balances from twenty-eight to zero.

(*c*) Much more important is the weakness, nay, the practical nonexistence, of a supranational authority among STEs. Suppose that three sovereign STEs, F, G and H, all agree upon a triangular deal. In conditions of planner's tension, low international liquidity, late deliveries, and latent economic war, they may each feel that a planned favorable balance with one partner is a hostage to fortune. Exports are on the whole unpopular in an STE (Chapter XV, Section 13); they exist only in order to ensure imports. So if F is supposed to overexport to G, and G to H, and H to F, what happens if G falls down on its deliveries to H? H cannot retaliate by delaying deliveries, for in this G has the whip hand. Nor can she threaten F in order to make F threaten G—that is not how international diplomacy works. So, in the strained conditions normal to STEs, we see both that G will want to underfulfill toward H and that H

has no weapon. Therefore, *H* will refuse to accept such a plan in the first place.

In other words, although it is not possible for an international liquidity crisis of the Keynesian type to originate in the domestic economy of one STE and spread to others, something similar can, indeed, spread: a goods crisis and a desire to hoard stocks. Through supply failures and the bottleneck effect the ancient 'policy of provision' (Chapter XV, Section 13) asserts its sway over the planners' minds, and they make whatever export cuts they can get away with. Among such cuts is obviously the reduction of export surpluses to other STEs. It is no accident that multilateralism begins to be spoken about among STEs at just the moment when the CMEA is being strengthened. For such a CMEA could truly penalize failure to fulfill export plans. We see, not for the first time, how centralization rationalizes, partial decentralization causes confusion.

It may or may not be the case that the new international bank (Section 16, below) plans multilateral trade among STEs. For the rest the only planned multilateral trade known to me is the series of Finnish-Soviet-third country triangles planned by the USSR in 1951–55. This exception proves the rule. Finland was at that time a 'non-Communist satellite', politically much under Soviet influence, and burdened by a structural export surplus with the USSR—due to the end of her reparations. In these circumstances the USSR functioned as the required supranational authority. The third country was, significantly, always an STE.[1]

(*d*) Then, where balances are not in convertible currency, a balance with one STE implies purchasing power over specific goods, probably unobtainable in most other STEs. Thus if a Bulgarian credit against Poland is suddenly transferred to Hungary all three countries may be rudely surprised. It might well be that in the next year Poland could have squeezed out more of her habitual exports to Bulgaria, and is not prepared to satisfy Hungary instead. Both client countries may also be disappointed. Even if

[1] To wit, Poland and Czechoslovakia. Cf. F. L. Pryor, *The Communist Foreign Trade System* (London, 1963), p. 194; Ilmari Hustich in *Ekonomiska Samfundets Tidskrift* (Helsinki), 1/1963; R. F. Mikesell and J. N. Behrman, *Financing Free World Trade with the Sino-Soviet Bloc* (Princeton, 1958), pp. 54–5. These arrangements came to an end in 1956. They even included a Soviet-Finnish-Chinese triangle, in which Finland's balance was unfavorable with the USSR, favorable with China. Trilateral balance is, of course, very much easier to negotiate and enforce than multilateral, so it may be of slight interest that any multilateral balance, resting upon any set of bilateral imbalances, can be expressed as a number of trilateral balances. Formal proof is available on request to the author.

the balance is offset against a Polish credit with Hungary, so that
Polish exports to Hungary do not have to rise, Poland may still be
upset at losing her claim on specific Hungarian goods. Any supranational planner must take all this carefully into account. It arises,
of course, from the extreme imperfection of the inter-STE market.

We might infer that a command economy is almost by definition
incapable of multilateralism and irreciprocity when dealing with
another of its kind. Certainly most writing on the subject gives one
this impression: no multilateralism without internal decentralization, it almost says. But in my view this is not so. STEs both can
and do trade irreciprocally, as we have seen, with MEs. So long as
the latter keep a convertible currency, i.e., are prepared to provide
multilateral finance, the thing is easy. Then why should not STEs
make their valuta currency convertible, so that other STEs are
willing to hold it? Why should not the USSR run a regular,
planned trade deficit with Bulgaria, and give her gold, or dollars, or
transferable valuta rubles, or even Cuban sugar?—for sugar, as we
have seen, is almost as liquid as gold.

If CMEA members can pile up a big enough stock of these international counters they can then by mere bilateral *tâtonnements* in the
market place, and without supranational planning, work out an
irreciprocal trade pattern that suits them. If a particular country is
running an overall deficit, it will be running down its stock of
'counters'. Then it should apply more or less the same percentage
cut to its imports from each other country, so as to preserve the
pattern of irreciprocity. No doubt it will be tempted to cut its
imports most where it is in import surplus. But this is the ordinary
temptation of any country that trades multilaterally; it need not be
greater for an STE.

The administrative complications to which we have referred arise
from the necessity to balance everything in directly usable goods.
But this in turn can only be due to a lack of acceptable 'counters',
or to stupidity. I am far from ruling the latter out, after reading so
much of the official literature, but I believe it built originally on
objective circumstances. The lack of international counters was
Europe-wide in 1946–49. The ACCs of Western Europe were just
as bilateral as the budding STEs of the East. But they then took time
out to build up gold and dollar reserves, while the STEs preferred a
breakneck pace of growth that permitted no such thing. The ACCs
also had a tradition, and skilled civil servants and bankers, to whom
the European Payments Union came naturally. I.e., they did not

simply acquire the necessary counters by the sweat of their export surpluses, but also by credit creation. In this the STEs are following them, as we see in Section 17, with a sixteen years' lag.

Ultimately, then, only one thing prevents uncentralized but planned multilateralism among STEs: a shortage of international liquidity. The new centralizing schemes (below) are not absolutely necessary: they are simply cheap ways of providing such liquidity, and ideological cover for what has accidentally come to seem unorthodox.

9

A final consideration, which requires lengthier analysis, is the terms-of-trade argument for bilateralism. To some it seems quite obvious that this argument is valid. Thus Messrs. Mikesell and Behrman simply say:

Bilateralism undoubtedly enhances the buying power of state buying and selling monopolies in dealing with weaker trading partners. This principle is so well known in domestic markets that it scarcely needs amplification.[1]

Amplification is certainly not provided, and the authors continue (their italics):

Thus bilateralism undoubtedly provides a means of *obtaining* more favourable terms of trade for bloc countries, especially in purchasing primary commodities, even though they appear to be *offering* more favorable terms of trade.

—a mysterious claim indeed, for how could the terms of trade be other than what they appear to be?

But domestic markets are not barter markets: firms buy and sell for money, which is 'transferable' or 'convertible' toward third parties. Monopoly and monopsony, with or without discrimination, are not the same thing as bilateral monopoly. This latter state of affairs is alone relevant to international bilateralism. Thus the monopolist of a commodity does well to split up the market for it if he can, and exploit the varying consumers' surpluses in each segment by varying price policies. The main condition for him is that the buyers must be unable to defeat him by reselling it among themselves. Is there some parallel here to, say, the Polish position in 1948: being the only country with a coal surplus in 1948 could Poland rationally prefer the bilateral Europe of that year to the multilateral Europe of 1958 as a market for her coal? The main

[1] Op. cit., p. 27.

condition for her would, of course, be so to ration her coal sales that no country bought enough to be able to re-export.

The short answer is twofold. First, while Poland might gain by bilateralism and reciprocity, her trading partners must then by definition lose; therefore, they would not adopt the policy (unless forced into it by some irrelevant factor). Secondly, even Poland would have done better in a multilateral market. Her power to discriminate is not, of course, increased by multilateralism, *but neither is it reduced*. Instead, the purchasing power of her earnings rises, since she no longer raises up export monopolists against herself. Bilateral monopoly (or in international terms, 'bilateralism') is not as good for her as unilateral monopoly. In this she does not differ from an enterprise.

It is instructive, however, to elaborate. So let us set aside multiplier, transfer and speculative effects, and assume that a country's export volume is not diminished by bilateralism and reciprocity. Then our case differs from price discrimination at enterprise level[1] mainly in that the markets do not all offer the same coin in return. The inconvertible Swedish krona and French franc are not as good as the convertible Swiss franc, and, furthermore, the two inconvertible currencies differ in that, say, Sweden can offer iron ore, much prized by Poland, while France cannot. Suppose that Sweden is short of coal and long on iron ore, so that the ore/coal barter rate is more favorable to Poland in kronor than in Swiss francs, i.e., on the world market. Then bilateralism and reciprocity have done Poland good, and her diplomats should urge it upon all Europe,[2] in order to be able to exploit the Swedes. But it is incomprehensible why Sweden should be selling her ore to Poland when she can get more coal for it with Swiss francs !

10

The case is not altered if Sweden obtains better terms from Poland for some other import or export by means of her unfavorable deal in ore and coal. Bilateral negotiations are notorious for 'full-line forcing' of this kind, which undoubtedly makes the empirical analysis of particular cases very complicated. Thus, this practice will

---

[1] In a world of MEs an enterprise can well discriminate between home and foreign markets. If currencies are convertible, this is a straightforward case of enterprise price discrimination like any other. If they are not, the situation becomes very complicated, and happily irrelevant here.

[2] U.N., Third Sessions of the General Assembly, Part I, *Second Committee on Economic and Financial Questions, Summary Record*, November 2, 1948 (Mr. Modzelewski).

redistribute incomes in Sweden: away from producers of ore and consumers of coal to those interested in other products. If this can be neglected, we have only to say that the more success Sweden has in negotiating over these other products, the less Poland's initial success is worth to her. If, on the average, the relative terms of trade favor either party, the other should break off the deal and sell and buy in Swiss francs.

Such full-line forcing has the disadvantage that its victim must sometimes re-export the inferior goods forced upon him. Poland would, of course, be very foolish to press too much coal on Sweden, as we have seen; for coal re-exports would result and break down her monopoly. But she may well use this monopoly not to get a high price for coal but to promote some other export, even welcoming the possibility of re-export. For she has now imposed on Sweden the sales effort required for this evidently not very useful good, and converted her own stock into cash here and now. Such re-exports, then, might even be planned and agreed by both sides. In the same way either country might not produce at home all its promised deliveries, but instead buy them in the world market and re-export them to the other country. We have here a re-export very different in origin and purpose from the financing kind mentioned above.

II

As to Poland's monopoly power, it depends ultimately on the scarcity of coal alone. Bilateralism and reciprocity might actually hinder her exercise of it. Thus let her simply ration coal out so as to get as much profit as she can in each market, *and spend her earnings where she will*; clearly, they will have greater purchasing power than if confined by irrational restrictions to particular markets. This could only be the wrong policy on two grounds. First, Sweden might have reacted irrationally to the original bilateralism. She might, for instance, miscalculate, and offer a barter deal even less favorable to herself than one for money. Thus, she may object to simply paying a high price that all the world can see, and prefer to wrap up her humiliation in the cloak of barter. Or, since private enterprises and the government in Sweden all have different interests, either coal importers or general exporters may persuade the government to subsidize exports to Poland; and in the play of interests this may turn out worse for Sweden than to pay a high price for coal and be done with it. Secondly, bilateralism might help Poland to differentiate her coal prices. Theoretically, this is not so: any monopolist, by carefully seeing to it that no customer in the low-price market gets more than he needs for his own purposes, can exploit the varying elasticities of demand to the limit. It is his customers' re-exports that defeat his purposes, and bilateralism cannot stop these. But I would not deny a psychological assistance from bilateralism; for it makes some kind of price differentiation almost inevitable, and this prepares men's minds for monopolistic discrimination in particular.

The argument is unaffected if prices in the bilateral market move out of line from world prices, so that national currencies, translated at the current rates of exchange, no longer mean the same thing. In this situation, we have to turn to the terms of trade in each market, i.e., to 'deflate' the money used in the bilateral market so as to render it comparable to that used in the world market. This deflation once effected, we find as before that both parties cannot gain: a very important result for the study of inter-STE trade. This is the 'relative terms of trade' concept discussed in Chapter IX. We learned there that nothing very simple can be said about the effect of bilateralism and reciprocity on the terms of trade of given STEs. It is not even obvious that the USSR gets better terms of trade from eastern Europe than from the world as a whole.

12

It is reassuring to note that once upon a time a power in a less imperialistic position, desiring bilateralism on 'Keynesian' (strictly Mercantilist) grounds, had actually to bribe her partners to get them to accept the practice. This, of course, was Nazi Germany, operating curiously enough in the same part of the world in the late 1930s. Her terms of trade under Schacht were noticeably worse than Britain's, which stuck to multilateral trading. Discriminatory exchange control was introduced in spring, 1934, and the terms of trade moved as follows:

TABLE X/5. The Effect of Schacht on the Terms of Trade
with Eastern Europe, 1934–38
(1933 = 100)

	1934	1935	1936	1937	1938
Germany .	95	89	85	82	90
UK . .	99	96	94	90	96

Source: Howard Ellis in *Quarterly Journal of Economics*, Supplement to Vol. LIV, Part 2.

Even very hostile observers admit the same fact.[1]

It is true that UDCs, ever sensitive on the terms of trade, favor bilateralism and reciprocity. We need not add here to what we have said in Chapter I on the Marxian and Prebischian doctrines that hold the terms of trade to be *a priori* unfair to UDCs; but do these policies in practice get them better terms of trade? I have complete confidence in the logic of the preceding argument, and say that under ordinary conditions they do not.[2]

First, note that such talk always dies down when raw-material prices rise—which is very often the case. It is *ad hoc* talk, much as we showed the doctrines of Marx and Prebisch to be. Secondly, it follows directly from what we have said that it pays to 'be bilateralized': if some great importer wants us to abandon the free disposal of our exports, a big enough bribe may make it worth our while. But no UDC should be so foolish as not to insist upon that bribe. Moreover, it is wise to ask why the importer is willing to pay it.

Thirdly, we must not confuse bilateralism and reciprocity with preferences, state trading and long-term contracts. In these days a UDC is in a strong position to bully a state trader diplomatically, and long-term contracts offer a stability that anyone might rationally prefer to the probability of greater gain combined with the possibility of loss. But such contracts are wholly compatible with multilateralism, and bilateralism notoriously *de*stabilizes prices, since it makes them dependent on the b.o.p. of a particular country.

13

Of less importance than the relative terms of trade, but still interesting, is the question of the general absolute level of prices in bilateral markets: will it normally be higher or lower than outside?

The initial tendency of these prices will depend on the historic causes of the bilateralism. The Sterling Area was founded on a devaluation in order to avoid deflation: it retained the original level of world prices while the outside level fell. Schacht, we saw, had to depress German prices while his East European partners retained their previous price level: that was his bribe. In Stalin's case all prices were meant to be the same as outside, but have, in fact, been higher. This may well be because of the accident that they started at

---

[1] Antonin Busch, *The New Economic Warfare* (London, 1942), pp. 26–30.

[2] I am confirmed by Pryor's estimate (op. cit. p. 183) of USSR's relative terms of trade with UDCs.

the Korean peak level and have been too sticky to fall fast enough; but I personally suspect the human tendency illustrated in the story at the head of the chapter. Bilateral markets are peculiarly subject to the 'money illusion' of which Keynes accused the trade unions.

Summing up on the terms of trade and bilateralism, it is simply as if a Polish peasant were to take his wheat to market and sell most of it for zlotys by auction; but reserve some to make a barter deal with the harnessmaker. Then if the wheat/saddle ratio in the barter deal is the same as the ratio of prices on the open market no-one gains, and the parties have lost only the time spent in concluding the deal. If it is not the same, one of the parties has been a fool. Moreover, the peasant has probably not got the precise kind of saddle he wanted, nor the harnessmaker the amount of wheat he wanted. This, indeed, is why perfect markets grew up out of the individual haggling of peasants—which *is* bilateralism and reciprocity.[1]

14

Bilateralism and reciprocity, then, cannot improve any country's terms of trade if its partner is a free, self-regarding agent. They cannot, where STEs are concerned, be a Keynesian policy. When an STE deals with an ME, they would appear to have only drawbacks for the former. Between STEs the only rational reason for them is illiquidity. So there is some mystery about the Communist devotion to these principles. Moreover, devotion is incomplete in practice. For it seems from Table X/2 that STEs trade multilaterally between ACCs and their dependents. Indeed the sophisticated Poles write in the planned valuta balances with particular ACCs as fully fledged, computable targets like any others. A short historical account is therefore in order.

The official Soviet story on bilateralism[2] is that the USSR did not trade bilaterally until 1929–33, when the currency restrictions introduced by certain ACCs forced bilateralism on her. It includes no explanation of inter-STE bilateralism, and no admission of the exceptions we have shown to exist in Table X/2. And while this account of the origin of the phenomenon is plausible, we have to remember that 1929–33 is precisely the moment of the First FYP;

---

[1] P. J. D. Wiles, *Price, Cost and Output* (2nd ed.), p. 25.
[2] A. M. Smirnov, op. cit., pp. 154–6; L. I. Frei, *Mezhdunarodnye Raschety i Organizovania Vneshnei Torgovli Sotsialisticheskikh Stran* (Moscow, 1960), pp. 145–65. The League of Nations agrees (League of Nations, *Trade Relations Between Free-Market and Controlled Economies* [Geneva, 1943], p. 74).

which may have had some tendency, however irrational and un-necessary, toward bilateralization of trade.

After the war, there was at first no choice: deprived of negotiable foreign currency, no state in any part of Europe could avoid bilateral-ism, indeed, in certain Soviet cases, physical barter. As the satellites were steadily Communized the administrative necessities discussed above (Section 8) added themselves to currency shortage as argu-ments for bilateralism among each other, though this never seems to have been publicly admitted. But trade with MEs might again have become multilateral, as the MEs relaxed their currency restric-tions, had the STEs so wished. Yet they loudly announced their intention at the United Nations in 1948 of sticking to bilateralism.[1]

The statements of Communist representatives on this point are exceedingly brief, and attempt no serious explanation. There are even indications that not everyone agreed on it. Thus the Soviet-Polish payments agreement of January 26, 1948, provided that a balance in the clearing account might, on agreement of both sides, be transferred to a third country, or vice versa;[2] and the celebrated Finnish–Polish–Soviet and Finnish–Czechoslovak–Soviet triangles date from 1949. Moreover, the Czechoslovak delegate at the UN never gave his assent to bilateralism, and there were hints that multilateralism might be a good thing under certain circumstances in both Soviet and Polish speeches.[3]

However, we have seen above many reasons why an ME should press bilateralism upon an STE, just as, in fact, happened in the 1930s. There is no doubt that these reasons still operate. Polish sources inform me that only Canada, the United States and Australia allow total convertibility of Polish balances without question. All other MEs exert one kind or another of pressure for bilateralism, indeed, for reciprocity. There is little doubt that since the war the 'blame' has rested with both sides, while before the war it rested only with MEs.

15

As to multilateralism among STEs, nothing was heard of it after 1948 until the UN Economic Commission for Europe tried to help

---

[1] E.g., U.N., op. cit., November 9, 1948 (Mr. Arutiunian) and November 2, 1948 (Mr. Modzelewski). For a handy brief account of these early years, see Henry Chalmers, *World Trade Policies* (Berkeley, Cal., 1953), which is a series of contemporary annual reports by a United States Department of Commerce official.

[2] I. Zlobin in *Voprosy Ekonomiki*, 2/1962, p. 78.

[3] E.g., U.N., op. cit., November 9, 1948 (Messrs. Arutiunian and Łychowski).

out in 1956. The Commission's scheme began to operate in July, 1957, and continues. It covers all European countries, and from 1963 also UDCs, and thus tactfully conceals the incapacity of STEs to be multilateral among themselves behind the screen of larger goals. The agent is the secretariat of the Commission itself, and its technique is to build closed chains of countries, each compensating the next by the same sum. Each chain is entirely voluntary and entirely *ad hoc*. The amounts cleared have run as follows:

TABLE X/6. MULTILATERAL CLEARINGS THROUGH THE UN ECONOMIC
COMMISSION FOR EUROPE, 1957–64
(July to June, mn. $)

1957–58	22·0	1960–61	6·7
1958–59	18·1	1961–62	7·9
1959–60	15·9	1962–63	3·7
	1963–64	More than 7·0[a]	

SOURCE: Z. Krolak in *Handel Zagraniczny* (Warsaw), 2/1964.
[a] July, 1963–September, 1963.

Most chains have involved an STE, but it is not stated that there have ever been two STEs. This would, of course, be necessary before we could say that the Commission had made multilateral payments between STEs possible. The fall until 1963 was due to the increased use of hard currency; the inclusion of UDCs in the scheme caused the subsequent rise. Clearly, if all West European currencies had always been convertible these chains could have involved only STEs until 1963; the scheme does not arise out of East European inconvertibility alone. Clearly, too, the main effect of the scheme has been on East-West trade; otherwise, the increase in Western convertibility would not have so sharply reduced the volume of business.

16

As to strictly inter-STE trade, there is no evidence that the Commission ever touched it. The CMEA signed an agreement on multilateralism in July, 1957, the same month that the Commission's scheme began to operate; doubtless this scheme had acted as a challenge. A settlements department was specially created in the Soviet Gosbank to handle the business. The system was not quite the same as the Commission's. With the agreement of both partners any bilateral balance might be transferred to a central multilateral pool, where the settlements department did whatever it could. To prevent a weak member flooding the pool, there was an upper limit to the amount transferable. By this method the balances did not cancel out multilaterally, but left net debtors and net creditors. So it was also made possible to settle them with goods; and these physical settlements were carried out by a commission of representatives of the ministries of foreign trade.[1]

Clearly, these arrangements were designed to deal with chance balances arising *ex post*, and not at all with planned multilateral trade. The agreement was much spoken of in 1958 and 1959,[2] but already in 1959 a Soviet writer adjudged it a failure.[3]

By 1962 this complaint was common,[4] and recent articles on the new multilateral bank (below), which should properly pay tribute to its predecessor, fail to mention it. Evidently, the agreement became a dead letter, or nearly so.

17

The new International Bank for Economic Co-operation (IBEC) opened for business on January 1, 1964. The principal change brought about has been of mere accountancy: each CMEA member has now one clearing account only—with the bank. All its commercial transactions with other members pass through this one account, which is kept in valuta rubles.

These rubles are thus automatically *transferable*: a Polish debt to Bulgaria and a Rumanian debt to Poland leave Poland owing the bank the net sum, and if Bulgaria should happen to owe Rumania the same happens. But the rubles are not *convertible* (Section 18), nor has the bank brought about any substantial multilateralism or irreciprocity. For all basic commercial agreements remain both bilateral and reciprocal, and the transferable ruble acts only to cancel (where possible) unplanned balances that arise *ex post*.[5]

Thus, a semiofficial Polish organ could write in July, 1963:

The new system will introduce the principle (*all bilateral agreements remaining in force*) of multilateral settlement: this will allow us to balance debts which *may*

---

[1] Marian Minkiewicz in *Handel Zagraniczny* (Warsaw), 11/1957.
[2] Cf. the sources quoted in Pryor, op. cit., pp. 195–6.
[3] O. Bogomolov in *Mirovaya Ekonomika i Mezhdunarodniye Otnoshenia* (Moscow), 4/1959 (see Alfred Zauberman in *Problems of Communism* [Washington], 4/1959).
[4] Cf. the sources quoted in Pryor, op. cit., p. 197.
[5] Adam Żebrowski (*Finanse*, Warsaw, 2/1964) is almost alone in implying the contrary; he can hardly be right.

arise in the turnover with one country against surpluses *existing* in the trade with another.[1]

And in October, 1963, the Director-General of the Polish Ministry of Finance said:

It has been established that every year, after a series of bilateral trade agreements (and they will continue to be concluded) there will be multilateral trade and finance talks. The objective of these will be to balance the accounts of each country with the remaining partners.[2]

All this implies that the new multilateralism will affect only unplanned balances, as and when they arise and are so distributed as to be convertible, but that no irreciprocal trade will be planned.[3] Thus, taking these sources *au pied de la lettre*, we infer that (where '—20'→ means 'has a favorable balance of 20 with'):

(i) If it turns out *ex post* in the first year that A—20→B—20→ C—20→A, the bank will cancel all the balances, but trade for next year will be planned to be reciprocal; i.e., instead of planning, as would have happened before:

(ii) A←20—B←20—C←20—A, the CMEA will plan:

(iii) A—0—B—0—C—0—A, since meanwhile the IBEC will have cancelled all the balances. But in a free market situation (i) could easily have turned out to be the most economical, and have continued indefinitely.

Or, to take another case, if trade turns out at

(iv) A—30→B—20→C—20→A, a rational supranational planner would infer that this was a natural pattern and plan

(v) A—20→B—30→C—30→A, in order to pay off B's debt to A, and in the third year to settle down with an equilateral triangle, doubtless embodying

(vi) some such expanded value as 25 a side. But, in fact, what will happen is that the bank will cancel as many balances as it can, and then CMEA will plan:

(vii) A←10—B—0—C—0—A.

It is clear that (iii) is better than (ii), and (vii) is better than the corresponding complete reversal of (iv); the bank will do much good. But it is also clear that (i) and (v/vi) are a lot better again.

---

[1] Editorial in *Polish Economic Survey* (Warsaw), 14/1963, p. 8 (my italics).
[2] Henryk Kotlicki in *Polish Economic Survey*, 20/1963.
[3] But other sources imply that some will; see Adam Żebrowski in *Finanse* (Warsaw), 2/1964.

Multilateralism means that we must grant short-term credit. The inter-trade of CMEA members in 1961 was $10,100 mn.,[1] implying about $12,000 mn. in 1963. The bank will have $75 mn.[2] at its disposal, or 0·6% of all relevant imports. The bank's lending power is officially stated to be small, but it is, in fact, quite trivial. The contrast with the IMF is very striking. Thus during 1959, before the recent enormous stand-by agreements had been negotiated, the IMF held, in gold and foreign exchange, 9·6% of all the imports of its members.[3] However, as Franklyn Holzman points out,[4] no one formula tells us the appropriate amount of international liquidity. One needs far greater reserves for irreciprocal than for reciprocal trade, for instance. Holzman makes out the combined reserves of the IMF and all MEs to have been 220% of such trade between them as was irreciprocal on the Michaely-Pryor formula in 1958. If IBEC is—and it surely is—planning for much less irreciprocity, it and its members will need smaller reserves. Again it will never need to make stabilization loans, since STEs do not allow resident convertibility.

Another way of looking at the importance of IBEC is to compare its strength with its members' strength. If Soviet reserves are about $2 md. today (Table V/3), total CMEA reserves might be $2.2 md. The promised $75 mn. is a mere 3·4% of this total, while the IMF had about 25% of its members' reserves in 1958–59.[5] Moreover, we must not assume that the IBEC will be as generous with its resources, whatever we may think of the IMF's record! On the other hand, and perhaps most important of all, IBEC is new, and the acorn gives us no clue as to the size of the oak.

Under present arrangements the IBEC will lend for the following purposes: to tide over random imbalances due to uneven delivery timing, to cover seasonal fluctuations, and in case of temporary b.o.p. difficulties. In each case there are upper limits, and interest is charged as various lower limits are passed. The bank also operates with non-members in transferable rubles, conducts arbitrage in convertible currencies, and invests in joint and other enterprises both

---

[1] Visible imports in 1961 were $8980 mn., including Albania but excluding Mongolia (U.N., *Yearbook of International Trade Statistics*, 1961, p. 24). Set these two countries off against each other and take invisibles to be 12% of visible trade (Chapter XIII, Section 3).

[2] Kotlicki, op. cit.

[3] Visible imports $101·3 md. (U.N., *Yearbook of International Trade Statistics*, 1961, pp. 20–21 taking the whole world except Communist countries to be members). These are taken to be 73% of total imports (Table XIII/2, the unweighted average). IMF reserves were $13·4 md.

[4] In ed. Henry Rosovsky, *Industrialization in Two Systems* (New York, 1966), p. 260.

[5] Holzman loc. cit., and footnote 3 above.

within and without CMEA territory.[1] It is a sort of Soviet-type combination of the IMF and the IBRD, while the nearest parallel to the GATT is, of course, the CMEA itself.

18

The most important issue in Soviet-type multilateralism, then, is whether it is to be *ex ante* or *ex post*; shall the irreciprocity be planned or shall it just happen in the inevitable course of trading planned to be reciprocal? If the latter, the balances to be settled will never be big. But the second biggest issue, equally unsettled, is the convertibility of the balances at the IBEC into hard currency. Certainly, in view of their chronic lack of it, STEs could not be expected to settle bilaterally in it, as they would become liable so often. In fact, hard currency transactions between them have been very rare, partaking of the nature of formal inter-state aid. But if the IBEC sets a tolerable upper limit above which a country's short-term debt with all CMEA members together must be settled in hard currency, this is a much less likely event than exceeding a 'swing' limit with a particular country.

Poland has consistently advocated this since 1963[2], saying, let the transferable ruble be converted into gold above certain limits. We must presume that it is pure selfishness on her part; certainly she admits to having a persistent surplus with the CMEA.[3] I attribute these base motives with such confidence because I do not see, from the Communist point of view, any special logic in the proposal. A preferential area exists in order not to trade with other areas; therefore, in order to economize in their currency. The Polish proposal tends to break down the preference.

If mere financial discipline is the aim, if Poland simply wants the IBEC to work well, there are other penalties for excessive indebtedness that would preserve the preferential bloc while yet rendering it multilateral. The obvious penalty is a stiff rate of interest (as opposed to the present one of under 2%); but commodity penalties and even price penalties could be devised. What is above all untrue is that the transferable ruble must be made convertible in order that trade with ACCs be multilateral. For, as we have seen, such trade is already multilateral; it suffices, for this to be possible, that capitalist currencies be convertible.

[1] Adam Żebrowski in *Finanse* (Warsaw), 2/1964.
[2] See references given by Henry W. Shaefer in *Osteuropäische Rundschau*, 4/1966.
[3] Henryk Kotlicki in *Trybuna Ludu*, April 27, 1965.

The Polish proposal would add only this to the existing degree of multilateralism, that Poland could run a surplus with the CMEA as a whole, and a deficit with ACCs as a whole. The scheme in force prevents such 'inter-bloc multilateralism'.

We must presume, on the always-plausible basis of self-interest, that Rumania has not supported Poland, although she is in matters of international trade much more independent, because she has 'hard-currency commodities' which sell well enough to ACCs. What Poland wants, in a nutshell, is to convert her transit services, which she can only sell to STEs, into dollars.

There is, then, beyond doubt a *drift towards convertibility*. The transferable ruble, good for debts among CMEA members, is no stopping place, nor is it ultimately tolerable that trade plans must always be reciprocal. There can be little doubt that one day USSR and the IBEC will set up a fully convertible currency that any CMEA member can earn by running a planned positive consolidated balance with the CMEA, and use to pay debts in the non-Communist world. Since Rumania has surely torpedoed the supranational organization for some time to come, such consolidated balances will arise from bilateral bargaining and be only nominally subject to the CMEA. They will be restrained, merely, by the IBEC rules. Moreover particular STEs, perhaps especially those not in CMEA, may introduce an administrative convertibility of their own currencies. But we can hardly expect resident convertibility; surely only Yugoslavia will undertake such a folly (Chapter VI, Section 15).

A convertible currency for general trade is, after all, a social service to the world. In the bad old days—which UK and USA madly seek to perpetuate—particular countries provided it. And there is some profit in this, provided residents are forced to hold a distinct, inconvertible, currency. Otherwise the domestic economy must be forever more deflated than is good for growth. The need for caution is much enhanced by the use of such trading currencies as bank reserve currencies—but this is not a Communist problem. In the future, however, it will be international organs like IBEC and IMF that provide both trading and—where needed—bank reserve currencies.

19

It is often not enough, in trading with an STE, to import as much as one exports overall; various parts of total trade, variously defined, must also balance exactly.

One case may be christened *enterprise reciprocity*: all exports to an STE must be matched by extra imports from it. Thus, during the great Czechoslovak b.o.p. crisis of 1962–63 a particular capitalist firm that had made a sale would be told that the deal was off unless it could spend the krona proceeds in Czechoslovakia itself. Alternatively, a special agency, *Transakta*, stood ready to find another capitalist customer to spend the proceeds—for a finder's fee of 5%! Occasionally, also, the STE imposes the task of reciprocity on its own foreign trade enterprise.[1]

Similar to this is *marginal reciprocity*: any sale to an STE over and above the existing plan must be matched by a purchase from it. A good instance is the Greek match transaction described in Chapter IX, Section 19. But in this case there was a subtle difference: not facing at that time a b.o.p. crisis, both the USSR and Czechoslovakia went out of their way to offer 'marginal reciprocity' as an attraction to Greece. And so it very well may have been;[2] the main point is the STE's institutional capacity to make such offers. No doubt, too, STEs have also on occasion had to insist on this kind of reciprocity when it was most unwelcome to their customers.

Then there is what we may call *processing reciprocity*: the STE delivers a raw material or semifabricate to its trade partner (STE or ME) to process and return. The payment is a certain amount of the raw material in question.[3]

Finally there is the commodity-group reciprocity of Chapter VIII, Section 19: trade in heavy industrial products should balance itself.[4]

Appendix to Chapter X

ON THE MICHAELY-PRYOR IRRECIPROCITY FORMULA

The meaning of the index J is best grasped by illustration. If the set k consists of a, b and c, and

$$\text{if } E_{ac} = 0, \quad I_{ac} = 100, \quad E_{bc} = 100, \quad I_{bc} = 0; \quad \text{then } J_{kc} = 1\cdot0; \tag{1}$$
$$\text{if } E_{ac} = 50, \quad I_{ac} = 50, \quad E_{bc} = 50, \quad I_{bc} = 50; \quad \text{then } J_{kc} = 0; \tag{2}$$
$$\text{if } E_{ac} = 45, \quad I_{ac} = 55, \quad E_{bc} = 55, \quad I_{bc} = 45; \quad \text{then } J_{kc} = 0\cdot10; \tag{3}$$
$$\text{if } E_{ac} = 42\cdot5, I_{ac} = 57\cdot5, E_{bc} = 57\cdot5, I_{bc} = 42\cdot5; \text{then } J_{kc} = 0\cdot15. \tag{4}$$

---

[1] There are several Western specialists in such activities (cf. *Observer*, London, February 5, 1967). Their work is by no means confined to STEs.

[2] But the extremely favorable terms of trade probably counted for more.

[3] For a recent case see *Süddeutsche Zeitung* (Munich), December 14–15, 1963: Dutch purchases of Soviet steel ingots in exchange for the sale of steel rolling services.

[4] But when Czechoslovakia practiced this against USSR under Stalin it was held to be sabotage! Cf. *Prozess gegen die Leitung des Staatsfeindlichen Verschwörerzentrums mit Rudolph Slánský an der Spitze* (Prague, 1953), p. 395.

But at few points in all economics is our devotion to the time-interval in which the earth circles the sun so misleading. Suppose situation (3) shows a group of STEs: then it will be usual for them to plan exact reciprocity and fail to achieve it. If C underfulfills its export plan toward A more grossly than its export plan toward B, and if at the same time A exports loyally but B less loyally, we get the particular 45–55–55–45 pattern shown. But precisely because of these events the next year's plan will be for 55–45–45–55. Suppose this second plan is exactly fulfilled, then *ex post* over the two years combined $J_{kc} = 0$; and this clearly expresses the planners' intentions, which are that precisely this should be true *ex ante*. It is true, but more than a little confusing, to be told that *ex post* J_{kc} was 0·10 in each year; or that *ex ante* it was 0 in the first year but 0·10 in the second!

Thus from 1955 to 1961 of all STEs only Poland and Mongolia had consistently one kind of visible trading balance with the USSR, Soviet exports exceeding imports in both cases.[1] This is clearly due in Poland's case to the large transit services she notoriously renders, so that we may doubt whether the Polish over-all trade balance had, in fact, consistently one sign. Mongolia, too, renders transit services, but undoubtedly the main factor in her balance is Soviet aid; i.e., we may assume that her over-all trade balance with the USSR is also negative. It follows that over a few years the Soviet J with other STEs is negligibly small.

A cursory examination of Polish trade figures with other STEs also shows J about zero.[2] We may, therefore, conclude that STEs are a great deal more reciprocal than the statistics of any single year indicate. Within so short a period, chance fluctuations, or the deliberate correction of previous chance fluctuations, give J an irreducible minimum value.

Would the same be true of MEs? It appears not. Thus, of Common Market countries in 1957–61:

Germany had a constant visible surplus with all 5 partners,
Italy had a constant visible deficit with all 5 partners except Holland in 1961,
France had a constant visible deficit with Germany and Holland,
France had a constant visible surplus with Italy and Belgium,
Holland had a constant visible surplus with France and Italy,
Holland had a constant visible deficit with Belgium and Germany,
Belgium had a constant visible deficit with France and Germany,
Belgium had a constant visible surplus with Italy and Holland.

Thus Mr. Pryor's $J = 0·10$ for each year is true also of a number of years. So he has correctly stated the degree of irreciprocity of the Common Market, but much overstated that of the CMEA. The difference is, of course, that the former countries genuinely trade on multilateral principles, while the latter, trading bilaterally, simply fail to achieve the reciprocity at which they aim within each 365-day period.

As the Polish case has already shown, invisibles present an awkward problem. Even the most advanced and publicity-minded Western countries seldom break them down by trading partners, yet quite small invisibles may be enough to reverse a visible trade *balance*, the numerator in the formula for J. Countries like Poland are, therefore, better excluded. In this connection, Mr. Michaely prices

[1] *Vneshnyaya Torgovlya SSSR* 1958 (Moscow, 1959); ibid., 1961 (1962); ibid., 1956 (1958).
[2] *Rocznik Statystyczny* 1963 (Warsaw, 1963); however, the expected visible deficit turns up with the USSR, the DDR and Czechoslovakia, for which Poland renders considerable transit services.

his imports c.i.f. without question, Mr. Pryor tries to reduce them to f.o.b. The latter is clearly right: the transport to A's frontier of goods from B might, for all we know, have been on the ships or rails of C, and we have no other ground for including it than lack of research funds.

If goods (or services) are rendered as part of an investment, or in order to amortize a debt, bilateralism is not disturbed, but irreciprocity is no longer evidence against it. Indeed, as we saw in Chapter X, one of the very principal reasons why a strong country D may impose bilateralism on a weak country E can be to collect a debt—by impounding the proceeds of E's exports instead of allowing them to be converted. And in happier circumstances D may be tempted precisely by the existence of bilateral ties to invest heavily in E, thus running a big trade surplus and piling up an inconvertible currency balance over many years. Nearly all Communist foreign aid is of this nature. Such considerations led Mr. Pryor, correctly, to exclude Albania from his reckonings of J; yet, of course, Albania trades bilaterally.

Finally we have to note a slightly different formula for J. Mr. Michaely's index of irreciprocity is:

$$J_{nj} = \tfrac{1}{2} \sum_{1}^{n} \left| \frac{E_{ij}}{E_{nj}} - \frac{I_{ij}}{I_{nj}} \right|.$$

This is the same as Mr. Pryor's formula if $E_{nj} = I_{nj}$, and this condition does approximately hold for the countries they take, since they both exclude countries with marked visible trade balances. We thus do no violence to either party if we compare their figures directly.

CHAPTER XI

IMPERFECT COMPETITION, DECENTRALIZED PLANNING, AND NATIONAL SOVEREIGNTY[1]

1 Purpose of chapter.
2 Sovnarkhozy versus countries.
3 Supranational versus national planning.
4 Competition versus computation.
5 Perfect computation implies a supra-national authority—
6 and a communications network out of this world.
7 Decentralization is inevitable in command economies—
8 but leads to irrational choices of both 'what' and 'where'.
9 Indeed, all decentralization makes irrational—
10 and particular command hierarchies do this in particular ways.
11 Decentralized planning must use broad categories, which are usually meaningless.
12 Inter-STE trade as an example of decentralized planning:
13 if such trade can be rationally ordered by a center there is no economic need for separate countries at all.
14 Epiphenomenal decentralization.
15 *A priori* sectoral allocations are therefore also irrational—
16 but mixed economies need not be.
17 Summing up.

I

THIS chapter contrasts two myths: perfect competition throughout a whole economy[2] and 'perfect computation' as defined in Chapter II. It maintains that the former is in some respects as centralized as the latter, and that decentralized computation, the only kind possible, resembles in many important respects imperfect competition. It follows that subordinate planning authorities are an evil, if a necessary one. Since the existence of separate Communist countries also

[1] A preliminary version of this chapter appeared in *The Economics of Planning* (Oslo), 1/1964. Many of the same points are made by R. W. Campbell in his 'On the Theory of Economic Administration' in ed. Henry Rosovsky, *Industrialization in Two Systems* (New York, 1966).
[2] In naturally monopolized industries this concept entails a public board operating according to Lerner's Rule, i.e., marginal cost = price. It is not to be inferred that I hold perfect competition in particular sectors of capitalism to be mythical; quite the contrary.

decentralizes computation, some gloomy conclusions are drawn for national sovereignty. Thus a rather flickering theoretical light is thrown upon the Rumanian-Soviet controversy.

2

The parallel must first be developed between nationally independent STEs and territorially defined bodies within an STE, such as the sovnarkhoz.[1] If supranational planning is tight, the only economic differences are likely to be monetary. For although the main physical targets are set by an outside authority, the separate country still has a separate currency, central bank and b.o.p. Clarity demands, then, that we first distinguish this normal kind of balance from the balance of payments of a sovnarkhoz or other area using the national currency. If all the sovnarkhoz's enterprises are profitable, it is highly probable that the balance of payments across its boundaries will favor it; as there is then no unit on its territory receiving any subsidy (from the central treasury) or borrowing at short term (from the central bank), which is what we normally mean by an adverse b.o.p. There will, of course, be a flow of taxes to the capital, and a flow of long-term funds and social services in the opposite direction. But we may treat the long-term capital in this case just as we do when the relation is international: the flow is 'normal' and is defined as a constituent part of the balance, resembling normal exports. As to the social services, they should figure as if they were pensions, etc., duly paid to emigrants by the country in which they had been earned. The taxes correspond to international tribute or reparations.

If, however, the separate area is a country, every enterprise within its borders can be profitable, yet the b.o.p. unfavorable. For prices can easily be such as to make exporting enterprises profitable while they underfulfill the plan, and importing enterprises profitable while they overfulfill it. Indeed, the plan itself might not have aimed at foreign balance. And all this is compatible with a balanced budget.

[1] In 1957 the USSR was divided, for the planning and operation of industry and construction, into about 100 territorial units called sovnarkhozy, in place of the approximately thirty previous ministries. Under these latter the economy was split up by products; now, it was split up by areas. Thus under the old dispensation all steel mills everywhere were governed by a ministry of ferrous metallurgy in Moscow. Under the new one a steel mill in Leningrad was governed, like all other factories in Leningrad, by the sovnarkhoz of that city. The territorial principle was also partly applied in Czechoslovakia and Bulgaria. The sovnarkhoz had no separate monetary system; it was not even a tax-collecting unit. When Khrushchev fell the sovnarkhozy were abolished and the ministries re-established.

Quite irrespective of the profits of enterprises or the state of the public revenues, the country's central bank will have to borrow from others. This is not to say that internal monetary balance will correct, or imbalance upset, the b.o.p.; we saw in Chapter III that this is not so for STEs. It is only to say that there is a consilience of internal monetary and external trade balance in the case of a sovnarkhoz, none in the case of a country.

3

Having mastered this distinction we can briefly show the similarities and divergences between supranational and national planning. First, all the planning is primarily physical in both cases, but there is also a strict monetary plan for the sovnarkhoz. So long as the country remains even nominally independent, it will surely retain its own currency, central bank and budget. So the cleft between monetary and physical planning is likely to be far greater in the supranational case. Secondly, in no case will b.o.p. 'crises' be entirely eliminated. Even a sovnarkhoz may have a bad harvest. Indeed, since international trade is normally planned to balance anyway between STEs it would seem that supranational planning will accomplish nothing new here. Only, perhaps, since it will be more strict and detailed it will be more effective.

Thirdly, just as it is possible to transmit orders via production-branch, not territorial, authorities within a country, so it is possible between countries. In the USSR the territorially-defined authority had until 1957 little to do with economic planning, which was built around ministries of ferrous metallurgy and the like. In the world at large the first successful supranational body was the European Coal and Steel Community, which similarly operated on a production-branch basis, giving orders not to countries but to the coal and steel industries within them. In 1964 a similar body was founded under the auspices of CMEA: Intermetall, which co-ordinates certain aspects of metallurgy and engineering (but not fuel) in the DDR, Czechoslovakia, Poland and the USSR. But, lastly, just as the territorial principle gives more weight to local feeling within the USSR, so supranational planning among STEs will appear to violate national sovereignty less if it at least works through the Gosplan of each STE. Even so, however, the production principle cannot possibly be neglected; the supranational authority is bound by mere technology to reckon up *how much* steel is produced as well as *where*, and therefore to instruct each country's Gosplan accordingly.

4

Contrast, now, perfect computation with perfect competition. Assume away for the moment the cost of organizing either system, and note in passing that perfect competition, with its brokers and tickertapes, is far from costless. *This latter system is in a sense very centralized*, in that knowledge of current scarcity conditions and access to both resources and outlets are universal. The perfect market and the rules of the game (especially the free-entry rules) are mechanisms specifically designed to ensure that everyone who needs to know knows, and that resources go to the highest bidder, i.e., in the direction most useful to the consumer, while outlets go to the lowest bidder, i.e., to the producer who uses the fewest resources. Thus decisions are invariably taken in the light of countrywide, even worldwide, scarcity conditions.

The decisions themselves are, of course, absolutely decentralized: there is no authority above the enterprise. But the huge majority of decisions actually taken will be the same as those taken under perfect computation. Where there are differences, presumably the latter is to be preferred, since it is immune from speculative hysteria and makes full allowance for external economies. In perfect computation knowledge is, or need only be, confined to the center, where alone it is needed; it is universal in the sense that the single decision-maker has it. Decision-making is, of course, centralized by definition, and the problem of individual access to resources and outlets falls away; for there is only one 'enterprise', and it has access to everything. It follows that the resource allocation resulting from universal free trade will be the same as that resulting from a supra-national command economy, provided that the decision-makers are animated by the same principles. In a general way, the most correct principle is, of course, that marginal cost should equal price.

Imperfect competition, on the other hand, results in a fragmentation of knowledge and of access to resources and outlets. To say that these things are fragmented is to say they have been monopolized; i.e., rendered costly or unobtainable to some—whether innocently or not, avoidably or not, is another matter. This is pretty much how imperfect competition is defined.

To such a definition there appear to be two principal exceptions, which we shall mention here only to clear them out of the way. The first is perfect oligopoly, in which marginal cost may still not equal price even though there is free knowledge and access. This special case is rare to the vanishing point.[1] The second is what we may call the mere 'allocative inefficiency' of the participants. Under this heading I include breakdowns of normal communications, and such intellectual errors as the use of average instead of marginal concepts; but not 'productive inefficiency' such as ignorance of, or failure to apply, modern techniques. 'Allocative inefficiency' is quite compatible with the ordinary definition of perfect competition. I single it out here only for the sake of comparative justice, since I wish also to abstract from its counterpart under computation. For the imperfections of computation are undeniably twofold: those due to allocative inefficiency and those due to a similar fragmentation of knowledge and access.

We do not speak here of the former; i.e., of the irrational criteria and procedures of Communist planners, so much more often stressed by Western economists than the corresponding allocative inefficiency of competing enterprises. It is the fragmentation of knowledge and access under computation that concerns us, *because in this case its name is decentralization*. When we say that in an STE knowledge and access are fragmented, we mean that some authorities know about particular scarcity relationships while others do not; some have access to resources denied to others; outlets are confined to particular suppliers, not the cheapest, etc. And all this, of course, is because there is not one authority but many. Even if a final super-authority exists, it is not exercising its powers in every instance; so sovereignty is fragmented *de facto*; and that, after all, is what de-centralization means.

5

Now just as nature, geography and technology conspire to make competition imperfect, quite apart from the evil machinations of men,[2] so do various given factors ensure that an STE should be decentralized, i.e., computation be imperfect. One of these is the sovereignty of the nation-state, our principal subject here. A federation, such as the USSR, can be entirely nominal: the Party is in no sense federal, and innumerable economic administrative organs either are central or, if regional, cut across the borders of the political sub-divisions. But not even Stalin could make the nation-state into a nominal entity. In particular, he never set up any

---

[1] See P. J. D. Wiles, *Price, Cost and Output* (2nd ed.), pp. 28–9.
[2] Ibid., p. 18.

supranational planning body. It is perfectly false that CMEA was such a body (Chapter XII); and the innumerable other channels of interference—advisers at all levels, normal diplomacy, Party emissaries—did not bring about anything like a co-ordinated and detailed plan.

Thus free trade and perfect competition, centralizing only knowledge of scarcity conditions and access to resources, and extruding national sovereignty from economic affairs, can achieve a rational international allocation of resources. But a group of STEs can only do the same by superimposing a supranational sovereignty. In both cases, the state feels its independence threatened, but in the latter far more so: since there is a personal authority in a defined place, there is 'someone to shoot'. In the absence of imperialistic developments (Chapter XVI) the free market preserves infinitely better the sensation and, indeed, the reality of political sovereignty. The inter-STE authority can, of course, be governed by a democracy of states, and subjected to a constitution. But it must still by definition be supranational, not merely international.

It is with this problem that Khrushchev struggled in 1962–64. Economic efficiency and the need to stop Chinese political penetration pointed the same way: to a tighter integration of the CMEA. Yet it was impossible to reduce the smaller Communist countries to their status before 1956, and Khrushchev surely did not mean to try. No doubt, he meant seriously to observe the CMEA's democratic constitution, even while giving it extra powers. Nevertheless, the memory of Stalin was green, and, indeed, democratic procedures are in a perfectly general way incompatible with Communist ideology and practice. Moreover, even in the most genuinely democratic[1] supranational setup a large country like the USSR would dominate by the mere nature of things. The result was the Rumanian split described in Chapter XII. The present chapter could be said to be the economic theory of the Galati steel-mill crisis, or the explanation why economic rationality is incompatible with the existence of Rumania. With sufficient idealism, humanity may eventually take the road of democratic supranationalism; or states may disappear by conquest. But as things are, the existence of states is an almost insuperable obstacle to perfect international computation.

---

[1] The reference is, of course, to a democracy of states, however undemocratic their internal affairs.

6

A second obstacle is at present quite insuperable: the total incapacity of human communications to bring enough data, punctually, to the computers. At this point we must drop our assumption that computation and competition are costless systems. As is well known, we are very far indeed from being able to collect data on supply and demand for all products and transmit them to one center. Moreover, computers are not yet advanced enough to perform the correct mathematical operations upon these incredible masses of data either accurately enough or quickly enough for use. And then the orders have to be sent back, enforced, and audited, which is also a very serious communication problem.

Universal perfect competition is also, but slightly less of, a pipedream. The administrative cost of really establishing it everywhere would, similarly, be very great, because of the mass of data required. We have not space to say very much about these costs, but broadly speaking, perfect competition requires only that knowledge of the price be communicated and centralized, though certainly it is an immense advantage if knowledge of the techniques of production is similarly treated. Perfect computation, on the other hand, requires also that knowledge of the supply and the demand curves be communicated and centralized. In the former, the requisite calculations are conducted by each enterprise; in the latter, by the center. We have extremely little idea what each system costs, but it seems fair to accept the standard *a priori* Western view that the administration of competition is very many times cheaper than that of computation; a cheapness for which, of course, we pay, for instance through neglect of external economies. But our ignorance of the comparative costs of the two systems is one of the most serious gaps in all economics.

7

Anyhow, an STE must, whether national or supranational, be partly decentralized. Detailed information need then only pass up a small administrative distance, and detailed orders can be worked out by a low-level body and passed down the same small distance. By dealing in broader categories the low administrative body can similarly inform and receive orders from a body at a higher level, and, similarly again, that body can deal with the center, or yet another intermediate body. The volume of communication passing between any two bodies, the volume of computation required of any body, and the span of command (number of people with whom a superior must deal directly) can thus always be manageable.

This span may not, of course, be the same between all levels, and there is no reason to suppose that fallible human beings will arrange these matters optimally. This is especially so because all power is political power. National minorities, like nation-states, object to being sunk within larger bodies and also to being split into smaller bodies. Personal empire-building will tend to enlarge bodies but also to multiply them. Thus, even if the administratively best size and number of bodies were known it would not be obtained. But some hierarchy of bodies there must be.

8

In the context of international trade and national minorities, we naturally think of the intermediate bodies as defined on the territorial principle, and controlling all economic activity within their geographical borders. Some STEs, notably the USSR under Khrushchev, have been slavishly divided up on the territorial principle even where national minority feelings are not affected—indeed, even where the boundaries drawn give them gross offense—and even as concerns 'octopoid' industries (e.g. railroads) where the principle is most inconvenient. These territorial bodies are, as we saw, the sovnarkhozy. But the principles remain the same if the 'body' is defined as a branch of production, like the old Soviet ministries and *glavki*. All the same decisions of what, where, when, how, and for whom to produce have to be taken in any case. Some of these decisions will be taken better, some worse, depending on the way the hierarchy of 'bodies' is drawn up.[1]

However, the mere existence of 'bodies' with powers of their own is an imperfection of computation. This can be illustrated first with regard to 'what', i.e., to the products chosen:

Suppose that two neighboring sovnarkhozes both use the established criteria of central planning correctly in view of the resources and needs of their territories. They will both produce racing bicycles for boys, and compete to sell them in a third sovnarkhoz. Either perfectly centralized planning, or a free market into which no higher body than an enterprise entered, would have resulted in only one sovnarkhoz specializing in such bicycles. The only way in which two independent

[1] Cf. P. J. D. Wiles, *The Political Economy of Communism*, Chapter VIII; and Campbell, op. cit.

sovnarkhozes could effect the same result would be for them to establish a perfect inter-sovnarkhoz market and compete in it, like very large firms. . . .
Whichever solution they adopted, they would have to use it all the time and in exhaustive detail. It would be useless, for instance, to have an inter-sovnarkhoz market in some such broadly defined commodity as 'steel', or to accept orders concerning 'steel' from the central computer, while filling in the details oneself. For economic life does not consist in making 'steel': it means making racing bicycles for boys. In such narrow categories are things bought and sold, over immense distances: and in such must they be planned.
The same is true if the subordinate unit we are considering is the enterprise, not the sovnarkhoz. The story of the nails is classic.
A factory was making nails, and its output target was expressed as a number of nails. In order to avoid excessive centralization all other details were to be settled by the factory. So it made the nails as small as possible. To remedy this the planners re-expressed the target in terms of a weight of nails. So the factory made them as large as possible. Then the planners abandoned decentralization and handed down a plan for kinds of nails, each of a different weight, and a number for each kind. But clearly an alternative improvement would have been to decentralize all decisions in a competitive market.[1]

This kind of thing explains the notorious pendulum between centralization and decentralization to which Communist planning has been subject. First we centralize, and pile up an excessive bureaucracy, inhibit initiative, etc. So, secondly, we decentralize, and find we are paying too heavy a penalty in irrationality. That irrationality is, indeed, the second pole of the pendulum has not been enough appreciated. Naturally, total decentralization would have very different effects, but that is, of course, ruled out by the institutions and ideology—and perhaps also by its effect on goals other than rational resource allocation.

The point can also be illustrated in the hardly less vital matter of 'where', i.e., the location of economic activity:

Then, too, regionalism is not only an intellectual standby, but also an administrative necessity. For the central planner has to think in broad categories, lest he be bogged down in details. So just as he must think of steel, not bicycle wheels, he must think of regions, not the location of a given plant. If his problem is to be administratively manageable he must delegate decisions about bicycle wheels to trusts; so also the placing of plants to regions. With ideal communications, indefinitely much information and good computers—i.e., with perfect computation—the central office can dispense with all such intermediaries and delegation, as we have already seen. It can deal directly with a given establishment, telling it to go to the north-eastern suburbs of Vinnitsa and make bicycle wheels. But life is not like that yet. Imperfect computation requires not only regionalism but regional *authorities*.

[1] L. Smolinski and P. J. D. Wiles, in *Problems of Communism*, November–December, 1963, pp. 24–5.

The necessity to think in such broad terms has very unfortunate results at the margin. The planner must lay down quantities of 'steel' and 'aluminium' without ever knowing whether the marginal bicycle wheel plant is as profitable as the marginal saucepan plant. Under perfect computation these two are directly compared, and production in each line is pushed until it is equally profitable; the demand for such general items as steel and aluminium is determined solely by the demand for such particular items as bicycle wheels and saucepans. But the use, under imperfect computation, of intermediate authorities for steel and non-ferrous metals limits the equalization of profit to alternative outputs within each branch separately. So also with regions: it may well be approximately right that Ukraine should have so many new factories, but we cannot tell whether specifically Vinnitsa should have a bicycle factory until we know what RSFSR is doing about bicycle factories. Ideally, under perfect competition and perfect computation alike, the regional distribution of new plants to Ukraine is visible only *ex post*. I.e., it merely results from the location of specific plants to specific places.[1]

9

All of this has obvious relevance to international economics; we need only change the names. Indeed, the point is very general and may be formulated thus: the view of every quasi-independent subordinate authority, or 'body', as we shall say, in every economic system is blinkered, and even given the very best general instructions it will not act in accordance with 'the social interest'. This may be demonstrated as follows.

A 'body' with no independence at all is a mere transmission belt for superior orders. It will, of course, pursue 'the social interest' as the center sees it; and that down to the very last detail. It has no need to be informed about conditions elsewhere, and access to the best supplies and outlets is ensured by the all-knowing center. But our proposition does not concern this kind of subordinate. We need only note our general assumption, common to the whole succeeding argument, that the center has, indeed, correctly perceived 'the social interest'.

The 'very best general instruction' is presumably to equate marginal cost with price, while using the cheapest technique. It can and should be elaborated to take account of this or that external economy. But in a free market profit is much the strongest activator (Chapter II, Section 3); and it does not pay the subordinate authority (in this case the enterprise) to take account of external economies or, indeed, to equate marginal cost with price. The subordinate is fairly

[1] Wiles, *The Political Economy of Communism*, pp. 149–50.

well informed (by the market) and has good general access, but he is ill activated (by private profit).[1]

On the other hand, he can receive *rather* detailed instructions from a central command post. These now become our 'very best general instructions', and we again assume them to be right. The subordinate is activated to carry them out by plan-fulfillment bonus, threat of imprisonment, etc. Let us assume a very large item: these stimuli are universally, efficiently and ineluctably applied. But they never activate him to do anything in particular, since the instructions are all about 'steel', not 'bicycle wheels'. Nor has he any longer general access to the cheapest supplies and most anxious customers, since many of these have been cut off from him *a priori* by the central planners' general instructions to other subordinates. So he blindly bargains his way along through a maze of *ad hoc* deals. It scarcely matters what activates him to do one particular thing rather than another. He might spontaneously choose his own micro-activator, say, profit; or it might be given him as part of his general instructions, say, a bonus based on gross sales. Similarly, his micro-criterion might or might not be given him. If he were free to choose, he would presumably equate criterion and activator, choosing the most profitable course in order actually to enjoy the greatest profit. But the center might easily lay down gross output, net output, some physical targets, customer's requirement, or, indeed, again profit. In all cases, cut off as he is from universal access and doubtless also information, the subordinate will do the right thing only by chance.

10

Then, too, the way in which the 'body' is defined leads to differing kinds of distortion. Innumerable 'grids' of subordinate command, both overlapping and mutually exclusive, can be placed over the economy. An infinite number of types of intermediate body results. Often different instructions are given to each type: technological bodies will modernize techniques, territorial bodies will locate enterprises, production-branch bodies will decide output magnitudes, etc., etc. But most economic decisions *can* be made by any

---

[1] There is an interesting and neglected possibility, which we have not space to pursue here: instruct the subordinate to act with complete freedom on the market in pursuit of social profit, but confiscate 100% of the private profit he makes, and reward him from the central treasury according to the auditor's judgment of how well he has fulfilled his instructions. The obvious flaw is the weight of responsibility placed upon the auditor.

body, however defined: the State Committee on Technology, for instance, could locate enterprises. Yet even if we give these various types of body the same activators and the same criteria, they will use them differently and violate them differently.

There are at least two possibilities. First, the whole system may be impregnated with some irrationality, which, however, will receive a significantly different content according to which hierarchy of bodies is used. Thus planner's tension leads in all STEs to the phenomenon I have called 'subordinate autarky'. For tension means that someone or other will have to do without planned, and, indeed, needed, supplies. So, mistrustful of suppliers they cannot command, bodies set up new suppliers of their own; and gradually each body becomes autarkic. This is, of course, one of the main reasons why a country, of Soviet or any other type, should be autarkic; and it was the principal vice of the sovnarkhozy.[1] But the production-branch ministry is by no means free of it: transport, repairs and minor construction were and no doubt are again all carried on in the same area by the auxiliary enterprises of each ministry. Ministries even used to make their own new machinery, including the most expensive and sophisticated kinds. These enterprises were well below optimal size, and their products were hauled over inordinate distances. The Sovnarkhozy on the other hand avoided even rational long hauls, and short hauls too if they led across their boundaries.

Now, clearly, subordinate autarky is not touched by reorganizing the hierarchy of command, but only by abolishing intermediate bodies or by relaxing tension. However, the location and transport patterns resulting from such autarky will differ very much according to the way in which bodies are defined. In the West we are only really accustomed to one 'body': the nation-state. So we think ef autarky as territorial by definition. But, in fact, this feature is known in capitalism, though it seems to be much less pronounced. Large capitalist firms, specializing on the whole in one branch of production, do reach out through *vertical integration* into other branches, where they establish small and inefficient plants. And they, too, do so in order to ensure supplies, especially in periods of inflation. Inflation, to repeat what we said in Chapter III, is the nearest an ME can get to planner's tension.

But, secondly, the very principle whereby the body is defined may give rise to a specific irrationality. For, clearly, the choice between one and another structure of the hierarchy is not *only* a

---

[1] It is, in fact, the medieval 'principle of provision' discussed in Chapter XV.

matter of administrative convenience. Khrushchev did not introduce sovnarkhozy without some notion that location questions were
being wrongly decided; nor give power to the State Committee on
Technology without some feeling that inventions were being
applied too slowly. I.e., the body's principle of definition is an
implicit, possibly an explicit, general criterion of action. By a sort
of *déformation professionelle* we maximize our eponymous interest,
be it Azerbaijan, steel production or the use of computers.

To give some examples both small and large, territorially defined
authorities, like sovnarkhozy and countries, unnecessarily diversify
their product range. Mere pride leads to this result in all systems,
even when special factors like subordinate autarky are absent. If
production-branch be the principle of definition, the authority will
be wasteful of its own product for internal use—compare the
enormous personal coal allowances that mines everywhere give to
miners, or the free holiday travel enjoyed by railroad employees
the world over. Such authorities will also locate new enterprises
near to headquarters regardless of cost. Then, again, there are
authorities with a purely technological function, which thus pursue
technical modernity regardless of cost or profit. Such are the
research departments of capitalist businesses, and—doubtless—the
Soviet State Committee on Technology (Gostekhnika).[1]

II

Thus, cost and administrative feasibility stringently dictate that
all detailed command planning be decentralized. But it seems that
from the point of view of rationality it must all be centralized. This
latter doctrine is new and strange, and seems unconscionably hard.
Let us confirm it by seeing in what circumstances it might be false.
This is the same as to ask: 'When in a market economy would it be
unnecessary to have a perfect market in a particular commodity?'
Let there be commodity categories A, B, C, like 'steel' or 'grain'.
These categories are not real economic objects at all, but mere
logical constructs. Real commodities, the specific components of
the *sortament*, are A_1, A_2 . . ., B_1, B_2 . . .; such things as steel tubes for
racing bicycles for boys. These are the things an enterprise indents
for, a merchant buys and sells, a production manager tells a foreman
to tell a workman to make.

[1] On all this compare Wiles, op. cit., 1962, Chapter VIII.

However, the resources required to produce A_1 and A_2 are often identical, so they can be allocated to 'A' in a general way. The allocation can even be quite detailed without the planners knowing what the specific *sortament* will be. There is, in fact, a 'law of increasing complexity of *sortament*': the fundamental factors of production are few and very adaptable, they produce many types of rather specific intermediate good, which in turn are rather less various and specific than finished goods. This law is merely empirical, and results from the simple fact that fabrication increases both variety and specificity. Nature, various and peculiar as she is, delivers to man but a few objects. These in turn he makes into very many. It need not be so: he could have chosen otherwise, but that is how things are.[1]

But is it a matter of indifference, from the input point of view, what the *sortament* of output is? That *sortament* becomes more complex with fabrication only proves that inputs are adaptable. It tells us nothing of the costs of such adaptation. Now, such adaptation sometimes really is costless, so that the planner really can express his orders in broad categories without loss. This is as much as to say that the optimal number of commodities of which the center should take cognizance under perfect computation, or for which perfect competition should provide a separate market, is smaller than the total number of commodities. We may try to prove this proposition first at the enterprise level. If between a particular producer and consumer either party (not necessarily both) is completely indifferent between two commodities, there is no call for outside control or competition. Thus, if the customer asks that his lot be delivered tomorrow, not today, or made up of fewer articles of a larger size rather than many of a smaller size, he obviously prefers his specification, or he would not have asked for it. If, on the producer's side, these changes have no repercussions on his other outputs, or on the inputs he uses, the rest of the economy has only to reckon with the customer's increased satisfaction.

A fortiori, when two articles are perfect substitutes from everybody's point of view (two bushels of Farmer Giles' wheat, two bottles of X's beer) there is no need for outside intervention, even in the strictest imaginable utopia of rationality.

These exceptions to the rule are probably not negligible at all,

[1] Cf. P. J. D. Wiles, *Price, Cost and Output* (New York, 1963), pp. 18–19. This is as much as to say that input-output matrices are, on the whole, triangular: some outputs are basic and enter into the production of many others; some are final and while they use many inputs they are not themselves inputs elsewhere.

for certain enterprises can, in fact, switch from one output to another with the very greatest ease. A farmer can select big or small apples from his crop, an engineering shop can alter minor specifications at the drop of a hat. The customer, to whom these changes are, of course, very important, can get what he wants from the producer with whom he is already in contact; there is no saving in going to another producer. Therefore there are kinds of inter-enterprise loyalty, of market 'good will', that do not lead to 'fragmentation' in the proper sense of the word, and the advantages of perfect competition or computation are not sacrificed. The same applies to the stickiness or unadaptability, within limits, of the *raznaryadka* in an STE.[1]

12

Turn now from the enterprise to the subordinate planning body or—in the international case—the country. If decentralized planning is rational, the center can dictate to the bodies so much A, B and C in rubles, or tons, or whatever, and each body can *independently* settle A_1, A_2, etc., without sacrificing any economy. We have, then, somehow to exclude the case that we should all be better off if body I chose to specialize all its A resources in A_1, and body II in A_2. This would not be the case if:

All the specific goods were produced under constant costs over the relevant ranges of output;

The comparative cost ratios[2] of these goods were the same in each body;

There were no external economies, stretching beyond the confines of one body, involved in the choice between A_1 and A_2; i.e., the body must be able to 'internalize' all the economies when it draws up its own plan, even if some of them reach beyond the enterprise;

The comparative cost ratios of the general categories were also the same in each body, so that it did not seem rational to the center to plan any exchange of the categories A, B and C in the first place.

Granted all these conditions, the bodies will be neither ordered to make exchanges, nor tempted thereto in defiance of orders, by the discovery of economies of specialization unobserved from the center.

---

[1] For the *raznaryadka*, or 'distribution', see Wiles, op. cit., 1962, Chapter IX.

[2] Since we are discussing product movements only, international trade theory applies. Factor movements between bodies will also be planned, and will no doubt eventually equalize incomes everywhere. But meanwhile, comparative-cost theory is still correctly applied to product movements.

13

However, it will almost certainly be rational to have some inter-body exchange. Let us suppose, for the moment without question, that the center can rationally allocate tasks in terms of large categories between bodies, implying 'exports' of A by I to II, and 'exports' of B in the opposite direction.

But now who is to decide the *sortament*? Clearly, the *sortament* in *inter*-body trade must be decided either administratively by the center or voluntarily among the bodies. In the latter case, it is inefficient if there is not a perfect inter-body market where the cheapest supplier can be found in each line.[1] To this solution there could only be ideological objections; it is obviously feasible and rational. The planning solution is also feasible and rational; if a command economy can be that at all it can be so in this case.

But could either solution be operated in abstraction from the *intra*-body *sortament*? If I is told, or finds it profitable, to export A_1, will this act affect its internal choice between A_1 and A_2? The answer is, yes, unless the first and third conditions listed above hold. If they do, additional output of A_1 is without repercussion. Such repercussions, however, are almost inevitable. By ordering I to export A_1 and II to export A_2, the center is indirectly deciding their internal *sortament*; e.g., if returns diminish all round I must produce less A_1 for 'home' use, and II less A_2, and vice versa if returns increase. It appears on reflection that this does not disturb the rationality of the final allocation, provided that the center orders inter-body trade in full knowledge of all repercussions. If it does so, however, it possesses all the knowledge required to order the intra-body *sortament* as well, and the authorities at body level become administratively superfluous. They are not, however, harmful if they actually do nothing, and it might be politically and psychologically wise to retain them as post offices for central instructions.

14

Seemingly this is what Kantorovich does when he recommends his version of perfect computation.[2] The Gosplan lays down a few

---

[1] If the bodies use a non-market procedure, they have by definition voluntarily subjected themselves to central command—perhaps to a center of their own devising, parallel to the original one.

[2] L. N. Kantorovich, *Ekonomicheski Raschët Nailuchshego Ispol'zovanja Resursov* (Moscow, 1959), p. 167; this has now been translated as *The Best Use of Economic Resources* (Cambridge, Mass., 1965).

basic shadow prices, and the rest are calculated independently by each sovnarkhoz in the light of its own conditions. Should any of these later be found to differ between sovnarkhozy, so that exchange might seem profitable, the center must rationalize such exchanges by setting uniform prices. It is not clear whether he realizes how constant such intervention must be, and that it implies enough knowledge and power to do away with sovnarkhozy. It is clear that Kantorovich has every interest in preserving the sovnarkhozy, since these bodies represent both the current Party line and innumerable vested interests. There are, indeed, many psychological and other arguments for what we may call *epiphenomenal decentralization*: the erection of intermediate bodies that act as fifth wheels in a coach. Thus undoubtedly Stalin would have liked to convert his governments of satellite states into 'epiphenomenal' bodies: sovereign authorities in form, but mere post offices in content. However, as we have seen, he was very far from succeeding.

The prime example of epiphenomenal decentralization in practice is the Slovak Board of Trustees. In view of the separate historical nationhood of Slovakia this body has to exist and to be involved in all decisions. Yet in periods of centralization, such as 1963, all decisions are, in fact, taken in Prague, and such effective decentralization as must necessarily remain reaches down from Prague not to Bratislava but to much smaller bodies, whose powers are uniform in the Czech and Slovak provinces.[1] The USSR, as a nominally federal country, has also had innumerable such bodies.

15

So if the center is capable of rationalizing inter-body exchanges it is administratively capable of doing without bodies. Our next point is almost a mere corollary. It is logically contradictory to posit a rational allocation of resources between A and B by an authority ignorant of the outputs of A_1, A_2 ..., B_1, B_2 ... A and B are, to repeat, mere logical constructs. The national output of A is simply the sum of the national outputs of A_1, A_2 ... Therefore, if the center knows these outputs, it has no call to be talking in terms of A and B; therefore no call to be talking to intermediate bodies.

This is an important point of very general application. The government of Pakistan, for instance, acts irrationally in making *a priori* sectoral allocations of development funds to 'water', 'roads',

[1] Pavel Korbel in *Hinter dem Eisernen Vorhang* (Munich), 5/1963.

'agriculture', etc., which must then be subdivided among particular projects by each subordinate authority. For in this way it is certain that the marginal road will be less, or more, profitable than the marginal irrigation channel; a conclusion that is not disturbed in the least by taking account of social profit, external economies, growth potential, etc. All projects should be compared with all others, and this means a centralized information system.[1] Only the usual shortage of administrators and channels of communication makes the existing system tolerable. In the same way, it is not enough to demonstrate the extreme profitability of 'education' or of 'medicine'. We must, in each case, consider particular schemes—and we may well find that something quite ordinary, like a bicycle plant, is still more profitable. 'Profit', to repeat, can be defined as widely or as narrowly as we like: the point is unaffected.

16

A misinterpretation must be guarded against. This is not an attack on mixed economies as such; it depends on the mixture. Indeed, we have already explicitly commended as rational a set of small bodies, each a 'perfect computer' at home, but dealing with each other on a market. What could be more mixed than that? In the same way, if one sector, say, heavy industry, is centrally commanded from top to bottom and another, say, agriculture, left quite free, our only query is how substitutions or trade between these sectors are effected. And this query might easily be answered to our satisfaction, since all the computed sector has to show is that it reacts rationally to the market sector, just as it would in any case have to show that it did to foreign trade. Again, if an economy is to be called 'mixed' when it is planned by mere restriction as opposed to positive command, it is obvious that a general tax on some activity also escapes our censure. Thus, if it is felt that the market (or, indeed, the computer) underestimates the value of residing in northern Norway, or overestimates that of alcohol, rational micro-decisions between Tromsö and Hammerfest, whiskey and gin, are not hindered by a proportional subsidy or excise.

In each case, the point is the same. We have mixed our model, but we have not decentralized knowledge and access. Everybody still knows all the details he needs and can make direct detailed

[1] P. J. D. Wiles, in *Economic Digest* (Karachi, Autumn, 1960).

comparisons. No-one has been boxed into a watertight compartment where the water level differs from that in other compartments.

17

We have sought in this chapter to prove three propositions:

A. The *sortament* of inter-body exchanges will be rational if there is a perfect inter-body market. The bodies are then small perfect computers, like large enterprises, which settle many of their interrelations in a quite uncentralized manner.

B. The only other way to make this *sortament* rational is for the center to have such extensive knowledge of intra-body conditions that it can plan them in every detail. The bodies are then unnecessary, and for all administrative purposes there might as well be central computation.

C. There is no such thing as a rational allocation of resources between large categories before the *sortament* has been rationally determined. *There is no such thing as 'steel'.*

Given these propositions, all practically likely decentralized computation is irrational. Yet, as we saw, no other kind is practically possible in a command economy.[1]

Naturally, as always, the losses due to imperfect current allocation must be empirically estimated, and weighed against the costs of perfecting it. In earlier writings,[2] I have insisted that 'Choice' is to some extent alternative to 'Growth', and that considerable imperfections of current allocation should be accepted if they are, for any reason, the unavoidable price of growth. This doctrine has twofold application here. The first is that imperfect computation may be so superior in growth that a country could rationally prefer it to both perfect and imperfect competition. But to pursue this very broad subject would take us too far afield, and I have little new to say about it. Secondly, however—and this is a conclusion from the reasoning in this chapter—perfect computation, with its necessary absence of intermediate authorities, might be so expensive in means of communication and/or so offensive to local, minority and national sentiment that we should again prefer imperfect computation. Indeed, we should clearly be right to do so at present, since

---

[1] Messrs. Janusz Zielinski and Aleksy Wakar use precisely this argument to argue for complete centralization, without consumers' sovereignty, in their *Zaryz Teorii Gospodarki Socjalistycznej*, Warsaw 1963.

[2] *Economic Journal*, June, 1956, and my op. cit. 1962, Chapter XI.

the cost of 'perfection' is still infinite at our current technical capacity. We have not even any guarantee that perfect computation will ever be feasible, for the number and complexity of products and sub-contracting relations might grow faster than the ability of the communications industry to carry information;[1] and it is by no means certain that humanity will ever abandon national sovereignty. Certainly for the time being the nation-state absolutely ensures that both computation and competition shall remain imperfect.

[1] For the rapid increase in this complexity, and the strain it puts on planners, cf. Smolinski and Wiles, op. cit. Perfect competition, however, is automatically rendered imperfect by the same phenomenon.

CHAPTER XII

THE POLITICAL ECONOMY OF
INTERNATIONAL INTEGRATION

1 Barrier abolition versus assimilation.
2 The integration of small countries.
3 The primacy of politics.
4 Is a 'Prussia' necessary?
5 The origins of the CMEA.
6 Stalin's substitutes for it.
7 CMEA: the middle period.
8 Bilateral substitutes for it.
9 Other economic models of international integration.
10 Consortia and STEs.
11 Legal models of international integration.
12 The Galati steel mill—
13 and its consequences.
14 Galati has no parallel in Western Europe.
15 Why they try to integrate heavy industry alone.
16 Integration can be irrational.
17 Why should *countries* specialize?
18 Monetary integration is irrelevant.
19 Migration.
20 Trade does not equalize incomes between nations—
21 nor even does the free flow of factors.
22 Soviet-type assimilation.

I

INTEGRATION has been defined in many different ways, and very often persuasively,[1] as something necessarily good. But one might not approve of completely free trade and migration, or of a total supranational command economy, or of leveling down rich countries to make them equal to poor ones, or of imperialism, or of large countries swallowing little ones—yet all these should bear the name of integration. We use here two morally neutral definitions. First, two countries are said to be fully integrated if they are

[1] Cf. P. P. Streeten, *Economic Integration* (2nd ed.; Leyden, 1964), pp. 14–17.

306

subject *without artificial distinction or barrier* to one market or one planner. Artificial imperfections of competition and computation are understood here to include not merely tariffs and exchange controls, but all legal procedures, restrictive trade-union practices, discriminatory rail tariffs, etc., that keep goods, services and people at home.

Natural barriers coincident with the national boundary are also a bar to this kind of integration, but on the definition of the word 'natural' there is little to be done about them. The sea is no different from a mountain or desert or mere distance; it is simply a question of the transport cost the barrier imposes.

By the second definition, two countries are integrated if their economies are *assimilated*. This means that the same real incomes are paid to people in the same position, that job qualifications, the tax structure, etc., are the same. In a word, the two economies resemble each other. In particular they have similar factor endowments; see Section 21.

The processes of barrier abolition and assimilation are pretty much independent. We can tear down all artificial barriers to the exchange of goods, capital, techniques and people, but still transport costs may reduce trade, while the language barrier and social habits keep out immigrants. The law of factor-price equalization will then tend to equate the relative but not the absolute real rewards of the factors of production in different countries. Pockets of depression may actually be perpetuated and increased by free trade. On the other hand, provided only that technical and cultural knowledge flow freely, two countries of similar factor endowment may come to resemble each other very greatly despite all manner of artificial barriers to trade.

Moreover, some professions and occupations can be integrated while others are very far from it. E.g., British dons in Singapore get British salaries and native dons get nearly as much, because it would be intolerable in such a situation to pay the native don only his opportunity cost; but the London taxidriver gets very much more than the Singapore rickshawpuller.

If integration normally calls to mind the abolition of these barriers, and if this is the main subject that international integration authorities have to negotiate upon, economic assimilation is nevertheless often the ultimate goal. If the perfect general integration of two countries requires both processes, an integration confined to economics can rest on the absence of barriers alone. Assimilation is a far

greater threat to national identity than barrier abolition. It characterizes above all the policy of a national majority toward a minority
within its boundaries. But the white nations of the British Common-
wealth are also assimilated—behind protective barriers.

2

We shall begin with the special problems of the small country.
In the not so distant past it was rather a good thing to be a small
country, or rather a small ACC, as Norman Angell kept insisting.[1]
It was not involved with imperialism, or at least, most small ACCs
were not; yet its standard of living was very high—a fact no Marxist
or imperialist was willing to face. It could more easily keep out of
wars. It stood to benefit by free trade more than a big country
(Chapter IX, Sections 1–7). It could easily attract very large enterprises.

But more recently things have gone wrong for the small ACC.
Neutrality has been so often and so grossly violated that it is clearly
no protection, unless one is both lucky and armed to the teeth. The
neutral small country needs, of course, defense forces in proportion
not to its own size but to that of its enemies. It holds—or more
likely held—colonies only on the sufferance of the great powers,
since treaties mean so much less. It cannot wage economic war,
even against another small country (see Chapter XVI).

Then there are commercial dangers. If the small ACC benefits
most from free trade, it loses most by other countries' protectionism
and by the trade diversion resulting from the integration of other
countries. These dangers are now much greater, both because
protectionism is commoner and because the economies of scale have
increased. Moreover, a Keynesian monetary policy cannot be
effectively pursued in so small an area.

Then, as Simon Kuznets points out,[2] in some ways every state,
and not merely an STE, corresponds to an enterprise. Its higher
education is somewhat of an economic unit and so, often, is its
literary world. If it has its own language these things are especially
true, and create endless problems for intellectual and scientific
workers. These considerations once affected belles lettres alone, but
now they affect technology: whole classes of people must study

---

[1] *The Great Illusion* (expanded ed.; London, 1914).
[2] In *The Economic Consequences of the Size of Nations*, ed. E. A. G. Robinson (London, 1960), pp. 25–7.

abroad, learn other languages, etc. They may not come back. There are also certain immensely expensive lines of research—atomic energy, subatomic physics, space, supersonic aircraft design—which rely mainly on government finance. Of these, a small nation can afford only one or no units. Could such research and development units attract enough private capital they could, of course, settle wherever it was cheapest, on the basis of comparative cost. But public capital is forthcoming for these cultural and scientific activities only on condition that they are pursued on the national territory.

3

The solution to these problems is, of course, to integrate the small countries. Before we consider the various ways in which this can be done, let us first make clear that *integration is a political act*. One does not integrate with one's enemy—or if one does, we call it imperialism (see Chapter XVI). To integrate, moreover, is to commit oneself to political friendship for a very long time. Coolly considered, the economic advantages are often quite small, as is notoriously the case in the Common Market, three of whose members are so large that they hardly require it. Moreover, the group, by the very act of forming itself, will almost certainly bring diplomatic and economic[1] disadvantage to its neighbors.

The economist has far too easily assumed—and outsiders have too readily agreed—that he is the principal expert witness in matters of integration. Let us admit that when governments integrate they direct the immense weight of their effort into abolishing economic barriers; let us even admit that, by grossly exaggerating the economic benefits, they set these before themselves as the principal motive (until, inevitably, they learn the contrary). The facts are that integration has essential political preconditions; that it cannot surmount the weary obstacles in its way without a strong political will; and that once the economic benefits have been seen for what they actually are the movement must also have a political motive to keep going.

Nevertheless, the smaller the country the greater the economic benefit. It is also characteristic of modern politics that small countries nowadays usually enter upon integration with the idea of going the

---

[1] Through trade diversion. This is only offset after a time, if the group's autarky does not continue to increase after the initial act, and its member economies grow more rapidly together than they would have separately—most debatable suppositions.

whole hog, i.e., of sacrificing sovereignty, in the long run. Indeed, one may say that *only* those small countries value their independence today that have some special political reason for it; e.g., Sweden, Switzerland, Yugoslavia. The European Common Market undoubtedly had its origin in just such feelings: the Six had lost the war and felt like 'small ACCs'. Three out of the Six, of course, were not, and now that they have begun to feel their own true strength they have begun to go their separate ways.

Such feelings also prompt small UDCs. In the 1780s, there were thirteen UDCs on the western shores of the Atlantic, which first confederated and then federated. The states of Central America are now trying to follow the same pattern, and there are also such stirrings in the Near East and Africa. UDCs, however, have not much to give each other, and amalgamations among them are of smaller economic importance. Their true motivation is very obviously political.

As to small STEs, innumerable ideas of Balkan federation and central European federation circulate among them. Being of their nature anti-Soviet, they have not surfaced often since the Yugoslav schism. Precisely one of the *casus belli* in the Yugoslav schism was Tito's (and Dimitrov's) urgent advocacy of Balkan federation soon. But this case was a little exceptional. We may not presume such loving-kindness among the peoples of Eastern Europe as reigns in other areas where federation has taken place or is being discussed. Integration is much easier where there is no history. Virtually every nationality in Eastern Europe hates each of its immediate neighbors.

4

For what we, in fact, have to deal with in the Communist world is a *bloc of one large and several small countries*—politically an altogether different animal. History records many federations or outright mergers between one large and one small state which can hardly be described as conquest: England and Scotland, Russia and the Ukraine, Belgium and Luxembourg. It records also many empires; imperialism, to repeat, is the unwilling integration of the weak with the strong. But only one even approximate parallel suggests itself to the position of the USSR within the CMEA: Prussia in the *Zollverein*. Both bodies took advantage of the small country's political skepticism of independence and economic need for integration, but both expressed in practice the imperialism of the single dominant power.[1] *Ceteris paribus*, the small country will naturally be more resistant to this type of bloc than to one that contains two large powers, or none. Nevertheless, these are, of course, the blocs that work best, since there is adequate leadership. If the successful federation of the Thirteen Colonies is an obvious exception to this rule, the slow advance of the Common Market seems to confirm it.

5

Now the paradox of the CMEA is that under Stalin the USSR had the power, but not the will, to impose any degree of economic unity short of outright annexation; while under Khrushchev it had the will but not the power. We saw already in Chapter I why Stalin balked at annexation. We can also see from his reaction to the federation of all satellites proposed by Dimitrov in 1947[2] that he would certainly not contemplate a powerful federation excluding the USSR. But one including it would have been rather too like annexation for his taste. He toyed instead with the idea of three partial federations: Albania, Yugoslavia and Bulgaria, Poland and Czechoslovakia, Rumania and Hungary.[3] After the Tito split he abandoned all of these. His whole object was to hold the satellites down, but at arm's length. Unreliable and Westernized, they must not be allowed too close. The upshot was that very peculiar system of control that was all his own: an empire like a wheel with a very large hub and thick spokes but hardly any rim. At the center sat the dominant power, connected by strong and intimate bilateral ties to its satellites. These had also bilateral connections with each other, but rather weak ones. This is shown in Table XII/1.

Thus the visible trade of these countries with each other and with 'Germany' showed no striking change. They and the DDR between them more or less filled the place that united Germany had previously filled. The real change is that from irrational avoidance of the USSR to irrational concentration upon her.

The foundation of the CMEA made no real difference. Its origin lay in the necessities of propaganda: something was needed to

[1] Jacob Viner makes nearly the same point in *The Customs Union Issue* (Washington, D.C., 1961), pp. 91–2.
[2] Text of Dimitrov's proposal and of *Pravda*'s leader in Vladimir Dedijer, *Tito Speaks* (London, 1953), pp. 322–3. It is not correct that Dimitrov proposed only a Balkan federation—which Stalin himself then favored. It was the size of the proposed federation, and Dimitrov's covert anti-Soviet tone, that angered Stalin.
[3] Ibid., pp. 314, 320, 325, 326, 327, 330, 331.

TABLE XII/1. TRADE DIRECTION OF CERTAIN SATELLITES, 1938, 1952, 1958
(per cent of total visible turnover)

	1938			1952a			1958		
	With other satellites	With Germanyb	With the USSR	With other satellites	With Germany	With the USSR	With other satellites	With Germany	With the USSR
Bulgaria	15	49	0	16	14	59	19	13	53
Czechoslovakia	11	18	2	21	5	32	16	15	33
Hungary	14	29	0	31	9	29	25	16	27
Poland	6	20	0	17	16	32	13	17	26
Rumania	21	25	0	19	9	57	13	12	51
Unweighted average	11	28	0	21	11	42	17	15	38

SOURCE: For 1938: League of Nations, *The Network of World Trade* (Geneva, 1942); 1952: UN Economic Commission for Europe, *Economic Survey of Europe in 1954* (Geneva, 1955), pp. 113, 292; 1958: UN, *Yearbook of International Trade Statistics 1961*. In 1958, West Germany accounted for 5% of the unweighted average, East Germany for 10%.

a Approximately.

b Figures for 1938 are for Germany; figures for 1952 and 1958 are for East and West Germany combined.

counter the Marshall Plan. It did not mitigate the prevalent bilateralism; it did not co-ordinate national plans of production and investment; it distributed no multilateral aid, indeed no aid at all; it was a mere epiphenomenon. In the words of the head of the Polish Planning Commission, 'In the initial phase of its existence the CMEA limited its activities to the sphere of trade relations, and took a marginal interest only in problems of production.'[1] But since the prime function of a Soviet-type government is to regulate production the CMEA was *ipso facto* unimportant.

Indeed, its foundation coincided with the great increase in the quantitative preferences between STEs of 1949 (cf. Table IX/2); i.e., with the withdrawal from East-West trade. And here it may well have been helpful as an information center. It is also certain that it dealt with above-plan surpluses available for current trade between STEs. This is a genuine and characteristic, if minor, problem. Inside an STE, products often show a surplus or deficit in one geographical area of the domestic trade network, and have to be redistributed. Also quantities produced above plan are released into the network from production in the first place, and other crises of various sorts are continually arising. The solution of these problems is often left to trade fairs and other procedures strikingly reminiscent of an ME.[2] So also, then, these things arose in the inter-STE market, and the CMEA was the obvious seat of attempts to deal with them.

Yet all this is very small beer, and one wonders whether the CMEA originated in anything at all except propaganda. The

[1] S. Jędrychowski in *Trybuna Ludu*, November 9, 1957.
[2] P. J. D. Wiles, *The Political Economy of Communism*, Chapter IX.

problem is genuine, and those who write about the CMEA should try to answer it. Romantic as it may be, I find Mr. Kaser's answer[1] wholly plausible. The CMEA was a carry-over from the aggressive, expansionist, forward-looking policy of A. A. Zhdanov, who had supported a forward, 'Leningrad-type' policy in Europe and treated the Communist Parties of both Eastern and Western Europe as responsible, semi-independent, agents.[2] He died conveniently, but perhaps naturally, immediately after the Tito-Stalin schism. In economics his protégé was N. A. Voznesenski, who survived him until his arrest in March, 1949. Voznesenski stood for a rational economy—it is unclear whether centralized or decentralized—that made use of sensible prices. For instance, one of his last acts was to raise Soviet wholesale prices (January, 1949); they were subsequently lowered again (twice, in January and July, 1950). It was also in 1950 that the ridiculous appreciation of the ruble occurred. That is to say, Stalin and Malenkov were consciously rejecting the use of the price mechanism, both nationally and internationally, in favor of continued physical planning.[3]

Now the CMEA was founded, amid much fanfare of trumpets, on January 25, 1949. Yet by 1950 it was scarcely ever mentioned in the press, even when the context demanded it.[4] The conclusion is therefore irresistible that its foundation was the last fling of the Zhdanov-Voznesenski policy, and that Stalin found himself saddled with an organ he had indeed allowed to be born, but could not personally work with.

In harmony with the unimportance of this organ, its council did not meet after the third session (November, 1950) until March, 1954. Serious work began in this year, i.e., at the very moment when the small STEs began to cease to be satellites.

6

We cannot speak, then, until 1954, even of attempts at international planning, still less of a supranational organ. Instead we

[1] Michael Kaser, *Comecon* (2nd ed., Oxford, 1967), Chapter 2.
[2] Franz Borkenau, *Der Europäische Kommunismus* (Berne, 1952), pp. 511–16. This passage is very convincing and free from Borkenau's ludicrous exaggeration that Tito and Zhdanov were in a successful, clandestine conspiracy against Stalin in 1947 (ibid., pp. 492, 495). Dedijer, otherwise so informative (op. cit.), is quite silent on the personality of Zhdanov. For a balanced view, cf. Ernst Halperin, *Der Siegreiche Ketzer* (Cologne, 1957), pp. 71–7.
[3] Table VI/1. Cf. Wiles, op. cit., pp. 104–6, 119; Gerald Segal in *Problems of Communism*, Washington, 1966; Martin Ebon, *Malenkov* (London, 1953), pp. 65–77; Wolfgang Leonhard, *Kreml Ohne Stalin* (Cologne, 1959), pp. 255–9; Kaser, op. cit., pp. 33–41.
[4] Ibid., p. 43.

must speak, borrowing a phrase of C. R. Fay,[1] of a Soviet 'informal empire'. This was held together by the uncoordinated and irregular system of oppressive devices described in Chapter XVI: 'advisers' at all levels, mixed companies, overweening ambassadors, Party channels, occupying troops, reparations agreements, etc. These were capable only of sporadic physical planning. Precisely because it was a formal body, established by treaty, with a democratic constitution based on national sovereignty and international equality, Stalin did not much use the CMEA.

In particular, it suffered from being a state and not a Party organ. The supreme authority being in each country the Party, a truly effective CMEA would be 'supra-Party', not supranational as non-Communists understand the term. But there has not been a supra-Party organ since the Cominform, which last met in plenary session in 1949 and was disbanded in 1956.[2] The nearest approach has been the irregular and *ad hoc* international conference of Parties, as notably the one of November, 1957, in Moscow, which brought together nearly all Communist Parties in the world. Even these conferences, often justly compared to the great *ad hoc* ecumenical councils of the Christian church before the Photian Schism, have only moral force. None of them has ever been occupied with anything so specific as a large investment project, though individual Politburos gaily handle such issues every weekday. Nor is it likely that such a conference should delegate sovereign power over several economies to an inter-state body, since Parties have always been sovereign over state planners. A supranational economic planning body with teeth would, to repeat, have to be an inter-Party body. Here, then, is an abiding problem, flowing from the essence of Communist political theory, for which Stalin cannot be blamed.[3]

It is true that the STEs under Stalin formed a trade bloc in so far as there was quantitative discrimination against outsiders and as they all used the same economic model, economic policy and trading procedures. They also changed their policies more or less in harmony, increasing investment during the Korean War, relaxing it in 1953, etc.[4] But these similarities hardly amounted to what we normally call a trade bloc. There was even very extreme and excessive

[1] *Imperial Economy* (Oxford, UK, 1934), pp. 23, 46.

[2] The Cominform was founded in 1947, and, as its name implies, was formally an information bureau. But its great anti-Tito resolutions certainly bound its members. Even the Comintern (1919–43) had no formal sovereignty over its member parties.

[3] There have been at least six economic conferences confined to CMEA Parties: cf. Kaser, op. cit., p. 234.

[4] Albeit they collectivized agriculture at very different rates.

similarity, but not integration. Just to take one example slightly outside our field, every frontier inside the bloc was guarded by barbed wire and armed men almost as closely as those with the outside world. There was, then, some approach to assimilation, but few barriers were abolished.

It has often been remarked how many domestic problems Stalin left his successors; allowing them to pile up during the years of his tyranny because he was aging and inert, because he knew his system would last his time, because he was so great a tyrant that in a sense he had no problems. The whole status of the satellites was also such a problem, and the neglect of international planning was a particular scandal, a thing absolutely contrary to Marxist psychology and sound reason alike. Stalin was able to dominate by informal violence; he seems even to have inspired respect in the Chinese. He required neither justice nor rationality nor ideological soundness nor even formality. His successors required all of these, and when they denounced him the dam broke.

7

The history of what happened may be briefly told. In March, 1954, new principles were laid down, including for the first time the coordination of FYPs and the specialization of countries. At the same time standing commissions of the Council on various subjects were founded. These commissions were a satellite proposal: as early as 1954 we can no longer speak of a Soviet monopoly of power or initiative. Indeed, one of the worst misunderstandings is to present the CMEA as simply an extension of Soviet power. It is, on the contrary, by its very nature a brake upon the more extreme manifestations of that power, as we have seen. From time to time this or that small STE has found the CMEA extremely useful for some purpose or other, the Rumanian example notwithstanding.

However, the new general economic concept in 1954 was undoubtedly Khrushchev's. Still at that time a 'metal-eater' and proponent of heavy industry, he had to offer something different from Malenkov's New Course. Malenkov had brought about a demotion of heavy industry, an increase in consumption and a general relaxation. He had applied this policy also to the satellites, but had kept their commercial and political status unchanged. Now Malenkov, as all Kremlinologists agree, had been Zhdanov's main enemy, and Khrushchev constantly used this point against him, honoring the memory of Zhdanov and imitating most of his policies—from crude outbursts against artists to flirtations with Tito. He was, in his 1956 Secret Speech, to rehabilitate Zhdanov's economist Voznesenski; but now already he rehabilitated his policy on the CMEA: the international division of labor was to be exploited within heavy industry. The abandonment of autarky would lower costs, so leave over a little bit more for consumption; it would also entail supranational planning by the CMEA.[1] Khrushchev was to return to this policy in 1962.

This was also the time when the mixed companies were resold to the satellites, the Control Commission withdrawn from the DDR, and reparations ended. But doubtless Malenkov and Khrushchev were agreed on this. There was no talk of specialization in consumer goods or agriculture.

But whatever the policy, more important was the new *interest in national plans*. Various countries prolonged their present FYPs into six- or seven-year plans, or inserted intercalary years, in order that every FYP should begin in 1956. In and among STEs an economic policy is only taken seriously, and an authority is only taken seriously, if it influences the plan. The point is not affected by the fact that plans are constantly altered, so that the plan that is under- or over-fulfilled at the end of the year is not the one that was set, and published, at the beginning of the year. It does not even matter that FYPs are still more cavalierly treated in the same way. For all these alterations are also plans, and come from the same all-powerful center.

It follows that almost whatever aspect of integration we are considering—criteria for current trade, investment criteria, technological policy, etc.—we must ask whether the instructions of the integrators have been entered in the plan of each country. If they have not, they are worth extremely little. If we insist upon this obvious point here, it is perhaps only to rub in the earlier insignificance of the CMEA, when plans were hardly discussed.

1955–56 were years of preparatory administrative activity, in which nothing practical happened. But at least the fifteen standing commissions, alluded to above, were formed—on Czechoslovak, East German and Polish initiative. In the event the amount of FYP coordination achieved was minimal, since 1957 was spent picking up the pieces after the events of late 1956. In addition to the tremen-

---

[1] Taken mainly from Fritz Schenk, *Im Vorzimmer der Diktatur* (Cologne, 1962), pp. 259–61. Cf. *Imre Nagy on Communism* (New York, 1957), pp. 106–7; I. T. Vinogradov in *Voprosy Istorii KPSS*, 3/1957.

dous shifts in the terms of trade that the Polish coup and the Hungarian revolution brought about, the USSR scrapped her sixth FYP, thus throwing all FYP coordination out of joint.[1]

In May, 1958, the *Parties* of the CMEA nations (indeed of all STEs) met, and the CMEA began at last to look really serious, laying great public stress on specialization and the international division of labor. The principle was not new, but the volume of publicity indicated that someone meant business. However, the lack of a permanent central authority was crippling: the CMEA council, consisting of vice-Prime-Ministers, used to meet about twice a year in one place or another, but there were no Ministers Resident. Since the organization lacked this authority at the top, still nothing happened on the ground.

8

Thus, in practice, 1957-62 were years of *bilateral negotiation and cooperation*. It would be tedious to list the enormous number of agreements put into effect. However, the careful researches of Radio Free Europe[2] give an idea of their scope in the case of two countries only: Poland and Czechoslovakia. A major 'Economic Convention' was signed in March, 1947, upon which little was built for ten years. Then, in May, 1957, the 'Polish-Czechoslovak Committee on Economic Cooperation' was set up, and in four years very much was achieved:

June, 1957	Czechoslovak credit for Polish sulphur development, to be repaid in sulphur.
October, 1957	Similar credit for coal.
March, 1958	Cooperation in border-area water systems.
November, 1959	Specialization in agricultural machines.
September, 1960	FYPs to be coordinated.
September, 1960	Oder-Danube canal to be planned.
September, 1960	Committee renamed: insert 'Scientific and Technical' after 'Economic'.
January, 1961	Credit for copper, similar to that for sulphur above. But Poland will use some of the credit for other purposes, while still repaying in copper.

[1] But there was at least an ill-fated agreement on multilateralism in 1957. Cf. Chapter X, Section 15.
[2] *The Background of Polish-Czechoslovak Economic Co-operation*, November 11, 1961; *Polish-Czechoslovak Economic Co-operation Since the Prague Declaration of 30 September 1961*, June 26, 1964.

May, 1961	Specialization in tractors; each country to produce different parts for a single agreed model.
May, 1961	Similar specialization in trucks.
May, 1961	Border-area water systems again.
June, 1961	Electricity exchange.
June, 1961	Transit of Czechoslovak overseas trade.
September, 1961	Big new general agreement.

Truly there is more—increasingly more—in international economics than flows of goods and money! Despite serious attempts to include other things in both this and the next chapter, I believe that in this and other books the surface only of these problems has been scratched.

Very much, then, was achieved in 1957–62. But it was not achieved by the CMEA, despite pious references in the preambles of inter-STE agreements, and horrendous generalizations in the first and last paragraphs of Western articles. Indeed, in the Polish literature, the only one with which I am even slightly familiar, pious references themselves are notably scarce. Thus Gomulka's speech in Prague on the occasion of the September, 1961, agreement, refers to the members of the CMEA, not to the Council as a separate body;[1] and an article entitled 'Investments and Foreign Trade' in the major ideological monthly[2] contrives not to mention the CMEA once, even in the paragraph on international coordination.

Clearly the CMEA, for all its large new bureaucracy, was still not pulling its weight. Meanwhile, the Common Market, contrary to every Marxist rule, had proved a great success. Capitalism had not fallen prey to its 'contradictions', while 'Socialism' had, even though the ideology admitted no possibility of serious contradictions under the more progressive system. The contrast became with every month more glaring. It would be folly to underestimate this element.

So in 1962 Khrushchev returned to the charge.[3] In June an executive committee of permanent representatives was founded, who were to reside in Moscow and enjoy vice-Prime-Ministerial rank in their own cabinets. But the individual national veto re-

[1] 'The Background . . .', op. cit.
[2] Stanislaw Kuzinski in *Nowe Drogi*, August, 1960. Cf. *Zycie Gospodarcze*, October 9, 1960, a two-page article on inter-STE aid; Stanislaw Albinowski, on the co-ordination of investments, in *Zycie Warszawy*, October 20, 1960.
[3] According to the leader in the Bratislava *Pravda*, October 10, 1962, the actual initiative was Polish, with Czechoslovak support. However, Arthur J. Olsen says in the *New York Times*, June 16, 1962, from Warsaw that Khrushchev's actual proposals went further still, and the role of these two countries was to force a compromise. Text of Khrushchev's proposals in *World Marxist Review*, September, 1962.

mained. Even so, it is no accident at all that in April, 1963, the crisis between Rumania and the CMEA was first made public (Section 11, below). So far, on the purely constitutional level, Rumania has had everything her own way. The individual veto remains, and the CMEA is still far less supranational than the Common Market.

9

But the Rumanian crisis requires a little preliminary theory on the different ways in which economic barriers can be abolished. For there is a 'modelology' of international integration just as there is of national planning.

(i) We saw in Chapter XI one extreme model: a centralized, supranational command economy, with no countries left. But as we saw there, this is the least possible of all models. There is a surprisingly wide range of alternatives, and our choice depends partly on the internal model used by the countries to be integrated, partly on what we want to do.

(ii) The pre-1956 Communist model was that each country was an STE, while above it stood no real supranational organ but an international imperfect market. Certain agreed rules governed the market: bilateralism, a quantitative preference for each other, etc. If there had been perfect computation within each STE, and a perfect multilateral market among them, and a price preference against the outside world, everything would have been more tidy and rational but the model would have been rather similar. It may be described as 'French' or 'indicative' planning among STEs, inasmuch as each country's plan was at least known to all others.

(iii) Another possible way of integrating is via the free market: each country is an ME, and they are bound simply by a price preference; i.e., they have a common external tariff, or at least a set of high ones, and a zero or at least a lower tariff among themselves. The Common Market and EFTA are both varieties of this conception, and so was Benelux.

(iv) Yet again we can integrate MEs on the basis of the regulated market. The supranational organ takes over the regulatory duties—investment licensing, monopoly control, etc.—from the individual states. The Common Market and the European Coal and Steel Community (ECSC) both have elements of this.

(v) Moreover, it is almost as easy to integrate by production-branches as territorially. Dealing with what are initially sovereign states, we naturally assume that these territorially defined units have the power and must cede it to another such unit. But a glance at the Western world shows that this is quite false. In an ME the state has less economic power than the enterprise, and the latter's authority quite commonly oversteps state boundaries. So the private international firm is in a very real sense an international integrator,[1] and it normally works on the production principle. Moreover, beside it stands the public international firm, which we here call the consortium. To take only recent cases, a good example is the Scandinavian Airlines System, jointly owned by the Danish, Norwegian and Swedish states;[2] or, on a more *ad hoc* level, the Anglo-French Concorde. Such firms, by the way, not only abolish barriers, they also assimilate people with exceptional efficiency.

(vi) Above the consortium stands the fully-fledged supranational authority, also operating on the production principle. Of all the peculiar institutional hybrids that mere logic can devise, it might be thought that this was the most obviously empty box, sketched out by *a priori* lucubration. Yet one such also has existed: the ECSC. And the reason is not far to seek: the High Authority is both more and less than an international firm. It is more in that it was set up by treaty, its officials have diplomatic immunity among the member states, and it can annul some of these states' legislative acts. It is less in that for the most part it can only regulate; it is just another cartel or antitrust authority, of the type that MEs know so well. It has, indeed, some power to command; e.g., it can initiate investment projects. But to this extent it is merely an international firm, however big, and it fits as easily into an ME as any other such firm.

10

What is more difficult to see is how international firms and authorities fit into the STE. In olden days the answer was obvious: one of the parties to the consortium was always the USSR, and its will prevailed. The old mixed companies never had any serious difficulty with the planners in the STE in which they were located, since the national plan was simply adapted to the plan of the company.[3] When national equality began to be seriously practiced

---

[1] Or, of course, if its managers are citizens of an ACC and it operates in a UDC it is an instance of imperialism.

[2] There happens in this case also to be a small private participation.

[3] This older group of mixed companies is further treated in Chapter XIV, Section 34.

among STEs it was only logical that mixed companies should disappear. No sovereign command economy can tolerate such foreign bodies on its territory.

However, today mixed projects (we can hardly say companies) are creeping back. They are mainly inter-'satellite', and do not involve the USSR. They are, in the absence of a single boss, more difficult than ever to fit into a command economy. Most of these projects originate in bilateral negotiations which have only the vaguest connection with the CMEA itself: that organ continues unimportant. Characteristically country A wants to ensure a supply of some mineral in country B, and has something directly relevant to offer B: capital or technique. Mostly this can be assured by simple treaty, without foreign ownership. But such ownership does occur in what is perhaps the first of the new wave of proper mixed companies: Haldex. This company in Poland obtains coal from coal wastes, and exploits the by-products. It uses half Hungarian and half Polish capital, Hungarian technique (gratis) and—of course—Polish coal waste (also gratis). Hungary and Poland each receive half the profit and one-quarter of the coal, for which they must pay prime cost. The rest of the coal and all the by-products are at Poland's disposal.

It will be observed that this is a very simple arrangement, scarcely more than an international loan such as those made by Czechoslovakia for the development of Polish sulphur, coal and copper (Section 8, above). Hungary's invisible income from the profits will presumably never exceed the amount she has to pay for the coal. Therefore, she gets cheap[1] coal, while Poland's b.o.p. cannot suffer. Even so, there are a million ways in which Poland can twist this agreement to her advantage: discriminatory freight rates, a turnover tax on the by-products, high prices for odd supplies, etc., etc. Both Hungary's profit and the price she pays for her basic share of coal are determined not by treaty but by current Polish action. The Czechoslovak loans avoided such involvements and dangers, since they were essentially trade treaties, not direct investments.

There are, of course, provisions for settling differences. The board of directors is mixed and the supervising council is mixed, and 'Matters exceeding the Statute competence of the enterprise organs are jointly decided on by the Minister of Mining and Power of

---

[1] Prime cost is expected to be 70% of that of Polish steam coal. For all this see Tadeusz Muszkiet in *Polish Economic Survey*, 20/1963. For other examples cf. Kaser, op. cit., pp. 127–8. For capitalist investment in STEs cf. Chapter XVIII.

Poland and by the Minister of Heavy Industry of Hungary'.[1] But it is perfectly evident that Poland has the whip hand since the enterprise is on her territory.

Moreover, among MEs we cannot say that foreign and mixed enterprises are similarly at the mercy of the territorial authority. For all the government has to do in such cases is not intervene, i.e., remain true to its general traditions. But here, if the Polish Government does not 'intervene' the enterprise will come instantly to a standstill. For instance, supplies and transport must be positively allocated by repeated acts of government will. It is permissible to take a gloomy view of the future of mixed companies, even now that Soviet imperialism is not a factor.

II

We may turn to the legal status of the international organ, setting out the main types only. (a) This could be something as simple as an inter-governmental treaty, binding the states to maintain such-and-such external tariffs, to permit the free movement of factors of production, etc., etc. Such a treaty needs virtually no supranational administration and yet can be very effective. (b) The consortium or supranational authority in a particular branch of production requires a special statute, but can thereafter operate (well or ill, as we have seen) without further sacrifice of national sovereignty. (c) There can be a permanent international civil service in a large building, and an agreement to send ministers there regularly for consultation only. The staff informs itself, advises and persuades. The ministers persuade each other. But that is all. Of such nature are the UN, OECD, EFTA and the Council of Europe. (d) A confederation sets up a new territorial government with Ministers Resident, but one that is only an emanation of the existing members. Sovereignty remains with the states, who therefore have the rights of veto and secession. The Common Market is still essentially a confederation. (e) A federation sets up an irremovable supergovernment. The old states have particular powers guaranteed to them by a constitution difficult to change. (f) Finally there is direct merger or annexation.

The obvious point at once emerges that *it is much easier to integrate MEs than STEs*. The free movement of products, factors and money *is* integration. So all that the governments of MEs need do is get

[1] Tadeusz Musziet, op. cit.

out of their way, combining the treaty form of organization (*a*, above) with the preference form of economic model (iii in Section 9). Since, however, all MEs regulate the market in some way, this regulation must itself be internationalized. Now the regulations may all along have been such that they can be fixed once for all, like tax rates, by legislative act. In this case, their enforcement requires few administrative powers or discretions, and a treaty, which is an international legislative act, will again suffice. Other matters—a common university, a common airline, atomic research—can mostly be delegated to consortia, operating on defined charters. These, too, operate far more easily within an ME than within an STE.

There are, however, types of market regulation that require the continuous administrative attention of the government itself. Material licensing, import quotas, and Keynesian monetary policy are good examples. These can hardly be delegated to any consortium or international authority operating on the production principle, as they affect the whole economy too nearly. A confederation or federation is the obvious organ; if we like we can call the authority by some other name, but it remains by definition a new super-government.

This is more than ever the case with STEs. There are two reasons for this. First, the STE's government has unlimited claims to economic sovereignty, which it also, in fact, exercises. If in such a context, with economic command being a definitional attribute of government, the CMEA or the Soviet Gosplan can say whether or not there shall be a steel mill in Rumania, that organ is the government of Rumania. It is true that the High Authority of the ECSC has nearly the same power in Belgium—it can both initiate and veto new investment—but this fact does not matter so much to such a government. The Belgian Government undoubtedly had such a sovereignty, but did not exercise it or set very great store by it, before resigning it by treaty to the ECSC. Secondly, it is not over large investment projects only that a supranational authority of the Soviet type is likely to exercise command, but also over innumerable details of current output. The mere volume of orders crossing the frontier, and the fact that the Rumanian planning commission would have to adapt itself to every one of them, would more surely reduce Rumania to a sovnarkhoz than any spectacular veto on a particular project.

Mutatis mutandis, then, the CMEA *is and is meant to be* a far less supranational organ than the High Authorities of the ECSC and the Common Market. It is formally by name and also in very deed a council, that is, an organ of type (c) above. In particular, it is an 'aegis' or 'umbrella' under which bilateral deals of all sorts are made. The truly integrative measures—mixed companies of the Haldex variety, technical collaboration, etc.—remain bilateral. Theoretically, such measures would be possible if the CMEA did not exist. Indeed, that is precisely the case: Poland and Czechoslovakia laid many abortive plans for economic union in 1947–48.[1]

Bilateral arrangements between small STEs have the supreme advantage that they involve no imperialism. Sovereignty is sacrificed, as in all international treaties, but voluntarily and to a body in which each country has equal weight.[2] Moreover, administratively all bilateralism is very much easier, as we show in Chapter X.

12

The delicacy and difficulty of integrating except through the impersonal forces of the market are best illustrated by the CMEA's greatest defeat to date: over the Galati steel mill in Rumania. Previous revolts of satellite governments (Yugoslavia, Poland, Hungary, Albania) had been mainly political, especially at their inception; where 'political' is a broad word covering opposition to Communization, insults to national pride, direct violations of national sovereignty, or disagreements on ideology and foreign policy. But the Rumanian revolt is due to the CMEA. We cannot call an economic event nonpolitical in an STE—indeed, we hardly can anywhere. But at least we must say that all subsequent 'non-economic political' events—the flirtation with China, the removal of Russian street names, the turn to French as a main language—in this case followed the 'economic political' event.

The story begins in 1957 at the latest. The CMEA—which still meant the USSR—was in its first wave of specialization within engineering. Rumania was producing a type of truck not allotted to it. The Soviet delegate asked for an interruption of the session. When it resumed he threatened to cease all steel deliveries to Rumania—not merely those for this truck.[3]

[1] Pryor, *The Communist Foreign Trade System*, p. 208; Margaret Dewar, *Soviet Trade with Eastern Europe, 1945–49* (London, 1951), pp. 15–16; Section 8, above.

[2] An Albanian would except bilateral arrangements with imperialist Yugoslavia, as he knew them before 1948. But then there is a big difference in size here too.

[3] Radio Free Europe, quoting its Berlin Bureau, February 3, 1968. This is obviously an interview with Fritz Schenk.

Our next firm knowledge concerns the Galati steel mill. I can do no better than pillage Mr. J. F. Brown's scholarly account:[2] on November 11, 1960, the USSR agreed, *inter alia*,

... to supply machinery and equipment to the value of about 500 million dollars, and to help the Galati Steel Works between 1961 and 1968 with the construction of a large steel shop, with an annual production capacity of 1–5 million tons equipped with a blooming-slabbing installation and continuous sheet rolling mill.... In the course of 1961 there must have been certain voices raised in Comecon councils urging a kind of international specialization which Rumania considered harmful to her interests. This idea of international specialization was obviously Soviet sponsored and had become the prevailing policy at the time of the 22nd CPSU congress in October 1961. Speaking at the Rumanian Party's central committee plenum held in November–December 1961 to hear Gheorghiu-Dej's report of the 22nd CPSU congress, the Rumanian planning chief, Gaston-Marin, cited the CPSU programme to support the Rumanian policy of the 'priority development of heavy industry' and continued:

Our Party has always resolutely opposed and has always combated from a Marxist-Leninist standpoint those erroneous 'theories' which, while defending the keeping of proportions between the branches of the national economy and the priority development of heavy industry on the scale of the whole socialist camp rather than within the framework of the individual socialist country, in fact deny the necessity of creating the technical and material base of socialism and present in a distorted manner the principles of specialization and cooperation within the framework of the socialist international division of labour.

This remark would hardly have been made if the Rumanians had not felt that in terms of this framework of the 'socialist international division of labour', there were interpretations, held probably by the most advanced economic powers, like the USSR, East Germany and Czechoslovakia, which implied a severe curtailment of the comprehensive industrial plans of the less advanced nations, such as themselves. They have never declared themselves against the specialization concept as such; on the contrary, they have declared their support for it quite openly. But, whereas it has evidently seemed to them that the advanced Comecon members interpret specialization as being by *industry or groups of industries*, the less advanced Rumanian interprets it as specialization by *branches of industry*. This would, of course, allow the Rumanians to go ahead with their many-sided development. . . . [In June 1962 came the crucial CMEA meeting described in Section 8.] Immediately after this Comecon summit, Khrushchev made his visit to Rumania for reasons which have never been very clear. But, perhaps impressed by the strength of Rumanian insistence on going ahead with their plans, he seems to have been anxious to allay some of the worst fears of his hosts. On the other hand, in nearly all his speeches Khrushchev emphasized the advantages of bloc co-ordination and specialization much more than his Rumanian counterparts did. On his return home he stated that 'the wish of the Rumanian comrades' to fulfill new and higher targets in the development of their economy was 'fully comprehensible

[1] In (Soviet) *Survey* (London), October, 1963, pp. 22–4. I only disagree in being unable to distinguish, as Brown thinks he can, between Khrushchev's integration policies in 1956 and in 1959. Cf. also Kaser, op. cit., Chapter VI; J.-M. Montias in *Soviet Studies*, October, 1964; J. B. Thompson in *Hinter dem Eisernen Vorhang* (Munich), 7–8/1964.

to us'. But he did not say that Rumania was fully capable of this. Instead he returned to the theme of Comecon coordination by saying that the Rumanian communists, 'like the fraternal parties of the other socialist countries, saw great possibilities for the growth of production in the unification of effort on the basis of the intensification of cooperation and the further improvement of the international division of labour'.

Neither on his return nor during his eight-day stay in the country did Khrushchev mention anything about the projected Galati Steel Works. His hosts, however, constantly referred to it in their speeches and have done so ever since, stressing their determination to go ahead with it.

13

Note that Khrushchev did not in so many words propose to make the CMEA supranational. Nor have I been able to discover anywhere a formal statement that Rumania, let alone Hungary and Bulgaria, must concentrate on raw material exports. Nevertheless, this is what was felt. In September, 1962, Ulbricht also visited Rumania, trying to press more integration on her. He failed. The breach was first indicated in a more straightforward manner in November, 1962, when steel machinery was ordered from the West, and in December, when a Rumanian historical journal attacked a Soviet historian for neglecting the role of the Rumanian Party in the armed uprising against Antonescu and the Germans.[1] From that point the quarrel escalated. Rumania turned westward for steel mill equipment, abolished the Gorki Institute of Russian, re-established French as the first foreign language, was sticky over trade with the DDR, sent her ambassador back to Tirana, flirted with China, etc., etc.

Naturally, she could not have gotten away with it had her b.o.p. with the West not been favorable. By a singular irony, it was her strong position in despised raw materials that permitted her to construct this presumable white elephant of industrialization. Contrast the position of Poland described in Chapter X. Without raw materials saleable in the West, but sitting athwart the transit lines of the East, Poland has a favorable balance within the CMEA. So she demands that it be strengthened—in ways that suit her.

It remains to be seen whether the mill is efficient or profitable. The *a priori* view of an outsider is that in this respect, of course, the CMEA—or the USSR and the DDR—were right and Rumania was wrong. The onset of supranationalism hit precisely Rumania because it coincided with the onset of economic rationality. No doubt a differently motivated supranationalism would have caused

[1] Cf. *Hinter dem Eisernen Vorhang* (Munich), 1/1963, pp. 34–5.

a row with some other country. But the trouble with rationality is that it strikes at one of the root ideas of Marxism: that it is imperialistic to trade machinery for raw materials.

After this incident the CMEA has perforce continued as before. Bilateral agreements of all sorts have been concluded between pairs of countries interested in them: it is their full right, and Rumania has no veto. Notably, the USSR has imitated since 1964 the type of intergovernmental, bilateral, commission of cooperation pioneered by Poland and Czechoslovakia (above).[1] But no great advance has been made in the integration of all the members, where Rumania has a veto. The freight-car pool (founded 1962–64)[2] and the IBEC (founded 1963; cf. Chapter X) remain the principal monuments of general integration. The 'Friendship' oil pipeline, which began in 1962 to deliver Soviet oil to various STEs, does not include Rumania, though it passes close to her border and she delivers a million tons a year to CMEA members. Curiously enough, her exclusion (as a supplier) does not figure in the literature on her quarrel; it appears she is not interested in exporting more oil to the CMEA.[3] Albania has, of course, been excluded from everything since December, 1961.

14

The Galati incident augurs very ill for integration within the CMEA. The Six have overcome many crises as great,[4] lurching slowly onwards to further success beneath the heavy burden of the Cross of Lorraine. It is tempting to try to compare the political situations within the two blocs, and say that one or other has more non-economic obstacles to overcome, irrespective of the economic model used. Among STEs the Stalinist past is a fearful incubus on a bloc with the USSR inside it, and every ex-satellite is tempted to pay a little back when opportunity arises. Again, in the general atmosphere of mutual isolation and insincerity created among individuals by Communism we cannot expect group rivalries and hatreds to subside; for members of these groups are, after all, indivi-

---

[1] Harry Trend, 'Recent Developments in Comecon', Radio Free Europe, March 14, 1964.

[2] Agreed on in general terms, December, 1962. In early September, 1963, Rumania ceased to be a participant. But on September 14 she rejoined. The pool opened for business on January 1, 1964. Cf. Harry Trend, 'The Proposed Joint Railway Car Pool', Radio Free Europe, September 16, 1963.

[3] *Petroleum Press Service*, London, 1964, p. 326; ibid., 1965, p. 471.

[4] E.g.: the coal crisis of May, 1959, when ECSC's proposals for cutting output in the coal slump were rejected by Council of Ministers; the French veto on British entry in January, 1963; the agreement on agricultural prices in 1962.

duals, yet do not meet each other and talk frankly. We thus have the absurd situation that Czechs and Poles, nay, Czechs and Slovaks, between whom history has shed so little blood, have worse relations than Frenchmen and Germans. Yet there are also unifying factors unknown in the West. Governing circles have a really paranoid fear of the outside world, a feeling of imminent imperialist aggression, to which few West Europeans are prone; a fear too of their own subjects that gives point to the proverb 'we must all hang together or we shall hang separately'. Moreover, they share an almost identical ideology in which integration figures very largely, and a Party training that teaches them to make personal sacrifices. Finally we miss among them the single charismatic leader who happens to be personally opposed to integration, as in the West.

It is thus tempting, though no more than tempting, to say that other things are equal and to attribute the quicker integration of the Six to their economic model; which integrates quietly and impersonally while prime ministers are in bed. Specifically the Galati steel mill crisis could hardly have risen in the ECSC. A crisis over a declining industry that needs an international subsidy, like Belgian coal, is indeed possible—though it was averted. But it either is or is not profitable for Belgium to put up a *new* steel mill, *under the given tariff and rail-freight rules*. We see at once how narrow are the tolerances within which Belgium can distort her argument, and how little she *can* do to protect her mill if it looks like a loser, or *need* do if it makes money. Moreover, steel is not nationalized in Belgium, so we have, further, to imagine a group of capitalists who will spend the time persuading the government to go to all this trouble for them.

15

The political issue, then, in the Galati affair, was that of national sovereignty: a not very surprising discovery. But the economic issue was not one that would have set the Common Market on fire: autarky in heavy industry. It would, however, strike a chord among any group of UDCs. For, as we saw in Chapters I and VIII, Prebisch and Marx are barely distinguishable. The USSR, and sometimes also the DDR and Czechoslovakia, have been accused of trying to hold back Yugoslav or now Rumanian development by monopolizing machinery exports and insisting that the aggrieved country be a source of raw materials alone. There is, however, a specifically Marxist twist: the 'Prebisch' quarrel with the ACCs is about the terms of trade between manufactures generally and raw materials generally, including consumer goods, while the Yugoslav or Rumanian complaint is only about machinery and industrial raw materials, including fuel. It is the terms of this trade, i.e., of trade within Marx' Department I, that obsess the Marxist mind; to the neglect of foodstuffs and consumer goods. Thus these quarrels are quite unlike those inside the Common Market.

The theory of imperialism, then, remains very much alive, not merely as a stick to beat the enemy with, but as a bone of family contention. Without any adequate theory of international values, Marxists cannot simply accept given prices and terms of trade, nor even given factor endowments. They have developed instead a compulsively political attitude to these things, which carries over into their mutual relations.

It may seem strange that the USSR, well known to be a net importer of machinery and exporter of raw materials, should be so passionately accused of exploitation by Rumania, a country in the same position. But first the USSR is a very large country to which trade is much less important. Secondly, in the trade directly between them Soviet machines are exchanged for Rumanian raw materials. And above all, Rumania regards the DDR, with much justification, as being still a satellite, a mere extension of the Soviet economy.

Trade in agricultural products has not pre-occupied the CMEA. The Common Market's fearful difficulties with prices find here no reflection. It is not that there are no farm subsidies—far from it. It is that there is in an STE no farm bloc, lobbying with skill and passion for higher prices. As everywhere else, a better international division of agricultural labor would cause large displacements, but food is so universally short that no acre and no peasant would go unemployed. Moreover, the turnover tax is so big and variable that although imports might lower retail prices, domestic procurement prices would be unaffected.

Besides, there has been no interest in international agricultural planning. As late as July 28, 1963, a CMEA communiqué 'admitted that it is necessary to expand multilateral co-operation in the provision of agricultural production', failed to mention specialization, and ended with a simple reference to 'further efforts by each country for an upsurge in agriculture'.[1] By the end of that year certain specializations in seed production had been agreed upon. It is reasonably clear that the medieval 'principle of provision' (Chapter

[1] My italics.

XV) has been at work: each STE had been frightened to export food, lest it get no imports in return. Merely technical co-operation, however, is as flourishing as in other fields.[1]

The failure to specialize in consumer goods, on the other hand, though equally pronounced, should be ascribed to ideological snobbery. They are beneath the notice of important international commissions. Yet supply and quality vary very much from country to country, and there are many traditional skills unexploited. Moreover, as Franklyn Holzman has ingeniously pointed out,[2] consumer goods are quite peculiarly easy for an STE to trade in, since such trade does not disturb the input/output matrix. Consumers, who do not figure in the matrix, can adapt themselves very easily to an efflux of the domestic goods to which they are accustomed, and an influx of new foreign goods. Further, as we saw in Chapter IV, consumer goods are a valuable b.o.p. cushion.

Dr. Holzman tells me that this idea was, so far as he knows, his own. However, the Chinese and the Soviet Co-operative Wholesale Societies made some such exchange in 1958, and Poland has bought Soviet watches in this way since at least 1965: 'not a normal transaction of the Ministry of Foreign Trade, but a so-called exchange transaction of the Ministry of Internal Trade'. A Polish economist even discussed several pricing principles which might govern such transactions in 1967.[3] By 1968 Hungary and Czechoslovakia, the most decentralized STEs, had a limited agreement to exchange certain, mainly consumer, goods freely. Any enterprise may import, the central bank *must* find the valuta. Tourists, too, barter and smuggle consumer goods on a massive scale.

16

Does *integration lead to more rationality* if the basic system of resource allocations is irrational? Can one irrationally integrate at all? The answer to both questions is yes. Like prosperity, rapid growth and social justice, integration is independent of rationality. Indeed, more rationality might actually mean less integration (in contrast to its effect on prosperity and growth). This would happen if the countries concerned were naturally autarkic or naturally traded with countries outside the bloc. Thus we are reminded of

[1] Kaser, op. cit., pp. 158–9.

[2] In ed. Henry Rosovsky, *Industrialization in Two Systems* (New York, 1966), p. 263.

[3] New China News Agency, June 14, 1958; G. Pisarski in *Zycie Gospodarcze*, June 6, 1965; A. Bodnar, ibid., July 9, 1967.

the very obvious point that trade diversion, which all blocs bring
about and which is perhaps their most significant feature, is irrational. Yet we would not wish to deny that the Common Market
was a step toward integration simply because it had diverted trade.
One thinks in particular of its agriculture: the integration of the
agriculture of the Six is strictly dependent on high protection. If
West German agriculture was even more protected before joining
the Six, Dutch agriculture was less. Yet Dutch agriculture also has
been 'integrated'.

It is not, then, for lack of a *rational* allocation system that the
CMEA has been marking time in matters of trade, but for lack of
an *agreed* system. Agreement might be easier with some irrational
system.[1] Indeed, world prices themselves are used not so much
because they are rational (though they may well be that too), as
because they are easy to agree on. But prices are not enough:
there has to be an agreed method of settling quantities, too. And
this, as we have seen, there will not be until plans are internationally
agreed.

The irrelevance of rationality is well illustrated by one of the
most impressive achievements of the CMEA to date: the specialization of the engineering industry in each member on particular
products.[2] The object of this is to benefit by the economies of scale.
Yet such benefits may be enjoyed, indeed, presumably are, without
any increase in rationality. Indeed, worse, we see below that they
may be canceled out by making the allocation less rational.

Let a specialization be ordered which contradicts comparative
costs, each country specializing in the wrong thing; then clearly if
costs are constant or increasing the bloc is worse off.[3] If costs
diminish, however, we can make no prediction. Thus let the gain
to the bloc be defined as quantities of factors released, quantities of
output throughout the bloc being constant. Then if country A is
ordered to produce more of commodity 1, and country B of commodity 2, although the 1 : 2 cost ratio is higher in A, the bloc as a
whole gains by the lowering, through the economies of scale, of the
cost of the amount of 1 that A was already producing. But it may
gain or lose a quite indeterminate amount by the transfer of factors
from A's erstwhile relatively efficient industry 2 to its less efficient

[1] The opposing point of view is commonly stated, especially by writers on the CMEA;
e.g., Kaser, op. cit., Chapter 2. But I have never seen discussion.
[2] Actual decisions listed ibid., p. 88.
[3] Of course, the position of individual countries is more complicated, but we shall not deal
with that.

but now expanded industry 1, in order to make the 1 that B previously made.

Thus express all values in a common currency, and assume constant factor prices, and let small letters stand for quantities, large ones for unit costs. Then:

Total cost used to be: $a_1A_1 + a_2A_2 + b_1B_1 + b_2B_2$

And now it is: $a_1xA_1 + b_2xA_1 + a_2\gamma B_2 + b_2\gamma B_2$;

where b_1 is now produced in A and a_2 in B, and $x,y < 1$ are the ratios of the unit cost after enjoying economies of scale to the unit cost under autarky. Then if the total of money expenditure indicated by the second line is lower than that indicated by the first line, fewer factors all told are being bought, for factor prices are constant. Now clearly $a_1xA_1 < a_1A_1$, $b_2\gamma B_2 < b_2B_2$. But the relations of b_1xA_1 to b_1B_1, and of $a_2\gamma B_2$ to a_2A_2, are anyone's guess. Despite the economies of scale, the new costs (e.g., b_1xA_1) may so far exceed the old (e.g., b_1B_1) as to outweigh the saving on the production that has not been reallocated. Yet even were that to happen we should still be forced to say that the two countries had been integrated.

In any case, a specialization that takes advantage of comparative costs is, of course, far better. Thus, in the above example, it is to be presumed that production functions are similar in the two countries, so that if 1 is allocated to B and 2 to A there will still be increasing returns. Then both types of gain are additive. But there is nothing in the price system of STEs to ensure this result. Integration can, then, occur in defiance of comparative costs. It probably has.

17

Besides, there is no reason why *countries* should specialize. It might be cheaper if selected enterprises in various countries concentrated on one product, and other enterprises in an overlapping but not identical group of countries on another. Or perhaps an activity should be concentrated in an area like Silesia, that straddles two countries.

Such effects are commonly achieved by free markets, and are doubtless rational. Specialization by countries is a mere administrative necessity that perfect central computation would also abolish. It is another example of the imperfection of computation discussed in the previous chapter: things must in practice be decentralized, but the intermediate body is bound to carry out its work wrongly. In general, we saw, the production-branch principle, with all its faults, is more rational than the territorial principle. It follows that international consortia would make better intermediate bodies from this point of view than countries. A consortium has clearly fewer axes to grind in the matter of location than a country; and specialization is essentially such a matter.

Again, how narrow or broad should specialization be—by sector or by production branch or by type? The use of categories broader than specific types is, of course, also irrational, since what applies to one type may or may not apply to another in the same category. And here, for once, administrative necessity hardly fights the other way. Different types really can be—and are—allocated to different countries. We may compare the correct use of tariffs in UDCs: they should not protect the whole of industry, but only selected industries. Sector-wide protection causes every production branch and, indeed, type to be produced without skill or scale; it prevents a specialization that would raise efficiency, while encouraging growth no more than would selective protection.

Evidently Gaston-Marin (Section 11, above) felt that Rumania was being threatened by proposals for sector-wide specialization which would exclude her from metal-working. We know that Czechoslovakia, trying to sell her superabundant machinery, did in effect propose this.[1] This would have been most irrational, as we have just seen. More important, it was contrary to the practical tradition of Marxism, which has always insisted, though with scant theoretical argument or textual basis in the master's work, that all heavy industry be developed everywhere. The offence to Rumanian nationalism was still more important.

Rumania, on the other side, proposed a more detailed breakdown by production branches. This would have enabled her to balance foreign trade in the sectors of heavy and light industry separately—which is precisely the 'structural bilateralism' of Chapter VIII, Section 19. The bilateralism itself is, of course, quite irrational, like all other bilateralism, but how about the general Rumanian position? Clearly, since it involved more detailed investigation and fewer large *a priori* categories, it was theoretically better than the counter-proposal. But that does not mean that the particular project, indeed, the particular choice of production branch, upon which Rumania insisted was rational. Indeed, Rumania was simply 'metal-eating', in Khrushchev's inimitable phrase (Chapter VIII, Section 20). The CMEA had every reason to accept the general principle while

[1] Cf. Montias, op. cit.

resisting the particular application. Indeed, this is just what it has done. Thus Rumania deserves credit, but possibly not sole credit, for insisting on specialization in narrow categories. But this does not justify the Galati steel mill, which probably remains a very uneconomic way of producing an obsolescent material. Petrochemicals would have suited her better.

18

Free trade in money, i.e., cash and bills, is a vital part of integration as known under capitalism, and should strictly be part of the integration of socialist MEs also. A bloc of MEs without hot-money flows is, of course, imaginable, but this would mean exchange control. Ordinary trade and long-term investment would both be subject to scrutiny, lest they disguise hot money; short-term flows, which are so very liable to be hot, would be forbidden. Such a state of affairs hardly deserves the name of integration, but otherwise there might be serious b.o.p. difficulties. For, of course, the absence of ordinary trade barriers, the standardization of stock exchange procedures, the comity of the law courts and a hundred other things encourage money to flow very freely indeed. Yet under such complete integration only the old remedy of differential bank rates is available to correct the flows. Deflation and unemployment[1] are thus more likely than if the countries had not formed a bloc. A fairly good solution is a large increase, by mutual credits, in the international liquidity of the bloc's central banks. A better and more radical solution is to go beyond integration to merger. Whatever the model of the economy, where there is only one currency and one central bank we can no longer properly speak of a balance of payments (cf. Chapter XI, Section 2), though there are still deficitary and surplus areas. But, more important, hot money gains nothing from moving around inside the bloc; so short-term flows are not speculative.

The STE has, as we have many times insisted, the advantage that there is no hot money in it at all, and no liquidity preference, so no Keynesian effects. In a banking system of the type described, short money would not flow speculatively from Moscow to Leningrad, let alone to Prague. Therefore, none of these difficulties attends integration of STEs, and there is no pressure for central-bank merger

---

[1] Inflation is more easily cured: by sterilizing the inflow of foreign money through open-market operations.

at an early date. Moreover, in so far as budgetary policy often creates hot-money flows, it cannot be independent in a bloc of MEs. But for good or ill, ministries of finance in STEs can pursue widely separate policies. Monetary integration is genuinely unimportant, not merely neglected—as in most blocs of MEs.

19

We defined integration above as including the *free movement o people*. It will be recalled (Chapter II) that the free or more or less free movement of capital has been assumed throughout; restraint on it is not regarded as part of the definition of a country, though, of course, should there be such restraint there is no integration. The abolition of national boundaries, then, means among other things free movement of tourists, temporary labor, and migrants. If tourism is a simple matter, the other categories require more than merely an assurance that employers will not discriminate in hiring. We may add such fringe benefits as easy transfer of pension rights and social service entitlements, rapid acquisition of citizenship, reasonably high priority on housing queues if any, and interchangeability of professional qualifications. It is, indeed, at this point that assimilation enters the picture. The free movement of people is not just a matter of national barriers like tariffs on goods; it requires an adjustment of the whole society.

These things are simply not discussed among STEs. There is, for instance, no commission of the CMEA for them. The movement of people between STEs is practically confined to experts, diplomats and tourists, i.e., to people on short-term assignments (cf. Chapter XIII, Section 9). If free movement is an essential part of integration, STEs are an exceedingly long way from it; so long, indeed, that it has been possible for the Rumanians to condemn it as 'unsocialist' (ibid.). Yet, since each labor market is fairly free, migration is not incompatible with the economic model.

20

Migration has raised the question of assimilation. Let us define assimilated countries as having not merely interchangeable degrees and examinations, and similar taxes, but also equal standards of living. It is entirely possible that nearly all conditions for work should be the same, and all barriers absent, yet standards of living should differ radically. For since one country can have a permanently depressed area, it is easy for separate countries in a bloc to be richer or poorer.

It is one of the great recent gains in economics that we have come to understand that perfect competition neither increases nor diminishes the relative backwardness of an area. One fallacious argument to the contrary, recently popular, is perhaps not so dead a horse but that it needs flogging again: perfect competition brings about 'factor-price equalization' between nations, and thus equalizes real incomes across national boundaries. In this way, the movement of goods would be an adequate substitute for the movement of factors. Of course, nothing of the sort is true. If the rent/wage ratios in several countries are equalized by the appropriate exchange of land- and labor-intensive goods (it is notoriously a big 'if', but let that pass), the efficiencies of the 'natural units' of these factors may still greatly differ, and therefore real rents and wages per such unit may be high or low. In one country acres of land will be less fertile, labor more idle and unskilled than in another; though the yield on capital, the most mobile of all factors, will be more nearly the same. True, we can no longer speak of precisely the same production functions in different countries, since a more detailed analysis of factor-classes into sub-classes, used in the same way in both countries, is no longer possible. But the same goods, broadly speaking, use more labor, land, or capital in most countries, and relative factor endowment does not lose all its meaning. It remains, then, true that appropriate international trade can equate or at least approximate relative factor scarcities, but it does not even begin to approximate the real rewards of the factors between countries. While relative scarcities converge, the gains from trade may still accrue mostly to the rich countries, though they are most likely distributed at random between rich and poor.

21

But there is worse to follow. Even the free movement of factors is insufficient to bring about assimilation. Let us guard against one misunderstanding here. If two areas, or two countries, fully integrated, differ *only* in the wealth of their natural resources, and the richer of the two has full employment, capital and labor will flow from poor to rich. Malthusian pressure in the poor area will be relieved and equal standards of living reign. It is quite certain that local pride will be much offended, and the erstwhile richer population will also suffer from the competition of the immigrant factors. The evacuation of northern Sweden has had such effects. Applied to the Scottish Highlands, evacuation has, again, worked wonders, but it threatens the very existence of a distinct national minority.

So evacuation, however unpleasant and defeatist, *is* assimilation. But the forces of competition are often not strong enough to make any serious change at all. Thus if not only the natural resources but also the schools and working traditions of southern Italy are inferior, there will be an excess of unskilled labor there. Some of it will find its way north, but in view of northern unemployment most will prefer to be unemployed at home. All such emigration is, of course, an excellent thing, as it relieves pressure on natural resources, but the northward flow is smaller than the natural increase in the south. Since cooperant factors and social overheads are scarce, this large reservoir of unskilled labor will not attract much capital, except where natural resources are outstandingly superior; not even at lower wages for equivalent grades. But the wage is, in fact, almost certain to be monopolistically high, owing to trade unions and the sentiment of national uniformity. So, on the contrary, the few skilled people there are in the south, and the little capital that is accumulated there, are likely both to flow north, following each other in a vicious circle. Thus the abolition of barriers has actually impoverished the south. Local tax-rates will rise, since local government has more poverty-stricken people to care for than before, but a narrower tax-base. Despair, corruption and illegality will increase (or, in the south Italian case, not decrease).

A truly competitive, starvation wage might break the circle, and all minimum wage laws are certainly a great disservice to backward areas. To reach prematurely for the fruits of assimilation will destroy the growing tree. But many elements of backwardness would remain even if skill and capital did flow south spontaneously. For they would come because of the low, unskilled wage, and use labor-intensive techniques. Skilled people would be rare, feel lonely and have to be extremely well paid. The social environment would be marked by extreme inequality, and this would hardly improve either local government or elementary education. The progressive north would remain a magnet for most of the capital and most of the skill, and long-run equilibrium would prevail with equal real returns to capital and all grades of skill, but most of the unskilled labor would remain in the south. Factor endowments still differing radically, this can hardly be called assimilation.

Nor is this only common sense. It is reassuring that theory tells us the same thing. For we meet here one of the very few practical applications of the theory of factor-price equalization, upon the importance of which we cast doubt in Section 20. Commodity exchange permits not merely factor immobility between countries, but also between areas within a country. Indeed, it is only within countries that factor-price equality becomes, eventually, absolute; for only within countries is it at all likely that production functions will become identical. So the unskilled wage is, indeed, eventually the same everywhere. But this discourages movement and keeps the large unskilled masses where they are, producing the least skill-intensive things. Similarly commodity exchange permits, even encourages, factor immobility between occupations. The unskilled find it more profitable to specialize in skill-extensive goods that they can 'export' than to improve their skills and make indifferently what someone else is already making well. In a separate nation or region there would be infant industries, and this would not be so.[1]

Assimilation, as we ordinarily use the word, implies that the social pyramid is much the same everywhere. This implies a similar factor endowment in every region. It is no argument against this usage that it implies that town and country can never be assimilated. For they cannot indeed; and that is why Marxists, the assimilationists *par excellence*, are so obsessed with the 'problem' of town and country. Of course, to those who do not want *everything* to look like everything else, there is no problem. We are not arguing for assimilation, we are merely explaining it.

There is, then, not much in the market mechanism that in practice leads all the way to assimilation. Countries and areas can differ for ever in the essential elements of capital, technique and education. In a general way the state or some supranational authority must always intervene.

All this is fairly clearly perceived in the Common Market. Special arrangements have been made for an artificial flow of capital and technique into southern Italy, over and above all arrangements of the Italian state. Greece's main motive for adhesion as an associate member would seem to be a lively expectation of capital and technique at low cost. In other words she appreciates that there is a spirit of assimilation abroad in the Common Market, and that a poor associated country stands to benefit from it. Again, both these

[1] The U.S. Negro, though not concentrated in any locality, suffers from just this effect, and this is the economic rationale of the programs of Marcus Garvey and Elijah Mohammed.

countries benefit by the free movement of labor, which facilitates emigration.

22

Now Communism, which defines its last state as the perfect indistinguishability of nations and areas, town and country (Chapter I), is dedicated as is no other creed to economic assimilation. This can be seen in practical domestic policy toward industrial location and national minorities. Industry is located most often on a basis of regional autarky, and particular care is taken to ensure that national minorities are brought up to the average level, both of industrialization and of living standard. Both capital and skilled labor, even also unskilled labor, are poured into these areas. If this leads to their cultural assimilation, so much the better, both because they are politically troublesome in the short run and because in the long they will and must in any case disappear.

The same tyrannical generosity has been at work *vis-à-vis* the smallest and poorest STEs.[1] Only across frontiers it is capital alone, and not labor, that moves, owing to the Soviet-type prejudice against migration (Chapter XIII)—though it is of course the more efficient means of assimilation. Now since the free market does so little to assimilate backward countries or areas, it need not surprise us that the marginal productivity of capital may easily be higher where development has already gone a long way, and labor is both dearer and more skilled. The determination to invest capital, even government capital, as productively and profitably as possible is highly inimical to backward areas. But Communism is almost completely free from such prejudices, and in this context that is merely an advantage. If its fear of migration hinders assimilation, its innocence of economic rationality is a help. Market socialism in Yugoslavia has hurt, and Czechoslovakia threatens to hurt, the backward areas.

Rather is it bad relations between Communist countries that have retarded the flow of capital toward the poorer ones. Nearly all the poor STEs were in the early 'sixties allied to China, itself as poor as they, and the flow of Soviet and East European capital has turned inward, or out to the non-Communist UDCs. As late as January, 1959, Khrushchev was implicitly promising astronomical quantities of aid to all poorer STEs, including China, when he said that all Communist countries would reach Full Communism at about the

[1] Mongolia, North Korea and Albania: Cf. Chapter XIV, Sections 12, 13.

same time. By October, 1961, however, this promise had implicitly been withdrawn.[1] If there is any promise now on the Soviet side it is that CMEA countries will all enter Full Communism together.

Appendix to Chapter XII
THE SOVIET GKES

ONE of the main reasons for the lack of official publications about Soviet aid, both in technology and in capital, is that it is administered by a rather secret organ of government, beholden neither to the Ministry of Foreign Trade nor to that of Finance. Both of these ministries have house organs (*Vneshnyaya Torgovlya* and *Den'gi i Kredit*) which give good information on their activities; but one searches in vain for very many hard data on aid.

The Chief Administration of Economic Relations with the Countries of People's Democracy (GUES) founded in 1946, and was led by A. I. Smirnov.[2] It was first known to exist via a chance announcement in *Pravda* of July 14, 1955. Its head was then K. I. Koval'; later P. V. Nikitin. By decree of July 25, 1957, it became the Chief Committee of the Council of Ministers for Foreign Economic Relations (GKES), and M. G. Pervukhin its chairman. This was in every possible way a step up. A Chief Administration is hardly more than a large department in a Ministry—the GUES was presumably independent of any ministry, as some of these administrations are. A Chief Committee of the Council of Ministers is as important as any of the old ministries—which were being abolished at precisely this time. 'Countries of People's Democracy' is, of course, far less inclusive than 'Foreign'. And Pervukhin is, or was, senior to Koval'. However, he had recently offended Khrushchev over the introduction of *sovnarkhozy*, and on February 21, 1958, was replaced by S. A. Skachkov. The latter is still (1967) only a candidate member of the Central Committee. Along with other bodies in the field of foreign trade, the GKES survived the administrative upheavals of 1963 intact.[3]

The GKES has commissions for scientific-technological cooperation with the CMEA countries and Albania, China, Finland, North Korea and Yugoslavia. It has four trading corporations of its very own.[4] It has no very obvious connections with CMEA. Occasionally Western observers confuse it with CMEA or a committee thereof, or, referring to it by its right name, treat it as an international or even supranational body. All this is incorrect. No doubt much foreign aid is discussed in CMEA, especially multilateral aid and aid between members; but each country must naturally have its own organ, and in the USSR this is the GKES.

One of the main functions of the GKES is intelligence, and this, beyond doubt, explains much of its secrecy. Alexander Kaznacheev,[5] who defected from the Rangoon Embassy in June, 1959, lists four intelligence groups: military (under

---

[1] Wiles, op. cit., p. 382.

[2] Information from a casual Soviet contact.

[3] Thus it was not subordinate to the Vysshii Sovnarkhoz or the SovnarkhozSSSR (organization chart in *Ekonomicheskaya Gazeta* (Moscow), January 4, 1964).

[4] *Pravda*, July 20, 1958; August 23, 1960; November 20, 1963; *Vneshnyaya Torgovlya*, 3/1959.

[5] In his *Inside a Soviet Embassy* (New York, 1962), Chapter XV and p. 98.

the GRU, the army intelligence), political, economic and embassy security (these three being under the KGB). The economic intelligence group operated within the two economic missions: GKES and trade. Kaznacheev goes on:

The Economic Mission (GKES), as was generally understood by all Soviet personnel, was the main base for the Economic Intelligence group's operations. This mission apparently had few other functions to perform besides those which under the Soviet system mentioned above could be entrusted only to Intelligence. The Trade Mission, on the other hand, had a great amount of ordinary trade business to handle, which required no special Intelligence methods. I also noticed that the number of people from the Economic Mission regularly coming to work inside the Referentura Section in the Embassy (only Intelligence personnel could work there) was much larger than that from the Trade Mission.

Earlier he says:

Economic warfare was the overriding purpose of the other big economic office—the Economic Mission. Its parent body, the GKES in Moscow, is the central Soviet agency for penetration into underdeveloped countries by means of economic assistance, i.e., loans, credits and gift projects. Such projects in Burma included a Technological Institute, a hospital and a hotel. Though the Burmese Government showed no eagerness to expand these ties with Moscow, the Economic Mission was staffed with highly qualified economists—some of them from the Soviet Academy of Science. Their main job was to gather and analyse information on the Burmese economy, and thus take part in long-range planning of Soviet economic policy in Burma. The mission's officers were also very active in penetrating Burmese Government economic offices and business circles. The head of the mission—Vasiliy Panov, whom I knew closely—told me once that his people were better informed about Burmese economy than were their Western counterparts and even the Burmese themselves. He asserted that they were kept in constant readiness to move as soon as a possibility for a thrust into the Burmese economy presented itself.

It is not obvious to me what a 'thrust into the Burmese economy' might mean. Nor, surely, is it clear to Kaznacheev. But he may be reporting correctly the language of his colleagues.

Furthermore, one of the Committee's deputy chairmen, G. S. Sidorovich, is a colonel-general.[1] His presence indicates an interest in military deliveries, and may be another cause of the faint odor of brimstone that the GKES manages always to give off. Thus its head, Skachkov, contributed to a book on Soviet foreign aid in 1962,[2] yet the name of his organization was not mentioned in it. Or, again, Mr. Marshall Goldman tells me that when studying foreign aid in 1963 he got nearly everywhere in Moscow except to the GKES, though their telephone number is published.[3] One cannot either escape the feeling that a name so elaborately casual as 'economic relations' conceals some sinister design. One is reminded of the Manhattan Project, or, indeed, of that threadbare Soviet code-name for atomic energy, 'Medium Machine-Building'. It appears from the subject-matter

[1] *Pravda*, July 29, 1958; August 23, 1960; November 20, 1963; *Vneshnyaya Torgovlya*, 3/1958.

[2] S. Skachkov, V. Sergeev and G. Shevyakov, *Pomoshch i Sotrudnichestvo vo Imya Mira* (Moscow, 1962). This 55-page, 6-kopek book deals with the export of factories, materials and experts including economic planners; construction jobs abroad; and the training of foreigners in the USSR.

[3] In *Moskva, Kratkaya Adresno-Spravochnaya Kniga*, 1958.

of Skachkov's book that the GKES does not deal with ordinary trade, be it never so political.

The executive representative of the GKES in China in 1965 was a Col. A. A. Shaitan. He was responsible for the transportation across China of Soviet military aid to Vietnam.[1]

China has a similar body: the 'General Bureau for Foreign Economic Relations', founded in January, 1960.[2]

Obviously such bodies are not responsible for the short-term aid that arises out of swings in the b.o.p. Possibly also medium-term credit, say for the commercial purchase of a machine, is beyond their purview.[3]

[1] *Jen-min Jih-pao*, January 16, 1966, translated in *Ost-Probleme*, April 22, 1966. This number covers well both sides of this whole controversy: China makes no charge for what she does transport, but prohibits overflights, insists on rail transport alone and delays acceptance of shipments at her frontier. She would prefer the goods to go by sea. Cf. also *Ost-Probleme*, December 2, 1966.

[2] Audrey Donnithorne, *China's Economic System* (London 1967), p. 330.

[3] Cf. Marshall Goldman, *Soviet Foreign Aid* (New York 1967), pp. 75–6.

CHAPTER XIII

INVISIBLES OTHER THAN CAPITAL

I

THE lack of a theory of invisible trade is one of the major scandals in the field of international economics. 'Invisibles' is a mere catch-all concept, not analysed in any way. The very word, meaning invisible to a customs officer, is obsolete in the days of the central banker and the national income statistician. But before we come to theory we must realize that the mere volume of invisibles is normally concealed from us by our bad habit of quoting, in b.o.p.statements, gross visibles and net invisibles. It would be as sensible to do it the other way round—with shipping and insurance appearing to bulk large on each side of the account, and dwarfing a small net visible balance.

If we gross up the invisibles of an ACC they come to about one fifth of total trade turnover in a normal case. For instance, see the figures for Sweden in Table XIII/1.

TABLE XIII/1. SWEDISH BALANCE OF PAYMENTS
(mn. kronor)

	All Countries	Communist Countries
1. Visible exports f.o.b. . .	14,198	634
Visible imports c.i.f. . . .	−15,151	−685
2. Nonmonetary gold . . .	−1	0
3 (a). Foreign purchases of Swedish transport		
Freight . . .	2519⎱	145
Passenger . . .	186⎰	
3 (b). Swedish purchases of foreign transport		
Freight . . .	−1139⎱	−19
Passenger . . .	−38⎰	
4. Other travel expenditures		
Credit	368	6
Debit	−560	−3
5. Investment income		
Credit	270	15
Debit	−124	−2
6. Diplomacy		
Credit	55	8
Debit	−42	−2
7. Insurance		
Credit	174⎤	
Debit . . .	−152⎥	
8. Commissions	⎥	
Credit	117⎥	
Debit	−173⎥ Credit: 20	
9. License fees, royalties and patents	⎬ Debit: −13	
Credit	102⎥	
Debit	−239⎥	
10. Other services	⎥	
Credit	239⎥	
Debit	−501⎦	
11. Merchanting transactions, credit (net)	10	
12. Donations and inheritances		
Credit	85	2
Debit	−88	0
13. Government contributions to international organizations, etc. .		
Credit	0	0
Debit	−49	0
14. Total trade turnover (items 1 to 10) .		
Credit	18,228	828
Debit	18,120	724
15. (1 + 2) as per cent of (1–10), credit plus deficit . . .	81%	85%
16. Share of industry and agriculture in national income . . .	48%	—

SOURCE: Sveriges Riksbank, Årsbok (Stockholm, 1962), pp. 36, 41, 42; International Monetary Fund, *Balance of Payments Year Book 1960*, Sweden, p. 2; ibid., 1959.

2

Thus Swedish invisible turnover is at least 19% of all turnover—I say 'at least' because item 11 is still given net, and we do not know what turnover is involved. But in most statistics we would simply see:

Exports	+14,198
Imports	−15,151
Invisibles (net)	+1072

Moreover, invisibles have shown a secular tendency to increase. Thus, in the United States b.o.p. 'travel' plus 'other transactions' rose from 1·7% of the total in 1869–73 to 4·3% in 1953–55. These items then, in contrast to commodities and freight, have been an expanding part also of the United States national income.[1]

Now since the total b.o.p. of an STE is a state secret, but visible trade is published, no STE reveals its invisibles.[2] An added reason for Soviet-type secrecy about invisibles is undoubtedly ignorance and neglect, not to say ideological snobbery. For the materialist definition of production excludes invisibles, and the b.o.p. as a concept is almost totally absent from the Marxist classics, as, indeed, from all works of that time. Communist authors habitually refer to invisibles as insignificant, although as Mr. Micawber so rightly said, small sums may be very important when large sums must balance: 'Annual income twenty pounds, annual expenditure nineteen nineteen six, result happiness. Annual income twenty pounds, annual expenditure twenty pounds ought and six, result misery.'[3] To this day invisibles other than freight are most misleadingly called 'non-commercial' items.

In the non-Communist world the proportions of visible to invisible trade, taking all items gross, are approximately as in Table XIII/2. Our interest here is to get, by whatever indirect means are

[1] Taken from Table XV/2 here, and from *Historical Statistics of the United States* (Washington, D.C.), pp. 562–3.
[2] Except when, in 1935 and 1936, the USSR revealed its figures to the League of Nations. These figures are still solemnly repeated in modern Soviet textbooks, e.g., A. M. Smirnov, *Mezhdunarodnye Valyutnye i Kreditnye Otnoshenia SSSR* (Moscow, 1960); L. I. Frei, *Mezhdunarodnye Raschety i Organizovania Vneshnei Torgovli Sotsialisticheskukh Stran* (Moscow, 1960). Compare Table V/1. Unfortunately the invisibles are presented net. Even in Poland in 1964 the author's blandishments could extract no figures. Recent Polish figures revealing the b.o.p. in domestic zlotys are in no sense a breach of this security. The domestic-valuta ratio not merely is not published: it varies between exports and imports, and from branch to branch. A deficit in domestic zlotys is wholly compatible with a surplus in valuta. Yugoslavia, however, publishes hers year by year; doubtless it is a small added attraction to capitalist lenders.
[3] Charles Dickens, *David Copperfield*, Chapter XII.

possible, at the unpublished invisibles of STEs. So we take only countries which also report separately their dealings with STEs:

TABLE XIII/2. GOODS AND SERVICES TURNOVER OF TWELVE MEs, 1960
(unweighted average, per cent of total)

	With STEs Credit	With STEs Debit	With Whole World Turnover
(i) Visible exports and imports, f.o.b.	85⎤	90⎤	73⎤
(ii) International freight, including	⎬ (91)[a]	⎬ (95)[a]	⎬ (87)[a]
port disbursements . .	4⎦	6⎦	5⎦
(iii) Other transport . .	2	1	2
(iv) All other services . .	8	4	11
(v) Interest and dividends on debt .	0	0	3
(vi) Public and private transfers .	1	0	4
Total	100	100	100

SOURCE: International Monetary Fund, *Balance of Payments Yearbook 1960*; ibid., 1959.

[a] Items (i) and (ii) cannot be distinguished for Burma, Sweden and Ceylon. The other countries are West Germany, Iceland, Japan, Denmark, Ethiopia, Indonesia, Brazil, France and Israel.

Next, here are two special cases of particular interest, of which Yugoslavia is not included above:

TABLE XIII/3. GOODS AND SERVICES TURNOVER OF CEYLON AND YUGOSLAVIA,

	China Credit	China Debit	Ceylon, 1960, with Other Communist Countries Credit	Other Communist Countries Debit	Whole World	Yugoslavia, 1959, with Whole World
(i) ⎫ (ii) ⎭	99	98.0	94	96	86.5	86.6
(iii)	0	1.5	1	0	3.5	0.7
(iv)	1	0.5	5	4	6.0	5.2
(v)	0	0.0	0	0	2.0	0.8
(vi)	0	0.0	0	0	2.0	6.6
Total	100	100.0	100	100	100.0	100.0

NOTE: See Table XIII/2 for identification of line numbers and source. The reader is urgently warned to read the methodological note on freight in the appendix to this chapter.

Seven other countries provide a fair amount of information, but are incomplete on the transport side. So, omitting item (ii) we may add them in as in Table XIII/4:

TABLE XIII/4. GOODS AND SERVICES TURNOVER OF 19 MEs, 1960
(per cent)

| | With STEs | | With Whole World |
	Credit	Debit	Turnover
(i)	92	95	81
(iii–vi)	8	5	19

NOTE: MEs include Pakistan, Norway, Austria, Belgium-Luxembourg, Finland, Greece, Netherlands, and the twelve in Table XIII/2. See Table XIII/2 for identification of line numbers and source.

3

Looking at these countries, some things strike the eye at once: STEs do far less invisible trade with MEs than MEs do with each other; this applies to every single item. STEs buy far more services from MEs than they sell to them. If we distinguish between types of ME we find, first, that UDCs do not have a notably smaller trade in services than ACCs, but their invisible balances tend to be very adverse. Not, however, with STEs: Ethiopia, Ceylon, Pakistan and Burma ran favorable invisible balances with them in 1960, while only Brazil and Indonesia bought more services than they sold.

What percentage, then, are invisibles in inter-STE trade? Yugoslavia points the way to a good guess. Yugoslavia is by origin and by many present inclinations structurally similar to an STE. Yet she engages in vastly more tourism, and takes out many more patents and licenses, than an STE. It would be very strange if Yugoslavia's invisible trade with the world under items (iii) to (v) were smaller than that of STEs with each other: it amounts to 8% of visible turnover plus freight. Yet it would also be strange if technical aid, diplomacy and tourism among STEs were not greater than in STE-ME exchange. This is also 8% of visible turnover plus freight. Since inter-STE technical aid is free and interest charges are very low, the larger volume of exchange need not entail larger payments. We may then settle on this percentage for these items, until the explosive growth of tourism in the mid-'sixties.

Item (ii), however, must be estimated for the individual STE. Thus Poland has a huge favorable balance on it: her transit trade and shipping earnings amount to about 20% of her commodity exports. Most inter-STE trade, however, goes by land without rail transit through third countries, for the simple reason that most of it is with the USSR. Freight should therefore be a smaller percentage of visible trade than in STE-ME exchange: say 3%. Item (vi) is also important and variable. There are next to no emigrants' remittances between STEs,[1] but public transfers are large and, of course, exceedingly various year by year.

We thus arrive at a general guess: all invisibles, except in Polish exports, ran at about 11 or 12% of commodity trade, where foreign aid was not involved, until the tourism explosion. The proportion among MEs was 37%.[2]

4

Turning to particular items, the IMF gives us many data for the proportion of freight and insurance to imports, which it needs to know in order to convert c.i.f. into f.o.b. Since freights are a perfect market with very flexible prices, we need more than one year, and all the countries we can muster:

TABLE XIII/5. RATIO OF IMPORTS C.I.F. TO IMPORTS F.O.B., 1960–62
(per cent)

	1960	1961	1962
Brazil	113	113	113
Ethiopia	110	114	114
West Germany	108	108	107
Iceland	111	109	109
Israel	112	112	112
Netherlands	111	116	115
Norway[b]	106	105	106
United States[a]	109	108	107

SOURCE: International Monetary Fund, *Balance of Payments Yearbook 1960*; ibid., 1959. Merchandise insurance included above runs at about 0·5% of imports f.o.b.

[a] Adding the 'freight received by United States ocean vessels on imports' to the other items of freight on imports.

[b] Excluding imports of ships.

These figures are reassuring by reason of their stability and their resemblance to each other. Although clearly freights vary with distance and mode of transport chosen, totals do not seem to differ widely as a result: doubtless the many rail freights across third

---

[1] But Poles living in ACCs remit sums about equal to 10% of commodity exports or 4% of the national income. All figures for Poland derive from an incomplete special study: details available on request.

[2] For the statistics of invisibles in ME/ME and ME/STE exchange cf. Ely Devons, *Lloyds Bank Review*, April, 1961. It may seem, incidentally, to the attentive reader of Table V/1, that the USSR in 1935–36 put a heavy weight on invisibles. But the truth is simpler. She was running fast into complete autarky, and found it easier to reduce commodity trade than, say, diplomatic representation or debt service. In 1898–1913 Russian invisibles were 1·5% of commodity exports and 56% of commodity imports (P. I. Lyashchenko, *History of the National Economy of Russia*, New York, 1949, p. 718).

countries[1] paid by West Germany and the Netherlands cover such short distances as to be comparable to the long sea hauls to Ethiopia and Brazil. What principally emerges, then, is that freights are of great importance by reason of their mere size. A b.o.p. reckoning based on visible trade alone is so much waste paper, even if all the trade is given f.o.b. in both directions.

It follows, too, that it matters very much whether a country buys its freight services from others or from itself; let alone whether it performs such services on a wide international scale. In any normal categorization of Norwegian or Polish exports, that was not slave to the ridiculous distinction between visibles and invisibles, freight services would have pride of place. Yet precisely Polish shipping provides a striking instance of prejudice against invisibles, and that not only in accountancy but also in the allocation of actual scarce resources:

TABLE XIII/6. POLISH SHIPPING

	1938	1946	1947	1948	1949	1950	1951
mn. tons carried	1.3	0.5	0.9	1.8	1.9	2.5	3.5
mn. ton-km.	—	—	—	—	3485	4908	10,100
mn. passengers carried	51.8	3.0	27.0	35.9	31.3	15.5	10.3
mn. passenger-km.	—	—	—	—	123.7	53.5	29.8
Shipping under Polish flag ('000 BRT)	95	94	156	160	159	171	237

	1952	1953	1954	1955	1956	1962	1964
mn. tons carried	3.8	2.9	2.6	3.0	2.9	8.8	10.5
mn. ton-km.	9246	8889	6745	8535	9390	25,034	29,818
mn. passengers carried	11.7	9.6	11.9	12.5	12.3	17.6	20.2
mn. passenger-km.	42.7	39.6	45.2	54.5	49.7	54.4	69.1
Shipping under Polish Flag ('000 BRT)	249	250	265	288	287	764	853

SOURCE: *Rocznik Statystyczny* 1965, p. xxxviii.

From 1956 onward everything is 'clear sailing', but the earlier post-war years show a sharp decline in output and a catastrophic one in productivity. In the early 'fifties freight performance is saved by the opening of the China run (note the great increase in average ton-distance), while passengers take a terrible knock. Even today passengers are at a half of the pre-war level, though freight is eight times as big. Yet all this curious evolution follows the acquisition of many miles of coastline, and the two great ports of Gdansk and Szczecin.

[1] The concept of f.o.b. includes a rail freight paid to the border of the producing country; hence between two neighboring countries f.o.b. is identical to c.i.f.

In STEs, freight transport, although unpublished like other invisibles, in fact enters the foreign currency balance of the Ministry of Foreign Trade, and is thus reckoned at the official, not the non-commercial, rate of exchange.[1] The 'non-commercial' currency balance is prepared by the central bank.

5

The remaining invisibles are less important in all economies. Items (iii) and (iv) in the previous tables include passenger transport, touring expenses other than transport to or from home, diplomatic representation, merchanting commissions, insurance other than on merchandise, license fees, royalties, patents. We have no official data for STEs, and have presented our guess as to their volume above. For the rather special case of tourism see also Section 15, below.

The pricing of invisibles other than freight is or rather was peculiarly stupid in STEs. For while visibles are exchanged at 'world-market prices' (Chapter IX), to which the domestic financial system has to adjust itself, it is deemed that invisibles have no such prices. They must therefore be exchanged at cost; so the rate of exchange is very far from irrelevant. In the bad old days, when STEs overvalued their currencies by a factor of five and then denied it, this was a very serious matter. The writer himself once contributed heavily to Soviet invisible earnings by sending a short telegram from Moscow to Oxford in 1952. There being no discount, I sent it at the official rate, paying about £3. In 1957—also an unsophisticated period in a way—Poles used to buy themselves air tickets to foreign parts at the official rate, thus benefiting where the writer lost. They could do so because foreign travel had just been liberalized but the bureaucracy had not yet perceived that the official rate was only tolerable if no resident were permitted to buy at it. Now that the new non-commercial rates are in force (Chapter VI), trade in these items is conducted on the same principles in STEs and MEs.

As to items (v) and (vi), they are historically determined, and we see in Chapter XIV good reason to despair of knowing how big they are. Finally, it would appear that in all Communist b.o.p. statements the official traffic in arms is excluded. I am not absolutely happy about this, since the official definitions are certainly so drawn

[1] Smirnov, op. cit., pp. 77–8; enquiries of Polish officials.

as to include arms. Moreover, the universal practice of 'civilized' powers is to include them in the total, but not to itemize them separately. Rather are they strewn around the various residual items. However, published Soviet exports to North Vietnam, to take but the most obvious example, cannot possibly include arms. This is far and away our most important field of ignorance.

In the presence of so much total ignorance, to which must be added all the ordinary inaccuracy to be expected of visible trade figures,[1] it is extremely foolhardy to estimate the b.o.p. of an STE. My attempts in Chapter V are, it will have been observed, of the crudest kind.

6

So much for the method of pricing and the statistical volume. Next: *Are invisibles subject to the law of comparative costs?* Some clearly are. Countries with a tradition of seamanship export shipping services: Norway, Greece, Britain.[2] Countries with a tradition of financial expertness export insurance: Britain. Both these occupations flourish where the necessary labor is comparatively, not absolutely, cheapest. Indian seamen and insurers, for instance, come cheaper, but India exports other products (visible or invisible) in which her comparative advantage is greater. Moreover, the labor in question embodies intellectual capital, which has been accumulated unevenly over the face of the earth, thus creating a very ordinary and obvious case of unequal factor endowment.

So far, so very reassuring. But the word 'invisibles' covers a multitude of sins. Shipping and insurance are *product services*, and thus distinguishable by not one economically relevant criterion from the ordinary material goods that flow in international trade. And so far at least as shipping is concerned, STEs seem to treat it neither more nor less rationally than commodity trade. Other invisibles are *factor services*, and these neither are nor should be amenable to the comparative-cost theory. For insofar as factors flow between nations they do so (when not on political grounds) simply because the absolute return is higher. Here, too, theory and practice coincide; so again there is no fundamental cause for worry.

[1] Such figures are surprisingly unreliable in all countries. In particular, country *A*'s account of its trade with *B* seldom agrees with *B*'s account. Cf. Oscar Morgenstern, *On the Accuracy of Economic Observations* (Princeton, NJ, 1963), Chapter 9 and for STEs, Robert L. Allen, *Soviet Economic Warfare* (Washington, DC, 1960), App. B.

[2] I refer here to beneficial ownership. The flag is, of course, a different question, one of tax avoidance.

7

The only real difficulties are of accountancy and definition, to which we now turn. For when a factor is transferred for a longish period we call it a 'capital' transaction, where 'capital' means 'not current'. Here we shall always say 'non-current', since this use of the word 'capital' is most confusing. For capital, meaning loanable funds or abstinence, is by no means the only non-current factor transfer. An invention can be licensed or patented, and a man can migrate.

Now any *money* payment made at the time of transfer is, of course, included in the b.o.p. accounts; e.g., the loanable funds themselves are recorded in the non-current account. But if there is no money payment, the factor is transferred without entering the b.o.p. Thus the immigration of a worker (or, for that matter, of a baby or a pensioner) is recorded only insofar as he brings in any cash. Similarly, the purchase of a patent or license will be recorded only for the down payment made; which may be very small indeed compared with the increases in efficiency. Again, in later years, the presence of the migrant factor of production will only affect the b.o.p. to the extent that money passes in respect of it. In this way amortization, interest, and dividends fully account for the use of loanable funds; but royalties only very partially reflect the use of patents and licenses, and leave out other ways of transferring knowledge; while immigrants' remittances are a very distorting mirror in which to view the profit and loss of migration.

Thus neither at the time of transfer nor later does the b.o.p. include anything like all the factor services that cross international boundaries. It is, after all, the balance of *payments*, and these things do not always attract payment. A country's foreign economic relations are, therefore, not all accounted for in our normal measurements, even by the most formal criteria.

These moneyless factor transfers are extremely important for the life of a country. When enterprise or skilled labor come in they spread activity and knowledge for years afterward.[1] Knowledge can, again, come in in a technical journal or a newspaper for virtually nothing. It can also come embodied in a prototype—a fact that accounts for many romantic smuggling episodes where the exporter is jealous of his technique; yet more usually the prototype comes in at the mere cost of mass production, since it is seldom still a

[1] And, *per contra*—a subject beyond our scope here—the immigration of babies and pensioners has a most deleterious effect, unless they bring with them a foreign income.

prototype in its native land. As to the immigration of ordinary labor, its exact short-run effects are controversial and depend on circumstances; yet in the longest run no nation would ever have come into being without it.

8

There are, then, 'visible invisibles' and 'invisible invisibles'. The first are product services, already discussed, and the movement of loanable funds. This movement deserves a chapter to itself (XIV). The *international movement of labor* may be taken here. Both STEs and MEs differ widely among themselves in their *immigration* policy. Such is the general dearth of analysis that a general theoretical excursus is in order. The economic considerations that they should take into account are (*a*) skill, (*b*) prospective length of working life, (*c*) net effect on the b.o.p., (*d*) net claim on the budget and welfare services, (*e*) impact on the labor market, (*f*) impact on plan fulfillment, and (*g*) the general operation of the law of diminishing returns.

Items (*a*) and (*b*) speak for themselves; but note that they only matter in so far as they affect the others. Item (*c*) refers first to people who retire on foreign pensions (Section 14, below), but it should also be asked of a worker-immigrant how much he intends to remit to his relatives back home; moreover he may have a different propensity to import from natives. This again speaks for itself, but we need also to know whether he intends to work in an exporting, import-saving, importing, or neutral industry. As we saw in Chapter V, there is a strong 'input-output' or technological effect here which is quite independent of monetary or fiscal policy: it is not true that Keynesian techniques can convert any and every increase of efficiency with equal ease into a b.o.p. surplus. Thus, the expulsion of the Huguenots provided Britain with a silk industry and improved her b.o.p.

Item (*d*) is, in the days when every state is a welfare state, about equally important. Skill and age apart, the fiscally ideal immigrant is an energetic, healthy homosexual who requires no more education. According as his family circumstances vary or are likely to vary, so is the immigrant more or less fiscally desirable. Moreover, his effect on the budget, however it arises, works indirectly upon economic growth and upon the b.o.p.

As to (*e*), the immigrant's impact on the labor market, this item is largely removed from rational consideration in an ME by trade union pressure. The union sees only the immediate consequences to its existing membership, and normally neglects the possibility of promotion for natives within the profession opened up by immigrants at the bottom—let alone all wider considerations. But, in fact, the combination of unskilled immigration and full employment virtually entails the opening up of better jobs for the natives. Moreover, a skilled immigrant brings free capital into the country, and may widen some bottleneck to the great advantage of everybody. The STE is very superior at this point, since with such powerless trade unions it becomes at least possible for authorities to consider these matters rationally.

Moreover, excess demand in the labor market of an ME will cause immigration: from which it follows that mere careless fiscal and monetary policy can permanently alter a country's factor endowment. Since, as usual, immigration is not rationally considered, it is quite likely, indeed common, for inflation to be pursued for some entirely different reason, while this unintended side-effect goes merrily forward. Although, as we have just seen, immigration holds out surprisingly good prospects for the natives, it may in given cases be very deleterious, notably through sheer diminishing returns to the country's natural resources.

If the STE has no real equivalent to the trade union it has an equivalent to excess demand, and this is (f) over-ambitious planning. The plan sets absolute, not *per capita*, targets. The temptation, then, is to import labor regardless, just as more commonly raw materials are imported regardless. But a less ambitious plan, based strictly on the available labor, would avoid diminishing returns and impose a smaller savings burden on the natives. This caveat has special force for Mongolia and the DDR, below.

In any case (g), the law of diminishing returns, is not so easily dealt with. The average productivity of labor may fall—in the extractive industries it virtually must fall—while all natives improve their situation as in (e) (and the migrants themselves get better jobs than they had at home).[1] Again the sheer volume of exports is almost certain to increase as well as that of imports, which should worsen the single-factor terms of trade, an effect similar to diminishing returns. But we must also take into account the things the migrants were producing and consuming before they arrived. These,

[1] Let the original labor force be n, the original average income be y. Let m workers immigrate, and accept an income $x < y$. The original n now work up the social scale, and average $z > y$. Returns diminish if $(nz + mx)/(n + m) < y$, which is, of course, entirely compatible with $z > y > x$.

at least, might have been very competitive with their new country's sales and purchases. Then, again, in manufacturing industries there are economies of scale, which the increase in both supply and demand makes attainable.

In only one respect is it certain that returns will diminish for all to feel: pressure on amenities and general space. In a highly-populated country this may be decisive. But a very sparse country, like Australia, can actually benefit from the increased 'cultural density' up to a point.

All the effects discussed under (g) are bound to be neglected by an orthodox Marxist state, since the law of diminishing returns is anathema. Rooted in Malthus's rejection of human perfectibility, and substituting the accursed margin for the good old understandable average, the law is anti-Marxian in origin, implications and methodology. It is not on such grounds that Communists fear immigrants.

But non-economic factors are almost always more important, in all countries: health—if that is indeed non-economic, security, race. We need not here ask whether these factors are rationally considered by any kind of state.

9

Turning to analysis by countries as opposed to motives, we shall confine ourselves to organized states capable of regulating migration. The most liberal country is clearly the very special case of Israel. Israel actually illustrates a general principle, that of 'in-gathering': a nation-state is founded by part of some race or nation, and the remainder is encouraged to come and settle in it. Next in order of liberality probably come, or came, colonies with an unsuitable local labor force. Thus under British rule Ceylon, Burma, British Guiana and Fiji were populated with Indian laborers. The great liberality of immigration policy here is simply caused by the absence of racial considerations in the mind of the imperial power: since Burma was for the British and not for the Burmese, why not use Indian labor if it worked better? The successor states, the UDCs of today, are exceedingly restrictive. But the metropolitan, ex-imperial countries retain curious pockets of extreme liberality: the United States and Puerto Rico, Britain and Eire, France and Algeria, Sweden and Finland. In each case, this is the hangover of an attempt to annex the particular dependency favored. The American continent and Australasia are also a special case: these countries, which were 'new', i.e., unoccupied after the invention of the nation-state, traditionally favor many kinds of immigrant. Although skill is a consideration in their immigration laws, security is a bigger one, and race often bigger still; but even so, there are today few places with more liberal immigration policies.

That brief and superficial rundown leaves few non-Communist countries out of consideration. An intermediate case was the USSR of the NEP, which was liberal enough to admit 30,000 seasonal laborers from China and Persia in 1925/26, and more in the next three years.[1] When Stalin had full power he only admitted a few such laborers from other STEs—when he had founded some.

By comparison, then, most STEs are and always have been very restrictive. All countries welcome really high skills, except, of course, where the native practitioners of those skills are well union-ized; and here, as we have seen, the unionless STE is at a great theoretical advantage. The USSR had just such an immigration policy in the first FYP, and attracted many unemployed German and American craftsmen.[2] But after that period the security angle was long uppermost, and STEs would accept hardly anybody.

One exception used to be the Soviet acceptance of prisoners. Immediately after the war, Stalin kidnapped a large number of politically hostile elements in the satellite states (which had not yet strictly been founded), and put them to work at forced labor.[3] He also retained many German and Japanese prisoners of war, and Polish citizens of one kind and another, beyond their stated term. But he did mainly allow these people to leave the country on expira-tion of sentence—doubtless a good security measure. He also used Bulgarian labor at harvest-time.

Then about 1963 there was an about-face, along with the explosion of tourism, the strengthening of CMEA and increased interest in a rational division of labor. Czechoslovakia in particular had plan targets demanding more labor than her infertile population chose to provide (cf. Chapter V). She took 6000–10,000 Polish miners in

[1] Birmingham Bureau of Research on Russian Economic Conditions, *Memorandum no. 4*, (Birmingham, 1932). But there has been no Chinese labor in the USSR in recent years, despite what is said by Yuan-li Wu, *An Economic Survey of Communist China* (New York, 1956), p. 503. On this compare Klaus Mehnert, *Pekin und Moskau* (Stuttgart, 1962), p. 355.

[2] 3000–4000 under contract in 1929–31, and 'a number' not under contract.—Birmingham Bureau, ibid.

[3] Some of these went to corrective labor camps (Jean Rounault, pseudonym for Rainer Biemel, *Mon Ami Vassia* [Paris, 1949]); some were merely deportees with a limited freedom (like the hero of Godfrey Lias' *I Survived* [London, 1954]). Some, like M. Rounault, who is French, were not even satellite citizens.

1964 and in 1966 was negotiating with Yugoslavia.[1] Negotiations with Bulgaria, however, came to nothing in 1965.[2] The DDR also showed an interest in Yugoslav labor in 1966.[3]

Thus recent interest has been great. The Rumanians, those paragons of economic nationalism, have actually denounced migration as unsocialist. On June 12, 1964, *Viata Economica* attacked the Soviet geographer, P. Alampiev, who

... proclaims the thesis concerning the 'Possibility and utility of the seasonal and permanent migration of the population between various socialist countries'. This notion of the international 'migration' of the population is incompatible with socialism. We know only too well that at the time of the *bourgeoisie* there were situations when the inhabitants of our country had to leave ... in order to look for jobs even beyond the Atlantic Ocean; we have seen only too well how things develop in the 'Common Market', which has secured the 'free circulation' of the labour force. ... We have never imagined that a thesis could be voiced concerning the 'possibility and the utility' of a similar process within the framework of the world socialist system.[4]

But for some time the most hospitable STE, and certainly the most economically rational, has been Mongolia, which has used much short-contract Chinese labor on civil engineering projects. *Toute proportion gardée*, Mongol policy here has been perhaps the boldest in the world; its only serious competitor is the United States importation of Mexican 'stoop labor' for the harvest. By coincidence both countries have reversed their policies recently: the United States in 1965, as part of the 'War on Poverty', Mongolia

TABLE XIII/7. MONGOL vs. U.S. IMMIGRATION POLICY

	Mongolia (approx.)	U.S. ('000)
Population of working age, 1957 .	450,000[a]	87,500
Average number of short-contract unskilled workers present in the summer, 1956–58 . .	10,000[b]	500[c]
Annual net permanent immigration of working age . . .	0	162

[a] The total population was 826,000. I take a slightly higher proportion than in the United States.
[b] The treaty with China was signed in 1955. Up to some time in 1958, 20,000 had entered. They had contracts for several years. The peak number was 13,000 (*The Economist*, February 15, 1964; Rupen, *China Quarterly*, October–December, 1963; Mehnert, op. cit., p. 326; Harrison E. Salisbury, *To Moscow and Beyond* (New York, 1959), p. 228).
[c] Legally 350,000. I have guessed 150,000 'wetbacks'.

[1] Harry Trend, 'The Manpower Crisis in Czechoslovakia', Radio Free Europe, Munich' June 13, 1964; *Borba*, Belgrade, January 31, 1966.
[2] Privately communicated.
[3] *Borba*, January 31, 1966.
[4] Taken here from Michael Kaser, *The Comecon* (Oxford, 1965), p. 166.

in 1964, owing to political tension with China. Of the two countries Mongolia has been the more hospitable (see Table XIII/7, p. 357).

The numbers of foreign students also indicate a highly restrictive policy:

TABLE XIII/8. NUMBERS OF FOREIGN STUDENTS IN INSTITUTES OF HIGHER
EDUCATION

	Number	Per cent of Enrolment
US, 1963	74,814[a]	1.7[a]
UK, 1963	14,117[a,b]	c. 11.5[b]
West Germany, 1963	25,155[a]	7.2[a]
France, 1962	30,442[a]	10.0[a]
USSR, 1964	21,000[c]	c. 0.9[d]
(of whom from STEs	11,000)[c]	
UDCs	10,000)[c]	
ACCs	200)[c]	

[a] United Nations, UNESCO, *Statistical Yearbook*, 1964.

[b] Apparently for universities only. If we add teachers' training, technical schools, etc., universities come to a little less than half the internationally comparable total of *all* students; it is not known what the effect would be on foreign students.

[c] *New York Times*, January 13, 1965 (speech of N. N. Sofinski, Deputy Minister of Higher Education).

[d] *Narodnoe Khozyaistvo SSSR* 1964, Moscow, 1965. Since all other enrolment figures are for full-time students only, but in the USSR part-time study is pursued with such particular energy, I have subtracted half the part-timers (1·878 mn.) from the official total (3·261 mn.), to obtain the internationally comparable figure of 2·320 mn.

These small numbers, be it noted, come after several years of sharp expansion.

For the rest, substantial immigration has rested on the principle of 'in-gathering'. In 1956–59 Poland gathered in all kinds of prisoners from the USSR and others claiming Polish citizenship on some ground.[1] The USSR has tried to gather in the old religious diaspora, such as the Old Believers and Dukhobors and victims of old political persecutions such as Armenians. Above all, China encourages Overseas Chinese to retire to the mother country, and trains and sends out again Overseas Chinese students. It would appear that no one enters an STE simply to settle and work, on economic grounds; but there are a few political refugees.

10

As to *emigration* the story is very different. One policy is that of the *political safety valve*. In its early stages a Communist government

[1] About 1% of the population. The immediate postwar figures were, of course, far bigger— about 12% of the population—but Poland was not then a properly Communist country, and her general policy cannot be gauged from so great a *Völkerwanderung*. Source: Polish statistical yearbooks.

is often anxious to let out his *bourgeoisie* and political opposition. Lenin did this in a small way, and Castro has done it on a scale with remarkable demographic consequences.[1] This was a brilliant if unorthodox security measure; with so large and so Americanized a *bourgeoisie* a Communist state could hardly be stable ninety miles from Florida. Much the same happened under Kadar, whose seizure of power in Hungary in 1956 may be likened to an original seizure of power. Other Communist governments, however, have refused to permit emigration from the very moment of seizing power; there seems to be no set policy. At much later dates, groups that have proved particularly indigestible or useless may be let out, e.g., elderly Jews from the USSR and Eastern Europe. Another policy is that of *straightforward normal permission*, as if a Communist country were a civilized country. For many years now the Yugoslav Government has covertly practiced this policy: no arrangements were made with foreign governments, and the thing was strictly illegal, but, in fact, large numbers left. West European firms even began in 1962 openly to recruit labor. On November 1, 1963, the *short*-term emigration of *unskilled* labor was officially regulated by the Ministry of Labor.[2] I know of no other Communist government, i.e., of no STE, that has ever had such a policy, though Poland comes very close to it.

Poland's policy is certainly different, since though few of her emigrants are as political as in Cuba, and few feel the necessity to break the law in getting out, she certainly does not expect them to come back, thus giving proof of a low level of self-confidence. It is difficult within a short compass to develop adequate measures of a country's liberalism in these matters, since if individuals do not wish to migrate a very liberal policy will have no *ex post* results. Let us, then, crudely lay down that gross yearly turnover per thousand of the population is the best measure available. We then arrive at the following figures, including a capitalist country very similarly placed for emigration (see Table XIII/9, p. 360). It must be borne in mind that a Pole faces far more difficulties of security clearance before getting into some other country.

In all three countries the emigrant's remittance is a much prized element in the b.o.p. (Section 13).

---

[1] According to official figures in the UN *Demographic Yearbook 1966*, 3% of the population must have emigrated in 1960–65.

[2] Radio Free Europe, *Background Information Yugoslavia* (Munich, November 18, 1963). This paper quotes *Borba*, October 24, 1963; *Neue Zürcher Zeitung*, November 14, 1963; *Komunist*, June 6, 1963.

A third item, falling outside the scope of an economic work since it is statistically insignificant, is that of the *individual compassionate case*: the Soviet bride of the American journalist, etc.

Two cases are unclassifiable. The first is the DDR, the only Communist country ever to have been compelled to keep a frontier open. The government could close the zonal frontier and all those with other countries, but that between East and West Berlin had to remain open by treaty. Therefore, it had either to break the treaty, or to close off East Berlin, the capital, from the rest of the country,

TABLE XIII/9. THE LIBERALISM OF CERTAIN EMIGRATION POLICIES

	Average annual emigration	immigration	Turnover as rate per 'ooo of population
Poland, 1960–62	22,400	500	0.8
Yugoslavia, 1955–58	51,250	2700	2.9
Yugoslavia, 1962–67	?82,300	?9600	?5.0
Italy, 1958–61	73,600	28,600	2.1

SOURCES: Statistical Yearbooks of each country; U.N. *Demographic Yearbook 1962*. Yugoslavia has released no figures for the period of her new and more liberal policy. The latter figures are my informed guess.

or to tolerate free emigration. For fourteen long years it took the third way out, no doubt under strong Soviet pressure. Then in August, 1962, it finally switched to the first solution and built the wall. The results in the meantime show the most remarkable demographic drain since the Irish famine: the country's losses exceeded its natural increase to bring about a decline of 0·7% per annum in 1947–59.[1] The other case is by comparison trivial: in 1962, in the third consecutive year of hunger, the Chinese government turned its back while a few of its citizens migrated to Hongkong and Soviet Kazakhstan.

We should note here the great losses poor countries sometimes suffer through emigration. A medical education, provided at great expense to the Indian government and people, is to many of its beneficiaries but a passport to New York City. A good undergraduate degree is similarly a stepping stone to foreign study and that again to emigration. The tragedy is that such 'brain drains' have nothing to do with comparative, everything to do with absolute, advantage. They are the product of poverty and attempts to develop actually worsen them. It is the best people with the newest

[1] Wolfgang F. Stolper, *The Structure of the East German Economy* (Harvard, 1960); statistical yearbooks of the DDR.

skills that are lost. Indeed, it is only such people that the countries of immigration will accept.

Such perverse phenomena are quite foreign to STEs as a world system. Admittedly they are all poorer than ACCs; so suffer each a 'brain drain' toward them according to their several degrees of liberalism. The Cuban and East German losses have been very great. But they are all suspicious of immigration; so the more advanced among them never drain the brains of the less advanced. However, the amount of education given to foreigners is very small compared with that rendered by ACCs: compare Table XIII/7.

II

So much for government policies. As to individual motivation, such Communist governments, principally the DDR and Yugoslavia, as make public utterance on the subject say that people go because they seek a higher standard of living. And no doubt wherever emigration is reasonably free many go who have only this motive. No doubt, too, it operates in every case where there are other motives: the desires to gain political or religious freedom, to rejoin one's family, to escape one's family, and to avoid punishment for straightforward crime. In fact, in every major case political or religious freedom and economic betterment have pulled together; even the Kazakhs who left Sinkiang for Kazakhstan went to a freer and a richer country. It is of interest that the DDR uses economic counter-inducements, raising the salaries of doctors and professors right to West German levels although the general standard of living is lower. But if we learn that money kept a man, we learn little about what made him want to go; only perhaps that political or religious freedom have not an absolute priority in his eyes.

In general the low level of migration is very easily explained: STEs are police states, so fear immigrants; STEs are earthly paradises, so are embarrassed by emigrants. But there is another element: migration is a very personal and individual matter, and it fits neither the ideology nor the economic model that individuals should take such large decisions. The labor market is not *supposed* to be free, the words 'labor market', let alone 'free labor market', are never used. The free disposal of goods produced, as, for instance, on the kolkhoz market, is ideologically far more acceptable than the laborer's free choice of job. Labor is in ideology both planned and free at the same time—a notion more compatible with the Hegelian notion of freedom than with common sense. The free domestic flows of labor that, in fact, occur, and are dealt with by changes in wage differentials, are a very great ideological, as well as practical, embarrassment. Yet to plan migration is to deport, and that is a legal punishment for a specific crime. So it is perhaps not surprising that the STEs which were politically most liberal in the early 'sixties, Poland and Hungary, allowed much less migration than the less liberal Communist country which was not an STE: Yugoslavia. For Titoism has come to terms with the self-betterment of the individual, even if unplanned. The essence of Titoism is the confident acceptance of human nature as it is, as a fundamentally socialist and progressive phenomenon. Orthodox Communism is extremely mistrustful of all 'spontaneity'. The Yugoslav security police were by no means less brutal and unscrupulous; but their range of interests was narrower.

12

A minor invisible, little known among modern non-Communist countries, is *ransom*. At least the following cases are well established:

1932: To help the Soviet b.o.p. crisis (Chapter V), anyone could buy an exit visa by persuading relatives abroad to pay an individually negotiated price in convertible currency. The police arranged the deal, but the practice was not supposed to be public knowledge.[1]

1960–64: Rumania sold exit visas to the relatives living abroad of prisoners and others. Many were Jewish. The whole operation was conducted through one non-Rumanian individual, who got into the game via ordinary trade with Rumania. Officials of the country were never directly involved, in contrast to the other cases listed here. At about $6000 a head on about 2000 heads, and subtracting about $1000 for the intermediary, this trade may have netted Rumania $2 mn. per annum for five years, or 0.3% of her visible exports.[2]

1962: Cuba ransomed, openly and publicly, the prisoners from the United States invasion. The deal, concluded in December,

---

[1] A case is described at length in R. O. G. Urch, *The Rabbit King of Russia* (London, 1939), Chapters 1, 2, 25, 26.

[2] Representative Michael A. Feighan, *New York Times*, October 7, 1964; sundry Rumanian exiles.

1962, bought back 1113 prisoners for $53 mn., or $48,000 a head. The money was raised semipublicly under the auspices of the United States government. The sum was about 2½% of the Cuban national income, or about 8% of exports.

October, 1964: West Germany purchased the release of about 800 captives in East Germany, secretly, at about $10,000 a head.[1]

An important technical necessity in the ransom business is a reputation for honesty. Moral feelings are so deeply stirred that deals tend not to stick. Again, world opinion is very hostile; so the trade has to be secret (Castro made the only exception). Both the Rumanian and the Soviet officials, then, kept strictly to their side of the bargain, refunding deposits when bodies were not delivered, etc.

13

Ransom is in a sense but a special case of the *emigrant's remittance*. We have already met these remittances in connection with tariffs (Chapter IX, Section 9). We now come to their effect on the b.o.p. In Poland, in addition to the private packages subject to tariff, one Polish and several foreign firms specialize in these parcels. The PKO (General Welfare Fund, *Powszechna Kasa Oszczednosci*) accepts money in, say, the United States and converts it into either zlotys or goods for the Polish addressee at a very high, indeed, a quite absurdly high, rate of exchange. This was ninety-six zlotys to the dollar in 1956–57, and in 1964, seventy-two zlotys to the dollar.[2] The foreign firm operates in the same manner as the PKO, and the Polish Government positively encourages this. For even though it is competing with a state enterprise, the foreign one is more likely to mobilize the foreign funds. The state's 'profit' is that it has acquired the dollars—unless, as I suspect, the rate has been set so absurdly low as to lose all possible profit (Chapter XV, Section 7).

The Chinese Government runs a scheme similar to the PKO,[3] rather sharply regulating the quantities transferable, lest goods get into the black market and inequalities of income arise. Standing at the other end of the Communist spectrum of Puritanism versus liberalism, the Polish Government seemingly sets no limit on

---

[1] C. L. Sulzberger, *New York Times*, October 26, 1964.
[2] Curt Poralla, *Die Reformen des Polnischen Binnen und Aussenhandels vor und nach dem Oktoberumbruch 1956* (Berlin, 1958), p. 60; and my personal observations in 1964.
[3] *Ch'iao-wu Pao* (*Overseas Chinese Affairs Bulletin*), 6/1962 (= SCMM, April 16, 1963).

transfers, nor on the inequalities that arise from them. Emigrants'
remittances, foreign pensions etc., amounted to no less than 4% of
the national income in 1960.[1] Emigration, after all, has been a
Polish profession for nearly two centuries, and a 'remittance base'
has been built up that is only exceeded by Israel's.

14

From the emigrant's remittance we turn to *retirement*. Retirement
is an industry similar to tourism in more than one country. Mexico
does well out of United States pensioners, and the Bahamas out of
British pensioners. These countries, being capitalist MEs, have one
indisputable advantage over STEs in the same line of business: they
can sell land, thus still further improving their b.o.p.[2] Poland
specializes in retirement, but owing to her foolishly generous rate
of exchange probably loses by it. Thus I met a Polish-American
from Dallas who was living in Warsaw and drawing his $100-a-
month United States pension through the PKO. He was living
handsomely, not merely in comparison with other Poles, but also
in comparison with his likely circumstances in the United States,
since he was getting seventy-two zlotys to the dollar when the dollar is
only worth, by my reckoning, about fourteen. The other STE that
has seriously entered the pensioner industry is China. Note that in
both cases the appeal is nationalistic, not climatic. The whole thing
is a sort of 'in-gathering'. In China it is also theological: it is important
to be buried with one's ancestors.

There is in China also a serious attempt to attract capital, as well
as current contributions on income account, from emigrants. We
shall deal with it here for convenience. The State-Owned Overseas
Chinese Investment Companies attract patriotic capital from abroad,
which receives a regular and rather high *but inconvertible* 'dividend'—
recently 8% per annum. In this manner 'the overseas Chinese can
contribute their share to the building of socialism in the fatherland on the one hand and acquire a good many benefits for themselves at the same time'.[3] This practice began at least as early
as 1954, and achieved the dignity of a State Council regulation on

---

[1] A. Wierzbicki in *Studia Finansowe*, 1/1965.

[2] Strictly, however, it should be possible for the pensioner's heirs to sell this land, perhaps
at a higher price, and repatriate the sum. In this case it is the net increase in the quantity of
land in foreign ownership that matters. Moreover, the country of residence can fairly tax
the site value both during the pensioner's life and at his death. On United States pensioners in Mexico cf. *Time*, May 22, 1964.

[3] *Ch'iao-wu Pao*, February, 1963 (= SCMM, April 16, 1963).

August 2, 1957. Purposes to which the dividends may be put include: the expenses of returned overseas Chinese students; the general maintenance of returned overseas Chinese families; tourism; public welfare undertakings in one's home town. As to capital, after twelve years the original 'venture' is over, and one may reinvest it. My source is wholly unclear as to any other use to which the capital may be put, but strongly indicates that it remains inconvertible.

15

In view of what we have learned about emigration it need not surprise us that Yugoslavia takes, or took, an entirely different view of *tourism* from the STEs. It was very much a part of the Titoist revolution (which, as opposed to the Tito-Stalin split, should be dated about 1950) that the Party could retire not only from microeconomic but also from cultural affairs and from the control of personal contacts. So socialist realism was abandoned, and Western popular culture flooded into the country. This politico-cultural about-turn was decisive in the admission of a flood of capitalist tourists, even though the actual motive was simply to make invisible exports. The Yugoslav Government has not willingly exposed its subjects to the West; it has simply not felt the disadvantages keenly enough, when the cost is an overstretched security police or an unfavorable b.o.p.

Only in 1963–64, when Stalinism was well and truly dead, the Sino-Soviet conflict had restored genuine sovereignty to each STE, and the b.o.p. crises described in Chapter V had initiated a general reconsideration, did the STEs follow the Yugoslavs' touristic example. The Czechoslovak case alone will suffice. Between 1936 and 1956 visible trade doubled while tourism virtually disappeared. There are signs of liberalization in the early sixties, but tourism only becomes a serious currency-earner in 1964. Note that, in contrast to the late 'thirties the tourist balance is now kept extremely favorable (Table XIII/10).

Tourism is, of course, a product service, and, indeed, *par excellence* an industry based on natural resources; hence the inferior performance of Poland, which we shall see in Chapter XV to be by no means behindhand in encouraging the activity, even to ridiculous extremes. Tourism is further proof of how irrelevant is the distinction between visibles and the product services for all economic purposes; in economic theory, a city like Prague is indistinguishable from a good coal-mine.

TABLE XIII/10. TOURISM IN CZECHOSLOVAKIA, 1935, 1936, 1957–64
('000 persons)

	1935	1936	1956	1957	1958	1959	1960	1961	1962	1963	1964
Foreign tourists entering country	1698	1924	35	82	80	133	176	219	276[b]	364[b]	3135[b]
All foreigners entering country[a] .	—	—	—	—	—	—	—	620	697	807	3600
Native tourists leaving country	1255	1850	53	73	89	116	157	188	193[b]	236[b]	1820[b]
All residents leaving country[b] .	—	—	—	—	—	—	—	430	447	503	2100
Visible trade turnover, 1953=100	69[c]	77[c]	144	156	171	201	227	248	263	282	306

[a] Excluding transit.
[b] The residual, assuming that non-tourist travel grew by 5% p.a.
[c] Prague Chamber of Commerce, *Facts on Czechoslovak Foreign Trade* (1965), p. 12, gives 1937 as 91·8. I have derived 1935 and 1936 from the import volume index in League of Nations, *Review of World Trade* (Geneva, 1938).

SOURCE: pre- and post-war yearbooks.

16

We pass from the tourist to his shop, or rather to the 'valuta retail outlet', to coin a phrase. For such outlets deal with more than tourists in STEs; they welcome anyone with foreign exchange. Thus, for instance, any Polish black marketeer with a dollar bill can go to the PKO, and no questions asked. It was the same with Stalin's *Torgsin* shops in the USSR in the early thirties. *Torgsin* stands for 'trade with foreigners', and the main object of these shops was to make tourism and diplomacy possible in a starving country by selling to foreigners for valuta. The quality and range of their goods was strikingly better than in ordinary shops, and the prices very flexible. They handled also emigrants' remittances as a by-product of their main task, converting them into superior consumer goods for the beneficiaries. They also tried to tempt valuta out of the pockets of the people; for natives also could come and buy—again, no questions asked.[1]

Most STEs have similar institutions, and it remains to draw attention to a special case: the gift shop at the airport. The difference between these shops in ACCs and STEs is extremely striking, and illuminates not merely the economic but also the basic political principles upon which these societies rest. The gift shop in the Western airport arises out of the chance fact that there is no sovereign

[1] The *Torgsin* should be distinguished from the wartime 'commercial' shops, which also sold at very flexible prices, but only for rubles. Their object was not to collect valuta but to give the state its cut of the very high inflationary profits to be made on the kolkhoz market.

to levy indirect taxes outside territorial waters. So from selling tax-free liquor in the air[1] we move, by extension of the bonded warehouse idea, to tax-free liquor at the airport for those travelling abroad. The institution receives further psychological support from the rebate of indirect taxes granted by many countries to tourists who buy in ordinary shops. It is not the same thing, since, for instance, the United States grants no such rebates, but still runs tax-free airport shops. Again, the UK resident, who enjoys no such rebate in his own town, enjoys it at the airport.

Thus, in an ACC, these shops are the product of private legal ingenuity and private business initiative. They have accidentally burgeoned into a huge vested interest, which it would surely cost votes to suppress. It is tempting to say that they do less good to the b.o.p. than harm to the budget, but this is not obvious. For as we saw in Chapter VII, taxes can always be levied in one way or another; so if the odd resident buys the odd bottle of tax-free Scotch at the airport the treasury can easily recoup itself elsewhere. But the shops do permit foreigners to evade taxes that they would often have been willing to pay; and this is indeed bad for both budget and b.o.p. together. If, however, the elasticities of international substitution are great, the shop loses no tax and brings in valuta. So it is worth while at least during a b.o.p. crisis—the only time when valuta should have priority (Chapter V).

In STEs, on the other hand, these shops are not tax free at all, and rest upon no legal gimmick. They are simply *Torgsin*-type shops, selling high-quality goods for convertible currency. It is still possible for an STE to undercharge, and no doubt many do, choosing an implicit rate of exchange that much undervalues their own currency.[2] But at least the whole institution is not grounded in irrationality and private tax evasion. Only the force of competition is common to both: all airports compete, Warsaw must rival Copenhagen, in a process which began, perhaps, at Shannon.

17

More important, perhaps, than the international movement of people is *the international movement of technology*. Its actual effect—

---

[1] Vertically outside territorial waters. Strictly the right to levy taxes extends vertically upward until we enter outer space—a distance not yet legally defined from this point of view. In practice the right is unenforceable, and nearly all international flights over land sell tax-free liquor. But no internal flights do, and neither do flights within certain customs unions, or near-customs unions, like Scandinavia.

[2] Compare my remarks on the zloty above and in Chapter XV, Section 7.

the most far-reaching and sometimes devastating of all the results of international economic relations—we discuss in Chapter XIV. Here we have only to confess our utter ignorance of its financial consequences among STEs.

We can, however, be sure that they are rather small. Our account may conveniently amalgamate patent and copyright payments. In Marxist principle knowledge is a free good, and on that basis the USSR refused to join the 1887 Berne Convention on International Copyright and the equivalent patent agreement, the 1883 Paris Convention for the Protection of Industrial Property. Her refusal was mitigated by the failure of the preceding Tsarist government to join: there were here no signatures to denounce. In any case, very many countries operated outside these agreements, and the USSR of the NEP had little difficulty in making her own patent and copyright agreements with foreigners, as did other MEs. After all, her own domestic laws did not greatly deviate from international norms; so any foreigner could apply for a Soviet patent. Foreigners had copyright for works published within the USSR, but not for works published in any other country unless it had a reciprocal agreement with the USSR.

In the Stalin period the international patent situation was much less satisfactory. Like so much other old legislation, the market-type patent law was kept on the books. But it was quite overshadowed by a new system resembling the inventor's award characteristic of a capitalist war economy. This was the 'inventor's certificate' awarded by the government. The invention became the government's property, and the certified inventor received a reward. While it remained possible for a foreigner to take out a NEP-type patent, it was much more usual for the government to pay rewards to domestic inventors and simply appropriate foreign technical advances. Since it was uninterested in licensing its own inventions, and had few to offer, this position was satisfactory to it. In the meantime authors' and artists' copyright continued to be neglected in international trade, and the texts of foreign books were simply appropriated. Domestic copyright, however, was observed as much as during the NEP.

Various factors are now bringing the Soviet position into line: the death of Stalin and the general thaw, the increase of all types of foreign trade, and the hugely increased number of Soviet inventors, authors and artists with something to sell abroad. International copyright is still not recognized, and the work of foreign authors and actors is still appropriated. But this situation can hardly last. For instance, Mr. Harold Berman of Harvard University was actually permitted to argue in the Soviet Supreme Court in August, 1959, that not to pay royalties was unjustly to deprive a man of the fruits of his labor, and therefore unconstitutional. He lost his case, but his action was surely a step on the road to victory. Cases have been reported of foreign authors collecting ill-explained amounts of royalty in inconvertible rubles, when they come as tourists.

The refusal to recognize international copyright has been particularly undermined by the USSR's joining the Paris Convention on patents (July 1, 1965). Curiously enough, the essential change was on the non-Soviet side: foreign recognition of the Soviet inventor's certificate as on a par with a patent. It is, then, these certificates that attract foreign royalties. On the Soviet side, little formal change occurred. The old NEP law remains, as ever, in force, but foreigners had successfully used it even before 1965. The basic change is informal: the USSR has (or has not?!) abandoned industrial espionage and taken up honest payments instead. But such espionage is, as we see below, no Communist monopoly.

The forward policy in patents and the lag in copyright are easily explained by self-interest. In both fields the Soviet balance of *exchange* is extremely negative, but accession to the patent convention has improved the balance of *payments* slightly while accession to the copyright convention would sharply worsen it. It is easy for an STE to conceal its abuse of a foreign patent, but it does want foreign recognition for its own patents. Accession has made the concealment no harder, but it has provided the recognition. Abuse of copyright on the other hand, is almost impossible to conceal, and accession would make its continuance impossible. So as long as Soviet authors are little published abroad and translation is a major Soviet industry, the USSR has no interest in acceding to this agreement.

The East European STEs nearly all went Communist after having recognized the Paris and Berne Conventions.[1] They have thus been in theory indistinguishable from any civilized power, though no doubt in practice while Stalin lived they violated their agreements. There is, of course, no institutional reason why an STE should not loyally observe these conventions, since it is both a country and an enterprise at the same time.

[1] China went Communist before recognizing either convention. The Formosan régime has not acceded either.

Many romantic stories are told of the *direct theft* of Western technical secrets—over and above the purchase and imitation of prototypes without royalty payments. It is certain that technical espionage is practiced by large capitalist corporations, and it is particularly endemic, if rumor is to be believed, in the United States and Japan. Since Japanese firms normally steal foreign knowledge they figure far more often in nationalistic or political accounts of technical espionage than United States firms, which mainly steal from each other. Communist technical espionage must be seen in the light of these facts, if facts they be; we have no proof that it is more widespread. The most celebrated source for it is, in fact, pseudonymous;[1] I cannot say how much credence this author deserves, since he neither gives his real name nor reveals that he is not giving it.

18

Among STEs technological transfer is free, in accordance with Marxist doctrine; though if experts are physically moved the host country pays their salaries.[2] It is obvious that there is a great deal of such transfer, and the propaganda lays much stress on it. Yet is there more or less than in the rest of the world? With UDCs, technological transfer is a one-way process and part of foreign aid. What concerns us here is to compare the normal workings of 'socialist brotherhood' between STEs of approximately equal development with the normal workings of competition and greed between ACCs. In no field is the difference of economic activation greater. In all other cases the Communists have reverted to direct individual payment for services rendered, since the extremes of War Communism and the Great Leap Forward; and this applies not only at the level of the individual (fully) but also in large part at that of the enterprise. Even invention is materially well rewarded. On the other hand technological transfer inside a country, from institute to enterprise or enterprise to enterprise, is not rewarded but is at least legally compulsory. Only international technological transfer depends so much on altruism.

The obvious result of such a system would be to enhance one STE's demand for the technology of another, but to depress the corresponding supply. If no activator other than profit in fact

---

[1] Joseph Novak, *The Future Is Ours, Comrade* (London, 1960), pp. 72–7.

[2] There are also charges for the copying and postage of documents! The Russians charged the Chinese 4 mn. new rubles on this account in 1950–62 (*Pravda*, May 7, 1964).

operated, the zero prices imposed by doctrinaire governments would yield zero supplies, and in consequence zero transfer despite the height of demand. But, in fact, prices are not really at zero, and all sorts of other motives operate; so transfers are very large indeed. Prices are not really at zero because STEs *swap* technology. They have an excellent reason to supply it: a lively expectation of reciprocity. Moreover, there can be little doubt that if a particular STE were unwilling to supply technology its ordinary commodity trade would suffer. It is also not impossible that machine prototypes—those notorious carriers of technical progress—are charged for at monopolistic prices, or at least at higher prices than the true cost of domestic mass production.

And, anyway, other motives than profit are very active. Let us list them in rough order of importance.

(i) Marxist principle, proletarian solidarity, or socialist brotherhood. He would, indeed, be impercipient who did not give pride of place to the official ideology.

(ii) Then, too, technological transfer is part of foreign aid, and the varied motivations to foreign aid operate very strongly between rich and poor STEs, as we shall see in Chapter XIV.

(iii) If these reasons are obvious the third is less so. It is technological, as opposed to economic, nationalism.

Economic nationalism demands in normal circumstances that we conceal our knowledge from the foreigner. A bird in the hand is worth two in the bush: better monopolize the new product than rely on the presumption that foreigners will use our invention to enrich themselves in a *general* way, and that that in turn will improve our single-factor terms of trade. Such, for instance, were the motives behind the British restraints, until 1824, on the export of 'Artisans and Machinery'. Technological nationalism is a horse of quite another color: it is mere pride in our own cleverness. Nothing so flatters such pride as foreign imitation. Even if the foreigner prefers espionage to royalties we are still flattered. Such an attitude normally leads to the export of technology even against the national economic interest: e.g., Britain had rather see Indonesia install an atomic power station of British pattern, which both the UK and Indonesia must subsidize, than the Americans get in first.

In the Communist world it is virtually inconceivable that narrow calculation of economic interest ('It'll harm our terms of trade') should outweigh technological nationalism. The latter has had two main practical consequences. First, there is the conflict between

German and Soviet technical specifications, in which East German engineers, representing a whole German tradition that is clearly superior, have so far refused to give in to Soviet standardization proposals.[1] Secondly, there is or used to be the Soviet use of political pressure to force Soviet technology on other countries. An outcome of this is the well-known fact that the number of technical documents exported by the USSR to the DDR and Czechoslovakia exceeds the reverse flow, even though both the latter are much more advanced. We discuss below other possible explanations, but one surely is Soviet technological nationalism, aided by Soviet political dominance.

It is still not obvious that these activators will effect as much technological transfer as there is in the capitalist world. Here the main spur is simply the knowledge that many foreigners would be delighted to pay one good money for one's invention. We must add, however, that there is very much more travel between ACCs, very much more student exchange, and very many more international enterprises; also the whole social tone is more open and friendly. We could, of course, only know which system of transfer was more effective if we could measure the volume of technical knowledge. This, however, is still out of the question. It is obvious that Communist statistics of the numbers of experts and technical documents transferred[2] are nearly useless. The volume of technical knowledge is an economic magnitude, and can only be measured in value, i.e., in the money it is worth to the purchaser. Cost figures would be hardly more useful since so very much research is a failure and so very many research costs are joint between projects. The existing value figures, e.g., for royalty payments between ACCs,[3] are only a little better, since so much technological transfer is barter, or is embodied in the prices of prototypes, or is paid for by market-sharing agreements and heaven knows what else.

Faute de mieux—and seldom did the obscurity of a foreign language hide a greater inadequacy—we can dare to make a few empirical assertions. Where document transfer statistics show Bulgaria as receiving far more documents from the USSR than she sends, or Belgium is seen to make far greater royalty payments to

---

[1] Or so it seemed at the moment when Erich Apel killed himself; compare Erich Honecker's speech to the Central Committee, *Neues Deutschland*, December 16, 1965. On Apel's suicide see Chapter IX, Section 21.

[2] Published very often in all sorts of places. Cf. Kaser, op. cit.

[3] Cf. C. Freeman and A. Young, *The Research and Development Effort . . .*, OECD (Paris, 1965).

the United States than vice versa, it seems reasonable to infer that the smaller country has an unfavorable *balance of technological exchange*. The word 'exchange' implies the values that would have been paid by each country had the other charged what the traffic would bear. The actual technological b.o.p.[1] is either grossly unrepresentative of the underlying exchange or—in the Soviet-type case—actually zero. From the financial point of view, again, it is merely one invisible among many.

It seems from the slender evidence available that, first, small countries have unfavorable balances of technological exchange with big ones on a more or less equal level of development: Bulgaria, Poland, Hungary and Rumania with the USSR, all West European countries with the United States. The evidence presented by Messrs. Freeman and Young does not enable us to say whether the Soviet balance with Czechoslovakia and the DDR is positive or negative. Secondly, UDCs have unfavorable balances with more advanced countries.

If the second point is too obvious to discuss, the first leads to a small perplexity. Mere size causes a country to possess more exportable knowledge, because all knowledge is exportable and it simply has more people to know things; how, then, in a technically progressive world, can a small country keep up? Some of the answer is that knowledge is partially divisible, and the small country can specialize in, and lead in, the technology of its commodity exports. It can also neglect, and save much expense by neglecting, the technology of its imports. Smallness is of no help here, but at least it is not a hindrance. But in some degree knowledge is also indivisible, and apt to be shared by those who live physically close to each other. This puts the small country at a great disadvantage, which it must try to overcome by good communications and personal relations, by technological consortia, and the like. If research is in the hands of big international firms, a branch of such a firm may well settle in a small country. But in so far as research is a state concern the outlook is poor.

In late 1966 USSR swung over to the view that other STEs must pay for her technical knowledge.[2] Self-interest was of course basic here too, but another factor was the increasing role of economic calculation in the management of research. Recently Soviet authors have developed a number of 'effectiveness' formulae for research

---

[1] With which Messrs. Freeman and Young operate in their pioneering work.
[2] O. Bogomolov in *Kommunist*, 18/1966.

projects, similar to those used for foreign trade (Chapter VII). Though rather bogus, these do at least bring up the question of who pays. And it becomes instantly unclear why, if an enterprise in Vladivostok must pay for research done in Moscow, an enterprise in Plovdiv need not.

As so often, we find that this new development was foreshadowed in 1948, only to be suppressed by Stalin. At the end of that year Czechoslovakia demanded, but did not receive, money from Poland for technical information.[1] It is not clear as this is written whether charges have yet actually been made for knowledge.

This is merely to repeat what we have said in Chapter IX: the economics of the modern world is against small countries. The law of comparative costs will keep them in business as exporters of commodities, and, indeed, they must export enough to pay for foreign technology, even in respect of these commodities. But they will always tend to be behind, and must either accept lower real incomes, or sacrifice more and more their separate nationhood. In the Communist context, the newly-won sovereignty of the smaller STEs is jeopardized by the nature of things, unless they succeed, for political reasons, in tapping more United States technology than the USSR can.

Appendix to Chapter XIII

ON THE ACCOUNTANCY OF FREIGHT CHARGES IN THE B.O.P.

The countries chosen for Table XIII/2 are all of those in the IMF's *Balance of Payments Yearbook* which fulfill the following conditions:
1. their b.o.p. figures appear to be reasonably accurate, and the regionally unallocated item is not too large;
2. they distinguish the 'Soviet area' as a region;
3. their imports are given f.o.b. or can readily be reduced thereto (except Burma, Sweden and Ceylon).

The third condition is important if items (ii) and (iii) in that table are to be distinguished. The IMF[2] explain the matter thus: exports are always f.o.b., and the earnings of our shippers from carrying them are as unambiguously identifiable as our shippers' earnings in cross-trade between other pairs of countries, or our railroads' earnings in transit trade. But if imports are c.i.f. the items, given for f.o.b. on the left (p. 375), must be rearranged as on the right.

A country will hardly publish b.o.p. statistics with imports c.i.f. if it has enough knowledge to set them out f.o.b. Consequently the figure for 'freight on imports

---

[1] *Prozess gegen die Leitung des Staatsfeindlichen Verschwörerzentrums mit Rudolf Slánský an der Spitze*, Prague, 1953, p. 436.
[2] *Balance of Payments Yearbook 1960*, 'Concepts and Definitions', p. 10.

TABLE XIII/A1. ILLUSTRATION OF THE ACCOUNTING PROBLEMS OF FREIGHT

	All f.o.b.		Exports f.o.b. Imports c.i.f.	
	Credit	Debit	Credit	Debit
(a) Merchandise . .	90	100	90	125
(of which freight on imports:				
earned by residents . .	—	—	—	(10)
earned by foreigners) .	—	—	—	(15)
(b) Freight on imports:				
earned by residents . .	—	—	10	—
earned by foreigners . .	—	15	—	—
Freight on exports:				
earned by residents . .	40	—	40	—
Transit and cross-trade freight .	45	—	45	—
Turnover, (a) + (b) . .		290		310
Balance, (a) + (b) . .	60	—	60	—

TABLE XIII/A2. TWO COUNTRIES' INTERNATIONAL TRANSPORT TURNOVER IN DETAIL, 1960

	W. Germany (mn. DM)		USA (mn. $)	
	Credit	Debit	Credit	Debit
Ocean Freight . .	1779	2459	564[1]	853
Time Charter . .	—	—	8	178
Rail Freight . .	151	—	—	—
Freight Car Rentals .	—	—	24	25
Canal and River Freight .	33	228	—	—
Air Freight . .	—	—	55	22
Other Freight[2] . .	258	18	74	31
Port Disbursements .	604	1019	895	370
Repairs to Ships, Aircraft, etc. . . .	121	6	na.	na.
Ocean Passenger Fares .	75	na.	19	212
Air Passenger Fares .	—	—	177	251
Railway Passenger Fares .	110	—	na.	na.
Other Passenger Fares[3] .	242	213	na.	na.
Misc. Services . .	53	129	na.	na.

[1] Of which 136 is cross-trade.
[2] Includes road, pipe-line, Great Lakes and freight items marked —.
[3] Includes passenger items marked —.

earned by residents' is not normally distinguishable where imports are given c.i.f.; and not only the turnover but also the balance is wrong. The figures for Burma, Sweden, Ceylon and Yugoslavia in Tables XIII/2 and /3 are therefore wrong. Such an item is, of course, only a corrective one anyway: we are not otherwise interested, in a balance of *foreign* payments, in a payment by one resident to another.

Since one of our interests is to distinguish transport connected with goods from other transport, I have been at pains to expand item (ii) in Table XIII/2 beyond the mere item 'ocean freight' to include railway transit and, above all, ships' port disbursements. These are a very big item in most countries' b.o.p.s: say ⅓ of freights, or 5% of turnover. Air freight not being distinguished from air passengers, I have left it in item (iii). Capital repair of foreign ships, which should perhaps really be (i), has similarly been left in (iii), along with other 'goods' items such as merchandise insurance[1] and canal transit. We can form a very rough idea of the general importance of these items from the figures for West Germany and the United States, which alone publish enough detail (see Table XIII/A2, p. 375).

It should be re-emphasized that some countries earn a great deal by transit and cross-trade freight. The proportion of item (ii) to item (i) in Table XIII/2 does not tell us the freight cost of that country's trade. If all imports were given both f.o.b. and c.i.f. we should know by definition; compare Table XIII/5. But, even so, payments made to foreigners for freight on imports might perfectly well not have been made to residents of the countries where the imports had originated.

[1] This item tends to be 0·5% of imports and 0·2% of exports.

CHAPTER XIV

CAPITAL TRANSACTIONS

Speaking generally from the commercial viewpoint, our economic and technical aid to the UDCs is even unprofitable for us.

—Khrushchev

In this book 'capital' means loanable funds, not fixed assets. The warning is appropriately repeated here.

I

However national economies are organized, capital movements between them are of two types: trade-induced and security-induced. The latter is what the nineteenth century meant by the movement of capital: we sell securities abroad, and the money flows in. At the moment when the securities are exchanged for money, gold reserves or, better, net international liquidity positions move accordingly, although the current trade balance is wholly unaffected. Thereafter, the money may or may not quickly generate an importation of goods. For the original object in selling the securities was either 'real' or 'financial'; e.g., on the one hand to pay for some investment project or to balance the government's budget; or, on the other, to enable some resident to switch his portfolio around or to solve the liquidity problems of the central bank. In the former cases, the money will certainly get out quickly into the income stream; in the latter, perhaps only after a while. If the specific initial investment project or government expenditure has no import content, the increase in imports will only follow in due course, according to the values of the multiplier and the marginal propensity to import (m.p.i.). If the initial expenditure has an import content, that much money goes straight out again and the multiplicand is smaller *pro tanto*.

A trade-induced capital movement is an essentially Keynesian concept, and must be rather sharply distinguished. A country runs an unfavorable current balance and finds that it has been borrowing abroad: there must have been capital importation exactly equal to the current deficit.

Characteristically of Keynesian economics, the trade-induced capital import is *ex post*, unintended and an accounting identity. Characteristically of classical economics, a security-induced capital import is concerned with the purposive redistribution of thrift by entrepreneurs and governments. The latter concerns long-term securities, the former either bills of exchange or medium-term export credit guarantees. The short- or medium-term securities that constitute the induced capital import must be exactly equal to the trade deficit: no trade deficit need accompany or precede, hardly even follow, a deliberate sale to foreigners of long-term securities.[1] Money deliberately borrowed at long term is mostly spent at home, and inflates. Money accidentally borrowed at short term or deliberately borrowed at medium term on a foreigner's export credit guarantee, is—or has already been—spent abroad on imports; these deflate.

An STE, as we saw in Chapter III, can indeed relieve home inflation by imports, though it is not bound to; but it could never

---

[1] There is, nevertheless, tautological equality even in this case: the cash flows one way, and the security flows the other.

be so short of mere money as to need to borrow it to finance an investment project. *An STE never borrows money, only goods and services.*[1] For its own money is hardly exchangeable into foreign money, so it does not need valuta for internal purposes. There is thus no question of currency stabilization loans, and as to budgetary support, only the import content of the budget is ever borrowed. The deficit as such is met by bank advances at home. Investment borrowing is of course a kind of budgetary support. So all agreed projects receive enough money, if necessary by inflationary means.

Why then should we borrow abroad? The answer is, either deliberately, to spare our citizens some part of the burden of abstinence entailed by its plan, or because we cannot export enough and are having a straightforward b.o.p. crisis. The latter alternative is precisely the Keynesian trade-induced capital import. The former is the nearest approach to the classical security-induced capital import, but it is not a close approach. For not only is there no hint of portfolio rearrangement—there is no 'portfolio' at all—but the investment project itself is only loosely connected with the amount borrowed. It is, to repeat, not money that a project in an STE would be likely to lack, but specific imported goods; for the population cannot grind out enough exports to buy them outright. All planned capital imports, then, are for *parts* of projects, with 100% import content; whole projects, which never have 100% import content, are never financed abroad, since the state always ensures that domestic money is available to cover at least the domestic costs. But more than that: there is only one 'enterprise', so only one borrower, in the whole country. So there is only one project: the national plan. It is the net import surplus of all the micro-projects taken together that has to be borrowed. Or in the jargon of the foreign-aid profession, 'project support' and 'program support' are one and the same thing in an STE.[2]

Things are a little different should an STE export capital. This might again be trade-induced, by the failure of the trading partner to meet his export commitments. 'Security-induced' money is also lent at long term, according to plan, to other STEs; but no doubt equivalent exports will follow in this case too. On the other hand,

[1] To be absolutely strict it may indeed borrow valuta from one country in order to spend it in another—but that is merely a multilateral borrowing of goods and services.
[2] An apparent exception is when medium-term credit is taken from a capitalist supplier of machinery. But such credit always goes into the national bank, which is the official borrower, to form a part of the nation's valuta reserves. The credit is taken in this form simply because it is offered in this form.

if money is lent to another type of economy—e.g., budgetary support to a pro-Communist UDC—then it is at least conceivable that physical trade will not respond to the full extent. In this case, however, the STE must have lent convertible money—which has, indeed, occasionally happened.

2

So much by way of definition and clarification. Next, consider the distinction between the enterprise and the country. In the days of *laissez-faire* there was no foreign aid, only foreign investment or, expressive phrase, the 'migration of capital'. Enterprises borrowed capital where they could find it most cheaply in the world, and lenders bought the cheapest securities, grade for grade, wherever they could find them. Let us imagine the perfect case, not too unlike the uncontrolled economic relations of Western Europe and North America in the nineteenth century. The gold standard functions smoothly. The existence of separate countries is from the standpoint of the world capital market an afterthought. The trade in securities is like the trade in any good or service: if enterprises in A export more products and/or securities, or, at any rate, more of the two combined, than they import, A's currency will rise above the gold point, gold will flow in. The foreign-trade multiplier also operates: A's prices and incomes rise, and the people and enterprises will begin importing products and/or securities instead. If in later years A residents cease for one reason or another to borrow, they will still have to service their foreign debt. Gold will flow out, A's prices and incomes will fall, and enough exports will be extracted or imports inhibited to service the debt. The b.o.p. is not a problem, and, indeed, in the nineteenth century nobody talked about it.

Let us forget whether we approve or disapprove of this system. The principal exception to the realism of the picture was that the borrowing might be very large in relation to the country. A large enterprise in a small country, or the government of any country, might incur debt service equal to the gold reserves. In this case alone we have to think of the nation as a whole, and we face again the divergence of private and social profit inherent in the smallness of a country. We saw in Chapter VIII that whatever the comparative cost position, fewer Cuban resources should have been specialized in sugar; similarly here, ASEA must be careful where it borrows or Sweden will lose her reserves. A region the size of Cuba in a large country, say, the Mississippi Delta, can specialize in one crop without disaster, and an American company the size of ASEA in Detroit can borrow in New York. For, on the one hand, the local multiplier is never as big as the national multiplier if the crop fails; the mere fact of national independence turns trade inward for psychological and administrative reasons. And, on the other hand, a drain of funds from Michigan banks cannot mean the same as a drain from the Riksbank. For since no central bank is involved the drain is enhanced by the leverage of only one bank's reserve ratio, not two superimposed, nor does it endanger the currency.

The smallness of countries is one of the principal arguments for market regulation in all matters of capital transfer. Instead of itself overloading the b.o.p. with its own borrowings, the government of a small country, even on the gold standard, should be continually seeing to it that enterprises do not do the same. It should also ensure what cannot in a small country be left to chance: that enough capital goes into export industries (Chapter IV). These duties are much more urgent when the Gold Standard is abandoned.

3

Enough has been said to show that we do not need to 'aid' countries: it might be enough to 'finance' enterprises. Now since an STE is a single vast enterprise the difference disappears, and our next task is to explore the consequences of this. First, the government's credit is automatically pledged when an STE borrows, even for a small and specific purpose. This much increases the credit-worthiness of STEs, and assists them in that kind of borrowing that most interests them: medium-term credit to finance the import of machinery. Secondly, all economies external to the enterprise in an ME, as explained above, are internalized by the planners of the STE. The borrower will not willingly jeopardize the country's b.o.p. since the borrower is the country. Thirdly, there is neither speculation nor the problem of the leverage of bank reserve ratios.

This shows that an STE is far better organized to accept capital, as far as b.o.p. problems go. It needs no long argument, then, to show that it is for the same reasons better organized to lend capital. One need only think of the danger to an ACC's b.o.p. that its stock exchange constitutes: in theory the foreigner may borrow any amount quite suddenly, thus doing any amount of damage.

4

But the very institutions that eliminate over-indulgence eliminate also the desire to indulge at all. The STE is rather inclined to *capital autarky*. The purely institutional reasons for this are, first, that an STE cannot accept foreign economic initiative on its territory; so the whole supply of equity capital from ACCs is cut off.[1] And since equity capital is cut off, so is the very important direct investment of companies that have already established a foothold. Secondly, there being no stock exchange there are no negotiable securities and, in particular, no government securities. So there is no foreign portfolio investment.[2] Thirdly, monetary stabilization is no more an argument for foreign borrowing by the central bank. An STE's money, being cut off from foreign money, can only be stabilized by currency reforms, fiscal policy or incomes policy. Nor will the Ministry of Finance borrow for budget support. For this authority also is *unable* to use foreign money internally; its nearest approach would be to import some physical object with borrowed money, and sell it to the population on government account. This, indeed, is what Stalin did with Lend-Lease and reparations.

Again, trade-induced borrowing is small, simply because trade is planned to be in balance. Deviations from exact balance are, of course, inevitable, and are by definition trade-induced borrowing. But the custom is to offset such balances by building surpluses or deficits into next year's trade plan. It thus comes about that cumulative trade indebtedness over a period of years is always known and—with exceptions[3]—always small.

5

The interest in, and control over, the cumulative trade balance is the technical counterpart of the general capacity to avoid b.o.p. crises referred to in Chapter V. In fact, we are here contemplating the central advantage of the Soviet-type economic model in the whole field of foreign trade; perhaps its central advantage altogether. It is

---

[1] The exceptions prove the rule. In the NEP, the USSR permitted foreign equity capital, but was not an STE. In 1957, it was proposed to found export businesses in Poland with the equity participation of *émigré* Polish-Americans; but the régime stamped on this proposal. Cf., however, Chapter XVIII on modern developments in this field.

[2] There is, however, nothing to prevent equity or portfolio investment by an STE in a capitalist country. But in practice this scarcely ever happens, even though it is a useful weapon of economic warfare (see Chapter XVI).

[3] E.g., Albania, below.

highly symptomatic that the cumulative trade balance is practically never mentioned by non-Communist economists or administrators. For there would be little point in knowing it, since it is the product of a million independent decisions, and represents no magnitude of debit or credit on the accounts of any single authority. Important as is the central bank of an ME, it is still only responsible for its own accounts with foreigners, and the change in the short-term indebtedness of other banks, or residents generally, is the precise thing for which statistics are hardest to find.[1]

Thus we can only admire when the Polish Government releases such figures as these as a matter of course:

TABLE XIV/1. POLAND'S CUMULATIVE TRADE BALANCE WITH OTHER CMEA COUNTRIES, 1960–62
(mn. valuta zlotys; June 30)

		Debit		Credit	Net
1960	(2 countries)	108	(5 countries)	74	−34
1961	(1 country)	46	(6 countries)	124	+78
1962	(3 countries)	185	(4 countries)	60	−125

SOURCE: Adam Żebrowski in *Finanse* (Warsaw), 2/1964.

Since Polish exports to the CMEA were about 3600 mn. valuta zlotys per annum at this time, the swings of net indebtedness are not trivial: a 3% gain in 1961 and a 6% loss in 1962. It is not suggested that the system is well managed; only that it is a good system.

Similar Soviet figures were published during the NEP and up to December 30, 1931 (Table V/1). The concept, and the statistical data, are a commonplace in Communist countries. The elementary distinction between the 'stock' and the 'flow' b.o.p. is stressed, for instance, in Soviet textbooks such as A. M. Smirnov.[2] Smirnov calls the 'flow' b.o.p. 'the balance of payments in the process of its equilibration', and distinguishes it from the 'accounting'[3] (our 'stock') b.o.p. But, he says, since the 'flow' b.o.p. is planned and

---

[1] Thus on the 'conventional' basis of calculations of the United States b.o.p. an increase in private United States liabilities to private foreign persons and institutions increases the current deficit; but an increase in private foreign liabilities to United States persons and institutions is not counted at all. The 'official settlements' basis, used by most other countries, omits both items! (First National City Bank, *Monthly Letter* [New York], April, 1965).

[2] *Mezhdunarodnye Valyutne i Kreditnye Otnoshenia SSSR* (Moscow, 1960).

[3] This is in Russian *otchëtni*. An *otchët* is an account rendered for a period of time, out of a continuing flow. The 'stock' b.o.p. including long debt is called *raschëtni*, where *raschët* is a final accounting (ibid., pp. 308–11).

does not disturb the rate of exchange, we need only consider the planned flow and the actual stock. Moreover, he is quite right: the difference between planned and actual flow is indeed unimportant. The flow is planned so as to correct the actual stock, and if it fails to do so it is the current state of the actual stock that matters. For this is what must influence the plan for next year's real flow.

Thus, as with any prudent enterprise or paterfamilias, the principle is that net short-term debt fluctuate about zero, and net long-term debt be carefully calculated. The tolerance among MEs of big and fluctuating short-term indebtedness must be seen as peculiar, as forced upon the ME's central bank by the circumstance that it is not the country's sole agent in the foreign field, and so can only make estimates, hold reserves and regulate flows.

In principle, there is nothing against *funding* intolerably large accumulations of short debt. In practice, however, in the twenty years of historical experience available to us, STEs seem never to fund. They prefer simply to write off.

6

Institutions are not the only factor limiting debt. Ideology is also a tremendous inhibition, since (Chapter I) the lender-borrower relation is held to be inherently exploitative under capitalism. It is, therefore, obvious that one must not borrow too much from ACCs, but by an easy psychological transition this view has carried over into inter-STE relations. Indeed, it is perfectly realistic if we remember that Stalin's USSR has so far been the principal lender—if 'lending' be the correct word for tortuous claims that other people owe you money. Then over and above this underground current of hostility is the weight of official tradition. For though Marx said nothing whatsoever about international lending under socialism, and Lenin actually favored borrowing from capitalists both in 1917–18 and again in the NEP, little was, in fact, borrowed.[1] And then came Stalin with his pathological hatred of foreigners. Until he had his own satellites to exploit, he carried out the greatest investment drive in world history on a little medium-term import credit, all punctiliously paid off. This feat is a source of immense

---

[1] S. Swianiewicz, *Forced Labour and Economic Development* (Oxford, 1965), Chapter VII. Money was also lent—a curious anticipation of latter-day aid to UDCs. If the Kuomintang received merely military assistance, Kemal's Turkey got capital for development: $8 mn. in 1934 to build a textile combine (L. I. Frei, *Mezhdunarodnye Raschëty i Organizovania Vneshnei Torgovli Sotsialisticheskikh Stran* [Moscow, 1960], p. 222).

pride to Russians, and they boast of it endlessly; how then could the North Koreans and the Chinese not want to imitate them?

The phrase 'capital autarky' refers to the ratio between foreign borrowing or lending and total investment. It must not be taken to imply a greater unwillingness to lend than to trade. Rather the contrary: considering the small volume of trade, the amount of capital movement is fairly high. Albania (Tables XIV/8, /9, /10, and /11) must have one of the highest borrowing-trading ratios in the world. The UDCs generally, it may be inferred from Table XIV/4, had in 1960 a borrowing-trading ratio of 13% with the STEs and 28% with the ACCs.[1]

The recent borrowing by STEs from ACCs is of such great economic, political and ideological importance as to merit special treatment in Chapter XVIII.

7

Capital autarky has also much economic rationality behind it. For why should foreign investment be helpful at all? Whether trade- or security-induced, it must eventually be paid back, so the volume of capital in the country will not in the end be bigger than it is now. If we draw any advantage from its temporary presence in the country, that is offset by our interest payments. The notion that a foreign loan—as opposed to a foreign gift—is somehow helpful needs the most rigorous investigation.

It may assist us to begin with Robinson Crusoe economics. Every prudent paterfamilias knows that there is a limit to the advantages of hire purchase. The durables one gets with it are not of unlimited utility, the interest one pays is high, the alternative of saving the money oneself is distinctly attractive. Very many families, to whom the opportunity to 'import capital' is open, do not avail themselves of it, and are right. Quite simply, their rate of futurity discount is lower than the interest on borrowed money.

Now Robinson Crusoe economics is quite specially applicable to STEs, since they are fully employed, and international hot-money flows do not complicate the analysis of their workings. It should not, then, surprise us that the view of the prudent paterfamilias is predominant. Capital transactions are small among most STEs, not

---

[1] Visible exports to UDCs were, respectively, $1230 mn. and $21,230 mn. (United Nations, *Yearbook of International Trade Statistics* [New York, 1961], Table B). I have crudely written up these figures for invisibles by 12 and 37% respectively, in accordance with Chapter XIII, Section 3.

merely because of their institutions and psychology, but also because of rational economic calculation. Truth to tell, we do not grow by borrowed capital but by increased capital; and if we have to pay the foreigner back the increase is very short-lived. It is as if some private native capitalist had demanded his money back and spent it on champagne. A gift is an excellent thing, and a growing stream of foreign borrowing that always outpaces amortization is a fair thing while it lasts. Short loans enable us to adjust to catastrophes and to the inevitable minor mistakes we all make, but of what good is the single long loan?—after all, it must be repaid with interest. The answer seems to be that its worth to the borrower is strictly the commercial profit he makes on it. It follows that foreign equity investment has at least this advantage over politically more desirable loans, that it need not be repaid. If the dividend is higher than the interest would have been, at least there is no amortization, and it is only transferred in good years, which may well be the same for the company's accounts and for the country's b.o.p.

More importantly, an exogenous improvement in the terms of trade probably does more good than a long-term loan, since it constitutes the largest and least painful gift imaginable. Southeast Asia has lost far more through the development of substitutes for rubber and jute than she ever got back in capital transfers. The most monumental transfer ever made over a long period by one country to another was due to the United States preference on Cuban sugar; about 6% of Cuba's national income, year in and year out, was a United States gift to her simply through the higher price her principal export earned in the United States than on the world market.

8

The view that gifts are good and loans almost useless seems strange because *we confuse capital with the technical progress it brings.* Technical progress tends to enter a country astride the machines it imports or the enterprises that foreigners set up on its soil. The first may, the second nearly must, involve foreign borrowing. But it is too often forgotten that machines, nowadays even whole plants, are often bought outright. Nay more, technical progress is imported in ways still less connected with foreign capital. Patents are bought outright (by the expenditure of home capital), or merely rented. Technical journals are skimmed. Imported machines are imitated. People go on courses abroad. Technical espionage runs the whole gamut from the legitimate use of one's intelligence to straight theft. Companies also exchange knowledge by pure barter.

Thus capital transfer is one thing and technological transfer another. We keep here these two concepts rigorously separate. In the normal case technology is ridiculously cheap at the price, if any, charged for it; so any transaction, capital or current, that does not also transfer technology is likely to bring far smaller gains than one that does. The producer's surplus may be no greater, but the consumer's is astronomically greater.

If a thing is a lot more or less valuable than its price indicates, we speak of consumer's surplus,[1] external economies, or the divergence between private and social profit. However we categorize it, what is special about technological transfer that makes it so much more valuable than its price? Compare it first with that old cliché, factory smoke, the damaging effects of which are not included in the price of the factory's product. These effects are not great in comparison with the price of the product, and the smoke ceases to be made when the product ceases to be made. Or take a more serious case, the investment of foreign capital (without innovation in technique) in a Malthusian UDC. The act of investment generates not merely the return on the capital, which need only be a little higher than in the lending country; it also generates the very wages the new workers are paid. The social return on such investment is thus several times as high as in a country without a Malthusian problem, where extra capital is worth merely what it earns. Yet even so, when the capital is repaid the enterprise must come to an end.

It becomes clear that the distinguishing features of technological transfer are that it is *unreturnable* and *indestructible*. Its effects broaden out forever into the future and are therefore indefinitely great.[2] It is nearly impossible for knowledge to be imported and then lost; there is almost nothing here that corresponds to the consumption and consequent disappearance of a good or service. Individuals can forget, as any teacher knows, but it is very hard for a whole country to forget. Nor can knowledge, by its very nature, be returned to

---

[1] Indeed, consumer's surplus is a static concept scarcely suited to the description of this gain. For we normally mean such a surplus as the consumer would, in fact, have paid to a discriminating monopolist. But technological transfer greatly enriches the consumer, so that after a few years he is able to pay much more. Looking forward, then, he knows he will be able to pay more than he now could, if forced.

[2] Not infinitely, since a futurity discount applies. Moreover, a particular line of technical progress may be cut off altogether by a superior competing invention, made without the use of the knowledge developed in that line. Cf. P. J. D. Wiles, *The Political Economy of Communism* , pp. 372–4.

its originator, like a sum of capital being amortized. For its originator never lost it, and its recipient cannot thus simply divest himself
of it.

Technological transfer is thus easily the most important thing in
international economics. Yet we know almost nothing of its volume
and precious little of its value (Chapter XIII, Sections 18 and 19). The
volume problem is clear: units of knowledge are not statistically
definable, let alone comparable. The value problem is more peculiar.
For technological transfer has, of course, its price or prices. One may
be asked to pay very much more for a machine that is a prototype
than for the same machine when it is so no longer. The use of patents
is paid for by royalties, and so on. It is thus by no means impossible
for the producer to capture the external economies involved; only he
does not normally do so. It is not absolutely clear why. Even in a
capitalist society there is some reluctance to charge what the market
will bear, and the consumer's surplus very much exceeds the producer's where inventions are concerned. There seems to be some ethical
difference between making profits out of knowledge and making
them out of goods; indeed, outside oligopolies knowledge is often
free. In Marxism this admirable trait is far more strongly pronounced,
and knowledge is very often dispensed free to other STEs or to
UDCs, though it is sold to ACCs and special licensing departments
exist to administer this.

9

'Foreign aid', then, is a vague and almost irrelevant concept we
can hardly define. For the moment it is enough that we have
made the essential distinction between technological and capital
transfer. We now turn to the statistical definition of the latter.
Capital is transferred by A to B when A runs a favorable current
b.o.p. with B. This remains so whether the transfer is financed
by gifts or short-, medium- or long-term loans. If previously
accumulated debt is forgiven or repudiated we count the loan as
having been repaid all at once in the year when this happens, and
re-enter the sum as a gift in that year. If B repays part of its debt
that is a negative item in the year of such repayment. It is statistically convenient, and does little violence to facts, to neglect short-term
loans: if they are repaid the transfer was of insignificant duration: if
they are 'funded' into longer-term loans, these latter may be regarded
as the proper object of study: if they are forgiven, they should be

recorded as a gift at the date of forgiving. There are, in any case, no reliable figures for short-term loans.

If these principles are simple and sane enough they are amazingly little observed. I make no apology for listing in the text the main statistical fallacies in speaking of capital transfers.

(i) Promise is held to be simultaneous with performance. This fallacy operates heavily in favor of STEs, which make long-term promises and publish no other figures. ACCs, on the other hand, give most publicity to performance, not promise. Indeed, the strict process of annual budgeting, demanded by parliamentary democracy, often interferes with all proper planning and makes long-term commitment impossible. This greatly reduces the practical value of, for instance, United States aid (see p. 519). It also gives a propaganda advantage to STEs that varies with the rate of growth of their promises. In 1955–60, in the first flush of enthusiasm, STEs promised more than ten times as much in aid as they were currently delivering. This was, of course, quite natural, since they never promised such early delivery dates. If the rate of making new promises were to level off, eventually drawings would catch up with it. But:

(ii) it is a fallacy that every promise once made is kept. Quite the contrary, there is every propaganda advantage for *A* to promise something to *B* and give this statement much publicity; but if then *B*'s legislature does not accept the scheme, or if it is found technically unviable, it can be dropped without hitting the headlines or even the business columns. So the rate of *pledge attrition* can be amazing, particularly when they are dropped for political reasons. Thus Berliner[1] applies the rate of loan utilization customary when the IBRD makes a promise to obtain the following results for Soviet loans. I subjoin the actual deliveries as reported in the b.o.p. statements of the borrowing countries, apparently unavailable to Berliner.

TABLE XIV/2. SOVIET CIVILIAN LOAN UTILIZATION: ESTIMATE VERSUS REALITY (mn. $)

	Date of loan	Amount	Utilization per year		
			1955	1956	1957
India	1/1955–11/1956	333.3			
	Estimated by				
	Berliner		6.0	16.5	47.0
	Reported in Indian				
	b.o.p. statement		0	2.3	23.7

[1] Joseph Berliner, *Soviet Economic Aid* (New York, 1958), p. 213.

India's total drawings on all Soviet loans, including those made after 1956, were $139.5 mn. by the end of 1960. The drawings reached a peak in 1958 and thereafter steadily declined. This case is quite non-political.

Syria	3/1956	?3		
	Estimated		1.0	2.0
	Reported in			
	b.o.p. statement		0	0

The chances of a Communist take-over in Syria declined sharply in February 1958, when Syria joined Egypt in the UAR. Neither the above loan nor one of $170 mn. reported to have been agreed in October 1957, seems to have been used at all.

Indonesia	9/1956	100.0		
	Estimated		0	10.0
	Reported in b.o.p.			
	statement		0	0

Indonesia's total drawings on this and any subsequent Soviet long-term loan were $28 mn. by the end of 1960. The drawings reached a peak in 1958 and thereafter steadily declined. The fundamental cause here was Indonesian insolvency, brought about by her military purchases from USSR.

Yugoslavia	1/1956–8/1956	281.5		
	Estimated		28.0	28.0
	Reported in			
	b.o.p. statement		53.7	7.1

Yugoslavia's total drawings on these loans (there were no others) were $69.6 mn. by 1960. The last substantial drawing was in 1958. Cold war broke out again between Yugoslavia and the Sino-Soviet bloc in May 1958.

It is thus evident that the rate of drawing on loans is wildly different from that experienced by the IBRD. Politics enters heavily into it. Yugoslavia in 1956 was even able to draw more quickly than the IBRD rates indicate. Compare Chapter XVII, Section 8.

The incapacity of STEs to deliver also leads to non-utilization, as Iceland shows. In this case the USSR pledged $3.1 mn. in 1958, to finance the purchase of East German fishing vessels.

The delivery in 1959 of several of these small trawlers was followed by mounting criticism of faulty construction, inferior aluminium linings in the holds, defective auxiliary engines, and poor-quality ballast. Iceland has drawn only about half of the credit, and it seems unlikely that the remainder will be utilized.[1]

[1] Joint Economic Committee of Congress, *Dimensions of Soviet Economic Power* (U.S.G.P.O., Washington, 1962), p. 473. Compare Chapter XVII, Section 11.

Until, then, Communist governments quote figures for actual drawings it is out of the question to use the totals of their promises as measures of the capital they transfer, even indirectly. We can only use, the whatever misgivings, the figures reported by the UDCs; or, *faute de mieux*, Communist statistics of the visible trade balance. For an incautious attempt of the latter kind cf. Table XIV/11.

We are bound as always to redress any political imbalance. We may be quite sure that any published list of investment schemes, projected at home or abroad by any government, would show great attrition. The disease of starting more projects than you can complete is particularly characteristic of Communist domestic investment; but every ACC is prone to it, and UDCs are very prone. The loans of ACCs to UDCs are also, of course, subject to attrition. An interesting special case was the great Swedish loan to the USSR in 1946 (Chapter XVIII, Section 14), only half of which was ever used. This seems to have been mostly the fault of the borrower.

(iii) A gift is not a loan. Both are capital transfers, and the amount of capital transferred in one year is, indeed, gifts plus loans minus amortization. But if we receive a gift we never have to plan for amortization: we can go right ahead without worrying about our b.o.p. in future years. Amortization is not a serious problem only if we can be sure that current loans will forever exceed it; i.e., that lending will grow year by year for ever.

(iv) Amortization does actually occur, and must actually be subtracted. This is worth insisting upon, as it is so astonishingly often forgotten. In particular, it is often assumed that public loans made to UDCs are commonly not repaid but forgiven. This is quite false: on the contrary, UDCs, and countries generally, have nowadays rather good records as repayers of debt,[1] and amortization is a serious burden on their b.o.p. This fact makes gifts superior in the eyes of the simple-minded; they are right.

(v) The sale of capital equipment for cash may well be 'aid', but it is not a capital transfer. It is a common Soviet fallacy to call such sales aid, especially in the context of Sino-Soviet trade, without explaining how 'aid' is defined.[2] Western propagandists also falsely claim that when Stalin bought foreign machines during the first FYP he accepted foreign 'aid'. Moreover, *any* loan or gift is a capital transfer and therefore 'aid', even if it be a gift of rice in kind,

[1] If we except the smaller STEs (Sections 12–14, below), and such United States 'soft' loans as the surplus food deliveries under Public Law 480, which are surely not intended to be repaid. But Poland is now repaying even her PL 480 debt.
[2] Cf. Marshall Goldman, *Soviet Foreign Aid* (New York, 1967), p. 27.

or money the borrower chooses to fritter away. It follows that China is in as good a position to give 'aid', i.e., transfer capital, as Sweden—indeed, in a better one, since her government can more easily screw the required funds out of the population.

(vi) Private loans and gifts are capital no less than public ones. This might seem too obvious to mention, but in a work on Communism it should perhaps be spelled out. To believe the contrary requires very peculiar Marxist reasoning. For while it is obvious that a public loan, especially from an STE, comes at a lower rate of interest, this only means that the borrower gets *more* benefit out of the same capital sum. Again, it is true that the private loan often develops an isolated enclave in the borrowing economy, more closely related in many ways to the lending economy; but still the enclave pays taxes and royalties and employs residents. Very likely, too, there are external economies and miscellaneous unintended technological transfers. I.e., the capital transfer embodied in setting up the enclave must be calculated on the same principles as before, and only the 'aid' is smaller.[1] Besides, the same standards of a strictness must be applied to public loans and grants. These characteristically employ more natives and cannot be reproached for setting up 'enclaves'. But they are also characteristically more wasteful, indeed sometimes downright useless, as many hair-raising stories about Soviet and United States projects testify. For private capital to be actually a disadvantage we have to believe, for instance, in a Marxist theory of exploitation (cf. Chapter I): two parties can both freely enter into a transaction yet in some mystical way it is not free and one of them always loses. Moreover, the loser is always the poor borrower, and the argument must be so phrased as not to touch the superficially identical transaction with an STE.

But this is beyond the power of the most ingenious Marxist. He is, therefore, thrown back on the political effects of private aid. Now when the enterprise that borrows or ploughs back is a foreign one,[2]

---

[1] Cf. G. M. Meier, *International Trade and Development* (New York, 1963), pp. 169-70 Gunnar Myrdal, in his *Vår Onda Värld* (Stockholm, 1964), pp. 131-4, would deny the name of aid to any transaction which brings profit to the lender. To this definition I would oppose my own: all transactions that benefit the borrower are aid. If we must have emotive definitions let them at least be so formulated as to encourage the rich to help the poor, to be persuasive, not dissuasive. Similarly John A. Pincus (*Review of Economics and Statistics*, November 1963) bases his excellent review of aid concepts upon the inappropriate moralism that a loan is only aid if it is made at a rate of interest lower than in the lender's home market. Aid, on the contrary, is what helps: resources from without. Moreover Pincus' definition is inapplicable to STEs.

[2] And is presumably not 'exploited' when it borrows! But how could this be argued without sapping the whole exploitation theory?

this is very precisely imperialism (Chapter XVI), and a bad thing even in my eyes. But it is also possible for native private enterprises, for enterprises undergoing nativization, and for the government, to borrow abroad from private persons; in which case political opposition to the loan depends upon prior disapproval of the borrower. This, however, is merely the judgement that capitalist enterprises and governments are bad as such—a judgment that cannot depend on their borrowing from foreigners. Alternatively, we may oppose foreign borrowing in these cases because we think it puts us in the power of the foreign lender. But plainly all foreign lenders at fixed interest have equal economic power, including STEs: the power not to lend again. If the IBRD has exercised such power against Turkey, so has the USSR against Yugoslavia. If the borrower does not want to borrow again it is, of course, he who has power over the lender: the far greater power of repudiation.

(vii) Transfers of capital for direct military purposes are normally omitted from figures, and held to be borne on the defense budget. Often, compilers fail to make clear how they have treated military aid. Exceedingly little is known about inter-STE military aid or even deliveries. One of the very first published figures was given, unsurprisingly, in the course of Sino-Soviet controversy over Vietnam: Soviet deliveries (presumably all aid) to North Vietnam (over and above those to the Viet-Cong) were worth $550 mn. in 1965.[1] Or, again, such aid comes out, vaguely and indirectly, in such ways as this: on October 13, 1960, the USSR cancelled a North Korean debt of $190 mn. arising from previous credits, and postponed the repayment of credits amounting to $35 mn. Identified credits to North Korea at that date totalled $82·5 mn. Some of them had doubtless been amortized in part. This implies that at least $142·5 mn. had been extended in military credits and in unannounced civilian credits, possibly arising out of unplanned trade deficits. But doubtless this is a great underestimate, since these credits, too, had been previously amortized or forgiven.[2] For comparison, United States military aid ran at about $3 md. per annum until 1960, exceeding all other gifts and loans.[3] It looks as if the same could be said of Soviet military aid.

Such aid is not at all the same thing, of course, as the trade in arms.

---

[1] Letter of the Soviet Central Committee to the ruling parties of Eastern Europe, leaked to *Die Welt*, March 21, 1966.

[2] Marcello Caiola in *I.M.F. Staff Papers*, July, 1963.

[3] Franklyn Holzman in *Comparisons of the U.S. and Soviet Economies*, Joint Economic Committee, 86th Congress, 1st Session (Washington 1959).

But we have very slightly better figures for the latter, and we should do well to use them:

TABLE XIV/3. INTERNATIONAL ARMS DELIVERIES

	$ md.	Annual average, $ md.
Arms exported by the U.S. gov't., Jan. 1949–June 1966:		
sold	16.1[1]	1.0
given away	30.2[1]	1.8
Arms sold by private United States exporters		0.2[3]
United States total		3.0
Arms exported on whatever terms by USSR:		
to Communist countries incl. Yugoslavia and Cuba, Jan. 1945–summer 1962	10[4]	1.3
to other countries, Jan. 1955–summer 1964	4[2]	0.4
Soviet total		1.7
Percentage that these totals are of published commodity exports:		
USA		16%
USSR		45%

[1] Neil Sheehan, New York Times, July 19–21, 1967.
[2] Prof. Uri Ra'anan of M.I.T., privately communicated. The figure for other countries has been written up by 43% to make allowance for the low prices charged.
[3] Guessed; Mr. Samuel Cummings, the principal private dealer in United States and British arms, sells well under $100 mn. a year (source as in 1).
[4] Various releases of the U.S. Central Intelligence Agency.

Since 1962, says Mr. Ra'anan, more sophisticated weapons have been delivered within CMEA, and Soviet exports to Communist countries have risen. All these exports, it seems, are excluded from Communist export figures, though the import figures include the civilian goods delivered in exchange. On the other side an undetermined proportion of capitalist arms is scattered here and there through capitalist export figures.

When we add in the efforts of the UK, France, West Germany, Belgium and Sweden on the one side and Czechoslovakia on the other, the non-Communist arms trade must outweigh the Communist very considerably.

(viii) Machinery exporters and civil engineers customarily give medium-term credit, which is thus essentially an inter-enterprise affair and quite likely to go unrecorded (e.g., by the Indian b.o.p. statements). But in certain cases it exceeds all other capital transfers: e.g., Indonesia, which is normally too bankrupt to borrow in other ways, but happily does publish her estimates of this form of credit.

Medium-term credit has a rather special position among STEs. It is in principle a trade credit offered by the seller of a capital good to its buyer, with a more distant maturity than other trade credit because the good takes longer to 'realize'. There are, of course, medium-term government bonds under capitalism, and as long-term bonds mature they must pass through this phase. Such credit, therefore, is almost unknown inside STEs, where enterprises are forbidden to give each other credit, and governments do not issue negotiable securities to the public. It is, in consequence, also unknown between STEs. But it is accepted when a capitalist enterprise offers it; indeed, it is positively demanded where competitive supply makes that possible. Only, as we have seen, it is the bank, not the enterprise taking delivery, that receives the credit. Similarly, when an STE exports capital goods to an ME its bank offers medium-term credit to the buying enterprise, since competition compels it to do so. In June 1966 Poland transferred the costs and benefits of medium-term credit from the bank to the account of the foreign-trade enterprise.

(ix) Direct investment by large international enterprises, whether capitalist or Soviet-type, also tends to go unrecorded.

10

We now turn to the magnitude of capital transfers between STEs and UDCs. Despite all the dangers listed above it is safe to assert that such transfers are minuscule. Subject to the innumerable qualifications adumbrated, here are the figures for capital transfers throughout the world in 1960:

TABLE XIV/4. NETWORK OF WORLD CAPITAL TRANSFERS, 1960
(public and private civilian gifts and long- and medium-term loans, net of amortization; millions of dollars)

From	United States	Other Capital-Exporting ACCs	Capital-Importing ACCs	STEs	UDCs	International Bodies	Total
United States	0	α^a	β^a	168b	4270c	256c	6142d
Other capital-exporting ACCs	$-\alpha^a$	e	γ^a	−20b	3224c	335c	2045d
Capital-importing ACCs	$-\beta^a$	$-\gamma^a$	e	17b	434c	59c	−2127d
STEs	−168	20	−17	e	186g	5f	6h
UDCs	−4270	−3224	−434	−186	e	−655i	−8769h
International bodies	−256	−335	−59	−5	655	0	0i
Total	−6142	−2045	2127	−6	8769	0	0

NOTE: The capital-exporting ACCs, in addition to the United States, are France, the United Kingdom, Switzerland, West Germany, Belgium-Luxembourg, the Netherlands and Japan. The capital-importing ACCs include Canada, Australia, New Zealand, Denmark, Norway, Finland, Sweden, Austria, Iceland, Ireland, Portugal and probably South Africa [cf. Organization for Economic Co-operation and Development, *The Flow of Financial Resources to Countries in Course of Economic Development in 1956–59* (Paris, 1961), Table 4]. The UDCs include Yugoslavia, Israel, Turkey, Cyprus, Greece and Spain (cf. ibid, *1961* [Paris, 1963] Annex Tables 8 and 9).

Continued at foot of p. 396

The faults and uncertainties of such a table are perhaps only fully evident to its compiler. In particular the totals cannot be reconciled (note *a*). Again, the OECD's series of compilations, on which I have mainly relied, have still not been fully reconciled with those of the United Nations (op. cit.).[1] Even so, the orders of magnitude can hardly be upset. In particular, we may doubt whether STEs as a whole actually imported capital, but we cannot deny that they were roughly in total balance, with a very small surplus *vis-à-vis* UDCs in particular. United States aid to Poland, of course, accounts for most of their capital imports.[2]

II

As to intra-bloc capital transfers, our ignorance is very great. There are no b.o.p. figures; only China gives budget figures for aid drawings and deliveries; pledge attrition can go on, in conditions of Communist secrecy, without our being the wiser; short-term credit, military credit and debt forgiveness are all common but unpublicized; amortization is swallowed up in the uncertainty about invisible trade as a whole.

The biggest item has in the past been reparations, for which a few figures do exist. In terms of burden perhaps the largest of all capital transfers in the world were the two East German items below. They were about 25% of the DDR's national income in the late 'forties[3]: surely a world record for the rendering of aid. Here are my estimates for 1950:

---

[1] Cf. in particular OECD, op. cit. *1961*, Section O.2. I am informed that the OECD principally relies on the CIA for its figures of Soviet-type aid.

[2] Net United States grants and credits to Poland in 1960 were $127 mn. and—incidentally—to Yugoslavia, $48 mn. (United States Department of Commerce, Office of Business Economics, *Foreign Grants and Credits*, December, 1961).

[3] P. J. D. Wiles in *Social Research* (New York, Autumn, 1961).

Footnotes to Table XIV/4.

[a] By subtraction from the totals, $\beta - \alpha = 2637$; $\alpha - \beta = 1448$; and $-\alpha + \beta = 1494$. This is self-contradictory. Therefore the totals are wrong, even spectacularly wrong. I have thought it best to leave this discrepancy unsmoothed. Much of it undoubtedly arises from definitional discrepancies in the sources used.

[b] United Nations, *International Flow of Long-term Capital and Official Donations, 1959–61* (New York 1963), pp. 10–11; Marcello Caiola in *I.M.F. Staff Papers*, July, 1963, p. 335 The figure 17 includes, Austrian reparations to the USSR, omitted in the original.

[c] OECD, op. cit., *1961*, Table 2, except that Finland is from United Nations, op. cit., Table 3.

[d] Ibid., p. 6.

[e] Some inter-aid went on within the category, but the net figure has, of course, to be zero for the purposes of this table.

[f] OECD, op. cit., *1961*, Section 1.1.

[g] $4.7 mn. in 1959 and $6.5 mn. in 1961 (loc. cit.; OECD, op. cit., *1956–59*, p. 29.)

[h] These totals are the sums of the items.

[i] The assumption here is simply that international organizations neither hoard nor dishoard cash.

TABLE XIV/5. SOVIET RECEIPTS FROM STEs ON REPARATION AND
SIMILAR ACCOUNTS, 1950 ($ mn. at 1950 prices)

DDR, reparations[2]	1400
DDR, occupation costs[3]	500
Hungary, reparations[4]	47
Rumania, reparations[4]	71
Poland, cheap coal[5]	120
Military transit and occupation costs, other than DDR[6] .	?250
	c. 2370

(There were, in addition, Finnish reparations, $28 mn.[1]; Austrian reparations started later.)

[1] *Bank of Finland Yearbook 1950*, p. 3.

[2] Erich Klinkmüller, *Die Gegenwärtige Aussenhandelsverflechtung der SBZ Deutschlands*, (Berlin, 1959), pp. 99, 178–9. This estimate is based on official Soviet figures and on the figures of the Bundesministerium für Gesamtdeutsche Fragen; these two authorities agree.

[3] Bundesministerium für Gesamtdeutsche Fragen, *SBZ von A bis Z* (Bonn, 1958), p. 262.

[4] The figure for Hungary is based on an original total of 200 mn. reparations dollars to be paid over six years, later extended to eight years; the outstanding amount was reduced by 50% on July, 1948. Assuming that delays had held down actual deliveries to 50 mn. reparations dollars by that date, annual deliveries in 1950 were 1/8 × (200–50). The same formula is applied in the case of Rumania, substituting an original reparations figure of $300 mn. for Hungary's 200 mn. Source for both countries: M. Dewar, *Soviet Trade with Eastern Europe*, Royal Institute of International Affairs, 1950. The 'reparations dollar' of 1938 is valued at 2·5 times the current dollar in about 1951 (Klinkmüller, op. cit., p. 99; Bank of Finland *Monthly Bulletin*, December 1952, p. 22). Nicolas Spulber (*The Economics of Communist Eastern Europe*, New York, 1957, pp. 112, 170) has a ratio of 4 for Hungary already in 1946. At this time U.S. wholesale prices had barely doubled, and I assume his sources err.

[5] As a partial offset to her share in German reparations, which she received solely through the USSR as intermediary, Poland delivered at a preferential price altogether about 60 mn. tons of coal to the USSR over the years 1946–53 inclusive, in addition to normal exports. In 1950 this price was $2 a ton, when its market price would probably have been $18, implying a gift of $120 mn.; i.e., 1/8 × 60 × $16. Figures from sundry Polish sources.

[6] Guessed at one half of the DDR's total.

The total of this table is all a gift, not a loan. Amounting as it does to 3% of the then Soviet national income (n.n.i.o.), it puts the USSR in the very forefront of aid receivers. Certainly among large countries at peace she cannot have been exceeded.[1] Moreover in 1946–9 capital goods were still being dismantled in East Germany. Dr. Förster tells me that no record was kept of this, so it does not enter into Dr. Klinkmüller's totals. Of course most dismantling was so unskilled that East Germany lost far more than USSR gained.

We must add to these receipts the profits from mixed companies. The Soviet share went to the Ministry of Foreign Trade,[2] and its further disposal is unknown to me. Presumably it was spent on

[1] She also bears the palm for large countries at war: in 1944 Lend-Lease was 10% of the Soviet n.n.i.o. (Abram Bergson, *The Real National Income of Soviet Russia Since 1928* [Cambridge, Mass., 1961], pp. 99–100).

[2] Vladimir Rudolph in ed. Robert Slusser, *Soviet Economic Policy in Post-war Germany*, Research Program on the USSR (New York, 1953), p. 58.

imports from the country concerned. I have no idea of the magnitudes involved.

But the period of sheer Soviet robbery ended with the death of Stalin. Indeed, reparations were already much reduced before that event. By 1955 all reparations were paid and the Soviet share in nearly all mixed companies had been sold to the other partner. In almost no time the USSR had left the confident, or tribute-taking, and entered the penitent, or paying-out, phase of imperialism. Here things become very obscure. My own informed guess is that the Soviet civilian aid balance with other STEs moved as follows, excluding short-term trade swings:

TABLE XIV/6 SOVIET CIVILIAN AID FROM OR TO OTHER STEs ($mn.)

	1950	1957
Net grants, including reparations and debts forgiven	2370	195.5
Loans net of amortization	150	−59

SOURCES: Table XIV/5 and Wiles in *Problems of Communism*, July–August 1959.

By 1962 penitence had worn off. After all, USSR is not the richest country in the bloc, she renders most of the extra-bloc aid, her defense burden is easily the heaviest in the CMEA, and finally she has to supply raw materials at very high cost. Already then, before the price controversy described in Chapter IX, Eastern Europe undertook to lend long-term capital to finance the mining of such goods.[1]

Yet in its own irrational way such a flow represents a 'normalization' of inter-STE capital transfers in comparison with previous periods. Even so it is difficult to get Soviet-type aid into proper perspective *vis-à-vis* the aid of ACCs. For 'STE' is a term including two rich nations (the DDR and Czechoslovakia), four middle-class nations (Poland, Hungary, Rumania and the USSR) and seven poor ones (China, Albania, Bulgaria, Cuba, Mongolia, North Korea and North Vietnam). Yet nearly all the aid is rendered by one rich nation (Czechoslovakia)[2], one middle-class nation (the USSR) and one poor one (China)!

This is not how capitalism distributes its international burden. The Development Assistance Committee of the OECD consists of the fifteen major aid-givers: Australia, Austria, Belgium, Canada, Denmark, France, West Germany, Italy, Japan, the Netherlands, Norway, Portugal, Sweden, the United Kingdom, the United States. Of these Portugal indeed stands out as an oddity, being 'lower

[1] *New York Times*, November 11, 1962.
[2] Cf. Wiles in *International Affairs*, London, April 1967, p. 370.

middle-class', and Japan is not exactly rich. The total net flow of civilian private and public aid to UDCs was as follows in 1965:

TABLE XIV/7 WORLD AID TO UDCs, 1965 ($md.)

From the 15 ACCs listed	10.15	
bilateral, public		5.80
private, including medium-term		3.69
via international lending agencies		0.75
From other ACCs and from UDCs		
via international lending agencies	0.15	
From STEs	0.67	
	10.98	

SOURCE: OECD as above, 1966.

The $10.15 md. were 1% of the national income of the fifteen countries, and describe exhaustively the aid they rendered. The $0.67 md. were 0.2% of the national incomes of USSR and Czechoslovakia, but they and the DDR were rendering very approximately as much aid again to poor countries within the bloc.[1] However, in order to arrive at so large a total we must add the terms of trade subsidies, as described in Chapter IX. Thus our figure for intra-bloc aid is not *in pari materia* with the OECD's. But it is still a fair one, since it appears that aid to poor STEs systematically includes a terms of trade subsidy, whereas aid to UDCs is mainly loans. Irregular debt forgiveness, of course, goes for both. Moreover, as we saw, the two rich STEs render such subsidies even to their middle-class neighbors.

As to the comparison between the USSR and China, such figures for gross pledges and donations as we have show China—taking into account the proportion between gifts and loans—to export more capital within the bloc than she ever received, quite apart from her exports to UDCs. Moreover, most of this capital was exported while the Soviet loans were being amortized, a very heavy burden.

12

China apart, the poor STEs have received very generous allotments, which compare well with the *per capita* aid of ACCs to UDCs. These countries at least present fairly clear cases, and point

[1] This is the merest guess. The principal elements are (R.mn.): Cuba 193 as in text; Bulgaria (a terms of trade subsidy of 5% on Soviet turnover plus 10% on East German and Czechoslovak turnover) 110; Mongolia, North Korea, North Vietnam (see text) 50+8+49. Total $451 mn.

a very important general moral. With Bulgaria we dealt in Chapter IX: she receives a 'terms of trade subsidy' of unknown size. A more striking instance is Albania, the only one of these really poor STEs that publishes statistics. Albania never was in visible balance:

TABLE XIV/8. VISIBLE TRADE OF ALBANIA, 1936–38 AND 1945–63 (mn. old valuta lek)

	Exports	Imports	Exports as % of Imports
1936	c. 253	c. 720	c. 35
1937	c. 355	c. 834	c. 43
1938	339.4	1004.4	33.8
1945	21.6	81.2	26.6
1946	95.4	102.4	93.2
1947	237.3	1513.4	15.7
1948	416.6	909.2	45.8
1949	291.1	644.7	45.2
1950	323.9	1102.8	29.4
1951	457.6	1977.9	23.1
1952	653.8	1589.7	41.1
1953	549.4	2001.4	27.5
1954	508.7	1291.7	39.4
1955	650.0	2141.3	30.3
1956	950.0	1940.0	49.0
1957	1451.6	2665.7	54.5
1958	1460.5	3930.3	37.2
1959	1700.6	4264.7	39.9
1960	2428.1	4053.9	59.8
1961	2429.9	3611.6	67.3
1962	2045.6	3229.4	63.4
1963	2404	3537	68

NOTE: The frank, or frank ar, had the rate of 1 to 32.7 United States cents. On July 11, 1946, 5 old franks were exchanged for 1 new, and many were blocked; this does not affect the statistical validity of foreign trade figures. In July, 1947, 9 franks were exchanged for 1 lek (L. I. Frei, *Mezhdunarodnye Raschety i Organizovania Vneshnei Torgovli Sotsialisticheskukh Stran* [Moscow, 1960], pp. 30–1). The old lek is worth 2 United States cents, or 8 old kopeks.

SOURCE: The figures for 1936–37 are in millions of 1958 lek, adapted by me from pre-war figures in current frank ar [League of Nations, *International Trade Statistics 1938* (Geneva, 1939), p. 16]. Figures for 1938 are in millions of 1958 lek (*Annuari Statistikor i Republikës Popullore të Shqipërisë* 1960 [Tirana, 1961], p. 239); 1945–59: ibid., in millions of current lek; 1960–63: Radio Free Europe (Research), *Albania*, September 17, 1964, and *Annuari Statistikor . . . 1963* (Tirana, 1964).

Albania's performance can only be described as a remarkable diplomatic achievement. It is not less remarkable if broken down by countries. Albania has always depended on some one imperial power. Before the war this power was Italy. In 1936–38 she accounted for about 29% of imports and about 71% of exports.

Albania thus achieved a moderate surplus with her, except in 1938.[1] But, of course, the direct visible surplus does not prove Italy was not financing most of Albania's general deficit. I have been unable to check this. Immediately after the war UNRRA took over, delivering $26 mn. worth of supplies between August 1945 and early 1947.[2] Then Yugoslavia succeeded to the privilege, and must have financed most of the extremely large deficit in 1947. Indeed, until June, 1948, Albanian foreign trade was the monopoly of a 'Yugoslav-Albanian export-import company'.[3] In mid-1948 Albania broke very violently with Yugoslavia when the USSR did, liquidated this company, and settled down to a slightly more modest deficit with the CMEA countries, all of which have been most generous:

TABLE XIV/9. ALBANIAN COMMODITY TRADE WITH SELECTED COUNTRIES, 1955–63
(mn. valuta lek)

| | 1955–59 | | 1960 | | 1961 | | 1962 | | 1963 | |
	Exports	Imports	Exports	Imports	Exports	Imports	Exports	Imports	Exports	Imports
USSR	. 2894·8	7871·0	1210·1	2283·4	1053·5	1124·3	—	1·3	—	—
Bulgaria	. 181·9	537·0	79·8	133·6	84·5	93·3	102·7	23·7	115	—
Czecho-slovakia	. 1099·7	1939·4	389·6	391·9	482·7	515·9	522·1	435·7	295	506
DDR	. 669·7	1437·5	235·4	272·2	230·5	201·8	242·3	121·0	157	181
Hungary	. 404·1	745·4	179·1	128·3	127·3	165·5	76·2	83·0	124	104
Poland	. 430·2	892·2	136·7	171·2	199·0	199·1	245·1	158·3	202	226
Rumania	. 113·7	497·2	32·4	107·3	18·5	64·8	58·1	45·7	91	81
China	. 152·8	450·7	104·1	348·6	138·5	974·0	585·1	2107·1	1168	2084
Italy .	. 141·8	375·9	24·6	144·7	28·4	209·8	63·4	55·0	89	123
Yugoslavia .	82·0	87·1	20·1	15·2	13·4	11·2	21·8	27·8	25	17
Switzerland .	28·9	34·4	—	—	—	—	—	—	—	—

SOURCE: *Annuari Statistikor i Republikes Popullore të Shqipërisë 1960* (Tirana, 1961), pp. 240–1; and ibid., *1963* (1964).

Note in Table XIV/9 the characteristic 'ex-imperialist' position of Italy, now running a sizable and regular surplus. However, we must again beware of giving this a confident interpretation: Albania may simply be financing other imports, in hard currency, via Italian banks. At the official rate of 2 cents per valuta lek the over-all visible deficit in 1959 amounts to $32 per head. The invisibles were probably favorable, but not enough to make much difference. Our last figures for Albania's invisibles date from 1933:

[1] League of Nations, *International Trade Statistics 1938* (Geneva, 1939), p. 16.
[2] ed. Stavro Skendi, *Albania*, London 1957, p. 228.
[3] M. F. Kovrizhnykh *et al.*, *Vneshnyaya Torgovlya Stran Narodnoi Demokratii* (Moscow, 1955), p. 290. For this little-known period, cf. also Chapter I, Section 8.

TABLE XIV/10. ALBANIA'S BALANCE OF PAYMENTS, 1931–33
(mn. old US $)

	Visibles	Interest and Dividends	Emigrants' Remittances	Other Services	Total
1931	−4.3	—	1.4	0.5	−2.4
1932	−3.6	—	1.2	0.5	−1.9
1933	−2.4	−0.1	0.8	−0.3	−2.0

SOURCE: League of Nations, *Balances of Payments 1937* (Geneva, 1937), pp. 13, 41.

There was evidently a deficit of some 333 mn. postwar lek even in the early 1930s, and invisibles were far from filling the gap. In particular, emigrants' remittances only amounted to about 1 new United States dollar per head. However far 1933 may be from us today, it is difficult to think of any circumstance that can have altered this fact. The Soviet submarine base at Valona can hardly have brought in $10 mn. but the visible deficit was $40 mn.

It is extremely probable that one Albanian tactic for extracting so much money is to agree on a trade plan with another STE that is almost in balance and then simply to underfulfill her export plan. Pryor collected this series:

TABLE XIV/11. PLAN VS. REALITY IN EAST GERMAN–ALBANIAN TRADE, 1952–59
(thousands of old valuta rubles)

	DDR Exports		Ratio: Actual to Contracted	DDR Imports		Ratio: Actual to Contracted
	Contracted	Actual		Contracted	Actual	
1952	9315	9530	102%	1160	1890	163%
1953	12,008	11,615	97	3291	2489	76
1954	14,179	8622	61	3941	2314	59
1955	22,880	24,232	106	9400	5070	54
1956	15,914	16,696	105	8074	6612	82
1957	24,027	17,068	71	11,195	9113	81
1958	24,668	21,969	89	18,710	10,150	54
1959	27,307	27,700	101	23,883	19,172	80

SOURCE: F. L. Pryor, *The Communist Foreign Trade System* (London 1963), p. 192.

Whatever her methods, the CMEA countries were under no necessity of competition for influence to give Albania so much aid. Yugoslavia was clean out of the running, Italy had lost its imperialist dreams, China did not begin to fish in the troubled Adriatic until late 1960. It is difficult to see anything other than straightforward generosity here. It is interesting that after the break Soviet trade was run down to nothing, while the East European STEs continued to trade at the old level, but refused to give more credit (Table

XIV/9). We do not know what role Albania's mounting debt first to Yugoslavia and then to the CMEA countries has played in her switches of allegiance. Suffice it that China has picked up the torch, promising $123 mn. in credits during Albania's FYP of 1961–65. Expressed in annual terms, this approximates to the previous visible deficit. It may be taken gross, since service on the new Chinese debt will be negligible at first, and the old debts are not being serviced at all.

Albania produced about $200 per head in 1960, to yield a net domestic product of about $300 mn.[1] Assume that her invisible income from military bases and emigrants' remittances does indeed exceed her expenditures on freight. It would, then, be reasonable to suppose that she has run in the last years a b.o.p. deficit of one-third of imports, or 10% of the national income. However disguised, and by whomever supplied, this sum is a gift. Put another way, net aid has been about $26 per head per annum both before and after the split with the USSR.

13

Cuba, too, is generously treated. Her diplomatic tactic is not to have perfervid loyalties and switch them, but to be so absolutely indispensable that her thoroughly discourteous neutralism between the USSR and China has to be overlooked.

TABLE XIV/12. SOVIET CIVILIAN AID TO CUBA IN 1965 (R.mn.)

Sugar subsidy		95[a]
Exports to Cuba f.o.b.	338	
Imports from Cuba f.o.b. (deducting 10% from c.i.f.)	277	
Visible balance		61[b]
Freight services rendered to Cuba (10% of exports, and assuming they are all financed by USSR)		34
Salaries of technical advisers minus Cuban contribution (guessed)		3[c]
Total		287=$316 mn.

SOURCE: U.N. Yearbook of International Trade Statistics, 1966, Vneshnyaya Torgovlya Soyuza SSR za 1965 god. It would appear from Cuba's balances of visible trade with all other countries that USSR neither makes nor receives any multilateral payments on her behalf—except of course via re-exports of sugar (Chapter X).

[a] The price was $129 per ton. Cuba realized $85 per ton elsewhere, Finland, Ireland and Japan (countries unconnected with preference schemes) paid $83 per ton on average to all suppliers. I have multiplied $45 by the 2·33 mn. tons imported.

[b] The balance is fairly stable year by year, so does not represent mere short-term swings.

[c] There were about 700 Soviet experts (Chapters XVII, Section 9). Put their salaries at R.7000 p.a. and let Cuba bear one-third.

[1] Michael Kaser in Analyse et Prevision (Paris), November 1967, pp. 766, 843. Cf. also Jan Prybyla in Munich Bulletin, March 1963 and Ost-Europaische Rundschau, 5/1967; Schwanke in Oesterreichische Ost-Hefte, 2/1962.

This is $28 per head of population, or, say 8% of the national income —a figure rather in excess of the United States sugar preference and net capital export in the bad old days. Moreover arms are extra.

The very generous treatment of the small Asian STEs stands out clearly from such (vague and incomplete) data as we have. Of course, there was always Sino-Soviet competition here, but some of the gifts are very large. A particularly striking case is Soviet-North Korean relations in 1960. We saw above that a loan of $190 mn. was retrospectively turned into a grant: a very strong indication that the weaker country had been falling down on her export commitments, i.e., pursuing the Albanian tactic. This aid alone was $17 per head, or possibly 10% of the national income. In 1965, however, Soviet aid seems to have been confined to the presumed terms of trade subsidy. At 5% of turnover this is R. 8 mn.

In 1961–3 North Vietnam netted about 6% of her national income in gifts and unamortized loans from all sources, according to her budgetary data.[1] More than half of these were Chinese, and the general picture is compatible with what is implied in Soviet official trade sources: a persistent visible deficit with USSR of R. 40 mn. p.a. To this we should add the presumed terms of trade subsidy— which will not be shown in the budget—which I guess at 10% on Soviet turnover, or R. 9 mn.

By reason, no doubt, of her loyalty Mongolia (population about 1 mn.) fared much worse until recently. Her terms of trade subsidy, guessed at 5% on Soviet turnover, is R. 8 mn. But there is now a seemingly persistent Soviet trade surplus of R. 50 mn. Probably the invisible balance runs the other way, owing to troop quarterings and transit services in Sino-Soviet trade: say R. 8 mn. Total, R. 50 mn. or c. 12% of the national income.[2] Moreover the future may put Mongolia ahead of Albania. Soviet gross aid to Mongolia in 1966–70 is to be $733.3 mn., which indicates a planned net aid of about $500 mn.,[3] or $100 per head per annum. This may be about four times as great as Albania's recent receipts.

Here, too, we may venture to generalize about the size of nations. If it is no longer quite so good as it once was to be a small ACC (Chapter IX), it seems to be better than ever to be a small UDC.

---

[1] Ngoc Khue in *Finansy SSSR*, 3/1964; V. Rastorguev, ibid., 9/1966, esp. p. 86. Calculations available from the author.

[2] Which I put at $440 per head in 1962-3. Workings available on request.

[3] The gross figure is from Agence France Presse, Ulan Bator, June 9, 1965. It is 143% of gross Soviet aid in 1956–60. If all debt service in 1966–70 = one half of gross aid in 1956–60, we arrive at the above net figure.

By a shrewd act of self-negation, Puerto Rico can attract rivers of capital. A larger country than Cuba would not have made such a good thing out of the United States sugar preference (Section 7). By strategic location and political fidelity, Taiwan can do almost as well. Mongolia bids fair to be the Taiwan of the next quinquennium. But it seems that by fairly frequent shifts of loyalty Albania is not far behind. The real point is devastatingly simple: they are so small that they are cheap to aid. Therefore, they will get more than big countries in similar situations. How much of the Sino-Soviet quarrel is due to this simple fact? The USSR could not aid China, but even China could aid Albania. Paul Klee has it in his diaries: 'The big animals sit mournfully round the table and are not filled. But the clever little flies climb upon mountains of bread and live in a city of butter.'

14

Even so strong a country as the DDR tries to play the Albanian game. Fritz Schenk describes graphically—but only from memory[1]— how the DDR's debt to the USSR piled up during its first FYP, to be written off early in 1956 simply by a retrospective increase in Soviet import prices from the DDR for uranium and other products. In view of the DDR's staggering reparations burden until 1953, and of the exploitatively low price for uranium (which was and is supplied by a Soviet company), we need not be too surprised if Khrushchev felt a bad conscience in 1956. But in these altered circumstances the deficit then began immediately to pile up again, so that for the second FYP (1956–60) a deficit of 750 mn. new rubles was calculated. The Soviet authorities promised this sum, but no one believed it would be forthcoming in view of their own difficulties. Mr. Schenk adds that the trade balance each year was settled at Ulbricht-Khrushchev level, and that very few German officials indeed knew the amount of cumulative indebtedness. These, then, are 'trade-induced capital movements' with a vengeance.

There is, then, a striking informality about Communist credit procedures. Loans are promised but not actually made ('pledge attrition'); debts are contracted but never paid. If boastfulness and an eye for publicity cause 'attrition', the regular *repudiation or*

[1] *Magie der Planwirtschaft* (Cologne, 1960), pp. 87, 88, 138. On p. 88 a Soviet promise of R. 7·5 md. is dated early in 1957; on p. 138, in July, 1956. I have taken Mr. Schenk's generalizations from this episode with a grain of salt.

forgiveness of debt has other causes, mainly ideological. There is something very capitalistic about punctilious debt collection; the sanctity of contracts is neither High Tory nor Labour, let alone Marxist. Inside the Soviet economy, for instance, government debt to the population has been canceled in exchange for the cessation of fresh loan 'sales', which is manifestly unfair between the older generation to whom such debt had already been 'sold', and the young who benefited by not having to 'volunteer' to buy. Again, the debt of kolkhozy to the banks has been canceled more than once, and as we saw in Chapter III, nationalized enterprises pile up short debt at the banks with impunity. The hostility to interest also speaks volumes.

Mere informality, however, and mere contempt for capitalist procedures are not all. Socialist brotherhood strongly indicates that rich STEs should not claim their pound of flesh from poor STEs, nor, indeed, from UDCs. The STE is a very poor debt collector, always excepting Stalin's USSR. In addition, there is the basic anti-capitalist hostility that tempts most STEs to repudiate whatever debt they owe to ACCs at the moment of revolution. Debt incurred to ACCs thereafter, by the new régime, is more punctiliously handled than any other debt, but the initial repudiation is worth a small excursus.

15

Repudiation is, as we have seen, the conversion of a loan into a gift by the debtor's *force majeure*. Should the creditor take the initiative we call it forgiveness; and in many cases there is an uneasy mixture, known to capitalism as a 'composition with the creditors'. These events are common between businesses and countries, but have received altogether too little attention from economists.[1] Analytically their effect is the same as when a gift is made—a point covered in the next section. But statistically they are out of all proportion bigger than gifts, and constitute great if irregular events in economic history.

A notable case is Lenin's repudiation of Tsarist foreign debt, along with domestic debt. Pre-revolutionary Russia, notably as a result of World War I, was 'all loaned up'. Foreign debt was about 60% of national income;[2] the service of this, at 10% per annum, would have demanded 6% of the national income, or about one quarter of

---

[1] But cf. Bronfenbrenner in *Economic Development and Cultural Change*, April 1955.
[2] Footnote see p. 407.

exports, in any hypothetical Tsarist or democratic postwar Russia. Indeed, a large part of this debt would undoubtedly have been repudiated or forgiven in any case. Lenin canceled it all. It is notorious that he thereby made it almost impossible to borrow abroad, which he ardently wished to do, and even made current trading difficult. But it is equally obvious, though scarcely ever pointed out, that he also conferred a huge boon upon his country. 6% of the national income is a proportion so immense as to repay the cost of virtually any foreign blockade—and to place a heavy question mark over the intrinsic, as opposed to the adventitious, growth capacity of the Soviet economy in the 1920s.

The treatment of pre-revolutionary debt has varied very much from STE to STE. Lenin at first repudiated all state foreign debt (December, 1917); he did not repudiate foreign private enterprise debts until he nationalized the enterprises (mainly the summer of 1918). In January, 1919, facing a near-general embargo, he offered to negotiate on pre-war state debt, and from time to time he offered compensation to entrepreneurs in the shape of concessions to set up new enterprises on Soviet territory.[1] But all this came eventually to naught; except for a very few concessions he substantially repudiated everything, in that his terms were never acceptable.

Castro, on the other hand, in 1959, when he was only a semi-Communist, offered compensation to foreign entrepreneurs—in 4·5% twenty-year inconvertible bonds. In July, 1960, after the cancellation of the United States sugar preference, he worsened the offer to 2% and thirty years, but made the bonds convertible.

[1] E. H. Carr, *The Bolshevik Revolution*, Volume II (London, 1952), p. 139; Volume III (London, 1953), pp. 355, 375.

Footnote from p. 406

[2] Arrived at thus. Foreign debt in md. gold rubles of 1913:

Private enterprise within the USSR boundaries, 1914	2·0
Government, municipal and government-guaranteed, 1914	5·5
Government, contracted 1914–17	7·7
Amortization of above, 1914–17	0·0
Less foreign gold deposits of State Bank, confiscated by Allied governments in 1918	−1·0
Less one seventh fairly attributable to East European successor states	−1·8
	12·4

In 1913, national income on Soviet territory was R. 16·5 md. (Table XV/1). Put R. 21 md. for 1916. The other figures are from Harold G. Moulton and Leo Pasvolsky, *World War Debt Settlements* (New York, 1926), pp. 60–2. Note that the successor states inherited railroads saddled with about R. 400 mn. of foreign debt (which they repudiated!) out of about R. 3·0 md.; I have arbitrarily applied this proportion to the whole public debt.

I.e., the United States was effectually to restore the sugar preference, and one quarter of the dollars derived from purchases in excess of 3 mn. long Spanish tons per annum, at a price above 5·75¢ per lb., was to be devoted to converting the bonds. But this offer was not accepted by the United States, and the subsequent great wave of nationalizations in October, 1960, promised indemnities 'to be governed by a future law'. Nothing has been paid.[1]

Poland and Czechoslovakia, on the other hand, have both recognized pre-Communist debt, state and private, and paid convertible money on it. There is, then, no set pattern. Lenin and Castro both felt particularly strongly about foreign capital owing to its immense role in their countries. Even so, both made its compensation a diplomatic bargaining counter. In the other two countries the pretense is maintained that the Communist seizure of power was legal; foreign capital was never a serious problem; and more weight has always been placed on tolerable relations with the West.

All STEs treat domestic pre-Communist debt less leniently.

16

Since gifts are more important than loans, the import (and to some extent the export) policy of the aiding country, which affects the terms of trade, matters more than its official loans or the access it permits to its capital market. First, note that we say import *policy*. Although a freely negotiated rise in import prices has the same effect, we are here talking about foreign aid as a conscious process. Secondly, in treating this subject from the point of view of the aiding country's imports, rather than the aided country's exports, we imply that if the latter country improves in some way its terms of trade that is self-help, ordinary development economics, and not part of our subject. We should add that if it simply raises its export prices or—unlikely case—exerts monopsony power to lower its import prices, the physical quantities are adversely affected, and so also may be the balance of trade. Such 'self-help' is very questionable.

For the quantities are, indeed, as important as the prices. The object of aid is to raise the national income, and if export prices are raised but quantities lowered we may not achieve this. Those who remain employed on exports in the aided country have, it is true, a larger surplus left over for saving, but the main problem is to put

[1] Cuban Chamber of Commerce in the United States, *Digest* (New York), July 14, August 25 and October 27, 1960. Non-United States capital continues to be serviced, however.

to work those laid off. This is easy in an STE, and an ACC can achieve it quickly given the will. But in a UDC—of which we naturally think when we speak of foreign aid—where so many elasticities and substitutabilities are so low, it may be all but impossible. The principal 'gift', then, that an aiding country can bestow upon a Malthusian UDC is employment: it must buy larger quantities of its exports, even at unchanged prices. Indeed, by doing so it kills two birds with one stone; for it also improves the all-important balance of trade.

An arithmetical example may help to fix our ideas. We can only be sure about the very simplest effects of the various kinds of aid—their 'formal incidence' on the b.o.p. and the extent to which they make funds easily available for nonconsumption. A country has a national income of 1000 rupees in year 1. In case I it receives a straight gift from an aiding country. The money is *ipso facto* available for investment, whether physical or intellectual, and there is no repayment problem. The formal incidence on the b.o.p. is the amount of the gift.

In case II the giver of aid introduces a preference for, or removes a discrimination against, the aided country's exports. Let their prices rise, *ceteris paribus*, by 5%. Exports were, say, 20% of the national income, and 15% of them, or 3% of the national income, went to the aid-giver. The preference increases the value of this figure by one third, or 10 rupees, to 4%. In case IIa the extra quantity of exports is diverted from other foreign trade; the formal incidence of the aid on the b.o.p. is 5% of 4%, or 2 rupees. In case IIb the extra exports are diverted from internal trade, and the formal incidence on the b.o.p. is $10 - x$ rupees, where x is whatever new imports the government permits to mop up the inflation so directly brought about by the new exports. As we saw in Chapter IV, it is not simple to calculate x. In case IIc the extra exports are produced by hitherto unemployed resources, and the b.o.p. gains $10 - y$ rupees, where y is whatever new imports are permitted in this less inflationary case and $y < x$.

There is in none of these three cases any repayment problem, since the aid is a gift as before; but it may be difficult to capture it for investment purposes. In cases IIb and IIc we shall not even expect to capture most of it, since in IIb this would imply reduced consumption, and in IIc underpayment for work rendered. But at least the element due to price increase may well be claimed. An STE would have no difficulty here at all; owing to the way its foreign trade is financed, and to the stability of its internal prices, the whole profit from the preference would flow automatically into the treasury. But in an ME, and especially if the government is weak, the profit may disappear into consumption. The classic case is, again, the Cuban sugar preference, which went initially into the profits of United States milling companies (this, of course, was why it was granted). Later it was siphoned off into Cuban wages and forced reductions in the rents Cuban farmers paid to the millers. Its effect on investment and even tax revenue, however, remained indirect.

17

In case III the country receives loans only. In year 1 it borrows the fairly plausible sum of 30 rupees (or 3% of national income). If the loans never increase the time will, of course, come when repayment = new borrowing, and it has simply incurred an interest charge. So to make this case even plausible as a good development policy let it be possible to borrow every year 3% more than in the previous year. Then in case IIIa the conditions of the loan are typical of those laid down for official lending by the United States:[1] repayment takes fifteen years, beginning in the loan's third year, and the rate of interest is 5%. We then get a sequence like this:

TABLE XIV/13. NET FINANCING UNDER TYPICAL U.S. CONDITIONS

Year	1	2	3	4	9	16	17	18
Borrowed	30	30.9	31.8	32.8	38.0	46.9	48.3	49.7
Repaid	—	—	2.0	4.1	15.4	34.4	37.4	38.5
Sum outstanding at beginning of year	—	30.0	60.9	90.7	c.224.5	c.352	c.364	c.375
Interest	—	1.5	3.0	4.5	11.2	17.6	18.2	18.8
Net financing	30	29.4	26.8	24.2	11.4	− 5.1	− 7.3	− 7.6

At first, while the repayment burden is incompletely built up, net financing is a large positive item. But by the end of the seventeenth year the borrowing in year 1 is paid off, and it is clear that from then on the sum annually repaid grows at 3% per annum.[2] Therefore,

---

[1] OECD, op. cit., 1956–59, tables 6 in text and 6 in annex.

[2] If k be the number of years over which a loan must be repaid, and t the date of the oldest loan still outstanding, repayment in the year $t + k + 2$ is $(1/k)(B_t)[(\alpha^k + 1 - 1)/(\alpha - 1)]$, where B_t is the sum originally borrowed at t and $\alpha - 1$ is the constant rate of growth of B. In the year $t + k + 3$ repayment is $(1/k)(B_t + 1)[(\alpha^k + 1 - 1)/(\alpha - 1)]$.

the annual interest bill also grows at 3% per annum.[1] Therefore, net financing does the same. But it so happens that on our choice of magnitudes this sum is negative (it became negative already in year 14). So not even the hypothetical capacity to increase borrowing annually has ensured a perpetual positive flow of net financing. On the other hand, there was no problem of capturing the money for developmental purposes.

Now turn to Soviet loan conditions. The lower rate of interest would have brought about a small positive total of net financing, which would, of course, eventually grow. But then the shorter period of repayment is also unfavorable, since it increases amortization at the beginning of the series. Thus in case IIIb we take repayment in 10 years beginning in the third year and 2% interest. We arrive at:

TABLE XIV/14. NET FINANCING UNDER TYPICAL SOVIET CONDITIONS

Year	1	2	3	12	13
Borrowed . .	30	30.9	31.8	41.7	43.0
Repaid . .	—	—	3.0	34.5	35.5
Sum outstanding at beginning of year .	—	30.0	60.9	c.237.0	c.244.0
Interest . .	—	0.6	1.2	4.8	4.9
Net financing .	30	30.3	27.6	2.4	2.5

From year 13 on, as previously from year 18 on, the net financing item grows at 3% per annum. Only this time it is positive.

The rate of interest is, in fact, a great deal more important than the duration of the loan. If interest and amortization begin in the year after a loan is made, the condition that net financing eventually be positive is simply $1 + i < \alpha$, where i is the rate of interest. Thus if X is borrowed in year 1, but in year 2 we must pay back the whole of it, we pay back $X + iX$ and borrow αX. The same inequality can be demonstrated by induction for all amortization periods.[2]

---

[1] The gross total of loans outstanding grows at the rate $\alpha - 1$ (previous footnote). But at the beginning of any year $k + 1$ the total of all repayments ever made on loans outstanding is: $(k - 1)(\alpha x/k) + (k - 2)(\alpha^2 x/k) + (k - 3)(\alpha^3 x/k) + \ldots + (k - k)(\alpha^k x/k)$, where x was borrowed in the year 0 and has just been fully paid off, while the first amortization of $\alpha^k x$ is due this coming year. At the beginning of year $k + 2$ the loan αx is fully paid off and the loan $\alpha^{k+1}x$ comes in at the other end. So there are still only k terms, and the only change is that for αx we must now read $\alpha^2 x$ throughout. It follows that net loans outstanding also grow at the rate $\alpha - 1$: therefore the interest bill does the same.

[2] I owe the general proof, too lengthy to reproduce here, to Mrs. Bakker-Jarness. Cf. Evsey D. Domar in *American Economic Review*, December 1950, *passim*, but especially p. 808.

All cases of aid discussed are effective against Malthusian unemployment if any. Only in case II were we compelled to spell this out.

18

It would seem that Communist propaganda is partly correct, and a course of borrowing at rates characteristic of ACC aid is far from being the best kind of aid. The net financing in the first years is attractively high, but nemesis follows. Case IIIb, with rates characteristic of STE aid, is much preferable, but even it leaves the borrower in a very awkward situation: he can only have any net financing at all by steadily increasing his debt. Nor is this mere theory. The foreign debt service of UDCs rose from $0·8 md. in 1955 to $5 md. in 1964, or from 8% to 30% of gross aid. It follows that debt service grew three times as rapidly as gross aid. This was in part due to the rapid growth of aid in the early fifties, and to the natural lag of debt service in those initial years. But it is certain that even with the more stable present volume of total aid, debt service will still grow a great deal.[1] Gifts and preferences on imports are vastly better than either kind of borrowing.

This is naturally not proof of which case is best, since we have excluded so many variables. Our principal assumptions were:

(i) Technological transfer is not greater through loans or straight gifts than through import preferences. This is in itself very improbable, but there is, as we have seen, nothing to prevent technology being transferred apart from all loans, gifts and preferences. Indeed, nearly all aiding countries do this.

(ii) The aider will, indeed, go on lending more and more forever. It is not, on the other hand, necessary that he *give* the same sum forever, or that his preference be similarly permanent. For even if given in one year alone the sum is indisputable aid. It is, moreover, more probable that preferences will be permanent than that lending will increase forever, especially in an ACC; for loans require the assent of parliament or the cooperation of a merchant bank whenever they are made, and the probability is high that these authorities will come to regard the borrower as a poor risk. But a preference in an ACC is a once-for-all act of parliament, normally needing no annual renewal. On the other hand, in an STE a preference, too, is a mere

[1] Report of the United States Agency for International Development, quoted in the *New York Times*, April 5, 1965.

administrative act,[1] liable to be revoked at any moment. This constitutional quirk of ACCs is an immensely important advantage for them in rendering aid.

(iii) The loan or gift is not precisely directed toward an export industry, but has only a generalized effect on the capacity to export. This is also somewhat improbable; cf. Chapter IV.

(iv) The conditions on which loans may be spent are the same. In fact, the STE is likely to recoup its low interest in low-quality goods, and it will hardly ever permit the loan to be spent in a third country. ACCs are from time to time fairly liberal about this. The bilateralism of Soviet-type aid is a natural psychological consequence of bilateralism in trade; though there is nothing at all in the logic of Soviet-type institutions that forces aid to be bilateral. Indeed from time to time, as in the Icelandic case (Section 9), it *is* multilateral, and this is one of the prime *raisons d'être* of the GKES (Appendix, Chapter XII). But even in such cases the original aider very seldom hands over gold or convertible currency. Rather does he plan a strict trilateral scheme, whereby he runs a positive balance with the actual deliverer, who is another, named, STE. Needless to add that, just as with ACCs, such bilateral and trilateral aid puts much less strain on the donor's b.o.p. In the absence of perfect competition and perfectly flexible resources, as explained in Chapter IV, it is never a matter of indifference to a country's b.o.p. exactly what goods are produced, let alone exported. There is nothing like a strict and unimaginative insistence on multilateralism for reducing the quantity of aid.

(v) The recipient's terms of trade have been unaffected. In fact, this could only hold in the case of a gift or a loan in kind. A money gift or loan clearly raises prices against its recipient as it is spent, wherever it is spent. But the effect of loan amortization is more difficult to predict. If the borrower is repaying in his own inconvertible currency his export prices rise; but if he has first to earn foreign currency the fate of his terms of trade depends on how he sets about it. Thus, an export drive will worsen them, but an import cut will improve them. But in any case the period of amortization is usually longer than that of original expenditure; so all price effects are smaller. It is thus fairly certain that the borrower's terms of trade will suffer, whereas, of course, the grant of a preference improves them—that is, indeed, its whole object.

---

[1] We discussed the exact meaning of an STE's import preference in Chapter IX.

(vi) Political conditions of all kinds were excluded from our purview. Compare, however, Chapter XVIII.

19

All in all, it seems that STEs lend on better principles than ACCs. If they lend only very small sums, this is not necessarily bad, since lending is not a very good idea. However, as givers of straight gifts ACCs are incomparably superior, for here the main thing is the amount given. Of the capital transfers to UDCs in Table XIV/4 very approximately the following percentages were gifts:[1]

United States	. 53
Other capital-exporting ACCs	. 47
Capital-importing ACCs .	. ?
STEs	. 15
International bodies . .	. 8

It will be seen that the proportion of gifts in STE aid is quite high, indeed, much higher than in normal accounts of this matter. This is simply because we have expressed gifts as a percentage of capital transfers actually made, not those promised. A gift, after all, is either made or not made: it is much less likely to suffer from 'attrition'. Hence, what figures as a small part of Communist intentions is a large part of Communist achievement.

20

So far we have discussed imports as a way of giving aid only under the aspect of preferences (case II). But price is not the only question here; various aspects of the quantity of imports are quite as vital in judging the performance of the aid-giver. Owing to the work of Mr. Egon Neuberger it is possible to compare ACCs and STEs, or more strictly seven ACCs and the USSR, in this way, too. He summarizes his results as follows: 'We find that, in the period 1955 to 1960, the Soviet Union represented (1) a very small market, both absolutely and *per capita*, (2) a very rapidly growing market, and (3) a market of average or below average stability.'[2]

---

[1] The data are derived from the United Nations, op. cit., *1959–61*, Tables 8 and 9, and from my own workings. All are very approximate indeed.
[2] *The USSR and the West as Markets for Primary Products* (Santa Monica, Cal., February, 1963), p. v.

First as to volume of imports, he gives the following indices for 1960 on 1955 = 100:[1]

USSR	.	.	145.2 (4.2)	UK	.	.	90.9 (59.8)
US	.	.	86.1 (19.1)	Common Market			117.5 (30.0)[2]

The figures in parentheses are average annual imports per head over the period, in current dollars.[3] These data sufficiently prove the smallness and the rapid growth of Soviet imports; their instability is a more complicated subject.

Mr. Neuberger provides two indices of stability as an importer. The first is a special version of the coefficient of variation $\sigma/\bar{y}$. $\bar{y}$ is, as usual, the mean, in this case of all six annual observations (1955–60), say, of Dutch copper purchases. But the deviations going to make up σ are not, as normally, the deviations from $\bar{y}$ but from a regression line fitted to take account of growth.[4] This makes the formula much fairer to the USSR, which exhibits the greatest growth and would consequently have a very big σ of the ordinary sort.

His second stability index[5] considers only years in which imports declined from the previous level. It is, therefore, an index exceptionally favorable to the USSR, with its rapid growth. But from the point of view of the exporter this index has much merit, since he will be apt to treat rises as a bonanza; it is declines against which he must guard like the plague.

The sum of all such percentage declines is averaged over all six years. Of the eight countries studied, the USSR ranked very low for stability:

TABLE XIV/15. RANK OF THE USSR AMONG THE EIGHT COUNTRIES

	Value of Imports	Quantity of Imports	Unit Value of Imports
$\sigma/\bar{y}$	7th	8th	6th
'Decline index'	4th	7th	4th

SOURCE: Neuberger, op. cit., pp. 53, 54.

This instability is in extremely sharp contrast to Soviet propa-

---

[1] p. 134. These are strictly value indices, but each country faced the same prices. The products imported were: copper, rubber, cotton, jute, wool, hides, tobacco, oils and oil seeds, coffee, cocoa, tea, meat, rice, sugar.

[2] Average of individual countries, weighted by myself. Belgium was merged with Luxembourg, making five countries in the Common Market.

[3] Ibid., p. 136.   [4] Ibid., p. 26.   [5] Ibid., pp. 26–7.

ganda. The reason for it is presumably the chaotic nature of the planning process, though at least three political events do fall within the period. These are the end of the boycott of Australia in 1959, which however hardly affected wool purchases (Chapter XVII); the Communization of Cuba and the beginning of sugar re-exports in 1960 (Chapter X); and the decline of trade with China in 1960—which, however, was also much influenced by the Chinese harvest failure.

The Soviet-type preference for long-term contracts evidently does little to stabilize trade. Characteristically the so-called contract is not binding, and both prices and quantities are renegotiated annually. In this way the STE wins glory for having signed a contract, yet retains the political and economic leverage of the threat to renew on less favorable terms. Bilateralism, to repeat, is quite separate from long-term contracts.

If, then, the USSR is an unstable importer, this is not only for technical or institutional reasons but also in part because she offers stable markets only to countries in a stable state of alliance or neutrality. As countries become, or cease to be, Soviet allies —or, indeed, anyone's allies—rather suddenly and rather often, this political motive is, in fact, an important destabilizer. In an ACC, trade is far less sensitive to every political *rafroidissement* or *réchauffage*: the government can only take big measures, at long intervals of time. Thus, the period 1955–60 includes the United States blockade of Cuba; yet still the United States is a more stable importer.

21

As to the actual granting of preferential prices, the manipulation of the Soviet tariff is by itself meaningless, since it may or may not affect the prices the USSR actually pays (Chapter IX). Under bilateralism, moreover, the preference is a matter of the 'relative terms of trade'; i.e., we may expect prices to be higher—or possibly lower—in both directions, and the UDC gets a preference, not through the mere prices of Soviet imports from it, but through better terms of trade in this exchange than in the outside world. We saw in Chapter IX reason to believe that the USSR, and still more the DDR and Czechoslovakia, treat Bulgaria in this way. But the policy is not officially proclaimed, so we cannot be sure. The Soviet preference on Cuban sugar is, however, publicly proclaimed; an attempt has been made to equal the old United States preferential price. Outside the bloc, UDCs generally complain rather bitterly of the terms of trade they get from STEs. This is largely due to inefficient trading, delay and bad quality;[1] the STEs seem to intend to buy and sell at world prices.

Nay more. With their distrust of free markets and preference for administered prices, they are doctrinally much more open than ACCs to the notion of aid-through-preference. Moreover, there is the doctrine of non-equivalent exchange (Chapter I). Whatever its logical fallacies, non-equivalent exchange is thus a powerful encouragement to the granting of aid-through-preference. However, the STEs have not in practice reacted positively to UNCTAD proposals along these lines, but have kept their preferences for each other.

It would, indeed, be a great mistake to end a passage on the STEs as importers on an unconstructive note. No instability, not even rigidly disadvantageous stability, no autarky, really hardly anything, outweighs the advantage that the STEs' market has *grown*. If buying the UDCs' exports is the principal form of aid, growth has only to continue long enough for STEs to render truly more aid than ACCs. Moreover, there are hardly any items in which autarky has been stronger than where cocoa, coffee and *Kolonialwaren* generally are concerned. Quite apart from normal growth there might well be a sudden change of policy here.

The present degree of autarky in these products has been elegantly demonstrated by Frederic Pryor:[2] their retail prices are exceptionally high. Let us remember that since, on the whole, retail prices clear the market, high prices betoken unsatisfied demand and restricted quantity just as in an ME. But in addition there are notoriously long queues for *Kolonialwaren* in STEs: the prices tend to be below the market-clearing level appropriate to the small quantities, so any result based on them is an understatement. Mr. Pryor detects six countries where the gap between the world price and the domestic retail price, minus the average sales tax on all retail trade, is less than 57%:[3] Spain, Yugoslavia, the United States, Switzerland, France,

---

[1] For examples cf. Robert L. Allen, *Soviet Economic Warfare* (Washington, D.C., 1960).

[2] In *Review of Economics and Statistics*, November 1966.

[3] The formula is: $\sum PQ/\sum prQ(1 + t)$, where P is retail prices, p world prices, r the official or—where appropriate—tourist rate of exchange, t the average ratio of net sales tax to net material production, and Q the world quantity of imports, used as a weight. The products are coffee, tea, bananas, oranges, pepper, chocolate, tobacco, rice and sugar. Prices were dated 1964. Note that where, as in Poland, for instance, the tourist rate of exchange underestimates the purchasing power of the zloty, a truer rate would increase the gap. But the Soviet case is the opposite, and Pryor's formula overstates the gap.

Austria. So small a percentage as 57 might well be entirely accounted for by wholesale and retail margins: it indicates that *Kolonialwaren* pay the average rate of tax. A moderate degree of discrimination is indicated for five countries where the percentage gap is from 102 to 136: United Kingdom, Italy, Greece, West Germany, Eire. The seven STEs bring up the rear: Rumania (150), Bulgaria (179), Hungary (184), USSR (246), Poland (247), Czechoslovakia (337), DDR (744).

CHAPTER XV

AUTARKY

1   Autarky defined; and the quantifiable determinants of trade volume.
2   Historical comparisons are often better.
3   The purchasing power par rehabilitated.
4   Wholesale and retail p.p.ps.
5   The p.p.p. and the volume of trade in an ME.
6   Hyperpoly in MEs —
7   and in Poland.
8   Rationality in choice of trade volume would not hinder investment.
9   The 'participation rate' and its meaning.
10   Some statistics of participation rates.
11   The truth in the charge of autarky.
12   Despite all temptations there is little of it.
13   Differing styles of autarky.
14   Popular attitudes.

I

AUTARKY in this chapter is like bilateralism, an *ex ante*, or policy, concept. It might be defined as unwillingness to enter into foreign trade, or as the difference between the existing volume of trade turnover and the one that there would have been, *ceteris paribus*, under perfect competition.

Now unwillingness cannot be quantified, but 'the volume there would have been' might possibly be. We can certainly not know enough to predict directly from the techniques, resources and markets available; but we might be able to make a stab at it through comparisons of more and less *laissez-faire* economies that are 'otherwise similar'. Only what ought 'otherwise similar' to mean in this context? Without very much research it would not be possible to decide which variables really determine the long-run volume of trade. The ones most commonly chosen are income per head and population, and we shall accept these here as the best *measurable* determinants. But some theoretical misgiving is in place, for few have asked just why these are the best.[1] A short excursus on this question is in order.

Speaking simple-mindedly, the population looks indeed like a good determinant of the volume of trade, since a large population can specialize in more lines than a small one. Indeed, in one important case, population increase has been so influential that even the proportion of trade to national income actually fell, despite respectable growth in income per head and even in trade per head. This case is the United States, over the whole period for which we have records (Table XV/2).[2] The case should not surprise us, since the 'economic center of gravity' of the United States has also shifted far inland. In general, all the statistical studies[3] show a negative correlation between population and trade volume for all countries.

As to income per head, while it is universally held to be a very important determinant of trade volume, it is not so clear which way it works. We define here the *participation rate* as the proportion of the national income earned by, or spent on, foreign trade (cf. Sections 9 and 10). It is reasonable to suppose that most subsistence economies produce their own subsistence, and do not get it by trade, if only because transport costs are so high. So when incomes first begin to rise trade should increase, simply because it was zero before. It is then normal for the country—now out of the 'anthropological' stage and properly speaking a UDC—to export a few raw materials and depend on imports for all the sophisticated products it can afford. But after this stage it is not obvious why trade should grow more or less quickly than national income.

In fact, in a rich country, population and income per head are both indices of the same things: the abilities to produce a variety of objects, to master many techniques and to dispense with foreign materials. We must, of course, expect trade per head to rise with income per head; the latter is obviously a determinant of sorts. But

[1] F. L. Pryor [*The Communist Foreign Trade System*, p. 279] uses industrial production per head instead of national income per head, though he does not make it clear why. H. B. Chenery (in *American Economic Review*, September, 1960, p. 634) uses national income per head. Both use population. Neither really discusses the choice of these particular variables. But to be fair to Chenery the question of degrees of autarky is not on his mind. Simon Kuznets (in *Economic Development and Cultural Change*, October, 1964, especially p. 30) uses total national income instead of population. He is very confident of the rightness of this procedure, but does not say why.
[2] The Swedish participation rate has been stable since the industrial revolution (c. 1870), while the British rate peaked in about 1880.
[3] Pryor, op. cit.; Chenery, op. cit.; K. Deutsch, C. Bliss and A. Eckstein in *Economic Development and Cultural Change*, July, 1962; and Kuznets, op. cit.

when it comes to the relative growth of the two magnitudes the connection must be purely empirical.

Thus apart from commercial policy and from the size of the population, international specialization arises from: (i) increasing returns to scale, (ii) the variety of consumer wants, (iii) the dependence of producers on natural resources, (iv) the uneven distribution throughout the world of capital, education, enterprise and technology, (v) a low ratio of transport to factory cost.[1] In the seventeenth, eighteenth and nineteenth centuries (i) began to be important as never before, while (ii) and (iv) increased mightily. Meanwhile, (iii) at least did not fall. That is, while primary production did not keep pace with national income, *exotic* minerals and plant products became vastly more necessary for secondary production. It is no surprise, then, that both pre-industrial economists like Adam Smith and the large majority of his post-industrial successors predicted and also recommended an increase in trade. At present, too, trade continues to outgrow national income nearly everywhere. Can this trend be extrapolated?

Consider our five economic factors making for trade:

(i) The economies of scale continue to increase. Certain very important new industries demand larger scale than almost any of the old, established ones. This is not an *a priori* argument at all. Technical progress can easily lower the minimum tolerable size of an enterprise;[2] and thus, without actually prejudicing large enterprises, make them less necessary. The reduction in the size of machinery, for instance, has this effect. It simply happens, however, that the economies of scale are, on the whole, increasing.

(ii) will surely increase for ever, but we have no *a priori* reason to suppose the variety, as opposed to the quantity, of wants grows more rapidly than the ability to satisfy it. Perhaps to be rich is to be versatile, to be able to manufacture, if not to grow, everything at home. Indeed, clearly one kind of thing rich people want is more easily made at home: services.

(iii), then, is diminishing rapidly, especially with the invention of substitutes and the move into 'high-tertiary' activity.

---

[1] It is not necessary that there be a differential fall in transport costs, favoring international transports. Almost any fall will do. Thus suppose factory costs are 90 abroad and 100 at home, and transport costs are 30 from the foreign factory, 15 from the home one. Then if home transport costs are halved to 7·5, while foreign transport costs fall by only 47% to 16, the foreign good replaces the home one.

[2] P. J. D. Wiles, *Price, Cost and Output* (2nd ed.), pp. 214–21.

(iv) is the object of attack by all development policy everywhere. If that policy succeeds it will eventually disappear. As this is written, however, STEs and ACCs are increasing their capital stock (and their incomes) far more rapidly than UDCs. On the other hand, the exchange of knowledge is becoming an increasingly adequate substitute for that of goods all over the world (Chapter XIII).

(v) is unpredictable.

As to the population, it is growing more rapidly than ever in UDCs. This is, of course, a considerable obstacle to the attack on item (iv). But it is perhaps wisest to predict both the successful development of UDCs and the continued, if slower, growth of population. In ACCs and STEs population growth is certainly slower than it used to be, and this, of course, encourages them to trade.

What, then, of commercial policy?[1] This is, of course, quite as important as all other factors combined, especially for STEs, but nearly impossible to predict. In particular, the spirit of bloc formation favors free trade on the whole; internal barriers fall, external ones rise but little. And among STEs the new drive for rational resource allocation is a very powerful argument for *freer* trade, but not necessarily for *more* trade, since perhaps there is too much already (Sections 6 and 7 below).

Yet here too we must be cautious. At no point is the over-emphasis on mere trade within the general field of international economics more absurd than when we come to consider *cartels and specialization agreements*. If several capitalist firms form an international cartel agreeing to split up the market into their respective countries, there is no trade at all; yet the thing is pre-eminently a part of our subject. If the same cartel specializes its members not by area but by type of product each of them sells in every country, and trade is maximized. To the cartel corresponds international planning among STEs. This too may reduce or increase trade, according to whether it specializes enterprises by production branch or by territory served. If in 1963–64 the stress is all on product-wise specialization, this merely corrects the bad old autarkic state of affairs. Cases can be imagined in which territorial specialization (another name for autarky) should be preferred, so that not only international but even supranational planning could be rationally

---

[1] The advent of national sovereignty leads to a more autarkic policy. Cf. Deutsch, Bliss and Eckstein, op. cit., for statistical confirmation. The richest ACCs in this source have a higher participation rate than all but the still-not-sovereign UDCs. But the scatter among them is very great, and it is proper to suspect their more liberal commercial policies.

AUTARKY 423

used to diminish trade, or at least the proportion it bears to national income.[1]

All this makes prediction extremely hazardous. I venture to predict that in the next decade the participation rates of the more populous ACCs will not grow much, if at all; that Hungary and the smaller ACCs will shortly have to set bounds by an act of policy to the frighteningly high participation rates they have achieved (Table XV/5); that other STEs, especially the USSR and China, will further relax their autarkic policies and raise their participation rates; and that most UDCs will do the same. It seems quite impossible to look beyond the next decade.

2

But how much autarky was there in STEs, and how much remains? If the measurable determinants of population and income per head were all there would be no objection to Pryor's procedure, of international comparison based upon a correlation between trade, income per head and population established for many countries at a period of time. Pryor obtains such a formula for Western Europe and applies it to Eastern Europe: the shortfall of foreign trade in the East from that expected according to the formula demonstrates the presence of a policy of greater autarky. And since the shortfall is about fourfold we cannot quarrel with the results as a demonstration of the mere presence of autarky at a moment of time (1955). But a rather more delicate approach points in exactly the opposite direction: *the greater autarky of Eastern Europe was strictly temporary.*

This approach begins by asking: how about all the other determinants that must surely be equally important? One thinks here of natural resources, the pattern of communications (which might, for instance, encourage trade across the frontiers rather than inside the country), and the pattern of demand in the world as a whole, but especially in neighboring countries. Since these determinants cannot be quantified, we must simply hold them constant, and the only remotely possible way to do this is to consider the same country over time. Our question then must be: did this country's trade

---

[1] I give two practical examples. First, Poland and the DDR have split up fishing on the Baltic coast between them. Secondly, fines are imposed on a country's railroad system for detaining the wagons of another country. Such fining systems have been negotiated in both ECE and the Comecon. They take up a great deal of negotiating energy and pay off handsomely in efficiency. Yet their effect is to reduce wagon-exchange, even perhaps to reduce payments for wagon-exchange.

grow as much as that other's, under a similar influence of the two measurable determinants, income per head and population? I.e., we establish a 'normal' growth of trade compared with two factors, and see whether the STE has behaved 'normally'. Timeless comparisons between countries, such as those of Pryor and Chenery, take far too little account of the special geographical position and natural resources of each.

Take the extreme instance: Czechoslovakia. The shape of the country is such as to encourage foreign trade: between Slovakia and Hungary, between Bohemia and the surrounding Germanic territories. However obvious and necessary an act of state it is to encourage Czech-Slovak trade, this is itself autarkic. Then, too, the country only existed for twenty peacetime years between the wars, during which she and her neighbors experimented with great changes in commercial policy; therefore, no correlation of national incomes with trade over that period will tell us much. She was always very protectionist during this period, but much more so toward the end. Moreover, the period was very brief, and distorted by a huge slump.

So the statement, 'Communist Czechoslovakia is very autarkic', can best be shown to be true or false by beginning with national income, trade, and population in some pre-war period of reasonable stability, and correlating the *change* of trade volume with the *change* of the two measurable determinants according to a formula derived from 'similar' countries. Then if Czechoslovak trade has grown less since 1936 than it 'would have', and if the nonquantifiable determinants have the same influence as they had, the country is *even more autarkic than it was*. Such measurements are attempted in Table XV/5. They dispose utterly of the charge that the small East European STEs are autarkic—though they undoubtedly were so in 1955.

3

Let us now examine more carefully the state of perfect competition, mentioned above, by reference to which the concept of autarky is defined. In this hypothetical (we shall not call it ideal) state both the general price level and the rate of exchange are flexible; so that *the rate of exchange equals the purchasing power parity*, and both have spontaneously adjusted themselves to such a point that exports plus net natural long-term capital flow equal imports. Moreover, all individual agents, in both foreign and domestic trade, are maximizing their profits. If there is less trade than this we say there is autarky, and if there is more—a less commonly considered deviation—we shall call it *hyperpoly*, or over-trading. We hope to avoid throughout the argument the least implication that autarky or hyperpoly are bad. For both might represent conscious and rational decisions not to allow macro-magnitudes to be simply the sums of micro-magnitudes, however rational the latter might be in their own terms.

Every condition for hypothetical equilibrium laid down in the previous paragraph is doubtless obvious, save only the equality of rate of exchange with purchasing power par (p.p.p.). The matter is important to us because no Soviet-type rate of exchange need have any relation to the p.p.p. Even rather rationally-minded STEs choose as trade criteria rates very far removed from the p.p.p., and, as we shall see, this leads to great dangers of autarky and hyperpoly. What we have to say on this subject will also seem strangely old-fashioned to many. Like the equation of exchange, the p.p.p. lost all credit during the Keynesian revolution, and it became *de rigueur* to neglect it in all discussions of international trade. Keynesians seek in general to explain foreign exchange rates by movements of aggregate demand and supply, without too much attention to micro-economics. Instead of trying to relate this new type of theory to the old p.p.p. theory, instead of using them to complement each other, they have simply pointed to undoubted deficiencies in the p.p.p. theory and left it at that.[1]

This will not do at all. It is too often forgotten that international trade, even between STEs, consists of individual goods and services, the movement of which is individually decided upon. However ridiculous the p.p.p. may look from the econometrician's stratosphere, it is life and death to the actual trader and the tourist who provide him with his magnitudes. Moreover, there is the whole question of international micro-rationality, discussed in Chapters VII and VIII. We saw there that unless the rate of exchange is at p.p.p., decisions on particular exports and imports cannot be rational. Such questions are not Keynesian, but they are not therefore unimportant.

Indeed, the rate of exchange is like the rate of interest: its allocative (or micro-) role has been swamped by its Keynesian (or macro-) role. Keynesian thinking has acquired such a monopoly that the use of either rate as an allocator seems shocking and obsolete. But both

[1] This is not an unfair account of textbooks in particular. Cf. Charles P. Kindleberger, *International Economics* (Urbana, Ill., 1955); Jaroslav Vanek, *International Trade: Theory and Economic Policy* (Urbana, Ill., 1962); Thomas C. Schelling, *International Economics* (Boston, 1958); and Paul T. Ellsworth, *The International Economy* (New York, 1958).

426 COMMUNIST INTERNATIONAL ECONOMICS

roles exist, and they conflict. One must not set these rates indefinitely high or low in order to keep employment full. Beyond
certain limits the allocation of resources becomes so bad that one
must search for other ways to one's macro-economic ends. It is
precisely Sovietology, where Keynesian problems are absent and
allocative problems all in all, that brings us back to sanity in these
matters.

4

No apology, therefore, is made for using this antiquated concept.
Note that there are in all economies two important p.p.ps.: a wholesale one for commodities and producers' services and a retail one for
tourists—hereinafter c.p.p.p. and t.p.p.p., respectively. In an ME
the former alone is likely to correspond to the rate of exchange.
Notoriously, it does so because most commodity prices are flexible
and *individually* conform to any rate that happens to rule. The more
perfect the market the more certain it is that massive arbitrage will
correct each several price divergence. The c.p.p.p. then, is composed
of conformist individual prices, and so will itself conform to the
rate of exchange, however these prices are weighted. Sometimes,
indeed, in monoculture UDCs, the rate follows the price of the
principal export, and it is the currency, not the export, that is subject
to arbitrage.

The tourist, on the other hand, is a marginal buyer in large
domestic markets: his effect could never be described as 'massive
arbitrage'. The tourist buys what are inaccurately called 'non-traded
goods'. The fact that he is an insignificant trader enables him to
enjoy advantages or suffer disadvantages, even in simon-pure MEs,
year in and year out.[1]

In STEs very great differences between the t.p.p.p. and the c.p.p.p.
are certain. To begin with, the latter does not govern international
trade, and prices are arbitrary. To go on with, the turnover tax,
overwhelmingly placed, as we have seen, on the final stage of production of consumer goods, greatly and systematically depresses the
t.p.p.p.

It is the necessary conformity of individual wholesale prices in

---

[1] It is true that there is in theory another equilibrating mechanism: flows of factors between
'traded' and 'non-traded' goods. Thus if two perfectly competitive MEs have identical
production functions, and in one a 'traded' commodity becomes more profitable, factors
will flow into it out of *all* other goods and services until international equilibrium is restored,
and this will keep the prices of non-traded goods in line. But the required degrees of market
perfection and technical identity are almost inconceivable.

different countries under perfect competition that has made people condemn the conformity of the c.p.p.p. with the rate of exchange as a tautology. One glance at an STE's prices will show it is certainly not that: where the arbitrage is not factually present there is no conformity. Indeed, imperfect international competition among MEs also provides us with innumerable examples of divergence. Moreover, tautologies are often very informative. The man has yet to live who knows every tautology, and the term is not, on the lips of the wise, one of abuse.

5

Our next question is, then, whether any other macro-criteria of over-all trade volume are as satisfactory as micro-equilibrium in every product, with a rate of exchange equal to the c.p.p.p. The 'volume' of trade we define as the average of visible and invisible exports and imports. Now while there are always good grounds for autarky, and STEs have undoubtedly practiced that, it is not enough appreciated that today STEs are tending so far away from it that they seriously incur the danger of trading too much. The reasons for trading 'too little' tend to be political, so some at least escape the economist's condemnation. But not so in the opposite case: the mistake seems to be purely economic, and the obvious check upon it is to see that the marginal cost of import substitutes does not fall below the opportunity cost of imports. This latter is simply the marginal cost of exports. Thus the last pound in the hands of the government or any other consumer should have equal utility whether spent on imports or import-substitutes. But the last pound in the hands of any producer should yield equal revenue, whether from exports or from import-substitutes; and at the margin that revenue is, of course, one pound. It follows that a unit of currency must have equal purchasing power over imports, import substitutes and exports. And this can only be so if the actual rate of exchange, or the notional one used by the planners, is equal to the c.p.p.p. This concept should therefore influence planners continuously, and not merely at great crises such as currency reform or runaway inflation.

It is naturally possible to have far smaller or far greater volumes of trade that balance, but not by simple profit maximization in a rational price system. Thus hyperpolistic balance could be achieved by subsidizing both imports and exports, and autarkic balance has been normal among STEs. It is also quite possible for the rate of exchange to correspond to the c.p.p.p. while there is no equilibrium of foreign payments. In an STE this would be due to the arbitrary quantitative decisions taken. In an ME it would not result merely from imperfections of competition, for by themselves these will simply distribute prices at random about a c.p.p.p. derived from homogeneous commodities alone; and this would not disturb the over-all equilibrium, except in improbably unlucky cases. The prime cause of such a disturbance is the combination, characteristic in an ME, of 'Keynesian' effects and a pegged currency. If the central bank supports some rate or other by gold operations in the open market, then prices will naturally conform to this rate and form a c.p.p.p. about it. But aggregate demand is not necessarily adjusted to these prices, and may by excess or shortfall cause disequilibrium of foreign payments.

Ordinary international trade theory has little to say about the volume of trade as opposed to its terms or balance. We have only space here for the very briefest and most dogmatic theorization, confining ourselves to what is relevant to STEs. Let us start, then, at the hypothetical perfectly competitive prices, rate of exchange, and volume, and assume that all the relevant elasticities of demand and supply are high—as they are in the long run, which is all that concerns an analysis of autarky. We also assume, as is appropriate to the long run, full employment and no Keynesian effects. Then in MEs:

(i) A devaluation is equivalent to taxing imports and subsidizing exports; it alters the balance and the terms of trade, but the volume much less.

(ii) An appreciation has the opposite effect.

(iii) A tax on imports and on exports reduces the volume, improves the terms and, slightly, the balance.

(iv) A subsidy on both has the opposite effect.

(v) A tax on imports alone at first improves the terms and the balance, but lowers the volume: but then the foreigner, deprived of our currency, spends less on our exports so that the terms of trade are at least partially reversed; the only certain end-result is lower volume.

(vi) A tax on exports alone at first improves the terms, worsens the balance, and lowers the volume; but then we ourselves are forced to spend less on imports, thus restoring the balance and at least partially the terms; the only certain end-result is again lower volume.

(vii) A subsidy on imports alone is the exact opposite of (v).

(viii) A subsidy on exports alone is the exact opposite of (vi).

6

It seems that hyperpoly is not an important problem in MEs. It would be very surprising if the general volume of trade in any ME were too big. But small practical instances do occur. The two with which I am familiar arise from subsidies.

The simpler case is Bolivian. It seems that in the middle 'ftiefis

... they had a multiple exchange rate with such favourable rates for imported raw materials ('to encourage Bolivian industry') that there was a lively trade to *smuggle out* Bolivian manufactures made with these cheap materials! Result: net loss [sc. of foreign exchange].[1]

But import subsidies are by no means as common as subsidies to domestic production.

The more complicated case, then, is British. The formal incidence of the egg subsidy was on the price of eggs, not on that of imported egg-inputs. Nevertheless it was so great in the middle 'fifties that it greatly increased the importation of feed-stuffs. This was by itself hyperpoly, and must be a very common case. But worse followed: eggs were sold to Germany, at a profit, for a price so low that their foreign-exchange content was not recouped![2]

Hyperpoly on a different definition is, of course, very common: there is too much trade for national independence, or for economic growth. But this is not our definition here; indeed such a state of affairs is compatible with mild autarky as we use the word.

In an STE very similar effects can be produced, but the corrective price mechanism is absent. Thus the writer formed in Poland in 1964 the suspicion that the country was swinging too far from autarky and, laying down large *a priori* import plans, forcing itself to export at a grave disadvantage in order to pay for them. This would be the STE's equivalent of case (vii) above.

7

There can, for instance, scarcely be a field where rational economic theory has penetrated practice more deeply than Polish foreign

[1] Professor Alec Nove, privately circulated document, November, 1965.
[2] *The Economist*, May 4, 1957.

trade.[1] But the theory and practice as presented to me were all micro-rational only, and offered no defense against hyperpoly. On the contrary, by taking an unrealistically low view of the p.p.p. of the zloty, or by refusing to think in terms of p.p.ps. at all and simply setting a very low shadow rate of exchange, the planners were actually encouraging the excessive exports that their excessive imports made necessary.

As we saw above, when the Polish state has optimized its situation, its marginal import per dollar is worth no more and no less to it than its marginal export per zloty, or its marginal import-substitute per zloty, for these are like two substitutable factors of production on the iso-product surface of a very large firm. If the zloty-dollar rate is at c.p.p.p., this condition is easily obtained. But if the zloty is undervalued the marginal cost of the export in zlotys seems less than the marginal revenue from selling the export in dollars, and the state is tempted to export more.

In an ME such an undervaluation would raise import prices, choke off imports, and force an upward adjustment either of the exchange rate or of internal prices. But as we saw in Chapter VIII, in an STE import prices are arbitrary, and the Preisausgleich can make them quite low whatever the value of the zloty. And, in fact, it is customary for imports to be priced very low in Poland. More-over, as we shall see below, imports are mainly investment goods, and the principal determinant of the volume of exports is simply the state investment plan. There is thus a strong element of high-level political will-power in the situation, and no check on over-importing, except from the export side. Quite the contrary, if Poland abandons autarky she is likely to import immense quanti-ties, owing to the habitual ambitiousness and tension of her plan. Her only check on her import plan is to be able truly to compare exports, imports and import-substitutes—which is only possible if the shadow rate of exchange = the c.p.p.p.

If the government adds a new item, with high priority, to its import plan, the correct response of the planner is probably not to increase exports but to knock out the marginal import. If this is not done Poland will shortly be importing the whole of its national expenditure and exporting the whole of its national product —which would be very wasteful indeed. If there was no *a priori*

[1] E.g., W. Przelaskowski in *Ekonomista*, May, 1963; M. Rakowski in *Gospodarka Planowa*, February and April, 1957; M. Kalecki and S. Polaczek in ibid., April, 1957; J. Zieleniewski in *Finanse*, August, 1957; and W. Trzeciakowski, *Theoretical and Practical Methods of Optimization of Foreign Trade in a Centrally Planned Economy* (Warsaw, 1964).

virtue in autarky there is equally no *a priori* virtue in its reversal.
The relation of c.p.p.p. to t.p.p.p. in Poland in 1964 was fairly
characteristic of all STEs, and worth illustrating. According to the
estimates of the writer and his wife,[1] the retail purchasing power of
the zloty for purposes of statistical comparison was 6 United
States cents by Polish weights and 9·5 cents by United States
domestic weights. The actual t.p.p.p., by the weights appropriate to
a tourist, was 7·0 cents.[2] Yet the rate offered a tourist was 4·0 cents,
and the shadow rate for foreign trade calculations was apparently
taken by Polish officials to be about 2·0 cents. The former rate makes
a very rich man out of every tourist, and the latter is surely quite as
bad. It is true that food, clothes, shoes and other manufactures,
which are the nearest the tourist gets to a tradable commodity,
retail for about 3 cents. But the turnover tax, even though it is
rather small, should raise the c.p.p.p. *above* this figure, and so should
the high probability that enterprises in the export trade are more
efficient than those in the home trade.[3]

It requires no small self-confidence to correct a whole ministry
of experts on the basis of a little window-gazing, but the scientist
is supposed to have confidence in reason; my confidence is enhanced
by finding that Mr. Alan Brown has virtually anticipated me.[4]
The fact is that Hungarian trade decisions, on which Mr. Brown
concentrates, are meant to be sensibly based on a p.p.p.,[5] while Polish

[1] For the role of the economist's wife in these matters, and for the extreme uncertainty of
all p.p.ps., cf. the author's essay in *Soviet Planning* (Oxford, U.K., 1964), ed. Jane Degras and
Alec Nove. The estimates presented here make savage quality discounts against the zloty.

[2] The relativities implied by these figures are rather striking, and fairly typical of any STE.
The retail parities were as follows (cents per zloty; the figures in brackets show weights
appropriate to a Polish consumer, a United States consumer, and a tourist):

Food . . . 4 (45/25/0)	Clothes and shoes . 3 (15/15/0)
Restaurant meals . . 7 (3/8/50)	Transport . . 7·5 (2/5/20)
Haircut . . . 10 (1/1/0)	Postage . . 4 (1/1/5)
Urban rents: ordinary . 50 (3/0/0)	Hotel room . . 6 (1/1/10)
cooperative 25 (0/20/0)	Souvenirs . . 8 (0/0/10)
Durables . . . 2 (5/8/0)	(Weights unallocated) . (24/16/5)

Unlike the USSR, Poland publishes fairly complete figures on her turnover tax, which seems
to be at the low rate of about 16% of retail price on average.

[3] In 1956–7 the c.p.p.p. for manufactures was reckoned at 3·25 c. = 1 zl. (J. Zachariasz,
Finanse, 6/1956; R. Wilczewski, *Gospodarka Planowa*, 6/1960). In 1956–64 the U.S. wholesale
price level rose by 8·5% and the Polish by 18% (workings available on request). On the
other hand the Statistisches Bundesamt puts the retail p.p.p. at 1 zl. = 5·4 c. in 1964, by West
German weights (*Preise-Löhne-Wirtschaftsrechnungen*, Reihe 10, Internationaler Vergleich der
Preise für die Lebenshaltung, Stuttgart 1967, pp. 25, 39). This is lower than my reckoning. I
owe these references to Mr. Heinz Machowski.

[4] In *American Economist* (journal of Omicron Chi Epsilon, the economics honor society),
November, 1961, pp. 12–13.

[5] We quote one such piece of Hungarian reasoning in Chapter VII, Section 7. But it is
not implied that the Hungarian government accepts such good advice: on the contrary, it
may well be more hyperpolistic than the Polish. Cf. Table XV/5.

decisions are based on a rate which looks like a p.p.p. but is in fact arbitrary.

The Polish shadow rate of 1 zloty = 2 cents, referred to above, is not called a p.p.p., nor thought of as such by those who actually use it. It is the rate required to make the marginal export profitable, granted the *a priori* import bill. In other words, just as in the bad old days of autarky, the *a priori* import requirement decides the export volume; only now, instead of being autarkic, the requirement is hyperpolistic. For instance, Brown summarizes Rakowski[1] as follows:

> He arrives at this rate by calculating the foreign exchange price of the goods that workers in Poland buy for their wages, earned in producing an export good. To illustrate this, let us suppose that export good A costs 50 zloty [and] could be imported for $1. In this case, he would set the real exchange rate at 50 to 1. If good A sells for $1, they would just cover the cost of production. This method incorrectly assumes that the $1 earned by exporting A is used to buy the wage goods. In fact, there are other goods which might be more efficiently imported, releasing a larger amount of factors of production than that which would be necessary to produce the wage goods domestically.

Thus Brown's criticism is that the zloty would be worth more dollars if *different* foreign goods had been imported. We must add that it would be worth more Polish goods if *fewer* of them had been exported (for on the whole returns diminish in any economy). Rakowski's procedure, then, is guaranteed to produce a shadow rate more unfavorable to the zloty than the c.p.p.p.

Brown continues:

> M. Kalecki and S. Polaczek calculated the equilibrium rate of exchange which they found to be 56 zloty per dollar[2] (not very different from Rakowski's result). To show how they define the equilibrium rate of exchange, let us assume that the country wants to import an additional $1's worth of goods. The equilibrium rate of exchange will be that number of zloty which is necessary to produce exports to equilibrate the balance of payments. J. Zieleniewski has a similar method. He also calls it an equilibrium rate of exchange which, for him, is a rate that would guarantee the balance of payments equilibrium in the long run.

These authors too, then, quite plainly invite hyperpoly, and offer no restraint upon the planners' *a priori* import bill.

8

In many discussions Polish economists have made two rebuttals. First, the 2-cent notional rate for the zloty applies only at the margin;

[1] Op. cit.   [2] Op. cit.

most Polish exports would have been planned for even at a much higher rate. In other words, supply is very inelastic. This reduces the practical importance of my objection, but seemingly does not touch its logic. There is not much hyperpoly, but there is some.

Secondly, they say, if we use the c.p.p.p. as a criterion of trade volume, we shall discourage the import of machinery, and therefore growth. But the 'Hungarian' policy here advocated only checks these imports to the extent that it faces us with their exact consequences. The detailed import demands of the investment sector should naturally be made rational in view of the size of that sector, and this is not in dispute. But the total volume of investment imports must be taken into account via the consequential volume of exports, when the highest authorities decide the total of investment itself. Too much exportation itself tends to retard growth, particularly since it diverts domestic resources from direct use in investment.

The decision to import is, as we saw already in Chapter VIII, not synonymous with the decision to invest. Imagine a perfectly competitive *laissez-faire* economy which produces no machines or wine. If tastes switch from beer to wine, wine prices rise, beer prices fall, the rate of exchange falls, the c.p.p.p. falls and exports are encouraged. So also if tastes shift from beer to machinery—there is no difference. But the fact that the c.p.p.p. does not fall indefinitely is indeed a limit on machinery imports: it encourages import substitutes. If these substitutes are very inelastically supplied, and 'tastes' (i.e. the planners' preference) for machinery are incorrigible, the c.p.p.p. will, of course, fall very low. It is right that it should do so. The low c.p.p.p. reduces other imports and brings the planners up properly against the consequences of their tastes. It is far from being an obstacle to the plan; it simply tells them what it costs, and reminds them of better ways of fulfilling it.

9

So much as to the theoretical danger of hyperpoly. In practice, of course, we cannot measure the hypothetical volume of trade if a country like Poland or Czechoslovakia were to go over, *ceteris paribus* (!), to perfect competition. So we must stick to our more modest measure of probable changes in the degree of autarky, as described in Section 2. This means that we must use participation rates. It cannot be too often repeated that a low participation rate is not autarky, nor a high one hyperpoly. Each country being a special case, only movements in the rate even begin to have significance.

Nor does the participation rate tell us how 'important' trade is to a country. Presumably trade is 'important' when small changes in it cause large changes in the national income. Then for the United States, which runs a reserve currency and a gold standard, her 6% participation in foreign trade is extremely important, while France's much larger rate is less important. As far as these financial matters go, any given rate is less important to an STE. Again a country might engage heavily in processing foreign semi-fabricates for re-export, or in mere merchanting for re-export. Then both imports and exports are a large part of the national income, but the domestic value added dependent on them is not; and trade is 'unimportant'. Or, finally, the USSR may cut its imports and therefore its exports to the bone; then it only imports vital necessities and is ex hypothesi subject to the bottleneck effect. India is in the same position, for being simply unable to export she too only imports vital necessities.

We need, furthermore, to be very clear what our statistics really mean. As was implied by the factual description in Chapter II, Soviet-type statistics do not provide us with an adequate measure of the resources devoted to foreign trade, since only one factor—labor—is fully valued at a price. Moreover, this price is not altogether a scarcity price. It is not that the scarcity has been created by the central plan rather than the sovereign consumer; that does not matter when the question is the meaningfulness of factor cost. It is that administrative compulsion is applied at many points: in USSR to keep people on kolkhozy or to get them to go east, in all STEs to allocate the graduates of schools and universities during their first three years, etc. This lowers the supply curve of labor to particular jobs—perhaps insignificantly in most STEs, but very significantly in the USSR and China. Then, too, long-term capital is, or was until very recently, without price in most socialized sectors, though cooperative and private agriculture have to pay for it; and land was free everywhere, except in Polish private agriculture. Nor is the rate of profit everywhere the same—very far from it indeed.

So if we take the GNP at market prices of an STE (having been careful to add in the services omitted), subtract turnover tax and depreciation allowances, and add subsidies—which it is usually possible, with some trouble, to do—we do not arrive at the true net national income at factor cost. We are left instead with the bastard concept here called *net national income originating* (n.n.i.o.). It consists of the wages actually paid out, socialized profits, cooperative and private incomes from production, and emigrants' remittances. Whatever interest or rent is paid by and to private individuals is included, and so are interest and rent paid to the state; for all[1] these items are simply part of production cost. Interest paid *by* the state (e.g., on small savings) is in Western terminology 'interest on the national debt' and, thus, a transfer payment only counted in 'disposable income'. The point, then, is not that the concept excludes or includes the wrong things. It is that the basic pricing arrangements misprice, or altogether fail to price, those things. Nevertheless, the n.n.i.o. does extrude the turnover tax and subsidies: it is a not appallingly bad substitute for factor cost. In particular, if we wish to know the engagement of an STE in foreign trade we are compelled to use it, since there is no turnover tax in foreign trade. As to the special tax-cum-subsidy that is the Preisausgleich, this must of course be reinstated in order to arrive at domestic factor cost, and that is not always easy. *Faute de mieux*, then, our working concept is:

$\frac{1}{2}$ (visible+invisible turnover at domestic factor cost)÷n.n.i.o.

The dividend is so defined as to eliminate surpluses and deficits, whether temporary or systematic.

Does the 'participation rate' so defined misrepresent the *proportion* of scarce resources devoted to exports? In most STEs there is more interest and rent in agricultural costs than in other costs, since most agriculture lies outside the socialized sector, and if it does not pay rent it at least pays interest on long-term capital. It would follow that grain and livestock exports, to which industry adds no value, would be overstated relative to other exports. But these are about the only such items, and they do not exactly characterize the export structure of an STE!

Moreover, as we have seen, in the USSR and China agricultural incomes are depressed by administrative force: what is the effect of that on agricultural costs? The administrative pressure both reduces wage rates and increases employment; its net effect on the wage bill is quite unclear. But that again is unimportant, for

[1] The new long-term capital charges to state enterprises in Hungary and the USSR appear to be accounted for as part of socialized profit. This is because there are ideological inhibitions against counting interest as a cost.

the effect of such pressure on *marginal* cost is unambiguous: it is to reduce it, since the extra labor is available and waiting on the farm.

There is, again, little interest or meaning in a participation rate not expressed in the prices of the year to which it refers. Thus let small letters represent exports and large letters the national income, let T be the participation volume index and Y the national income volume index. Then we might try to discover the Soviet participation volume in 1937 by applying to that for 1928 the relevant Laspeyres indices of volume:

$$\frac{\Sigma p_o\, q_o}{\Sigma P_o\, Q_o} \times \frac{T_l}{Y_l} = \frac{\Sigma p_o\, q_l}{\Sigma P_o\, Q_l}\; .$$

But the right-hand expression is not in the factor costs of 1937. It is the Paasche indices of volume that give us what we want:

$$\frac{\Sigma p_l\, q_o}{\Sigma P_l\, Q_o} \times \frac{T_p}{Y_p} = \frac{\Sigma p_l\, q_l}{\Sigma P_l\, Q_l}\; .$$

But, as the equation makes evident, they do so only after the labor of revaluing all quantities of 1928 at 1937 prices. Clearly if we have enough information to know T_p and Y_p we can work out $\Sigma p_l\, q_l /\Sigma P_l\, Q_l$ direct. The use of volume indices is very definitely a *pis aller*, but it is one to which ignorance of other data may force us. In the Soviet case, below, I have preferred a direct calculation of the participation rate in 1937, in the prices of that year, however risky, to extrapolation by index numbers from 1928. For it is precisely in 1928–37 that index-number problems are most severe. The alternative calculations for 1959 show how great the error can be.

The factor cost of exports, and the equivalent value for imports, are also a problem. For the special Chinese case see the next section. In other STEs the Preisausgleich is large and secret, with the result that the domestic values of foreign trade are hardly known, even to the authorities. As this goes to press this is still true, for instance, of Czechoslovakia and Rumania. Our solitary Czechoslovak estimate rests on an informal Communist volume comparison of visible exports with national income. Our Rumanian estimate is an informed guess. Our Soviet estimate for 1937 rests on the bare assumption that there was no Preisausgleich in that year; for subsequent years we have extrapolated by means of volume indices, as above. But if the 1959 input/output table is expressed in new rubles it yields an export factor cost of R. 5·3 md. (Table XV/1 note 25)—very close to the official valuta figure of R. 5·0 md. Only, however, Poland and Hungary give us official input/output tables with exports and imports in domestic prices.

10

Turning now to actual participation rates, we find (Tables XV/1–6) that STEs used indeed to be very autarkic. There are too few large countries by which the USSR may be judged, so I have simply juxtaposed its case with that of the United States, a very protectionist country. The record speaks for itself. In 1938–40 the Soviet rate fell well below 1·0%; surely a record of sorts. Even by 1962 the USSR, albeit with a larger population than the United States, was still getting much less of her national income by foreign trade. The fact that this national income is much smaller than the American exercises no doubt an influence one way or another on the participation rate—but we have found no means of being sure which way. At even approximately this income and population there are only these two countries. We can only say that Soviet autarky has much diminished but still exceeds the United States.

Note that the USSR has twice changed its boundaries, in 1917–21 and 1940–45, as is shown in Table XV/1. However the effect of economic policy quite overwhelmed this factor: when area shrank the participation rate fell, when it expanded the rate rose. Nor should we give as much weight as in the United States case to the shift in the 'economic center of gravity' away from Europe. For, first, the center did not in fact shift much: there was no very great movement of population except during the war. Secondly the land distances across the USSR are far longer than in the United States, and the sea connection between the east and the west coasts is much nearer, and Japan and China are much closer to the new parts of the country. We should, therefore, expect an actual rise in foreign trade to follow the movement east. It is a striking sign of Stalin's autarky—and of the political tension of the times—that this did not happen. In 1965, however, a special bureau was formed to promote trade between Japan and the Far East.[1]

It is similarly instructive to juxtapose China and India. Few previous students have really accepted the fact that China's dis-

[1] T. Shabad in *New York Times*, February 13, 1965.

TABLE XV/1. PARTICIPATION RATES, USSR
(md. old R., current prices and boundaries)

	(i) n.n.i.o.	(ii) Visible Trade Turnover as published, current Valuta Rubles[23]	(iii) All Trade Turnover at Domestic Factor Cost	(iv) Participation Rate (%)	(v) Real Growth of (i)[4]	(vi) Real Growth of (ii)[15]	(vii) Population (mn., mid-year)[4]
1913	21·0[16]/16·5[20, 9]	2·89[16]	3·11[12, 16]	7·4[16]	45·2[7, 9]/76·6[7, 9]	354[16]	162[16]/141[9]
1925	16·4[24]	1·49	1·72[13]	5·3	27·7[7]/47·0[7]	86	144
1928	27·3[2]	1·68	2·57[13]	4·7	39·7[5]/67·2[6]	139	151·5
1932	c.67[22]	1·28	—	?2·5[1]	56·1[5]/75·7[6]	179	157
1937	218·1[3]	3·07	3·84[14]	0·9	100	100	165
1938	—	2·80	—	—	—	87·5	—
1940	353·4[17, 10]	2·86[11]	—	—	—	—	173[9]/195[10]
1950	675[18]	13·00	—	?1·7[1]	137[8]	265	180
1955	928[18]	25·92	—	?2·4[1]	182[8]	475	196
1959	1311[19]	42·06	?2·8[1]/4·9[25]	?2·9[1]	237[8]	761	211
1963	1585[21]	56·90	—	?3·3[1]	292[8]	1073	225

[1] Extrapolating from (v) and (vi) on the base of the 1937 figure.
[2] Oleg Hoeffding, Soviet National Income and Product in 1928 (New York, 1954), p. 47.
[3] Abram Bergson, Soviet National Income and Product in 1937 (New York, 1953), p. 76.
[4] Various sources as specified in Wiles in ASTE Bulletin, University of Pennsylvania, October, 1967.
[5] Using 1928 weights.   [6] Using 1937 weights.
[7] Using 1926–27 weights, and reckoning backwards identically from each of the two results of 1928.
[8] The choice of weights here is more or less indifferent.
[9] For inter-war boundaries.   [10] For the larger boundaries.
[11] For inter-war boundaries.

[12] Visible exports plus 2%. P. I. Lyashchenko, History of the National Economy of Russia (New York, 1949), p. 718, gives invisible earnings as 1·5% of visible in 1898–1913, but increasing.
[13] Table V/1. I have inflated the commodity turnover of 1928 by 32% to allow for the PAG, which had developed by that year. Cf. Holzman, in ed. A. Bergson and S. Kuznets, Economic Trends in the Soviet Union (Harvard, 1963), p. 327.
[14] Table V/1. Since the gold export shown for 1937 is clearly exceptional, I have taken R. 375 mn. as the relevant exports. For the rest, I have multiplied all figures by 4·38 to allow for the devaluation, and followed Holzman in assuming there was no PAG.
[15] Chaining together the various official indices of export growth, mainly from Holzman, loc. cit. I have preferred exports alone since they present far fewer index number problems, being of more stable quality. 1938 is included for convenience, since it is a common base-year.
[16] Boundaries of Russian Empire. Source: Falkus as in note 20.
[17] Abram Bergson and Hans Heymann, Soviet National Income and Product (New York, 1954), pp. 70, 190.

[18] The gross n.i.o. was 694 and 977 respectively: Nancy Nimitz, *Soviet National Income and Product, 1956–58* (RAND, 1962), p. 16. Depreciation was 14 in 1948 (source as in note 17), 80 in 1958 (Abraham S. Becker, *Soviet National Income and Product, 1958–62* [RAND, 1965], p. 14). I have interpolated as follows: 19 in 1950, 49 in 1955.

[19] Becker, op cit., p. 33, gives g.n.i.o. as 1406. I have deducted 95 for depreciation (source as in note 25).

[20] The preliminary and tentative estimate of my colleague Mr. Malcolm Falkus (LSE). He has detected many errors in the work of S. N. Prokopovich (Birmingham Bureau of Research on Russian Economic Conditions, *Memorandum* no. 3 [Birmingham, 1931], p. 13).

[21] Increasing the 1960 figure in the proportion (169·1/146·6) by which the official n.m.p. increased.

[22] My own dangerous interpolation.

[23] Holzman, op. cit., p. 288, unless otherwise stated. 1963: 12·9 md. new rubles.

[24] Prokopovich, op. cit. He seems reliable for post-war years. The original figures are for net national material product at factor cost, but including trade and passenger transport. I have added 5% for the omitted services. The series reaches 1928, and coincidence with Hoeffding is fairly exact.

[25] The input/output table of L. Ya. Berri, F. N. Klotsvog and S. S. Shatalin in *Metody Planirovania Mezhotraslevykh Proportsii* (Moscow, 1965), p. 97, puts the factor cost of exports at 53. Add 12% for invisibles as per p. 348 here. Their import figure of 91 is useless because it includes turn-over tax.

TABLE XV/2. PARTICIPATION RATES, USA
(md. current dollars)

	(i) National Income at Factor Cost[1]	(ii) Visible Trade[5] (half of turnover)	(iii) All Trade[5]	(iv) Participation Rate (%)	(v) Real Growth of (i)[6] (index, 1869/73 = 100)	(vi) Real Growth of (ii)[7] (index, 1869/73 = 100)	(vii) Population (mn.)
Average, 1854 and 1859	c. 2·75[1]	0·327	0·373	13·6	c. 68[1]	82	28·62
1869–73	5·73[3]	0·540	0·632	11·1	100	100	40·94
1897–1901	14·6[4]	1·10	1·27	8·5	389	371	74·80
1922–26	74·9[4]	4·24	5·31	7·1	916	736	114·1
1953–57	330[4]	15·10	21·15	6·4	2380	1535	165·3
1961–62	436	18·54	26·59	6·1	2782	1535	185·2

SOURCES: *Historical Statistics of the United States* (Bureau of the Census, Washington 1960; hereinafter 'HSUS'); current yearbooks.
[1] Value added by material output (HSUS p. 139) plus 11%. This addition is derived from comparison of this series, which is all we have for 1854–59, with 1869 and 1874, where it overlaps with source (3), below.
[2] My deflator here is 71, on 1869/73 = 100. Where the first figure is the price index and the second the weight, the components are: metal prices 75, 4%; building material prices 64, 7%; building wage rates c. 52/9%; consumer prices 73, 80%. Cf. HSUS pp. 90, 115, 127, 143.
[3] The net national product was 6·20 (HSUS p. 143). I have taken the same proportion to national income as in 1897–1901.
[4] HSUS p. 140.
[5] HSUS pp. 562–3.
[6] HSUS p. 139 col. F3, except for 1854 and 1859. 1869–1926, prices of 1929; from then on, prices of 1954. From 1960 includes Alaskan and Hawaiian rates of growth, but not the jump due to their inclusion.
[7] Deflating by the wholesale price index in HSUS pp. 115, 117.

orderly official cross-rate overvalues her trade with other STEs (Chapter VI, Section 13).[1] Although the required adjustment bulks large in foreign trade, it is unlikely to affect the national income, which takes account only of the trade balance.

Our object is, as always, to value exports at domestic factor cost or its nearest Communist equivalent. We saw in Chapter VI that the yuan-dollar rate is indeed about mid-way between the yuan-dollar p.p.ps. on Chinese and on United States weights; and that both the historical course of events and recent Chinese statements combine to condemn the yuan-ruble rate as the disorderly one. So in the absence of Chinese figures for the domestic factor cost of exports a first approximation is to accept the official yuan value of exports to non-STEs, but to write down that of exports to all[2] STEs by the factor:

$$\frac{\text{Yuan-ruble official rate (1 to 1)}}{\text{Yuan-dollar-ruble crossrate (1 to 1·52)}}[3]$$

This is done in Table XV/3. The result does not absolutely exclude a Preisausgleich, but it at last reduces it to manageable size, and makes the Preisausgleich probably the same for all trade.

In so far as its figures can be trusted—a qualification of over-whelming importance—the table shows that China was less autarkic in 1933, but that the normal post-revolutionary process was taking place in the 1950s, trade outstripping income. But there is little reason to have faith in the 6·5% figure for 1933. Every constituent item in it is unreliable, and it is also conceptually misleading, in that one third of the total concerns the then separate country of Manchuria. Had Japan not occupied Manchuria, China's national income might have been about the same (no war, but no forced development) while her trade would surely have been smaller. India on the other hand has always had a higher participation rate. The effect of independence cannot have been great by 1949–50,

[1] E.g. Li Choh-ming, The Economic Development of Communist China (Berkeley, Cal., 1957); Wu Yuan-li, An Economic Survey of Communist China (New York, 1956); Alexander Eckstein, The National Income of Communist China (New York, 1961); William W. Hollister, China's GNP (Cambridge, Mass., 1958)—all of whom wrote before Kang Chao's article in China Quarterly, July–September, 1964, originally made the point. In Wu Yuan-li et al., The Economic Potential of Communist China (Stanford, Cal., 1963), Volume I, Table 68 accepts the valuta yuan at face value; Tables 70 and 71 use neither the dollar-ruble cross-rate as here nor the valuta rate of one to one, but 1 yuan = 2 old rubles.
[2] Let us repeat: we do not actually know how China accounts for her trade with STEs other than the USSR.
[3] Where 1·52 = 4 (rubles = $1) ÷ 2·617 (Yuan = $1).

TABLE XV/3 PARTICIPATION RATES, CHINA, 1933, 1953, 1954, 1956
(mn. yuan, current prices)

	Visible Only				Invisible Turnover (very approx.)	True Total (half of adjusted turnover)	N.N.I.O. or National Income[b] (approx.)	Half of All Turnover as Per Cent of National Income (approx.)	Population, Mid-year (mn.)	Real National Income[e] (index)	Real Income per Head (index)
	Total Trade Turnover as Given[a]	Turnover With non-STEs[a]	Residual in Valuta Yuan	Residual at Domestic Factor Cost							
1933[d]	3061[e]	2960(?)		101(?)[f]	721[e]	1801	29,000	6·5%	500[g]	82	96
1953	8090	1980	6110	4020	262[h]	3131	81,000	3·9	583[i]	100	100
1954	8470	1697	6773	4450	267[h]	3207	86,000	3·8	621[i]	122	114
1956	10,870	2717	8153	5360	317[h]	4197	94,000	4·5			

NOTE: This table is confined to years which yield a moderate degree of certainty. According to imprecise reckonings by Professor Ronald Hsia (*China Mainland Review* [Hong Kong], September, 1965, p. 26), the peak year for the participation rate was 1955. It declined steadily until 1962 and then picked up again a little. The peak year for real income per head was probably 1959. For another estimate cf. Joint Economic Committee of Congress, *An Economic Profile of Mainland China*, February 1967, pp. 638-9. This also treats the exchange rates correctly.

a Table VI/5.

b Liu Ta-chung and Yeh Kung-chin, *The Economy of the Chinese Mainland* (RAND Corp., 1963), pp. 94-5, using where necessary the GNP deflators implicit in Hollister, op. cit., pp. 2, 12-13.

c As in sources (b). 1933-53: geometric mean of 1933 and 1952 weights. 1953-56: ditto, 1952 and 1957 weights.

d Including Manchuria and Mongolia, excluding Taiwan.

e League of Nations, *Balances of Payments* (Geneva, 1934). This makes arbitrary allowances for contraband and semi-arbitrary ones for invisibles. I have added in Manchuria's visible turnover (813), which excludes trade with China proper, from the League's *Statistical Yearbook*, 1934-35. China proper's invisibles (616) were 27% of her visibles; I have put Manchuria's at 13% of hers, or 105 (it was 285 including China—League of Nations, *Balances of Payments*, 1934). I have taken the movement of silver net (14), not gross (174); and excluded half China proper's debt service item as amortization (46 not 92). I assume that the League counted narcotics under contraband.

f China proper's turnover was 82, taking one half of her turnover with Korea and one third of her turnover with Germany. In view of Manchuria's proximity to North Korea and the USSR, I have put her turnover with these countries at one half of that of China proper, which was 38.

g Source (b), p. 254; very approximate.

h Derived as follows. Positive: emigrants' remittances—$36 mn. per annum (Wu et al., op. cit., p. 333; Szczepanik in ed. E. F. Szczepanik, *Economic and Social Problems of the Far East* [Hong Kong, 1962], p. 117); illegal export of narcotics—zero (Wu et al., op. cit., p. 333), say $50 million, quoting *Kung Shan Kuan Ch'a*, a paper connected with the Hong Kong bullion market and allegedly free of Formosan propaganda. Mah Feng-hwa, in ed. C. F. Remer, *Three Essays on the International Economics of Communist China* [Michigan, 1959], says $25 mn. But Mr. Dwight W. Perkins puts opium exports at zero, and believes the other figures are inventions; newly-mined gold and silver—$10 mn. (Hollister, op. cit., p. 52; Szczepanik, loc. cit., seems to have underestimated); tourism and official representatives—$5 mn. (Wu et al.'s guess); freight on exports—o (there is next to no Chinese merchant marine; overseas exports leave on foreign ships or via Hong Kong; there is no transit trade); port expenditures of foreign shipping—Y.20 mn. (1% of trade turnover with non-STEs, since in 1933 this item was 1% of all trade turnover); local expenditures of Soviet bases—Y.100 mn. (guessed at one third of the real value of the equivalent item in 1933). Negative: debt interest from Table XVII/4; foreign technicians' remittances $2 mn. (Szczepanik loc. cit.); tourism and official representatives $4 mn. (my guess).

i The official census figure.

j Official, from T'ung-chi Kung-tse (*Statistical Bulletin*), November, 1957.

so the rate for that year must reflect her colonial position. So it seems as if independence had no effect.[1]

So India's participation rate is slightly bigger, as befits a smaller country, and has probably been falling, owing to an incapacity to export. There can be no doubt that China's participation rate also fell in the early 'sixties, for the same reason. We see in Chapter XVII no reason to attribute this fall to Soviet economic warfare.

For the smaller countries I had hoped to be altogether more sophisticated; to evolve a West European formula, based on population and income per head, which tells us how much more East European STEs 'should' be trading than in the base year if their

TABLE XV/4. PARTICIPATION RATES, INDIA
(md. rupees)

Year	(i) Net National Income at Factor Cost	(ii) All Trade	(iii) Participation Rate (%)	(iv) Population, mid-period, mn.	(v) N.I. Real Growth Index	(vi) Visible Trade Real Growth Index
April, 1948– April, 1951	90·6	6·9	7·6	c. 353,000	76	80
1953–57	105·5	8·5	8·0	381,690	90	94·5
1957–59	123·1	10·1	8·2	413,334	98	107
1959–60	135·7	10·5	7·7	424,110	106	112
1961–62	151·0	10·9	7·2	442,466	114	117

SOURCES:
(i) U.N. Statistical Year Book, 1962.
(ii) I.M.F. Balance of Payments Year Book; Reserve Bank of India Bulletin.
(v) & (vi) U.N. Statistical Year Book, 1962; but note that the use of the cost of living as a deflator gives a mere 32·5%, not a 50%, rise over the period in the national income.
1948–51: (i) & (ii) from Dept. Economic Affairs, Final Report of National Income Committee, Feb. 1954, pp. 106, 110.
(vi) from U.N. Year Book of International Trade Statistics, 1963, p. 323, esp. footnote 4.

commercial policy and situation had changed in the same direction. But the Western figures proved recalcitrant, and yielded nothing that could seriously be called a correlation. It must be enough, then, to list the participation rates of certain small ACCs and STEs.[2]

The principal wartime changes affecting the performance of the STEs are as follows. Poland acquired a very large coalfield, and 35% of her exports were coal in 1956. She also lost 11 mn. people, or 32% of her population, and vastly increased her coast line and port facilities (cf. Chapter XIII, section 4). All these items argue for very great 'participation' in 1949–56, and less in 1962, when population had regained the pre-war level and coal bulked less large in a more sophisticated economy. In fact we do find a participation

[1] The inclusion of Pakistan's national income and foreign trade, and the exclusion of Indo-Pakistani trade, would make little difference to the results in 1949.
[2] Workings for b.o.p.s of STEs, and for the failed correlation, available from the author on request.

rate well above the 1937 rate in 1949 and 1956, but nothing prepares us for one double that level in 1962. In this latter year the contribution of coal to exports fell to 12%, while that of shipping remained about constant at 5%, as in 1937 and 1956. Yet the participation rate was double what it was even in the peak pre-depression year of 1929.

In Hungary nothing much happened to population or territory that would justify any great change, yet no post-war figure available to us is less than double that for 1938. It is unfortunately not possible to work out the participation rates for early post-war years, since no figures for trade volume have ever been published, whereby we

TABLE XV/5. EUROPEAN PARTICIPATION RATES (%)

	1929	1938	1947	1948	1949	1955	1956	1959	1963
Czechoslovakia .	34	23[1]	18	17	—	—	16	—	?19
Hungary . .	—	?10	—	—	—	?28	—	?25	?36[4]
Poland . .	14	?8	—	—	?10	—	12	—	27[5]
Rumania . .	—	—	—	—	—	?11	—	?11	?15
Belgium . .	—	45	—	38	—	44	—	—	49
Denmark . .	—	32	—	24	—	40	—	—	39
Finland . .	46	33	—	25[2]	—	28	—	—	30
Greece . .	—	29	—	—[3]	—	22	—	—	22
Netherlands .	44	34	—	36	—	53	—	—	55
Norway . .	—	—	—	54	—	55	—	—	56
Portugal . .	—	—	—	—	—	29	—	—	32
Sweden . .	27	21	—	23	—	28	—	—	31
Switzerland .	—	—	—	—	—	36	—	—	40

[1] 1937. [2] Excluding reparations. [3] Civil war. [4] 1964. [5] 1962.

might extrapolate from 1955.[1] But the whole account of Rakosi's foreign-trade policy in Chapter V indicates that the rate was little lower than in 1955. Thus already in 1953, when the official and semi-official attacks on Hungarian autarky began (see below), Hungary's participation rate was far greater than before the war! Seldom was there a sharper distinction between *ex ante* intention and *ex post* performance.

Czechoslovakia is the only country of the three with a participation rate lower than before the war. In view of her b.o.p. crisis in 1962 this may surprise us, but she still trades more than enough to be seriously affected by such a crisis. Her low participation rate is doubtless due to export failure. Agricultural exports have been hindered by collectivization, and the traditional exports of consumer

[1] On the method and the danger of such extrapolation cf. section 9 above. On Hungarian trade volume see Chapter V, section 10.

goods were simply abandoned. Machines were inefficiently produced, and could not make up the whole difference. Furthermore
by producing the whole range of machinery Czechoslovakia
rendered herself rather autarkic in this category, that bulks so large
in Soviet-type imports. All the same the course of the Czechoslovak participation rate *is* very peculiar, and is rendered much more
so by the tremendous fall in population: the annexed Ruthenes and
the expelled Germans amounted to some 23%.

Of Rumania we know too little to make any sensible statement.

The West European countries follow mostly a single pattern. A
high in 1929 precedes a low in 1938, which is hardly surpassed in
1948. Subsequently there is a gentle rise to about the 1929 position.
Finland, however, follows the Czechoslovak pattern, for reasons
equally mysterious.

II

Clearly the prime lesson of the preceding five tables is that
countries are individuals, ill adapted to generalization. A second
lesson is that Soviet-type autarky is in some cases a myth from the
start (Poland, Hungary) and in others rapidly on its way out (USSR
and Czechoslovakia, where trade is now outgrowing national
income).

What, then, remains of the charge of autarky? For USSR it is
largely true, not merely in *ex post* statistics but also in *ex ante*
expressions of intention. Thus, in the first, 1954, edition of the
official *Political Economy* textbook we read (p. 515):

Foreign trade under socialism is used for the fuller satisfaction of the growing
needs of society. It serves as an additional resource base for the development of
production and improvements in the supply of the population with the objects
of consumption.

This stands in a paragraph by itself, the first under the heading
'Foreign Trade'. It is followed by an institutional passage. It is
alleged that this was one of the most criticized passages in Eastern
Europe. Anyhow, in the 1955 edition (p. 539) the following lines
precede those quoted above:

The socialist economy demands a broad development of foreign trade—the
exchange of commodities with foreign countries, which permits us to exploit
the international division of labor. All outputs of socialist production entering
into foreign trade are, as we said, commodities. In the conditions of socialist

---

[1] Cf. Table VIII/5, and Chapter V, section 12.

society the development of foreign trade is subordinate to the basic economic law
and to the other economic laws of socialism; further it proceeds according to
plan, taking into account the influence of the law of value.

The standard Communist phrase, by the way, is 'economic independence', not 'autarky'. The difference is genuine.

But even USSR follows a common pattern with the rest. At
the moment of Communist take-over, or in the absence of other
Communist countries, STEs restricted their dependence on MEs.
Thereafter—from the moment that there was a 'socialist world
market' to play in—trade with other STEs grew faster than national
income. Nay more, once it had been reduced to a suitable proportion, trade with the rest of the world grew equally fast, keeping the
proportion constant. The initial phase is illustrated in Table XV/6:

TABLE XV/6. AUTARKY, ALL STEs
Export Indices 1952, on Base 1948 = 100
(current prices)

Exports of		Index 1952 on 1948	1948 Volume (mn. current $)	1952
USSR and Eastern Europe[b] to world	.	193	3170	6070
USSR to Eastern Europe	. . .	276	475	1310
Eastern Europe to Eastern Europe	. .	263	930	2440
USSR and Eastern Europe to world, excluding STEs	. . . . .	91	1615	1470
Asian STEs[a] to world	. . .	183	520	950
„ „ to USSR and Eastern Europe	.	1000	61	610
„ „ to world, excluding STEs	.	74	459	340
All STEs to each other	. . .	298	1466	4360
All STEs to world	. . . .	191	3670	7020
World to world	. . . .	140	57,500	80,400

SOURCE: United Nations, *Yearbook of International Trade Statistics*, 1961, Table B. A suitable
deflator for 1952 might be to deduct 5% from each index figure.
[a] North Vietnam, North Korea, Mongolia, China; excludes their inter-trade.
[b] Excludes Yugoslavia, and trade between East and West Germany.

The basic reason for this initial phase is clearly the ideology of
hatred of capitalism. To this we may add the character-structure
that goes with the ideology: simple suspicion, aggression and fear
govern the leaders' actions even when, as does happen, their régimes
are in no danger of attack. The Communist's world picture is like
his own personality: everybody is against everybody except if he is
under the command of a Communist state. Non-Communist
states are aggressive if strong enough, and in any case contact with
them is corrupting. Hence Stalin's astonishing decision not to trade
with the UDCs, his failure to use up the Swedish loan, etc.

In the 1930s, when Stalin introduced autarky, this fear of capitalism was justifiable. Though the particular alarums and excursions were often foolish, even a sane Soviet leader would have found it irresponsible not to reduce dependence on foreign countries. It was at this time that the policy, if not the slogan *we import in order to be autarkic*', was launched. The First FYP, as we saw in Chapter VIII, was attended by a sharp increase in imports of machinery. This was seen as a risk that the single proletarian state simply had to take, and it did indeed make possible a subsequent reduction to below the absolute levels of the NEP.

The same policy, and this time also explicitly the slogan, was used by Yugoslavia in her brief Stalinist period. The policy also governed the commerce of the other satellites at that time. If autarky vis-à-vis the West is meant, these small countries certainly succeeded in keeping down the volume of East-West trade while all other magnitudes rose. Since, too, they kept up machinery imports while other purchases sank (Table IX/1) we may again say that the early imports were the reason why trade did not grow later. However, there is here an interesting difference from the USSR. These small countries never suceeded in substantially reducing East-West trade in the way Stalin had, even though they proceeded rapidly to increase trade with the USSR and each other (Table XV/6). One reason may be that they were simply less determined about it. But another is surely that a small country cannot in fact 'import in order to be autarkic'. As it industrializes, its factories' need for this and that foreign raw material and machine grows, and rising consumer incomes increase the number of types of finished imports demanded. Nay more, very many installations of fixed capacity entail the importation of raw materials to feed them. Development that looks autarkic ('we shall produce our own steel') can have so large an import content, and be so inefficient, that it even raises imports. Thus Hungary's pride and sorrow under Rakosi, the Sztalinvaros[1] steel mill, needed to import both iron ore and coke! The raw materials are alleged to have cost more foreign exchange than the finished steel would have, since the mill itself was also very inefficient and used inordinate quantities of these materials. Such attempts to diversify Hungary may have been subjectively autarkic; objectively, they were the opposite. As Mikoyan told the Hungarians in June, 1953:

[1] Now called Dunapentele.

The matter of economic planning shows a certain adventurist spirit, particularly the excessive development of your own iron smelting industry. Hungary has no iron ore, nor coke. All this must be imported. No one in Hungary has yet figured out exactly the price of a ton of iron ore and steel in Hungary. Hungary is building foundries for which no one has yet promised to supply the ore.[1]

Thus for a small country development entails more imports and probably a worse balance. But a large country blessed with a good mineral base exploits domestic minerals, and its large industrial labor force can increase the variety of manufactured consumer goods *pari passu* with demand. Food shortages, of course, are as likely to arise in the one as in the other case, and do not affect the comparison.

12

For the rest, as we have seen, hyperpoly is the main danger. Yet previous authors have urged in addition good practical arguments for autarky derived from the STE's economic model itself. No doubt we should not have thought of them (I have played this game as enthusiastically as any) had we not supposed that STEs were in principle and fact very autarkic. However, the reasons are very convincing, and must be seen as in fact operating to restrict trade; so the Communist will to expand trade is all the more impressive for the obstacles it must overcome. Foreign trade, then, it is commonly said, is difficult to fit into a command economy, since where we are not sovereign we cannot command. If we are dealing with MEs, we have no guarantee of fulfilling our basic export plan: to hit the global foreign currency target. Unless our trading partners are very fully employed we shall always be able to fulfill the basic import plan—to procure the exact physical quantities required—but perhaps at excessive cost, which means a change in next year's export plan. If we are dealing with other STEs, we can be sure of selling whatever it is planned that they shall buy. But we cannot be sure of the physical imports, since planner's tension renders all deliveries uncertain. Better, then, thinks the Soviet-type planner, rely on your own enterprises, which you really can command. Besides which, the mere process of international negotiation is most exhausting, and must use up scarce administrative talent to an extent unknown in MEs. And again, each negotiation is, as we have seen, a diplomatic act, the failure of which has political consequences. At a personal level, too, Communist countries are deeply

[1] *Imre Nagy on Communism* (New York, 1957), p. 106.

suspicious of each other (section 14 below); and all the old national-isms simmer beneath the surface, unaired and uncured.

For capital autarky, reasons have already been given in Chapter XIV. For the refusal to let people move around—or to move them around—see Chapter XIII.

Convincing as all this may seem, trade in fact grows quickly. Indeed, even trade with MEs grows quickly once it has been reduced to the desired proportion. We can, then, discern a consistent policy: trade is in general good, but dependence on capitalist countries is bad. However simple, this explains practically everything: the reduction of trade with MEs in 1932 in the USSR; the similar reduction at the moment of takeover, around 1948, in East Europe, in 1950 in China, in 1959 in Cuba; the stagnation of Soviet trade until 1940[1]—for there were no other STEs to trade with; the instant expansion of inter-STE trade in every case at the moment of takeover.

Between STEs, the ideology of proletarian brotherhood is strongly and genuinely felt. Equally important is the ideological commitment to equal development, which as we saw in Chapter XII, section 18, might not, but probably does in fact, imply an increase in trade. Nor is the ultimate goal of a single world state without influence (Chapter I). These things have evidently out-weighed the factors listed above, that diminish trade.

On balance, then, *it is simply not true that STEs are autarkic by ordinary human standards.* Even though they trade irrationally little with MEs, they make such great efforts to trade between themselves that all in all they do their 'duty' by our subject very well. Three countries in particular—Hungary, Poland and the USSR—are considerably less autarkic than they were just before the war. The others will reach this Utopia, if Utopia it be, before very long. Poland especially is doing its best, by the use of an incorrect theory.

The Communists' own self-criticism has contributed to the uni-versal contrary impression. In particular, since the middle 1950s the Hungarians have criticized the 'autarky' of STEs.[2] What, however, on examination they mean is the planners' insistence on setting up *capacity* in every branch of industry, especially of heavy industry. But capacity does not imply a domestic raw material

---

[1] With the exceptions mentioned in Chapter VIII, section 15.

[2] Imre Nagy, in *For a Lasting Peace, For a People's Democracy* (Bucharest), July 17, 1953; Tibor Liska and Antal Máriás in *Közgazdasagi Szemle*, 1/1954. English extracts of the last are in United Nations' Economic Commission for Europe, *Economic Survey of Europe in 1954* (Geneva, 1955).

supply, as we saw above, and may actually increase one's net imports.

Similarly my own previous interpretation must be controverted:

> Notoriously planning leads to autarky, but Communists are exceedingly sensitive to the charge; for it not only reflects upon the excellence of their economic system but also upon their professions of peace and friendship. Yet the things said to us by those in charge of international trade could only have been said by men with a fundamentally autarkic bias: 'The fundamental determinant is our need for imports. We plan imports and then plan to export enough to pay for them.' This, from a departmental head of the [planning commission], was also referred to by Professor Lange as the 'first basic principle of socialist international trade'. It follows that there is no *will to export*, no desire to undersell the foreigner; yet without this the international division of labour will never be fully exploited.[1]

Suppose there is a 'will to import'? In that case, as we have already seen, the Polish doctrine that we should export just enough to cover imports is the reverse of autarkic.

13

There are styles of autarky that differ according to the economic model. Schematically, ACCs like exports, STEs like imports, UDCs are uncertain. An autarkic ACC fears imports, because these directly hit vocal vested interests: land, labor, and capital in the import-competing sector. Individual exporters cannot show themselves directly harmed by tariffs; so the protectionists tend to win. Then, too, as we saw in Chapter III, the foreign-trade multiplier exaggerates the impact of more imports into an all-round deflation. But exports are a direct source of personal income, and sought as such by individual enterprises. The STE on the contrary fears exports. Planner's tension makes it exceedingly difficult to do without goods at home, and there is reluctance at all levels to see anything leave the country. Imports are disagreeable, but much less so. They relieve planner's tension and raise consumption. They even, quite usually, break input-output bottlenecks of the kind discussed in Chapter IV. They are often of greater economic sophistication than can be produced at home, and thus are 'developmental'. They threaten no deflation, only the inevitable loss of foreign exchange.

The import-competitor, perpetually badgered to produce more himself, is never threatened by actual surplus capacity as a result of imports. The planners, struggling against permanent b.o.p. trouble, never permit such foolish expenditure of foreign exchange.

[1] In *Oxford Economic Papers*, June, 1957.

I once had the opportunity to ask a very plain-speaking and intelligent man in charge of the current trade plan if he ever had angry telephone calls from the managers of import-competing enterprises. The question had to be repeated to him three times, with different wording and much explanation, before he got it at all. He then said that such a thing was wholly beyond his experience. But where plant extensions are concerned there are pressures from managers, it seems; and of course when the CMEA tries to specialize a whole industry out of existence we see protectionism on the highest level, as virulent as any among MEs. The Galati steel works affair (Chapter XII) was nothing but protectionism, and there was much of it in the original Tito-Stalin quarrel. Moreover, it is fair to read protectionism, as known in the West, into the statements of Georgian politicians about tea. This traditional crop, they say, should be expanded to satisfy the whole Soviet demand; i.e., they resent tea imports.

The UDC is in an intermediate situation. For lack of imports it perpetually suffers from bottlenecks, just like an STE. It is also even more dependent on them for its further development. But it does suffer from all the ordinary multiplier effects, and vested-interest pressures, that plague an ACC. Moreover, the 'infant industry' argument is overwhelmingly important. Desperate for growth, the government might well hesitate between increasing and diminishing imports were it not for its chronic shortage of foreign exchange.

These two styles of autarky have each their historical precedent. In the Middle Ages and the sixteenth century, men's attitude to foreign trade was governed by what Eli Heckscher[1] called the 'policy of provision'. Men feared exports because of the extreme shortage of goods at home. Moreover, foreign trade was so uncertain that a ship, leaving the country full of exports, might come back with a valueless cargo after a very unfavorable barter deal, or simply sink. The STE has some of the very same reasons for its similar attitude.

The policy of provision yielded to Mercantilism, in which autarky consisted in a fear of imports, a love of exports and a passion for gold. This attitude does not merely resemble, it stands in direct continuity with, the protectionism[2] of the modern ACC. It was

---

[1] *Mercantilism*, trans. Mendel Shapiro (London, 1955); cf. Chapter XVI here. The reference in the Middle Ages was, of course, to staple foodstuffs and to raw materials. The 'policy of provision' continues to operate in famine time everywhere to this day.

[2] Note this significant word. We have so long forgotten the sixteenth century, and are so ignorant of STEs, that we use 'protectionism'—which means the fear of imports—as a synonym for autarky.

merely driven out of theoretical economics in the Anglo-Saxon world in the nineteenth century. Even in that world it flourished, of course, on a practical level. So strong is the tendency of the nation-state to autarky that seemingly one reason or another is always found for it.

14

An additional reason for Communist autarky is little appreciated in the West: the steady pressure of *popular* discontent at exports. We have seen that it is in the nature of the STE model that planners and managers should prefer imports to exports; to this is added an almost pathological popular distrust of these same planners and managers, who are always assumed to be bartering away their country's substance, and especially to other STEs and UDCs. Many jokes and sayings testify to this attitude:

'Why do all Polish cows face West?—because they graze in Poland and are milked in the USSR.'—Many forms of this joke circulate in all countries.
'The Russians take our coal, the Chinese have got our steel, and the East Germans are eating up our butter.'—Said to the writer by a chance acquaintance during the Poznań riots, June, 1956.
Many still cherish the idea of an autarkic Poland and criticize the government for an allegedly exaggerated forcing of international trade, especially with socialist countries. These people demand the export only of surpluses. But what have we in surplus? We must also undertake a thorough campaign of enlightenment on the activity of Comecon, which is so valuable for us and the other member states, also on our comprehensive economic and technical contacts with the underdeveloped countries of Asia, Africa, and Latin America; for there are also prejudices and doubts about that. From time to time, too, there still crops up some of the old mistrust against the USSR, the DDR and their peaceful and democratic intentions, also Czechoslovakia.[1]

In 1962–63 the Czechoslavak press was full to overflowing with 'enlightenment' of the sort implied by the last quotation. This was the period of the bad winter, the b.o.p. crisis, and the cutback of planned growth to almost zero (Chapter V). Ordinary people evidently believed the most damaging rumors about the CMEA and aid to UDCs. One even penetrated to Czech émigré circles in Boston and New York, where it was believed that the CMEA had moved a shoe factory (of all things!) to Hungary, leaving the workers unemployed.

Imports, on the other hand, whatever the official pressure for

---

[1] *Dziennik Ludowy,* July 26, 1963; shortened text here from *Hinter dem Eisernen Vorhang* (Munich), September, 1963, p. 35.

autarky, are welcomed by the population with equally absurd exaggeration. In particular, imports from the West form the object of a sort of 'Cargo Cult'.[1] Thus when I attended the International Economic Conference in Moscow in 1952 people were saying: 'Ah, now there will be black nylons.'

It follows, of course, that there must be exports to the West. The population seems to understand well enough the distinction between hard and soft currency. It is for them personally, as tourists, the distinction between freedom and captivity. Since they will do anything for dollars, they show understanding for the state's similar proclivities. This attitude seems to be most strongly developed in Poland. The columnist K. T. Toeplitz describes it well:[2]

Not such a long time ago, there existed in our ideological vocabulary an offensive term, the 'cult of the dollar'. This epithet covered, I believe, two emotions. The first was condemnation of an attitude in which money was held above all else, above human, ideological, cultural values; the second, condemnation of the idolization of foreign currency based on a capitalist, American economic system.

I do not maintain that the mistaken means of conducting the campaign for foreign currency inevitably lead to a 'cult of the dollar' in its former meaning. Our campaign is aimed at gaining the currency for our economy and for our common good, so its character is social, not egoistic. I do fear, however, that its effect is sometimes a 'cult of the dollar' in the latter sense, i.e., a belief that the dollar is something better, something infinitely more precious than our zloty. Let us not be misled into thinking that it is just a question of common calculation of foreign exchange rates. It is enough to note the admiration for the 'green stuff' one hears in casual conversations, to realize that the thing is far more important and far-reaching, including the sphere of civic education, including the scale of values which each one of us carries within himself and which constitutes the basis of our world philosophy.

Let us glance at a few current examples. Some time ago, the press informed us that we have caught and exported 'for precious currency' a certain number of pigeons from Warsaw's Old Town. In itself, the thing is not particularly startling. There are enough pigeons in the Old Town, and their activities are as decorative as they are destructive, if we consider the chemical properties of their droppings and the zeal with which they redecorate the old frescoes. If someone has decided to buy these pigeons and pay for them in dollars—why not sell? But there is no cause for trumpeting the fact about, turning it into a national holiday and presenting it as a success of our socialist economy. . . .

I switch on my TV set. A discussion among high school graduates is in progress. A young boy declares that he is ideologically engaged, that he is ready to take up any work for the social good. He has even picked out his work, as a result of which, he thinks, he might do justice to the ideological fire burning in his bosom—he wants to work in foreign trade and gain 'precious currency' for his

---

[1] The reference is to the curious religion of the Solomon Islanders, which centers upon the apocalyptic hope that a ship full of free goods will one day arrive.

[2] In *Kultura*, March 26, 1967. I quote Radio Free Europe's version.

country. I watch him in amazement. Perhaps this is simply a wise guy, who has found an ideological foundation for the attractive vision of an apartment in Valparaiso or Brussels, for the use of small conveniences there which make life easier than in Sieradz or Kutno and are at the same time surrounded by an aura of service to the country? But perhaps, on the other hand, he is the victim of too eager listening to radio and TV, and press readership, who has been persuaded by the above media that anything in our life which cannot be translated into dollars is sham? . . .

Note the importance of the fact that foreign trade officials go abroad: such jobs are much coveted.

So the popular attitude takes after the 'principle of provision' where UDCs and other STEs are concerned, and the 'Cargo Cult' where ACCs are concerned. But it has another, more historical and less hysterical, element: the subject masses agree with their rulers that heavy industry must be built up at home. The 'techno-logical snobbery' of Chapter VIII unites the people and the Com-munists. Eastern Europe's pre-war stagnation and dependence are not forgotten—or in the Soviet case Count Witte's efforts are simultaneously imitated and most unfairly traduced. Thus when I questioned a highly intelligent Polish exile on the general autarky alleged against his country's government, he automatically confused this with its stress on heavy industry, and launched into a patriotic defense of the latter. This is not the vested-interest protectionism of the British nineteenth century, which has colored our textbooks. It is List's developmental protectionism, a far different and more patriotic affair.

It is naturally not implied that every citizen of an STE shares these attitudes, or that they are coherent, or wise. I only insist upon them as part of the sociological background, without which we cannot explain the economic facts.

CHAPTER XVI

THE ECONOMIC THEORY OF ECONOMIC WAR AND IMPERIALISM

Who would bribe if he could bully?
—Sir Lewis Namier
'The political economy of war' might well be regarded as a contradiction in terms.
—Edwin Cannan, *An Economist's Protest* (London, 1927), p. 49.

1   The neglect of economic warfare by economists.
2   The main categories of economic warfare.
3   The bottleneck effect.
4   Its disuse under Mercantilism.
5   Nineteenth century economic pacificism.
6   Twentieth century total warfare includes economics.
7   The abuse of convertibility.
8   The assault on the enemy's terms of trade.
9   All goods and services may be strategic, or not, according to circumstances—
10   including capital.
11   But technological transfer is always strategic.
12   The principle of relative gain.
13   It is quite irrelevant whether or not we are waging military war.
14   Economic war is only for big, rich countries.
15   More rational warfare means less warfare.
16   Neutrals in general.
17   Neutrals and capital.
18   Threatening neutrals: boycotts, blockades and re-export bans.
19   Waging warfare on neutral territory.
20   Bribing neutrals.
21   Free trade as a war preparation.
22   Free trade in opponents and neutrals.
23   The STE's capabilities for economic warfare.
24   Imperialism as the economic means to domination.
25   Portfolio and direct investment.
26   Bribery.

27 Luring into bankruptcy.
28 Imperialism as economic exploitation: tribute.
29 Tribute, the transfer problem and the STE.
30 Tribute and the banking system.
31 Tribute, the banking system and the STE.
32 STEs and MEs as tribute-takers.
33 Reparations from current production.
34 Mixed companies.
35 Other forms of Soviet-type exploitation.

I

By what economic means can one country either harm or gain political domination over another? Having got such domination, what economic benefits can it draw? These questions delimit the neglected, because purely economic, aspects of economic warfare and imperialism. This neglect arose, not from the absence of the two phenomena before Communism—very far from it indeed—but from the narrowing and unscientific tradition of 'purity' among economists; who suppose that they should only ask questions to which economics alone has the answer. This habit leads to both timidity and rashness: to withdrawal from many areas where economics is a necessary partner, and to exclusive claims on other areas where economics has not in fact the sole key. There is a fair amount of descriptive literature in this field, but the bite of theory has been very feeble.[1]

In featuring these subjects so widely, then, I have no wish at all to imply that they are specially necessary in a book about Communism. If there is any implication it is that previous studies of international economics have been too timid. My aim is not by any means to show the whole of the relation between international politics and economics, but to hold up the flickering candle of economic theory to some of the dark patches. This chapter sets up the rudiments of a general theory and fits the STE into it. The next chapter describes factually certain episodes of Communist economic warfare. As to the neighboring subject of economic imperialism,

---

[1] Apart from the works directly referred to in other footnotes, I should mention W. B. Medlicott, *The Economic Blockade* (London, 1952)—a legal and descriptive work on the Ministry of Economic Warfare, 1939–41; Edmund Silberner, *The Problem of War in Nineteenth-Century Economic Thought* (Princeton, N.J., 1946)—an excellent work of *Dogmengeschichte* in the nineteenth century [this author has also written *La Guerre dans la Pensée Économique du XVIe au XVIIIe Siècle* (Paris, 1939)]. For the same in the twentieth century, see Walter M. Stern, 'Wehrwirtschaft', *Economic History Review*, December, 1960.

it has been often enough empirically described, so such little factual material as is neccessary is supplied in this chapter as it becomes relevant.

2

We begin, then, with economic warfare, including cold warfare. We treat it first as a bilateral affair, concerning only the two belligerents, hot or cold.

We classify the weapons of economic warfare as follows:

(i) Exploiting the bottleneck effect of Chapter V: an embargo is laid on an export of ours that the enemy needs in order to be able to produce;

(ii) What might be called geo-economic warfare: the closing of transit facilities to an enemy who happens to be unfavorably placed by geography (e.g., Egypt will not allow Israel to use the Suez Canal);

(iii) Worsening the enemy's terms of trade by monopoly of what he wants to buy, or monopsony of what he wants to sell;

(iv) Causing him unemployment by dumping in his country, import prohibitions in ours;

(v) Upsetting his currency by speculation;

(vi) Worsening his terms of trade by dumping in his foreign markets, or pre-empting what he wants to buy there;

(vii) Causing him an actual bottleneck by such pre-emption.

There are innumerable other weapons, which however are so bound to particular circumstances that they can hardly be discussed in any general manner. We therefore omit them all except in so far as they have historically been used by Communist countries (Chapter XVII).

3

In Chapter V we introduced the bottleneck effect, contrasted it with the multiplier, and examined their interactions. Now, the obvious application of the bottleneck effect is to economic warfare. It is natural, when restraint is imposed on imports by the planner anxious to do his country good, or even by the blind but neutral market, that bottleneck materials should be the last to suffer. So the effect rarely takes virulent form in peacetime. But when the planner is a hostile foreigner anxious to do as much harm as he can he naturally starts on bottleneck materials first of all. The 'geo-economic' exploitation of the enemy's vulnerable transit points is merely a special case of the bottleneck effect. For, strictly construed, the use by *A* of a port or canal in the territory of *B* is an invisible import by *A*. If *A* can find no substitute the lack of the facility becomes a bottleneck, just as if, say, oil had been cut off.

The bottleneck effect is the main weapon of twentieth century economic warfare, and so it also was in the seventeenth and earlier centuries. In those pre-Mercantilist times what Eli Heckscher[1] called the 'policy of provision' ruled. Since there was scarcely any internationally valid money, and barter was the rule, and since both goods and gold were perennially short in every country, all export should be forbidden in any crisis. The principle of provision governed not only the peacetime regulation of the corn trade—a very sensible thing, with famine just round the corner—but also the wartime regulation of trade with the enemy. That is, it was applied to him in reverse: the quantity of goods and gold in his country was diminished by a prohibition of all export to him. If he was fool enough to export to us, it seems, that was his business.[2]

4

But curiously enough in the eighteenth century, when economic warfare was the sport of kings and people wrote and thought about it more than today, the bottleneck effect was not the main thing. The eighteenth century and its doctrine, Mercantilism, were a very Keynesian century and doctrine.[3] Indeed, we may say of the Mercantilists that the discovery that money could replace barter in international trade went to their heads. They were the greatest monetary economists of all time. So it was through gold flows and the foreign-trade multiplier that the hostile foreigner mainly sought to do damage. I.e., he sought to deprive the enemy of gold by running a favorable balance. The principle of provision, so to speak, was confined only to gold, and other exports were now encouraged as a means of acquiring it. The logic of this was that the gold loss in turn made it impossible for the enemy to import war materials,

---

[1] *Mercantilism*, trans. Mendel Shapiro (London, 1955), III, 1, 3.
[2] Carl Rothe, *Schriftenreihe der deutschen Wirtschaftzeitung*, Heft 6, 'Wirtschaftskrieg' (Berlin, 1938); Heckscher, op. cit., II, 98; Georg von Below, *Mittelalterliche Stadtwirtschaft und Gegenwärtige Kriegswirtschaft* (Tübingen, 1917), pp. 26–31, 35–6, 40.
[3] As the master recognized; see J. M. Keynes, *General Theory of Employment, Interest, and Money* (London, 1936), Chapter 23. The eighteenth century is here deemed to include Napoleon and Pitt.

shook credit in his paper currency (if any), and caused unemployment, hence civil discontent.

Thus arises the too little regarded paradox, that in the eighteenth century belligerents tried desperately to sell things to each other, and the more the enemy imported the better, whereas in the twentieth such sales are forbidden, and the less the enemy imports the better. The eighteenth century attitude is more paradoxical but also more logical, for in those times:

(a) the state found the foreign-trade multiplier exceedingly difficult to offset by internal reflation;

(b) nor could it easily itself re-employ those put out of work, or even keep them alive. E.g., if Napoleon prevented British textile exports Pitt could not mobilize the population of Lancashire into the army, and the Old Poor Law could ill afford to feed them;

(c) if the action of the foreign-trade multiplier was mainly upon prices, not employment, there was no mechanism for price supports. E.g., if Pitt prevented French grain exports the peasants rioted and Napoleon was faced with a new Vendée;

(d) the population was unused to paper currency, and the mere thought of it lowered morale;

(e) anyhow the population was right: the banks and government were not to be trusted; bank closures and galloping inflations did, in fact, occur.

Bottlenecks, however, were curiously little exploited within this framework: there were few strategic export prohibitions alongside the general drive to export to the enemy. Thus, most strikingly, Napoleon never exploited a bad British harvest to prevent the export of European—or at any rate of French—corn; he was so obsessed with the French and British bs.o.p. that even the prospect of actual famine in Britain did not divert him from pure Mercantilism.[1] The only common cases of export prohibitions were, first and obviously, precious metals—*this* prohibition was of course the quintessence of the system as it stood; and, secondly, artisans and machinery. This latter prohibition had the same logic then as now: it was a denial to the enemy of the general prospects of

---

[1] J. Holland Rose, *Napoleonic Studies* (London, 1904), Chapters 7, 8. Eli Heckscher, *The Continental System* (Oxford, U.K., 1922), pp. 348–9, however, mentions a British grain blockade which nearly brought Norway to starvation. Tsar Paul also imposed a grain blockade of Britain in 1800, but no-one followed his example (Mancur Olson, *The Economics of the Wartime Shortage* [Durham, N.C., 1963], pp. 51–4). It has, furthermore, been argued in defense of Napoleon that he was in competition with other grain exporters outside, or partly outside, his control; so he might as well have taken the money; see *ibid.*, pp. 65–6.

development and growth, an attempt to avoid the transfer of technology described in Chapter XIII. Indeed, it was in its way an attempt to reduce the degree of the enemy's autarky and to keep up one's own exports.

5

Thus eighteenth century economic warfare was on the whole admirably adapted to the then structure of an economy, to wit a free market with no real central bank. Before we turn to the comparatively poor adaptation of the twentieth century we must spare a superior smile and a nostalgic tear for the intervening period, which hoped to outlaw economic war without touching military war. We inherit many of our contemporary misunderstandings from this attempt.

The nineteenth century, culminating in the Hague Conference of 1907, saw war as an affair of armies and governments, which would touch the citizen and his property as little as possible. 'Contraband' was restricted to imports, and at that to actual arms. This was an evident absurdity, since one import is a substitute for another, and exports are the means whereby they are earned. The notion was a lawyer's, not an economist's, concept. Contemporary economists, however, mostly followed Cannan, whose *ohne mich* stands at our chapter heading.

Property rights above all were protected by the international lawyers into whose hands economic war had fallen. The sanctity of private international contract was to be maintained: e.g., trade debts, insurance policies, etc., were to remain valid between the citizens of belligerents. In certain notable instances, e.g., the Russian state debt during the Crimean War, international contracts remained valid even when one party was the belligerent state itself.

I am extremely far from denying the idealism of the nineteenth century's hostility to economic war; or from suggesting that a rigorous application of these doctrines would not in practice mitigate a few of the minor horrors of war. Indeed, the attack on war has to begin somewhere, and perhaps then it was most tactically advantageous to begin it here. But it is permissible to wonder at the economic naïveté of this approach, and to point out its utter insufficiency in the succeeding century of socialism and planning. This whole train of thought rested on a false view of humanity: that states and armies are mere epiphenomena, while enterprises and people and property, united by capitalism, the gold standard, and free trade into one world system, are the *pays réel*.[1]

6

Events have re-educated the twentieth century, but only in part. Our attempts to outlaw war are primarily political, and supranational rather than international. But we still like to practice the art, where nuclear weapons are excluded. On the other hand, we have developed a quite new total, emotional refusal to trade with the enemy, which reflects our surrender before the fact that war is total, and cannot exclude economic affairs. Yet to define trade with the enemy as a crime, be he ME or STE, is only moderately well adapted to the purpose of harming him. There remain arguments in favor of such trade,[2] and economists have served both peace and their countries' interests ill in not putting them forward (cf. Chapter XVII, section 1).

7

In a cold war, for instance, the eighteenth century ploys can still be used effectively against an ME devoted to free trade and sound money. It is unlikely that one could effect a sudden flood of sales in an enemy country, for anti-dumping laws are now nearly universal and very effective. But one can suddenly stop buying its goods, thereby causing the same unemployment and drain of gold. Nay more, the modern international banking system adds a refinement, entirely in the old tradition, which would have delighted the Mercantilists of the first age: the exploitation of the foreign bank balance. If A has a large balance in B, and B's monetary institutions are basically those of the eighteenth or nineteenth centuries—gold standard, convertibility, free trade in money—an excellent gambit for A is to convert this large sum. Later in the war it is quite possible that B will have pulled itself together and will simply suspend convertibility, at least of A's funds. But as a surprise initial move, or as a move at any time in a cold war, the 'abuse of convertibility' is unrivaled.

This weapon played no part in the Napoleonic or previous wars, since foreign bank balances were extremely small. But the mere

---

[1] Cf. Herbert Luethy in *Encounter*, March 1965.

[2] In governing circles, they made themselves heard briefly in the House of Commons on January 26, 1916 [speech of Sir Henry Dalziel; cf. Paul Wiel, *Krieg und Wirtschaft* (Berlin, 1938), p. 26].

attempt to push exports was not so very different. Thus, having no bank balance to withdraw, Napoleon 'abused convertibility' by simply selling goods. The decline of the paper pound led to the Bullion Committee (1811), who urged upon the government such measures to restore the gold value of the pound as must have made it impossible to carry on the war. The Bullion Committee's report was the direct result of Napoleon's Mercantilism. He could not have foreseen that Parliament would reject the report, thus permitting wartime inflation to continue and victory to be won.

The abuse of convertibility has often played a role in internal politics. Thus, Francis Place used it against the Duke of Wellington in 1831-32: 'To Stop the Duke Go For Gold.' His notion was that the population could withdraw their deposits from all banks, and that the chaos would bring down the Prime Minister. It did. The foreign bank balance begins to play a big role in the time of Bagehot, who feared that Germany might wield the weapon unintentionally by withdrawing her London balances in gold in order to set herself up on the gold standard.[1]

This did not happen, but his fears were justified in the long run. For the heyday of the abuse of convertibility was of course the period when there was a great deal of convertibility: from about 1873 (when Germany went on to gold) to 1914. To go off gold was then thought of as an unmitigated disaster, although no-one was clear why (the real disaster of course would be not to go off gold in time, and so face bank closures). Furthermore, by a curious mixture of Social Darwinism with sound money, a nation was judged not only by the strength of its currency but also by the rate at which its government could borrow abroad. This was held to be an index not merely of its diplomatic strength but of its citizens' prosperity.[2]

This weapon therefore depends very greatly—much more than the others—on economic belief as opposed to economic fact. It was exceedingly powerful in 1911, changing the German government's attitude over Agadir.[3] On this occasion the weapon *may* have been used in all its purity: French banks may have deliberately withdrawn funds from Germany, causing a financial panic in that country that made German businessmen bring successful pressure on their government for peace. But of course had the funds simply fled, without

---

[1] Walter Bagehot, *Lombard Street* (London, 1873), Chapter XII.
[2] Even Norman Angell contrived to believe this: [*The Great Illusion* (London, 1914), expanded edition]. Hence the disastrous doctrine that war was economically impossible; cf. Chapter XVIII, section 3; Paul Einzig, *Economic Warfare* (London, 1940), pp. 10-13.
[3] Louis Baudin, *Free Trade and Peace* (Paris, 1939), p. 41. Chapter XVIII here, section 3.

the instigation of the French government, the result would have been the same.

In 1963 it was feared that General de Gaulle might use this ploy against the United States. There is no recorded case of its use by an STE, though there is no reason why such a country should not use it.

As an economic war heats up, however, these things are no longer possible. The free market yields to the regulated market, and there is in these matters as in few others a strong resemblance between the latter and the STE. We can obviously no longer cash our balances in enemy banks and take them away in gold. All that remains of the speculative weapon is to forge and circulate enemy banknotes—a fairly frequent measure in wartime;[1] and to circulate by radio rumors of devaluation, note recall, bank stops, and the like. On the whole these things have nuisance value only. One has either to exploit the bottleneck effect, or to resort to the third main kind of economic warfare, encompassed by the third and sixth items of section 2: turn the enemy's terms of trade against him.

8

To do this we must of course raise prices and cut sales wherever we are monopolists of his imports, and lower prices and cut purchases wherever we are monopsonists of his exports. That in itself is banal, although it will become slightly less banal when, later, we remove the assumption of bilateralism, or no neutrals. The interesting point at present is to see how these measures compare with the two categories previously discussed, the 'Mercantilist' and the 'bottleneck'.

(i) On the export side, 'Mercantilist' measures, aimed at the enemy's balance, incidentally improve his terms of trade by dumping on his territory, and this improvement must be reckoned as an offset to the harm done. On the other hand to worsen the enemy's terms of trade we must restrict exports. Funnily enough this will, if the elasticities are right, also hurt his balance—a possibility not allowed for by Mercantilism. It follows that dumping is ill advised where the enemy's elasticity of demand is low: his terms of trade will improve very rapidly, and even his balance may improve. And export restriction is ill advised where the enemy's elasticity of demand is

---

[1] Cf. Yuan-li Wu, *Economic Warfare* (New York, 1952), pp. 141–4. This weapon was also used by Stalin purely for b.o.p. reasons, and with no reference to economic war, in 1928–32 (Chapter V, section 9).

high: his terms of trade will not change much, his balance will improve, and we shall be left with unemployment.

(ii) On the import side 'Mercantilist' warfare and the assault on the terms of trade are identical. In both, imports are restricted, and the enemy suffers both in the balance and in the terms of trade.

(iii) Turning to the bottleneck, on the export side to inflict one on the enemy is nearly the same as to worsen his terms of trade. Clearly, we can only create a bottleneck in a thing for which the enemy has inelastic demand, i.e., where his terms of trade are vulnerable. The results of the latter shade off into those of a bottleneck, according to how far it is carried: we proceed gradually from raising the enemy's costs and maybe increasing his volume of employment (albeit at low productivity), through still further rises in costs that reduce his output sharply, to the final infinite rise in costs which makes it impossible for him to produce at all.

(iv) As to imports, the converse of imposing a bottleneck on the enemy is evading the one he imposes on us. In buying up by devious channels, or perhaps in a rush before hostilities really begin, the thing he wishes to deny us, we of course improve his terms and his balance of trade. But this may be worth our while.

9

Here, then, are our various weapons, so far as it is worth while to classify them. Before we begin to make allowances for neutrals there are a few further theoretical points to make. First, everything we have said applies to civilian products, too. For what, after all, *is* a 'strategic export'? Clearly not only an armament—a staple foodstuff is an equally good case. When Canada and Australia sold wheat to China during the Indian border war of 1962, they were as surely taking sides as if they had sold arms. They, and possibly China too, entered this transaction like somnambulists. The whole Western world, indeed also the Soviet bloc, reacted with a culpable lack of interest and awareness. The reason seems to be intellectual error: since Mercantilism went out of fashion no one knows the meaning of the words 'strategic export' any more.

Indeed, all 'bottleneck' products are 'strategic', even if superficially unimportant. For it is almost certainly to belligerent A's advantage to be able to reduce B's civilian production below the level desired. Such a reduction may force a diversion of resources from the war effort, and must lower civilian morale. It will probably also lower the supply of labor to the war effort.[1] The notion of international lawyers, that some goods are contraband, some 'relative contraband', and some not contraband at all, makes no economic sense except in the very short run.

Going still further, an armament might not be a 'strategic good'. Thus an oil-poor country A with a large engineering sector might fool an enemy B into swapping oil for rifles. But A would be able to replace even modern rifles with equally good ones, whereas without a stock of oil it could not go to war at all. If oil is not elsewhere available, and B will only take rifles, A gains.

10

Capital is a special case. It is universally believed to be a strategic good, or should we say strategic factor of production. But as we saw in Chapter XIV it has to be repaid, and must be considered separately from the transfer of technology (below). This granted, it becomes plain that even capital might not be necessarily strategic. If we lend to our enemy when he has had a bad harvest we indeed do him more good than the interest does us; for he borrows when his need is great and the means to repay accrue to him automatically, as the next harvest comes in. In the meantime he has had a considerable consumer's surplus out of the loan. But if we could rule out such distress borrowing, and also the fact that capital is par excellence a carrier of technical progress, there is nothing strategic about a loan in the ordinary course of business. Indeed, on occasions, lending, not borrowing, is the correct ploy: to lend excessively to an unwise borrower is a prime way of dominating him (section 27).

But it is insane to make a loan that will certainly be repudiated. It would pay a would-be belligerent excellently to borrow up to the hilt, and then to *begin* the economic war by defaulting. It would similarly pay him to confiscate his enemy's equity capital and all physical enemy property within his reach. And this indeed, through the institution of the Custodian of Enemy Property, is what every belligerent does. Default, repudiation and confiscation are, in fact, within the field of capital transfer, the main weapons of economic war. They are debtor's weapons: the debtor usually has the whip hand.

[1] The only exception is if the B government is politically feeble, and would welcome the release of resources for the war effort by *force majeure*, being unable to bring it about by its own taxation or planning. Such a possibility takes us back to the much purer MEs of the eighteenth century.

II

When we come to technology, however, the orthodox Philistine view really has to be accepted. The transfer of technology nearly always brings greater advantage to the recipient (Chapter XIV, section 8); royalties and other payments would have to be great indeed if the originator were to gain in an economic war from such transference. But the prohibition of technology transfer brings with it the embargo on the technology carrier, whatever it may be. For instance, Mercantilist Britain, as we have seen, was right to forbid the export of 'artisans and machinery'. Patents, of course, which are nothing but technology carriers, should have been added.

Moreover, capital, mere loanable funds, is also often a carrier, and not only in the simple sense that the loan often specifies a technology transfer (a machine, an expert) in the contract. More indirectly, all loans carry in new techniques since they set free resources that the nation or enterprise can use on research or development. In this way the borrower, provided he does take the required decision, can catch up. Here too, of course, the mere logic of loan amortization is inexorable: the converse must happen when the loan is repaid, a point too often forgotten. But since the loan is normally of a fixed capital sum at fixed interest, the borrower is likely to have bettered himself irretrievably. The lender, if hostile, has acted unwisely. The period of repayment will of course give him an advantage of ¦the same kind, but if he is—as is likely —more developed anyhow he will find it harder to exploit his advantage.

Mutually profitable trade, on the other hand, enables both countries to set aside resources for research and development at the same time. But even here the more backward country gains more, since the money can be more easily used.

12

We conclude that, apart from technological transfer, there is no permanent category of strategic goods,[1] that it varies extremely from circumstance to circumstance. We must prevent, not all transactions, but such as will strengthen the enemy relatively to ourselves. And this *principle of relative gain* is our second large theoretical proposition. It is not irrational to do the enemy absolute good, provided we do

[1] In the same way there is none of 'growth-inducing commodities': P. J. D. Wiles, *The Political Economy of Communism*, pp. 299–300.

ourselves more good; nor again to do ourselves harm, provided we do him more harm. The concentration on absolute gain and loss is a carry-over from peacetime, when our own absolute gain is all that concerns us.

This is of course easy to say. To put it into practice, however, we must calculate the direct profits made in each country by the trade, the change in tax yields, the change in employment levels, the net flow of gold, the effect of this on the two banking systems, the change in the terms of trade, and much else besides. To refuse to trade altogether is equivalent to saying that the bottleneck effect must hurt the enemy more than us, and that we could not improve on this by bringing in all the other effects, which of course depend on there being some trade.[1] But this is a blanket assertion which there is no a priori reason to believe.

Obviously, a true view of so complex a whole will be extremely difficult to achieve. In the face of so much uncertainty, what should the rational belligerent do? If he judges that his economists and traders are better than the enemy's, the uncertainty is much reduced and he should proceed in accordance with their advice. If he judges them inferior it is safer not to trade at all than to believe them. For the danger of being outsmarted rises with the volume of trade. If he judges them equal he will probably in fact play safe. For rightly or wrongly men in fact dislike uncertainty, and in fact blame action that goes awry more than opportunities missed through inaction. That the embargo should be our preferred weapon of economic war today is due mainly to intellectual inertia and administrative fear of responsibility and complexity.

The fear of complexity, at least, is sound. Take the case of sanctions against Italy in 1935. Clearly so loose a union of 'allies' as the League of Nations could not have been brought to apply a more complicated policy than the straight embargo demanded by Article XVI of the Covenant. No doubt one of the reasons for Napoleon's failure was that, driving a mixed team of doubtful allies against Britain, he permitted variations upon, and loopholes in, the Berlin Decrees.

13

Our third proposition, too, is made interesting or paradoxical only by intellectual inertia. This is that trade with the enemy is as

---

[1] Except for pre-emption and dumping on third markets, which are compatible with a refusal to trade directly.

good or as bad as it happens to be whether the war is a cold or a shooting one. This needs no long discussion. However surprising, it is perfectly obvious. The export of arms to an actually fighting enemy might itself be justifiable. Physical hostilities alter the principle of the thing in no way.

14

Fourthly, economic war is only for large or rich belligerents. One must begin with a considerable share in the enemy's trade, considerable credits in his banks, or a considerable export surplus to dump in third markets. Failing the right orders of magnitude, nothing can be done. A poor country, facing a rich enemy, should make every possible appeal to international law and morality against the whole concept of economic war. That two small belligerents should slap embargos, etc., on each other is a waste of effort: the officials concerned would serve their countries better at the front. It follows that small belligerents should normally not even pursue autarky. If they can rely on neutral supplies they should keep the peacetime structures of their economies, which, being more efficient, release more resources to the direct military effort. They have, in any case, little territory to lose and are more concerned with the sheer occupation of real estate—another argument for concentrating on physical warfare.[1] At no place in the whole of international economics is the distinction sharper between the small and the large country. The only exception is the 'geographical bottleneck': clearly, one small country might have a transit stranglehold upon another. In this manner Argentina could crush Paraguay without firing a shot; and the Suez Canal was the only serious element in the Arab blockade of Israel, even though the Arab countries are in local terms quite a large trading bloc.

15

So trading with the enemy, if you are cleverer than he, is a very wise thing. But that small conditional clause is crippling, and one can but wonder at the boldness of Napoleon and Pitt, slinging their exports at each other: were they so absolutely confident each of his own intellectual superiority? E.g., when French armies marched in British uniforms was it so obvious that Britain had won a battle? Even so, the mere fact that such trade is not a crime, but may on the

---

[1] Wiel, op. cit., p. 22.

contrary be high patriotism, is of the utmost political importance. The belligerent who fully understands it is at an immense advantage. The extent to which Communists in particular understand it we discuss in Chapter XVII; here we offer such more general remarks as are possible.

The first is that humanity as a whole must surely benefit if this view is widely accepted. If trade with the enemy *can* be good for us, there will be more of it. True, the enemy will not trade with us unless he expects to reap a relative advantage. But he may be wrong. It is thus possible for a cold war, even for a hot though non-atomic war, to proceed with both sides making faster economic progress, or slower regress, than at present.

This possibility is strengthened by some practical considerations. Most states, including recently the USSR, are not pure belligerents, hot or cold—especially not cold. They are not maximizing hostility alone but also their own future and present civilian welfare, their standing at the bar of world opinion, their general economic strength in case of a *renversement des alliances*, etc. etc. There is, therefore, ordinarily little place for extremism, and our rational belligerent may be induced to apply some less rigorous criterion to trade with the enemy, such as 'only stop trade if you're *sure* it gives your enemy a relative advantage'. A priori, much trade seems to be neutral in terms of economic warfare, i.e., to benefit both sides equally. Even so complicated a case as the recent (1963) Soviet purchases of wheat in Canada was probably about neutral. The USSR can eat, but the liquidity base of Western trade is expanded, and the burdensome United States wheat surplus reduced by sales in Canada's erstwhile markets. The scientific economic warrior begins seriously to worry only when transactions are far more one-sided, e.g., when technology is transferred and, as usual, not fully paid for.

Moreover, no state, and especially no belligerent, is rational in the first place. The mere introduction of rational discussion, the mere notions that economic warfare can be improved, and that relative gain is what counts, are almost bound to moderate hostility. Unthinking hostility is mostly more hostile than carefully thought out hostility, preferring the short-term gesture that relieves its feelings to the long-term policy that gains its ends. If American dockers refuse to unload Soviet crab, and the John Birch Society runs a smear campaign against shops that sell Polish ham, who can doubt that the RAND Corporation will think up good reasons for eating both?

16

So far we have been bilateral; we must now introduce third parties. By this we shall mean neutrals. A reliable ally is not worth treating as a separate belligerent; an unreliable ally raises too many complications for an elementary theoretical account. The addition of neutrals to the picture does not alter it basically. The 'Mercantilist' and the 'bottleneck' methods of economic warfare remain the principal ones. It becomes improbable that 'bottleneck' warfare will achieve much, simply because the neutrals are likely to present an alternative source of supply. This is particularly true in perfect competition: there is scarcely any point in a United States refusal to buy Cuban sugar at world market prices[1] if it has to buy some sugar at world market prices but wants to blockade Cuba. For other sugar simply replaces Cuban sugar in the United States and Cuban sugar replaces other sugar elsewhere. Again, there is scarcely any danger of Italy becoming dependent on the USSR if she buys Soviet oil; at the first Soviet attempt to exploit the bottleneck effect, Italy can buy other oil. The United States oil companies must think up other arguments.

In the same way, dumping or discriminatory tariffs, the principal 'Mercantilist' weapons, will have little effect, since it is now less likely that the belligerents were conducting a very large trade with each other in the first place. Here, again, perfect competition reduces the weapons' effectiveness: there is no point in belligerent *A* dumping on belligerent *B* a good freely traded and exactly similar to that made by a neutral. For *B* will simply re-export this article—indeed, in an ME no government intervention is required to ensure re-exports.

Only perhaps one weapon is made sharper by the presence of neutrals: the 'abuse of convertibility'. It is, as before, possible for a substantial belligerent to have built up an adequate bank balance in an enemy country. But now he can do more than merely upset domestic credit, he can also do his enemy's international credit great harm by suddenly converting it. Only if neutrals exist can international credit be spoken of. Indeed, in the modern world we can really only speak of international credit. Thus when Britain went off gold in 1797 the main damage was to internal credit; but a modern population is monetarily too sophisticated to worry much.

[1] The cancellation of the sugar preference is, of course, a quite different matter.

17

But if the 'abuse of convertibility' is made more serious, the refusal to lend capital becomes less so. This is simply because capital is competitively provided, like sugar. A simple private capital blockade by one country can be easily broken by a respectable debtor; for instance, the USSR gets British and German export credit in default of American. A refusal of public aid is about as easy to compensate, since aid is normally a political act on the part of one side or other in the Cold War, and the other side or sides are likely to step into the breach.

But the belligerent who is a debtor gains, for in the presence of neutrals his default may be less painful to him. If the default was ideologically motivated, it even endears one to the enemies of the creditor one has victimized. In this respect, foreign lending is more complicated than in the nineteenth century, when all lending was capitalist and most of it private too; so that an international lenders' cartel was built up against defaulters. It is really surprising under modern circumstances how little default there is. The greatest economic disincentive to default today is simply that the United States is overwhelmingly the largest supplier of public and private capital, and penalizes all defaults on her own loans, public or private.[1] Moreover, the next biggest lender, the IBRD, penalizes all default whatsoever, except possibly default against an STE. In a shifting international scene almost any country might wish at a later date to tap these two sources again. Curiously enough STEs have shown themselves to be bad, perhaps worse, debt collectors than ACCs, whether among themselves or vis-à-vis UDCs (Cf. Chapter XIV, section 14).

Thus neutrals on the whole soften the effect of economic war, in a way that they can hardly affect proper war. It is essential, for the weapons of economic war to have effect, that the influence of inter-belligerent trade on national income be great[2] and that neutral-belligerent trade be a poor substitute for it.

18

The belligerent must then try to draw the neutrals in. His object

---

[1] United States soft currency loans, notably the counterpart funds of surplus food delivered under Public Law 480, can only by courtesy be called loans at all.

[2] Not necessarily that the average ratio of trade to income be high, for that is a poor guide to its importance (Chapter XV, section 9). We have in mind a high marginal ratio.

is to get them to take such measures against his enemy as he does himself: so these measures need no further discussion. His means of persuasion might or might not be those of economic warfare: he might also threaten proper war or use yet other diplomatic means. In so far as these are non-economic they fall outside our competence. In so far as they are economic we have already discussed them. That is to say, A can bully the neutral N into participating in economic warfare against B by the use of precisely the weapons he is using against B. Only perhaps the phraseology is new and worthy of mention. When A persuades N to join him in exploiting the bottleneck effect, or in a total refusal to trade with B, we call it a *boycott*. When he uses physical force to stop or diminish N trade with B, we speak of a *blockade*.

In particular he will insist that his own exports to N be not re-exported to B. There is, as so often, no very impressive logic behind the preference for this particular prohibition; it is simply more acceptable to N by psychology and tradition. For the particular goods might not be, on any definition, 'strategic' for B. Quite other N exports might be 'strategic', and it might pay A to use yet other weapons of economic warfare in order to stop them. Nevertheless, the re-export question is of the greatest political and historical importance, and deserves a short excursus.

In order to embargo B's exports A commonly exacts a *certificate of origin* in all dealings with N. On the side of A's own exports the corresponding device is the application of the '*normal needs*' concept to N: A refuses to sell to N more than he needs for the ordinary workings of his economy, minus exports to B, if any.

The difficulties of the re-export problem will be sufficiently illustrated by examining the latter case alone. First, N's 'normal needs' are extremely difficult, both technically and diplomatically, to define. Secondly, N can evade the agreement by producing substitutes, which he exports to B while continuing for home consumption his prewar imports of the original good from A. He can also evade by further fabricating A's goods before reselling them to B, in a manner hitherto uncustomary. Only if A did not previously export the commodity to N at all is the embargo simplified. For in this case A should simply not begin to export it.

If this is the correct technique for coping with the re-export of neutrals, nevertheless, as we saw, re-exports are often not the main thing. A may be far more threatened by the normal trade between N and B than by any re-exports. For instance, quite simply, N might be selling arms to B that the latter cannot make. In such cases, which are surely more common, the important thing is not at all to prevent N re-exporting A's goods to B, or B's to A; it is to prevent N's own trade with B. A's trade with N is merely a weapon, and possibly not the best one; and if it is used the question is not at all of N's 'normal needs', but rather of pre-empting N's exports to B, or of threatening N with a blockade, or with dumping. Moreover, quite other weapons might be superior, such as straight diplomatic bullying.

All this can be inverted. If that attitude pays belligerent A, probably the opposite one will pay B, who will encourage N to break A's rules in every possible way. Here again, B's best weapon may not be the actual offer to N of good terms of trade, i.e., a high profit on re-exports between A and B; but some perfectly irrelevant weapon.

19

So much for bullying the neutral. Next, however, he might be too strong for us to change his commercial policy. Then his economy can still be a field of economic warfare for the belligerents. We try to *pre-empt* neutral exports of value to the other side, a process exceedingly painless to the neutral. We may also dump, or, rather, *outdump*, the enemy's exports to the neutral; and this may well be less popular. For in each case some neutral interests are adversely affected: the domestic consumers of his exports and the producers of import-substitutes. But in the latter case N's b.o.p. also suffers, and there may be unemployment.

Again, if the neutral himself cannot be bullied, perhaps enterprises on his territory can be. This is the *blacklist*. It is one of the supreme illustrations of the difference in normal international economics between an enterprise and a country, that blacklisting is possible at all. When the neutral is an STE it is, of course, impossible. For the essence of the blacklist is merely that enterprises in MEs are sovereign unless and until the state intervenes. If it does not intervene—which is very likely if it wants to preserve neutrality—the belligerents can attack the enterprises directly. Strictly, to blacklist an enterprise is to embargo all dealings with it, but many of the other tricks of economic war can also be used against it, notably dumping and pre-emption. The mere threat of blacklisting is, of course, often enough, since a country is so much more powerful than an enterprise.

20

A much more economically constructive, though surely less politically effective, approach to economic war is bribery,[1] i.e., doing good to neutrals, not harm to the enemy. The theory is that the neutrals will be most grateful to the belligerent who does them most good, and take up a more friendly stance than otherwise—which does not, of course, mean any specific degree of friendliness, because the initial position occupied by each neutral is different. We must leave to others the answering of the question whether in the long run there is any gratitude among nations; i.e., does a nation 'stay bought'? Here we need only observe that in the short run bribery is beyond question effective—a point very important for belligerents competing for a neutral's favors in a hot war. For the rest we must concentrate on the technical means of carrying out such a policy.

These means are all very obvious. There is the transfer of capital, and the very separate transfer of technology. There is the grant of better terms of trade; this affects not only prices but also quantities, not only the neutral's exports but also his imports. Pre-emptive buying (above) is by indirection also bribery. There is also the relaxation of a strategic export ban: the belligerent can bind the neutral quite closely to him by supplying arms.

21

Free trade has some unexpected connections with economic warfare, and is even on occasion a weapon thereof. When Adam Smith said 'defence is of much more importance than opulence',[2] he has always been understood, and probably understood himself, to mean that free trade enriched the country but lowered its defenses. But, in fact, this celebrated sentence came only in the context of the Navigation Acts—where it was certainly true—and much goes to show that Smith understood well enough that these things are too complicated to generalize about. For free trade is also very good for defense in several ways. First, and very reminiscent of the ancient 'principle of provision', is Hirschman's 'supply effect':[3] the belligerent *prepares* himself for war by the general enrichment that maximally free trade brings. In particular it enables him to stock

---

[1] Cf. A. O. Hirschman in *American Economic Review*, March, 1964; comments in December, 1964.   [2] *Wealth of Nations* (1776), Book IV, Chapter II.
[3] Albert O. Hirschman, *National Power and the Structure of Foreign Trade* (Berkeley, Cal., 1945), pp. 14, 34, 36.

up and acquire the latest techniques. In the epigrammatic Communist phrase, 'he imports in order to be autarkic' (Chapter XV, section 11).

The advantage of free trade in this respect can be illustrated by an arbitrary arithmetical example. A prospective belligerent expects a two years' war during which he must consume double the peacetime amount of certain imported materials, yet will be entirely unable to import them. Suppose that these materials are 33% of peacetime imports and 10% of the national income. Then wartime expenditure on them will be 20% of national income. We can then illustrate the contrast between a policy of autarky and one of free trade, consigning all further assumptions to a footnotes:

TABLE XVI/1. STOCKING UP VERSUS AUTARKY
Year

	1 (full peace)	2	3 (preparation for war)	4	5	6 (war)	7	(Total Cost in Years 2 to 7)
Physical quantity to be consumed	q	q	q	q	q	$2q$	$2q$	
Policy of autarky and no stocking up								
Imported	q	$0.9q$	$0.6q$	$0.1q$	0	0	0	—
Produced at home	0	$0.1q$	$0.4q$	$0.9q$	q	$2q$	$2q$	—
(Average cost of home output)		(20)	(17)	(15)	(13)	(16)	(15)	
Total cost	10	11	13	14.5	13	32	30	(113.5)
Policy of free trade and stocking up								
Imported	q	$2q$	$2q$	$2q$	$2q$	0	0	
Cost of importing	10	22	22	22	22	0	0	
Physical stock at end of year	0	q	$2q$	$3q$	$4q$	$2q$	0	
Interest and other costs of storage	0	0.5	1.5	2.5	3.5	3.0	0.5	
Total cost	10	22.5	23.5	24.5	25.5	3.0	0.5	(99.5)

NOTE: I have made arbitrary allowances in the costs of home production for diminishing returns to scale and improvement over time; and assumed a worsening of the country's terms of trade as its imports are doubled. Interest and storage costs are set at 10% of midyear stocks, valuing q at 10. All costs are in percentage points of the national income.

The policy of free trade and stocking up is much riskier, in that the length of the war may be underestimated. But it is cheaper *in toto*, and above all the time-pattern of its effort is a great deal better, for in wartime much fewer resources are devoted to acquiring these materials even than in full peacetime. Moreover, if q is some nuclear or other absolute weapon, the prospective war may, indeed, be very short. Merely to have the weapon may bring victory without one casualty. It could only be right to engage in the expensive autarkic production of such a weapon if some special extra premise held. Notably, one might lose one's sovereignty to the supplier of the weapon. Note that this is a kind of 'importing in order to be autarkic' in the sense of Chapter XV.

22

Before there is economic warfare at all there must be trade. The volume and geographical distribution of trade are clearly of the first importance; and they are themselves much affected by the use of tariffs, preferences, and free trade. A prospective belligerent should not, strictly speaking, want free trade in general, but only along those channels that will later enable him to wage effective economic war, and the opposite elsewhere. Indeed, he may actually impose a greater volume of trade than pure freedom makes possible. This was Stalin's policy vis-à-vis Finland.[1] Thus, if his potential enemy is economically weaker than himself he should urge free trade between the two of them, at the expense of his enemy's internal exchanges and his exchanges with third parties. Precisely the same applies to allies, to neutral markets and sources of supply, indeed, to all countries whatever; the prospective belligerent wants to get the maximum political leverage out of his trade, and therefore to concentrate it on countries economically weaker than himself. This was Hitler's prewar policy in East Europe, and Stalin's in the same region after the war.

Whether by chance or by design—I suspect equal parts of both—free trade between the United States and Cuba led to the same dependence. Vis-à-vis third countries this trade was *preferential*. Between the partners it was free almost to the point of economic hyperpoly. Every spare part to a machine was summoned by telephone from the mainland, to arrive within forty-eight hours. This is a classic case of free trade being a good preparation for economic war; without this long previous period the present United States embargo would not have been anything like as effective.

Vis-à-vis the strong, however, a belligerent has two rational courses of action. If they are likely to be inimical he must protect himself and cut down his trade with them. But if they are likely to be neutral he should insist upon the principles of free trade, indeed, he should do so even while he is preparing to break them himself. He can then draw the maximum economic benefit from

[1] It can also happen, in an STE, quite independently of economic warfare. Cf. Chapter XV.

them, while they have bound themselves to exercise no political leverage over him. Such was the commercial policy of Hitler before the war vis-à-vis the ACCs, and such in particular is Soviet policy today.

Free trade, then, if we are cynical enough, is a principle that may sway others' actions if we appeal to it. Sometimes we should, and sometimes we should not, so appeal. If we do not we do not bind ourselves; if we do we may yet be able to get away with hypocrisy.

Thus we arrive at a most curious and depressing contradiction of the doctrine that free trade is essential for peace: only when countries are really intimately related can they do each other any damage. If A and B are too entangled to quarrel without hurting each other the aggressor A may still hurt himself less than the victim B, which is all that is required for war. Only if they had had no economic relations would they have had no weapons of economic war. Indeed, as we see in Chapter XVIII, they might well then have no reasons for any kind of war.

Let us avoid misunderstanding. We have not said that free trade leads to war. We have said that free importation is a good way of stocking up before military war, and that maximum trade is the best preparation for economic war. Preferential trade among the future belligerents is thus the best, and autarky the worst, preparation. Free trade, moreover, may or may not make nations love each other; and the same dusty answer applies to trade as a whole (Chapter XVIII).

23

Now let us examine the relation of the STE to economic warfare. In every one of the six principal ploys of economic warfare listed in section 2, an STE ought to be more efficient than an ME. The advantages are so plain that we can run through them quite briefly and dogmatically.

(i) The STE's control over its own exports is superior, so it can better exploit the bottleneck effect against an enemy. Indeed, in the case of a cold war it can make the embargo secret, in that its foreign-trade enterprises can just 'happen' not to export certain things. Since embargoes and, indeed, economic warfare as a whole are not respectable, this is an immense propaganda advantage. On the other side, the STE may or may not be more vulnerable to such tactics itself. For if, in general, autarky reduces its dependence on imports, such imports as remain are likely to be indispensable.

(ii) Geo-economic warfare is, as we saw, merely a special case of the bottleneck.

(iii) The STE is plainly in a better position to use what monopoly or monopsony power it has. In an ME the competition of individual exporters or importers seriously blunts this weapon; the use of export or import taxes is much clumsier and less discriminatory than the STE's control over both price and quantity.

(iv) An STE, with its irrational price system and secretive finances, finds it particularly easy to dump. As to import prohibitions designed to hurt the enemy through his inelasticity of supply, it can, just as in the case of the embargo on exports, simply 'happen' not to buy things. Nor, above all, can anyone dump on the domestic market of an STE. Again, if its trading organs do buy up unexpected quantities of foreign goods they will not cause unemployment.

(v) Clearly, with all banks and foreign-trade enterprises under one command, the STE can mobilize its foreign balances more suddenly and completely, and therefore 'abuse convertibility' more effectively. However, it is not characteristic of an STE to have foreign balances on the scale required. As to the inverse situation, we cannot, of course, 'abuse convertibility' against an STE because its currency is not convertible in the first place.

(vi) If the STE is a better dumper in the enemy's market, so also it is better equipped to destroy his sales in a neutral market by dumping there.

It is similarly clear that an STE should be better at bribing and bullying neutrals, and better at resisting this if neutral. It is also completely immune to the blacklist of enterprises.

Moreover, the STE is superbly equipped to play the role of hypocrite about free trade. Thus the USSR can and often does arraign the ACCs before the court of world opinion for the various preferential and protectionist practices whereby they increase their political power: the Common Market, imperial preference, etc. But her own far more drastic practices of the same kind are shrouded in the mists natural to a command economy.[1]

Yet we have throughout felt constrained to say 'can' or 'should'. The reason is that the over-centralized STE is in practice so ill administered. Many and many a foreign merchant, or, indeed,

---

[1] Cf. Chapter IX, passim. For a recent instance of this type of propaganda see the Soviet proposals to the United Nations' Geneva Conference on Trade and Development (A. Ognev and Yu. Ogarev, 'The Foundation of an International Trade Organization is the Most Important Task of the Conference', *Vneshnyaya Torgovlya*, February, 1964).

trade representative of another STE, says, 'Oh, no, I don't like doing business with *them*.' It is far better to have a rather wrong decision now than the right decision too late; and economic warfare demands even more speed and flexibility than ordinary trade. There is also the more neutral point that it is very hard to reckon absolute or relative gain from foreign trade when prices are irrational.

24

From doing harm to foreign countries we turn to dominating them, i.e., to imperialism. We distinguish, and discuss successively, the attainment of political dominance by economic means, and the exercise of that dominance, however arrived at, for economic ends. The distinction reminds us that the easiest way to come to dominate a country is to defeat it in war, a subject beyond our purview.

A attains political dominance over *B* by economic means when, *inter alia*:

(*a*) He puts himself in a position to threaten successful economic war;

(*b*) He acquires the ownership and/or management of things on *B*'s territory, and uses them for political ends;

(*c*) He puts important *B* figures in the world of politics, press, or culture on his payroll;

(*d*) He puts the government hopelessly into his debt, and it wants to reborrow.

We are here, of course, right at, if not over, the edge of what may be called economics. Moreover, in strong contrast to the case of economic war, we can point to a large and competent literature, at least on the descriptive side. There are also at least two good theoretical works.[1] So our task in this chapter is only to relate these means to the economic model in countries *A* and *B*.

As to point (a), we have already listed the weapons of economic war, and the preconditions for it. We have also discussed the extent to which STEs are better capable of waging economic war than other countries. They are to the same extent better able to prepare conditions for, or take precautions against, dominance through the threat of such war.

---

[1] Hirschman, op. cit., 1945; Eugene Staley, *War and the Private Investor* (New York, 1935).

25

They appear even better placed when we consider the next two roads to political dominance by economic means. For clearly (b) no person or authority can acquire the ownership or management of anything on the territory of an STE; or at least not without its express permission and full knowledge.[1] But it needs special defenses to stop an STE acquiring, particularly through straw men, a controlling interest in the equity of a capitalist enterprise. Such an interest is also a profitable acquisition in its own right: it is one of the least costly ways of waging economic war.

An STE can also build up property abroad from scratch in various ways. It can found an enterprise, and plough back its profits. It can also subsidize this enterprise directly, or—more conveniently— by rigging in its favor the prices of the exports it sells to it, or the imports it buys from it. It can grant it straightforward monopoly and monopsony rights, and divert licensing revenues, consular fees, etc. etc. In all this line of possibilities we meet again the striking resemblance between an STE and a large enterprise. We are, in fact, describing direct investment in a foreign subsidiary. For most political purposes, however, 'portfolio investment' is better, i.e., operation through a straw man, who pretends not to be Communist-owned or managed. But it is difficult to imagine that such a secret could be kept for long.

Having set up or acquired its business the STE can use it for very various political ends. One is to acquire secret knowledge, especially knowledge of the defense industry, with which the business should try to have commercial dealings. Another is to exercise the political influences that ordinary large businesses can exercise in the existing political conditions—a large matter into which we need not enter. The business can be a refuge for native Communists, or subsidize the local Party. It can sabotage legislation that directly or indirectly hurts Communism. It may perhaps be in a position to do economic harm, say by boycott, to people and organizations that oppose Communism, or 'objectively' render the ground unfavorable for it. If not itself an organ of the press, the business can yet influence the press by restricting its advertising to fellow-traveling journals. But it is tedious to enumerate: in fine, everything that an American corporation does or is alleged to do, whether in the Caribbean or in France, can be done by a Soviet corporation. Nay more so, for the

[1] For the exceptions—which prove the rule—cf. Chapter XIV, section 4; Chapter XVIII, section 16.

Soviet corporation is directly under command of the Soviet goverment and so can be co-ordinated with other such corporations and with Soviet foreign trade. Moreover, it enjoys far more direct diplomatic support.

We see in the next chapter how astonishingly little STEs avail themselves of all these possibilities, and speculate on the historical reasons.

26

Our third economic road to political domination (c) was through the bribery—or shall we say the lucrative employment?—of influential figures in the victim's territory. This is very close, conceptually, to the outright support of one party or other in a civil war, which we do not call an economic weapon but rather a military one with an economic cost. Now such bribery is by all odds the cheapest way to acquire dominance, if the beneficiary stays powerful and stays bought. In a small and backward country it might cost as little as $100,000 p.a.: an average of $20,000 for five important people. Of course the price can rise astronomically as foreign powers compete for influence, but the thing remains so cheap it is the one single economic way in which small and poor countries can influence the policy of rich and large ones. The classic case is the quite trivial investment in Washington that a Caribbean country has, or had, to make in order to enlarge its United States sugar quota; or that Taiwan had to make in order to freeze United States policy towards China.[1] It is noteworthy that China, the poorest of all contemporary imperialist powers, has used bribery extensively in Africa. Her principal rivals prefer honest foreign aid, and the debacle of Chinese foreign policy in 1965–66 seems to show them wiser.

Like other policies, this one is very difficult to operate inside an STE. For even apart from the personal morality of top Communists —a consideration decisive in itself—no bank account is private and there is little upon which a large fortune can be spent. Indeed, the large fortune automatically attracts suspicion. Essentially the corrupted leader of the STE must spend his fortune abroad; he must plan to retire into emigration. More than any other kind of corrupt person, he needs a Swiss bank account.

In contrast, an ACC or UDC is open at every pore. Rich men are not suspect, it is worth while to have money, the bribe can be

---

[1] *The Reporter*, April 15 and 29, 1952.

currently spent, the prospect of emigration is smaller because discovery is less likely, the morality of leading citizens is in this respect a good deal more pliable, the penalties of discovery are less horrendous.

27

Finally (d), we may dominate a country by getting its government hopelessly into debt; or we may do so inadvertently, if the borrower's improvidence is none of our plan.[1] It is essential here either that the borrower should wish to re-borrow (cf. Chapter XIV, sections 14, 15) or that there be some internationally recognized debt-collecting mechanism. In the late nineteenth century it was moral, and militarily possible, for an ACC to send troops to collect from a defaulting UDC; a fortiori if the latter was its colony. But even then the better sanction was that a defaulter could not re-borrow. Permission to re-borrow was granted only if he 'put his house in order'—a wide concept extending from mere debt repayment to the acceptance of various extraterritorial devices. Of all this the twentieth century knows almost nothing. The contrast could hardly be greater between the United States marine in Nicaragua or British customs officer in China and the discreet adviser from the I.M.F. The determination of the rich to aid the poor, however badly they behave, seems almost unshakable. The STE seems to be at no advantage here. Alongside the blind and persistent generosity of ACCs we must set the fantastic forbearance of the USSR towards Albania, set out in Chapter XIV; or towards Indonesia, as is known to every newspaper reader. The Marxist ideology is, as we have seen, peculiarly unfavorable to debt collections, especially where the debtor is poorer than the creditor.

'Luring into bankruptcy' is, on an international scale, a technique more often spoken of than used. Even the Khedive probably was not lured into bankruptcy, but inadvertently fell. At most, if anyone lured him it was strictly private intermediaries, who in no way represented any state. But in the modern world it is no longer moral to land marines, and the international creditors' cartel is for the moment non-existent.[2] This technique, never much alive, is now definitely dead.

---

[1] Perhaps the best description of such a case is David Landes' account of the Khedive of Egypt, *Bankers and Pashas* (London, 1958).

[2] I do not wish to rule out a United States–USSR–IBRD cartel as a thing of the future; but if it came into existence it would most certainly lure no one into bankruptcy.

28

We have now seen how countries make economic war on each other, and how they use economic means to gain *political* dominance over each other. That leaves imperialism, the economic exploitation of this political power, however it was gained. For, clearly, had we gained it by military war it would still be the same political power, and we could still use it for economic gain. We have been careful in Chapter I to define exploitation, and shall continue with that definition here.

The most ancient, simple, and basically important form of exploitation is *tribute*: the mere unrequited transfer of money or goods from the colony to the metropolis, or from the conquered to the victorious power. Tribute is the taxation of one government by another, and is exceedingly similar to the taxation by a colonial government of whole villages and tribes under indirect rule: the subordinate government is permitted to gather the tax from its subjects in any way it wishes, provided only that it pays.

All ancient empires, from the Athenian to the Mahratta, were based on tribute, but in these more squeamish days we usually call it something else, justifying our receipt of it by something other than sheer conquest. Characteristically, tribute is nowadays called *reparations*, a word implying that the victor was innocent and the vanquished guilty of starting the war. However, hypocrisy is the homage paid by vice to virtue, and the use of the reparation concept has the effect of limiting the payments in time, until some notional bill for damages has been cleared. Tribute, of course, is forever. Going to the other extreme, there are also *theft and booty*: very considerable items in war and its immediate aftermath. Different from all of these, and often representing enormous sums in the b.o.p., is the quartering of troops, now renamed *occupation costs*.

29

This brings us to the *transfer problem*, to which Western economics has devoted so much ingenuity.[1] Now this literature devotes far too little attention to the possibilities that the transfers may be in kind, and that one or both economies involved may be an STE. Suppose first that the conquered country is an ME, and take first the case that the tribute was a piece of informal theft, uncompensated

[1] Cf. Charles P. Kindleberger, *International Economics* (Urbana, Ill., 1955), Chapter 16, and the sources quoted there.

by the conquered government. Then the domestic purchaser who would otherwise have bought the article now seeks to buy something else. Moreover, the victim of the theft, lacking compensation, dishoards whatever money he happens to have. All this is inflationary,[1] and the b.o.p. will suffer in accordance with the strictness and promptness to re-act of the conquered monetary and fiscal authorities.

Next, the tribute is extracted in a more formal way, but still in kind, via the defeated government, which in turn pays for it. This is far more inflationary than when the victimized producer or owner simply dishoards in order to compensate himself. But still monetary and fiscal policy can of course restore both the external and the internal balance. More serious, however, is the fact that the conqueror has now set up a precise bill of goods that must be produced. The conquered government may be able to procure just these goods by free-market procedures, but it also may not—especially in the straitened postwar circumstances. As we see in Chapter XVIII, section 14, this demands a system change in the tribute-paying country. Soviet-type elements are introduced at once, since the government may have to resort to command.

Then, thirdly, the conqueror may be receiving a budgetary grant in inconvertible money. In this case the victim is relieved of the necessity of adapting his economic institutions, since the conqueror has *ex hypothesi* accepted market procurement procedures. But most state procurement procedures have an element of command about them, even when the case is not that of a victorious government in a conquered territory. However freely these purchases are bargained they will make prices rise. Most probably, then, the defeated government, in order to avoid having to raise the budgetary grant in monetary terms, will keep the weapons of command in reserve.

But if, fourthly, the tribute is in convertible money it may be taken directly out of the conquered country's reserves. While the formal and immediate effect on the b.o.p. is the same as in the previous cases, there may now be no internal inflation at all, since a simple reduction of foreign exchange reserves is only inflationary to the extent that it reduces imports. Rather the contrary, the conquered power is more likely to deflate in order to replenish its reserves.[2]

Should it, however, be an STE that is paying the tribute, we must

---

[1] On the other side, he may well work harder and for lower pay.
[2] The classic instance is the French reparations to Germany after 1871.

bring into play the analysis of Chapter V. A tribute siphoned off in consumer goods will indeed be inflationary, but without effect on the b.o.p.[1] One taken in producer goods will however necessitate imports, and hinder exports, on input/output grounds. It will not be very inflationary, since inter-enterprise money is passive, and may in theory only be spent with government permission. A tribute consisting of convertible money may, as above, fall simply on reserves. But more likely the victim will respond by an export drive and an import cut. These, in contrast to the previous case, are inflationary, but as we have seen such monetary matters are now less important.

The terms of trade between the two countries will in either case be affected and in a quite easily predictable way. Since the goods and services transferred are presumably the same, at least in part, as those entering into normal trade between the two countries, the terms of trade should move against the conquered country. And this at least is true whether we are dealing with MEs or STEs, since international relations always resemble those on a market.

30

A smoother method of exacting tribute is to get control of the victim's money supply. This is, of course, a far more modern technique even than the exaction of budgetary support, if only because central banking is a recent invention. However, in practice, the difference between tribute financed by the central bank and that financed by the budget lies only in the monetary institutions used.

The essence of this weapon is very simple: let the victim's money be excluded from your own territory, but issue it yourself and to whom you please. Then he cannot use it for claims on you, but you can use it for claims on him. Thus in 1941–45 Franco-German trade was financed by a clearing account. There was, however, no provision for balancing this clearing in real terms; so the Reichsbank could provide inflationary marks for German importers (automatically convertible into francs), and French exporters would find no francs in their side of the clearing (resulting from German exports). The French clearing was then obliged to borrow from the Banque de France. Thus the inflation was transferred from

---

[1] Except if the government decides to replace these goods by imports, or if the will to work is seriously affected.

Germany to France, and the goods from France to Germany.[1] The mark was not legal tender in France.[2] But Germany did eventually compel the Banque de France to hold, as so-called foreign exchange reserves, the frozen mark assets of the French clearing office. In theory, French businessmen could also buy unlimited quantities from Germany, and thus run down these assets. But German export controls made this impossible. This part of the system was thus a development of prewar German practice in South-east Europe, and identical to the wartime operation of the Sterling Area, if for France we read Egypt and for the Reichsbank the Bank of England. The main distinction lay in the ultimate will to repay these balances.

The striking thing about these arrangements is their flexibility. Germany did not have to submit a fixed bill of goods, or even a fixed monetary claim, on France. Nor did France have to pass her reparations through any kind of budgetary procedure. Moreover— and this applies with particular force to the wartime Sterling Area— a budgetary obligation on the colony or defeated power looks bad. It is bad publicity and becomes a focus of resistance. Tribute seeps instead discreetly through the banking system, by small day-to-day decisions. It can even be called 'building up our foreign exchange reserves'.

31

But these advantages are closed if the defeated country is an STE; for then the reparations have to be included in the plan, whatever the bank or the budget may say. They were also left unexploited by Stalin even while East Germany was still an ME, which she remained for a longish period in the hope of reunifying all Germany and then Communizing the whole. The omission was no doubt partly due to Soviet unfamiliarity with Western banking techniques, but the main cause was undoubtedly the Soviet preference for a detailed plan of deliveries, co-ordinated with the Soviet plan. To this we return below.

The nearest Soviet approach to the use of banking and monetary mechanisms appears to have been a very simple, low-grade abuse of the note issue. Soldiers were given their back pay, withheld during the war, in 'occupation marks', which they carried around in sacks and tried to exchange for watches. Considerable sums were

[1] For a brief general review of German financial policies in occupied countries, cf. Pierre Arnoult, *Les Finances de la France et l'Occupation Allemande* (Paris, 1951) and Paul Einzig in *The Banker*, September, 1940, pp. 156–9, and October, 1941, pp. 32–5.
[2] Though it nearly came to that in the occupied zone: ibid., October, 1940, p. 66.

evidently involved,[1] but Soviet organizations were not given similar privileges at the Deutsche Notenbank. That is, the distinction between active money in the hands of consumers and passive money in the hands of enterprises and local authorities was extended to the reparations field. The Soviet soldier, as a consumer, got money that he could use as he pleased; the Soviet enterprise got indents for goods physically specified in a plan. These goods were financed by the East German budget.

Perhaps the most remarkable case of Soviet rigidity in this respect is Finnish reparations. Finland was by some historical accident not Communized in 1945–46, when the moment was ripe. The reparations agreement, permitting the USSR to specify detailed commodities, was signed in 1944, at a moment when it was perhaps not yet obvious to the Soviet authorities that they would in the long run have to deal with an ME. But for years later they continued along the old lines, specifying commodities that Finland could ill produce, instead of accepting convertible currency, and thus acquiring them more cheaply elsewhere.

32

We thus approach the question of the economic model in the tribute-levying country, and its effect on the manner of levying. In the main the effects are merely the opposite of those enumerated above. Inflation is now required in an ME where deflation was before; an importation of producer goods into an STE requires, on input/output grounds, that similar imports from third countries be cut, etc. etc.

But why did the USSR insist on defined lists of goods in this way, when she could have taken Ostmarks or Finnmarks as the case may be, or even convertible currency, and then procured what she wanted at lower prices and higher qualities? As far as procurement actually on the territory of the defeated power goes, the difference between global amounts of money and long lists of specific commodities is not very great. For the former must in any case soon be translated into the latter. Indeed, detailed specification, by avoiding the problem of rising prices, gives the tributary power less chance

---

[1] Much of the ultimate burden rested on the United States, not Germany. For there was nominally only one occupation mark, and very often the Soviet soldier bought his watch from an American soldier. The latter could convert such marks into dollars—a privilege that the United States authorities rapidly restricted when they saw what was happening. It had originally been the Allied intention to print only a fixed number of occupation marks in the United States, and distribute them among the powers. But Mr. Harry Dexter White, of the United States Treasury, later plausibly accused of being a Communist spy, arranged for the official transfer of the plates to Moscow, for a separate Soviet issue to be printed.

to cheat. It is a clear advantage of the STE as tribute-taker that it can make these specifications, and take delivery in the names of its enterprises. The government of an ME that specified lists of goods would be forced to resell them on the open market at home, and would be exposed to charges of inefficient trading and corruption. Its only alternative would be—as happened in West Germany in 1945–46—to allow individual enterprises to go foraging and then take payment in home currency from them. This procedure is certainly no better. The ME, then, should take tribute in a global sum of money via the central bank or budget.

But the Soviet failure to take convertible currency is, indeed, culpable, since many specific items could have been bought more cheaply elsewhere, and the resources of the conquered powers more profitably used in exporting to pay for them. In part we must put this down to the general Soviet failure, copiously illustrated in these pages, to appreciate problems of scarcity and comparative cost. But in part the decision was logical, for the alternative would have made the USSR dependent on deliveries from non-Communist, indeed, from NATO, powers. Although it could not have been known in 1946, the United States embargo was to begin in late 1947, to be followed by the general CoCom embargo. So *ex post facto* Stalin was justified in a general way, though beyond doubt his procedures were extremely inefficient at the micro-level.

33

Next, we must not take too simple a view of the precise nature of the thing transferred. For the booty ranges not merely from producer to consumer goods, as already mentioned, but all the way from the farmer's goose, 'liberated' by the honest soldiery for their Christmas, to a valuable patent. Now clearly a patent raises wide-ranging and long-run issues quite other than inflation or input-output; and those issues we have already discussed in Chapter XIV. But the previous analysis does throw light on the contrast between 'dismantling' and 'reparations from current production'. At the end of World War II the Western powers wanted to take out their reparations by dismantling, i.e., the physical removal of German industrial capacity. For on the one hand this coincided with the Morgenthau plan for 'pastoralizing' Germany, and on the other it brought technical progress to the dismantling power, since, as we have seen, knowledge tends to ride on the backs of machines. An adequate monetary policy could have covered (indeed, did cover) the transfer of capacity as easily as that of current production.[1]

In the Soviet case, there being no monetary problems, the task of absorbing reparations of either kind was easier. The question was as to the physical efficiency of the Soviet reparations-collecting organs. Originally set to dismantle particular plants on the orders of Soviet ministries, they failed to pack, label, or despatch properly. Very many priceless assets were simply destroyed or lost. Meanwhile, the ministries quarreled vehemently over who should have what, and the military government found it impossible to set any upper limit to dismantling. Hence a party arose within the military government and the Ministry of Foreign Trade headed by Mikoyan, that favored the better organized and less destructive process of taking reparations out of current production, principally from the mixed companies described below, which were accordingly part of the Mikoyan scheme. Though contrary to Allied agreement, and bitterly opposed by the individual ministries and their requisition teams, this proposal found favor with Stalin.[2]

So the 'transfer problem' of the textbooks affects only reparations between MEs or between an ME and an STE. For it is evident that its complications are due to the 'Keynesian' actions of money. We are therefore not bound to discuss them here. Transfers among, to,

---

[1] Let R be reparations in consumption goods, r in capital goods. Then if full employment in the conquering country would have entailed an output of $C + I$, where C is consumption, I investment, it is now required that:

expenditure = $C' + R + I' + r'$,
where $C + I = C' + I'$.

This is the very simple full-employment condition. In addition, balanced growth requires that:

$$C' + R = jC, I' + r = k I$$

even if $R = 0$ or $r = 0$, where j and $k > 1$ and represent some balanced growth path. E.g., if reparations are in capital goods this will somewhat depress domestic investment but still increase total investment, etc. Note that strictly the conquered country might have supplied r out of the current production of its capital goods industries. The fact that $r > 0$ does not logically entail any dismantling. Similarly, R might be derived from confiscated stocks of consumption goods.

[2] Vladimir Rudolph in Robert Slusser (ed.), *Soviet Economic Policy in Post-War Germany* (New York, 1953). Note that Mikoyan's opponents, who included such super-ministers as Beria (in charge of concentration camps and atomic energy) and Kaganovich (who had a special responsibility to break the cement bottleneck) were in breach of the Leninist principle of the State's foreign-trade monopoly. They were treating East Germany as a private raiding ground, and a costly and chaotic free-for-all had resulted. It is not recorded by our source that Mikoyan stepped so far out of character as to appeal to Marxist-Leninist doctrine. Probably his eventual victory was by appeal to sheer common sense. He was resisted on the ground that to pass all reparations through his hands would give him too much power.

or from STEs are essentially transfers in kind, without multiplier effect. Indeed, tribute in the form of a list of specified goods is the most obvious method of exploitation, and a very efficient one. Here the STE has two advantages: it can speak for its enterprises, and it can more easily adapt its physical resource allocations to making or receiving transfers in kind.

Perhaps for these reasons, perhaps because of his peculiar ruthlessness, crudity, and grasp of essentials, Stalin showed himself a vastly more efficient extractor and recipient of direct tribute in 1945–52 than France and Britain in 1919–31. Indeed, since Mercantilism there has been nothing like it. The very notion that there was some difficulty in absorbing tribute would have seemed utterly astonishing to him: an example of the 'internal contradictions of capitalism' too comical to be true. His own problems, although they were very grave and caused terrible waste, affected only his procurement machinery. Once he had reformed that, reparations paid off handsomely.

34

Finally there is the Soviet-type mixed company. For the essential theory of this institution see Chapter XII, Section 10. The mixed company is, or ought to be, only a socialist international enterprise, owned by more than one STE and operating in one or possibly more than one STE. Its trouble, we have already seen, is that, while paying profits to both its owners, it is wholly at the mercy of the central planning organ of the STE on whose territory it is situated.

Stalin's use of mixed companies, then, was an aberration. They were always located on the territory of a satellite, and the central plan of that country was adjusted to the plan of the company, not vice versa. The fiscal advantages they received were a simple scandal, even though 49% of the profit reverted to the satellite government. It would be tedious to enumerate here the various forms of chicanery: enough to refer the interested reader to other sources.[1]

But Stalin's companies aroused such intense indignation that they have often been misrepresented, and some of the grosser misunderstandings should here be set at rest. First, the companies were not

[1] Vladimir Rudolph, op. cit.; Vlas Leskov and Nikolai Grishin in the same volume; Gisela J. Conrad, *Die Wirtschaft Rumäniens* 1945–52, Deutsches Institut für Wirtschaftsforschung, Sonderhefte, Neue Folge, nr. 23 (Berlin, n.d.); Nicolas Spulber, *The Economics of Communist Eastern Europe* (New York, 1957), Chapter 6.

solely engaged in the current delivery of reparations. Thus even in the DDR the so-called SAGs (Sowjetaktiengesellschaften) also sold to the internal market and exported normally: from the end of 1947 only 70% of their output had to go in reparations. Reparations were paid for by the satellite's budget, whether they had been produced by a mixed company or a purely resident company; and were thus formally delivered by the state, not the company.

But, secondly, the Soviet contribution to the company's capital did nearly always originate in some claim to reparations. Thus in the defeated satellites other than the DDR the Soviet claim to all German property was converted into a 51% share of various going concerns—after the initial period of reckless dismantling described above. In the DDR itself a part of the claim to reparations was so converted. In both cases actual reparation deliveries from current production, though paid for by the satellite's budget, were physically produced for the most part by the mixed companies. In the satellites that had nominally won the war (Poland, Yugoslavia, Czechoslovakia, Bulgaria) there were, of course, no reparations, so very few mixed companies. The USSR proposed some to Yugoslavia, but was refused.

Thirdly, 49% of the profit really did accrue to the satellite. But it was spent on local technical improvements and welfare services, much as is profit in all Soviet-type enterprises. It appears that the Soviet 51% was not so spent, but was used for purely Soviet purposes; and that the 49% was not fully subject to the satellite's profit tax. So the satellite appeared to derive no benefit. In any case, profits were arbitrary.

Lastly, the East German SAGs were not wholly owned by the USSR. Formally they were ordinary mixed companies, and their German name is thus a misnomer. However, Wismuth A.G. (the Soviet uranium-mining enterprise in Saxony) was wholly owned, and is not a SAG. When the SAGs were sold back it remained in Soviet ownership. This company seems to be unique. There is justification for its ownership status in that it was developed *ab ovo* by Soviet geologists; there was nothing to confiscate in 1945.

There is a parallel here to capitalist international firms. In, say, Britain, a United States company would neither ask for nor receive any favors. Similarly, Hungary can get no favors for its Haldex company on Polish soil (Chapter XII, section 9). But Stalin got favors in Hungary, and so do United States companies in the Caribbean; and that, too, is imperialism. There are, of course, many differences. For instance, the Caribbean country is nominally an ME and has no plan; so there is no problem of adjusting the host country's plan to that of the enterprise. The company will also employ fewer natives, since it cannot rely on the supranational control mechanism of the Communist Party. Moreover, it may well employ much less than 50% native capital, for under capitalism the percentage holdings of equity capital are a deadly serious matter.

There are also many minor similarities. The United States company will pay better wages than native companies, and be more technically progressive; both because of its superior financial backing. This was also true of Stalin's mixed companies.

However, there is also an essential difference. The United States company gets its privileges by corruption and monopoly-monopsony power, with minimal diplomatic support; but Stalin relied almost wholly on 'diplomacy'. I.e., Soviet imperialism was wholly the fault of the Soviet government, and the enterprise's privileges were not even paid for by bribes; whereas United States imperialism arose out of the capitalist *nature des choses*. The enterprise has the initiative, and operates in a market, however imperfect, where it cannot command. So it pays for many if not most of its privileges in kickbacks to local legislators. The United States government is more guilty of complicity than of any definable action.

Colonialist imperialism, again, differed from both, in that the colony was not even a 'satellite': it had no nominal sovereignty. The metropolitan government favored metropolitan enterprises more in the Soviet than in the United States way: by law, not corruption. But these enterprises operated in markets, and receive very few fiscal preferences over native enterprises. The principal use of metropolitan sovereignty was to prevent native protectionism. It is entirely possible that the United States firm in the Caribbean buys, or bought, more privileges than the British Raj ever gave free to any British firm in India.

How much exploitation has resulted? A true answer would require a large research institute. Stalin was the most ruthless exploiter since Leopold II of the Belgians, and this accident of personality leads me to suppose that therefore he took more out of his victims than the various forms of Western imperialism, at least on average. But Stalin was more a fortuitous than a sociologically determined phenomenon. It is not in the nature of Communism that the enterprises of one STE should operate on the soil of another; indeed, it is rather abnormal. Again, the ideology of universal brotherhood is deeply felt, whereas capitalism operates on the whole without ideology, and its entrepreneurs seek their profits where they may.

The imperialistic international firm is under capitalism the product of unequal development, under Communism of unequal power. But it is a foreign body in both the institutions and the ideology of the latter, and did not last long.

35

Apart from tribute and mixed companies there are the terms of trade. Exploitation through these may or may not have continued in Eastern Europe long after the end of reparations. We have nothing to add here to our account in Chapter IX.

Allegations are also often made that the USSR sites steelworks in her satellites in such a way as to make them dependent. At Sztalinvaros (Dunapentele) and Nowa Huta Hungary and Poland built immense works. The first was and is utterly dependent on imported (Soviet) ore and even coke.[1] The second relies on native coke; with its excellent water communications Poland undoubtedly has two good reasons for a large domestic steel plant. But instead of being located on the Baltic, whither both Silesian coke and Swedish ore could come by water, the plant is on the Vistula near Cracow and must rely on Soviet ore that comes a long haul by land.[2] Now was all this a subtle form of Soviet imperialism?—for of course since both works are dependent on Soviet ore their owners have been rendered subject to the bottleneck effect. I greatly doubt it: many of the phenomena that we ascribe to imperialism all over the world are due to the folly of the dependency itself. Quite possibly in the Nowa Huta case Soviet negotiators were reluctant to supply so much ore, while Polish negotiators feared dependence on capitalist Sweden, remembering the anxieties that even Nazi Germany had had on this score. In the Sztalinvaros case USSR is known to have been critical.[3] Indeed in Hungary the combined cost of imported ore and coke exceeds even that of imported steel.[4]

More certainly, a large and uneconomic steel plant is of the essence of planning in STEs and UDCs alike. Steel, the symbol of power,

[1] In 1959–60 Hungary imported 74% of all her ore consumption and 33% of her coke from USSR.
[2] In 1959–60 Poland imported 61% of all her ore from USSR.
[3] *Imre Nagy on Communism*, New York 1957, p. 106.
[4] F. L. Pryor, *The Communist Foreign Trade System*, London 1963, pp. 28–9. Even in the DDR this combined cost exceeds that of imported pig-iron.

modernity, capital-intensity, investment, the primacy of heavy industry, etc. etc., is the prime fetish-object of such planners, even if not Communist.

In one notorious instance, admittedly long after the Stalin era, the Soviet government actually turned down a request for support in building such a steel works: at Galati in Rumania. We saw in Chapter XII what shattering political results this had *for USSR*. If the steel plant had not been built Rumania would have been better off and even more independent; her insistence is an obvious case of small-country steel worship, not different from Norway's or Ghana's.

CHAPTER XVII

ECONOMIC WARFARE IN COMMUNIST PRACTICE

The foreign trade policy of the USSR is part of the overall foreign policy of the USSR. —*Bol'shaya Sovetskaya Entsiklopedia*

I

IN economic as in military war there are national *styles*. By this I mean a choice of weapons not dictated by objective necessity or calculation but by tradition, emotion or other subjective leaning. In military war we can by no means leave national and even personal style out of account, but in the economic case science has been so much less applied, and objective necessity so little studied, that there seems to be little else but styles. A few of these can be distinguished.

Styles have been most seriously affected by theories of war itself. In particular, who is supposed to be at war: governments and armies, or whole peoples? If the former view is taken there will *ceteris paribus* be far less economic war, of whatever particular style. It is one of the great paradoxes of the subject that the eighteenth century, the century of Mercantilism, saw also the high point of an attempt to civilize war. And this meant, of course, to de-totalize it: to distinguish between the soldier and the civilian. Even the soldier conducted himself according to rules of the 'gentlemen, you shoot first' type. But the civilian was meant to be altogether exempt: to the point of being neutral. His very property was inviolate. There was no such thing as a Custodian of Enemy Property, and all contracts between citizens of enemy states, down to and including payments on insurance policies, were valid and enforceable in enemy courts. Thus it was that Britons moved freely about Paris during the Napoleonic War, *and thus it was that one might trade with the enemy*: civilians were not at war. The regulation of such trade had always seemed natural to Mercantilists, and they continued to regulate it in war much as they had in peace, only, of course, much more sharply.

The nineteenth century moved in two directions from this policy. Military war became more awful and more cynical; but the free-trade-cum-*laissez-faire* obsession simultaneously built up a tremendous prejudice against economic war. The quite obvious facts of imperialist clashes, say, over the Baghdad Railway, were denied by many respected economists.[1] To this we must add the beginnings of a genuine international peace movement. The climax was the Hague Peace Conference of 1907 which, while completely unconcerned with imperialism, practically outlawed many kinds of economic war. Thus while the army had become a *levée-en-masse* of conscripts *à la* Robespierre, led by generals who derived their theory from Clausewitz and Bernhardi and their practice from Sherman, the international lawyers decreed that war did not affect the civilian economy, scarcely even trade with the enemy. War was to be the pastime of the effete feudal upper classes; meanwhile the bourgeois *pays réel* was to trade where it wished.

It was Britain in 1914—as the power most likely to benefit—that exploded the 1907 agreement, though possibly not violating its letter.[2] The German propagandists of the interwar period were quite right in contending that Britain thus made war much more total, and undid the good of the previous trend.[3] Of course, economic warfare came back, as we have seen, with a new non-Mercantilist slant. In the eighteenth century war was not total, so trade with the enemy was permitted while current economic theory governed the type of state interference therewith; in the twentieth

[1] As is shown by Albert O. Hirschman, *National Power and the Structure of Foreign Trade* (Berkeley, 1945).

[2] Eberhard Schmidt in *Die deutschen Vergeltungs-Massnahmen im Wirtschaftskrieg*, ed. Friedrich Lenz and Eberhard Schmidt (Bonn, 1924), p. 7.

[3] Out of a very large though not always impressive literature I have relied mainly on Schmidt.

century war was total, so such trade was forbidden. But that was merely a psychological, not a logical, inference from the notion of total war; had economists interested themselves in the problem they could have suggested more effective devices than total embargoes.

The between-war period was dominated by yet another notion: that economic war could be a substitute for military. The absurdity was now perceived of controlling the lesser evil while letting the greater loose. On the contrary, the new international authority, the League—so infinitely stronger, for all its weakness, than such declaratory devices as the resolutions of the Hague Peace Conference—would prevent military war by waging economic war: sanctions against the aggressor. This was again a simple, crude refusal to trade with the enemy (Article XVI of the Covenant). It would seem that Sanctions did not work simply and only because the League did not work. I can find no fault with the notion itself; not even with its unimaginative selection of weapons from the armory of economic war. For how else could an unwieldy congeries of sovereign states, each with different attitudes toward the accused aggressor, be induced to cooperate? Certainly not in any of the subtler types of warfare discussed in Chapter XVI, which presuppose clear thinking and unified command.

During the Abyssinian War (October, 1935–May, 1936), Italy defeated Sanctions. If ever an economic war was ill organized, it was that of the League of Nations against Italy: oil was never embargoed, nor the Suez Canal closed. So craven and foolish was the application that the idea itself seems hardly to have lost respectability. It has no explicit place in the United Nations Charter, but we are still in the Age of Sanctions.

For it is in this spirit that the United States, the great modern practitioner of economic war, operates; perhaps in part out of a guilt-feeling at having wrecked their first application. The notion is no longer of two nations waging war with this or that weapon, but of a world order, reacting with dignified restraint to a moral leper. And the USSR wages economic war on other Communist countries in just the same style. Sanctions are the style most suited to an ideological age, in which nationalism may no longer appear naked, and military war has become a little dangerous.

2

But not only periods have their style. We must analyse the

phenomenon also country by country. The United States has a very ungainly and ineffective style, springing from her political isolationism, moral absolutism, weak government, and *de facto* economic autarky. Trading with the enemy is automatically bad. To import from him is like allowing a political infiltrator or a dog with rabies into the country. To export to him is to drain our own life-blood. While in individual transactions business is business, it is an ethical question whether there should be any transactions at all. Commercial recognition is a pass degree in that great moral examination of the foreigner, where honors is diplomatic recognition. So primitive a spirit demands the battle-axe, not the rapier: the embargo is almost the only weapon. It is even a popular, grassroots affair, as Polish ham, Soviet crab, and Yugoslav furniture testify. The spirit of exclusion here is a psychological extension of the boycott spirit that marks so strongly the relation between national groups in the United States: a Czechoslovak ping-pong ball in the drugstore is like a Negro house-owner in the suburb. The pressure comes, then, from the consumer, the trade unionist, the right-wing crackpot; the government follows. It is as if military strategies were decided by referendum. There can be no scientific economic warfare this way. The result is, moreover, that the United States is almost always engaged in some economic war or other; it is the only remaining country on earth where the pastime is popular.

The richness of the country is important here: there are other sources for ping-pong balls. It is this richness, moreover, that turns the United States government in wartime—when it really can wage economic war to its own prescription, without electoral interference—toward the expensive method of pre-emption, and away from the use of mere threats to neutrals.[1] Poorer countries, notably Britain, have taken cheaper weapons into their arsenal. In its heyday (1914–18) British economic warfare was the admired and feared example in the world. Pre-emption had, of course, its role, but more reliance was placed on diplomatic bullying, or threats to extend the blockade to neutrals, or acts of piracy disguised as changes in international law, and—cheapest of all—the blacklist of individual firms. This, then, was the more excellent style of a coldly rational government, possessed of a good navy and a good intelligence service, but not infinitely rich. But even it was seriously blemished by the failure to grasp the 'principle of relative gain', and by the consequent blank refusal to trade with the enemy.

[1] Cf. Yuan-li Wu, *Economic Warfare* (New York, 1952), pp. 299, 378.

Now contemplate the style of a weak country, or rather group of countries: the Arab League. It would be folly for this weak group to boycott a country, but it is or ought to be effective to boycott individual enterprises that trade with Israel, even individual tourists who visit the place. Thus they have very rationally chosen the blacklist and the geographical bottleneck (Suez) for weapons. If the war is, in fact, ineffective, it is due not to the conception but to the execution, and to the strength of the enemy. Here, too, we can begin to speak less of style and more of reason, but the refusal to trade with the enemy is still a blemish.

3

Can we distinguish a Soviet, or Communist, style? To my surprise it seems impossible. For all its splendid opportunities the STE uses the same weapons, just as crudely. As an aggressive and disagreeable government with large imperial interests, the USSR is, of course, constantly engaged in some economic war or other. But there is no published theory of economic war, and little evidence of a private one either. One main reason is that hitherto Communism has been on the receiving end of these weapons. Its main struggle is with the ACCs as a whole, and here it has been in no position to challenge. Subversion and espionage are where the Communist comparative advantage lies, though the opportunity has often been taken to make military advances when they are safe. To all this the ACCs have replied precisely with economic war, which is where *their* comparative advantage lies. The position of the USSR today is much like that of Germany in 1914–18: that of injured innocent.

STEs have historically needed technological and capital transfer; ACCs have historically tended to embargo such items (1918–21, 1947–date). From time to time, STEs have conducted export drives to earn currency, as in the first Soviet FYP; or, as recently in the UDCs, to gain influence. The ACC's reply has always been a boycott, however half-hearted; in which, however, there are large elements of ordinary protectionism, so that here the STE's position is much like that of any other up-and-coming commercial rival, say Japan or Hong Kong. With this general background it is not surprising that the general commercial policy of Communist countries has been *not economic warfare at all but free trade on their own terms*. This means, with no awkward questions asked about their own discriminations (Chapter IX, and access to foreign technology and as much foreign capital as they from time to time think wise (Chapter XIV, section 4).

They have everything to gain from this, since technological transfer favors them, and trade helps espionage and subversion. Their characteristic reaction to embargo has not been so much counter-embargo, though there has been that,[1] as smuggling and attempts to break the embargo diplomatically. *They have almost never blacklisted capitalist firms,*[2] and thus have renounced a major weapon, which they could have wielded more effectively than the Arab League.

We may, indeed we must, speculate on this failure. The distinction between firm and country is vital to the understanding of both imperialism and economic war. Common sense and true Marxism admit the distinction, and so reject the conscious-conspiracy theory of history in favor of social science. Vulgar Marxism, which finds many adherents also outside the Party, rejects the distinction, and so arrives at a generally paranoid and inaccurate view of capitalism. It is possible, then, that vulgar Marxism is one of the things that inhibits STEs from using the blacklist.

It is perhaps this experience with ACCs that makes the USSR so inept at economic warfare when it does turn that way. Only the Finnish case (section 7) can be considered a success, with the weapons correctly chosen and the desired result, or at least some positive result, achieved. Let us, then, examine individual instances of Soviet economic war since 1945.

4

The *first Yugoslav*, and the *Albanian*, cases may be taken together, since they are both similar and simple. In 1948 Yugoslavia, and in 1961 Albania, incurred severe Soviet political displeasure, for reasons too notorious to mention. In both cases the USSR simply cut off all trade—and, of course, aid.

[1] Thus the traditional Soviet exports of manganese were cut off in reply to CoCom; and Margolius, the former Deputy Minister of Foreign Trade in Czechoslovakia, suffered at the Slánský trial for exporting television tubes to Britain. (*Prozess gegen die Leitung des Staatsfeindlichen Verschwörerzentrums mit Rudolf Slánský an der Spitze,* Ministry of Justice [Prague, 1953], p. 429.) Oil, on the other hand, has been exported to CoCom countries though embargoed by them! A good account of the atmosphere and techniques of smuggling through the CoCom embargo is given by the pseudonymous J. Bernard Hutton, *The Traitor Trade* (London, 1963), and by Fritz Seidenzahl, *Geschäfte mit dem Osten,* Düsseldorf, 1957. For the detailed legal side cf. H. J. Berman and J. R. Garson in *Vanderbilt Law Review* 1967; and more generally G. Adler-Karlsson, *Western Economic Warfare,* Stockholm 1968.

[2] One exception is the eleven British companies represented in Moscow by the British spy Greville Wynne, who was caught in 1963 (*New York Times,* September 26, 1964).

It is possible that Stalin, who dealt with Yugoslavia (in 1948), thought that he would bring that country to heel in this way. And, indeed, since this was the first open dispute between two Communist countries there was no experience to guide the Kremlin. Besides, Stalin was in some matters so paranoid as not to be sane, and his godhead was in question. But, in fact, Yugoslavia turned to the West, and after a very unpleasant period of readjustment traded fairly profitably, in addition to receiving, instead of giving,[1] aid. She also remained a Communist country, if only 'in her fashion'. In addition the complete refusal to trade made nonsense of the Soviet attacks on the United States embargo; and looked bad in a very general way.

One can hardly speak of a blockade in either case. The Arabs have tried to prevent third parties from trading with Israel, the United States has tried to do the same against Cuba and North Vietnam, and the United Kingdom against Rhodesia, but Stalin made no serious attempt to blockade Yugoslavia. His satellites, of course, copied his embargo, but at least Hungary, Bulgaria, and Albania had good independent reason to do so, and were somewhat reluctant to see this episode brought to an end by Khrushchev in 1955.[2] Khrushchev did so in a manner wholly to vindicate Tito, and wholly to condemn Stalin. That Tito survived to win this total victory is in large part due to the ineffectiveness of the trade war.

In the Albanian case the East European STEs, no longer satellites, continued to trade (cf. Table XIV/9). By 1961 they were quite civilized and, separated from Albania by Yugoslavia, had no quarrel with so obscure a country. They did, indeed, cease to provide aid, but they appear to have written off all previous loans. So, indeed, apparently, has the USSR, which alone of European STEs has a total embargo.[3] The USSR has also effectively—though not formally—broken off diplomatic relations. Neither she nor her satellites did this to Yugoslavia; the connection of diplomatic relations with trade is discussed below.

This embargo has been equally ineffective. Depending mainly on China, Albania has also expanded ties with the capitalist world. She gets rather less aid from China than she used to from European STEs, and the Soviet embargo greatly damaged her at the time. But, like all other countries, she has preferred her independence.

---

[1] I refer to the aid she formerly gave Albania (Chapter XIV, section 12). It seems improbable that she was exploited by the USSR through the terms of trade (Chapter I, section 8).

[2] In fact, trade was resumed in 1954.

[3] Yugoslavia has always done some trade, even with Albania, since 1955.

5

Of far less importance, but of greater interest and less well known, is the embargo on *Australia*.

On April 3, 1954, the spymaster at the Canberra Embassy, Vladimir Petrov, deserted with a number of very damaging documents. On April 20, Mrs Evdokia Petrova was on her way back to the USSR, lest she too defect. Immigrants from Eastern Europe made an emotional scene at Canberra airport, but the embassy couriers, alias security policemen, got her successfully aboard the 'plane. At Port Darwin the Australian authorities persuaded or permitted her to telephone her husband. The couriers got into another scuffle, only this time with the Australian police; they were disarmed. Mrs. Petrova decided to seek asylum with her husband, and on April 23 the USSR broke off diplomatic relations and virtually stopped all trade, as shown in Table XVII/1.

TABLE XVII/1. AUSTRALIAN TRADE WITH THE USSR, 1952–62

	Imports from USSR		Exports to USSR	
	Value (£A '000)	Proportion of Total Australian Imports (%)	Value (£A '000)	Proportion of Total Australian Exports (%)
1952–53	731	0·1	1642	0·2
1953–54	734	0·1	26,146	3·2
1954–55	911	0·1	154	0·0
1955–56	758	0·1	—	—
1956–57	262	0·0	19	0·0
1957–58	535	0·1	34	0·0
1958–59	428	0·1	102	0·0
1959–60	525	0·0	12,580	1·3
1960–61	850	0·1	8198	0·8
1961–62	850	0·1	11,767	1·1

SOURCE: Bureau of Census and Statistics, *Overseas Trade*. Years ending June 30.

Thus the USSR continued to export—doubtless she needed the sterling. But she switched her wool purchases to South Africa. Wool being a perfectly competitive commodity, South Africa did not benefit and Australia did not lose. The matter was so trivial from the Australian point of view that the lengthy article 'Petrov' in the *Australian Encyclopedia*, which makes much of the diplomatic events, never mentions wool or trade at all. Diplomatic and trade relations were re-established on March 17, 1959, and wool imports from Australia figure in Soviet trade returns again from 1959 on.

Soviet actions in all this may seem childish, and ill proportioned to the aim of damaging the enemy. The latter they certainly were, but what else could the USSR have done? Australia is a very rich country a very long way away, trading negligibly with the USSR in any case, importing virtually nothing and exporting only a perfectly competitive product. There was thus no economic way of doing damage, and it so happens that there was also no political or diplomatic way. Presented with a problem like this, the technician might well reply, 'Forget it or you will look foolish; consult your dignity and pretend the *casus belli* never happened.'

The trouble with this advice is that the *casus belli* was more serious than the layman might suppose. The right to kidnap one's own diplomats is absolutely vital to a totalitarian country. Indeed more, it is in fact vital to any belligerent. If it had been possible to kidnap Burgess and MacLean in the USSR, we need have no doubt at all that the British government would have done it. The right is, of course, no part of the diplomatic immunities extended by international custom, but the USSR has valiantly tried to make it so.[1]

Now in the other instances listed, the body of the erring diplomat was never physically snatched from the hands of his or her Soviet escort. Gouzenko and Kaznacheev escaped quickly and without violence. Kasenkina leaped from the consulate into the street, where no Soviet guard could get her. Only in the case of Strygin was the Soviet escort physically threatened, but they in fact beat off the threat and took him successfully away. The case of Evdokia Petrova was thus the most serious of them all, and it may have seemed best to the Soviet government, by making a spectacle of itself in the matter of Australian trade, to prove to *other* governments the firmness of its intentions. And this example may indeed have been salutary to states in a weaker economic position.

From the narrow economic point of view, however, the whole thing was a farce.

6

Three cases of total embargo are not a large sample from which to generalize. Yet such is social 'science', so let us risk it. In each case, then, the embargo was highly counter-productive: international goodwill and prestige were lost, while the victim was driven into

[1] The following incidents are relevant: Oksana Kazenkina in New York, August, 1948; Igor Gouzenko in Ottawa, February, 1946; Col. Strygin in Rangoon, April, 1959; A. U. Kaznacheev in Rangoon, June, 1959; Mrs. A. Golub, Amsterdam, October, 1961.

the arms of the enemy. The cause seems to be in each case the same: the break was both diplomatic[1] and commercial indeed total, so the victim could only protect himself by turning to other supporters. These violent moves are not the way to obtain concessions: they are the prelude either to a Soviet invasion or—as it always turned out—a Soviet defeat. The lesson is very appropriate to the United Kingdom–Rhodesia case.

Did trade have to cease? It is by no means a settled principle that where a Communist state has no diplomatic representation neither shall it trade. History is replete with instances of the *prior establishment* of commercial relations. But in every case the Communist state wanted, and the other State refused, diplomatic recognition. So economics and politics alike indicated trade with the citizens of the power refusing recognition. The USSR in peace-time has only broken off existing diplomatic relations, it seems, with Albania and Australia as related above; history records no other cases. Thus the Soviet Government may possibly have felt a trade embargo to be an ontologically inescapable part of the diplomatic action they held necessary. If so, this is a great and rather unexpected disadvantage of being an STE; for naturally an ME can always withdraw its embassy and yet permit its enterprises to continue to trade.

7

A striking case of successful economic warfare is that against *Finland in late 1958*. The reader needs perhaps only the following background. Finland's visible trade with the USSR is about 20% of her total, as shown in Table XVII/2.

TABLE XVII/2. FINNISH TRADE WITH THE USSR, 1957–61
(mn. mark)

	1957	1958	1959	1960	1961
Total Imports	227,927	233,303	267,300	340,300	369,021
From USSR	40,356	41,937	47,548	46,966	50,268
Total exports	212,385	247,934	267,322	316,474	337,405
To USSR	42,433	43,782	44,793	45,012	40,877
To USSR, Oct.–Jan.	14,494	15,944	10,302	14,672	n.a.

SOURCE: Finnish Statistical Bureau, *Finland Officiella Statistik 1A* (annual). I am also indebted to my colleague, Mr. Altti Majava. The figures entitled 'Oct.–Jan.' stretch from October in the year of the column in which they appear to the next January, inclusive.

[1] Though the Soviet embassy was not closed in Belgrade in 1948, the language used, and the troop mobilizations, made the situation much more threatening for Yugoslavia than most more formal breakages of diplomatic relations.

By 1958, reparations and even the triangular arrangements referred to in Chapter X, section 8, had ceased. So the large Finnish engineering industry, built up to send reparations to the USSR and continued thereafter by the triangles, was very dependent on its Soviet market.

Based on memories of the civil war in 1918, the Communist Party in Finland is strong. It gets nearly a quarter of the votes but did not take part in the government from 1948 to 1966. Among the other parties, attitudes to the USSR vary from firm but conciliatory to conciliatory but firm. Each attitude is represented in all parties, but the Agrarians tend to the latter. The very active president, Kekkonen, is such an Agrarian. The Soviet question looms very large over Finland, but since agreement is so widespread and the situation so surprisingly stable Finns can afford to relax: politics is normally about the terms of domestic trade between industry and agriculture.

At the beginning of 1958 Finland's relations with the USSR were peaceful and normal. If on April 1, TASS declared its 'anxiety' over the anti-Soviet thinking of the Finnish right wing, that too was normal; that kind of minor pressure occurs all the time, and Finnish governments know how to deal with it. On May 23, President Kekkonen was very cordially received by Khrushchev, who promised a credit of R. 400–500 mn. for the purchase of Soviet goods, and transit rights for fifty years through the Saimaa Canal.[1]

In the general elections of July 7, the Communists[2] did unexpectedly well, obtaining 50 seats out of 200, a gain of 7. Apart from them only the Conservatives gained. The Agrarians, who had been the main government party, lost 5 seats. This was quite contrary to their expectations, since they had hoped by a very conciliatory Soviet policy to win votes from the Communists. Feeling deprived of a popular mandate on the above ground, and because of their unpopular choice of a price of butter, they stayed clear of the negotiations over a new cabinet. On July 31, Kekkonen asked the Communists to form a coalition cabinet. Everyone knew that this was a matter of form, and in two days they failed.

At about this moment the Agrarians took the view that softness on Communism had not paid, and they might as well join a general coalition provided the price of butter was right. Izvestia (August) expressed concern over this change of heart. Finally on August 29,

[1] Important for the transport of timber, over half of this canal now lies in Soviet territory.
[2] Strictly, Democratic League of the People of Finland, a front organization.

the Social Democrat Fagerholm formed a cabinet of all parties except the Communists and Independent Socialists. The presence of Conservatives, and of Mr. Leskinen, a right-wing Social Democrat, in this cabinet was particularly irritating to the USSR.

Meanwhile, pushed somewhat unwillingly by China, the USSR had attacked Yugoslavia in May, and found herself further constrained by Chinese and East German pressure to take a more forward line in September. For if China could make so loud a noise as she then was making over Formosa, why was there quiet over Berlin? Already on September 3, Ulbricht had pointed out the parallel between Berlin and Taiwan, and finally on November 10 Khrushchev delivered his famous 'slow ultimatum' to the Western powers to get out.

The atmosphere in Northern Europe being thus newly heated, and in face of the unusual irritation caused by recent Finnish political events, Khrushchev could not but get tough with Finland too. Articles in *Izvestia* had achieved nothing. So he turned to economics. By October 9, he had still not begun discussions of the loan promised in May, nor implemented his promise about the Saimaa Canal. A fishing agreement, completed in August, had not yet been signed. On October 12, Mr. Lebedev, the Soviet ambassador, was withdrawn and not replaced.

In mid-November, certain Finnish exporters were told that for the rest of the year, regardless of contracts, their deliveries to the USSR must be curtailed. By November 22, the Agrarians began to pull out of the cabinet, containing as it did *personae non gratae* in Moscow. They finally did so on December 4, feeling that they should never after all have deserted their traditional conciliatory policy. Meanwhile, negotiations for next year's trade protocol had not yet begun, though they normally did so in November. Part-time working was now widespread, owing to the slowdown in exports to the USSR, and on December 9, the Communists staged a big demonstration against unemployment and in favor of the USSR— and of their own participation in the cabinet.

On December 16, Parliament resolved that the government should use its powers to increase imports from USSR, so as to finance more Soviet-bound exports. Apparently the USSR had excused the slow-down of its purchases on b.o.p. grounds, with at least this much good reason, that the lag of Finnish imports is a perennial problem. After all, as Finnish businessmen say, what is there to buy?

The forms were preserved, and the Communists were consulted this time again. But the cabinet that emerged on January 13, 1959, was almost purely Agrarian. With President Kekkonen's next visit to Khrushchev on January 22, the crisis was over.

So what had USSR gained? Mr. Leskinen and the Conservatives were out of the cabinet, and she had shown her strength. How much more strength than that reflected in this cabinet change, it is difficult to say. For instance the Communists had got nowhere near the cabinet, but perhaps that was their aim, not Moscow's. It would need very detailed knowledge of things that subsequent Finnish governments wanted to do but did not do, for us to estimate the total political benefit to Moscow of this episode. Moreover after 1960 Finland has dropped her Soviet-bound exports from one sixth to one eighth of the total, and also in absolute terms, so that the threat through economic warfare is diminished. Nay more, the original threat was not only to refuse to buy exports but also to withhold concessions: the loan and the Saimaa Canal. In other words had not the concessions been promised in the first place we hardly know whether the threat to exports alone would have sufficed. The original promise of these concessions, be it noted, had only a chance relation to the crisis.

From the point of view of technique, two points are worth noting. First, the USSR, like all STEs, has a chronic shortage of convertible currency and a chronic difficulty in selling to economies that are—let us not say more advanced, but—used to good-quality manufactures, with assurance of spare parts and servicing. Her exports to Finland are thus largely raw materials, and there is nothing Finland would like better than permission not to buy (Chapter VIII, section 16). So on the one hand the USSR could not use the bottleneck effect, because all her exports have Western substitutes, and on the other she was, and always is, in genuine if only bilateral b.o.p. difficulties. But, secondly, Finland cannot sell her manufactures elsewhere, since they are not of specially good quality and are designed for Soviet use. Consequently the USSR could and did use the unemployment effect, as described in the previous chapter. The whole thing was by no means a farce, as in the Australian case.

The presence of Communists in the Finnish cabinet of 1966 is altogether too remote to be attributable to this quarrel of seven years previously. In the interval Khrushchev the bully has given way to Kosygin the diplomat, and the Finnish Communist Party has evolved into a position of almost Italian liberalism.

8

The economic wars with Yugoslavia 1958–60, and China 1960–date, are better called commercial quarrels. There was no embargo, but a slow reduction of trade, in both cases strikingly unselective. There is thus a distinct resemblance to the contemporary war with Finland; the main difference being the lack of any positive outcome. This lack is so notable that I feel the name of economic war would imply too clear a sense of purpose. In other words, Khrushchev was even more half-hearted about these things than Stalin. We can guess a plausible reason also for this: he was pretending to himself that he was not waging war at all, that he was simply reacting to the bad commercial practices of his opponent. So instead of a swift and ruthless cut-off all along the line, or at least of bottleneck commodities, there was a slow erosion of all trade year by year.

This is nowhere more clear than in the case of Yugoslavia, 1958–60. When Khrushchev liquidated Stalin's campaign against Tito in 1955, he also promised aid, i.e. loans, and increased trade from zero to a very respectable figure. Then in 1956 Tito supported Imre Nagy, and in 1957 he refused to attend the fortieth anniversary conference of ruling parties in Moscow, let alone sign its rather dogmatic resolution. Mao Tse-tung, already at that time toying with his new extremist line, took it into his head in Moscow that Tito was the arch-enemy. When in 1958 the Yugoslavs brought out a 'revisionist' new Party Programme, and opposed the execution of Imre Nagy, Mao's cup of anger overflowed. In May 1958 he attacked Yugoslavia root and branch, and forced Khrushchev reluctantly to follow suit. In that month, USSR reneged upon her aid promises, as shown in Table XVII/3, and demonstrated again that Soviet aid is no less political than the United States.

However, it could hardly be said that USSR declared economic war on Yugoslavia, when their inter-trade turnover dropped, in 1957–58, by a mere 20% in current prices. Turnover, on a non-aid basis, rose again after 1958, even before the public outbreak of the Sino-Soviet quarrel in 1960. From this point on, of course, Yugoslavia was not taboo at all. Moreover the satellites, if that is the correct word for them in 1958, took very little notice of this brief refroidissement: for the most part their trade with Yugoslavia (again, in current prices) continued to grow at a moderate rate. They had entered in 1956 into agreements to resume reparations (in the Hungarian case), and to settle other debts outstanding from Stalin's

TABLE XVII/3. YUGOSLAVIA'S VISIBLE TRADE
(mn. dinars, 1 dinar = $0·00333)

		1953	1954	1955	1956	1957	1958	1959	1960	1961	1962	1963
Bulgaria .	E	+	+	+	+	1234	570	2409	2565	2536	1872	2677
	I	+	+	+	+	1257	1600	1402	2174	2972	3129	2871
Czechoslovakia	E	−	866	2177	2455	2584	5853	4918	7724	5067	6404	6958
	I	−	332	2197	3616	5685	8213	6946	7873	5943	7728	12,916
Hungary .	E	−	269	833	1902	3597	4231	3919	6129	5405	3316	3687
	I	−	266	845	1918	5915	10,694	9469	10,975	9851	6279	7600
DDR .	E	+	275	622	1308	3122	7907	8000	13,915	9052	10,601	11,363
	I	+	67	662	950	2278	7881	8661	11,207	11,286	10,906	14,775
Poland .	E	−	−	1156	2684	4853	6604	10,157	6627	12,142	12,693	11,466
	I	−	−	1257	2361	5763	10,764	6081	11,344	8583	9634	9948
Rumania .	E	+	+	+	+	1318	706	536	1792	3201	2198	1501
	I			+	+	1110	1401	1104	2689	2512	1064	1998
USSR .	E	−	439	5385	12,669	14,675	10,922	14,154	15,803	15,209	12,988	25,612
	I	−	318	4334	21,139	20,799	17,345	17,288	17,081	9601	17,742	21,860
USA .	E	7801	6870	8311	8223	10,022	9889	9344	11,589	10,961	15,669	13,893
	I	40,754	28,446	43,250	38,767	52,121	40,197	42,004	26,549	54,357	54,862	55,833
Total .	E	55,794	72,113	76,976	97,011	118,533	132,419	142,995	169,848	170,670	207,146	237,103
	I	118,591	101,819	132,288	142,243	198,394	205,504	206,156	247,916	273,087	266,317	316,986
Soviet aid promises .					90,000[2]							−
Drawings on Soviet aid .		−	−	−	16,120	2140	2460	−451[1]	−	+	+	+

SOURCE: *Statistički Godišnjak*, various years; IMF, *Balance of Payments Yearbook*.
[1] Net repayment.
[2] Department of State, *The Sino-Soviet Economic Offensive in the Less Developed Countries* (Washington, 1958). Other figures for this promise differ within 10%.
− Sign for zero or negligible, as in source.
+ Presumed zero or negligible by me, nothing given in source.

economic war. Beginning payment in that year, they continued to service these debts satisfactorily. It will be remembered that they have also failed to go along with the Soviet embargo on Albania. Things were very different in 1948–53.

For Yugoslav-Chinese trade itself we have, it seems, no figures.

9

The *Sino-Soviet quarrel* has led to much unpleasantness but to few acts of economic warfare. It might almost be enough to say that: (i) through political faults on either side, Soviet experts were no longer usable in China, so the Chinese no longer demanded the machinery exports that went with them; (ii) commerce in general had been irrationally big when we consider transport costs (Chapter IX, section 25), so that 1960–61 simply saw a reduction to more rational levels; (iii) it is impossible to do much business with someone you hate, and who hates you.

There are many mysteries, but so far as the course of events can be reconstructed, it was as follows. In his life-time, Stalin did almost nothing for China. His two publicized loans, both of them economic, amounted, on an annual basis, to about 0·07% of the Soviet national income and 0·15% of the Chinese. At any time about 0·1% of his active male graduates were in China as advisers.[1] With this number compare the following totals of East European and Soviet technicians in the first half of 1962:

Afghanistan 2325, Guinea 1080, Egypt 960, Cuba 950, Iraq 830, India 665, total *c.* 10,000. Of these USSR provided about 70%.[2]

Stalin's military support in 1952 had been a substitute for direct Soviet military intervention in Korea: instead of which he *lent* money to China to do the fighting he had started! In 1953–58 China *bought* back certain mixed companies, and the military stores and installations of Port Arthur. This was on credit, hence the enormous loans of 1954–55. She received in this period no further economic loans, but on the contrary in 1956 was forced, or herself

[1] He lent $430 mn. in 1950–56, or $70 mn. per annum. The Soviet national income was R. (old) 1184 md. in 1955, and I estimate the ruble's wholesale purchasing power at 8 United States cents. The Chinese national income was Y.86 md. and the yuan was worth about 55 United States cents. There were 1390 economic and military advisers to be withdrawn in August, 1960, and altogether 10,800 visited China during 1949–59 (Sidney Klein, *The Road Divides* [Hong Kong, 1966], pp. 53, 76). These two figures are compatible with a slight build up over time, and an average stay of one year. There were 1·9 mn. Soviet males with a completed higher education in January, 1959, including those who had retired.

[2] Edward Taborsky in *Hinter dem Eisernen Vorhang*, Radio Free Europe (Munich, February, 1964), quoting the United States State Department.

decided, to begin to amortize all this borrowing. Her quarrel with USSR began in 1958. It was mainly non-economic, and broke out for reasons that hardly concern us here: the Soviet refusal to deliver atom bombs, the Soviet failure to intervene against the United States invasion of the Lebanon, the Yugoslav Party Programme, the execution of Imre Nagy, the Chinese claim to be, through the People's Communes, nearer to Full Communism.

TABLE XVII/4. CHINA'S ECONOMIC RELATIONS WITH THE USSR

	China's Visible Civilian Exports[a]	China's Estimated Civilian Trade and Freight Balance[b]	China's Publicized Long-term Civilian Borrowings[c]	Drawings on All Long-term Borrowings[d]	Estimated Amortization[d]	Interest[d, f]
	(mn. dollars)				(mn. domestic yuan)	
1950	180	+20	300	244	0	0
1951	310	−140		625	0	−5
1952	420	−140		1305	−320	−15
1953	470	−230		438	0	−25
1954	560	−170	130	884	−100	−30
1955	640	−420[g]		1657	−400	−80
1956	740	+10		117·4	−400	−80
1957	740	+180		23·3	−400	−80
1958	880	+220		0	−560	−70
1959	1100	+140		0	−560	−70
1960	830	−10		0	−660	−60
1961	560	+180		1460[e]	−700	−40
1962	510	+270		0	−1140	−20
1963	420	+230		0	−920	−20
1964	320	+180		0	−800	0
1965	220	+20		n.a.	n.a.	0
			Total	6754	6960	

SOURCES: [a] Read from graph in Joint Economic Committee of Congress, *An Economic Profile of Mainland China* (Washington, 1967), p. 595. Since there is a contiguous land frontier, we need no adjustment for f.o.b. and c.i.f.
[b] Balance of trade with USSR, ibid. Subtract from this 10% on China's imports from E. Europe (op. cit., p. 594) to allow for Soviet freight charges (from 1952, 10% on one half, assuming the rest went in Polish ships).
[c] The two items often publicized.
[d] As in Chinese budget statements through 1959.
[e] A Soviet funding of short indebtedness incurred during the Great Leap Forward (op. cit., p. 640; see end of Section 9 here).
[f] Put at 1% on the balance of the first loan (which was stated to be at 1%), and 2% on the balance after 1955 (op. cit., p. 658). The unpublished military loans seem to have been at 2%. I have distributed the consolidated figures in op. cit., p. 640 to individual years according to my own rough calculation.
[g] Includes the transfers of mixed companies and perhaps some military installations.

Nevertheless, we may sympathize with China for feeling economically quarrelsome. However, she was in a weak position to wage economic war, so in fact preferred other methods of controversy. *Until the summer of 1960 the USSR took no economic reprisals.* On the contrary, trade expanded, and, in the words of Oleg Hoeffding[1] :

Both in 1958 and 1959, the level of trade was considerably in excess of what had been provided for by the annual trade protocols for those years. The excess reflected Soviet willingness to meet supplementary Chinese shopping lists, presented in a helter-skelter fashion that must have been quite irksome to Soviet economic planners. In August, 1958, and again in February, 1959, the USSR still proved willing to add substantially to its earlier commitments to support Chinese industrialization by selling more or less complete sets of equipment for industrial plants to be built with Soviet technical aid. Under two agreements concluded at those dates, the USSR undertook to assist with construction of an additional 125 projects.

As shown in Table 2, the value of deliveries described in Soviet statistics as 'complete sets of equipment' reached a peak in 1959, accounting for 42% of total exports to China.

Moscow, it is true, extended no credits to China to finance this import expansion. It made the Chinese pay promptly by concurrently stepping up their exports to the USSR. However, Moscow showed itself accommodating by accepting payment, increasingly, in Chinese manufactured consumer goods, a class of goods traditionally low on the Soviet scale of import priorities. . . . The principal items in this class—fabrics, clothing and footwear—represented more than one-third of total Soviet imports in 1959, running a close second to agricultural raw materials and foodstuffs which earlier had been the mainstay of China's exports to the USSR. China would have been hard put to find other markets in which to exchange such quantities of consumer goods for capital equipment vital to its industrialization ambitions.

Soviet responsiveness to China's needs, however, had its reverse side in attitudes which the Chinese may have found predatory and cynical. Far from granting new credits, the USSR insisted on punctilious discharge of China's debts.

However, in summer 1960, the USSR withdrew her all-important experts. It is alleged that her excuse for so doing was that China had insisted on taking over their political education.[2] If the Chinese really did make this move, it was of course an appalling breach of Communist principle, amply justifying the withdrawal of the threatened persons. But it does not seem to be true. I base this judgment on the very valuable personal account of the Soviet chemist, M. A. Klochko,[3] who was one of those hastily withdrawn, and later defected in Canada. A Ukrainian, Klochko is

---

[1] *Sino-Soviet Economic Relations 1958–1962*, RAND Corporation, RM-3787-PR, 1963, pp. 7–8.

[2] ed. Geoffrey Hudson and R. McFarquhar, *The Sino-Soviet Dispute*, China Quarterly publication, 1961, pp. 226–7, suggests that both sides agree this happened.

[3] *Soviet Scientist in China* (New York, 1964), pp. 65–9, 137–8, 143–5, 151, 166–7.

distinctly pro-Chinese. He says that the *casus belli* was the acrimonious public debate between Khrushchev and Peng Chen at the Rumanian Party Congress in June. He also reports no serious attempts to subvert his Party loyalty—quite the contrary, he was bound at all times to attend Soviet Party meetings. But he does not deny that China was most wastefully disregarding Soviet technical advice, just as she was disregarding native technical advice. He also states that since late 1959 Soviet advisers were literally not allowed out of their hotels or institutes alone. He effectively compares this withdrawal with Stalin's equally sudden withdrawal of his experts from Yugoslavia in March 1948.

Thus, USSR had much provocation to withdraw her experts, but was still surely in the wrong. In any case, it was this, and no purely economic act, that was the *casus belli*. But the economic effects on China were very serious.

China reacted, for instance, by reducing her demand for Soviet machines. There were in any case better machines available in Western Europe, so China bought them instead, and Soviet offers were not taken up. As she said in one of her innumerable letters:

Your sudden withdrawal of all the Soviet experts working in China upset the schedules of construction and the production arrangements of many of our factories, mines and other enterprises and establishments, and had a direct impact on our need for the import of complete sets of equipment. Such being the case, did you expect us to keep on buying them just for display?[1]

This is an admission that China could have continued to buy. Indeed we may further ask why, if China could buy West European machinery without admitting experts, she could not buy Soviet machinery, with which she was more familiar, when the experts were withdrawn.

So little real Sino-Soviet economic war was there that nonmachinery imports kept up very well (see Table XVII/5, p. 513).

Indeed between 1958 and 1961 the decline in machinery, etc., hardly exceeded the decline in China's agricultural exports, brought about by the Great Leap Forward. Even without the withdrawal of Soviet experts, it might have been a natural thing. Again the all-important oil item kept up; yet its reduction was a 'natural' for USSR, had she seriously been waging economic war. For however competitive is the oil world in general, here the USSR had almost a monopoly. Her sole soft currency competitor was Rumania, which sold a quarter as much to China in 1961, and only equalled her

[1] *Peking Review*, May 8, 1964.

sales in 1963, when they had dropped off considerably. The Far East does not abound in any oil, let alone soft currency oil, and China would have had to pay exorbitantly to replace Soviet supplies. Moreover Rumania's 'declaration of independence' came only in 1962, and she might not have cooperated. As to domestic oil, China's new oil field did indeed make her autarkic by 1965, but in 1961 it had only just been discovered. These facts alone make the phrase 'economic war' unacceptable.

TABLE XVII/5. CHINA'S TRADE WITH USSR IN DETAIL
(mn. new valuta rubles)

	1958	1959	1960	1961	1962	1963	1964
Imports							
Machinery and equipment .	286	538	454	97	25	38	52
Iron and steel . . .	55	43	53	31	25	10	19
Crude oil and petroleum products	83	106	102	109	73	55	19
Foodstuffs . . .	1	0	0	57	19	0	0
Other	146	178	127	36	68	65	32
Total apart from machinery, etc.	285	321	281	234	185	130	70
Total	571	859	735	331	210	168	122
Exports							
Agricultural . . .	351	403	236	45	—	—	—
Fabrics, clothing, footwear .	198	352	338	287	—	—	—
Other	244	236	189	164	—	—	—
Total	793	990	763	496	465	372	283

SOURCE: Soviet foreign-trade yearbooks.

Nor was Chinese retaliation lacking, though here too we are forced, *faute de mieux*, to rely on Soviet data:

'Since 1960 the Chinese have severely cut the supplies of tin, mercury, tungsten and molybdenum concentrates to the USSR; also, products such as tantalum and beryllium concentrates, piezoelectric crystals and the like were removed from the list of supplies to the Soviet Union. At the same time there are data available that these strategic raw materials are being exported from the Chinese People's Republic to imperialist countries.'[1]

Further to complicate the story, USSR was comparatively generous to China after her harvest failure of 1960. As Table XVII/4 shows, China, bound by agreement to amortize her previous debts, failed altogether to do so in 1960. Her shortfall from her obligations in 1960 alone was said by the Russians to be (new valuta) R. 288 mn.,[2] implying that a favorable balance of c. R. 291 mn. had been planned. This debt, it was agreed, would be paid off in 1961–65, beyond doubt over and above all other debts. But at least there was no

[1] *Izvestia*, June 4, 1964.
[2] *Vneshnyaya Torgovlya*, May, 1961, pp. 17–18. Cf. Ye Chi-shuan, *Pravda*, April 9, 1961.

interest, and the Soviet action appears neither generous nor un-
generous in itself. It was, however, most unfriendly when we compare
the Soviet treatment of a North Korean debt in November 1960.
The very big sum of R. (new valuta) 203 mn. was forgiven or newly
promised as aid; whereas China got no debt forgiveness and no
new loans or gifts at all.

China, however, has paid or even pre-paid her debt. In bad years
like 1960, when her balance was unfavorable, she must have used
convertible currency.

10

We turn to that more pleasant branch of economic warfare, the
attraction of neutrals. Here first is a case of gross failure, falling
mostly within Stalin's lifetime: *Iran, 1951-53*.[1]

On April 28, 1951, Moussadegh became Prime Minister on a
program of nationalizing the Anglo-Iranian Oil Company. The
British government, owning 50% of the shares therein, pointed
out that this would be a breach of treaty, and offered to renegotiate
on royalties and taxes. The two sides were very far apart on both
issues, and on September 27, Iranian officials occupied the premises
of the AIOC. Between April and September Soviet reaction seems
only to have been to fear a British attack. On May 16, the newspaper *Dad* feared that in that case Soviet troops would cross the
border. This would have been legal by the Iranian-Soviet Treaty
of 1921, which gives the USSR the right to send troops whenever
Iran is invaded by a third power. *Dad* also reported Soviet troop
concentrations, which an Iranian officer confirmed on June 6.
Meanwhile the line of Radio Free Azerbaijan, a Soviet station pretending to be in Iranian Azerbaijan, was: 'Be patient, the hour of
freedom is near.' It did, however, also have the sense to offer Soviet
technicians to replace British ones.

This suggestion was not, however, taken up by Iran, which
proceeded to operate the refinery itself, very lamely and at much
reduced output. It was unable to sell the output, since the international oil world, a small and tight-knit circle, refused to buy, and
threatened with boycott anyone who did buy.

It would be difficult to exaggerate the hatred of the Iranian people,
under Moussadegh's inflammatory leadership, for the AIOC and
Britain, or the atmosphere of world crisis engendered by the dispute.
Meanwhile, the USSR, instead of profiting by this xenophobia,

[1] I have used mainly Utrikespolitisk Institutets *Kalendarium* (Stockholm, annually).

drew much of it upon herself. Thus the United States, seeking very naturally both stability in the area and its own profit, intervened to offer both mediation in the dispute and economic aid to Iran. On May 12, 1952, the USSR told Iran that acceptance would contravene the 1921 treaty, a rather sinister threat implying that the USSR might exercise the right under that treaty already described. On July 1, Iran rejected the argument in this note, and United States influence continued to increase. On August 2, it is true, the Senate resolved that United States military advisers should leave, but it far more importantly resolved to terminate the Soviet fisheries concession in the Caspian. Originally granted in 1927, this concession was to run out in October, 1952; it involved a Soviet station on Iranian soil. On August 14, Fascist rioters destroyed the Soviet information office in Teheran.

On January 2, 1953, the oil crisis continuing to steal the headlines, Moussadegh in fact denounced the fisheries concession, and on February 2, the USSR tamely accepted this. It was only after this that the first break occurred in the front of the international oil cartel.[1] The Italian company Supor sent its chartered tanker the *Miriella* to Abadan, where it picked up oil at half-price. The oil was landed in Venice on February 14, and on March 11, the Venetian court rejected the AIOC's contention that the oil was stolen. The *Miriella* was meanwhile on a second trip. On May 27, a Japanese court protected the Indemitsu Company in the same way. In neither country had the AIOC exhausted the possibilities of appeal when on August 16, 1953, Moussadegh fell to Zahedi's *coup d'état*, and the oil crisis was as good as over. The new and more rational government got a settlement very favorable to Iran, and Moussadegh had succeeded in excluding not only the British but also, almost by accident, the Russians.

I conclude that here was an ideal opportunity for Stalin, which by his inflexibility he muffed badly. He alone could offer courts of law in which the AIOC's suits for repossession could be guaranteed to fail. If he could not supply the tankers himself, nor even afford to charter them, at least he could permit the 'rogue elephants' of the oil world to pick up the oil and sell it to him. Instead, he at first behaved as if the British would invade; concentrating troops, using his bogus Azerbaijani radio, and preparing to invoke the 'imperialistic' 1921 treaty. When in October, 1951, he perceived

---

[1] The tanker *Rose Mary* had been forced into Aden in December, 1952, by an act, presumably, of British piracy. The Aden court handed over the oil to the AIOC on January 9, 1953.

that Britain would use no force, he should instantly have switched to economic warfare. This he notably failed to do: Soviet-Iranian trade did not greatly increase in 1952, and in particular no oil was bought. Even token purchases would have won him warm applause and friendship. Nor was the USSR an oil exporter (even within the bloc) herself at that time,[1] so such purchases would not even have been uneconomic. So great was Stalin's failure here that Iranian xenophobia turned partly against the USSR as well, though she had been a wholly innocent bystander; and the fishing concession was lost.

The relevant trade figures are as follows:

TABLE XVII/6. IRAN'S TRADE WITH USSR

(mn. rials; 32·25 rials = $1)

	1948	1949	1950	1951	1952	1953	1954
Visible exports to all countries[1]	19,007	17,175	25,747	11,232	2657	3196	5886
Visible exports to USSR[1]	28·4	n.a.	24·1	973	689	381	593
Visible imports from USSR[1]	21·8	n.a.	329·3	807	722	307	542
Exports in b.o.p. statement:[2]							
Caspian Fisheries	42	65	65	69	70	79	36
Direct	263	287	240	871	728	n.a.	381

[1] From the trade accounts.
[2] Persian solar years: thus the figures under 1948 are from March 21, 1948 to March 20, 1949. It would appear that the earlier trade figures have counted exports to USSR as going to some intermediate destination.
SOURCES: U.N. *Yearbook of International Trade Statistics*; I.M.F., *Balances of Payments*.

Thus trade with the USSR did increase sharply, but oil was not among the objects traded.

II

In the case of *Iceland 1956* a neutral was indeed wooed, but not won. Though the economic wooing was quite efficient, the USSR had bad political luck at the end, when the Hungarian Revolution shook Icelandic politics to their depths and undid all the good of Soviet fish purchases irretrievably.

[1] *Narodnoye Khozyaistvo SSR 1961* (Moscow, 1962), pp. 545–6. The flood of extra-bloc oil exports, which converted the USSR from a net importer to a net exporter, was, indeed, a major policy change made on Stalin's death [Leonard M. Fanning, *Foreign Oil and the Free World* (New York, 1954), pp. 255–8]. It involved, of course, greatly accelerated production increases. Such exports, beginning under Malenkov in 1953, are irrelevant to the situation in 1952 under Stalin.

The tangled story goes back to the last war. The Icelandic people had always bitterly resented the British invasion of 1940 and the United States NATO base that was its ultimate outcome. Britons and Americans were easily the most unpopular foreigners. In March, 1952, the government unilaterally extended its territorial waters for fishing purposes, by drawing the line between promontories rather than hugging the coast, and by anyway expanding the then usual 3 miles to 4 miles. Thus, many valuable fishing grounds were denied to foreigners. This was a breach of international law,[1] and it led to an embargo at Grimsby and Hull against Icelandic landings. But the trawler owners of Grimsby had forgotten, if they ever knew, the trauma of 1940.

The cup of this basically neutralist people thus ran over. In 1953 the USSR stepped in and began to buy fish. She exchanged it for her oil, newly made available for export. Her policy must have been to use the extreme unpopularity of the British to get rid of the United States base. The general elections of this year gave the Communists only 7 seats out of 52 (previously 9). But the two seats they lost went to the National Defense Party, non-Communist and petty bourgeois but opposed to the base. Altogether the anti-United States vote may be said to have risen from 20% to 25% of the poll. In 1954, the Russians made significant gains: the United States–Icelandic defense treaty was revised. The United States was to employ more local labor, and to confine her personnel to her bases. In 1955 STEs promised aid for the first time, but of course deliveries

TABLE XVII/7. ICELAND'S VISIBLE TRADE AND OFFICIAL AID
(mn. krónur, 1951–59, 16·32 krónur = $1)

	1951	1952	1953	1954	1955	1956	1957	1958	1959
Total exports	727	641	706	846	848	1032	988	1070	1060
To USSR			89	128	156	203	213	176	194
To UK	170	89	74	79	71	96	93	81	90
To US	133	158	108	144	99	128	91	133	179
Total imports	924	910	1110	1131	1266	1469	1362	1398	1542
From USSR			22	132	173	243	279	245	248
From UK	265	189	128	129	138	135	158	142	138
From US	121	185	295	229	283	245	181	194	242
Fuel oil, gasoline and lubricating oil (thousands of tons):									
Total	177	237	283	242	268	293	315	344	392
From USSR	0	0	39	218	232	265	294	322	347
Official aid, net drawings:									
Total	0	0	0	0	0·2	82·6	144·5	98·9	52·8
From US	0	0	0	0	3·4	62·5	98·4	35·3	76·8
From STEs	0	0	0	0	0	0	17·6	29·6	−6·8

SOURCES: Icelandic statistical yearbooks; IMF, *Balance of Payments Yearbook*.

[1] Iceland quoted the Norwegian precedent, but Norway had made no unilateral move.

did not occur for many months, as shown in Table XVII/7. The total promised was krónur 408 mn.;[1] in the event nothing like that was delivered, as we saw in Chapter XIV, section 9.

The year 1956 was the high point of Soviet influence. On March 28, the Alting resolved (31 to 18, 3 abstentions) that the base must go. The elections of June gave the Communists one more seat, but wiped out the National Defense Party. Nevertheless, the Independence Party (conservative) had alone supported the base in the campaign, and a coalition government was formed of all parties except the independents, with the first Communist in the cabinet. This was Mr. Ludvik Josepsson, who took over precisely the portfolio of Fisheries and Foreign Trade. Increasing slightly her position over 1955, the USSR became top trading partner.

Hungary (October, 1956) changed the whole picture. In November, the Social Democrats switched their position on the base. At the same time the fishing dispute with the UK was settled by an Icelandic victory. In December the United States was able to announce that the Icelandic Government had withdrawn its request for the removal of the base. In 1957 the United States in her turn promised more aid, but as the table shows she was always well ahead in this respect. The STEs' aid promises were grossly underfulfilled, and deliveries petered out as shown.

The electoral position has not much changed since 1956, but from the next general elections (1959) the country has been governed by a coalition of Independents and Social Democrats. The USSR is left with her memories, and a large ongoing exchange of fish for oil which she has tactfully and—no doubt—profitably not cut back. The odd Soviet car appears on the streets. It is not too much to say, but it cannot be proved, that had it not been for Hungary there would now be no base.

12

Our next instance is again one when the weapons of economic war were not used, although they surely might have been. On September 6, 1961, diplomatic relations were broken off between Pakistan and *Afghanistan*[2] in the course of a border quarrel. Trade with Pakistan and transit trade both ceased. This transit trade comprised 'most of Afghanistan's imports and some of her exports'.[3]

---

[1] $25 mn.: Robert L. Allen, *Soviet Economic Warfare* (Washington, 1960), p. 265.
[2] I have mainly used the *New York Times* and the *Yearbook* of the *Bol'shaya Sovetskaya Entsiklopedia*. For the background cf. Peter G. Franck, *Afghanistan* (New York, 1960).
[3] *New York Times*, September 29, 1961.

Afghanistan was thereby placed almost wholly within the economic power of the USSR. Now at this time, as both previously and subsequently, the Communist Party was prohibited in Afghanistan, albeit its agents had a great deal of factual freedom. Nevertheless, here was an issue about which a powerful Communist neighbor might well feel strongly, and even bound in proletarian duty to act. No doubt, too, there were dozens of other issues, as there might be between any neighboring states. The Soviet opportunity was, of course, geographical. Afghanistan borders essentially upon three countries: Pakistan, Iran, the USSR.[1] Communications with Iran are negligible, so in September, 1961, the USSR was presented with a 100% stranglehold on Afghan foreign trade. To be precise, only rail transport is a serious factor for transit trade, and at the crucial moment of time there were four practical railheads. The first is at Kushka in the Turkmen Republic, and there is one other railhead on the Soviet border at Termez in the Uzbek Republic. There are also railheads at Chaman and the Khyber Pass in Pakistan. Of the three main cities, Kabul is 150 km. from the Khyber Pass, Herat is 100 km. from Kushka, and Kandahar 100 km. from Chaman. On the Persian side, the nearest railhead is 500 km. from Herat.

Incidentally—it is of less importance—there were in 1961 as good as no railways in Afghanistan, the first 5 km. being built in 1959–60 from Kushka south to Turgundi. For the rest, all internal transport, and all connection to foreign railhead, was by road.

The direction of Afghanistan's visible trade moved as shown in Table XVII/8 on p. 520.

As to aid, the USSR in 1961 was outspending the United States two to one, but Harrison Salisbury held that psychologically the United States was holding its own (*New York Times*, November 26, 1961). Nevertheless, the prestige of the United States as an aider was shaken by her refusal to commit herself more than one fiscal year ahead (*New York Times*, June 12, 1962), whereas already on October 18, 1961, the USSR had signed an 'economic and technical co-operation agreement' covering the whole of the second Afghan five-year plan.

The moment the Pakistani transit trade ceased, United States aid began to pile up in the Himalayas, and official circles in the United States became very gloomy. The Merchant mission, sent out to re-open the transit, failed, and on November 7, 1961, the *New York*

---

[1] The Chinese stretch of frontier is a remote snippet of Sinkiang desert. Next to it comes a similar frontier with Kashmir, in the part occupied by Pakistan.

Times practically wrote Afghanistan off to Communism. Afghan traders urged the mission to ship its aid via the USSR; it was discovered that West European deliveries took 45 days on this route, against 75 days via Pakistan, at comparable cost (*New York Times*, November 13, 1961). Characteristically, the United States refused to use this route.

TABLE XVII/8. VISIBLE TRADE OF AFGHANISTAN, 1959–63

(mn. Afghans)

Imports

		1959	1960	1961	1962	1963
Total	. .	3650	3392	4124	5841	6303
Czechoslovakia	.	156	114	140	263	227
West Germany	.	106	123	151	202	193
India	. .	361	364	328	444	524
Iran	. .	—	—	—	73	—
Japan	. .	336	220	208	373	434
Pakistan	. .	109	96	94	9	94
USSR	. .	1687	1734	2189	3654	3201
UK	. .	63	71	42	71	98
US	. .	612	496	788	550	1122

Exports

		1959	1960	1961	1962	1963
Total	. .	2722	1949	2222	2967	3459
Czechoslovakia	.	85	115	84	130	289
West Germany	.	175	202	233	215	140
India	. .	488	268	214	401	455
Iran	. .	—	—	—	(0·09)	—
Japan	. .	—	—	—	—	—
Pakistan	. .	173	185	59	—	196
USSR	. .	725	427	695	1161	1066
UK	. .	415	299	362	381	474
US .	. .	579	401	418	452	560

SOURCE: United Nations, *Yearbooks of International Trade Statistics.*

One fascinating possibility is that what we have here is an Afghan or a Pakistani trick; that one or both sides were trying to frighten the United States with the bogy of a Soviet-Afghan trade war, and thus bring United States pressure to bear on the other side to make border concessions. It is certain that the United States was frightened in this way, and intervened vigorously to settle the border dispute, or at least to get transit rights for her trade and aid. The view that it was all or mostly an Afghan trick is, of course, Pakistani (*New York*

Times, October 5, 1961); it has this to support it, that in some sense Afghanistan closed her own border. She even re-opened it on January 23, 1962, for eight weeks to admit the United States aid piled up on the other side. But naturally she denied this version and attributed the whole cessation of transit trade to her enemy (*New York Times,* November 13, 1961). In any case, the final responsibility is not of much interest to us here.

On January 29, 1962, Afghanistan, having made a transit agreement with Iran, requested the United States to ship all her aid that way, but in March difficulties were reported owing to the poor roads (*The Times,* London, March 21, 1962). Nevertheless, on June 14, Afghanistan asked the United States for $350 mn. more aid over the next five years—the figure the USSR was reported to have offered.

United States diplomacy was active throughout, but achieved only Pakistan's permission for United States aid to pass. It at no time opened the frontier to normal trade with other countries. Soviet diplomacy seems to have been wholly passive. It is perhaps too much to ask that the USSR should have conciliated a quarrel that was so great a godsend, but it is more noteworthy, and less consonant with Western notions, that neither was it exacerbated or exploited. It was, in fact, the Shah of Iran who pressed his good offices (July 4, 1962)—again contrary to his country's interests, since he had stood to gain a new railway and a slice of the transit trade.

Eventually the Shah succeeded, and the border was finally re-opened on September 15, 1963, as part of a general re-establishment of relations.

13

The general lesson—to which the brilliant Finnish case is an important exception—is that the USSR is neither very skilled at nor very keen on economic war. Her weapons are crude, and she nearly always loses. In keenness especially she would seem to fall below United States standards. Moreover, as we see from earlier chapters, economic imperialism in any direct sense has practically ceased with Stalin. On the contrary, the USSR has moved from the tribute-exacting to the post-imperialist paying-out period in one decade. *She has never 'sent a gunboat'.* Debt collection and property protection rank miles behind politics for her.

But the USSR is not the only STE one might accuse of such practices. Yugoslavia, while she was an STE, behaved most imperialistically toward Albania, and China today is in a strong position to do the same. She could also, perhaps, 'exploit' North Vietnam and North Korea, though Soviet competition here is keen. However, China's allies and small neighbors (except Mongolia) give her a clean bill of health in this respect. It is not economic but political warfare that has got China into trouble (1966) round the world. The main reason is doubtless her own poverty: her factor endowment compels her to make war, if at all, either with masses of ill-armed men or with extremist political doctrines—she has nothing else to 'export'.

Finally we have to try to answer the fascinating question, Why do Communist economic wars usually occur between Communist states, and not with their principal and common enemy? One answer we have already given: in the general Cold War each side uses its best weapons, and that of economic war favors the side which is at present economically stronger. Communism is traditionally and continually trying to stop the great economic war. But as to quarrels between Communist states, what other weapons have they? The most comradely, ideologically correct weapon is to build up a friendly faction in the other country's Party. The trouble with this is quite simply that Communist security police forces are very efficient, and always liquidate such factions. Open propaganda is also much used. The Chinese, in a manner consonant with their labor-intensive economy, even spread it by hand from the Trans-siberian Railway. Espionage is certainly used, as we know from the Yugoslavs.[1]

But military war really cannot be used. There is no single instance of such a war between Communist states. Stalin was on the brink of it against Tito, troops being mobilized in Hungary and Yugo-slavia. Unarmed combat has broken out at various places along the Sino-Soviet border. Poland threatened war against the USSR in October, 1956. The Albanian-Yugoslav border used to be about as peaceful as Kipling's North-West Frontier. But real formal shooting on the grand scale would be too deep a disgrace. The Brotherhood of Man is a perfectly genuine part of Communist doctrine, deeply and sincerely held. If the intolerance, violence and mendacity of the creed—in all its sub-forms—makes brotherly feeling impossible among the comrades, nevertheless, some appearances simply must be preserved.

It is easy, then, to see why economic warfare is almost endemic

---

[1] Vladimir Dedijer, *Tito Speaks* (London, 1953). Cf. also *The Penkovsky Papers* (New York, 1966).

among Communist states: faction-building and propaganda are unsuccessful, and military action morally impossible. This leaves only economic warfare. Besides, you can always accuse the other side of being grasping, or of delivering bad-quality products—there are endless possibilities of chicanery, of pretending you are not at war when you are.

Finally, because among STEs each country is an enterprise, all trade is political: all quarrels about prices, etc., automatically rise to cabinet level if not settled lower down, involving both the state machine and national pride. Moreover, STEs are few; they would at best form an oligopoly, and in fact choose to be a series of bilateral monopolies. Yet oligopoly is in any case a state of economic war.[1]

[1] P. J. D. Wiles, *Price, Cost and Output* (2nd ed.), pp. 98–101.

CHAPTER XVIII

TRADE AND PEACE[1]

It would spread Christianity and lead to an outflow of precious metal.
—Japanese decree rejecting a Russian trade proposal, 1804

The Bolivians have never fought the Persians.
—EUGENE STALEY, *War and the Private Investor* (New York, 1935), p. 458

Torgovlya—torgovlya, a druzhba—druzhba (trade is trade and friendship is friendship).
—Phrase of Soviet foreign trade officials, according to Milentije Popović, Tito's Minister of Foreign Trade, *Über die Wirtschaftlichen Beziehungen Zwischen Sozialistischen Staaten* (Mainz, 1950), p. 30

All the true love that money can buy.
OSCAR BROWN, JR.

> With gold and fear and hate
> I have harnessed state to state.
> —RUDYARD KIPLING, *The Peace of Dives*

1 Smith and Mercantilism.
2 The Anglo-French example.
3 Is trade good for peace?—Constant, Cobden, Angell.
4 Is autarky better?—Fichte, Keynes.
5 Perfect competition and the relations between people and states.
6 An imaginary no-trade world.
7 Prosperity does not cause peace.
8 The effect on public opinion of international economic exchanges.
9 The same, cultural exchanges.
10 Foreign travel and personal impressions.
11 Trade the result, not the cause, of peace.
12 The bad results of ACC-UDC trade—
13 and even of STE-UDC trade.
14 However STE-ACC trade is happier. It influences ACCs—
15 but not greatly.
16 It is extremely important to STEs—

---

[1] I owe much to two excellent books on this subject: Louis Baudin, *Free Trade and Peace* (Paris, 1939) and Edmund Silberner, *The Problem of War in Nineteenth Century Economic Thought* (Princeton, N.J., 1946).

17 so they even adapt their institutions to it—
18 with even ideological consequences.
19 Capital flows used to be the most exacerbating of all relations—
20 but now only technical dissimilarities remain.
21 The new capital flows between ACCs and STEs.
22 Communist views on cause and effect.
23 The answer is to abolish national sovereignty.

I

How, if at all, do international economic relations promote peace?
The attempt to answer such a question lowers the tone of the whole
book. It is disgraceful to present such woolly and unproven generalizations on a subject not one's own. But whose subject is it? We
all want peace, and we all want trade; we all believe that there is
some relation between them. If the relation is not all economic,
neither is it all political or sociological. So everyone shies away from
it. Yet the subject is and always has been one of the most important
in public affairs; so the fool that broaches it deserves at least tolerance.

In the absence of basic literature, before turning to the specifically
Communist side of this subject we shall have to present its general
development. The best place to begin is at the attack on Mercantilism in the late eighteenth century, when it first began to be seriously
urged by economists that trade is good for peace.

Adam Smith has been interpreted to say that through free trade
(a) individual citizens of different countries develop so much friendship and mutual respect that they will not wish to go to war, and
(b) countries' economies become so entangled that they cannot go
to war. Such views may, indeed, be attributed to the inferior
geniuses of Cobden and Bastiat, but I cannot trace them in Smith.
In no passage in his *Wealth of Nations* does he say, or even really
imply, that trade inevitably brings peace. He certainly says—and
very rightly—that Mercantilism exacerbates international relations;
but in general his objections to it are economic. He seems to touch
most directly upon our theme in his well-known observation on the
Navigation Acts:

> The act of navigation is not favourable to foreign commerce, or to the growth
> of that opulence which can arise from it.... As defence, however, is of much
> more importance than opulence, the act of navigation is, perhaps, the wisest of
> all the commercial regulations of England.[1]

[1] *Wealth of Nations* (1776), Book IV, Chapter 2.

Here, indeed, is a cold realism not to be found in Constant and Cobden, who are surely the true protagonists of the view we are examining (below).

2

For the relation between trade and peace is very complex. It was, indeed, precisely these ideas, read by others into Smith, that caused such bad blood between Britain and France in his own time. Smith's book appeared in 1776. Its influence was so instantaneously great that already in 1777–78 he was an honored guest in governing circles in London. Smith quite specifically mentioned France as a country with which trade should be freer.[1] Meanwhile, in France, the Physiocrats had long been active. They believed as ardently in free trade as Smith, and in addition, attributing all wealth to the land, were particularly keen to encourage French agriculture. This combination of views led them in particular to favor the export of corn and wine.

These two streams of thought easily mingled with the economic interests involved, to produce the so-called Eden-Vergennes Treaty (1786), which greatly reduced tariffs each way. France's traditional exports—corn, wine, etc.—benefited somewhat, but this hurt British products only to a limited degree since it was mainly other imports that they replaced.[2] On the other hand, Britain's highly developed new industries—principally cotton textiles—made havoc of France's similar but younger industries. The treaty was mildly popular in Britain and southern France, but so intensely unpopular in northern France that it is fairly regarded as a principal, not a subsidiary, cause of the Napoleonic Wars. J. Holland Rose writes:

> It is interesting to reflect on the influence of Pitt's commercial treaty of 1786–87 with France, in producing the jealousy felt by the French extremists for our industrial and commercial supremacy. In the misery and turmoil of 1789–93 that treaty appeared to be the prelude of Pitt's deep-laid conspiracy to enrich England at the expense of France. At any rate, the triumph in 1792–93 of the extremists of Paris and the manufacturing north over the men of the wine-growing south, where alone that treaty had been popular, had this among its many results, that in place of a commercial intercourse approximating to free trade, France rushed to the opposite extreme of commercial prohibition. The premature attempt of 1786, made under the old monarchy, and the reaction which it caused under the republic, have done much to identify in France a prohibitive or strictly protective policy with popular government.

[1] *Wealth of Nations* (1776) Book IV, Chapter 3, Section i.
[2] C.-E. Labrousse, *Crise de l'Economie Française* (Paris, 1944), pp. 585–6.

Bonaparte, in his skilful selection and use of all the Jacobinical ideas and aims which could establish his power, found none more ready to hand, none more popular, than commercial jealousy of England, and the determination to make our wealth our ruin. The land of Quesnay and Turgot reverted to mediaeval ideas about commerce and national prosperity. Never had the frenzy for prohibition been more general, more popular in France than in 1800, at the time when Napoleon took the helm of affairs.[1]

This, then, was the direct effect of Adam Smith's book, and the doctrines attributed to it. Smith perceived that Mercantilism was an ideological irritant: that so long as governments were obsessed by the notion that trade is war by other means there would be no peace. This service to humanity can scarcely be overestimated. But if we agree that trade is just trade, not war, we do not have to plump for free trade. What Smith should have said is that if only there were peace between nations free trade would follow. Then, as now, the doctrine that free*r* trade *makes* nations love each other is absurd. Indeed, twice more in history have attempts to bring about free trade between Britain and France caused bad blood: the Cobden-Chevalier treaty of 1860, and de Gaulle's exclusion of Britain from the Common Market of 1962. Each time it was supposed that freer trade would bring about greater friendship; each time the attempt to get it stirred evil passions.

3

It is characteristic of the poverty of our modern specialized thinking that these large issues are very seldom seriously studied any more. At the dawn of the social sciences people were not so timid, and the works of Benjamin Constant and Johann Gottlieb Fichte probably represent, *faute de mieux*, that 'up-to-date bibliography on the subject' dear to those who want to be in touch with the latest developments.

Benjamin Constant (1814) was less moderate and sensible than Smith. He did hold that trade was good for peace:

Commerce has modified even the nature of war. Mercantile nations were once on a time subjugated by warlike peoples. Today they resist them with success. They have auxiliaries right among these same peoples. The infinite and complicated ramifications of commerce have placed the interest of each society outside the limits of its territory, and the spirit of the times conquers the narrow and hostile spirit which men used to dignify with the name of patriotism.

[1] *Napoleonic Studies* (London, 1904), pp. 167–8.

Carthage, fighting with Rome in antiquity, had to succumb: the nature of things forcibly overwhelmed her. But if there were today a war between Rome and Carthage, Carthage would have the world's prayers for her. The spirit and customs of latter-day mankind would be with her.

So the situation of modern peoples prevents them from being bellicose.[1]

Even though he wrote in 1814, Constant was not thinking very carefully about the causes of the late war, and much exaggerated the peaceful inclinations of both the modern and the ancient Carthage. In the same passage, however, he did also teach the much simpler lesson, that trade is simply more profitable than war, and try to divert the aggressive instincts of his countrymen into this channel:

War and commerce are but two different means of arriving at the same aim, which is to possess what is desired. Trade is nothing but a homage paid to the strength of the possessor by him who aspires to the possession; it is an attempt to obtain by mutual agreement that which one does not hope any longer to obtain by violence. The idea of commerce would never occur to a man who would always be the strongest. It is experience, proving to him that war, i.e., the use of his force against the force of others, is exposed to various resistances and various failures, which makes him have recourse to commerce, that is, to a means more subtle and better fitted to induce the interest of others to consent to what is his own interest.

War is thus anterior to commerce. The one is the savage impulse, the other the civilized calculation.

But his next sentence is very controversial:

It is clear that the more the commercial tendency dominates, the feebler the war-making tendency must be.

In the sense that cavalry officers are uninterested in profit and loss, while merchants think discretion the better part of valor, this is both true and highly important: a country governed by cavalry officers will certainly be more bellicose than one governed by merchants. But our question is whether, keeping the psychology of the government constant, the country is not less exposed to friction the less trade there is. The merchant psychology is quite compatible with autarky: e.g., the United States. And contrariwise, the whole eighteenth century is witness that a government can love at once both foreign trade and war.

After Constant, a still more straightforward statement of the doctrine here called in question comes from Richard Cobden:

[1] *De l'Esprit de Conquête et de l'Usurpation dans leurs Rapports avec la Civilization Européenne* (1814), I/2.

If I were not convinced that the question comprises a great moral principle, and involves the greatest moral world's revolution that was ever yet accomplished for mankind, I should not take the part I do in this agitation. Free Trade, what is it? Why, breaking down the barriers that separate nations . . . those feelings which nourish the poison of war and conquest, which assert that without conquest we can have no trade, which foster that lust for conquest and dominion which sends forth your warrior chiefs to scatter devastation through other lands, and then calls them back that they may be enthroned securely in your passions, but only to harass and oppress you at home.[1]

That trade is more profitable than war, that war does no good, was precisely the view of Norman Angell seventy years later.[2] To anyone familiar with the universal bellicosity of 'civilized' men in the years 1890–1914,[3] it will seem no small service to have rubbed in this simple point. While perfectly correct, it does not, of course, prove that trade is good for peace, a view Angell did not originally put forward. However, after his first edition came out, the Agadir crisis (1911) caused a run of French capital from German banks, which was generally believed, by well-informed journalists in Berlin, to have so much frightened German capitalists that they brought successful pressure on the German government to keep the peace. This episode very much impressed Angell, who in his 1914 edition included a rather foolish speech on how trade has made war almost impossible.[4] The speech rests, if examined, on no other historical or economic fact than Agadir. Thus, Angell cannot be altogether acquitted of misleading the world, as he was so often accused.

4

Fichte (who wrote in 1800) would doubtless have replied to Constant and Cobden that the diversion of, say, Napoleon's interests from war to trade would, if possible, be a good palliative. But the basic remedy is more radical; since trade would lead us back to war in the end, it too must be stopped. Fichte goes much further than I, seeing in his proposals an ultimately though not an immediately practicable policy.[5] To quote him is not to sanction his economics

[1] Speech to the Anti-Corn Law League, London, September 28, 1843, *Speeches* (London 1870), p. 79.
[2] *The Great Illusion* (London, 1914, expanded edition), *passim*.
[3] On this exceptional bellicosity cf. Angell op. cit.; I. F. Clarke, *Voices Prophesying War* (London, 1966) Chapter 4. Note in particular the notion that war is self-sacrifice, and therefore anti-materialist.
[4] Angell, op. cit., I/9.
[5] *Der Geschlossene Handelsstaat* (1800), from the dedication (I have used the text in *Sämmtliche Werke* [Berlin, 1845]).

or his (quite moderate) nationalism. I select some of the more reasonable passages.

But it is at once clear that the moment a government begins publicly to take these measures, and seeks for itself and its nation exclusive benefits from its co-existence in a common Trade Republic [This is Fichte's phrase for a freely trading world—P.J.D.W.], all other governments that suffer from this must take the same measures . . . and that if they cannot do so easily against the dominant nation they will happily do so against another still weaker. To the hostile attitude that all states have anyway towards all others because of their territorial boundaries is added a new, commercial, hostility; and a general, secret commercial war.[1]

A state that is in the process of closing itself off from commerce must first advance or retire, as the case may be, into its natural boundaries. In order to satisfy the demands of its citizens put forward in the previous chapter, it needs in part a spacious territory that could contain within itself a complete and closed system of the necessary production. In part, too, under the influence of general law and order, and continuous domestic prosperity, the citizens will no longer need to be oppressed by that army of taxes that is required by standing defence forces and a perpetual readiness for war.[2]

Keynes made a much more moderate statement of the same position:

I sympathise with those who would minimise, rather than maximise, econ-omic entanglement among nations. Ideas, knowledge, science, hospitality, travel—these are the things which should of their nature be international. But let goods be homespun wherever it is reasonably and conveniently possible and, above all, let finance be primarily national. Yet, at the same time, those who seek to disembarrass a country of its entanglements should be very slow and wary . . . a greater measure of national self-sufficiency and economic isolation among countries than existed in 1914 may tend to serve the cause of peace rather than otherwise.[3]

5

Let us descend toward particulars. The commercial relation between human beings is not an easy one. If one buys from or sells to a man on a perfect market, even if one competes with him in

---

[1] Ibid., II/6.

[2] Ibid., III/3. I find that Lord Robbins, *Economic Planning and International Order* (London, 1938), p. 322, is altogether too hard on Fichte. It is true that he said, 'Every state must receive what it intends to obtain by war and what *it alone* [Robbins' italics] can reasonably determine, that is its natural frontiers. When that is accomplished it will have no farther claims on any other state since it will possess what it had sought.' And it is true Fichte was thinking primarily of Germany, and that he is an ancestor somewhere in the Nazis' intellectual tree. But that does not diminish the scientific validity of his statement: take away 'it alone' and we have an obvious historical truth. Nor can Fichte's economic autarkism be brushed aside because he was nationalistic about German frontiers; this would be to argue so much *ad hominem* as hardly to argue at all.

[3] In *Yale Review* (1932–33), p. 758.

buying or selling, no enmity results, but also no friendship. For this kind of market is 'impersonal': not that it does not consist of people—to suggest that is metaphysical—but it appears to the participants that none of them is to blame for what goes on.[1] The case for not hating your customer or competitor is so strong that even a Marxist blames only 'the system'. The only human passion able to withstand the cooling influence of perfect competition is nationalism: North Americans like to blame foreigners from whom they buy raw materials when prices are high, and Latin Americans like to blame North Americans to whom they sell raw materials when prices are low.

But perfect competition is the least exacerbating of commercial relations! The more personal they become the worse they are. We can hardly have good relations with oligopolistic competitors, who are individually able to do us harm by direct decision, and relations with customers are bound to deteriorate when the price is a matter of bargaining.

If individual relations deteriorate as competition becomes less perfect, state relations deteriorate as controls are applied. Clearly, the least hostile inter-state economic relations are no relations, i.e., *laissez faire*. Note that 'least hostile' is not the same as 'best', for *laissez faire* encourages imperialism (Chapter XVI, section 22) which may lead in the long run to relations still more hostile than those that would have arisen from, say, autarky. But protectionism, devaluation, export subsidies, quotas, and exchange control, the devices characteristic of the regulated market, all also lead to bad relations between states. If supranational computation be substituted, in the way some STEs want the CMEA to function, state relations again deteriorate, as the Rumanian case shows. The supersession of commerce by command has, of course, made things worse, not better. The consilience of all individual interests in a planned society, however respectable its lineage through Marx back to Rousseau, is plain rubbish.

We are driven toward a pessimistic conclusion: all economic relationships are unhappy, but the less personal and political they are the more tolerable they are. The point is well made by an author less reluctant to make it, Wilhelm Röpke:

Gold currency thus illustrated the saying of Adam Ferguson . . . that 'peoples find themselves unexpectedly in possession of institutions which are indeed the

[1] P. J. D. Wiles, *Price, Cost and Output* (2nd ed.), pp. 31–9.

outcome of human action, but not the result of human intention'. . . . The obligations, namely, which a conscientious conformity with the rules of the gold standard imposed upon all participating countries formed at the same time a part of that system of written and unwritten standards which, as we have seen, comprised the liberal *ordre public international*. . . . The increase of political direction in economic life must necessarily result in the destruction of the monetary order, which rested on the principle of freedom of economic affairs from political direction. . . . The liberal idea, by creating an *ordre public international* which was kept together by manifold institutional links, achieved the closest possible approach to the (unreachable) goal of setting up an international equivalent of the national state which was indispensable to international relationships. At the same time the separation of the political and economic spheres . . . was not only a decisive aid in the creation of this quasi world state, but also limited the burden placed upon this framework of the international economy, so that this international substitute set-up sufficed for the actual requirements of an international order.[1]

But even Röpke does not go the whole hog. For, of course, he is unwilling to admit that perfect competition and free trade themselves bring about situations that must in the fullness of time breed war. Colonialism and imperialism, as we have already seen, become eventually such monstrous political evils that no government, whatever its economic policy, can ignore them any more. It is untrue that free trade binds countries so close that they can no longer get into the correct posture to draw the sword. On the contrary, it binds them so close that willy-nilly the large and rich come to dominate the small and poor; the latter are then so irritated beyond all bearing that they very frequently draw the sword, at whatever cost to themselves. And history also shows trade between equipollent countries to be an irritant, if only because they always in fact try to control it, and always will. So behind our pessimistic conclusion lurks one yet more pessimistic: trade is always bad, in all its forms, for international friendship. Or in Fichte's words:

So long as all are quiet next to each other, they do not fall into strife; only when they arouse themselves and move around and are up and doing, do they bump into each other.[2]

ᴧ

6

Imagine that, *per impossibile*, nation-states had grown up first and humanity stood before the choice: to have free trade or protectionism or supranational planning or no trade at all. Beyond the least doubt the safest course, though not the superficially attractive course, would be no trade at all. For that way international relations

[1] *International Order and Economic Integration* (Dordrecht, 1959), pp. 76–7.
[2] Op. cit., I/1/i.

would be minimized, and international relations are the cause of war, and war is an incomparably great evil. World government is a fine thing—a complete world government in which there is no Rumania any more to quarrel with a USSR. But the path toward it would seem to a wise man fraught with every possible danger. Let all countries remain isolated instead, and then perhaps they will not attack each other.

All of which is as unhistorical as the Social Contract, but like that myth it is useful. It both sobers and illuminates. It is irrelevant, of course, to our real situation because we already have a great deal of trade and indeed other kinds of international relation. A *decline* in trade would cause a decline in prosperity, and in nations' knowledge of each other, without actually abolishing their contacts with each other. This might have very different effects on peace.

For two of the ways in which trade is supposed to influence international relations are that it increases prosperity and our knowledge of foreigners. Now both it undoubtedly does, though I can think of exceptions. But what do we do with this prosperity, and what kind of knowledge do we gain about what kind of foreigner? Seemingly these questions are so large that no one can answer them. Let us, however, try.

7

History provides no evidence that prosperity causes peace. Walt W. Rostow[1] argues that a country's period of 'take-off into sustained growth' leads to disturbed politics and possibly war; while the period of industrialization itself is so absorbing that countries have no energies left for aggression; but in the ensuing period of 'mass-consumption' a country has seemingly a choice between guns and butter it did not previously have. I have shown elsewhere[2] that neither the United States nor France was at all peaceful during the period of industrialization, and Rostow himself excepts Germany. He might also have excepted Tsarist Russia, which annexed eastward as aggressively as the United States did southward. But take away the intervening period of pacificism, and we are left with no theory at all of how growth is related to peace.

Another candidate theory, often put forward these days, is based on evolution in the USSR and China: the poorer Communist

[1] *The Process of Economic Growth* (2nd ed.; New York 1960).
[2] In *Encounter* (London), November, 1959.

countries are, the more aggressive they are. This too crumbles at the approach of the flat-footed empiricist. Semi-industrial USSR was exceedingly pacific in the latter part of the NEP, when Trotsky had been excluded from power; but when in the throes of violent industrialization at once committed aggression (Finland, 1939) when it looked easy. Still industrializing madly, she then occupied Eastern Europe and revolutionized it at bayonet point. Pre-industrial China, for all her braggadocio, has never attacked any country except India;[1] in 1955–56, the 'Bandoeng' period, her foreign policy was more peaceful than the USSR's. But the theory has at least some present-day plausibility: there is a striking contrast between the Russian with his TV set, his 'someting to lose', and the Chinese with his half-empty ricebowl. It gains appeal when we consider also the aggressive behavior of the Albanian leadership. Yet three instances[2] are a very shaky base for a generalization. Before 1958 nobody thought of it, and its inapplicability to non-Communist countries is a most serious defect.

Truth to tell, the history of sovereign groupings of men is largely that they attack their neighbors when opportunity offers, and the attacker's stage of development, rate of growth, or absolute level of productivity would seem to be related to this tendency in no way whatsoever. What does matter is that the neighbor be held to be weaker, and the campaign technically possible. A good ideological pretension helps, of course: Liberate the Holy Places, *Drang nach Osten*, White Man's Burden, Manifest Destiny, Permanent Revolution. But such ideologies have a way of appearing when needed, and disappearing when the policies they indicate become too expensive.

8

Prosperity, then, and economic growth have no certain or stable causal relation to peaceability—though of course peace promotes them. So there is no causal connection running from trade to peace along this indirect route. What of getting acquainted with people of other nationalities? We shall take first trade and aid, leaving tourism till later. Through trade and aid there come into contact

[1] Counting, as we must, since we are dealing with the Chinese point of view, Tibet and Taiwan as part of the national territory.
[2] It would be very wrong to include North Korea and North Vietnam as evidence, since these countries are split, an abnormally exacerbating state of affairs. For that matter, the DDR is much more aggressive toward her Western neighbor than any other European satellite.

merchants, planners, and other people who have to conduct commercial negotiations. We have already dealt with this: the less personal these negotiations are the better. In general, perfect competition is best, and supranational planning worst. Let us only add that the natural antagonisms of the market place or planning bureau flourish also within a country, and it is at least possible that in comparison with one's compatriots a foreigner may shine. Where it occurs, this lesser antagonism is presumably a weak factor for peace.

Trade and aid also establish contacts between technicians, and these are generally held to be among the most fruitful of all international contacts. Certainly in my own experience, respect and friendship nearly always increase as a result of professional contacts. No doubt it is a backhanded compliment to this tendency that Chinese and Soviet—but not other Communist—technicians keep themselves strictly to themselves in foreign parts. To technicians may be amalgamated the special case of students.

Tourism, and indeed the after-hours behavior of technicians and negotiators, are another matter. The local inhabitants nearly always dislike holiday-makers, and if they are foreign so much the worse. It is surely beyond doubt that if no Swede ever took a weekend in Copenhagen, or Dutchman in Antwerp, international relations would be better. Even in such a complicated case as Anglo-Saxons in Paris, of whom the natives rather demand ludicrous behavior so as to enhance their own feeling of superiority, the net effect is surely negative. For this contemptuous affection is not a healthy feeling, and on the other side the Anglo-Saxon tourist feels he is being overcharged all the time. It appears that his suspicion is correct, but even if it were not it is most irritating.

Sport, of course, is worse than trade, for it is deliberately intended to be competitive in a very personal manner, an outlet for aggression, on the part of spectator and even sometimes performer. The planner or merchant does not meet his opposite number in a floodlit stadium, and play continuously to the public gallery. A feeling of mutual respect does grow up among sportsmen, since this is a kind of professional contact; but this can hardly outweigh the damage done among spectators.

9

To deal briefly with cultural exchange and peace is bold, but books are visible and pianists invisible exports, they cost money and they shade off into ordinary trade. So we can hardly omit them. So, staying on the level of personal acquaintance, exchanges of cultural *performers* are always welcome. I cannot recall an instance, even where the performer was mediocre or the genre unpopular, in which a foreign dance, exhibition of antiquities, or concert did not improve international relations. These things are non-competitive, and very like professional and technical contacts.

But what of the general knowledge of the foreign country acquired by these channels? Among free societies nearly all exchanges of culture and information make for peace. Indeed, this is a basic principle upon which these societies are constructed. But not so with STEs. Taking first high culture, it is safer to import foreign performers than original modern works. Clearly Western abstract painting offends Communist principle and to some extent popular taste. Free trade in literature with Communist countries is unthinkable, and Western attempts to promote it worsen relations. This is even more true of information. To be sure, if the West had its way here Communism would die and the prospects of peace in this case improve: which is as much as to say that there can be no true peace without a cold war first. But the more short-run view is that one cannot live peacefully with a totalitarian society and be continually threatening its long-term existence. 'Trade' here is simply political: an attempt to infiltrate ideas. Indeed, STEs do not live on such free terms with each other, let alone the outside world.

Much the same may be said of mass entertainment. Communism, other than Yugoslav, has been vastly suspicious of capitalist pop culture, and its importation has definitely worsened relations between governments. Even in free societies an influential minority may object to such imports, on the ground that they are more corrupting than the home product, or tend to destroy those national manners and traditions that they consider appropriate to the lower classes. If occasionally this is serious, on the whole the fact that the masses themselves enjoy the import must have greater weight. If they get a distorted view of the country of origin, so often do the importers of its high culture; and the distortion may easily be a flattering one.

Here again I find that Fichte was before me, though not to my total liking:

In the wide system of world commerce much acclaim has gone to the advantages of international acquaintance through travel and trade, and the many-sided education that they give. Maybe: if only we were peoples and nations in the first place; and there were somewhere available a solid national formation of the individual which through international contact could pass over into an all-round formation of mankind, and so fuse itself.... There is nothing that completely removes all differences of situation and nationality, or belongs only to the human being and not the citizen, save knowledge. Through this and only through this will and should men continue to be connected.... Only this remains their common possession, after they have divided everything else up among them. This connection will be destroyed by no closed state; it will on the contrary be enriched, for the enrichment of knowledge through the united strength of humanity even forwards its separated earthly goals. The treasures of foreign literature will be imported by subsidized academies, and exchanged for domestic ones. No state on earth, after this system has become general and perpetual peace well founded between peoples, has the least interest in keeping its discoveries from one another.[1]

10

So free cultural exchange is an excellent thing. But as well as the direct exchange of 'cultural objects', culture rides the backs of travelers much as technology rides machines. But what culture? For we must expect all visitors to a country—negotiators, technicians, students, tourists—to gain a distorted picture. It can hardly be as distorted as that formed by those who do not travel, but it may, in contrast to the picture given by a 'cultural object', be actually more unfavorable than the truth. Thus it is possible, indeed quite common, for people to view France from a distance through a romantic glow, but to be converted by their reception in Paris to Francophobes. Similarly, travel behind the Iron Curtain makes many a peace-loving capitalist into a paranoiac: his prior knowledge that things have much improved—a correct impression that anyone can derive from reading—is quite overlaid by the actual sight of the remaining drabness of all material life, and the fact that he was tailed by the police.

Then too we must consider what actual influence at home have the particular people who travel. Among them are the very influential indeed, not only in *esse* but also in *posse*. Consider Chiang and Nehru in Moscow in the 1920s, Chou En-lai and Ho Chi Minh in Paris, de Gaulle in London, etc. The opinions formed by actual and future rulers are of course incalculably important, but not only for good, nor only for peace. Against this ordinary merchants and tourists may over a long period help to change the public image of the foreign country. But they are only one tributary out of many, and they too may well be a poisoned one. Moreover, a nation's public image itself, good or bad, is only one influence out of many upon its neighbors' foreign policy.

[1] Op. cit., III/8. It will be observed that Keynes might have been quoting him (section 4).

11

Our conclusion on all this must be thoroughly destructive. There are reasons enough for encouraging trade, cultural contact, personal contact, and tourism, without dragging peace into it. Prosperity, consumer's sovereignty, personal freedom, the pure right to knowledge, self-development, often family affection—all demand that we be permitted to trade, travel and transfer capital. A political system that refuses its citizens the right to these things is *ipso facto* bad; though it must naturally be allowed to control the b.o.p. and this is no minor derogation from the general principle. But that such contacts make also for peace is questionable. No hard-headed answer can be given to that in general. Every country's relation with every other is a special and highly complicated case.

Peaceful international relations, of the various types here described, *are the result not the cause of good feeling.* Indeed, good feeling is sometimes thus 'corrected', as it were, by a feedback: it brings about so many contacts that relations deteriorate. The notion that the more relations there are the better relations will be is derived from no observed facts but from the eighteenth-century assumption that men are naturally good; it is on a par with the notion that prosperity makes people peaceful. But that too rests, as we have seen, on no observed fact—unless the contrasting cases of the USSR, China, and Albania in the early 1960s be accepted as a basis for a theory of human history. In fact, life is more complicated. Many people are naturally bad, and natural badness helps one in a political career. Many whole nations or states are bad; ignorance of them and isolation from them might be excellent if at all practicable.

12

In particular, trade between ACCs and UDCs causes bad blood on both sides. It is characteristic of Adam Smith and the Enlightenment that this relation was not thought of as a special one, since all men are equal, even though the devil has a tendency to take the hindmost. Indeed, the West African Negro kings who kidnapped the slaves for the slave trade were well received in Europe, much as if they had been white potentates. Even in this traffic neither side felt, evidently, inferior. There were no doctrines of racial inferiority then, and economic inferiority was a simple fact of life, to be lived with and overcome by fair means or foul. A deal was a deal, and there were no left-wing economists to call it exploitation.

Today, or at least until ten years ago, the opposite is true. Ideas of racial superiority often poison personal relations and obscure true knowledge of the other country. The fact of economic superiority is rubbed in by every contact. On the one side, it reinforces the notion of racial superiority; on the other, it gives rise to envy, malice, and the notion of exploitation (Chapter I). Even eighteenth-century optimism would surely be shaken by the everyday facts of modern trade between ACCs and UDCs.

Let us be specific. Who would deny that Cuba would never have gone Communist but for free trade with the United States? The country was rich by Latin American standards, United States equity capital was fast being bought out by Cubans, both rent and tenure had long been frozen in favor of the peasant on the great latifundia, the trade unions had a more complete stranglehold on the labor market than perhaps anywhere in the world. But the peso was still hardly more than a dollar certificate, so that every financial wind in Wall Street blew through the island; free trade had specialized the country in sugar and then the preference had tied it specifically to the United States market; and above all the tone of Havana was set by the worst type of United States tourist and his hangers-on, for whose sake the town was given over to brothels, blue films and gambling dens. Revolutions come and go, of course, in Cuba as in other places. But that Castro's revolution took an anti-United States turn is beyond question due to the 'close contact with and knowledge of' the United States brought about by free trade.

13

These phenomena also have their parallels in STEs. We saw in Chapter XV that the citizens, though not the rulers, of Communist countries are profoundly suspicious of exports to other Communist countries, and of the foreign aid their government renders. This exacerbates their contacts with ordinary citizens of UDCs and of other STEs, sometimes with public and explosive effects. We may instance the hostile reception of Negroes in Bulgaria (1963), and of Chinese (since many years) and Negroes (1963) in Russia.[1] All these cases are primarily conflicts of color, but all observers agree that there is the contributory feeling that 'we' are doing too much for 'them'; 'we' can ill afford it, and 'they' are not grateful. Nor is this

[1] I write 'Russia' deliberately, since this is mainly a racial feeling among Great Russians: Soviet citizens of Mongoloid features are sometimes mistaken for Chinese in Moscow, and cold-shouldered.

feeling absurd: some African countries have a *per capita* income not much below the USSR's, when allowance is made for the low defense burden and the warm climate. Moreover, foreign students receive very high stipends by Soviet standards, and are apt to be richer than the average of their own country.

A further parallel is that since the very institutional model of the UDC is malleable, the STE imitates the ACC in trying to mold this model, by trade, after its own. Political reactions to this can be very fierce. We saw already in Chapter XIV how capital transfers are used in this way. We must now add that Soviet-type bilateralism induces UDCs to set up state trading corporations. For this is the easiest way in which they can deliver the stated quantities, at stated prices, required in the trade protocols.

14

Realism demands, however, that one optimistic note be struck. Trade between ACCs and STEs is conducted in conditions of mutual respect that do little harm to personal relations. Indeed, so absurd have been the views of the other party commonly entertained on each side that at least in this case personal acquaintance has usually improved attitudes. But more than that, *such trade tends to deform and 'bourgeoisify' Soviet-type institutions*, whereas hitherto its effect on the institutions of ACCs has been transitory.

Take the latter case first. Suppose that the ACC guarantees specific deliveries under the annual trade protocol. Attempts have occasionally been made to do this, and they all indicate one thing: such a guarantee, if successful, means a change of institutional model, the ME ceases to be purely that and takes on aspects of a STE.

One remarkable case is Sweden in 1946. The Swedish loan to the USSR was a fairly large one,[1] so large firms in the relevant sectors thought that they would be particularly hard hit. Deprived of any of the legal apparatus of a command economy, the government could only use such indirect controls as it had. One class of such controls included the nationalization of existing enterprises, the establishment of new public enterprises, and the encouragement of foreign competitors to set up shop in Sweden. Another was discriminatory raw material licensing. Finally, there was the only species of direct command legally possible: the direction of labor. Even in the labor market, there were more important indirect means

[1] 1000 mn. kr., or, if used up over 5 years, 0·8% of the national income in 1946.

available; e.g., creating local unemployment in favor of enterprises fulfilling the Soviet credit or throttling other activity through licensing. Whether such indirect controls were threatened, or even contemplated, we need not here inquire, and so may avoid the question of fact.[1] What concerns us is that only such thoroughly ineffective means were open to the Swedish government, and that these means had manifestly not been designed for the purpose of regulating trade with the USSR, so that their actual use would have roused even stiffer opposition than did the suspicion they were going to be used. In fact no such means were employed, largely because Stalin did not use up the whole loan.

15

An even more striking case was that of Finnish reparations. These were expressed, not as in the Swedish case, as so much money, likely to be spent within certain sectors, but as exactly specified goods worth so and so much. I.e., Stalin incorporated the Finnish reparations-producing sector within his command economy. For our purposes here it is quite incidental that he wanted reparations; had he done the same to normal requited exports the lesson would be the same.

Finland, then, included during the reparations period a Soviet-type enclave. How, in a capitalist parliamentary democracy, did this work?[2] First, the economy was accustomed to government powers of a similar kind in wartime, and the Commission of War Reparation Industries was set up even before the reparations treaty was signed. As far as the Finnish people were concerned, the war was not over until the reparations were paid. Commanding universal consent, the Commission had a nonpolitical chairman, and included businessmen, labor representatives and civil servants. It had powers to take over management and give orders as to production, to order a firm going bankrupt to continue in operation, and to requisition tools and materials. Seemingly the only powers it lacked but might have been happy to have were to set up new firms

[1] The question became a violent political controversy, even on the level of bare fact. Cf. Herbert Tingsten, *Mitt Liv* (Stockholm, 1963), pp. 124–39; L. I. Frei, *Mezhdunarodnye Raschëty i Organizovanie Vneshnei Torgovli Sotsialistocheskikh Stran* (Moscow, 1960), pp. 214–15.

[2] Being unable to read Finnish, I am indebted to my colleague, Mr. Altti Majava, who is in turn in part indebted to Jaakko Auer (*The Finnish War Reparation Deliveries to the Soviet Union*, Helsinki, 1956). The English summary in this book is too brief. Cf. Bank of Finland, *Monthly Review*, December, 1952.

and to direct labor; in fact, not even the government had these powers.

The Commission bought the reparations just as a belligerent ministry of supply might buy munitions, and delivered them to the USSR. There was, of course—this is, after all, Scandinavia—an *Ombudsman* to see if prices were reasonable. In nearly all cases investigated they were, characteristically, too high. There was also an arbitration committee to hear the complaints of firms or of the Commission. The latter's great powers were almost invariably kept in reserve: one delinquent enterprise was taken over, one enterprise was forced not to close down, and one direct command to produce a particular thing (a kind of small ship) was given.

What can we make of the contrasting Swedish and Finnish experiences? The Swedish case is very imperfect not only because of the dispute as to fact, but also because the loan was, once promised, not fully utilized. The expected strains on the Swedish economy did not, then, materialize. Nevertheless, the cases show the strong difference between a guarantee of delivery of money and a guarantee of delivery of specified goods. In the wildest imagination of its opponents, the Swedish Government contemplated nothing more than such measures of mere regulation and prohibition, not Soviet-type command, as would keep the real purchasing power of the loan intact. Had the loan been made to an ME there would still have been a case for such measures; indeed, the internal organization of the borrowing economy had nothing to do with them. What was very relevant was the government's refusal to use general, 'quantitative' methods of monetary and banking restraint upon prices as a whole. Instead there were—or were not!—specific, 'qualitative' restraints on prices in the particular sectors where Soviet purchases were expected.

The Finnish case, on the other hand, demonstrates that if an ME is to trade with an STE according to inter-STE methods, with a specified bill of goods, it must introduce at least so much of the command economy as is implied by its own weapons acquisition process in time of war. Powers to command must be there, though persuasion and even bargaining occupy the forefront of the stage. The powers were abandoned when reparations were paid off; Finland is now again an ordinary ME.

In addition to these special cases, we saw in Chapter X a general effect of ACC-STE trade: it tempts the ACC into bilateralism. This has not hitherto brought about a spread of state trading, but it has exposed the government to every kind of protectionist pressure.

16

But when MEs trade with STEs it is mainly, and more permanently, in the latter that the model tends to change. STEs have made great adaptations in order to export to ACCs, since it has historically been from these countries that they have got the machinery, technology and food they most need. This trade is to them economically the most important of all. Indeed, we can go further: there is nothing in central planning that says one STE should prefer another as a trade partner. Inter-STE trade seems not to be marked by any special stability in comparison to STE-ACC trade.[1] Other STEs are neither more nor less reliable suppliers or customers. On the contrary, a large free world market is an admirable thing for an STE, mainly as a source of emergency supply but also as a market for unpredictable surpluses. The *theoretical* predictability of *total* supply in a planned economy is a very long way from the *practical* predictability of the *surpluses and deficits* that enter into foreign trade.

The free market at home, and the large semi-planned kolkhoz reservoir, play a similar role. No STE is without them. But in the foreign field the clearest acknowledgment of such necessities is the Chinese toleration of Hong Kong: a colonialist vestige right on the doorstep, a nest of spies, a haven for refugees, a center of conspiracy and rumor—all for a favorable balance settled in hard currency! The mere existence of Hong Kong is the greatest single adaptation made by any STE to the necessities of trade with ACCs.

In these markets the buyer is king. The good simply has to be delivered on something approaching the due date, and to very nearly exactly the right specifications. These latter nearly always imply a better quality than that customary at home, so that an absurd 'quality hierarchy' grows up: goods for home use, exports to other STEs, exports to UDCs, exports to ACCs. Were it not for this hierarchy it is scarcely to be believed that any quality would be as good as it is; through it some breath of ordinary competition penetrates the STE, and the effect must be presumed to be tonic.[2]

The 'quality hierarchy' has its parallel in MEs as well. Indeed, it belongs to the snobbery we all feel about international trade (cf. Chapter VIII), and is a too little regarded phenomenon. It is impossible in perfect competition, but it might seem that transport cost

[1] This is the preliminary result of a rather lengthy investigation of my own.
[2] Cf. Antoni Gutowski, 'The Art Called Export' in *Polityka* (Warsaw), January 4, 1964; K.T.T., 'The Oedipus Complex', in *Kultura* (Warsaw), October 1, 1967. Characteristically, both my references for this important economic phenomenon are from non-economic journals!

rendered it rational elsewhere. But even if the weight of transport in c.i.f. cost falls as quality rises, demand might easily still be such as to render the lower quality a preferable export. Another rational explanation might be that the more advanced the country the better the quality it demands. But while this may explain the difficulties felt by STEs selling to ACCs, it does not explain why these same ACCs tend to export only their best goods to each other, or why STEs sell better goods to other STEs than they use at home. The fact that international trade is more competitive is neither here nor there, since it does not explain why it is worse to sell bad products very cheap than good products rather cheap. My inclination is to put a large part of the phenomenon down to technological national-ism; we sell our best goods abroad much as we are more polite to foreigners.

17

Be that as it may, Soviet-type institutions as well as productive efforts have been adapted in order to trade with MEs, in ways both great and small. Thus there is the comparatively trivial matter of departments of foreign relations in Soviet Sovnarkhozy.[1] Their role was—for the Sovnarkhozy are no more—consultative only, like that of so very many other Soviet committees. Not all Sovnarkhozy had them in 1962. On a slightly more important level, old capitalist trade-marks are used in exports to MEs: e.g., 'Gdynia-Amerika Line' instead of 'Polskie Linie Oceaniczne'. Different again is the adaptation to the market shown by the Soviet fur industry, which has long run its own auctions in Leningrad.[2] These date from before the war and have recently grown in importance and frequency. There is, of course, nothing less Stalinist than an auction.

There are also very many export incentives more redolent of the market than the production incentives for home use. Thus East German enterprises making certain exports have been permitted since June, 1954, to retain 1 or 2% of the foreign currency earnings, and spend them more or less at will.[3] This very common practice, known also in Yugoslavia and in most MEs that have exchange control, implies a certain freedom from the plan for the exporter. A more radical version is the eight Hungarian export enterprises

[1] Cf. L. Baulin in *Vneshnyaya Torgovlya*, May, 1962, for RSFSR; I. Vakhrushev in *Vneshnyaya Torgovlya*, July, 1962, for Ukraine.
[2] *New York Times*, January 26, 1965.
[3] R. F. Mikesell and J. N. Behrman, *Financing Free World Trade with the Sino-Soviet Bloc* (Princeton, 1958) p. 64.

which have been permitted since 1958 direct contact with the foreign buyer, to the exclusion of the Ministry of Foreign Trade.[1] In this way very fine details of the *sortament*, including delivery dates, are settled directly by the enterprise. The plan, however, apparently still governs—or governed—the grosser categories of the *sortament*. Similarly since 1962 thirty Polish enterprises have supposedly worked for export outside the plan. That is, their general categories are laid down centrally, but they produce the exact *sortament* that the foreigner—capitalist or Communist—happens to order, and maximize their profits.[2] The Hungarian joke circulates about these enterprises: '. . . and thirty cars will drive on the left-hand side'. And indeed, such a formal and direct contradiction between *laissez faire* and central command has not been avoided. The thirty enterprises are supposed freely to decide their own *sortament*, but in fact the Planning Commission has often intervened. The choice of *sortament*, again, affects an enterprise's inputs—which, of course, are the outputs of some other enterprise enjoying no such freedom from the central plan.

A yet further 'escalation' is permission to the exporting enterprise to give, or to the importing enterprise to receive, credit. Normally, as we saw in Chapter XIV, credit is arranged and paid for by the Ministry of Foreign Trade (short-term), the central bank (medium-term) or the treasury (long-term). In Poland since June 21, 1966, medium-term credit is charged or paid to the enterprise itself.

We saw in Chapter VII that it is primarily through foreign trade that economic rationality has entered the STE. The first practical step is to rationalize the choice of customer and price for exports *already produced* and imports *already decided upon*. The last stage is when every imported input and every exported output is rationally decided upon, which, of course, entails the rationalization of all inputs and outputs in the whole economy. Poland has passed through the first stage, and her thirty enterprises are an intermediate point. That the large output categories and the very identities of the enterprises should be decided by the center is not necessarily irrational, but in Poland in the 1960s it is so in fact. For, as we saw in Chapter XI, in the current state of the arts the only way to rationality is as yet via the free market.

At least, however, this scheme leaves the *sortament* more or less

---

[1] Jerzy Jaruzelski in *Życie Warszawy*, May 16–17, 1965.
[2] Information from Stanisław Grużewski in *Handel Zagraniczny* (Warsaw), March, 1964, and sundry conversations in Poland.

to the market—clearly in the hope of rationalization without too great disturbance. If the Polish government continues to be illogical it can in fact stop at this point. Occasional interference with the *sortament*, an incapacity to supply the exact inputs required, and a refusal to increase the number of enterprises under the scheme, all present an untidy picture. But the economic gain is real, while the basically Stalinist structure of contemporary Polish planning is hardly touched.

18

The *malaise* that this kind of thing produces in the Soviet-type mind is very great. For direct contact between the exporting enterprise and the foreign buyer violates the sacred Leninist principle of the government's foreign-trade monopoly. Forgetting that all their enterprises are now 'socialist', and that Lenin asserted his principle as part of the 'capture of the commanding heights' in a mixed economy, the orthodox react like frightened rabbits.[1] Thus Jaruzelski (op. cit.) tries to reassure them that the Hungarian scheme does not 'undermine the state's trade monopoly'—but it does, and that is just why it is good. For today, now that all the uncommanding heights are also in safe hands, the government's foreign-trade monopoly is simply a bureaucratic nuisance. In particular, while Lenin lived the USSR made very few sophisticated or custom-made exports, to which the process of fabrication necessarily gave individuality. An intervening wholesaler or bureaucrat does little harm to a product by nature perfectly competitive; not so to one by necessity heterogeneous, such as a machine. In such a case there should be not only free contact but even free contract between the producer and the foreign client.

Bad organization, then, is not the least cause of the failure of Soviet-type machinery exports. Administratively speaking, the result of the government's foreign-trade monopoly is that the foreign buyer sees the trade agreement with the STE, but not the STE's production plan. The agreement specifies the quantities, and is public; the plan specifies the enterprises producing, and is private. Genuine adaptation to foreign importers' demands weakens the plan.

So the convergence of the economic if not social systems of capitalism and Communism is helped along by foreign trade. Moreover, like most of the internal convergence that has hitherto occurred,

[1] Even in Yugoslavia 80% of foreign trade went through the state's regular foreign-trade organizations until the reforms of 1965–66 (*Privredni Pregled*, Belgrade, October 4, 1965).

it has mainly affected STEs, not ACCs. Where Finland has fallen back into her pattern the USSR continues to move out of hers. Not surprisingly, too, foreign-trade-induced convergence affects small STEs more than big ones, and particularly those that export heterogeneous goods. That North Korea, North Vietnam, Mongolia, Cuba and Albania seem not to be converging has many better explanations. But at least they would be in serious difficulty if they exported machines.

It is worth while to warn again that the convergence of the economic models of ACCs and STEs will not inevitably make them friends. Similarity of economic institutions has not in the past prevented states from tearing each other apart.[1] In this case, however, there is the special feature that dissimilarity of economic model has been a cause of the fundamental hostility. When necessity dictates a rapprochement there is a loss of confidence in Leninist dogma that can only be good.

Even so, it is perhaps of greater importance that ACC/STE trade weakens the accursed political solidarity of both sides. The diplomatic wanderings of France and Rumania surely count for more than the Polish deviations from the Soviet model.

19

It is not, however, only goods, people and ideas that move. The migration of capital is the only side of this subject which has been at all seriously studied, doubtless because Marxists are interested in it. After all, the Marxist has the virtue that he is not afraid of large and serious subjects. We do not have to agree, however, with what he says. No detailed refutation need be attempted here, since many admirable empirical studies have already provided it. The basic truth is that the migration of private capital invariably exacerbates the relations between labor and capital and government and capital; but not between countries unless the capitalist receives support from his own government. For without that support the migration does not bring about an interstate relation of any sort. Extremely often, particularly before the 1880s, the government did not intervene. When it intervenes it is because capital *happens* to be present and *happens* to claim diplomatic protection at a time and place convenient for its government's imperialistic aims. Cases of conspiracy, of a government encouraging the capital to go there, or to lodge

[1] Cf. Wiles, in *Encounter*, June 1963.

complaints when there, are rather rare. The exception is German capital, which was so encouraged in the early 1900s.[1]

When state capital moved, however, things became worse—much worse. Let the reader consider the latter ends of Disraeli's Suez Canal investment, or of Anglo-Iranian Oil. The Panama Canal and Stalin's mixed companies were obvious examples of the same genre. It is evident that the movement of state capital is a diplomatic affair and a very dangerous one. Imperialism, then, is hardly motivated at all by the original export of private capital, but it does use its repudiation and default as an excuse; state capital, however, is its weapon not its motive. Imperialism is primarily due to the uneven military strength of countries, the love of power, and the facility of the human mind for inventing excuses. Beside this fact particular motives pale into insignificance. Thus Mercantilist imperialism was a struggle for markets and power, to which high industrial imperialism did indeed add the desire to place its capital profitably. Communist imperialism on the other hand seeks ideological conversion and power, though Stalin also sought economic tribute.

Must we not, then, particularly condemn the ever-increasing export of state capital in the form of public civilian aid? Now that it is about three times as large as that of private capital, has it not brought us nearer to war than ever in the nineteenth century? In particular does not the open public competition in aid exacerbate the cold war? When Soviet-type aid began in late 1953 the United States was still under the spell of McCarthy, and a panic resulted. Soviet propaganda, with its quarter-truths about imperialism and its downright mendacity on the economic effects of capitalist aid, did nothing to help. Other ACCs, however, always took a more level-headed view, and the United States has now fallen into line. Soviet, though not Chinese, propaganda has become slightly more reasonable. Competition in aid has in fact made strongly for peace: a thing that would have astounded any intelligent student of international relations up to 1953.

The initial United States panic was not, historically speaking, absurd; it simply missed the changed climate of opinion. Competition in civilian aid-giving might have led to further strains or even war. The involvement of the United States and the USSR in

---

[1] The best general empirical work on this subject is Eugene Staley, *War and the Private Investor* (New York, 1935). For the special case of Egypt, see David Landes, *Bankers and Pashas* (London, 1958).

one country might have led, indeed sometimes has led, to pro-American and pro-Soviet parties inside a given UDC, which as one or other side wins elections or coups lead in turn to whole countries having a particular bias. The mere competition between the principal aid-givers is likely to worsen their relations, as all competition does. If, Fichte would have said, international relations are ipso facto bad, why invent a new kind of international relation?

But much of this would have happened anyway. Trade, diplomatic support and above all military aid set up innumerable pressures of this kind. It was the benign features of competition in civilian aid that showed up more strongly. For one thing it has simply diverted public funds from military expenditures, at least in the countries that give. Private investment would not have done that.

But the main thing is the changed *motivation* in the export of public capital, not merely since Disraeli and Theodore Roosevelt but also since Stalin, whose death was probably the turning point. We no longer speak of the migration of capital but of *aid*: the publicly professed motive is no longer profit for us but help to others. As there is no smoke without a fire, so there is no hypocrisy without genuine feeling. The unprecedented proportion of gifts in all this aid is evidence enough. The British Voluntary Service Overseas, the international youth brigade in Yugoslavia, and now the United States Peace Corps are part of the same tremendous shift of opinion.

With such motivation competition cannot be very deadly. When German capital went competing in the Near East in the 1900s, no doubt it contributed as much to local economic development as does any aid today. But its effect on British and French capital, and therefore on diplomacy, was infinitely worse than is, say, that of Soviet capital in India today on United States capital or diplomacy. For the German projects were meant to thwart other projects, and to exclude British and French capital from both power and profit; but the Soviet projects are meant only to please India. There is, ordinarily, room and to spare for them and their rivals.

Nay more, actual cooperation ensues. On a simple level, Congress was shocked to discover in 1962 that some United States aid materials had been used in Soviet projects, and vice versa[1]. On a more complicated and important level, Polish and British economists have sat on the same Ghanaian planning committee. If the alleged goal is the same for all parties, and the bare minimum of hypocrisy can be relied upon, cooperation is inevitable.

[1] *New York Times*, March 25, 1962.

This leads us to the multiplicity of aid-givers. Aid involves many other countries than the two cold-war principals, and most of these have been unable to hope for political influence through aid. If the ex-imperial powers have mixed motives, Czechoslovakia, West Germany and above all the Scandinavian countries have been fairly disinterested. In addition international aid-giving authorities have sprung up; which of course would be the ideal solution if only nationalism were not the main part of the will to contribute.[1] The resulting political complications have been so great as to blur the hard edges of diplomacy.

20

As to the impact of aid upon its recipients, that is not the subject of this book, unless the recipient be an STE. A book about Communism should in particular not be asked to deal with the impact of Communist aid on UDCs—a subject far more appropriate for experts on UDCs.[2] We may, however, appropriately recite some of the main peculiarities of STEs as aid-givers.

(i) One we have already met in Chapter XIV: since five-year plans for physical output take precedence over annual budgets, they have no difficulty in entering into commitments of more than one year. This puts them at a distinct advantage over at least the United States, where the executive has been unable to overcome Congress' insistence on its power to control supply by means of annual budgets.[3] Other ACCs are more flexible here, however, and so is the IBRD.

(ii) The STE finances the project that the UDC demands, without too many questions. In this it differs *toto coelo* from both the United States and the IBRD, which fuss endlessly over the project's direct justification, the way it fits into the borrower's general plan, etc. etc. The distinction is truly paradoxical: the champion of laissez-faire capitalism insists on plans it can verify, while the great domestic

---

[1] If the STEs have also international bodies (the CMEA and the IBEC) and engage in various *ad hoc* multilateral schemes through the GKES, it is surely for technical economic reasons and not in order to ease international tensions. On the GKES cf. appendix to Chapter XII. Note that multilateral aid is an ambiguous term. I here use it to indicate that more than one nation has deliberately cooperated in giving aid. But it might also mean that a single aid-giver gave convertible currency, to be spent by the recipient in any country at its discretion.

[2] Cf. however my contribution to *The Soviet Impact* (Royal Institute of International Affairs, foreword by Arnold Toynbee, 1967), and the references therein.

[3] Cf. the Afghan case, p. 519. Some two-year funds were obligated in 1966, however.

practitioner of the command economy asks no questions and indeed permits riotous folly. At bottom lie two different psychologies. ACCs feel a sense of economic responsibility for what they do in the aided country, while STEs respect first of all its political sovereignty. One party suffers a hangover of imperialism, and must justify its aid before a critical and vocal public opinion at home; the other has preached national sovereignty so long—as an antidote precisely to imperialism—that it hardly dare even give advice. If the aid recipient is another STE, however, unlimited 'advice' is forthcoming. The USSR so adjusted her aid to, even merely her trade with, Yugoslavia in 1948 and Rumania in 1961, as to modify their FYPs, even their whole development strategy. The Galati steel mill crisis (Chapter XII) shows the USSR acting in a way of which she would never dream when faced by a non-Communist UDC.

(iii) STEs like to finance specific, visible, durable projects—and this is in part a corollary of the second point. Not for them food loans: where, indeed, would they get the food? Nor stabilization loans: for these imply acceptance of the capitalist monetary system, and are ideologically most unattractive. They are also perhaps of all aid the least politically rewarding, since they demand of the borrower that he deflate. Small wonder, then, that no ACC makes a stabilization loan on its own, but all shelter behind the common whipping-boy, the IMF. STEs also avoid the even more ambitious 'program support', where the lender provides the miscellaneous imports necessary for an agreed general national plan.[1] Less interference is necessary, and more kudos is gained, by building a dam or factory. Ideology further demands that the project be in heavy industry, or Marx' Department I; i.e. Communist aid should contribute to the 'production of the means of production' and not the 'production of the objects of consumption'.

(iv) Program support, then, is an inherently imperialistic relationship, before which ACCs do not hesitate when rendering foreign aid. They even control the use of the counterpart funds which characteristically result from food aid and program support. Even the Polish use of PL 480 counterpart funds was at least checked by the United States. While all STEs are careful to confine themselves to project support alone in their dealings with UDCs, the USSR makes free use of program support vis-à-vis other STEs. She does so not only

[1] Instances of this are the Marshall Plan itself, and the United States loans made since 1962 to Chile and Colombia: New York Times, July 20, 1964, p. 37.

in rendering aid, but even in planning balanced trade, as the Galati steel mill shows.   This, then, is more imperialist than even United States behavior.   On the other hand capital flows between other STEs are project support again.

(v) There being no counterpart funds, the merely monetary problem of immense foreign-owned balances does not arise.

(vi) The aid is normally bilateral, and bilateralism is not admitted to be state of sin.   As always, it increases the volume of aid.

(vii) Enthusiasm on both sides and bad planning by the borrower sometimes lead to a factory being built that needs imported raw materials, for which however the Communist aid, concentrating on fixed assets, has made no provision.   The aided country must then either let its nice new factory stand idle or borrow elsewhere to finance the imports necessary to run it.   This mistake characterizes also Communist domestic planning, as we saw in Chapter V.

(viii) Communist aid is to governments, and insistence on specific projects expands the nationalized sector. Capitalist aid may or may not be to governments, and even when it is, the devices of program support and stabilization loans use the borrowing government as a channel whereby the money may well reach private enterprise.   It is an official and open aim of U.S. public aid to help the development of capitalism.

(ix) STEs charge, as we saw in Chapter XIV, lower interest rates—a very great advantage.   It is also commonly alleged that they are wise not to make so many gifts, since a gift is insulting.   Now that their repayment burden is growing, UDCs surely cannot continue to indulge such idiotic sentiments.

(x) Lastly STEs are poorer than ACCs, so their aid-giving is more meritorious.

Without entering deeply into the economics and politics of UDCs it would be folly to generalize confidently about the effect of these differences.   On balance they seem to do STEs neither good nor harm; perhaps more important is the on the whole inferior quality of the goods provided, and the lateness of deliveries.   It is the similarities of the two aid systems, and especially in their motivation, that are more impressive.   Convergence is at work in this field also.

21

It is even more obviously at work in the new capital transfers between ACCs and STEs: perhaps the most hopeful and exciting of all the post-Stalin developments in our field. Let us first repeat that such transfers are by no means ideologically unorthodox. They were constantly sought by the USSR in 1917–18, before War Communism, and again during the NEP. Apart from short- and medium-term credit, some quite complicated transfers, involving technology and land concessions, actually took place.[1]

But if ideology is no bar, detailed central planning surely is. Domestic enterprises work not for profit but for plan-fulfillment: how could foreign enterprises act differently? It is no accident that all concessions came to an end within six years of the beginning of the first FYP; politics cannot, surely, have been the sole cause. Trade credit and even general inter-governmental 'program support' remain entirely possible. But ordinary capitalist long-term invest-ment is difficult to envisage.

Yet it is precisely what is envisaged. The bell-wether is as usual Yugoslavia, which has been experimenting since 1964. But hers is a market economy, and her inhibitions are ideological alone: how can 'ownership by the whole people' and management by workers' councils be compatible with foreign equity participation? Would not such a thing be the 'exploitation of man by man?'[2] Virtually every European STE has by now followed suit. The easiest and commonest system is merely to buy a license to imitate some capitalist product, and import technicians. The Soviet-type enterprise has then a monopoly of its home market, and is fully subject to the com-mand economy. As to exports, its capitalist patron may give it sole rights to sell to particular countries, notably other STEs; subject to this limitation it must behave like any other exporting enterprise. The co-operant capitalist firm sells the initial plant and takes a royalty in cash, or so many units of output; it does not own anything on the territory of the STE, and is thus not at all in the same position as Lena Goldfields Ltd. (footnote 1).

So far as one can see into the rather secret negotiations of Poland with Fiat and Krupp, and the USSR with Fiat, the agreements[3] are

[1] The two most notable were the Red Army's agreement to cooperate with the Reichswehr on Soviet soil, and the Lena Goldfields Ltd. The Reichswehr used its agreement to test weapons in violation of the Versailles Treaty; the Red Army provided the secret sites and the unskilled labor, and shared the knowledge gained. Cooperation began in 1921 and ended on Hitler's advent to power in 1933. Lena Goldfields Ltd. got its concession in 1925, as compensation for its expropriation in 1917. Although the concession ran for thirty years, the terror trials of foreign technicians brought it to a halt in 1934, when the company accepted £3 mn. to cease business.

[2] Cf. my article in *Lloyds Bank Review*, October, 1967.

[3] Signed in December, 1965 and June and May, 1966 respectively. On the whole non-Yugoslav side of this matter cf. Michael Gamarnikow in *Osteuropäische Rundschau* (Munich), 12/1965.

of this kind; so they violate neither the ideology nor the institutions. More contrary to both, and reminiscent of Lena Goldfields Ltd., is direct capitalist investment on the territory of the STE. Cases of this appear to be exceedingly rare, just as Haldex, Hungary's direct investment in Poland (Chapter XII, section 10), has very few parallels. A genuine example seems to be the new Intercontinental Hotel in Bucarest, under the management of Pan-American Airways. But here too the institutional fit is not impossible. A hotel sells its services to consumers, especially foreign tourists, who are unplanned anyway. The ratio of value-added to bought-in inputs is particularly great, so the sphere of independence open to a Soviet-type manager is great, and his dependence on the central planner unusually small (it will be borne in mind that labor is hired in a market). Add that some of this particular hotel's bought-in inputs will surely be imports financed by its valuta earnings, and what we have is almost an importing-processing-and-re-exporting business whose sole Rumanian input is labor. This labor, however, must be being exploited— were it not in a service trade, so by Marxist definition immune!

There are also now similar investments by STEs in ACCs: Moskvich assembles cars in Belgium and Skoda in Austria. These enterprises, surprising as they are, involve serious ideological but no institutional problems. There is precedent for them in the various Communist banks long established on foreign soil, to which we referred in the preface.

It is true that all these transfers of capital are small.[1] It is true that they are less indigestible by Soviet-type institutions than might be thought. I.e., on the institutional side the move from War Communism to NEP, which made Lena Goldfields Ltd. possible, was very much bigger. It is true that the orthodox precedents are ample. Nevertheless NEP caused little change in ideology or ultimate intentions, whereas today all is in flux. NEP was a commonsense reaction to a domestic crisis; the Krupp and Fiat deals, infinitely smaller though they are as concrete events, betoken a changed basic attitude to the enemy. The Moskvich and Skoda deals are smaller again, but they are still stronger evidence of basic change.

22

Communists have always maintained that trade is good for peace,

---

[1] Thus Italy will receive plant orders of $75 mn. per annum in the first four years of the Fiat deal, which is much the biggest (*The Times*, London, May 23, 1966).

though they never explain in detail why this is so. Their practice is the same as anyone else's: when STEs are at enmity among each other they reduce trade; when in friendship, they increase it (Chapters XVI, XVII). But trade in every case is effect and not cause.

Undoubtedly however what Communists have in mind when they make this propaganda is not their internal trade wars. Rather are they looking outwards at the NATO embargo. But here again trade is effect, not cause. Political hostility, entirely mutual, preceded the embargo, and the latter was simply the weapon of the economically stronger side. The removal of the embargo would have to be, and indeed its partial removal has been, preceded by a political improvement. The most we can say is that governmental actions making for more trade—or less embargo—are probably good *gestures*. A *détente* has to begin with a concrete expression of good will, a concession by one or both sides. An expansion of trade is one such measure, but this is very far indeed from proving that peace has some economic base. Rather the contrary, it is yet another demonstration of the extent to which the economic relations of states are a political football.

Similarly, socialists of every hue have always maintained that world socialism would bring world peace.[1] A not much emphasized corollary of this is world free trade. But here the ideology itself is correct in putting the horse before the cart.

23

We may phrase our conclusion on trade and peace thus. There were three fundamental answers to mercantilism. The first was Smith's: stop it by having free trade. The second was Fichte's: stop it by having no trade. To Smith we reply: look at what happened when your doctrines were taken seriously—they also made for war; anyhow free trade *is* a kind of mercantilism, the mercantilism of the strongest power, and it leads to imperialism almost as surely as a thought-out commercial policy; moreover, you will never root out mercantilism; it is too logical and natural a consequence of having states. For instance, it revived quickly enough in the 1880s, when other great powers than Britain began to export capital and manufactures. From then to now great-power rivalry has covered the globe with mercantilist tensions. Moreover, if we

[1] Silberner, op. cit.; Elliot R. Goodman, *The Soviet Design for a World State* (New York, 1960).

lower tariffs the hydra develops other heads: exchange control, competitive foreign aid, customs unions, state trading. The period from Waterloo to the 1880s was quite abnormal, in that there was only one great economic and naval power in the world. War, of course, there was, but it had other origins and methods.

For Fichte a briefer reply suffices: the system renders foreign aid impossible. There is also force in Constant's position: states will try to get by war the materials they cannot get by trade. Moreover, Fichte also fails to perceive that the main thing is the spirit of pure nationalism. He errs precisely as did Constant and Cobden, in supposing that wars are primarily economic. He errs even more seriously in actually liking the nation-state.

For when we asserted above that 'international relations are the cause of war', the operative word in the sentence was, we can now see, 'international'. If there must be states, it would perhaps be better if they had never established relations. But there are indeed states, and they do have very intimate and active relations, which it would now be impossible to reduce below the threshold of serious friction. And in any case states border upon each other, and the quarrels that arise from their geographical contact are more important, by and large, than those that arise from their economic contact.

There is, then, no way back; if peace is a supreme value, mankind can only take flight forwards. The third answer to mercantilism is: abolish the nation-state. World government is the only real solution. It has the advantage, too, of attacking all causes of war, not only the economic ones. But the way to this solution may not be through the maximization of economic contacts; that, to repeat, would be to confuse cause and effect. It might be best in particular cases to 'play it cool' in all matters of trade, aid, and tourism. States will not truly merge until they trade freely, but that is not to say by what means the vicious system of national sovereignty will soonest be dissolved.

INDEX

Activators, 33
Adler-Karlsson, G., 499
Afghanistan, 509, 518–21, 550
Agriculture, 37, Ch. VIII, 329, 331, 435
Aizenberg, I., 141, 144, 147
Alampiev, P., 357
Albania, 7, 17, 18, 28, 38, 41, 141, 211, 214, 280, 285, 311, 324, 327, 339, 382, 400–5, 481, 499, 500, 509, 521, 522, 534, 547
Albinowski, S., 176, 318
Alekseyev, A., 249
Algeria, 355
Allen, R. L., 148, 219, 261, 351, 417, 517
Al'ter, L., 44
Altman, O. L., 123
Alton, T., 112, 117
Ames, E., 137
Amortization, 391
Anderson, O., 459
Angell, N., 308, 461, 529
Antonescu, I., 326
Apel, E., 241, 247, 372
Arab League, 498, 499, 500
Argentina, 40, 192, 260, 467
Armenia, 358
Arms, 103, 115, 350, 351, 393–4
Arnoult, P., 485
Arutyunian, A. A., 276
Assimilation, 307, 335
Athenian empire, 482
Atlas, S., 127
Australia, 276, 416, 501–2, 506
Auer, J., 541
Autarky, 22, 207, Ch. XV.

Baade, F., 181
Bagehot, W., 461
Bahamas, 364
Bakker-Jarness, D., 163
Bakker-Jarness, L., 411
Baksht, M., 193, 197
Balance of payments, 'trouble' and 'setback', 82–91
Balassa, B., 23, 105, 170

Bankruptcy, 48
Banque Commerciale pour l'Europe du Nord, 53
Barrier abolition, 307
Bartha, F., ix
Bastiat, F., 525
Bateson, E., 98, 217
Batyrev, V., 49, 126
Baudin, L., 461, 524
Bauer, O., 19
Baulin, L., 175, 544
Baykov, A., 197
Becker, A., 111, 439
Behrman, J., 237, 238, 260, 268, 270, 544
Belgium, 205, 284, 310, 328, 347, 372, 394, 554
Below, G. von, 457
Benelux, 319
Bentham, J., 3
Berg, M. von, 111
Bergson, A., 70, 131, 195, 397, 438, 439
Berliner, J., 389
Berman, H., 369, 499
Beria, L., 488
Bernhardi, F. von, 495
Berri, L. Ya., 439
Bialer, S., 2, 12, 27, 242
Biemel, R., 356
Bilateralism, 40, 120, 168, 173, 174, 211, 240, Ch. X, 413, 416, 419 (see also 'Reciprocity')
Bilateralism, structural, Ch. VIII/19, 333
Birch, John, 468
Blacklist, 472, 477, 499
Bliss, C., 420, 422
Blockade, 471
Bloom, G., 9
Bodnar, A., 330
'Body', defined, 31
Bogomolov, O., 25, 243, 248, 249, 278, 373
Boguslavski, M., 5
Bolivia, 429
Borkenau, F., 313